MCSE: PHR/SPHR: Professional in Human Resources Certification® Study Guide, Second Edition

HRCI Test Specifications

RESPONSIBILITIES	CHAPTER
STRATEGIC MANAGEMENT	
Interpret information related to the organization's operations from internal sources, including financial/accounting, business development, marketing, sales, operations, and information technology, in order to contribute to the development of the organization's strategic plan.	3
Interpret information from external sources related to the general business environment, industry practices and developments, technological developments, economic environment, labor pool, and legal and regulatory environment, in order to contribute to the development of the organization's strategic plan.	3
Participate as a contributing partner in the organization's strategic planning process.	3
Establish strategic relationships with key individuals in the organization to influence organizational decision-making.	3
Establish relationships/alliances with key individuals and organizations in the community to assist in achieving the organization's strategic goals and objectives.	3
Develop and utilize metrics to evaluate HR's contributions to the achievement of the organization's strategic goals and objectives.	3
Develop and execute strategies for managing organizational change that balance the expectations and needs of the organization, its employees, and all other stakeholders.	3
Develop and align the organization's human capital management plan with its strategic plan.	3
Facilitate the development and communication of the organization's core values and ethical behaviors.	3
Reinforce the organization's core values and behavioral expectations through modeling, communication, and coaching.	3
Develop and manage the HR budget in a manner consistent with the organization's strategic goals, objectives, and values.	3
Provide information for the development and monitoring of the organization's overall budget.	3
Monitor the legislative and regulatory environment for proposed changes and their potential impact to the organization, taking appropriate proactive steps to support, modify, or oppose the proposed changes.	3
Develop policies and procedures to support corporate governance initiatives (for example, board of directors training, whistleblower protection, code of conduct).	3
Participate in enterprise risk management to prevent and/or mitigate loss and ensure business continuity by examining HR policies to evaluate their potential risks to the organization.	3
Identify and evaluate alternatives and recommend strategies for vendor selection and/or outsourcing (for example, HRIS, benefits, payroll).	3
Participate in strategic decision-making and due diligence activities related to organizational structure and design (for example, corporate restructuring, mergers and acquisitions [M&A], offshoring, divestitures). **SPHR ONLY**	3
Determine strategic application of integrated technical tools and systems (for example, HRIS, performance management tools, applicant tracking, compensation tools, employee self-service technologies).	3

Sybex®
An Imprint of

WILEY

RESPONSIBILITIES	CHAPTER
Develop/select and implement/administer occupational injury and illness prevention, safety incentives, and training programs. **PHR ONLY**	8
Develop/select, implement, and evaluate security plans and policies to protect employees and other individuals, and to minimize the organization's loss and liability (for example, emergency response, evacuation, workplace violence, substance abuse).	8
Communicate and train the workforce on the security plans and policies.	8
Develop and monitor business continuity and disaster recovery plans.	8
Communicate and train the workforce on the business continuity and disaster recovery plans.	8
Develop internal and external privacy policies (for example, identity theft, data protection, HIPAA compliance, workplace monitoring).	8
Administer internal and external privacy policies.	8

CORE KNOWLEDGE REQUIRED BY HR PROFESSIONALS

Needs assessment and analysis	2
Third-party contract management, including development of requests for proposals	2
Communication skills and strategies (for example, presentation, collaboration, influencing, diplomacy, sensitivity)	2
Organizational documentation requirements to meet federal and state requirements	2
Adult learning processes	2
Motivation concepts and applications	2
Training techniques (for example, computer based, classroom, on-the-job)	2
Leadership concepts and applications	2
Project management concepts and applications	2
Diversity concepts and applications	2
Human relations concepts and applications (for example, interpersonal and organizational behavior)	2
HR ethics and professional standards	2
Technology to support HR activities (for example, HRIS, employee self-service, e-learning, ATS)	2
Qualitative and quantitative methods and tools for analysis, interpretation, and decision-making purposes (for example, metrics and measurements, cost/benefit analysis, financial statement analysis)	2
Change management methods	2
Job analysis and job description methods	2
Employee records management (for example, electronic/paper, retention, disposal)	2
The interrelationships among HR activities and programs across functional areas	2
Types of organizational structures (for example, matrix, hierarchy)	2
Environmental scanning concepts and applications	2
Methods for assessing employee attitudes, opinions, and satisfaction (for example, opinion surveys, attitude surveys, focus groups/panels)	2
Basic budgeting and accounting concepts	2
Risk management techniques	2

Sybex®
An Imprint of
WILEY

RESPONSIBILITIES	CHAPTER
Develop, implement, and evaluate performance management programs and procedures (for example, goal setting, job rotations, promotions).	5
Develop/select, implement, and evaluate programs (for example, flexible work arrangements, diversity initiatives, repatriation) to meet the unique needs of employees. **SPHR ONLY**	5

TOTAL REWARDS

Ensure that compensation and benefits programs are compliant with applicable federal, state, and local laws and regulations.	6
Develop, implement, and evaluate compensation policies/programs and pay structures based upon internal equity and external market conditions that support the organization's strategic goals, objectives, and values.	6
Administer payroll functions (for example, new hires, deductions, adjustments, terminations)	6
Conduct benefits programs needs assessments (for example, benchmarking, employee survey).	6
Develop/select, implement, and evaluate benefit programs that support the organization's strategic goals, objectives, and values (for example, health and welfare, retirement, wellness, employee assistance programs [EAP], time-off).	6
Communicate and train the workforce in the compensation and benefits programs and policies (for example, self-service technologies).	6
Develop/select, implement/administer, and evaluate executive compensation programs (for example, stock purchase, stock options, incentive, bonus, supplemental retirement plans).**SPHR ONLY**	6
Develop, implement/administer, and evaluate expatriate and foreign national compensation and benefits programs. **SPHR ONLY**	6

EMPLOYEE AND LABOR RELATIONS

Ensure that employee and labor relations activities are compliant with applicable federal, state, and local laws and regulations.	7
Assess organizational climate by obtaining employee input (for example, focus groups, employee surveys, staff meetings).	7
Implement organizational change activities as appropriate in response to employee feedback.	7
Develop employee relations programs (for example, awards, recognition, discounts, special events) that promote a positive organizational culture.	7
Implement employee relations programs that promote a positive organizational culture.	7
Evaluate effectiveness of employee relations programs through the use of metrics (for example, exit interviews, employee surveys).	7
Establish workplace policies and procedures (for example, dress code, attendance, computer use) and monitor their application and enforcement to ensure consistency.	7
Develop, implement/administer, and evaluate expatriate and foreign national compensation and benefits programs. **SPHR ONLY**	7
Resolve employee complaints filed with federal, state, and local agencies involving employment practices, utilizing professional resources as necessary (for example, legal counsel, mediation/arbitration specialists, and investigators).	7
Develop and direct proactive employee relations strategies for remaining union-free in non-organized locations.	7

RISK MANAGEMENT

Ensure that workplace health, safety, security, and privacy activities are compliant with applicable federal, state, and local laws and regulations.	8
Identify the organization's safety program needs.	8

Sybex®
An Imprint of
WILEY

RESPONSIBILITIES	CHAPTER

WORKFORCE PLANNING AND EMPLOYMENT

Ensure that workforce planning and employment activities are compliant with applicable federal, state, and local laws and regulations.	4
Identify workforce requirements to achieve the organization's short- and long-term goals and objectives (for example, corporate restructuring, M&A activity, workforce expansion or reduction).	4
Conduct job analyses to create job descriptions and identify job competencies.	4
Identify and document essential job functions for positions.	4
Establish hiring criteria based on job descriptions and required competencies.	4
Analyze labor market for trends that impact the ability to meet workforce requirements (for example, SWOT analysis, environmental scan, demographic scan). **SPHR ONLY**	4
Assess skill sets of internal workforce and external labor market to determine the availability of qualified candidates, utilizing third party vendors or agencies as appropriate.	4
Identify internal and external recruitment sources (for example, employee referrals, online job boards, resume banks) and implement selected recruitment methods.	4
Evaluate recruitment methods and sources for effectiveness (for example, return on investment [ROI], cost per hire, time to fill).	4
Develop strategies to brand/market the organization to potential qualified applicants.	4
Develop and implement selection procedures, including applicant tracking, interviewing, testing, reference and background checking, and drug screening.	4
Develop and extend employment offers and conduct negotiations as necessary.	4
Administer post-offer employment activities (for example, execute employment agreements, complete I-9 verification forms, coordinate relocations, schedule physical exams).	4
Implement and/or administer the process for non-U.S. citizens to legally work in the United States.	4
Develop, implement, and evaluate orientation processes for new hires, rehires, and transfers.	4
Develop, implement, and evaluate retention strategies and practices.	4
Develop, implement, and evaluate succession planning process.	4
Develop and implement the organizational exit process for both voluntary and involuntary terminations, including planning for reductions in force (RIF).	4
Develop, implement, and evaluate an AAP, as required.	4

HUMAN RESOURCE DEVELOPMENT

Ensure that human resource development programs are compliant with all applicable federal, state, and local laws and regulations.	5
Conduct a needs assessment to identify and establish priorities regarding human resource development activities. **SPHR ONLY**	5
Develop/select and implement employee training programs (for example, leadership skills, harassment prevention, computer skills) to increase individual and organizational effectiveness.	5
Evaluate effectiveness of employee training programs through the use of metrics (for example, participant surveys, pre- and post-testing). **SPHR ONLY**	5
Develop, implement, and evaluate talent management programs that include assessing, developing, and placing high-potential employees. **SPHR ONLY**	5
Develop/select and evaluate performance appraisal process (for example, instruments, ranking and rating scales, relationship to compensation, frequency).	5
Implement training programs for performance evaluators. **PHR ONLY**	5

NOTE Exam specifications and content are subject to change at any time without prior notice and at the Human Resource Certification Institute's sole discretion. Please visit HRCI's website (www.hrci.org) for the most current information on their exam content.

PHR®/SPHR®
Professional in Human Resources Certification
Study Guide
Second Edition

PHR®/SPHR®
Professional in Human Resources Certification
Study Guide
Second Edition

Anne M. Bogardus, SPHR

BICENTENNIAL

1807

WILEY

2007

BICENTENNIAL

Wiley Publishing, Inc.

Acquisitions and Development Editor: Maureen Adams
Technical Editors: Cynthia Erickson and Laura Owen
Production Editor: Martine Dardignac
Copy Editor: Sally Engelfried
Production Manager: Tim Tate
Vice President and Executive Group Publisher: Richard Swadley
Vice President and Executive Publisher: Joseph B. Wikert
Vice President and Publisher: Neil Edde
Media Development Specialists: Kit Malone and Steve Kudirka
Book Designers: Judy Fung and Bill Gibson
Compositor: Jeff Wilson, Happenstance Type-O-Rama
Proofreader: Ian Golder
Indexer: Nancy Guenther
Anniversary Logo Design: Richard Pacifico
Cover Designer: Ryan Sneed

Library of Congress Cataloging-in-Publication Data

Bogardus, Anne M.

  PHR/SPHR : Professional in Human Resources certification study guide / Anne M. Bogardus. -- 2nd ed.

    p. cm.

  ISBN-13: 978-0-470-05068-2 (paper/cd-rom)

  ISBN-10: 0-470-05068-3 (paper/cd-rom)

  1. Personnel management--Examinations--Study guides. 2. Personnel departments--Employees--Certification. I. Title. II. Title: Professional in Human Resources/Senior Professional in Human Resources.

  HF5549.B7583 2007

  658.30076--dc22

                          2006036641

Sybex®
An Imprint of
WILEY

To Our Valued Readers:

Sybex® is excited to be publishing the PHR/SPHR: Professional in Human Resources Certification Study Guide, Second Edition the first of its kind for the increasingly critical business area of Human Resources. The skills and concepts covered here are certainly different from the technical topics one usually finds in Sybex Study Guides, but the relevance and importance to businesses of all kinds will be immediately evident to all who peruse this invaluable book.

Just as the Human Resource Certification Institute is committed to establishing measurable standards for certifying human resource professionals, Sybex is committed to providing those professionals with the skills and knowledge needed to meet those standards. The author and editors have worked hard to ensure that this study guide is comprehensive, in-depth, and pedagogically sound. We're confident that this book will meet and exceed the demanding standards of the certification marketplace and help you, the PHR or SPHR exam candidate, succeed in your endeavors.

Good luck in pursuit of your PHR and SPHR certifications!

Neil Edde
Vice President & Publisher
Sybex, an Imprint of Wiley

For Kit, who taught me to love reading; Bob, the best manager of people I've ever known; and to both of them for their unwavering support and love.

—With love and gratitude

and in loving memory of Don and Gerry Cottle, beloved uncle and aunt.

Acknowledgments

Having dreamed of writing a book for a very long time, I was thrilled when this opportunity was presented to me. The team at Sybex provided the encouragement, cheerleading, and whip-cracking that got me through the process. Thanks to Maureen Adams for helping to shape the book, and to Jeff Kellum for stepping in at the last minute. To Martine Dardignac, *merci tellement* for making sure that the final product was the best it could be. Thanks also to Sally Engelfried whose attention to detail was immensely helpful and to Jeff Wilson and Happenstance Type-O-Rama who made the pages of this book so accessible. I'm grateful for the level of professionalism and expertise that each of them brought to the project.

I am most grateful to the book's technical editors, Cynthia Erickson, SPHR, and Laura Owen, JD, SPHR. Cynthia—thanks for reminding me when to stop and for asking the right questions to help me clarify some of the information. Aside from that, your support and encouragement were always there when I needed them. Laura, thanks for taking this on, and for your encouragement and support. You are both awesome!

Thanks also to my clients, from whom I learn more every day. Finally, thanks to my friends for their understanding and patience while I finished this project—all of you are the best!

About the Author

Anne M. Bogardus, SPHR, began her human resources career in compensation at a public multinational corporation, Castle & Cooke, owner of the Dole food brand, and later at First Nationwide Bank. Currently she is founder and principal of S.T.A.R. HR in northern California, which specializes in building human resource functions that serve strategic business needs. Her practice includes small- to medium-sized businesses in a wide range of industries including biotechnology, mortgage lending, high technology, public relations, retail, nonprofit, and construction. Ms. Bogardus is also the author of an introductory book for non-HR business professionals, *Human Resource Jumpstart*, also published by Sybex.

HR is a dynamic profession requiring practitioners to keep up-to-date with current trends and changes to employment law. The PHR/SPHR exams are updated annually to reflect these trends and changes. For information updates between revisions of this study guide, log on to www.starhronline.com and click PHR/ SPHR Certification to view changes or ask questions about content.

Contents at a Glance

Introduction   *xxiii*

Assessment Test   *xxix*

Chapter 1   Certifying Human Resource Professionals   1

Chapter 2   Core Knowledge Requirements for HR Professionals   23

Chapter 3   Strategic Management   89

Chapter 4   Workforce Planning and Employment   127

Chapter 5   Human Resource Development   195

Chapter 6   Total Rewards   247

Chapter 7   Employee and Labor Relations   329

Chapter 8   Risk Management   381

Appendix A   Case Study   431

Appendix B   Federal Employment Legislation and Case Law   437

Appendix C   Resources   457

Glossary   465

Index   *507*

Contents

Introduction   *xxiii*

Assessment Test   *xxix*

Chapter   1   Certifying Human Resource Professionals   1

The Human Resource Profession   2
Development of the Human Resource Body of Knowledge   3
    Defining the Functional Areas of the BOK   5
    Core Knowledge Requirements of the BOK   6
    Certification Levels   7
    Eligibility Requirements   9
    Recertification   10
The Test   10
    It's *Experiential* and *Federal*   12
    What the Questions Look Like   13
    Preparing for the Exam   14
    Taking the Exam   18
Summary   20
Key Terms   21

Chapter   2   Core Knowledge Requirements for HR Professionals   23

Needs Assessment and Analysis   25
    Third-party Contract Management   26
Communication Skills and Strategies   28
    Employee Communication   28
    Professional Communication   30
Documentation Requirements   30
    Documenting Employment Actions   30
    Documenting Performance Issues   30
Adult Learning Processes   32
Motivation Concepts   33
    Abraham Maslow: The Hierarchy of Needs (1954)   33
    Fredrick Herzberg: Motivation/Hygiene Theory (1959)   34
    Douglas McGregor: Theory X and Theory Y (1960)   35
    Clayton Alderfer: ERG Theory (1969)   35
    David McClelland: Acquired Needs Theory (1961)   35
    J. Stacy Adams: Equity Theory (1963)   36
    Victor Vroom: Expectancy Theory (1964)   36
    B. F. Skinner: Operant Conditioning (1957)   36
Training Techniques   37
Leadership Concepts   38
    Behavioral Theories   38

Situational Theories	39
Contingency Theories	40
Leadership Styles	40
Project Management Concepts	41
Diversity Concepts	42
Human Relations Concepts	43
HR Ethics and Professional Standards	44
Human Resource Technology	45
HRIS Systems	45
Qualitative and Quantitative Analysis	49
Data Collection	50
Analysis Tools	50
Qualitative Analysis	54
Metrics and Measurement	54
Change Management	55
Job Analysis and Description	56
Job Analysis	56
Job Descriptions	57
Employee Records Management	58
Interrelationships among HR Activities	66
Organizational Structures	68
Environmental Scanning Concepts	71
Environmental Scanning Tools	72
Employee Attitude Assessment	75
Basic Budgeting and Accounting	76
Accounting	76
Budgeting	77
Risk Management	79
Summary	80
Exam Essentials	80
Key Terms	81
Review Questions	84
Answers to Review Questions	86
Chapter 3 Strategic Management	**89**
Strategy	92
Organizations	92
Organization Functions	93
Strategic Planning	98
Organizational Structure and Design	104
Strategic HR Planning	107
Building Strategic Partnerships	108
Management	108
Enterprise Risk Management	110

Legislative and Regulatory Processes 111
   Legislative Process 111
   Administrative Law 112
   Lobbying 113
Corporate Governance 113
   Organization Values and Ethics 114
   Code of Ethics 115
   Codes of Conduct 116
   Ethics Officers 118
HR Metrics—Measuring Results 118
Global Considerations 119
Summary 120
Exam Essentials 120
Key Terms 122
Review Questions 123
Answers to Review Questions 125

Chapter   4   Workforce Planning and Employment   127

Federal Employment Legislation 129
   Civil Rights Legislation 130
   Age Discrimination in Employment Act of 1967 132
   Americans with Disabilities Act of 1990 134
   Civil Rights Act of 1991 134
   Federal Contractors, Subcontractors, and Agencies 136
   Annual EEO Survey 138
   Affirmative Action Plans 141
Strategic Workforce Planning 143
   Workforce Goals and Objectives 143
   Job Analysis and Description 144
   Qualified Employees 145
   Translating Organization Goals into Staffing Plans 148
   Labor Market Analysis 150
Staffing Programs 151
   Sourcing and Recruiting Candidates 151
   Candidate Selection Tools 157
   Employment Offers 173
   Post-Offer Employment Activities 175
Organization Exit Processes 179
   Voluntary Exit Processes 179
   Involuntary Exit Processes 180
Metrics—Measuring Results 183
Global Considerations 184
Summary 186
Exam Essentials 187

Key Terms	188
Review Questions	190
Answers to Review Questions	193

Chapter 5   Human Resource Development   195

Federal Employment Legislation	196
Copyright Act of 1976	197
U. S. Patent Act	198
Organization Development	198
Strategic Interventions	199
Techno-Structural Interventions	202
Human Process Interventions	208
Human Resource Management Interventions	211
Employee Development	211
Management Development	213
Employee Training Programs	214
Analysis	215
Design	218
Development	221
Implementation	224
Evaluation	227
Performance Management Programs	228
Performance Appraisal	229
Elements of Performance Appraisal	230
Timing Performance Appraisals	230
Performance Appraisal Methods	231
Training Performance Evaluators	233
Unique Employee Needs	236
Diversity Initiatives	236
Flexible Work Arrangements	236
Repatriation	236
Metrics—Measuring Results	237
Global Considerations	238
Summary	238
Exam Essentials	239
Key Terms	240
Review Questions	242
Answers to Review Questions	244

Chapter 6   Total Rewards   247

Total Rewards Defined	249
Total Rewards Philosophy	250
Total Rewards Strategy	252

Compensation   253
  Federal Employment Legislation   256
  Types of Compensation   265
  Traditional Pay Structures   272
Benefits   283
  Involuntary Benefits   285
  Voluntary Benefits   294
  Health and Welfare Benefits   305
Payroll   313
  Payroll Systems   313
  Payroll Administration   313
Communicating TR Programs   316
Metrics—Measuring Results   317
Executive Compensation   317
  Stock Options   318
  Board of Directors/Outside Directors   320
  Total Rewards Budgets   320
Global Considerations   321
Summary   321
Exam Essentials   321
Key Terms   323
Review Questions   326
Answers to Review Questions   328

Chapter   7   Employee and Labor Relations   329

Federal Employment Legislation   330
Employee Relations   331
  Employer Rights and Responsibilities   331
Organization Climate and Culture   342
  Employee Involvement Strategies   342
  Communicating with Employees   344
Employee Relations Programs   345
  Positive Employee Relations Strategies   345
  Workplace Policies and Procedures   346
  Employee Feedback   348
Performance Improvement   349
  Disciplinary Terminations   351
  Workplace Behavior Issues   352
Dispute Resolution   353
  ADR Methods   353
Labor Relations   355
  Labor Laws and Organizations   356
  Employee Rights   357

Union Organization	360
What Can an Employer Do?	360
The Organizing Process	361
Collective Bargaining	366
Union Avoidance Strategies	372
Metrics—Measuring Results	373
Global Considerations	373
Summary	373
Exam Essentials	374
Key Terms	375
Review Questions	377
Answers to Review Questions	379

Chapter 8	**Risk Management**	**381**
	Federal Employment Legislation	382
	Occupational Safety and Health Act of 1970	384
	Mine Safety and Health Act of 1977 (MSH Act)	394
	Drug-Free Workplace Act of 1988	394
	Other Legislation Impacting Risk Management	395
	Risk Assessment	396
	Safety and Health Risks	396
	Security Risks	405
	Loss Prevention	409
	Injury and Illness Prevention Programs	410
	Injury and Illness Compensation Programs	413
	Business Continuity	415
	Safety Training Programs	417
	Workplace Privacy	417
	Workplace Investigations	421
	Metrics—Measuring Results	422
	Global Considerations	423
	Summary	424
	Exam Essentials	425
	Key Terms	426
	Review Questions	427
	Answers to Review Questions	429

Appendix A	**Case Study**	**431**
	The Scenario	432
	The Challenge: Create an HR Plan	434
	Case Study Answer Key	436

Appendix   B | **Federal Employment Legislation and Case Law** | **437**

Additional Cases | 447
  1968: *Rosenfeld v. Southern Pacific* | 447
  1969: *Weeks v. Southern Bell Telephone Co.* | 448
  1973: *McDonnell Douglas Corp. v. Green* | 448
  1978: *Regents of California v. Bakke* | 449
  1979: *United Steelworkers v. Weber* | 450
  1981: *Texas Department of Community
    Affairs v. Burdine* | 450
  1987: *Johnson v. Santa Clara County
    Transportation Agency* | 451
  1987: *School Board of Nassau v. Arline* | 451
  1989: *Martin v. Wilks* | 452
  1992: *Electromation, Inc. v. NLRB* | 452
  1993: *E. I. DuPont & Co. v. NLRB* | 453
  1993: *St. Mary's Honor Center v. Hicks* | 454
  1995: *McKennon v. Nashville Banner Publishing Co.* | 455
  2001: *Circuit City Stores v. Adams* | 456

Appendix   C | **Resources** | **457**

Strategic Management | 459
  Books | 459
  Professional Associations | 459
Workforce Planning and Employment | 460
  Books | 460
  Professional Associations | 460
Human Resource Development | 460
  Books | 460
  Professional Associations | 461
Total Rewards | 461
  Books | 461
  Professional Associations | 461
Employee and Labor Relations | 462
  Books | 462
  Professional Associations | 462
Risk Management | 463
  Books | 463
  Professional Associations | 463

Glossary | **465**

Index | *507*

Introduction

Congratulations on taking the first step toward achieving your Professional in Human Resources (PHR) or Senior Professional in Human Resources (SPHR) certification! The process you are embarking upon is rewarding and challenging and, as more than 83,000 of your fellow human resource colleagues have already discovered, it's an excellent opportunity to explore areas of human resource management with which you may not work every day. In the next few pages, you will find some general information about human resource certification, some suggestions for using this book, information about what to expect in the following chapters, and a discussion of the organizations involved in certification.

Before we begin, a word about what you should already know. This study guide was designed to serve as a refresher for experienced professionals who have practiced HR for a minimum of two years. I assume that those who are pursuing certification have the basic HR knowledge that comes not only from education in human resources but also, more importantly, from exempt-level experience. If your daily work is truly generalist in nature, you likely have touched upon many of the topics I cover, but you may not have in-depth knowledge in all of them. Conversely, if you specialize in one or two areas of HR, you probably have extensive experience in those areas but may need to refresh your knowledge in other areas.

The goal of this study guide is to provide enough information about each of the functional areas of human resource management to enable candidates in either situation to find what they need to prepare themselves for successfully completing the exam. There are more than 22,000 books related to human resources listed on Amazon.com alone, and there is obviously no way that I can cover all the aspects of HR in a single book. So I've organized the information around the test specifications (test specs) established by the Human Resource Certification Institute (HRCI), the certifying body for our profession. I'll talk more about the test specs in Chapter 1, but for now, suffice it to say that the key to success on the exam is a thorough understanding of and ability to apply the test specs when answering questions on the exams.

About Human Resource Certification

What exactly *is* human resource certification? Briefly, let's just say that certification is a way of acknowledging individuals who have met the standard of competency established by HR practitioners as that which is necessary to be considered a fully competent HR professional. To understand if this book is for you, you'll want to know why you should become certified and how the certification process works.

Who Certifies HR Professionals?

There are three organizations involved in the certification of human resource professionals: the Human Resource Certification Institute (HRCI), the Society for Human Resource Management (SHRM), and the Professional Examination Service (PES).

The Human Resource Certification Institute

HRCI is the certifying body for the human resource profession. It was formed by the American Society of Personnel Administrators (ASPA) in 1972 when it was known as the ASPA Accreditation Institute (AAI). In its early stages, HRCI was financially dependent upon SHRM, but it is now financially independent. Both HRCI and SHRM have individual boards of directors that govern their operations. While HRCI and SHRM have a long history of affiliation and mutual support, the certification process is a separate and distinct function of HRCI, and SHRM has no more control over or access to the certification process than does anyone else in the profession.

You can find HRCI's organizational mission statement at www.hrci.org/ AboutUs/MISVIS/.

The Society for Human Resource Management

SHRM is the largest organization of human resource professionals in the world, representing more than 200,000 members worldwide in 2006. From its beginning in 1948 as the American Society for Personnel Administrators (ASPA), SHRM has been a leader in the endeavor to gain recognition for the human resource profession. Today's certification program is a direct result of efforts by the first volunteer members of SHRM who recognized the need for a defined body of knowledge and set about to develop it along with a certification process that evaluates the abilities of practitioners in the field.

Professional Examination Service

PES is a nonprofit organization that conducts license and credential examinations for a wide variety of professions, including psychology, pharmacy, real estate appraisal, and security management, among many others. PES maintains the database of test items developed by HRCI and is responsible for ensuring that applicants for the PHR and SPHR exams meet the eligibility requirements, administering and scoring the tests, and notifying candidates of the results. In 2005, PES conducted the most recent review of the body of knowledge, called a practice analysis study, to ensure the continued relevance of the credentialing process to current business practices.

I will refer to these organizations frequently in Chapter 1 as I discuss the body of knowledge and the certification process.

Why Become Certified?

Over time, the certification offered by HRCI has become the industry standard for determining competence in the field of human resources. There are many reasons that individuals may decide to seek professional certification. Let's talk about just a few of them.

First, certification is an acknowledgement that you have met the standards of excellence determined by other HR professionals to be those which are necessary to be fully competent in the field. Because the standards are developed by working professionals, not just by those who teach and consult in the field, this credential demonstrates that you are a fully competent HR practitioner based on a standard set by your peers.

Second, certification is a way to increase your marketability. In difficult economic times, when there is tough competition for jobs, certification provides an edge that can be advantageous in your job search. With an abundance of job seekers for a limited number of jobs, whatever you can do to set yourself apart from the crowd can give you the edge when potential employers are making the final hiring decision.

Third, those who spend the time to advance their own knowledge and achieve certification have demonstrated their ability to continue learning and growing as times and business needs change. A person who is willing and able to set a significant goal and do what is necessary to achieve it demonstrates characteristics that are in great demand in business today: results orientation, technical competence, commitment, and excellence.

Finally, certification enhances your credibility with coworkers and customers. It demonstrates to those with whom you come in contact during your work day that you have met the standard that has been determined by others within the field to be that which is required to demonstrate competence.

Whether your reason for seeking certification falls into one of these categories, or you are motivated to do so for some other reason, it can be a great opportunity to validate how much you already know about the practice of human resources as a profession.

How to Become Certified

To become a certified HR professional, you must pass either the PHR or SPHR exam, both of which have been developed by HRCI in a comprehensive process described in Chapter 1.

HRCI uses a computer-based testing (CBT) process during two time periods each year: between the beginning of May and the end of June and from mid-November through mid-January. One advantage of the CBT process is that exam candidates know before they leave the testing center whether or not they are certified.

Each exam, PHR and SPHR, consists of 225 questions. Of these questions, 200 are scored to determine whether or not you pass the exam. The additional 25 questions are being "pretested" in order to determine their reliability and validity for inclusion in future test cycles. A detailed discussion of how the questions are developed and scored can be found in the HRCI *PHR & SPHR Certification Handbook*, which can be viewed and/or downloaded at the HRCI website (www.hrci.org), or you can request a hard copy from HRCI by calling (866) 898-4724. The handbook is an essential guide to all aspects of the exams and includes test dates, application deadlines, fee information, and answers to frequently asked questions about the certification process, as well as the full list of test specifications.

Chapter 1 explains in greater detail how much and what kinds of experience are required for each exam level and how the questions differ on each level.

How This Book Is Organized

I've talked a little bit about Chapter 1, which provides information about requirements for certification and the testing process. Chapter 1 also provides some suggestions on the best ways to study for the exam.

Chapter 2, "Core Knowledge Requirements for HR Professionals," provides a brief discussion of the knowledge requirements with implications in multiple functional areas. Reading this chapter first gives exam candidates a base for understanding topics covered in subsequent chapters.

Chapters 3–8 get down to the specifics of each functional area and discuss the test specifications in detail. Each of these chapters consists of a list of objectives, an overview of the functional area, the federal employment laws applicable to that area, and a discussion of the test specs, including appropriate court cases.

I have also provided three appendices to facilitate your study. Appendix A is a case study that gives you an opportunity to pull information from multiple functional areas to develop an HR plan for a fictitious company.

Appendix B, "Federal Employment Legislation and Case Law," is a chronological listing of the federal legislation appearing throughout the book, as well as significant court decisions with implications for human resources. In this appendix, I've also included additional court decisions that were not discussed in the chapters but have significance for HR practice and with which you should be familiar, so be sure to review these. They are included in a separate section of the appendix.

Appendix C, "Resources," is just that: a list of additional sources of information about each of the functional areas of human resources.

Finally, I have included a glossary, an alphabetical listing of all of the key terms throughout the book with their corresponding definitions.

The Elements of a Study Guide

You'll see many recurring elements as you read through the study guide. Here's a description of some of those elements.

Summary   The summary is a brief review of the chapter to sum up what was covered.

Exam Essentials   The Exam Essentials highlight topics that could appear on one or both of the exams in some form. While I obviously do not know exactly what will be included in a particular exam, this section reinforces significant concepts that are key to understanding the functional area and the test specs HRCI has developed.

Key Terms   Throughout each chapter, I've identified and defined key terms that exam candidates will need to understand.

Chapter Review Questions   Each chapter includes ten practice questions that have been designed to measure your knowledge of key ideas that were discussed in the chapter. After you finish each chapter, answer the questions; if some of your answers are incorrect, it's an indication that you need to spend some more time studying that topic. The answers to the practice questions can be found after the last question in each chapter. The chapter review questions are designed to help you measure how much information you retained from your reading and are different from the kinds of questions you will see on the exam.

What's on the CD?

The CD provides some essential tools to help you with your preparation for the certification exam. All of the following gear should be loaded on your computer when studying for the test.

The Sybex Test Preparation Software

The test preparation software, made by experts at Sybex, prepares you to pass the PHR/SPHR exams. In this test engine you will find all the review and assessment questions from the book, plus four additional bonus exams that appear exclusively on the CD. You can take the assessment test, test yourself by chapter, or take the practice exams. Finally, you can be graded by topic area, so you can assess the areas where you need further review.

> Just as on the certification exams, the bonus exam questions on the CD draw upon your experience as an HR professional. Be on the lookout for questions based upon your everyday activities in HR and not just on the material in the PHR/SPHR study guide.

Electronic Flashcards for PC and Palm Devices

Sybex's electronic flashcards include 150 PHR and 150 SPHR questions designed to challenge you further for the PHR and SPHR exams. Between the review questions, practice exams, and flashcards, you'll have a wide variety of materials to help you prepare!

PHR/SPHR Study Guide in PDF

Sybex offers the *PHR/SPHR: Professional in Human Resources Certification Study Guide* in PDF format on the CD so you can read the book on your PC or laptop if you travel and don't want to carry a book, or if you just like to read from the computer screen. The latest version of Adobe Reader is also included on the CD.

How to Use This Book and CD

This book has a number of features designed to guide your study efforts for either the PHR or the SPHR certification exam. All of these features are intended to assist you in doing the most important thing you can do to pass the exam: understand and apply the test specs in answering questions. This book helps you do that by listing the current test specs at the beginning of each chapter and by ensuring that each of them is fully discussed within the chapter. The practice questions at the end of each chapter and the practice exams on the CD are designed to assist you in testing your retention of the material you've read to make you aware of areas in which you should spend additional study time. I've provided web links and other resources to assist you in mastering areas where you may require additional study materials. Here are some suggestions for using this book and CD:

1. Take the assessment test before you start reading the material. These questions are designed to measure your knowledge and will look different than the questions you will see on the exam. They give you an idea of the areas in which you need to spend additional study time, as well as those areas in which you may just need a brief refresher.

2. Review the test specs at the beginning of each chapter before you start reading. Make sure you read the associated knowledge requirements in HRCI's *PHR and SPHR Certification Handbook* as these may help you in your study process. After you've read the chapter, review them again to make sure you understand and are able to apply them.

3. Answer the review questions after you've read each chapter; if you missed any of them, go back over the chapter and review the topic, or utilize one of the additional resources if you need more information.

4. Make sure you understand the laws that apply to each functional area, the information covered in each of them, and to which companies or government agencies they apply.

5. Download the flashcards to your handheld device and review them when you have a few minutes during the day.

6. Take every opportunity to test yourself. In addition to the assessment test and review questions, there are bonus exams on the CD. Take these exams without referring to the chapters and see how well you've done—go back and review any topics you've missed until you fully understand and can apply the concepts.

Finally, find a study partner if possible. Studying for, and taking, the exam with someone else will make the process more enjoyable, and you'll have someone to help you understand topics that are difficult for you. You'll also be able to reinforce your own knowledge by helping your study partner in areas where they are weak.

Assessment Test

1. According to the WARN Act, an employer with 200 employees is required to provide 60 days' notice of a mass layoff when:

   A. The employer is seeking additional funding and will lay off 70 employees if the funding falls through.

   B. A major client unexpectedly selects a new vendor for the company's products and the company lays off 75 employees.

   C. The employer lays off 5 employees a week for 3 months.

   D. A flood requires that one of the plants be shut down for repairs and 55 employees are laid off.

2. An employee has come forward with an allegation of quid pro quo harassment by her supervisor. As the HR manager, you are responsible for investigating the complaint. The supervisor in question is someone with whom you have become quite friendly. In this case, the best person to conduct the investigation is

   A. You

   B. The corporate attorney

   C. The direct manager of the accused supervisor

   D. A third-party investigator

3. As of September 1, 1997, the federal minimum wage is set at:

   A. $5.15 per hour

   B. $7.16 per hour

   C. $5.75 per hour

   D. $6.75 per hour

4. During the union organizing process, the bargaining unit is determined

   A. By the union organizers

   B. Jointly, by the union and the employer

   C. By the National Labor Relations Board

   D. By the employees during the election

5. The motivation theory that suggests people are motivated by the reward they will receive when they succeed and that they weigh the value of the expected reward against the effort required to achieve it is known as:

   A. Vroom's Expectancy Theory

   B. Adams' Equity Theory

   C. McClelland's Acquired Needs Theory

   D. McGregor's Theory X and Theory Y

6. The most effective method of performance evaluation is

   A. A field review process

   B. A continuous feedback process

   C. A forced ranking process

   D. A behaviorally anchored rating scale process

7. An example of a nonqualified deferred compensation plan is

   A. An excess deferral plan

   B. A target benefit plan

   C. A money purchase plan

   D. A cash balance plan

8. Which of the following is an example of a passive training method?

   A. Vestibule training

   B. Demonstration

   C. Distance learning

   D. Self-study

9. The OSHA consulting service

   A. Helps employers identify the OSHA standards that apply to their workplace

   B. Fines employers for violating OSHA safety standards

   C. Does not require compliance with OSHA standards

   D. Is a one-time service

10. One purpose of a diversity initiative is to:

   A. Increase workplace creativity

   B. Increase the effectiveness of the workforce

   C. Increase the organization's ability to attract customers

   D. All of the above

11. When workplace conditions pose a threat to an unborn child, the company must:

   A. Do nothing. It is up to employees to protect their unborn children.

   B. Move the employee into a different job that does not pose a threat to the unborn child.

   C. Advise the employee of the potential threat and allow the employee to make the decision.

   D. Allow only sterile employees to work in jobs that pose a threat to unborn children.

12. The Health Insurance Portability and Accountability Act

    A. Prevents HR from investigating claims issues

    B. Requires continuation of health benefits

    C. Established EPO networks

    D. Limited preexisting condition restrictions

13. The concept that recognized businesses as social organizations as well as economic systems and recognized that productivity was related to employee job satisfaction is known as:

    A. Human resource management

    B. Strategic management

    C. Human relations

    D. Human resource development

14. Before selecting an HRIS system, which of the following questions should be answered?

    A. What information will be converted to the HRIS?

    B. Who will have access to the information stored in the HRIS?

    C. How will the HRIS be accessed?

    D. All of the above.

15. The correlation coefficient is a statistical measurement that is useful for:

    A. Determining whether or not one variable affects another

    B. Compensating for data that may be out of date

    C. Determining which variables are outside acceptable ranges

    D. Describing standards of quality

16. The process of identifying risks and taking steps to minimize them is referred to as:

    A. Liability management

    B. Risk management

    C. Qualitative analysis

    D. Risk assessment

17. When an employer wants to obtain insight into employee goals, job satisfaction, and provide career counseling to those in the work group, the most effective method to utilize would be

    A. An employee survey

    B. A skip-level interview

    C. An employee focus group

    D. A brown-bag lunch

18. Examples of workplace ethics issues include:

   A. Workplace privacy

   B. Conflicts of interest

   C. Whistle-blowing

   D. All of the above

19. Which of the following statements about substance abuse policies is *not* true?

   A. Substance abuse policies identify who will be tested.

   B. Federal law requires all employers to implement substance abuse policies.

   C. An effective policy describes when tests will occur and what drugs will be tested.

   D. An effective policy describes what happens to employees who test positive.

20. Which one of the following statements is true of a hostile work environment?

   A. When a single incident of unwanted touching occurs, a hostile work environment has been created.

   B. A hostile work environment may be created when an individual witnesses the ongoing harassment of a coworker.

   C. A hostile work environment can only be created by a supervisor.

   D. A grievance procedure and policy against discrimination protect employers from hostile work environment claims.

21. An HR audit is designed to help management

   A. Improve employee morale

   B. Analyze HR policies, programs, and procedures against applicable legal requirements

   C. Improve HR effectiveness

   D. All of the above

22. Which of the following is a productivity type of statistical HR measurement?

   A. Turnover and retention

   B. Cost per hire

   C. Revenue per employee

   D. Job satisfaction

23. Which of the following is an example of a strategic OD intervention?

   A. Leadership development

   B. Total quality management

   C. A learning organization

   D. Teambuilding activities

24. A statement of cash flows is a financial report that tells you:

   A. The financial condition of the business at a specific point in time

   B. Where the money used to operate the business came from

   C. The financial results of operations over a period of time

   D. How much money is owed to the company by its customers

25. According to the Copyright Act of 1976, which of the following is most likely to be considered a fair use of copyrighted material?

   A. Distributing 30 copies of a chapter in a book to a study group

   B. Copying a book for 10 staff members of a nonprofit organization

   C. Distributing 30 copies of a paragraph in a book to a study group

   D. None of the above

26. A PEST analysis is used during the strategic planning process. PEST is an acronym for:

   A. Political, environmental, strengths, threats

   B. Political, economic, specific, timely

   C. Political, economic, social, technology

   D. Product, environment, social, technology

27. Which of the following is a characteristic of the Delphi technique?

   A. It is a quantitative tool used to build consensus.

   B. It is a structured meeting format.

   C. The participants never meet.

   D. It requires a facilitator to guide the process.

28. The Occupational Safety and Health Act of 1970 grants employees the right to do all of the following *except*:

   A. Be advised of potential safety hazards

   B. Speak privately to an OSHA inspector during an inspection

   C. Observe the employer when measuring and monitoring workplace hazards

   D. View detailed reports of all workplace accidents

29. Which of the following alternative staffing methods would be *most* appropriate for a company with ongoing yet sporadic needs for a specific job to be done?

   A. Intern program

   B. On-call worker

   C. Seasonal worker

   D. Temp worker

30. A standard employment practice that seems to be fair, yet results in discrimination against a protected class is a description of:

    A. Disparate treatment

    B. Disparate impact

    C. Adverse impact

    D. Unfair treatment

31. The Economic Growth and Tax Relief Reconciliation Act of 2001

    A. Requires pension plans to account for employee contributions separately from employer contributions

    B. Allows employers to contribute a percentage of company earnings to retirement plans each year

    C. Allows employees over 50 years old to make catch up contributions to retirement accounts

    D. Requires employer pension contributions to be funded on a quarterly basis

32. Measuring staffing needs against sales volume could be done most effectively by using which of the following techniques?

    A. A multiple linear regression

    B. A ratio

    C. A simulation model

    D. A simple linear regression

33. Which of the following points is important to effective lobbying, that is, attempting to influence or persuade an elected official to pass, defeat, or modify a piece of legislation?

    A. Learn how the legislative and political process works.

    B. Begin by using persuasion to convince the elected official to accept your position.

    C. Make big financial contributions.

    D. Let the elected official choose a solution rather than present a proposal solution.

34. The Vietnam Era Veterans Readjustment Assistance Act (VEVRAA) requires that

    A. All contractors list all job openings with state employment agencies

    B. All employers list all job openings with state employment agencies

    C. State employment agencies give preference to Vietnam veterans for senior-level management position referrals

    D. State employment agencies give preference to Vietnam veterans for positions lasting three days or longer

35. The FLSA requires employers to pay nonexempt employees for time spent:

A. At home while waiting to be called to work

B. At work reading a book while waiting for an assignment

C. Attending a voluntary training program

D. Commuting to work

36. The _____ seating arrangement is best for case discussions where everyone can observe each other and a trainer.

A. theater style

B. U-shaped style

C. classroom style

D. banquet style

37. A process for reducing the impact of bias during performance reviews by using multiple raters is known as:

A. Inter-rater reliability

B. An MBO review

C. A rating scale

D. Paired comparison

38. According to the OSHA inspection priorities, which type of workplace hazard receives first priority for an inspection?

A. Catastrophes and fatal accidents

B. Programmed high-hazard inspections

C. Imminent danger

D. Employee complaints

39. A lockout occurs when

A. The employees shut down operations by refusing to work.

B. The employer refuses to allow the union to unionize the workplace.

C. The employer shuts down operations to keep employees from working.

D. The employees patrol the entrance to the business.

40. Total quality management focuses all employees on producing products that meet customer needs. This is done by:

A. Eliminating processes that waste time and materials

B. Developing a high level of expertise in all employees

C. Sharing information with all levels in the organization

D. Balancing the needs of all stakeholders in the organization

41. A high-involvement organization is an example of what type of OD intervention?

    A. Human process

    B. Human resource management

    C. Techno-structural

    D. Strategic

42. An employee earning $22,500 per year supervises three other employees and spends 35 hours per week on essential job duties that require discretion and independent judgment. This employee is

    A. Exempt, based on the executive exemption test

    B. Exempt, based on the administrative exemption test

    C. Nonexempt, based on the salary basis requirement

    D. Nonexempt

43. Health and wellness programs are beneficial for employers because they:

    A. Increase productivity, reduce medical costs, and attract top-quality job candidates

    B. Provide nutrition counseling, exercise programs, and health education programs

    C. Require employees to lose weight, stop smoking, and avoid substance abuse

    D. Provide on-site opportunities for physical fitness

44. An effective progressive disciplinary process begins with

    A. A written warning

    B. A verbal warning

    C. A suspension

    D. Coaching or counseling

45. Which of the following would be considered an extrinsic reward?

    A. Challenging work on a new project

    B. A 10 percent salary increase

    C. A feeling of accomplishment after completing a tough assignment

    D. Recognition by the CEO at a company meeting

46. "Thanks for such a great presentation! You'll always have a job with us." This is an example of

    A. The duty of good faith and fair dealing

    B. An express contract

    C. An implied contract

    D. Fraudulent misrepresentation

47. Samantha is hiring an outside sales rep for a new sales territory. Part of the selection process included an assessment test that measures successful sales characteristics. Samantha scored particularly high on the test. During the interview, Christopher, the hiring manager, had some concerns about how well Samantha would fit into the company culture, but when he learned how high she scored on the test, he immediately decided to hire her. What bias could be at work in this situation?

A. Halo effect

B. Knowledge-of-predictor effect

C. Cultural noise effect

D. Stereotyping effect

48. The Excelsior list is

A. A list of all employees in the bargaining unit provided by the employer to the union

B. A list of the employees who do not want the union to represent them

C. A list of the employees who have signed authorization cards for the union

D. A list of all employees in the bargaining unit provided by the union to the employer

49. Which of the following activities is *not* a responsibility of the operations function of a business?

A. Designing the product

B. Scheduling production runs to coincide with customer demand

C. Ensuring that products or services meet quality standards

D. Determining what new products will be produced

50. Which of the following activities does *not* contribute to ergonomic injuries?

A. Awkward postures

B. Extended vibrations

C. Falling down stairs

D. Contact stress

51. A target benefit plan

A. Uses actuarial formulas to calculate individual pension contribution amounts

B. Requires an actual deferral percentage test to be performed each year

C. Provides a means for employees to become owners of the company

D. Uses a fixed percentage of employee earnings to defer compensation

52. To increase the chances for successful repatriation of employees, the process should include:

A. Development of a qualified pool of candidates for global assignments

B. A formal repatriation program that includes career counseling

C. Setting expectations for repatriation before employees begin global assignments

D. All of the above

Answers to Assessment Test

1. C.   The WARN Act requires employers to provide 60 days' notice when 500 employees or 33 percent of the workforce are laid off, and it requires the number be counted over a period of 90 days. Five employees a week for 3 months is a total of 65 employees (5 employees times 13 weeks) which is 33 percent of the workforce. There are three exceptions to the WARN Act: the "faltering company exception" (A), when knowledge of a layoff will negatively impact the company's ability to obtain additional funding; the "unforeseeable business circumstance" (B), when unexpected circumstances occur; and the "natural disaster" (D) exception. See Chapter 4 for more information.

2. D.   In this case, the organization will be best served by a third-party investigator. The most important consideration in an investigation of sexual harassment is that the investigator is seen as credible and impartial. Since you (A) have become friendly with the accused, it will be difficult to maintain impartiality during an investigation. While the corporate attorney (B) may be selected to conduct investigations, this solution can lead to conflict of interest issues. The direct manager of the accused supervisor (C) may not be viewed as impartial by the accuser or by regulatory agencies. See Chapters 2 and 8 for more information.

3. A.   The federal minimum wage was raised to $5.15 per hour on September 1, 1997. The minimum wage in some states and other localities may be different. Although legislation to increase the minimum wage was defeated by Congress in 2006, when Democrats assume control of both houses in 2007 as a result of the mid-term elections, this legislation will likely be reintroduced. Check the DOL website at www.dol.gov/dol/topic/wages/index.htm for the current minimum wage. See Chapter 6 for more information.

4. C.   The National Labor Relations Board (NLRB) determines which jobs will be included in the bargaining unit based on the "community of interest" shared by the requirements of the jobs. See Chapter 7 for more information.

5. A.   Vroom explains his theory with three terms: expectancy (the individual's assessment of their ability to achieve the goal), instrumentality (whether or not the individual believes they are capable of achieving the goal), and valence (whether or not the anticipated goal is worth the effort required to achieve it). Adams' Equity Theory (B) states that people are constantly comparing what they put into work to what they get from it. McClelland's Acquired Needs Theory (C) states that people are motivated by one of three factors: achievement, affiliation, or power. McGregor's Theory X and Theory Y (D) explains how managers relate to employees. Theory X managers are autocratic, believing that employees do not want to take responsibility. Theory Y managers encourage employees to participate in the decision-making process, believing that they respond to challenges. See Chapters 2 and 5 for more information.

6. B.   A continuous feedback review process is most effective because it provides immediate feedback to employees, enabling them to correct performance issues before they become major problems. In a field review (A), reviews are conducted by someone other than the direct supervisor. Forced ranking (C) is an evaluation method in which all employees are listed in order of their value to the work group. The BARS process (D) identifies the most important job requirements and creates statements that describe varying levels of performance. See Chapter 5 for more information.

7. A.   An excess deferral plan makes up the difference between what an executive could have contributed to a qualified plan if there had not been a limit on contributions and how much was actually contributed because of the discrimination test required by ERISA. These plans are nonqualified because they are not protected by ERISA; they are limited to a small group of executives or highly compensated employees. A target benefit plan (B) is a hybrid with elements of defined benefit and money purchase plans. A money purchase plan (C) defers a fixed percentage of employee earnings. A cash balance plan (D) combines elements of defined benefit and defined contribution plans. See Chapter 6 for more information.

8. C.   Distance learning is similar to a lecture in that a presenter provides information to a group of participants but does not require active participation. Vestibule training (A) is a form of simulation training. Demonstration (B) is an experiential training method. Self-study (D) is an active training method. See Chapters 2 and 5 for more information.

9. A.   OSHA consultants provide free services to assist employers in identifying workplace hazards and the standards that apply in their workplaces. The consulting service requires employers to abate any hazards that are identified during the consultation but does not fine them for violations. To receive a free consultation, employers must agree to advise OSHA of changes in operating processes that may require additional consultations. For more information, see Chapter 8.

10. B.   The purpose of a diversity initiative is to increase the effectiveness of an already diverse workforce by educating the employee population about the benefits of a diverse workforce, which include increased creativity (A) and an enhanced ability to attract customers (C). See Chapter 2 for more information.

11. C.   The Supreme Court determined in *Automobile Workers v. Johnson Controls, Inc.* that it is the responsibility of prospective parents to protect their unborn children. While employers must provide information about potential hazards, the employer may not decide for the employee whether or not to work in a job that poses a risk to an unborn child. For more information, see Chapter 8.

12. D.   HIPAA prohibits health insurance providers from discriminating on the basis of health status and limits restrictions for preexisting conditions. HIPAA does not prevent HR from investigating claims (A) issues as long as the employee provides written permission. COBRA requires continuation of health benefits (B). EPO networks (C) are established by physicians connected to a hospital. See Chapter 6 for more information.

13. C.   The concept of human relations was first introduced in the 1920s and challenged previous assumptions that people work only for economic reasons and could be motivated to increase productivity simply by increasing monetary incentives. Human resource management (A) is the business function responsible for activities related to attracting and retaining employees, including workforce planning, training and development, compensation, employee and labor relations, and safety and security. Strategic management (B) is the process by which organizations look for competitive advantages, create value for customers, and execute plans to achieve goals. Human resource development (D) is the functional area of human resources focused on upgrading and maintaining employee skills and developing employees for additional responsibilities. See Chapters 2 and 5 for more information.

14. D. A needs analysis will provide answers to these questions as well as whether or not the HRIS will be integrated with payroll or other systems and what kinds of reports will be produced. See Chapters 2 and 3 for more information.

15. A. The correlation coefficient is useful in determining whether or not two factors are connected. For example, the correlation coefficient will tell you whether an increase in resignations is related to a change in location of the worksite, and if so, whether the change had a strong impact on resignations. See Chapter 2 for more information.

16. B. Risk management identifies areas of possible legal exposure for the organization and reduces those risks with preventive actions. Liability management (A) occurs after a liability is incurred, while risk management seeks to prevent liability. Qualitative analysis (C) covers several subjective tools for analysis. A risk assessment (D) is used to determine how likely it is that an emergency will occur. See Chapters 2 and 8 for more information.

17. B. A skip-level interview provides an opportunity for a manager's manager to obtain insight into the goals and satisfaction of employees in the work group. An employee survey (A) is best used to gather information on various issues that can be collated and summarized. A focus group (B) can be utilized to involve employees in the decision making process. A brown bag lunch (D) is an effective way for senior managers to meet with small groups of employees to answer questions about the company goals and mission and to obtain feedback about operations. See Chapter 7 for more information.

18. D. Workplace privacy, conflicts of interest, and whistle-blowing are all examples of workplace ethics issues. Ethics are considered a standard of conduct and moral judgment defined by the processes that occur and the consequences of these processes. See Chapter 3 for more information.

19. B. The Drug-Free Workplace Act of 1988 requires only federal contractors and subcontractors to establish substance abuse policies. A fair and effective policy will describe which employees will be tested (A), whether it is all or specific job groups. The policy should describe (C) when tests will be done (pre-employment, randomly, upon reasonable suspicion, or according to a predetermined schedule), what drugs are included in the process, and the consequences for employees who test positive (D). For more information, see Chapter 8.

20. B. A coworker who witnesses the ongoing harassment of another individual may have an actionable claim of a hostile work environment. A single incident of unwanted touching (A), unless it is particularly offensive or intimidating, will not reach the threshold of a hostile work environment established by the courts. A hostile work environment may be created by any individuals in the workplace, including customers, vendors, or visitors, in addition to supervisors or coworkers (C). In the case of *Meritor Savings Bank v. Vinson*, the Supreme Court held that the mere existence of a grievance procedure and anti-harassment policy (D) does not necessarily protect an employer from hostile work environment claims. See Chapter 7 for more information.

21. D. An HR audit is an organized process designed to identify key aspects of HR in the organization such as employee morale, HR policies, programs, and procedures, and HR effectiveness. See Chapter 3 for more information.

22. C.   There are three types of statistical HR measurements: employee measures, such as turn-over/retention (A) and job satisfaction (D); productivity measures, such as revenue per employee and OSHA incident rates; and HR activities measures, such as cost per hire (B) and ratio of total employees to HR staff. See Chapter 3 for more information.

23. C.   Learning organizations and knowledge management are examples of strategic OD inter-ventions; TQM (B) is an example of a techno-structural intervention; leadership development (A) and teambuilding activities (D) are examples of human process interventions. See Chapter 5 for more information.

24. B.   A statement of cash flows provides information about the money that flowed through the business. It identifies whether the cash was received from customers, loans, or other sources, how much cash was spent to operate the business, and how much was reinvested in the busi-ness. A balance sheet describes the financial condition of the business at a specific point in time (A). The income, or profit and loss statement, tells you the financial results of operations over a period of time (C). An accounts receivable ledger describes how much money is owed to the company by each customer (D). See Chapters 2 and 3 for more information.

25. C.   Four factors are considered in determining whether or not use of published material is a fair use: the purpose of the use, the nature of the work being copied, how much of the work is copied, and what economic effect copying the material will have on the market value of the work. For more information, see Chapter 5.

26. C.   A PEST analysis is used to scan the political, economic, social, and technological condi-tions in the external environment to determine what impact those conditions will have on the success of the organization. See Chapter 3 for more information.

27. C.   The Delphi technique is a qualitative tool for building consensus using a consecutive round of questions that are collated and distributed for review in subsequent rounds. Participants in the process never meet, so this is an advantageous method to use when participants are geo-graphically separated. See Chapter 2 for more information.

28. D.   Employees have the right to review accident reports without information that identifies the employees involved in the accident. For more information, see Chapter 8.

29. B.   An on-call worker is the best solution for situation in which the employer needs the same job to be done on a sporadic basis. This allows the employer to rely on the same person to do the job, reducing training requirements. An intern program (A) would not be appropriate because it is a short-term training solution. Seasonal workers (C) are generally only required at specific times of the year. Temp workers (D) provided by agencies may not be available when needed because they may be on other assignments. See Chapter 4 for more information.

30. B.   Disparate impact occurs when an employment practice that seems to be fair unintention-ally discriminates against members of a protected class. Disparate treatment (A) occurs when a protected group is treated differently than other applicants or employees. An adverse impact (C) is any negative result of a change to any of the terms or conditions of employment. Unfair treatment (D) can refer to any perceived difference in how employees are treated. See Chapter 4 for more information.

31. C. EGTRRA made changes to pension contribution limits and allows employees over 50 to make catch-up pension contributions. See Chapter 6 for more information.

32. D. A simple linear regression measures one variable against another. Multiple linear regression (A) measures more than one variable against others. A ratio (B) compares one number to another. A simulation model uses a computer program (C) to predict the possible outcomes of different business scenarios. See Chapters 2 and 4 for more information.

33. A. To be effective, most experts agree that it is best to first do your homework, that is, learn how the legislative and political process works. In this way, you can participate effectively in the process. Persuasive skills (B) are useful in presenting your point of view. Big financial contributions (C) are often used by lobbyists to ensure elected representatives will listen to their points of view. Elected officials often choose solutions proposed by a variety of constituents (D), while lobbyists prefer to present a proposed solution to elected officials. See Chapter 3 for more information.

34. D. VEVRAA applies to government contractors and requires that all job openings be listed with state employment agencies *except* those that will be filled from within, are for senior-level management positions, or will last less than three days. See Chapter 4 for more information.

35. B. A nonexempt employee who is waiting for an assignment while at work must be paid for the time spent waiting. See Chapter 6 for more information.

36. B. Theater style (A) is best for lectures, films, and so on, while classroom style (C) is best for listening to presentations. Banquet style (D) is best for small group discussions, and the U-shaped style (B) is best for case discussions where everyone can observe each other and a trainer. For more information, see Chapter 5.

37. A. Inter-rater reliability seeks to reduce bias by having multiple reviewers rate an individual's performance and averaging the ratings. Management by objectives (B) establishes goals at the beginning of a review period and rates how well the goals were achieved. A rating scale (C) is one method of performance appraisal. The paired comparison (D) method compares all employees in a group to each other. For more information, see Chapter 5.

38. C. OSHA inspections that will prevent injury or illness receive first priority for OSHA inspections. An imminent danger hazard (C) is one that has a reasonable certainty of death or serious injury occurring before normal enforcement procedures can occur. Catastrophes and fatal accidents are given second priority. Programmed, high-hazard inspections (B) receive fourth priority, and employee complaints (D) have third. For more information, see Chapter 8.

39. C. A lockout is an action taken by the employer to stop employees from working. A strike occurs when employees refuse to work (A). An employer that refuses to allow the union to conduct an organizing campaign (B) is committing an unfair labor practice. Picketing occurs when employees patrol the entrance to the business (D). See Chapter 7 for more information.

40. A. The TQM concept reviews processes to eliminate waste, relies on teamwork, and involves all members of the organization in meeting customer needs. Personal mastery, a high level of employee expertise (B), is one of the five disciplines of a learning organization. Information sharing (C) is one characteristic of a high involvement organization. The ability to balance stakeholder needs (D) is a requirement of a change agent. See Chapter 5 for more information.

41. C.   Techno-structural interventions address issues of how work gets done in an organization. A high involvement organization is one in which employees at all levels are involved in making decisions about how work is accomplished. Human process interventions (A) are designed to build competencies at the individual level of the organization. HRM interventions (B) focus on HR processes and programs such as selection procedures or performance management that address individual employee needs. Strategic interventions (D) are used to execute changes to an organization's vision, mission, or values. For more information, see Chapter 5.

42. C.   Effective in 2004, employees must be paid a minimum of $455 per week to be exempt from FLSA requirements. This employee earns only $432.69 per week ($22,500/52 weeks = $432.69). While (D) is also correct, the *best* answer is the one that explains why. See Chapter 6 for more information.

43. A.   Employers look for benefit programs that add value to the bottom line. Health and wellness programs do this by increasing productivity and reducing costs. These programs are attractive to job candidates and enhance recruiting efforts. For more information, see Chapter 8.

44. D.   An effective progressive discipline process begins with coaching or counseling, acknowledging good performance, and providing guidance on performance that needs to be changed. Providing ongoing feedback, both positive and negative, reduces the stress level for both employees and supervisors when serious performance issues arise and must be addressed. A written warning (A) is the second step of a formal disciplinary process. A verbal warning (B) is the first step. Suspensions (C) are usually the last step prior to termination. See Chapter 7 for more information.

45. D.   Extrinsic rewards are nonmonetary rewards in which self-esteem comes from others, such as formal recognition for a job well done. Challenging work on a new project (A) is an intrinsic reward. Salary increases (B) are monetary rewards. A feeling of accomplishment after completing a tough assignment (C) is another type of intrinsic reward. See Chapter 6 for more information.

46. B.   An express contract can be oral or written and states what the parties to the contract agree to do. In the absence of an offer letter with an at will statement that says it can't be modified except in writing by the CEO or some other high level executive, statements meant to convey appreciation can sometimes create this type of contract. The duty of good faith and fair dealing (A) is a common law doctrine that parties to an oral or written contract have an obligation to act in a fair and honest manner to facilitate achievement of the contract goals. An implied contract (C) can be created by conduct and doesn't have to be stated explicitly. Fraudulent misrepresentation (D) occurs when an employer makes false statements to entice a candidate to join the company. See Chapter 7 for more information.

47. B.   The knowledge-of-predictor effect occurs when an interviewer is aware that a candidate has scored particularly high or low on an assessment test and allows this to affect the hiring decision. The halo effect (A) occurs when the interviewer allows a single positive characteristic of the candidate to overshadow other considerations. Cultural noise (C) occurs when a candidate gives answers they think the interviewer wants to hear. Stereotyping (D) occurs when the interviewer makes assumptions about a candidate based on generalizations about the group the candidate belongs to (for example, women). See Chapter 4 for more information.

48. A.   Once an election has been scheduled, the employer must provide a list, known as an Excelsior list, containing the names and address of all employees in the bargaining unit determined by the NLRB. See Chapter 7 for more information.

49. D.   Marketing (or in some companies, product management) is responsible for determining what new products will be produced based on market research designed to find out what products customers are willing to purchase. See Chapter 3 for more information.

50. C.   Ergonomic injuries are caused by repeated stress to a part of the body. A fall down the stairs is a single occurrence and therefore not an ergonomic injury. For more information, see Chapter 8.

51. A.   A target benefit plan is a hybrid plan that has similarities to defined benefit pension plans and money purchase plans. These plans use actuarial formulas to calculate individual pension contribution amounts. Deferral percentage tests (B) are required each year for 401(k) plans. An ESOP provides a means for employees to become owners of the company (C). A money purchase plan (D) defers a fixed percentage of employee earnings. See Chapter 6 for more information.

52. D.   Organizations that are able to successfully repatriate employees after global assignments do so by carefully selecting candidates for those assignments, setting appropriate expectations before the assignment begins, and establishing a formal program to assist employees in reintegrating into the home office after a global assignment. See Chapter 5 for more information.

Chapter

1

Certifying Human Resource Professionals

Human resources. Ask ten different people what human resources is or does, and you'll get at least eight different answers. Management advisor, recruiter, employee advocate, paper pusher, union negotiator, counselor, policy police, coach, mediator, administrative expert, corporate conscience, strategic business partner, and the dreaded "party planner"—these are just a few of the roles that those both inside and outside of the profession think we play. Some of these descriptions are based on misperceptions from nonpractitioners, others describe the roles we aspire to attain within our organizations, and some describe what we do each day. The HR body of knowledge (BOK) provides the means by which we define ourselves to the larger business community and communicates to them what roles are appropriate for the human resource function in an organization. This chapter provides you with an overview of HR certification: the growth of human resources as a profession, a little history about the certification process, a discussion of the types of professional HR certification (there are three), and the required and recommended eligibility standards for each. You'll also learn about the HR body of knowledge and a few tips to assist you in preparing for the PHR and SPHR exams.

The Human Resource Profession

By the end of the nineteenth century, the industrial revolution had changed the nature of work—businesses were no longer small organizations that could be managed by a single owner with a few trusted supervisors. As a result, many support functions were delegated to individuals who began to specialize in specific areas. One of these functions became known as industrial relations or personnel and evolved into what we know today as human resources. As businesses continued to become even larger entities, standards began to develop as practitioners met and shared information about the ways they did their jobs. The need for more formal training standards in various aspects of this new function became apparent, and colleges began to develop courses of study in the field. By the middle of the twentieth century, the personnel function was part of almost every business and numerous individuals worked in the field. A small group of these individuals got together in 1948 and determined that personnel was developing into a profession and was in need of a national organization to define it, represent practitioners, and promote its interests in the larger business community. Thus, the American Society for Personnel Administration (ASPA) was born.

For the first 16 years of its existence, ASPA was a strictly volunteer organization. By 1964, membership had grown from the small group of charter members in 1948 to over 3,100 members—enough to support a small staff to serve the members. With membership growing, the discussion quite naturally turned to the topic of defining the practice of personnel as a profession. While there are similarities in the characteristics of established professions, such as a code of ethics, a specific and unique body of knowledge, and an education specific to the profession, there are aspects to most professions that set them apart from each other, and personnel was no different. To solicit the contribution of practitioners in this process, ASPA cosponsored a conference with Cornell University's School of Industrial Relations to determine how best to define the characteristics that made personnel a profession. This conference spawned a year of consideration and debate among ASPA members.

According to the HRCI website, the culmination of this process was an agreement on five characteristics that were needed to set personnel apart as a profession. The original characteristics were only slightly different than the following characteristics currently listed by HRCI:

1. The HR profession must be defined by a common body of knowledge which must be the subject of courses of study at educational institutions.

2. There must be a code of ethics for the HR profession.

3. HR as a profession must be the focus of ongoing research and development to move it forward in keeping with changing business needs.

4. There must be a certification program for HR professionals.

5. There must be a national professional association that represents the views of practitioners in the larger business community and in the legislative process.

Once ASPA had a clear definition of what was required for the practice of personnel to be considered a profession, the members knew what needed to be done to make this a reality: develop a body of knowledge and a certification program to evaluate the competence of practitioners.

Development of the Human Resource Body of Knowledge

With their goal clearly set, ASPA members went about the process of developing a body of knowledge for the profession. ASPA created a task force to study and report on the issues involved and recommended a course of action. The ASPA Accreditation Institute (AAI) was formed in 1975 with a mandate to define a national body of knowledge for the profession and develop a program to measure the knowledge of its practitioners.

As a first step in the process, AAI created six functional areas for the BOK:

- Employment, Placement, and Personnel Planning
- Training and Development
- Compensation and Benefits
- Health, Safety, and Security
- Employee and Labor Relations
- Personnel Research (later replaced by Management Practices)

Over time, as personnel evolved into human resources, ASPA changed its name to the *Society for Human Resource Management (SHRM)* to reflect changes in the profession. At that point, AAI became the *Human Resource Certification Institute (HRCI)* for the same reason. These associations exist today to represent and certify the profession.

HRCI ensures the continued relevance of the BOK to actual practice with periodic codification studies. The first of these occurred in 1979; subsequent studies were conducted in 1988, 1993, 1997, 2000, and 2005. These reviews enlisted the participation of thousands of human resource experts in ongoing assessments of what a human resource generalist needs to know to be fully competent.

As with all previous codification studies, HRCI began the most current review in January 2005 with the question, "What should a human resource practitioner know and be able to apply to be considered a competent HR generalist?" HRCI commissioned the Professional Examination Service (PES) to conduct a *practice analysis study* to obtain information from a variety of sources on the existing state of human resource practices as well as trends predicted for future needs of the profession. Under the guidance of PES, additional information was collected through the use of critical incident interviews and focus groups. Finally, approximately 6,000 certified professionals were surveyed to obtain their views on the current and future needs of the human resource profession.

The most recent practice analysis study culminated in a major revision to the BOK announced in 2006. The resulting six functional areas constitute the current human resource body of knowledge:

- Strategic Management
- Workforce Planning and Employment
- Human Resource Development
- Total Rewards
- Employee and Labor Relations
- Risk Management

Clearly, the nomenclature has changed over the past 30 years, yet the basic functional areas of HR have remained fairly stable. Significant changes have occurred, however, within the six functional areas, ensuring the relevance of human resource practice to the changing needs of business in the twenty-first century. A major change occurred with the 2001 practice analysis to ensure that HR professionals understand, and are conversant in, the language of business when "Strategic Management" replaced "Management Practices" as a functional area. This change reflects the increasing need for practitioners to not only fully understand the traditional operational and administrative requirements of human resources, but to also have a broad understanding of other functional areas in business organizations. The 2005 practice analysis resulted in two more changes to the BOK: "Total Rewards" replaces "Compensation and Benefits" and "Risk Management" replaces "Occupational Health, Safety, and Security."

Initially, the certification process was a series of exams, one for each level of certification in each of the six functional areas that was identified by the AAI task force. A few years later, HRCI added a generalist exam. The intent of the process in this early stage was to serve the needs of both specialists and generalists. Because there were two levels of certification for each functional area, the process was quite cumbersome and not a little confusing. Eventually the popularity of the generalist exam led to elimination of the specialist certifications, which left just two: Professional in Human Resources (PHR) and Senior Professional in Human Resources (SPHR). These are the certification levels in existence today.

As the practice of human resources continues to evolve to meet the needs of international business operations, more emphasis is being placed on the area of global human resources. In response, HRCI developed a new certification, the Global Professional in Human Resources (GPHR). The first GPHR exam was administered in spring 2004. As of March 2006, 396 practitioners have been certified in global practices.

 The *GPHR: Global Professional in Human Resources Certification Study Guide* will be available from Sybex in spring 2007.

As it continues to advance certification opportunities for HR professionals, HRCI announced in the summer of 2006 that a BOK for the first state certification, for California, is being readied for the spring 2007 exam cycle.

Defining the Functional Areas of the BOK

Once HRCI collated the information from the practice analysis study, test specifications were developed to define each functional area. The test specifications have two parts: responsibilities and knowledge requirements. The responsibilities describe areas of practice with which a fully qualified generalist must be familiar. For example, one of the areas of responsibility for Risk Management is "Develop and monitor business continuity and disaster recovery plans." The knowledge requirements describe the information needed to master the responsibilities. Continuing the example from Risk Management, knowledge of "Business continuity and disaster recovery plans (for example, data storage and backup, alternative work locations and procedures)" is needed for full understanding of the Risk Management function.

For the 2007 BOK, HRCI has identified some responsibilities as "PHR Only" or "SPHR Only" within the functional areas. As you are reading Chapters 2–8, look for these icons in the margins:

PHR ONLY   **SPHR** ONLY

While the body of knowledge is the same for both exam levels (PHR and SPHR), the functional areas in each test are weighted differently to distinguish the different experience requirements of candidates for each level. To understand how this works, let's take a look at what each functional area covers.

Strategic Management   Looks at the "big picture" of the organization and requires an understanding of overall business operations, basic knowledge of other functional areas in the organization, and the ability to interact and work effectively with those functions. Strategic Management ensures that traditional HR activities contribute to and support organization goals through the HR planning process, incorporating change initiatives when needed to move the organization forward and providing tools to measure HR effectiveness.

Workforce Planning and Employment   Covers activities related to planning for and managing entry into and exit from the organization to meet changing business needs.

Human Resource Development   Utilizes training, development, change, and performance management programs to ensure that individuals with the required knowledge, skills, and abilities are available when needed to accomplish organization goals.

Total Rewards   Concerns the development, implementation, and maintenance of compensation and benefit systems to support organization goals.

Employee and Labor Relations   Addresses the employment relationship in both union and nonunion environments.

Risk Management   Covers programs that reduce or eliminate organizational risks from health, safety, and security issues.

Core Knowledge Requirements of the BOK

In addition to the six functional areas of the BOK, HRCI identified 22 core knowledge requirements for the HR body of knowledge, all of which have implications in all six of the functional areas. Among the core knowledge requirements are topics such as needs assessment and analysis, liability and risk analysis, and motivation concepts and applications to name just a few. I'll discuss each core knowledge topic in more detail in Chapter 2, "Core Knowledge Requirements for HR Professionals."

In the meantime, as an example, let's take a look at how one of the core requirements, "Communication skills and strategies," applies in each of the six functional areas:

Strategic Management   Building consensus among senior managers for communicating a reorganization to the workforce

Workforce Planning and Employment   Communicating a sexual harassment policy to new hires

Human Resource Development   Introducing a new performance management process to the workforce

Total Rewards   Communicating company benefit plan changes to employees affected by the changes

Employee and Labor Relations   Advising management on appropriate responses to a union organizing campaign

Risk Management   Introducing an emergency response plan to the workforce

As you can see, each of these scenarios requires a different strategy in order to effectively communicate necessary information to the intended audience. These core knowledge requirements can be the basis for exam questions in any of the functional areas, so it is important to not only be familiar with them in general terms but also to understand how they apply to each area.

Now that I've introduced the six functional areas in broad terms, let's look at what each exam is intended to measure and how the weightings reflect this in each exam.

Certification Levels

The questions asked most often by those considering taking the step toward certification are, "Which level should I choose? Is the PHR easier than the SPHR? What is the difference?" Choosing an exam level is an individual choice—if you meet the eligibility requirements (which will be discussed in the next section), the choice is really up to you. As to whether one is easier than another, I doubt that anyone who has taken them would say that either test is easy. They are equally difficult, but in different ways. Let's take a look now at what each of the certifications is intended to measure.

Professional in Human Resources (PHR)   The PHR certification measures a candidate's ability to apply HR knowledge at an operational or technical level according to the HRCI website. This exam tests a candidate's ability to apply HR knowledge to handle situations occurring on a day-to-day basis. PHR candidates are skilled in implementing processes and procedures and are knowledgeable in the requirements of employment legislation for problems or situations with a narrow organizational impact. They are able to develop solutions by drawing on a variety of sources and knowledge that apply to a particular situation.

The functional areas in the PHR exam are weighted to reflect its emphasis on the operational, administrative, and tactical application of the elements of the body of knowledge. Table 1.1 shows the functional area weightings for the PHR exam.

In the PHR exam, then, the bulk of the questions (48 percent) are related to operational and tactical application of the responsibilities and knowledge for Workforce Planning and Employment and Employee and Labor Relations.

TABLE 1.1   PHR Functional Area Weighting

Functional Area	Exam Weight
Strategic Management	12%
Workforce Planning and Employment	26%
Human Resource Development	17%

TABLE 1.1 PHR Functional Area Weighting *(continued)*

Functional Area	Exam Weight
Total Rewards	16%
Employee and Labor Relations	22%
Risk Management	7%

Senior Professional in Human Resources (SPHR)   The SPHR certification measures a candidate's strategic perspective and ability to pull information from a variety of sources to address issues with organization-wide impact. This exam measures the candidate's ability to apply HR knowledge and experience in developing policies that will meet the organization's long-term strategic objectives and have impact on the entire organization.

The SPHR exam measures a senior-level candidate's strategic ability to integrate HR processes into the "big picture" of an organization's needs and to develop policies to support the achievement of business goals. Table 1.2 demonstrates how the weightings for the functional areas reflect this.

TABLE 1.2 SPHR Functional Area Weighting

Functional Area	Exam Weight
Strategic Management	29%
Workforce Planning and Employment	17%
Human Resource Development	17%
Total Rewards	12%
Employee and Labor Relations	18%
Risk Management	7%

From these weightings, you see that 47 percent of the questions on the SPHR exam are related to the senior candidate's ability to develop effective strategic plans for successful business operations (Strategic Management) and policies to guide employment relationships in the organization (Employee and Labor Relations).

The *PHR/SPHR/GPHR Certification Handbook* contains the most current listing of the HRCI test specs. Because both the PHR and SPHR exams are built around them, I strongly urge those preparing for the test to review the *Handbook* and familiarize themselves with the test specs for each functional area prior to reading the related chapter. The HRCI website www.hrci.org provides information on downloading or ordering this free publication.

Eligibility Requirements

As I've mentioned, complete information on eligibility requirements for the exams is available in the *PHR/SPHR/GPHR Certification Handbook*, and HRCI, of course, makes the final decision as to whether or not a candidate meets them. In this section, I will provide a broad overview of the requirements, along with some suggestions based on the experience of successful candidates.

Any individual with two years of experience in human resource management at the exempt level meets the minimum requirement for either exam. (If you are unsure what this means, see Chapter 6, "Total Rewards," in which I discuss exemption status in some detail.) In order to meet the two-year experience requirements, candidates must spend 51 percent of their work time on exempt-level human resource activities. It's important to note that almost all supervisors and managers perform some HR functions as part of their daily requirements but because these activities are not usually the major function of the position and constitute less than 51 percent of their time at work, this experience most likely would not meet the requirements established by HRCI.

So, the minimum requirements are pretty simple. Let's be realistic for a moment, though. The PHR and SPHR exams do not just measure book knowledge. They measure your ability to apply that knowledge in work situations. The more experience you have in applying knowledge at work, the greater your chances of passing the test. To give candidates an idea of what is needed to be successful (as opposed to what is minimally required), HRCI recommends PHR candidates have 2–4 years of experience prior to taking the exam; for SPHR candidates, they recommend 6–8 years. HRCI provides profiles of the ideal candidate for each of the exams, which can be found in the *PHR/SPHR/GPHR Certification Handbook*.

Recommendations for PHR candidates   To summarize the ideal PHR profile, HRCI suggests that candidates have between two and four years of professional-level, generalist HR experience before they sit for the exam. PHR candidates generally report to a more senior HR professional within the organization and during the course of their daily work focus on implementation of programs and processes that have already been developed. PHR experience focuses on providing direct services to HR customers within the organization.

Recommendations for SPHR candidates   According to HRCI, the ideal SPHR candidate has six to eight years of increasingly responsible HR experience. An SPHR needs to be able to see the "big picture" for the entire organization, not just what works best for the human resource department. This requires the ability to anticipate the impact of policies and decisions on the achievement of organizational goals. SPHR candidates are business focused and understand that HR policies and processes must integrate with and serve the needs of the larger organization. While a PHR's decisions and activities have a more limited effect within narrow segments of the organization, decisions made by SPHR candidates will have organization-wide impact.

Student or recent graduate requirements   HRCI has a program that allows college students who will graduate in one year or less and those who have graduated less than one year ago to take the PHR exam without having met the experience requirement. However, students or recent graduates who pass the exam may not use the PHR designation until they provide documentation of having met the two-year minimum experience requirement.

Recertification

Up until 1996, HRCI awarded lifetime certification to individuals who successfully recertified twice. At that time the policy was changed to reflect the need for professionals to remain current with developments in the field. As a result, the lifetime certification program ended and, with the exception of those who were awarded lifetime certification prior to 1996, all PHRs and SPHRs are now required to recertify every three years.

There are a number of ways to be recertified; they fall into two basic categories: recertification by exam or professional development.

Recertification by exam   HR professionals may retake either exam to maintain certification at that level. Information on recertifying by exam is available in the *PHR/ SPHR/GPHR Certification Handbook*.

Professional development   To recertify on this basis, PHRs and SPHRs must complete 60 hours of professional development during the three-year period. These 60 hours may be accomplished in a variety of ways. One of the more common is through attending continuing education courses, including workshops and seminars related to HR functions. Another way to earn recertification credit is by developing and/or presenting HR courses, seminars, or workshops. Recertification credit for teaching a specific course is awarded only for the first time it is taught.

On-the-job experience can also be the basis for recertification credit: the first time you perform a new task or project that adds to your mastery of the HR BOK, you may earn credits for the work if it meets criteria established by HRCI.

Professionals who take on leadership roles in HR organizations or on government boards or commissions may earn certification for those activities if they meet the criteria established by HRCI.

Finally, certified professionals receive credit for membership in SHRM and other national professional associations or societies. HRCI publishes the *PHR/ SPHR/GPHR Recertification Guide* to provide detailed information on the various methods of recertifying and the amount of credit that can be earned for the different activities. This guide may be downloaded at www.hrci.org, or you may request a copy by calling HRCI at (866) 898-4724.

The Test

Now, just a little bit of information about the test.

One question asked of me frequently by candidates preparing for the exam is, "What are the questions like?" The HRCI website provides a very detailed explanation of testing theory and question development. In this section, I've summarized what I think is the most practical information for those preparing to take the exams. Those of you who are interested in the details will find more than you ever wanted to know about it on the HRCI website at www.hrci.org/faq/faq_3.html#1.

The questions in these tests are designed to measure whether candidates meet the objectives established by HRCI as the standard required for a minimally qualified human resource professional to achieve certification. The exam questions are designed to assess the depth and breadth of candidates' knowledge and their ability to apply it in practice. Questions at the basic level examine a candidate's ability to not only recall information but to comprehend it as well. Questions designed to measure knowledge and comprehension constitute the smallest percentage of questions on both the exams, but there are slightly more of them on the PHR exam. Questions at the next level, application, are more complex and require the candidate to apply their knowledge in practical situations that require the ability to differentiate which information is most relevant to the situation and will solve the problem. Questions of this type are the ones most prevalent on both the exams. Questions at the highest level of complexity, synthesis, require candidates to use their knowledge in multifaceted situations by drawing upon information from different areas of the body of knowledge to create the best possible result. They require the ability to review actions taken in a variety of situations and evaluate whether or not the best solution was implemented. This type of question appears on both the exams but is more prevalent on the SPHR.

The exam questions, which HRCI refers to as "items," are developed by two panels of volunteers, all of whom are SPHR-certified professionals trained to write test items for the exams. These panels meet twice a year to review items that each member has written between meetings. Each volunteer generates about 50 questions annually that are then reviewed by the whole panel. Questions that make it through the item-writing panel process move to an item-review panel for additional consideration. As a question travels through either panel, one of three things can happen to it:

1. The item can be rejected as not meeting the criteria for the exam.

2. The item can be returned to the writer for additional work.

3. The item can be forwarded to the next step in the process.

When an item is accepted by the review panel, it moves on to the pretest process for inclusion as an unscored pretest question.

Each item consists of the stem, or premise, and four possible answers: one of these is the correct or best possible answer, and three others are known as distractors. There may be two answers that could be technically correct, but one of them is the best possible answer. As part of the item development process, HRCI requires that the correct answers are documented, and they take great care to ensure that the best possible answer is one that is legally defensible.

Each of the exams consists of 200 multiple-choice test questions (which are used to determine your score) and 25 pretest items (which are not scored), for a total of 225 test items. The exams are four hours long. This means that you will have 1.07 minutes to answer each question. You'll be surprised at how much time this gives you to consider your answers if you are well prepared by your experience and have taken sufficient time to study the test specifications. As you answer practice questions in preparation for the exam, be sure to time yourself so you can get a feel for how much time it takes you to answer each question.

Test candidates often ask why the pretest questions are included on the exam, and the answer is simple: these items are included to validate them prior to inclusion on future exams as scored questions. While the 25 pretest items are not scored, you will not know which questions are the pretest questions while taking the exam, so it's important to treat every question as though it will be scored.

The more you know about how the questions are designed, the better able you will be to focus your study, which leads us to the next section: some tips on preparing for the exam and what to expect on test day.

If you are anything like the tens of thousands of HR professionals who have taken the certification exam since 1976, you are probably a little nervous about how you will do and what is the best way to prepare. In this section, I will provide you with some hints and tips gathered from my experiences as well as from others who have generously shared their experience in taking these exams.

It's *Experiential* and *Federal*

The most important thing to keep in mind, and this can't be stressed enough, is that these exams are *experiential*. That means they test your ability to *apply* knowledge, not just the fact that you *have* knowledge. For this reason, memorizing facts is not all that helpful. With a few exceptions, it is far more important to understand the *concepts* behind laws and practices and how they are best applied in real life situations.

Another crucial factor to keep in mind is that these exams test your ability to apply knowledge of *federal* requirements, so you should be aware of legislation and significant case law that has developed since the 1960s. As experienced professionals are aware, federal law is very often different from the requirements of a particular state. This brings us to our first bit of advice from previous test candidates:

> Do not rely on your past experiences too heavily. Just because you have done it that way at one company doesn't mean it is the right (or legal!) way.
>
> —*Becky Rasmussen, PHR*

> Don't necessarily think of how you would do it at work. It is possible the way your company is doing it is wrong so you will answer the question wrong. Look for the most correct answer and take plenty of practice tests. The more you take, the more familiar you will become with test taking.
>
> —*Susan K. Craft, MS, PHR*

This tip applies to several situations: your state requirements may be different from the federal requirements that are the subject of the test, your company practice may not be up-to-date with current requirements and, in some cases, you may be operating on the basis of a common myth about legal requirements or HR practices that is not, in fact, accurate. One way that HRCI tests the depth of knowledge of candidates is to provide one of those commonly held myths as one of the distractors for a question. It's not really a trick question, but a candidate with minimal experience may not know the difference. As you study, think about why you do things in a particular way, how you got that information, and how sure you are that it is the most current and up-to-date. If it is current, great! You're a step ahead of the study game. If you aren't sure it's the most current, do a little research to find out if it will apply on the exam, if it's a state requirement, or if it's possibly some misinformation that you picked up somewhere along the way.

What the Questions Look Like

As mentioned earlier, the HRCI website goes into a fair amount of detail on the technical aspects of test development. Much of that technical information won't help you in developing a study plan. However, you may find it useful to know the types of questions that the item-writing panels are trained to develop.

In the previous section, I discussed the different parts that make up a test item. Each item begins with a stem, which presents a statement or a question requiring a response. The stems will either ask a question or present an unfinished statement to be completed. Within that context, the stem can be categorized in one of the following ways:

Purpose   To answer these questions, you need to demonstrate that you know the objective of a particular law, regulation, or HR practice.

Ordering   These questions require that you know the sequence of a multipart process or practice. A question may require that you are able to identify what needs to happen before or after any step in the process.

Recognition of error   These questions require you to be familiar with HR practices and federal laws in order to identify practices or actions that are incorrect and to understand why they are.

Cause and effect   To answer a question phrased in this way, you will need to understand the consequences of a practice or action.

Similarity   To correctly answer these questions, you must be able to identify the common elements of two or more practices, ideas, or concepts.

Association   These questions require candidates to form a connection between two concepts or ideas.

Definition   These questions may provide a definition and require that you select the correct term, or they may provide a term and provide four possible definitions.

Finally, SPHR candidates in particular should prepare themselves for scenario-type test items. These items are preceded by a short description of a typical HR situation and are followed by two or more questions that relate back to the same scenario. These items are well suited to test concepts at the synthesis level of complexity.

> My experience was that the actual test differed from any of the prep materials or sample tests that I had seen. The exam questions were differentiated by nuance rather than clear distinctions. Studying from multiple sources helped me be better prepared for this unexpected approach.
>
> —*Lyman Black, SPHR*

Preparing for the Exam

There are a number of options available to assist candidates in preparing for the exams. One option is a self-study program that you put together for yourself based on the test specifications. Another option, depending on your location, is to attend a formal preparation course. In the last few years, informal online study groups have become popular and effective ways to prepare for the exam. Regardless of the option you choose, the most important step is to know what you already know. Then figure out what you need to learn and develop a study plan to help you learn it.

Develop a Study Plan

While many are tempted to jump in and immediately start reading books or taking classes, the best thing you can do for yourself at the outset is to identify where you are right now and what study methods have worked for you in the past and develop a study plan for yourself.

> The study technique that worked best for me was simply making preparation for the test a priority! I outlined a realistic study schedule for myself and stuck to it as much as possible. Plus, I studied away from my everyday environment in order to avoid distractions. For me this was a local bookstore cafe, a table covered with notes, a latte in one hand, and a pack of flashcards in the other...and it worked!
>
> —*Julie O'Brien, PHR*

Where are you right now?   The best way to answer this question is to take the self-assessment test immediately following the Introduction to this book. This will help you to see where your strengths and weaknesses lie. Based on the assessment test and on your work experience, make a list of areas in which you will need to spend the bulk of your time studying (your weaknesses) and the areas you simply need a refresher review (your strengths).

What study methods have worked for you in the past?   This may be easy or hard to determine, depending on how long it's been since you took a class. Make a list of study methods that you have used successfully in the past.

Develop a study plan.   With your list of strengths and weaknesses and the study methods that work for you, create a study plan:

Develop a timeline.   Decide how much time you need to spend on each functional area of the body of knowledge.

Working back from the test date, schedule your study time according to your strengths and weaknesses. You may want to leave time close to the test date for an overall review—be reasonable with yourself! Be sure to factor in work commitments, family events, vacations, and holidays so you don't set yourself up for failure.

Get organized!   Set up folders or a binder with dividers to collect information for each functional area so you know where to find it when you are reviewing the material.

Plan the work, then work the plan!   Make sure you keep up with the plan you have set for yourself.

> Keep up with the reading; do it every week, faithfully. Take notes on what you don't understand, then ask someone about them.
>
> —*Becky Rasmussen, PHR*

> Make sure you don't cram; at least a week before the test, take some days off or make extra time available to study so that you're not cramming the night before.
>
> —*Rose Chang, PHR*

When creating your study plan, did you do the following?

- Assess your strengths and weaknesses by taking the assessment test at the beginning of this book?
- Review the HRCI test specifications?
- Identify study methods that will work for you such as self-study, working with a study partner, using a virtual (online) study group, or taking a formal preparation class?
- Identify useful study materials such as this study guide and CD contents, online HR bulletin boards, current HR books and magazines?
- Develop a study time line?
- Plan to start studying three to four months before the test?
- Allow more time to study weaker areas?
- Allow refresh time for stronger areas?
- Schedule weekly meetings with a study partner?
- Set up a file or a binder with space for each functional area to store all your study materials, questions, and practice tests?
- Allow time two to three weeks before the test for a final review of everything you've studied?
- Simulate the test experience by finding a place to study that is free from distractions and giving yourself 1.07 minutes to answer each bonus exam question from this book? Challenge yourself further by setting a timer to see how well you do?

> Stop studying two days before the test. Rest. Relax. You've done everything you can. Now it's time to prepare mentally and physically for test day.

Study Options

There are several study options available for exam candidates: study partners, self-study, and formal preparation courses are the most common. Whichever option you choose, be sure to review the *PHR/ SPHR/GPHR Certification Handbook*, specifically Appendix A, to ensure that you cover all areas of the test specifications.

Study partners   No matter which study option works best for you, many have found that partnering with someone else is a critical part of the process. Find one or two others who are studying, develop a group study plan, and meet each week to review the material for that week. Working with a reliable study partner makes the process more enjoyable and helps you to stay focused. The ideal study partner is one whose areas of strength coincide with your areas of weakness and vice versa. One effective technique is to prepare the material and "teach" it to your study partner. Teaching your partner one of your weaker areas results in a deeper understanding than just reading or listening to someone else talk about it.

> **Online study groups**   If there is no one local for you to partner with, try an online study group. If you are a member of SHRM, you can find others interested in forming an online study group on the HRCI/Certification bulletin board at `www.shrm.org/forums`. There are also a number of other online communities where you may find study partners, including HR-Man at `www.hr-man.com/`.

> I'd advise anyone to form a study group and meet on a regular basis to read, compare notes, quiz each other, and lend moral support! Not only did I learn a lot from my study partners, I gained some wonderful professional friendships—and we ALL passed!
>
> —*Julie O'Brien, PHR*

> Present the material yourself! Don't just listen, participate. If you teach it, you think of it much differently than if you are sitting passively and listening.
>
> —*Alicia Chatman, SPHR*

> I set up a very small study group; three people. We met once a week until a month before the test, when we met twice a week. It was good to have someone say, "Listen to the question." This made me slow down and review the phrasing and some key words like "most," "not," "least," etc.
>
> —*Patricia Kelleher, SPHR*

Preparation materials   There are several publications designed to prepare candidates for the exams. This book (of course!) is an intense, very focused overview of material you may find on the exam.

Other helpful publications include the SHRM Learning System, available online from the SHRM Store at `www.shrm.org` and the Human Resource Certification Program (HRCP) available at `www.hrcp.com/`.

At the end of this book, Appendix C, "Resources," is a list of additional materials that focus on specific functional areas, and there are many other excellent sources available.

> I think there was a synergistic benefit from applying several approaches rather than using just one technique or single source of information. I used several approaches to prepare: two study guides, a review course, and flash

cards. I also found that my kids enjoyed quizzing me during our times driving to school, sports, etc.

—*Lyman Black, SPHR*

Self-study   Self-study provides you with the greatest flexibility in deciding what areas to focus on. If you go this route, developing a study plan is crucial in keeping you focused (and be sure to use Appendix A of the *PHR/SPHR/GPHR Certification Guide* when you set up your plan). Equally important to this method is finding a study partner to share questions and ideas.

> Capitalize on your resources. Look to guidance from peers, bosses, consultants, subject matter experts, textbooks, white papers, and articles, and anyone/anything else you can find that will complement your knowledge. I made my own flash cards on specific topics where my knowledge was weaker. Those helped a lot, too.
>
> —*Shirley Pincus, SPHR*

Formal preparation courses   A number of organizations sponsor formal preparation courses designed specifically for the exam. These are offered by colleges and universities and by local SHRM chapters in some cases. Contact your local SHRM chapter for information on courses in your area.

Preparation Techniques

To begin with, the best preparation for the exam is solid knowledge of human resource practices and federal employment law combined with broad generalist experience. Because it is experiential in nature, your ability to use HR knowledge in practical situations is the key to success. This is not a test that you can "cram" for, regardless of the materials you use.

> Rewrite the book in your words! Use your experiences to explain the lesson. It will help you remember the lesson.
>
> —*Alicia Chatman, SPHR*

Preparation materials can help provide an organized way of approaching the material. In many cases, you already have the information, you just need a refresher of where it came from and the reason it is appropriate for a particular situation.

> A friend of mine used the practice tests to give me oral exams on the material. This was very helpful because I was not reading the questions, just listening to them and answering them, marking of course the ones that I answered wrong to emphasize my study on that specific topic.
>
> —*Marcela Echeverria*

> I found an "SQ3R" technique (Survey, Question, Read, Recite, Review) effective in studying the materials.
>
> —*Lyman Black, SPHR*

Possibly the best advice to give you is this: don't rely on a single source of information in your preparation. If you have a limited budget, make use of the library to check out books about the various functional areas. If you are financially able and so inclined, take the opportunity to build your personal HR library (and don't forget to read the books while you're at it!). Take a preparation course. Form a study group. Ask questions of your peers at work. Find a mentor willing to answer your questions. Make use of online HR bulletin boards to ask questions and to observe what others ask and the responses they receive.

WARNING A word of caution about HR bulletin boards: although they can be a great source of information and provide a wide range of responses, in some cases, the answers provided are *not correct*. If you make these bulletin boards part of your preparation, make sure you verify the information you receive with other sources.

None of the people who create the preparation materials for the PHR/SPHR exams have special access to the test. The best any preparation materials can do is to provide you with a review of HRCI's test specifications. It is to your advantage to utilize as many sources of information as you can to obtain the broadest possible review of the HR body of knowledge.

Answer as many questions as possible! Whether or not they are the same format as the questions on the exam, they will assist you in recalling information, and that will benefit you during the exam. Aside from the practice questions provided with this book, a great source of questions is the *HRCI Certification Guide*, by Raymond B. Weinberg (SHRM and HRCI, 2005) (not to be confused with the *PHR/SPHR Certification Handbook*). This little book provides 125 practice questions and answers and is available from online booksellers.

> Knowing the material isn't always enough. Many people sitting for the exam have been away from test-taking for a long time. I think it helped me a lot to practice taking tests with time limits. Practice evaluating similar answers and identifying the best of the lot (not always the very best answer, but the best one presented).
>
> —*Judy Wiens, SPHR*

HRCI now also provides a sample test online. There is a fee to take this test, but it does include questions that have been retired from HRCI's test item pool, so it will give you an idea of what to expect.

Taking the Exam

One of the comments heard most often by candidates as they leave the test site is that the information in their preparation materials did not bear any resemblance to what was on the test. None of the questions in this book or in any other preparation materials will be exactly like the questions on the exam. The broader your preparation and experience, the greater will be your ability to successfully answer the exam questions.

Knowing the kinds of questions that may be asked, as described earlier in this chapter, can help you focus your study and be as prepared as possible.

One of the best pieces of advice I've heard about getting ready for test day is to stop studying two or three days before the test. By then, if you've been diligent about your study plan, you will be well prepared. The night before, get a good night's sleep. Allow yourself plenty of time to get to the test site.

> Go to bed early the night before and have a light breakfast the morning before the test, so you are alert...unlike me who kept falling asleep during the test!
>
> —*Rose Chang, PHR*

On Toot Day

The PHR/SPHR exams are administered as a Computer Based Test (CBT) by Prometric. This provides candidates with greater flexibility in scheduling the test and has other benefits as well.

The following list provides some time-tested hints and tips for exam day gathered from many who have gone before you and were willing to share some of what they learned in the process. For the day of the exam:

- Get a good night's sleep the night before the test.

- Plan to arrive at least 15 minutes before your scheduled test time.

- Bring your ID (your driver's license, passport, or any other unexpired government-issued photo ID with a signature) and the test admission letter, along with any other required documents.

- Bring only items you must have with you. You will not be able to take anything into the testing area except your ID.

- Don't overeat in the morning or drink a lot of caffeine before the exam.

While taking the exam:

- Read the entire question carefully; don't skim it. Taking the time to do this can make the difference between a correct and incorrect answer.

> I am a speed reader and missing one little word could change the entire question. Slow down and read every word.
>
> —*Marie Atchley, SPHR*

- Read all of the answer choices carefully; don't skim them or select an answer before you've read them all.

- If you are unsure of the answer, eliminate as many "wrong" answers as you can to narrow down your choices. Remember: one of them is the correct one!

- Very often your "gut" instinct about the correct answer is right, so go with it.

- Don't over-analyze the questions and answers.

- Don't look for patterns in the answers. A myth has been circulating for a number of years that the longest answer was the correct one—it's just not true.

- If you don't know the answer to a question, *guess*. If you don't answer it, it will be counted as incorrect, so you have nothing to lose, and you might get it right.

> I was not surprised by the test at all. Everyone said it was hard; it was! Everyone said that it was subjective; it was! Everyone said that you will feel like you flunked; I did! (But I actually passed.)
>
> —*Patricia Kelleher, SPHR*

The Aftermath

The best thing about CBTs is that you will have a preliminary test result before you leave the test center. If you pass, knowing immediately relieves you of the anxiety of worrying and wondering about the results for four to six weeks until they arrive in the mail. If you don't pass the test, knowing immediately will probably not make you feel any better about it, but there are a couple of consolations:

1. The time and work you put into studying has already benefited you by increasing your knowledge about your chosen profession—congratulate yourself for investing in your career.

2. While the test is important to you, put it in its proper perspective—it's only a test about HR, it's not your life. People take tests every day and not all of them pass on the first attempt.

If you plan to take the test again, review HRCI's advice on retaking the exam at `www.hrci.org/`. Click on the Certification tab, then on "How Exams are Developed," then on "Retaking an Exam." Browse through the entire HRCI website—there is a lot of information about how the test is constructed and scored that may help you refine your study plan for better success.

Summary

Certification for HR professionals is a process that has been evolving for more than 50 years. The HR BOK was first developed in 1975 to define the profession and provide the basis for certification. Over the years, HRCI has updated the BOK to reflect current business needs and trends to ensure its viability in business. Both the PHR and SPHR exams are based on federal legislation and case law and are experiential, meaning that in order to pass them candidates need to have exempt-level experience in the field.

Questions on the exams are developed by certified HR professionals who volunteer their time to produce 50 questions per year. The questions go through two levels of review prior to inclusion as unscored pretest questions on an exam. A question that is validated in this process goes into the pool of questions that are available for testing purposes. Questions that do not pass this rigorous process are either discarded or returned to the writer for additional work.

There are a number of methods that can be used to prepare for the exam. The most important preparation methods are to use as many sources of information as possible and to study with a partner or group.

Key Terms

Before you take the exam, be certain you are familiar with the following terms:

employee and labor relations

Human Resource Certification Institute (HRCI)

human resource development

risk management

Society for Human Resource Management (SHRM)

strategic management

total rewards

workforce planning and employment

Chapter

2

Core Knowledge Requirements for HR Professionals

THE HRCI CORE KNOWLEDGE REQUIREMENTS COVERED IN THIS CHAPTER ARE:

- ✓ Needs assessment and analysis
- ✓ Third party contract management, including development of requests for proposals
- ✓ Communication skills and strategies (for example, presentation, collaboration, influencing, diplomacy, sensitivity)
- ✓ Organizational documentation requirements to meet federal and state requirements
- ✓ Adult learning processes
- ✓ Motivation concepts and applications
- ✓ Training techniques (for example, computer based, classroom, on-the-job)
- ✓ Leadership concepts and applications
- ✓ Project management concepts and applications
- ✓ Diversity concepts and applications
- ✓ Human relations concepts and applications (for example, interpersonal and organizational behavior)
- ✓ HR ethics and professional standards
- ✓ Technology to support HR activities (for example, HRIS, employee self-service, e-learning, ATS)
- ✓ Qualitative and quantitative methods and tools for analysis, interpretation, and decision-making purposes (for example, metrics and measurements, cost/benefit analysis, financial statement analysis)

- ✓ **Change management methods**
- ✓ **Job analysis and job description methods**
- ✓ **Employee records management (for example, electronic/ paper, retention, disposal)**
- ✓ **The interrelationships among HR activities and programs across functional areas**
- ✓ **Types of organizational structures (for example, matrix, hierarchy)**
- ✓ **Environmental scanning concepts and applications**
- ✓ **Methods for assessing employee attitudes, opinions, and satisfaction (for example, opinion surveys, attitude surveys, focus groups/panels)**
- ✓ **Basic budgeting and accounting concepts**
- ✓ **Risk management techniques**

As we discussed in Chapter 1, "Certifying Human Resource Professionals," the BOK for HR consists of six functional areas plus the core knowledge requirements. These core areas have been identified as knowledge and skill capabilities that are essential to competency as an HR professional. Because each of these knowledge areas may have implications for practice in two or more of the HR functional areas, I am introducing the basic concepts in this chapter. These introductions are brief, designed only to provide a refresher for each of the concepts.

Needs Assessment and Analysis

Needs assessment and *needs analysis* are terms used interchangeably to describe methods for obtaining the information necessary to make decisions that will best accomplish an organization's goals. These methods can measure needs in any area of business; in HR they are often employed in the areas of training and development, staffing projections, and benefit planning, but they can be utilized to gather information for any program.

There are many models for needs assessment. The common elements involve the following steps:

1. Describe the objective.

This step answers the question, "Where do we want to be?" and looks at the various elements necessary to accomplish that objective. It is important to obtain relevant information from all the possible stakeholders to ensure a full understanding of what is needed, as well as to ensure buy-in when recommendations are presented. In developing the objective, consider elements such as strategic business goals, department goals and objectives, budget constraints, available resources, and any other factors that impact the situation. These include the people, skills, or materials necessary to meet the objective.

2. Define the current situation.

This step answers the question, "Where are we now?" and looks at each element described in Step 1 to determine what is already available within the organization and create an inventory of skills, people, equipment, technology, and whatever assets are already in place.

3. Conduct a gap analysis.

A *gap analysis* compares the objective to the current situation and results in a list of people, actions, or items needed to attain the objective described in Step 1. As part of this process, it's important to gather as much information as possible about the gaps so that they are clearly understood and to identify any constraints that may inhibit efforts to close them.

4. Set priorities.

   In a world of limited resources, it may not be realistic to expect to go out and obtain everything that is needed to fill all of the gaps immediately. Prioritizing identifies the gaps most
   critical to achieving the objective and focuses on closing them first.

5. Investigate and develop options.

   This step answers the question, "What is the most effective way to fill this gap?" Be as open-
   minded as possible when developing options and collect data from as many sources as are
   available. Involve others in brainstorming sessions as appropriate and look for ways in
   which similar needs have been met in and outside of the organization.

6. Evaluate options and determine budget impact.

   Determine which of the possible options will be the most effective way to fill the gap. A
   crucial element of this step is the cost of implementation. It is important to consider both
   direct and indirect costs: the impact on the company's bottom line in the short term, as
   well as the return on investment (ROI) and long-term costs and savings. Another budgetary consideration is the cost of not implementing the option: in the long run, will it cost
   more or less to operate without it?

7. Recommend solutions.

   Whether you or someone higher in the organization is the final decision maker, it's important to document the reasons for selection of a particular solution.

Third-party Contract Management

A *contract* is a legally enforceable agreement between two or more parties in which all parties
benefit in some way. Generally, one party makes an offer to do or provide something of value
(a product or service), and the other agrees to do or provide something in return (payment).
Contracts can be formal or informal, oral or written. While an oral contract can be legally
enforceable, written contracts provide more protection for the parties involved.

In a *third-party contract*, some part of the transaction is provided by an entity other than
those who have signed the contract. There are many examples of third-party contracts in business; perhaps the best known for HR professionals is an agreement with a temp agency in which
the company agrees to pay the temp agency for services provided by an employee of the agency.

As an increasing number of HR functions are outsourced, the need for practitioners to
understand the issues involved in effectively managing third-party contractors becomes more
important. A critical factor for a successful contractor relationship is a clear understanding of
the product or service to be provided, along with clearly defined expectations for quality and
service levels. This information is best communicated through a process known as a *request
for proposal (RFP)*.

In many organizations the RFP process is handled by a purchasing group or is outsourced
to someone who specializes in preparing them, but it's important to understand what information is needed to develop an RFP that satisfies both parties. A well-constructed RFP serves
as the basis on which the product or service is obtained, a guide to ensure that the delivery
meets the organization's requirements, and a means of evaluation at the end of the project.

While there is no standard RFP format for use in all situations, the elements for developing one are similar.

Conduct a needs assessment   Whether you are requesting bids for a one-time project or an ongoing outsource relationship, you must be able to describe your objectives and budget clearly so that vendors will provide an accurate and appropriate proposal.

As part of the needs assessment process, a client may conduct informal "pre-proposal" meetings with possible vendors. This is particularly useful when the client has little direct experience with the project or wants to learn more about the product or service in order to describe it more clearly in the RFP. This is sometimes known as "scoping" the project, and can become a more formal process with the use of a scoping document that solicits information from a variety of possible vendors before the RFP is written.

Developing the RFP   The format of an RFP varies with each organization. In general, the following components are included:

1. A brief description of the organization, including information that will help vendors provide an accurate bid, such as number of employees, locations, and so on.

2. An overview of the project summarizing what is needed.

3. Administrative details about the process, including submission deadlines, how to request an extension, the format requirements for submissions, and what happens if there are errors or omissions in the RFP. Information about how the proposals will be evaluated should be included here as well (for example, will the project be awarded to the lowest bidder or will other criteria be more important?). Any penalties for late delivery and how to handle work that is beyond the scope of the RFP are included here as well.

4. A clear, complete, and detailed description of the project (also known as the scope of work, technical description, or project specifications) that contains information significant to the ability of the vendor to prepare a bid and that can be measured during the evaluation phase.

5. The name of the contact person for additional information about preparing the proposal.

Proposal formats   As per Step 3, the RFP provides vendors with a format to follow when submitting proposals. This serves two purposes. First, it makes an evaluation of the proposals easier, and second, it ensures that vendors provide all the relevant information for an evaluation of the project. While the format will vary between organizations and different projects, the following elements will make it easier to compare and evaluate the proposals:

Executive summary   A brief overview of the vendor's qualifications to provide the product or service needed by the client.

Vendor qualifications   Includes references from other clients.

Project management plan   Describes specifically how the vendor intends to supply the product or service.

Project team   Includes personnel who will be supplied by the vendor as well as the client's employees who will be involved.

Roles and responsibilities   Includes information about members of the project team.

Delivery schedule   Provides a timeline and milestones for the completion of specific events.

Pricing information   Includes how the project will be billed and whether it is based on project completion, time and materials, or completion of specific milestone events. The vendor should also provide pricing information for any requested work that is beyond the scope of the proposal.

Evaluate the proposals   Once the proposals have been submitted, the evaluation process can begin. There are many factors to consider, including the reputation of the vendor, the qualifications and experience of the project team, the size of the company and whether or not it has the capability to complete the project, how flexible the vendor can be in terms of schedule or other issues, the proposed cost, whether the schedule submitted meets the needs of the organization, and whether the vendor's approach to the project is compatible with the organization's culture.

Select a vendor   When the evaluation has been completed, notify the successful vendor, along with those whose proposals were not accepted.

Negotiate the contract   Formalize the agreement and sign a contract with the successful vendor.

Execute the agreement   Implement the project. Initially, gathering together all the members of the project team, both those who work for the vendor and those who work for the organization, is important to ensure that the project gets off to a good start. It is also important to maintain contact with the vendor during the implementation phase to ensure that it stays on track and meets your expectations.

Evaluate the project   Whether this is an ongoing outsource function or a one-time project, an evaluation ensures that the project continues to meet organizational needs and provides useful information for future projects.

Communication Skills and Strategies

HR professionals must develop expertise in communicating information to a variety of stakeholders, from top executives to production workers, customers, and vendors. This requires the ability to determine which strategies will most successfully communicate different types of information to these various audiences.

Employee Communication

An effective employee *communication strategy* provides opportunities for "top-down" communication by management and "bottom-up" communication from employees. It must balance management's need to ensure the confidentiality of sensitive company information with the need of employees to know, understand, and feel part of what is happening with the company. An effective strategy builds employee trust in the organization during the communication process by sharing meaningful information with them. The more employees know about the company's vision, goals, and operations, the more engaged and productive they are. Employees who feel connected to the success of the organization become good-will ambassadors, enhancing its reputation in the community and effectively referring qualified candidates for open positions.

There are many options for providing or exchanging information with employees. Some of the methods to consider are listed in Table 2.1.

TABLE 2.1   Possible Communication Delivery Methods

Top-down Communication	Bottom-up Communication
Intranet	Open door policy
Public address system announcements	All-hands meetings
Posters	Staff meetings
Newsletters	Brown bag lunches
Individual letters to employees	One-on-one meetings
Flyers	email
Bulletin board postings	Webcasts

An effective communication strategy delivers the same information in several ways; determining the best mix of methods begins with a clear picture of what management hopes to achieve. Once the objective is clear, answers to the following questions determine which delivery methods are most appropriate for a particular situation:

- What information will be provided?
- Who is the intended audience?
- Who will provide the information?
- Is the information time sensitive?

To select the best delivery mechanisms for a particular organization and message, it is also important to consider the organization's culture. The most effective strategies are a reflection of the culture, whether it is very formal or informal and laid-back. Another consideration that guides the selection of communication methods is the employee base: is the workforce computer savvy or are employees accustomed to receiving information from their managers in small group meetings?

"Bottom-up" communication methods help employees feel that their concerns are heard and addressed, which adds to their investment in the organization's success. There are, of course, many messages that are most appropriately delivered "top-down" as well. Mechanisms to enhance both types of communication will contribute to the effectiveness of the overall strategy.

Professional Communication

Because HR professionals must communicate a variety of messages to differing audiences, it is likely that multiple communication strategies will be developed to ensure that each audience receives necessary information in the way that best meets its needs and that gets the HR message across effectively. To achieve this, HR professionals need skills for a wide variety of purposes, including presentations, collaboration, influencing, diplomacy, and sensitivity.

Documentation Requirements

Documentation requirements fall into two basic categories. The first is the collection and main-tenance of required employment records, such as application forms, tax documents, and benefit records. These requirements are described in the section on "Employee Records Management" later in this chapter. In that section, Table 2.5 provides a detailed list of most employment doc-uments that must be maintained for legal purposes along with the required retention period required by each federal law.

The second category is the maintenance of appropriate documentation for employment actions.

Documenting Employment Actions

Traditionally, the HR department has been charged with responsibility to ensure that all the "i's are dotted and t's are crossed" when it comes to documenting employment relationships. As the *subject matter experts (SME)*, HR professionals are those most qualified to ensure the maintenance of proper documentation and to safeguard the privacy of personal employee information. The maintenance of these records is important for two basic reasons: some are required to be maintained to comply with federal, state, or local employment laws and others provide information necessary for effective management of the organization. In some cases, the records are needed to meet both of those requirements.

Documenting Performance Issues

There are two sides to this topic. The first is the need for managers to address performance issues when they occur in order to effectively manage the employees who report to them. All too often, line managers are reluctant to confront employees about performance issues and neglect to advise them of any problems until either the annual performance review or when the situation becomes so untenable that the manager's only thought is immediate termination of the employee. In either situation, the employee is taken completely by surprise at the seri-ousness of the situation and will not have had the opportunity to rectify the problem. This side of performance management will be fully discussed in Chapter 5, "Human Resource Development."

The other side of this issue concerns the creation and maintenance of written documentation for disciplinary actions described here.

1. Verbal warning

While it may seem contradictory to state that a written record of a *verbal warning* should be maintained, it is not. The verbal warning includes specific examples of the unacceptable performance or behavior and notice of the consequences if it does not change, that is, further disciplinary action, up to and including termination. The written record of this conversation can be as simple as a contemporaneous note by the supervisor that describes the date and time of the warning, the name of the employee involved, what was discussed, and any agreements that were made about future changes in behavior or performance.

2. First written warning

At this stage, the written record becomes more formal. In some companies, forms are provided for managers to fill in with the appropriate information. In companies without specific forms, the *first written warning* is a memo to the employee describing steps that have already been taken, exactly what the performance problem is, steps that need to be taken to avoid future consequences, and any agreements that have been made about performance changes. This document should be signed by the employee. When employees balk at signing a warning with which they disagree, the supervisor can advise them that signing does not indicate agreement, just that the warning has been discussed. If employees still will not sign, the supervisor can make a note indicating the date and time of the discussion and the fact that the employee refused to sign the document.

3. Final written warning

A *final written warning* is similar to the first, with the addition of a statement advising the employee that continued inability or refusal to make necessary performance changes will result in termination of employment.

4. Decision-making day

As a final step prior to termination, some companies provide a decision-making day at this point. Employees are sent home, usually with pay, and asked to think about whether or not they are willing to make the changes and keep their jobs. If they are, they return to work the next morning and make a commitment to make the necessary changes. It is made clear to employees that if the changes are not made, immediate termination will result without additional disciplinary steps. If they come back to say that they are not willing to conform to the performance requirements, they are terminated without further disciplinary action.

5. Suspension

Some companies take an additional step prior to termination and suspend employees for varying periods of time depending on the seriousness of the offense and other considerations. A *suspension* is accompanied by a written document spelling out all the steps previously taken to resolve the issue, the reason for the suspension, and a statement that continued nonconformance may result in termination.

6. Termination

At this stage, employees are well aware of the issues leading up to the *termination*. Depending on the circumstances, prior to taking this step it may be advisable to have counsel review the existing documentation and provide guidance for the final termination letter.

Some of the additional documents that must be provided and maintained when employees are terminated include agreements for severance (with accompanying releases) or for compliance with the ADEA (discussed in Chapter 4, "Workforce Planning and Employment"), along with documentation of compliance with COBRA requirements (discussed in Chapter 6, "Total Rewards") and state unemployment documentation (if required).

As experienced HR practitioners are aware, including a disciplinary process in an employee handbook can abridge the doctrine of at-will employment (to be fully discussed in Chapter 7, "Employee and Labor Relations"). This presents a dilemma: without documentation of adverse employment actions, employers are unable to defend against claims of discrimination. With a published disciplinary process, employers are vulnerable to claims of discrimination if the process is not followed in all cases. To address these conflicting issues, some employment attorneys recommend that this disciplinary process be used as a guideline for managers to follow in addressing performance issues, but that it not be published in an employee handbook.

Maintaining contemporaneous records as just described can make the difference between a summary judgment in the employer's favor and a large jury award to a former employee. This process, or one similar to it, should be familiar to all candidates for the PHR/SPHR exams; it covers most performance issues.

Adult Learning Processes

The concept that adult learning processes were different from those of children was developed in the United States by Eduard Lindeman during the 1920s. Lindeman first promoted the idea that, for adults, the methods of learning were more important than what was being taught. His belief was that the most effective learning for adults took place in small groups where knowledge could be shared based on the life experience of the participants. Malcolm Knowles expanded on Lindeman's theories in the 1970s when he identified characteristics that set adult learning apart from the way children learn. The work of Lindeman and Knowles is the basis for the study of how adults learn known as *andragogy*. The definition of andragogy evolved as researchers sought to further define adult learning; today it has come to mean education in which the learner participates in decisions about what will be taught and how it will be delivered. This approach is in contrast to *pedagogy*, the study of how children learn, which is defined as education in which the teacher decides what will be taught and how it will be delivered.

Much of Knowles' work centered on identifying characteristics of adult learning that would make the process more productive for learners. Knowles promoted the idea that, with

maturity, people grow into new ways of learning, described by the following five characteristics, which form the basis of andragogy today:

1. Self-concept

    An individual's self concept moves from dependency on others to autonomy and
    self-direction.

2. Experience

    An individual builds a wealth of knowledge that grows with each new experience. This
    information reserve can then be drawn upon for further learning.

3. Readiness to learn

    Individuals become increasingly interested in the relevance of information to specific
    needs and how directly it applies to their current situations.

4. Orientation to learning

    The ability to apply information immediately to solve current problems is increasingly
    important to learners.

5. Motivation to learn

    The motivation to learn is based more on personal needs and desires than on expectations
    of others.

These basic characteristics of adult learners are important concepts with implications
beyond traditional training and development. Understanding the best ways to provide information in work situations can enhance productivity and job satisfaction for the workforce.

Motivation Concepts

From the beginning of the industrial revolution, business owners have sought the key to improving productivity. This search prompted scientists to study the work environment, businesses, and
the relationship of people to organizations. These studies led to many theories about work, some
related to the physical environment or organization structures and others that looked at why
people work and what motivates them. These traditional theories of motivation center either on
the need for employees to be self-motivated or the need for managers to motivate them. They
provide a basis for understanding what drives employees to perform at peak levels of productivity, which can help managers understand the reasons for lowered productivity. Each functional area of the HR body of knowledge is impacted by whether or not employees are motivated
or demotivated at work. Incorporating these concepts into the planning stage of HR programs
and initiatives can increase the value of the end result.

Abraham Maslow: The Hierarchy of Needs (1954)

Maslow, a behavioral scientist, developed his *hierarchy of needs* to explain how people meet their
needs through work. This theory describes needs that begin with the most basic requirements for

life—food, shelter, and basic physical comforts—and progresses through stages of growth as people strive to fill higher-level needs. Maslow identified five levels of needs that motivate people:

Physiological needs   These are the most basic needs. Individuals striving to find enough food to eat or a place to live are motivated by attaining those things. People at this level are motivated by actions that provide the basic necessities of life.

Safety needs   Once people have food and shelter, they look for ways to ensure that they are safe from physical and emotional harm.

Social needs   At this level, people are motivated by the desire for acceptance and belonging within their social group.

Esteem needs   At this level, people are motivated by recognition for their achievements.

Self-actualization needs   When people are confident that their basic needs have been met, they become motivated by opportunities to be creative and fulfill their own potential. They do not look outside themselves for these opportunities but depend on themselves to find and act on them.

Fredrick Herzberg: Motivation/Hygiene Theory (1959)

Herzberg's *motivation/hygiene theory* (also known as the *two-factor theory*) began with a study on job attitudes that he conducted in Pittsburgh in the 1950s. He began the study believing that the causes of job satisfaction would be the opposite of the causes of job dissatisfaction. However, his review of several thousand books and articles on job attitudes did not prove his premise; in fact, the results were so vague that it was not possible to draw any conclusions. This led Herzberg to conduct a study in which he asked the participants to identify the work experiences that resulted in positive feelings about their jobs and the ones that resulted in negative feelings.

The result, as Herzberg himself described it in an interview, was that "What makes people happy is what they do or the way they're utilized, and what makes people unhappy is the way they're treated" ("An Interview with Frederick Herzberg: Managers or Animal Trainers?" *Management Review*, 1971). Both factors can motivate workers, but they work for very different reasons. The satisfaction (motivation) factors motivate by changing the nature of the work so that people are challenged to develop their talents and fulfill their potential. For example, adding responsibilities that provide learning opportunities to a receptionist performing at a substandard level can result in improved performance of all duties assigned if the poor performance is related to boredom with repetitive tasks. The dissatisfaction (hygiene) factors motivate to the extent that they allow people to avoid unpleasant experiences. For example, as long as employees continue to perform their assignments at an acceptable level, they continue to receive a paycheck. Hygiene factors provide only short-term benefits to employers, while factors related to motivation lead to longer-term job satisfaction.

A result of Herzberg's theory is the concept of *job enrichment* in which the significance of the tasks in a job is increased to provide challenging work and growth opportunities.

Douglas McGregor: Theory X and Theory Y (1960)

McGregor expanded on Maslow's work to describe the behavior of managers in their relationships with their employees. McGregor identified two distinct management approaches, *Theory X* and *Theory Y*.

Theory X managers have a world view of employees as lazy and uninterested in work and needing constant direction to complete their assignments. Theory X managers believe that employees do not want to take responsibility and are interested in job security above all else. Theory X managers are generally autocratic, utilizing a "top-down" management style.

In contrast, Theory Y managers believe that, given the opportunity, people will seek out challenging work and additional responsibility if the work is satisfying. Theory Y managers are more likely to invite participation in the decision-making process from their subordinates.

Clayton Alderfer: ERG Theory (1969)

The *ERG theory* developed by Alderfer builds on Maslow's work as well. Alderfer identifies three levels of needs: existence, relatedness, and growth.

Existence   Relates to Maslow's definition of physiological and safety needs as those that are required to maintain basic life needs.

Relatedness   Similar to Maslow's descriptions of social needs and the esteem we find from others.

Growth   Based on the self-esteem and self-actualization concepts Maslow described.

The premise for Maslow's theory was that people move sequentially through the levels one at a time. Alderfer's theory allows for the possibility that people can work on multiple levels simultaneously. It also describes the concept of frustration-regression, which occurs when an individual falls back to a lower level in frustration at the difficulty of a higher level.

David McClelland: Acquired Needs Theory (1961)

The premise of McClelland's *acquired needs theory* is that experiences acquired throughout their lives motivate people to achieve in one of three areas:

Achievement   Those motivated by achievement take moderate risks to achieve their goals, respond to frequent feedback, and generally prefer to work as sole contributors or with others interested in achieving at the same level.

Affiliation   Individuals who need affiliation look for acceptance within the work group and need regular interaction with their coworkers or customers.

Power   These individuals are either looking for personal power or institutional power. Those interested in institutional power are often effective managers who are motivated by coordinating work groups to achieve organization goals.

J. Stacy Adams: Equity Theory (1963)

The basic concept of Adams' *equity theory* is that people are constantly measuring what they put into work against what they get from work. If their perception is that it is a fair trade, they are motivated to continue contributing at the same level. When they perceive there is an imbalance and they are putting in more than they are getting back, they become demotivated and lose interest in their work, decreasing productivity and quality.

Victor Vroom: Expectancy Theory (1964)

Vroom's *expectancy theory* maintains that people are motivated by the expectation of the reward they will receive when they succeed, and that each individual calculates the level of effort required to receive a particular reward to determine if the reward is worth the effort that is required to attain it. Vroom uses the following terms to explain this theory:

Expectancy   According to Vroom's theory, motivation starts with an assessment by individuals about their capabilities to successfully complete an assignment.

Instrumentality   If individuals believe they are capable of completing an assignment, they next assess "what's in it for me"—that is, will their effort to complete the work be the instrument for obtaining a reward for the work?

Valence   This is the result of calculations as to whether the possible reward is worth the effort required to successfully complete the work.

B. F. Skinner: Operant Conditioning (1957)

The results of Skinner's work on *behavioral reinforcement* are more commonly known as behavior modification. His basic theory is that behavior can be changed through the use of four intervention strategies:

Positive reinforcement   Encourages continuation of the behavior by providing a pleasant response when the behavior occurs.

Negative reinforcement   Encourages continuation of the behavior by removing an unpleasant response to a behavior.

Punishment   Discourages future occurrence of the behavior by providing an unpleasant response when the behavior occurs.

Extinction   Discourages future occurrence of the behavior by ceasing to reinforce it. For example, when a parent praises a child for doing his homework each night and the child starts doing it without being reminded, the parent may stop praising the child. If the child then reverts to the previous behavior of forgetting to do his homework, the behavior has become extinct.

🌐 Real World Scenario

Operant Conditioning in Customer Service

The customer service manager at Wright Sisters, Inc., Susan Sherwood, has a problem employee, David Rogers. David can be charming and has a knack for calming down disgruntled customers on the phone. In fact, his coworkers often rely on him for assistance with unhappy customers who are difficult to please. David has worked for WSI for three years and is for the most part productive and cooperative. There are times, however, when he has snapped at coworkers, and he is often disruptive in staff meetings. Recently, Susan has observed him being rude to some customers during customer support calls. She has also noticed that coworkers have stopped giving him work that he is supposed be doing; instead they are doing it themselves to avoid dealing with him. Susan, who has been working on her MBA, just finished a course in industrial psychology and decides to give Skinner's theory of operant conditioning a try to see if it will work in a practical application. She comes up with the following interventions to use with David:

Positive reinforcement   At the end of each meeting in which David exhibits professional behavior, Susan will thank him publicly for his contribution during the meeting.

Negative reinforcement   When David behaves professionally during the day and does not create any disruptions, he will not have to meet with Susan at the end of the day.

Punishment   Whenever David is rude to a customer or coworker, Susan will reprimand him.

Extinction   Coworkers will no longer do his work for him when David becomes confrontational with them.

Training Techniques

Training techniques are used throughout the HR BOK for programs specific to each area, such as:

- Strategic Management: ethics, Sarbanes-Oxley compliance
- Workforce Planning and Employment: new hire orientation, interviewing
- Human Resource Development: skill development, performance appraisal
- Total Rewards: salary increase guidelines
- Employee and Labor Relations: union avoidance, supervisory skills
- Risk Management: safety training

Training techniques are fully discussed in Chapter 5 along with all other aspects of training and development.

Leadership Concepts

Much has been written about leaders and how they develop: are they born or made? There is little agreement in research about where leaders come from. Does the effectiveness of a leader depend on the situation? Which is more important as a function of leadership, the ability to develop structures or the ability to develop people? One thing is certain: however they do so, effective leaders are able to inspire the people around them to do their best work and influence people to follow them in achieving a common goal. In this section, I'll introduce you to some of the theories researchers have developed to explain leadership; as you will see, none of the theories are able to explain all its aspects. While some theories are currently more popular than others, all of them are the subject of ongoing study as researchers continue to try to explain leadership ability.

The study of how leaders become leaders was first addressed during the nineteenth century when Thomas Carlyle suggested the "great man" theory; that is, that leaders are born with innate qualities that set them apart from other "mere mortals." It was Carlyle's premise that leadership could not be learned but was instead the result of the superior qualities of some few men. Early in the twentieth century this premise became the basis for trait theories of leadership that look to the personality, intellect, and physical traits of individuals to explain their ability to lead others.

Several drawbacks to trait theories became apparent over time. The first and most significant of these was that each researcher identified different leadership traits, which resulted in multiple lists of relevant traits. The second was that research showed there was little difference between the traits exhibited by leaders and those of followers. For example, traits such as courage and intelligence were found in followers as often as in leaders. Finally, trait theories did not explain how leaders were successful in different situations using very different methods. As the limitations of early explanations for leadership development became clear, researchers turned to other areas for investigation, including behavioral, situational, and contingency theories of leadership.

Behavioral Theories

During the 1940s, researchers moved to a new area of research and focused on the ability of leadership to be taught: anyone could become a leader with the right information. This view of leadership moved the research focus from personality traits to what leaders did to inspire people to follow them. Two aspects of behavior became apparent in the research. The first was behavior that focused on the structural elements of the job, such as establishing rules and guidelines for employees. The second was behavior that considered the needs of employees, such as standing up for them and explaining decisions. Douglas McGregor's Theory X and Theory Y provide an example of a behavioral theory of leadership.

As with trait theories, there were leadership characteristics that were not explained by behavioral theories, most notably, how or why one behavioral aspect worked in one situation but not in others. This led to a new avenue for research: the impact of leadership in different situations.

Situational Theories

Situational theories of leadership seek to explain leader effectiveness in different situations. The elements that are considered in situational theories are how the leader and followers interact and how the work is structured. Several well-known theories fall into this category:

Blake-Mouton Managerial Grid, 1968   Robert R. Blake and Jane S. Mouton developed a grid to explain the characteristics of different leadership styles. The grid considers two aspects of leadership: concern for people and concern for production, as shown in Figure 2.1.

The grid uses nine levels to measure each aspect. Leaders at the lowest extreme (1,1) show no concern for either people or production. At the highest extreme (9,9), leaders show maximum concern for both production and people, and according to Blake and Mouton, are the most effective leaders.

FIGURE 2.1   Blake-Mouton managerial grid

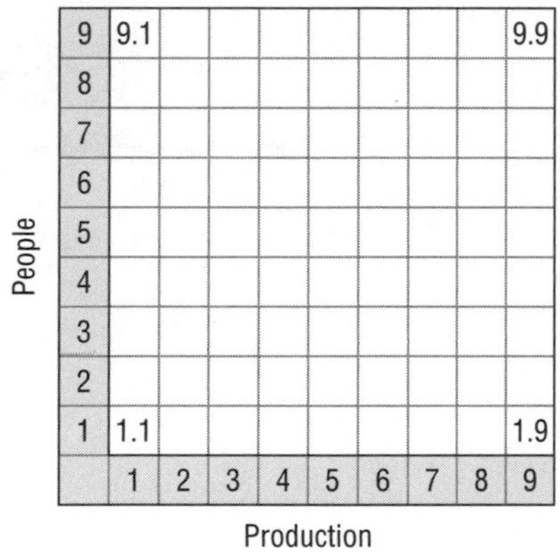

Path-goal theory, 1971   The path-goal theory of leadership was developed by Robert House, a professor at the Wharton School of Business. This theory proposes that a leader can impact the behavior of a group by establishing goals and providing direction on reaching those goals. House describes four leadership styles that may be used to accomplish this, based on the specific situation: directive, which specifies what is to be done; supportive, in which the leader provides encouragement for the group members; participative, in which the leader involves the group in the decision-making process; and achievement, in which the leader establishes a difficult goal and encourages the group to accomplish it.

Hersey-Blanchard theory, 1977   Paul Hersey and Kenneth Blanchard describe leadership in terms of the maturity level of the followers. In this theory, maturity refers to psychological maturity (or motivation), and job task maturity (or level of experience). The model provides four styles of leadership appropriate in different circumstances:

Telling   When followers are immature or inexperienced, the leader must be more directive by providing guidelines and defining roles for them.

Selling   When followers have some experience, the leader is still directing them but in a more general sense. Greater emphasis is placed on encouraging followers who have the motivation but lack sufficient experience to do the job.

Participating   At this level, the followers have progressed in terms of their ability but may lack the necessary motivation and require support to encourage them to act on their own.

Delegating   At this level, followers have both the experience and motivation to accomplish their tasks. The leader identifies the goal, and followers are accountable for producing results.

While situational theories address issues that were missing in both the trait and behavioral theories, they are criticized for being two-dimensional and not allowing for multifaceted situations that occur in the real world of business. In addition, these theories do not account for differences in culture and gender in explaining leadership.

Contingency Theories

To address some of these criticisms, Fred E. Fiedler developed a model known as Fiedler's Contingency Theory to address the shortcomings of situational theories. Fiedler's theory begins with an assessment of the leader's style. Fiedler uses a method known as the "least preferred coworker" scale to determine this. Leaders identify the coworker, past or present, with whom they had the most difficulty working and rate this person on a scale of 1 to 8 on a series of measures such as the coworker's level of cooperation and friendliness. The result is known as the least preferred coworker (LPC) score. A high LPC score indicates that the leader has a greater concern for people than for tasks, and a low score indicates a greater concern for tasks. Fiedler proposed that the LPC score could be used to predict the situations in which a leader would have a better chance for success.

Fiedler then describes situations in terms of three aspects:

Leader-member relations   The relationships leaders have with members of the group are the key factor in determining the level of influence the leader has within the group.

Task structure   Jobs that are highly structured provide a leader with greater influence than do those that require less structure.

Position power   Situations in which a leader has the discretion to assign tasks or to reward or punish members of the group provide the leader with a greater chance of success.

Each of these theories provides a different perspective on leadership and helps to explain something about it. They are the basis for many of the discussions in subsequent chapters; in particular, Chapters 3, 5, and 7 consider different aspects of the interactions between employees and managers, and these theories may provide the basis for a deeper understanding of the ways in which managers and leaders are able to influence employees.

Leadership Styles

Everyone has experienced leaders with different styles: the authoritarian leader who tells employees what to do, the democratic leader who involves employees in the process, the laissez-faire leader who abdicates responsibility and leaves employees to figure things out without guidance or support, and the coach who prepares employees to take on additional responsibility. There are different situations when all of these styles may be appropriate.

Authoritarian or directive   These leaders are effective in situations requiring immediate action or those that are life threatening. When productivity is the highest concern, authoritarian leadership may be the best style.

Democratic   These leaders are most effective in environments of highly skilled professional employees who are self-motivated and accomplish tasks on their own. When relationships in the work environment are of primary concern, this style is most effective.

Laissez-faire   These leaders allow group members to operate on their own. This leadership style provides no direction or guidance and can lead to chaos if members lack confidence in their abilities. For individuals who are highly motivated and can work independently, this may be an acceptable style. In general, it results in lower levels of productivity.

Coaching   These leaders work with group members to develop skills and abilities so they will be able to operate independently.

There are two other leadership styles to keep in mind: transactional leadership and transformational leadership.

Transactional   *Transactional leadership* focuses on getting the job done and seeks to do this by offering a reward in exchange for accomplishing organization goals. Transactional leaders manage by exception, either by seeking out areas where rules are not being followed and making a correction, or by taking action when the goal is not met.

Transformation   *Transformational leadership* focuses on the relationships in the group, building them to achieve organization goals. These leaders set the ideal for the group and act as role models, inspiring excellence within the group and stimulating new ideas and perspectives. Transformational leaders are coaches who work with individuals to develop their skills and abilities and improve their performance.

Project Management Concepts

Project management (PM) describes the process of initiating, planning, executing, controlling, and closing an assignment that is temporary in nature. The assignment may involve designing a new software program, constructing a building, implementing a new marketing strategy, or any other activity that is not part of the ongoing operations of a business. In *Project Management Jumpstart*, Kim Heldman, a certified project management professional (PMP), describes the five phases of a project life cycle.

Initiation   During the initiation phase, project requests are evaluated and selected for implementation. Those who will be affected by the project, the stakeholders, such as the project manager, sponsor, team members, customers, and others, meet to discuss the proposed project. Once a project is selected, a project charter is created by the sponsor to sanction the project and commit resources to its completion. The charter also identifies the goals and appoints the project manager.

Planning   The planning phase is led by the project manager (PM) and lays out how the project will be accomplished. The plan describes the deliverables, budget, and scope of the project, then develops specific activities and KSAs required to execute the activities. Finally, a timeline for completing the project is created.

Executing   During this phase, the project plan is implemented. A project team is created and other resources are acquired. Activities identified in the planning phase are completed during this time, and the PM manages the timeline, conducts status meetings, and disseminates information to the sponsor and other stakeholders as needed.

Controlling   The PM keeps the project on course and on budget by comparing accomplishments to the original plan and making course corrections as needed. As the project progresses, stakeholders may request changes to the original scope and the PM will review and incorporate them into the project as appropriate.

Closing   The closing phase is the point at which the sponsor/customer acknowledges achievement of the project goals. The PM collects information from stakeholders to improve future projects, stores documentation of project activities, and releases resources for use in other projects or activities.

For HR professionals, the ability to manage projects is critical to success. The following list shows how HR projects can occur in any of the functional areas:

Strategic Management   Integrating the cultures of two organizations after a merger

Workforce Planning and Employment   Developing a new hire orientation program

Human Resource Development   Creating a career development program

Total Rewards   Developing a stock option program

Employee and Labor Relations   Developing an employee handbook

Risk Management   Developing an emergency response plan

Each of these activities is a short-term assignment that will result in a program that will become part of the organization operations when it is complete, but the process of designing the program is not an ongoing operation.

The Project Management Institute maintains a website with additional information about projects and how they are managed at `www.pmi.org`.

Diversity Concepts

As businesses become global entities employing individuals with diverse cultural, racial, and ethnic backgrounds, understanding *diversity* in the workplace becomes more critical to organizational success. Organizations implementing programs to increase diversity realize benefits such as improved productivity and bottom-line results for shareholders. There are many other business reasons to make workplace diversity a priority:

A diverse workforce is more creative   Increasing the variety of perspectives available to an organization brings new points of view to decision-making processes, challenging conventional wisdom and creating an atmosphere that encourages the synergy of ideas.

A diverse workforce reflects the population   When businesses increase the diversity of their workforces, they increase their ability to attract customers. Customers are attracted to organizations when they feel comfortable with its representatives, and employees who understand and communicate well with customers help increase the customer base for a company's products or services.

A diverse workforce increases the candidate pool   The Department of Labor predicts an increasing shortage of qualified candidates for available positions in the near future, with a projected shortfall of about five million workers by 2010. Increasing the candidate pool by including a wide diversity of applicants will be essential to fill open positions.

Workplace diversity presents challenges that organizations look to HR professionals to address, including the difficulty associated with change and the need to do things in new ways. It is challenging for individual employees to work with people who behave and communicate differently than what is perceived as normal. For example, something as seemingly simple as differences in the amount of "personal space" that are customary in different cultures can create uncomfortable situations, such as one person backing away from another to increase the space between them while the other moves closer seeking to decrease the space.

Difficulties also arise for employees whose backgrounds are dissimilar to the group. They may feel uncomfortable in situations requiring them to make major adjustments in order to be accepted by a group whose culture is different from their own. The comfort level for all involved can be improved with *diversity training*, which seeks to educate all groups about the cultures, needs, and attitudes of other groups in the workforce to ensure the inclusion of all groups in workplace activities.

A *diversity initiative* seeks to increase the diversity of the workforce or to increase the effectiveness of an already diverse workforce. As with any company-wide objective, top management support is essential for success of the initiative, as is a clear picture of the challenges that the initiative will address. Communicating the purpose of the initiative and providing feedback mechanisms for employees to ask questions will help to ease any fears about the changes taking place in the organization. The initiative may begin with training designed to educate employees about the need for and benefits of diversity for the organization and to explain the benefits of diversity to them as individuals. As with any HR program, an evaluation of its effectiveness should be conducted at an appropriate time.

Human Relations Concepts

The concept of human relations covers a broad spectrum of ideas that concentrate on the importance of the human element at work, including interpersonal characteristics and organizational behavior.

This approach to workplace relationships, introduced in the 1920s, challenged traditional assumptions that people work only for economic reasons and that monetary incentives provided sufficient motivation for increased productivity. Human relations theories recognized that businesses are social as well as economic systems and looked at the impact of formal (management) and informal (work group) social connections in the workplace and the impact these connections have on work processes. For the first time there was recognition that employees are complex individuals, motivated at different times by different factors, and that increased productivity could be tied to employee job satisfaction.

Human relations theories classify intelligence into several types; of interest here are the two types of personal intelligence: intrapersonal and interpersonal. Intrapersonal intelligence refers to self-knowledge or how well individuals know themselves. Interpersonal intelligence refers to emotional intelligence and social aptitude. Emotional intelligence (EI) is characterized by individuals who are aware of their emotions and are able to control how they react to them. Emotionally intelligent individuals are able to motivate themselves to achieve goals and are sensitive to the emotion of others and able to manage relationships with them.

Over time, a number of tests have been developed to identify how individuals react in different situations, for example, are they confrontational or do they attempt to mediate situations? These tests are used in some organizations to help employees work together more effectively. For example, the Myers-Briggs test identifies personality types with four-letter codes; the explanation of the code provides a description of the individual's personality. These tests are used in organizations to improve organizational effectiveness and increase understanding between coworkers.

HR Ethics and Professional Standards

Both the Society for Human Resource Development (SHRM) and the Human Resource Certification Institute (HRCI) have developed standards for professional behavior for the human resource profession.

The SHRM Code of Ethical and Professional Standards in Human Resource Management consists of six core principles summarized here:

Professional responsibility   HR professionals represent their profession to their organizations. As such, they must hold themselves accountable for their decisions and ensure their actions further the credibility of the profession.

Professional development   HR professionals are expected to continuously expand their knowledge of the profession and the organizations in which they work.

Ethical leadership   HR professionals are expected to model ethical behavior in their organizations and act as an example and guide to develop other ethical leaders.

Fairness and justice   HR professionals bear a responsibility to ensure that all those with whom they come in contact and all those within their organizations are treated with dignity and respect and afforded equal employment opportunities.

Conflicts of interest   To maintain trust within their organizations, HR professionals must avoid even the appearance of conflicts of interest and prevent situations where they appear to or actually do receive personal gain from their positions.

Use of information   HR professionals are privy to confidential information related to their organizations and the employees who work for those organizations. As such, HR professionals have a responsibility to protect this information from inappropriate uses.

The complete text of the SHRM Code of Ethics is available at `www.shrm.org/ethics/code-of-ethics.asp`.

HRCI's Model of Professional Excellence sets a high standard of professional integrity and excellence for practitioners with expectations for honesty, reliability, fairness, and cooperation at all times. The complete text is on the inside back cover of the *PHR/SPHR Certification Handbook*.

Human Resource Technology

With the reams of paper generated during the course of an employment relationship, the advent of the *human resource information system (HRIS)* was a clear benefit for HR professionals. An HRIS serves two purposes: first, as a repository of information, and second, as an aid to effective decision making.

HRIS Systems

As a repository of information, the HRIS provides an electronic means of storing employment documents, thereby reducing the need to maintain physical files. In firms with multiple locations, both national and global, the ability for employees to access information through the company's intranet or via the World Wide Web reduces delays in payroll processing tasks and ensures instant access to the information for those with the authority and need to access it. For companies required to produce reports for the Equal Employment Opportunity Commission (EEOC) or the Office of Federal Contract Compliance Programs (OFCCP), electronic access to the data needed to compile reports has increased accuracy and reduced the time required to produce them.

As an effective decision-making tool, the HRIS provides access to a wealth of information that is needed to make strategic decisions, such as analyzing turnover trends, creating succession plans, or projecting staffing needs.

Selecting an HRIS

As with any project, the first step in selecting an HRIS is to conduct a needs analysis and identify:

- What information will be converted to the HRIS, and how is it currently maintained? Table 2.2 lists some uses to consider for an HRIS.
- Will the system need to integrate or share data with other company systems?

TABLE 2.2   Uses for HRIS

Applicant tracking	COBRA administration
Automated benefit administration	EEO/AA reporting
Tracking recruitment efforts	Administering training programs
Eliminating multiple data entry	Compensation administration
Tracking service awards	Tracking time and attendance
Sharing payroll information with finance department	

- Who will have access to the information and how many levels of access will be needed (for example, view and change individual records, view and change workgroup records, view payroll information, and so on)? Table 2.3 displays what a typical access hierarchy could look like.

- What kinds of reports will need to be produced based on the information?

- Will the HRIS be accessible via the intranet or the Web? If so, what security will be in place to protect the privacy of employees and prevent identity theft?

Once this information has been collected, research can begin on the availability and cost of a system that fulfills the requirements. This analysis should include the purchase cost for the system with a comparison to the cost of continuing to use the current system.

TABLE 2.3   Typical HRIS Access Hierarchy

HR Access (global information)	
Maintain employee records	Coordinate payroll administration
Administer employee benefits	Administer labor relations program
Post jobs	Administer safety programs
Administer compensation plan	Track applicants
Administer FMLA leaves	Administer employee relations
Track attendance/vacation time	Manage recruiting
Track applicants	Complete EEO/AAP reports
Manage relocations	Administer training programs

TABLE 2.3   Typical HRIS Access Hierarchy *(continued)*

Payroll Access (restricted information)

View payroll information	Administer payroll

Management Access (restricted to work group)

View budget/forecast reports	Manage performance
View succession plans	Administer service awards
Track attendance/vacation time	View compensation
Manage training needs	View recruiting status

Employee Access (restricted to personal information)

Change address and family status	Change payroll tax withholding
View company policies	View attendance/vacation tracking
View benefit enrollment information	Open enrollment benefit changes
Bid for internal job openings	

Implementing an HRIS

Once the HRIS installation project has been approved, some practical considerations need to be worked into the implementation schedule. If the HRIS software vendor or a third party will be handling the implementation phase, the RFP should include information about this phase of the project. If the implementation is to be done with internal IT staff, it's important to establish a timeline that works for both departments and allows the organization's HR information needs to be met during this stage.

When implementation is complete and the system has been tested to ensure it is functioning correctly, the new service can be rolled out to those who will be using it; if an employee self-service component is included, this means providing the necessary level of training for all employees. Utilizing some of the training methods described in Chapter 5 could mean this happens via small group trainings with demonstrations, with self-study CBT training, or by some other means that ensures those who will need to access the system are able to do so.

Employee Self-Service

Employee self-service allows employees to access their own records through some type of automated system. This could be a company intranet, through the Internet, an automated phone system, or a computer kiosk. Providing employees with the ability to access and make changes to routine information frees HR staff to perform other mission-critical functions and gives employees 24/7 access to their information.

Table 2.3, shown previously, identifies the kinds of access typically provided in employee self-service applications.

Applicant Tracking Systems

An applicant tracking system (ATS) provides an automated method for keeping track of job applicants from the time they first apply to an organization to the point when the position is filled—and beyond if the database is searched as new openings occur. These systems range from Excel spreadsheets to sophisticated database systems that track applicant qualifications, are easily searchable based on different criteria, and provide reports that can be used for annual EEO-1 reports or affirmative action plans. Table 2.4 presents the types of information typically captured in an ATS.

Hiring Management Systems

If ATS systems ease the administrative burden of the hiring process, hiring management systems (HMS) take the technology to the next level. An HMS makes use of technology to carry the employer brand throughout the application process. It integrates with corporate recruiting websites to simplify the candidate's experience by moving data directly from candidate input to the database. This reduces errors and improves relationship management with faster response times. HMS systems can prescreen by providing questions that will help candidates self-screen out of the process if they do not meet minimum qualifications, thus reducing the time recruiters spend reviewing resumes of unqualified candidates.

An HMS also provides additional recruiter support with templates to standardize candidate communication and facilitate communication between recruiters in large organizations. Most HMS systems include customizable report writers that can be used to answer questions about specific jobs or the recruiting system in general.

TABLE 2.4   Typical ATS Capabilities

Applicant Information	Open Positions	Recruiter Needs
Resume upload	List of open positions	Applicant contact information
Application upload	Job descriptions	Search by applicant information
Applicant profile	Hiring manager access	Search by qualifications
Applicant auto response	Job posting	Information security
Comments		EEOC report information
Link resume to profile		Report generator

Qualitative and Quantitative Analysis

Making business decisions requires accurate and reliable information; without it, for example, a decision can result in excess inventory rather than increased profits because demand for the product was less than projected. Since there are no crystal balls in the board room, business leaders must rely on the judgment of experienced managers and an analysis of historical data to predict possible future trends.

There are two types of research, primary and secondary. *Primary research* is original, meaning that the researcher has performed the research. *Secondary research* is based on information that has been collected or reported by others, such as books or articles by primary researchers, industry standards, or analysis of trends within an organization.

One very formal method of primary research is known as the *scientific method*, and although it is not generally identified as such in analyzing business problems, the process is very similar to the way in which business problems are analyzed prior to making decisions. There are five steps to the scientific method. A common business problem, absenteeism, shows how these steps can be used in solving HR problems:

1. Identify a problem:

   Absenteeism is too high.

2. Create a hypothesis:

   The absentee rate is higher with new employees.

3. Decide how to test the hypothesis:

   A correlation analysis of length of employment and attendance data will confirm or not confirm the hypothesis.

4. Collect data to verify the hypothesis:

   Review employee files and attendance records. Correlate hire date and number of absences for each employee.

5. Draw conclusions/analyze the data:

   Does the correlation analysis verify or not verify the hypothesis?

The result of the analysis will either prove the hypothesis, that absences are higher among new employees, or disprove it. Sometimes, the process of analyzing data may shed light on other factors that contribute to the problem.

Another issue to consider is whether or not there will be a control group in your test. Using a control group tells you if the hypothesis being tested causes the result you are looking for, or the result is the same with both the group being tested and the control group.

In many situations, secondary research also provides valuable insights for HR professionals looking for ways to solve problems in their organizations. For example, the SHRM website offers a variety of white papers and toolkits created by practitioners to solve problems encountered in specific organizations. Accessing these tools provides insight into how other professionals have solved various problems common to many organizations and can be used to develop solutions without reinventing the wheel.

Data Collection

Collecting data is an important element of the analysis process; if the proper data is not collected, any decision based on it, regardless of the method of analysis used, will not be an accurate decision. So how do you find reliable data to use in analyzing HR problems? Here are some sources to consider:

Personnel records   Personnel records provide information that can be used for analyzing trends. For the absentee example, personnel records tell you how long each employee has worked for the company as well as how often the employee is absent from work.

Observations   The hypothesis for the absentee example could have been based on the observation of a general manager who noticed that several new employees were frequently absent.

Interviews   Interviews provide direct information about problems. The HR department can interview some new employees to find out how often they are absent and why. This data collection method can provide more information than records, but its relevance depends on the frankness of the people being interviewed and their willingness to share information. In addition, interviews are time consuming and may not be cost effective for that reason.

Focus groups   Focus groups are often used to find out how people feel about products or advertisements. They can also be effective methods for gathering information for HR analysis, but again, they are subject to the willingness of participants to open up. In a focus group, this willingness may be inhibited by the presence of coworkers or supervisors.

Questionnaires   Questionnaires can be an effective means of gathering information from large groups of geographically dispersed employees but are limited in the types of data that can be collected.

Once data has been collected, there are two basic categories of data analysis tools: quantitative analysis methods based on mathematical models and qualitative analysis methods based on the best judgment of experienced managers or SMEs.

Analysis Tools

There are a number of different tools available for data analysis, and they fall into two basic categories: quantitative tools and qualitative tools. There are benefits and drawbacks to both types of analysis; reliance on a single method may not provide the most comprehensive analysis. Using several different tools helps to minimize errors.

Quantitative Analysis

Quantitative analysis tools are based on mathematical models for measuring historical data. Several of these measures provide useful data for HR decisions. Some quantitative analyses commonly used to analyze HR and other business data include the following:

Correlation   A *correlation* measures two variables to determine if there is a relationship between them. For example, if the HR department posts a quarterly reminder of the referral bonus that is paid for new hires, a correlation analysis could be used to determine if there is an increase in referrals in the weeks after the reminder.

Correlation coefficient   The *correlation coefficient* describes the relationship between two variables and is stated as a number between −1.0 and +1.0.

For example, say the HR department wants to find out what factors contribute to absenteeism in the company. One of the factors they decide to analyze is length of time at the company, so one hypothesis they might use is "The absentee rate is higher with new employees."

To analyze this, they would collect two numbers for each employee: how many months employed and how many days absent. The numbers are then plotted on a graph for analysis.

If this hypothesis is correct, they would expect to see a *negative* correlation coefficient, that is, the shorter amount of time employed, the higher the absentee rate would be. This would be reflected by a negative number, for example, −.2. Figure 2.2 shows how this looks.

A *positive* correlation coefficient would tell HR that the opposite is true, that the absentee rate is actually higher when employees have longer tenure with the company. This would be reflected by a positive number, for example, +.8. Figure 2.3 shows what this would look like.

If there were no correlation at all, that is, if length of employment had nothing to do with absenteeism, the correlation coefficient would be 0.0, as shown by Figure 2.4.

The steeper the trend line (the higher the absolute number), the greater is the connection between the two variables. In the absentee example, the positive correlation (+.8) reflects a stronger connection between a longer amount of time with the company and more absences than the example of negative correlation (−.2).

FIGURE 2.2   Negative correlation

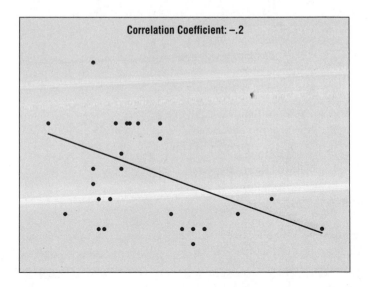

FIGURE 2.3   Positive correlation

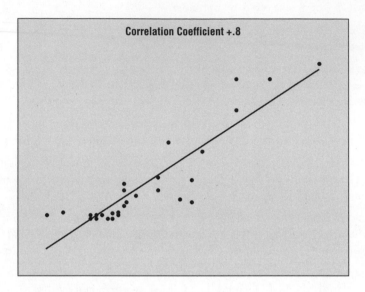

FIGURE 2.4   No correlation

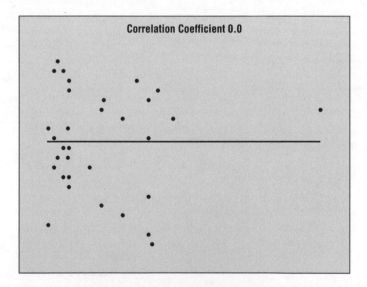

Measures of central tendency   Often referred to as the "average," there are several measures of central tendency that can be used in analyzing data:

Mean average   The *mean average* is the sum of the values in a set of numbers, divided by the number of values in the set.

Mode   The *mode* is the number that occurs most frequently in a set of numbers.

Median   The *median* can be found by putting the numbers in a set in sequential order. The median is at the physical center, so half the numbers are below it and half are above it.

Moving average   Sometimes called a "rolling average," the *moving average* is used to calculate an average for a specific period, for example, to calculate the average number of new hires each month for the past 12 months. As the number for the most recent month is added, the oldest number is dropped.

Weighted average   A *weighted average* is used to compensate for data that may be out of date; the more current data is multiplied by a predetermined number to better reflect the current situation.

Weighted moving average   The *weighted moving average* calculation assigns more weight to current data with the use of a predetermined number as well as dropping the oldest data when new data is added.

Time series forecasts   There are several *time series forecasts* that can be used to measure historic data and provide a basis for projecting future requirements. One example of HR uses for these tools is in the area of staffing levels, but they are useful in analyzing many other areas as well, including benefit utilization, compensation trends, or the effectiveness of a recruiting system. For purposes of discussion, staffing level analysis is used to demonstrate how each of the following tools is used.

Trend analysis   *Trend analysis* compares the changes in a single variable over time, and, over a period of years, they generally move upward or downward. For example, this tool can reveal information on seasonal staffing requirements, which are periods of time within a one-year period that regularly vary from the general trend. *Cycles*, periods of time during which a pattern of performance (growing, peaking, declining, and plateauing at the lower level), also become apparent in a trend analysis.

Simple linear regression   *Simple linear regression* measures the relationship between one variable (for example, staffing) against another variable (such as production output) and allows prediction of one variable from the other. For example, measuring the number of units produced against the number of employees producing the units over a period of years would allow the analyst to forecast the number of employees needed to meet an increase in demand.

Multiple linear regression   *Multiple linear regression* measures the relationship between several variables to forecast another. An application of this model in workforce planning would be to determine if there is a relationship between lower staffing levels, absenteeism, and production output.

Simulation models   Simulation models allow several possible plans to be tested in abstract form. For example, an organization that wants to know the predicted results of different staffing alternatives can use a simulation model to determine which is the most cost effective.

Ratios   Ratios provide a benchmark based on the historic relationship of one variable to another. For example, the average HR staffing ratio is generally considered to be 1:100. As an organization's workforce increases or decreases, this ratio can provide an estimate of the number of staff required to provide services for the general employee population.

Qualitative Analysis

Qualitative analysis tools are subjective evaluations of general observations and information and include various types of judgmental forecasts. These tools can be as simple as an estimate made by a knowledgeable executive (for example, an experienced sales manager may be able to predict quite accurately by the end of the first month of a quarter whether or not the sales goal will be met). In other situations, the tools can be as involved as formalized brainstorming using a Delphi or nominal group technique.

The *Delphi technique* obtains input from a group of individuals who provide their expertise in succeeding rounds of questions about an issue or problem. After each round, the results are collated, prioritized, and returned to the participants in the form of additional questions for further analysis until a consensus is reached. An important factor of the Delphi technique is that the participants never meet but provide their input in written form. There are several benefits to this technique, including the fact that it is a viable alternative when participants are geographically separated and that it encourages a wide variety of ideas that might otherwise not be considered.

The *nominal group technique* is a structured meeting format designed to elicit participation from all members of the group in order to arrive at the best possible solution to the problem at hand. The process requires a facilitator and begins with a period of time for individuals to think about and write down all their ideas about the issue. After that, each participant presents one idea, which is recorded by the facilitator for later discussion. When all of the ideas have been presented, the process of prioritizing and consensus building takes place, until a resolution has been agreed upon.

Choosing appropriate tools for data analysis provides the HR professional with a comprehensive view of what is needed to accomplish department and organization goals.

Metrics and Measurement

Metrics provide a standard of measurement that can be used to compare results over a period of time. The value of this measurement for HR is that it can be used to quantify activities and programs to demonstrate the value added to the organization. The most important factor to consider in determining which metrics to use in a specific organization is a simple one: measure what is relevant and meaningful to management and will add value to the decision-making process.

Determining which specific metrics will add value to any particular organization is best done by those who work in the organization and know how it operates and what metrics will be useful to assess past experience and project future needs. There are two types of metrics that are useful for HR professionals: those that measure business impact, and those that measure tactical accountability. At the end of each of the following chapters, a section titled "Metrics—Measuring Results" provides some commonly used metrics for that functional area.

Business impact measures   Business impact measures demonstrate how a particular HR program or activity adds value to the bottom line. Two metrics that are useful in measuring business impact are return on investment and cost/benefit analysis.

Return on investment   One of the most commonly-used business metrics is *return on investment (ROI)*. ROI is calculated by dividing the benefits realized as a result of a program by the total related direct and indirect costs.

Cost/benefit analysis   A *cost/benefit analysis (CBA)* compares all costs of a proposed program to the benefits that will be realized if it is implemented and forecasts the net impact on the bottom line. CBA can be used to evaluate the cost-effectiveness of several alternatives and recommend a preferred course of action. The difference between CBA and ROI is that CBA includes soft costs in the calculation, while ROI generally includes only hard costs.

Tactical accountability measures   Tactical accountability measures provide relevant information for evaluating the effectiveness of specific HR programs. These measures identify how well programs for workforce management issues, productivity, and other HR activities are working. Some measures commonly used for this purpose include:

- Job satisfaction
- Organizational commitment and involvement
- Training cost per employee
- Cost per hire
- Turnover and retention
- Absenteeism and sick leave use and frequency
- Grievance rates
- Terminations as a percent of population

Building a business case   A business case is used to evaluate the possible consequences of taking (or not taking) a particular action, such as implementation of an HRIS system, for example. A business case identifies what criteria will be used to determine success, proposes alternative ways to execute the action, and describes possible risks that could result from implementing and not implementing the proposal. An extended time line demonstrates the impact of the program on cash flow, identifying where cost reductions or gains are to be expected. An important element is the description of the basis for quantifying benefits and costs so that those reviewing the proposal clearly understand the assumptions that led to the final recommendation or decision.

Change Management

Change management is another concept that will be more fully developed in Chapter 5. Its reason for inclusion as a core knowledge requirement is simple: change is everywhere. Processes change constantly to meet changing business needs. People change jobs. Economies change. Government regulations change. All of these changes and many others must be addressed with HR programs that are flexible enough to take in the changes while continuing to serve the needs of people within the organization.

Major changes in an organization occur as the result of restructuring, mergers or acquisitions, "right-sizing," and work-force expansions. All of these changes require the workforce to adjust to new ways of operating.

For example, when mergers or acquisitions occur, two organizations, two sets of processes, two cultures, and two groups of people doing similar jobs must acclimate to each other to ensure the success of the business. The process is stressful for employees because, almost inevitably, some people will lose their jobs as the organization eliminates redundancy from its operations. Maintaining morale and productivity during this process often presents a monumental challenge for organizations and HR professionals.

A key element of managing change is ensuring that employees receive current information as soon as possible. While management is often tempted to "wait until we have all the answers," the absence of information creates added stress and apprehension that hinders the acceptance of change by employees. Keeping employees abreast of a situation in flux, even by telling them that all decisions have not been made yet, builds trust that they will not be left in the dark about what is happening.

In general, people resist change for many reasons, some of which can be explained by the motivational theories discussed earlier in this chapter. Change removes the underlying sense of safety and impacts the social structures people create around them within organizations. This makes it difficult for them to accept change, particularly when there is a lack of certainty about the future. Balancing the organization's need to continually adapt to changes in the business environment with the employee's need for clarity and direction presents challenges for every functional area of human resources.

Job Analysis and Description

Job analysis and job descriptions provide the foundation for much of what happens within the employment relationship. The job description compiles all the information collected during the job analysis into a document that is used for multiple purposes in the organization, beginning with the hiring process:

- Based on the job description, the recruiter screens applicants to ensure that their *knowledge, skills, and abilities (KSAs)* are appropriate for the position.

- The applicants for the position use the job description to find out what they will be required to do if the position is offered to them.

- The job description is the basis for performance management and appraisal.

- The job description is the basis for determining the appropriate level of pay for the work that is done.

- The job description includes the essential job functions and provides a guideline for employees who request reasonable accommodation for disabilities.

Job descriptions are also used to determine competitive compensation, to classify employees properly for equal opportunity and affirmative action reports, and for many other aspects of employment. It is essential, therefore, that these processes produce full and complete information about the jobs in the organization.

Job Analysis

The purpose of job analysis is to define a job so that it can be understood in the context of accomplishing organization goals and objectives. To do this, information that describes the work to be done must be collected. There are several ways to collect information during the job analysis process:

- Interview the incumbent if available.
- Interview the supervisor or a group of coworkers.
- Complete a structured or an open-ended questionnaire.
- Complete a task inventory.
- Observe incumbents and make notes.
- Utilize work logs kept by incumbents.

The information gathered during the analysis is summarized in a job description that is used for the various purposes described previously.

Job Descriptions

Job descriptions are written documents that contain information about a job. The description includes the following information.

Identifying information   The job description is identified with the title of the position, department, supervisor, exemption status, salary range or grade, and the date it was created.

Supervisory responsibilities   If the position has responsibility for supervising others, those positions are listed in this section.

Position summary   The summary is a short description of the job, usually two to five sentences.

Essential functions   Essential job functions are the reason the job exists and must be performed by the incumbent. This information is required to comply with the Americans with Disabilities Act (ADA), to be discussed in Chapter 4. Each function should include a description of the level of complexity and the frequency of tasks. As appropriate, the functions describe relationships that the incumbent will have, including supervisory, coworkers within the work group, coworkers in other departments of the company, any external relationships with vendors or customers, and the level of interaction that will take place in these relationships.

Nonessential functions   Nonessential job functions are those which could be performed as part of another job in the organization. For ADA purposes, these functions could be moved into other jobs as a reasonable accommodation for a disabled employee who is fully qualified to perform the essential job functions.

Equipment operated   This section lists tools or equipment that will be used and the frequency of use. This includes use of the computer, telephone, production equipment, any hazardous equipment or tools that will be used, and protective gear or uniforms that will be required.

Job specifications   Job specifications state the minimum qualifications needed for successful performance. Depending on the job, some or all of the following may be required specifications:

Education, licenses, or certificates required   Minimum required qualifications are described in this section. The requirements must be related to the essential job functions, again, to comply with the ADA.

Communication skills required   A description of the level of communication skills necessary to do the job is included in this section. Will the position be writing reports, making presentations internally or externally, or communicating orally?

Experience required   The minimum level of experience required to successfully perform the position is identified.

Skills   Any skills necessary for successful job performance are included in this section.

Physical requirements   Any physical requirements must be described to comply with the ADA. The physical requirements must be related to the essential job functions.

Mental requirements   For ADA purposes, describe the level of mental acuity required to perform essential job functions.

Work environment   The work environment is described, whether it is in an office setting or includes any hazardous equipment or locations that will impact the employee. If stairs or ladders must be utilized, or the job will require work in confined spaces, this must be included as well.

Approvals   The job description should be signed by the manager to verify its accuracy.

During the job analysis process, it is important to keep in mind that the analysis focuses on the *job*, not the *person*. Particularly when a high-performing employee has been in a particular job for any length of time, it is can be difficult to separate what the employee brings to the job from the job's main purpose.

Employee Records Management

Not surprisingly, mounds of paperwork are generated in the employment process: resumes, applications, references, government forms, and performance evaluations are just a few of the many documents created for each employee. In enacting employment legislation, Congress has mandated retention requirements for various documents which, unfortunately, are not consistent. In addition, many state and local governments have retention requirements that differ from federal requirements.

Table 2.5 lists federal document retention requirements for the PHR/SPHR exams; these may be different from the state and local requirements where you practice, so keep that in mind while you are studying. As with any other conflicting requirements, documents should be retained in accordance with the strictest requirement.

TABLE 2.5   Federal Employment Document Retention Requirements

Federal Law or Regulation	Document(s) Covered	Retention Period	Covered Employers
Title VII of the Civil Rights Act of 1964 (Title VII)	Records of all employment actions: employment applications, resumes, hire, rehire, layoffs, recalls, terminations, promotions, demotions, transfers, compensation	1 year	15+ employees
	Apprentice selection records		
	Name, address, social security number, gender, date of birth, occupation, job classification		
	Compensation records (direct and indirect), tax forms, records of hours worked, benefit payments, tax deductions		
	Current EEO-1 Report		
Title VII of the Civil Rights Act of 1964 (Title VII) Americans with Disabilities Act (ADA) Age Discrimination in Employment Act (ADEA) Rehabilitation Act of 1973 (RA)	Personnel records related to discrimination charges	Required: until resolution Best practice: 7 years after employee leaves (for use in future litigation)	15+ employees (ADA/Title VII) 20+ employees (ADEA) Federal contractors and subcontractors with contracts of $10,000+
Americans with Disabilities Act (ADA)	Job announcements, advertisements, and job orders sent to agencies or unions	1 year	15+ employees
	Records of all employment actions: applications, resumes, promotions, transfers, demotions, layoffs, terminations		
	Reasonable accommodation requests		
	Name, address, social security number, gender, date of birth, occupation, job classification		
	Compensation records (direct and indirect), tax forms, records of hours worked, benefit payments, tax deductions		

TABLE 2.5   Federal Employment Document Retention Requirements *(continued)*

Federal Law or Regulation	Document(s) Covered	Retention Period	Covered Employers
Age Discrimination in Employment Act (ADEA)	Compensation records (direct and indirect), tax forms, records of hours worked, benefit payments, tax deductions	3 years	20+ employees
	Name, address, social security number, gender, date of birth, occupation, job classification		
	Employee benefit plans	1 year after plan ends	20+ employees
	Written merit plans		
	Temporary employee records	90 days	20+ employees
	Job announcements, advertisements, and job orders sent to agencies or unions	1 year	20+ employees
	Records of all employment actions: applications, resumes, promotions, transfers, demotions, layoffs, terminations		
	Pre-employment records for temp positions		
	Employment test results		
	Physical examination results		
	Training records		
Consolidated Omnibus Budget Reconciliation Act (COBRA)	Written COBRA procedures	6 years (required by ERISA)	20+ employees
	Payment records and correspondence		
	Documentation that COBRA notices are sent within specified time period		
Davis Bacon Act	Name, address, social security number, gender, date of birth, occupation, job classification	3 years from end of contract	Federal construction contractors and subcontractors (contracts over $2,000)
	Compensation records (direct and indirect), tax forms, records of hours worked, benefit payments, tax deductions		

TABLE 2.5 Federal Employment Document Retention Requirements *(continued)*

Federal Law or Regulation	Document(s) Covered	Retention Period	Covered Employers
Employee Polygraph Protection Act (EPPA)	Reason for test administration Test results	3 years	All employers
Employee Retirement Income Security Act of 1974	Dated and signed documentation of employee receipt of plan reports and disclosures Beneficiary designation and distribution elections—beneficiary distribution Documentation for eligibility determinations (age, length of service record, marital status)	Indefinitely	All employers except churches and governments
	Copies of summary plan descriptions and annual reports, COBRA notices, and other plan reports-Wage and hour records used to determine retirement benefits	6 years after filing date	All employers except churches and governments
	Beneficiary designation and distribution elections—participant distribution	3 years	All employers except churches and governments
Equal Pay Act (EPA)	Date of birth for employees under 19 Gender Occupation Payroll records (time cards, wage/salary rate, deductions, explanation for difference between rates for men and women)	3 years	All employers
Executive Order 11246	Affirmative Action Plan and supporting documents	Update annually	Federal contractors and subcontractors with 50+ employees and contracts over $50,000

TABLE 2.5   Federal Employment Document Retention Requirements *(continued)*

Federal Law or Regulation	Document(s) Covered	Retention Period	Covered Employers
Fair Labor Standards Act (FLSA)	Collective bargaining agreements	3 years	All employers
	Individual employment contracts		
	Sale and purchase records		
	Date of birth for employees under 19		
	Payroll records, including record of name, birth date, gender, occupation		
	Basis for salary calculations for exempt employees		
	Written training agreements, job and selection criteria, records of minority and female applicants		
	Regular pay rate	2 years	All employers
	Beginning of work week, start time		
	Straight time and overtime earnings calculations (day/week)		
	Total wages for pay period		
	Pay deductions		
	Pay period and date of payment		
	Basis for payment of wages		
	Work schedules		
	Job announcements, advertisements, and job orders sent to agencies or unions	1 year	All employers
	Certificate of Age	Until termination	All employers
Family and Medical Leave Act (FMLA)	Basic employee information (name, address, title, compensation, employment terms, hours worked, wage deductions)	3 years	50+ employees within a 75-mile radius
	Employee notices and description of policy		
	Records of leave dates and hours of intermittent leave		
	Benefit premium payments		
	Documentation of disputes about FMLA leave		

TABLE 2.5   Federal Employment Document Retention Requirements *(continued)*

Federal Law or Regulation	Document(s) Covered	Retention Period	Covered Employers
Federal Insurance Contributions Act (FICA)	Income tax withholding information	4 years	All employers
Federal Unemployment Tax Act (FUTA)	Income tax withholding information	4 years	All employers
Immigration Reform and Control Act (IRCA)	I-9 signed by employee and employer	3 years from hire date *or* 1 year after termination (whichever is longer)	4+ employees
National Labor Relations Act (NLRA)	Collective bargaining agreements	3 years	All employers
	Individual employment contracts		
	Sale and purchase records Written training agreements, job and selection criteria, records of minority and female applicants		
	Straight time and overtime earnings calculations (day/week)	2 years	All employers
	Basis for payment of wages		
	Total wages for pay period		
	Pay deductions		
	Pay period and date of payment		
	Work schedules		
	Certificate of Age	Until termination	All employers
Occupational Health and Safety Act (OSHA)	Safety and health training records	3 years	11+ employees
	Illness and injury logs	5 years	11+ employees
	Supplementary injury and illness records		
	Employer records of adverse reaction to chemical substances		
	Medical exam records for exposures to toxic substances	30 years	11+ employees
	Medical exam records for exposures to blood-borne pathogens		
	Hazardous material exposure records		

TABLE 2.5   Federal Employment Document Retention Requirements *(continued)*

Federal Law or Regulation	Document(s) Covered	Retention Period	Covered Employers
Rehabilitation Act of 1973 (RA)	Job announcements, advertisements, and job orders sent to agencies or unions	Retain for 2 years (1 year if less than 150 employees)	Federal contractors and subcontractors with contracts of $10,000+
	Records of all employment actions: applications, resumes, promotions, transfers, demotions, layoffs, terminations		
	Employment test results		
	Physical examination results		
	Training records		
	Name, address, social security number, gender, date of birth, occupation, job classification		
	Compensation records (direct and indirect), tax forms, records of hours worked, benefit payments, tax deductions		
Service Contract Act (SCA)	Name, address, social security number, gender, date of birth, occupation, job classification	3 years from end of contract	Federal service contractors and subcontractors with contracts of $2,500+
	Compensation records (direct and indirect), tax forms, records of hours worked, benefit payments, tax deductions		
	Wages and tax deductions		
Social Security Act	Employee name and ID number	4 years from tax due date	All employers
	Social security number		
	Employee home address with zip code		
Toxic Substance Control Act (TSCA)	Documentation of hazardous material exposures	30 years from report date	Manufacturers, importers, processors or distributors of toxic chemicals
	Documentation of significant adverse reactions to work environment		
	Claims of occupational disease or health problems		

TABLE 2.5   Federal Employment Document Retention Requirements *(continued)*

Federal Law or Regulation	Document(s) Covered	Retention Period	Covered Employers
Uniform Guidelines on Employee Selection Procedures (Guidelines)	Applicant race and sex Employee race and sex Veteran status Disability status	2 years for 150+ employees; 1 year if less	Employers subject to Title VII, EO 11246, and other EEO laws (ADEA and PA are exempt)
Vietnam Era Veterans' Readjustment Act (VEVRA)	Affirmative Action Plan for current and prior year Documentation of good faith effort to comply with AAP Job announcements, advertisements, and job orders sent to agencies or unions Records of all employment actions: applications, resumes, promotions, transfers, demotions, layoffs, terminations Employment test results Physical examination results Training records Name, address, social security number, gender, date of birth, occupation, job classification Compensation records (direct and indirect), tax forms, records of hours worked, benefit payments, tax deductions	2 years	Federal contractors and subcontractors with contracts of $25,000+
Walsh-Healey Public Contracts Act (PCA)	Name, address, social security number, gender, date of birth, occupation, job classification Compensation records (direct and indirect), tax forms, records of hours worked, benefit payments, tax deductions	3 years from end of contract	Federal contractors and subcontractors with contracts of $10,000+

Interrelationships among HR Activities

It has become increasingly important for HR practitioners to understand how individual HR programs, processes, policies, and functions interact with each other. Particularly for SPHR candidates, the ability to link together various aspects of best practices and legal requirements from a variety of functional HR areas, along with being able to evaluate the impact of these activities as a whole, is crucial to exam success.

For example, let's consider the possible consequences of changing an organization's compensation strategy.

 Real World Scenario

Changing the Compensation Plan

Wright Sisters, Inc. (WSI) manufactures garden equipment and employs about 3,000 people, most of whom work on the production line. WSI prides itself on the quality of its products and the loyalty and dedication of its workforce. For many years, WSI has been considered one of the best places to work in the community; as a result, they were able to be selective about who they hired. About six months ago, a new plant opened in the area, and WSI now faces unaccustomed competition in the labor market. Candidate quality has declined noticeably in recent months and line managers are having some problems maintaining product quality. Senior management is considering a number of options to solve the problem.

While the pay being offered by the new company is about the same as WSI's pay plan, the new plant is located in a brand new building with many amenities that WSI's building doesn't offer. Making changes to the building would require a lengthy remodeling process, and WSI's management wants to take some immediate steps to increase the quality of the candidates they are attracting. As a result, management has decided to increase the starting pay for new hires. At the same time, they are unwilling to make any changes to pay rates for current workers. As the VP of HR contemplates this decision, she foresees some problems:

- Because management is not willing to consider a change to the pay ranges even though they are increasing the starting pay, compression will become an issue within a very short period of time.

- Once word gets out that new employees are making more than employees with more seniority, the VP foresees an increase in employee relations issues, most notably morale problems among the production workers. As she is well aware, morale problems generally lead to decreases in productivity and quality.

- While WSI's workforce has remained loyal to this point, with only a very few defections to the new plant, the VP is concerned that there will be an increase in turnover when employees feel their loyalty is not appreciated.

- Management has always been very open and responsive to employee concerns, so employees have not been susceptible to union organizing efforts. The VP is concerned that this change will open the door for an organizing campaign.

- Finally, the VP is concerned about possible claims of discrimination, as much of WSI's workforce is older than the average age of applicants for these positions.

As she considers these issues, the VP begins work on a presentation for management to ensure that they understand all the implications of this change prior to its implementation; while this change may temporarily solve the recruiting issue, it could easily lead to increased costs in a number of areas.

Probably the best example of the way HR programs and activities connect to each other is the area of talent management. This activity unites the HR functions that build, retain, develop, and manage a workforce capable of taking an organization into the future. The talent management approach incorporates several human resource activities—planning for future workforce needs, recruiting, retaining, and developing employees, managing their performance, and creating a positive, supportive culture.

Chapter 4 describes how workforce planning, including recruitment and retention, is used to attract individuals with the right skills. One of the tools used to retain key employees is development, discussed in Chapter 5. Another element of talent management is an effective performance management program that provides ongoing feedback to employees so that they can continue to improve their skills and knowledge. Chapter 7 discusses the importance of a positive organization culture and the impact it has on the qualified, productive employees that are essential to achieving organization goals.

There are two schools of thought developing about which employees are included in talent management initiatives. In some organizations, a very narrow view is taken, and talent management focuses on high-potential employees being groomed for leadership positions. Other organizations take a broader view, recognizing the need to retain talented individuals at all levels. While it is crucial to have talented, effective individuals at senior organization levels, front-line employees are often more visible to customers and end-users and the impact they have in one-on-one interactions affects organization success. Management philosophy and budget constraints have an impact on which philosophy is embraced in different organizations.

Understanding the impact of individual programs on the HR function, as well as on the organization as a whole, is key to increasing the strategic value of HR to organizations. As you study the material in this book, keep in mind the possible impact of the various principles, theories, laws, and regulations on HR activities and programs. In this way, you'll gain a better understanding and appreciation of their role in HR.

Organizational Structures

Keeping a large group of people with different perspectives and assignments moving in the same direction is a challenge for organizations. *Organizational structures* were designed to provide a framework that keeps information flowing to the functions and employees who need it to keep the organization moving forward. Some structures are more successful at this than others, and over time, as the business environment changes, different structures were developed to solve the shortcomings of traditional structures. In some cases, organizations may use different structures in different business units. For example, the VP of Sales in an organization with a functional structure reports to the CEO, but the sales organization may be organized with a geographic or product structure for the most efficient management of the sales operation.

Functional structure   This is represented by the traditional pyramid-shape organization chart with which most people are familiar. It is a hierarchical structure in which communication moves from the top down and from the bottom up. These structures are more formal and rigid than some other structures and are appropriate for businesses with a single product line where specialization is an advantage. In this structure, each functional area reports to the CEO. Functional organizations are generally very centralized. Figure 2.5 depicts the traditional functional structure.

Product-based structure   A product-based organization structure, also known as a customer-oriented structure, is organized by product line and is appropriate when the company has well-defined product lines that are clearly separate from each other. In this structure, each product line reports to the CEO; these structures lend themselves to either centralized or decentralized decision-making processes. Figure 2.6 displays a product-based structure.

Geographic structure   In a geographic structure, executives of regional areas are responsible for all the business functions in their assigned region; the regional executives report to the CEO. Structuring an organization in this way is appropriate when there are common requirements in the region that are different from the requirements in other regions. Geographic structures are decentralized, with most decisions being made at the local level. Figure 2.7 depicts a geographic structure.

FIGURE 2.5   Functional organization structure

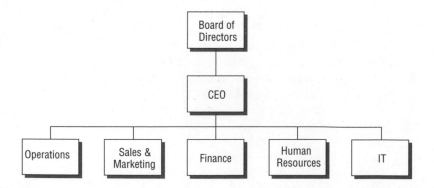

FIGURE 2.6   Product-based organization structure

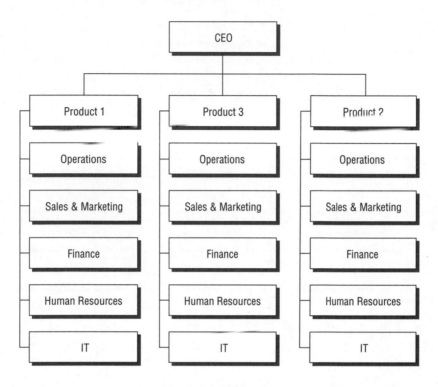

Divisional structure   A divisional structure has characteristics similar to that of the geographic structure, but the divisions may be based on criteria other than geography, such as the market or industry. Like the geographic structure, divisional structures are characterized by decentralized decision making. A sample division structure can be seen is Figure 2.8.

Matrix structure   In a matrix structure, employees report to two managers. Generally, one manager is responsible for a product line and the other has functional responsibility. For example, the VP of marketing and the production manager for a specific product would both supervise the marketing coordinator who is creating collateral for the product. A matrix organization is advantageous because it encourages communication and cooperation; it requires a high level of trust and communication from employees at all levels to ensure that contradictory instructions are minimized. A matrix structure is depicted in Figure 2.9.

Seamless organization   A seamless organization is one in which the traditional hierarchies do not exist—it is a horizontal organization connected by networks instead of separated by the boundaries that characterize other organization structures. The purpose of this structure is to enhance communication and creativity. Seamless organizations would not be possible without the technology that allows employees to connect with each other via email and the Internet from anywhere in the world. This technology enables employees to meet with coworkers who have specialized knowledge without the expense of traveling.

FIGURE 2.7   Geographic organization structure

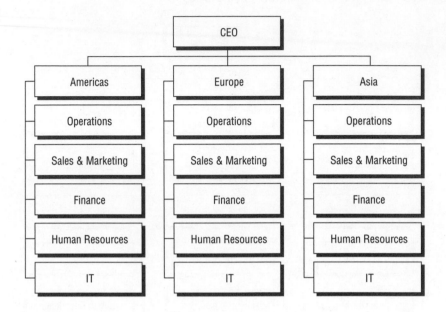

FIGURE 2.8   Divisional organization structure

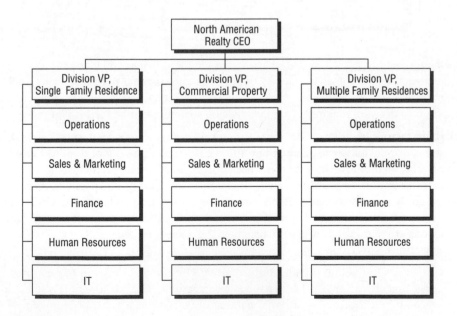

FIGURE 2.9   Matrix organization structure

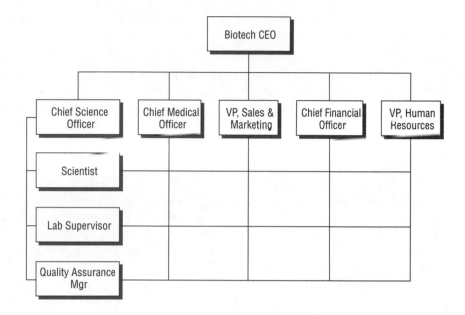

Environmental Scanning Concepts

In order to develop a strategic plan and set the future direction of a company or develop human resource programs to support its growth, leaders need to know what is going on within the organization, in the industry, and the marketplace and how technological developments will affect operations. An *environmental scan* provides the framework for collecting information about factors relevant to the decision-making process and can help management make decisions that take advantage of existing opportunities and avoid pitfalls. There are two elements to the scanning process: internal assessment and external assessment, and there are a number of planning tools available for use in collecting the information.

Conducting a comprehensive environmental scan can be a challenge; there is a great deal of information available from many sources, and finding the information that is relevant to the specific business can be time consuming. In addition to the information available from industry associations, government agencies, and trade organizations, customers and suppliers are excellent sources of information for a specific business. Many business-focused cable television channels present in-depth program segments on pertinent topics such as unemployment and inflation (among others), and business publications also provide in-depth examination of some topics. There is a wealth of information available—the challenge comes in finding what is most appropriate for a specific organization's needs.

Environmental Scanning Tools

There are a number of tools available for use in the scanning process. Let's take a look at some that are commonly used.

Statistical models   A number of quantitative analysis models that can be used to identify trends were described earlier in this chapter. These are useful internally (to analyze turnover rates, for example) and externally (to analyze customer buying habits).

SWOT analysis   A *SWOT analysis* looks at the strengths, weaknesses, opportunities, and threats that are facing the organization. Strengths and weaknesses are internal factors that can be controlled by the organization; opportunities and threats are external factors that may impact an organization's plans.

   Strengths   Strengths are internal factors that will support the organization's plans. These can include people (perhaps your workforce is highly trained in a unique skill not available to other businesses in your market), machinery and equipment (a recent upgrade of manufacturing equipment that allows you to produce more high quality products at a lower cost), technology (a state-of-the-art order processing system), and other factors that give the organization an edge in the marketplace.

   Weaknesses   Weaknesses are also internal factors, but these represent obstacles to the organization. Weaknesses can include workforce issues such as poorly trained workers, old machinery or equipment that is inefficient and costly to operate, outdated technology, and any other factors that make it difficult for an organization to achieve its goals.

   Opportunities   Opportunities are external factors that will aid the organization in the marketplace. These can include a wide variety of factors such as economic upswings, demand for the product, a competitor whose product quality has declined, and other factors that are discussed more fully in the next section.

   Threats   External factors that the organization must overcome or turn to an advantage are threats to its ability to achieve success. These can include strong product competition, economic problems, low unemployment rates, and other factors that make it more difficult for the organization to compete.

PEST analysis   A *PEST analysis* (also sometimes referred to as a STEP analysis, depending on how the words are arranged) scans the external environment to identify opportunities and threats as part of the SWOT analysis. PEST is an acronym for political, economic, social, and technological factors. I'll discuss PEST in more detail in just a minute.

Porter's 5 Forces   This analytical tool was created by Michael E. Porter, PhD, a professor at Harvard Business School who has written extensively on business planning and strategy. In his book, *Competitive Strategy: Techniques for Analyzing Industries and Competitors,* first published in 1980 by Free Press, he described five forces that are found in all industries. These forces include new competitors, suppliers, buyers, alternative products available to consumers, and the type and level of competition in the industry. The importance of these factors in strategic planning will be more fully discussed later.

Internal Assessment

Leaders need a firm grasp of the talent and resources currently available within the organization. Some areas to consider in an assessment of strengths and weaknesses could include the following:

Credibility of executive team	Market penetration
Strength of management team	Customer service reputation
Organization culture	Market share
Workforce diversity	Customer loyalty
Current product quality	Level of sales
Time to market	Employee loyalty
State of technology	Turnover rate

The areas to be reviewed will depend to a certain extent on the nature of the business but should include an assessment of performance in every function of the business.

There are a number of ways to collect this information: questionnaires, qualitative analyses, focus groups, surveys (of customers, suppliers, and employees), stakeholder interviews, and other information collection techniques as discussed earlier in this chapter.

External Assessment

Scanning the external environment presents more challenges than does an internal assessment because the vast amounts of information available must be sought in a wide variety of locations. Tools such as the PEST analysis and Porter 5 Forces analysis can assist in narrowing down what kind of information needs to be collected. The PEST analysis provides a guide for collecting information related to the general business environment:

Political

The political environment includes such things as increased government regulations and events that influence them, such as massive business frauds. A recent example of this is the impact of the Sarbanes-Oxley Act of 2002 enacted by Congress in response to the Enron and WorldCom scandals. Less spectacular but equally important considerations for business planning purposes include changes in employment regulations such as the changes to overtime regulations proposed by the Department of Labor in 2003–4.

For multinational corporations, consideration must be given to political situations in each country of operation, including the stability of the government in some countries, restrictive trade policies, and the friendliness of the government to foreign investment.

All countries and businesses are now faced as well with the threat of terrorism that has negatively impacted sales in the travel industry; products related to security, on the other hand, have a wider market in this situation.

Economic

The most obvious example of economic concerns has to do with the strength of the economy—can customers afford the organization's products? The unemployment rate is a key factor here, along with interest rates, inflation, and changes in fiscal policy.

For investment and expansion purposes, the stock market impacts the ability of a business to raise capital, and the price of real estate can add to the cost of purchasing or leasing new facilities. The strength of the dollar and the rate of inflation must both be considered when creating a long-term strategy.

Social

The demographics of the target market must be considered in long-term planning as well. If an organization's products are targeted at young adults, for example, and that population is static or decreasing, the organization must either change its products or find new markets for them. For multinational corporations, analyzing the social factors of widely diverse markets around the world can prove challenging, but it is essential to ensure that the long-term planning will result in a strategy that increases the success of the business.

Technology

The rate of change in technology varies in different industries, as does the cost of purchasing new technology. Technology affects the level of automation in an organization, and that impacts the overall cost of products. From cell phones to hand-held computers and robotics on production lines, advances in technology impact how work is done and must be considered in the environmental scanning process.

Porter's 5 Forces Analysis

While the PEST analysis provides a guide for scanning the general business environment, Porter's 5 Forces analysis hones in on issues specific to the industry in which the organization operates. It is critical to understand these industry-specific factors and address them during the planning process. Some questions to ask in the analysis include:

How likely is it that new competition will enter the market?   A market with great demand for a product that is inexpensive to produce and requires little initial investment will encourage new competition. This puts pressure on the organization to maintain a competitive price or to differentiate its product on some basis to maintain market share.

How reliant is the organization on its suppliers?   When an organization produces a product requiring a unique part that can only be obtained from one supplier, the organization may find itself at the mercy of the supplier should it decide to raise the price of the part, discontinue it, or change it substantially.

How diverse is the organization's customer base?   A company reliant on one or only a few customers may find itself being pressured to lower prices, particularly if the product is easy to obtain from other sources.

Are comparable replacement products available to customers at a reasonable cost?   A serious threat to the organization's customer base will be present if a product is generic and similar products made by competitors are easy to obtain at a similar or lower price.

What is the level of competition in the marketplace?   The level of competition in the market will, to a certain extent, limit the strategies available to an organization wishing to enter that market. A market dominated by one or two large competitors holding the bulk of the market share presents quite a different challenge than a new, untapped market with a few small competitors.

There is a more detailed discussion of Porter's 5 Forces at www.quickmba.com/strategy/porter.shtml.

Employee Attitude Assessment

Gathering information about employee attitudes and opinions provides information about how well the organization is meeting employee needs and the level of engagement in the employee population, and it provides input for changes to a benefit package or other HR programs. Employee attitudes impact productivity and conducting an assessment can help an organization diagnose what is causing low productivity or morale. Once problems are identified, programs can be designed to address the issues and improve productivity. Various methods are used to collect this information, including surveys, interviews, and focus groups.

Employee surveys   Employee surveys can be used to gather information on any number of issues and are effective for large numbers of employees. Surveys can be developed in-house or outsourced to companies which specialize in developing and conducting them regularly. Outsourcing a survey can result in more honest feedback because the identity of participants can be protected.

Interviews   One-on-one interviews are used to gather in-depth information about individual attitudes and perspectives. This method of collecting information is best for collecting detailed information about, for example, a complex work process. When information must be gathered from large groups of employees, however, interviews are an inefficient and time consuming method.

Employee focus groups   When it is impractical to solicit input from all employees, a focus group consisting of a cross-section of employees from various departments and levels in the organization can be used to solicit employee input.

Whichever method is selected, it is important to give all employees an opportunity to be heard and to collect information on a wide variety of topics, from the effectiveness of individual managers to organizational climate and specific policies. Employees must feel safe to provide honest feedback, and this is most often accomplished by making the survey anonymous. The most important result of employee attitude assessment is the ability to identify trends that are impacting morale and productivity.

Basic Budgeting and Accounting

The finance function is responsible for creating and maintaining accounting records and managing organization budgets. HR professionals at the management level are often expected to participate in the budgeting process not only for HR-specific expenses, but by providing compensation and benefit information that is incorporated in the overall organization budget. While closely related, accounting and budgeting activities have different goals.

Accounting

The accounting function creates reports to summarize the results of business activity, including the balance sheet, income statement, and statement of cash flows. All accounting reports are produced at the end of accounting periods, which are generally monthly, quarterly, and annually. The annual reporting period can be defined as any 12-month period and does not necessarily coincide with a calendar year (January through December). An annual reporting period that is different from a calendar year is known as a *fiscal year*. Many companies, for example, have fiscal years that begin on July 1 and end on June 30 of the following calendar year.

The *balance sheet* is a picture of the financial condition of the organization on a specific day, usually the last day of the accounting period. Information on the balance sheet includes the company's assets, liabilities, and equity. This report is known as a balance sheet because the total of the liabilities and the equity must equal the total of the assets as represented by the balance sheet formula:

Assets = Liabilities + Equity

The *income statement*, sometimes referred to as the *profit and loss statement (P&L)*, provides information about the financial results of operations during the reporting period. The report tells you how much revenue was produced from various sources, how much it cost to produce the goods or services, what the overhead expenses were, and what the profit or loss for the period was.

The *statement of cash flows* provides important facts about the money that flowed through the business during the accounting period: where it came from and what it was used for. This statement shows how much cash was a result of sales, how much was spent to produce the products that were sold, how much money was borrowed or came in as a result of new capital investments, and how much was invested in assets.

HR professionals need to understand some basic accounting terminology and be able to read and understand financial reports in order to be effective strategic partners in their organizations. Table 2.6 provides definitions for some common accounting terms.

TABLE 2.6 Common Accounting Terms

Term	Definition/Description
Accounts receivable	Money owed to the business by customers
Accounts payable	Money owed by the business to its suppliers

TABLE 2.6 Common Accounting Terms *(continued)*

Term	Definition/Description
Accrued expense	Expenses, such as vacation leave, that have been incurred but not yet paid
Assets	Tangible or intangible items of value owned by the business
Audited financial statements	Financial statements that have been examined by an independent auditor (not affiliated with the company) to determine if they fairly represent the financial condition of the business
Budget	A projection of revenue and expenses used to control actual expenses
Cost of goods sold	Money spent on supplies and labor to produce goods or services
Equity	Value of the business to owners after all liabilities have been paid
Expense	Money spent to operate the business
GAAP (Generally Accepted Accounting Principles)	Standards established by the Financial Accounting Standards Board (FASB) for recording financial transactions
Gross profit	Sales revenue less cost of goods sold
Liability	Money owed by the business to others, such as lenders or the government (for payroll taxes withheld), or to employees (for unused vacation time)
Net profit	Gross profit less operating expenses
Profit	Money earned by the business after all expenses have been paid
Retained earnings	Net profits that are not distributed to owners but remain in the business as equity
Revenue	Money received from customers for products or services

Budgeting

The budgeting process is used to determine how many and what kind of resources will be required to accomplish goals and objectives generated by the strategic plan. Whether the plan requires additional employees, funds to outsource elements of the plan, new technology, or new equipment, these elements determine how much cash is needed to achieve the goal. There are two basic ways to create a budget; the first is based on historical budget information and the second is known as *zero-based budgeting* (ZBB).

Budgets based on historic information   A budget based on historic information bases the current budget on the prior year's budget. Past budgets and expenditures are reviewed and the new budget is based on the historical trends. In some cases, the amounts in the budget are increased by a flat percentage rate, based on inflation or anticipated salary increases. This method assumes that operationally, nothing will change from the last budget.

Zero-based budgeting (ZBB)   The concept behind ZBB is very simple: assume you are starting from scratch and determine what is needed to achieve the goals. How many people will be required? How much will you need to spend on outsourcing? What will be the cost of new technology or equipment? Unlike the historic budget process, ZBB requires that the need for each expenditure be justified in terms of the new goals and action plans.

As part of a zero-based budget planning process, HR examines all the programs offered to employees to determine if they are still adding value to the organization. Programs that no longer add value are dropped and replaced with those that do add value; or, if cost cutting is required, are dropped and not replaced.

Regardless of the way in which the budget is developed, it can be created from the top down, from the bottom up, or with a combination approach.

Top-down budgeting   The top-down budget is created by senior management and imposed on the organization. Managers with operating responsibility have little input on how much money they will have to achieve their goals. This process is advantageous to senior management because they have complete control of how and where the money is spent. The disadvantage is that those creating the budget are generally far removed from actual operations and may not have full knowledge of what will be needed to achieve the goals they establish. This method often results in political battles as mid- and lower-level managers lobby senior management for additional funds for their particular departments.

Bottom-up budgeting   The bottom-up budget includes all managers with budget responsibility in the budget creation process. Managers with direct operating responsibility for achieving goals develop a budget based on their knowledge of operating costs and provide the information to senior managers who have a view of the big picture for the organization. One advantage of this process is the commitment of operating managers to a budget they helped to create. Disadvantages include the amount of time required, the lack of awareness of the organization's big picture on the part of operating managers, and initial budget requests that may be unrealistic.

Parallel budgeting   A parallel budget includes elements of both the top-down and bottom-up approaches: senior management provides broad guidelines for operating managers to follow in creating budgets for individual departments. This approach gives operating managers a context for developing individual budgets that are more realistic.

The end result of the budget process is a projection of expected revenue and costs needed to generate the revenue. Budget reports also include a cash flow projection which is used to prepare for short- or long-term shortfalls of cash, such as might occur in a seasonal business when the cash that comes in during the sales period (such as Christmas or Mother's Day) must support expenses that occur over a longer period of time. A separate report, known as a capital budget, is used to project asset purchases, such as buildings, machinery and equipment used in manufacturing, or computers.

Risk Management

Risk management is the process of identifying possible threats to achievement of an organization's goals and taking steps to reduce the impact of those threats. Risks to an organization come in many forms, including failure to comply with government regulations and inadequate internal controls. In the human resource function, risks are often in the form of liability for questionable employment actions. Liability is a legal term that refers to a duty or responsibility owed by one party to another. A *liability* can result from an agreement or a contract or can be created through a tort. A *tort* is another legal term that describes an action that injures someone. Torts are not related to laws or contracts but can result in legal action: the party who has been injured is able to sue the wrongdoer and collect damages for the injury that has been done.

As will be discussed in Chapter 7, liability for wrongful actions in employment relationships costs businesses millions of dollars in judgments for many different types of torts, from wrongful termination to sexual harassment and discrimination. HR professionals can help managers understand the legal exposure that may result from making adverse employment decisions without first understanding the possible consequences, including the costs of defending a lawsuit.

One way to mitigate against risks is through insurance coverage, and an important policy for businesses to maintain is *employment practices liability insurance (EPLI)*. EPLI protects employers against lawsuits brought by current or former employees. During the application process, an insurance company evaluates the employer's human resource policies and any lawsuits or claims filed by employees or former employees. These factors, along with considerations of the employer's operations and size, are used to determine whether or not an EPLI policy may be issued and the amount of the premium to be paid.

Managing risk involves taking steps to reduce the legal exposure created by poorly written policies or unlawful practices in an organization. This can be done by assessing the risk:

1. Identify possible exposures to legal action (for example, inconsistent policy application).

2. Audit the organization's employment practices. Educate managers on the possible risks that could result from unlawful employment actions.

3. Develop a plan to reduce the risks, and obtain top management support for the process.

4. Analyze the costs of purchasing insurance versus self-insuring, and recommend a course of action.

5. If losses related to employment issues have occurred in the past, develop a way to present a plan for reducing the costs of these losses to top management.

Once a risk assessment is completed, there are three possible ways to reduce the risk: the organization can obtain insurance, decide to self-insure, or mitigate the risk by replacing equipment or providing training to reduce possible hazards to employees.

Summary

This chapter provided an overview of the core HR knowledge requirements, which have implications in all of the HR functional areas and are the basis for understanding responsibilities in those areas.

Each of these requirements is the subject of many books, articles, and seminars, and some are even the basis for entire professional associations or certification programs in their own right. If, after reading this chapter, you feel the need for additional information about any of these topics, the Internet or your local library will provide additional resources to enhance your knowledge. Appendix C, "Resources," at the end of this study guide also provides some resources that may be helpful.

Keep in mind that it's most important to understand the concepts introduced in this chapter and the way they apply to the functional areas of the body of knowledge.

Exam Essentials

Be able to describe how HR programs interact.   It is important to understand the ways programs or policies developed for one functional area impact others. For example, the compensation policy will affect the quality of candidates attracted by the company, turnover rates, the ability of the company to maintain union-free status, and employee job satisfaction.

Be able to describe the needs assessment and analysis process.   Needs assessment and analysis refers to a process used to obtain information about what a business needs to meet its goals. There are seven steps in a needs assessment: describing the objective, defining the current situation, conducting a gap analysis, setting priorities, developing options, determining the costs, and recommending the solution.

Understand the uses of a third-party contract.   Third-party contracts are used for various functions in the HR department. Choosing a third-party contractor begins with a needs assessment to determine how best to serve the needs of the organization. The RFP process provides an organized way to select the best option for the needs of the business.

Be able to describe communication strategies.   To ensure that the right information is provided to employees when they need it and that there is a mechanism for senior management to hear from employees, a communication strategy must be developed based on what information is needed, who needs to hear it, who will provide it, and when it will be delivered.

Understand the basic concepts associated with andragogy (adult learning theory).   Andragogy, also known as adult learning theory, is built on concepts that say adults are autonomous, self-directed, goal-oriented, relevancy-oriented, and practical, and that they need respect. Also, adults build new knowledge on a foundation of life experiences. Adult participants react either positively or negatively to training as a result of the presence or absence of these characteristics.

Be able to recognize and describe various motivation theories.   Motivational theories help HR professionals and managers understand why employees behave the way they do and develop programs that result in highly motivated, productive workers.

Understand the uses for qualitative and quantitative analysis methods.   Quantitative analysis is based on mathematical models, such as correlation and measures of central tendency. Qualitative analysis is based on more subjective judgments based on secondary research.

Be able to describe the benefits of workplace diversity.   A diverse workforce is more creative and better reflects the customer population. Increasing diversity in the work force provides access to more qualified candidates; this is important due to the projected shortfall of qualified workers over the next decade.

Understand the HR Code of Ethics.   The HR Code of Ethics developed by SHRM requires HR professionals to maintain standards of professional responsibility and development, provide ethical leadership in their organizations, ensure fairness and justice within their organizations, avoid the appearance of conflicts of interest, and use confidential information appropriately.

Understand the difference between job analysis and job descriptions.   Job analysis is the process used to identify and determine duties associated with a particular job; job descriptions are the end product. Typically, job descriptions document a job's major functions or duties, skill and physical requirements, and working conditions.

Understand metrics and how they are used in HR practice.   Metrics provide a means for quantifying HR programs and activities to exhibit the value added to organizations. The best metrics are those that provide relevant information to management and add value to the decision-making process.

Key Terms

Before you take the exam, be certain you are familiar with the following terms:

acquired needs theory	multiple linear regression
active training methods	needs analysis
andragogy	nominal group technique
balance sheet	organizational structures
behavioral reinforcement	pedagogy
case study	performance-based training (PBT)
change management	PEST analysis
communication strategy	presentation

computer-based training

conferences

contract

correlation

correlation coefficient

cost/benefit analysis (CBA)

cycles

Delphi technique

demonstration

distance learning

diversity

diversity initiative

diversity training

employment practices liability
insurance (EPLI)

environmental scan

equity theory

ERG theory

expectancy theory

experiential training methods

fiscal year

gap analysis

hierarchy of needs

human resource information system (HRIS)

income statement

job enrichment

knowledge, skills, and abilities (KSAs)

liability

mean average

primary research

profit and loss statement (P&L)

programmed instruction

project management (PM)

qualitative analysis

quantitative analysis

request for proposal (RFP)

return on investment (ROI)

scientific method

secondary research

simple linear regression

simulation training

statement of cash flows

subject matter experts (SME)

suspension

SWOT analysis

termination

Theory X and Theory Y

third-party contract

time series forecasts

tort

transactional leadership

transformational leadership

trend analysis

two-factor theory

verbal warning

vestibule training

weighted average

median

mode

motivation/hygiene theory

moving average

weighted moving average

written warning

zero-based budgeting

Review Questions

1. A department manager advises you that the productivity of his data entry operators is unsatisfactory and asks you to develop a training program to improve their data entry skills. What is your first step?

   A. Conduct a needs assessment.

   B. Develop a lesson plan.

   C. Talk to other managers to validate the situation.

   D. Select a training method.

2. For several months, the management team has been struggling to come to grips with the need for a formal succession plan. About 30 percent of the workforce will reach retirement age within 10 years, and little has been done to prepare for the loss of knowledge in key roles that will occur as employees begin to retire. The team has come to a consensus that what is needed is a comprehensive plan, one that includes a mentor program for each of the key positions, identification of key skills that will need to be replaced, a recruiting strategy that attracts qualified candidates who are looking for longevity, and creating a more open culture. Which of the following can be used to accomplish these goals?

   A. Create a succession plan

   B. Create a knowledge management program

   C. Create a talent management program

   D. All of the above.

3. Based on an analysis of the industry and labor market trends, a VP of Human Resources has determined that the best course of action for her company is to change from a narrow to a broadband salary structure. The current structure has been in place for more than 15 years, and the VP is anticipating strong resistance to making the change. Which of the following tools should the VP use to convince the executive team to make the change?

   A. Calculate the return on investment

   B. Build a business case

   C. Calculate the cost-benefit analysis

   D. Conduct a SWOT analysis

4. Maslow's hierarchy of needs does *not* include the following need:

   A. Social

   B. Safety

   C. Growth

   D. Self-actualization

5. Rachel has worked in accounting for six years. She has always been a steady performer, but recently she has made several costly errors in her work. The accounting manager, Rachel's boss, has talked to her several times, but no improvement has taken place. What is the most appropriate action the manager should take?

    A. First written warning

    B. Verbal warning

    C. Decision-making day

    D. Coaching

6. What is the purpose of a diversity initiative?

    A. To educate all employees about other groups in the workforce

    B. To increase the diversity of the workforce

    C. To increase organizational creativity

    D. To increase the comfort level of employees

7. Which of the following is *not* an appropriate use of an HRIS?

    A. Tracking applicant data for the EEO-1

    B. Tracking time and attendance

    C. Tracking employee expense reports

    D. Maintaining employee records

8. The middle value when values are arranged in order from high to low is the

    A. Mean

    B. Median

    C. Mode

    D. Moving average

9. A basic principle behind job analysis is that

    A. The analysis focuses on the job, not the person.

    B. The analysis focuses on the person doing the job, not the job.

    C. The analysis is limited to task inventories and questionnaires.

    D. The required qualifications should include everything the manager would like the employee to have.

10. After conducting a risk assessment, what can you do to protect the company against any identified risks?

    A. Identify policies that are applied inconsistently throughout the organization.

    B. Obtain employment practices liability insurance.

    C. Develop a plan to reduce the risks.

    D. Present management with a plan for reducing the risks.

Answers to Review Questions

1. A. A needs assessment is conducted to determine what is required to solve a problem, including whether or not training is the appropriate intervention. If, for example, network crashes are the cause of the low productivity, training will not solve the problem. Lesson plans (B) are created during the design stage of training discussed in Chapter 5. Talking to other managers to validate the situation (C) may be included in the needs assessment along with other factors. The training method is selected (D) during the development phase discussed in Chapter 5.

2. C. A talent management program is a comprehensive strategy for workforce management. This approach includes planning for future needs, recruiting qualified candidates, creating compensation and retention strategies, developing employees, managing performance, and cultivating a positive culture. A succession plan (A) is part of the workforce planning element of a talent management program. Knowledge management (B) focuses on building systems that retain corporate knowledge accessible as needed by the organization.

3. B. A business case lays out the desired result of an action or program, presents alternative solutions, describes possible risks from both implementing and not implementing the action, and defines the criteria used to measure success. ROI (A) and CBA (C) may be included as part of the business case and a SWOT analysis (D) may have identified the need for a program or action.

4. C. Maslow's hierarchy of needs is a theory developed to explain what motivates workers. The levels are physiological, safety, social, esteem, and self-actualization. Growth is a need level identified by Alderfer in the ERG theory, which is based on Maslow's work.

5. B. Assuming that the nature of the previous conversations with Rachel has been informal, the most appropriate step is a verbal warning, where Rachel is advised that this is the first step in the disciplinary process and failure to improve will lead to further disciplinary action, up to and including termination. The first written warning (A) takes place after a verbal warning. A decision-making day (C) is usually the final step prior to termination. Coaching (D) is an informal means of talking to employees about performance problems and generally occurs prior to a verbal warning.

6. B. A diversity initiative is designed to increase diversity in an organization. Diversity training educates employees about the cultural and social differences in other cultures and is designed to increase the comfort level of employees (A and D). A benefit of diversity is increased organizational creativity (C).

7. C. Data for employee expense reports is maintained by the accounting department, although the employee data in the HRIS may feed finance's expense reporting tool. An HRIS system can be used to collect and track employee data for various uses, including EEO-1 reporting (A), time and attendance (B), and other employee records (D).

8.   B. Median is defined as the middle value when values are arranged from high to low. Half the numbers are higher than the median; half are lower. The mean (A) is calculated by adding up the values and dividing by the number of values. The mode (C) is the value that occurs most frequently in a set of numbers. The moving average (D) keeps data current by dropping the oldest data when new data is added.

9.   A. The correct focus of a job analysis is the job itself, not the incumbent in the job. Performance management focuses on the person in the job (B). An analysis may utilize a number of sources in addition to task inventories and questionnaires (C), including interviews, observation, and supervisory input. The required qualifications should be related to the essential functions of the job to avoid complaints of discrimination (D).

10.   B. As part of the risk assessment, inconsistent policies have been identified (A), a plan for reducing risk has been developed (C), and management has reviewed the plan for reducing risks (D). After the assessment is complete, the company may decide to purchase insurance, self-insure, or mitigate the risk by making operational changes.

Chapter

3

Strategic Management

✓ **Interpret information related to the organization's operations from internal sources, including financial/ accounting, business development, marketing, sales, operations, and information technology, in order to contribute to the development of the organization's strategic plan.**

✓ **Interpret information from external sources related to the general business environment, industry practices and developments, technological developments, economic environment, labor pool, and legal and regulatory environment in order to contribute to the development of the organization's strategic plan.**

✓ **Participate as a contributing partner in the organization's strategic planning process.**

✓ **Establish strategic relationships with key individuals in the organization to influence organizational decision-making.**

✓ **Establish relationships/alliances with key individuals in the community to assist in achieving the organization's strategic goals and objectives.**

✓ **Develop and utilize metrics to evaluate HR's contributions to the achievement of the organization's strategic goals and objectives.**

✓ **Develop and execute strategies for managing organizational change that balance the expectations and needs of the organization, its employees, and all other stakeholders.**

✓ **Develop and align the organization's human capital management plan with its strategic plan.**

- ✓ Facilitate the development and communication of the organization's core values and ethical behaviors.

- ✓ Reinforce the organization's core values and behavioral expectations through communication and coaching.

- ✓ Develop and manage the HR budget in a manner consistent with the organization's strategic goals, objectives, and values.

- ✓ Provide information for the development and monitoring of the organization's overall budget.

- ✓ Monitor the legislative and regulatory environment for proposed changes and their potential impact to the organization, taking appropriate proactive steps to support, modify, or oppose the proposed changes.

- ✓ Develop policies and procedures to support corporate governance initiatives (for example, board of directors training, whistleblower protection, code of conduct).

- ✓ Participate in enterprise risk management to prevent and/or mitigate loss and ensure business continuity by examining HR policies to evaluate their potential risks to the organization.

- ✓ Identify and evaluate alternatives and recommend strategies for vendor selection and/or outsourcing (for example, HRIS, benefits, payroll).

- ✓ Participate in strategic decision-making and due diligence activities related to organizational structure and design (for example, corporate restructuring, mergers and acquisitions [M&A], offshoring, divestitures. **SPHR ONLY**

- ✓ Determine strategic application of integrated technical tools and systems (for example, HRIS, performance management tools, applicant tracking, compensation tools, employee self-service technologies).

The current business environment, with its emphasis on the ability to compete in global markets and respond to rapidly changing conditions, requires more of its leaders and managers than ever before. They must seek and develop competitive advantage in their marketplaces and continuously create new processes, products, and services to meet the ongoing challenges presented in a global business setting. As each challenge is met, successful managers are already forecasting the next challenge on the horizon, looking for an advantageous market position. This ongoing process of innovation, advantage, value creation, and reassessment is known as strategic management. HR professionals seeking certification must understand what strategic management means, how the process impacts HR policies and practices, and how HR can add value in the organization's quest for market advantages.

To lay the groundwork for our discussion of strategic management, this chapter examines the interaction of human resource activities with organization functions and looks at how HR policies are developed to meet organization needs established by the strategic planning process. Because a major factor in business operations is constant change, this chapter also looks at managing change in organizations and discusses the roles of HR and management in that process. This chapter also examines core values and ethics and how HR can influence ethical standards in organizations. I'll take a look at corporate governance, and finally, examine the legislative and regulatory environment and how HR practitioners can influence changes in that arena.

As you begin this chapter, be sure to refer to the knowledge requirements for Strategic Management in the *HRCI Certification Guide* described in the introduction to this book. In addition, several sections in Chapter 2, "Core Knowledge Requirements for HR Professionals," have particular relevance here: a review of the discussions on needs assessment, development of RFPs, communication strategies, leadership concepts, HR ethics and professional standards, technology, quantitative and qualitative analysis tools, change management, employee records management, types of organizational structures, environmental scanning, employee attitude assessment, basic budgeting, and risk management techniques will enhance your review of the material in this chapter.

Strategy

What is business strategy, and how does it impact HR professionals? A business strategy is developed by the executive management team led by the CEO, president, or other leader of an organization. The purpose of the strategy is to clearly identify the goals to be achieved by the organization, create an implementation plan, and distribute assets and other resources needed for success. HR professionals contribute to business strategy as the subject matter experts (SMEs) for attracting, retaining, and managing a workforce qualified to implement the strategy and achieve organization goals.

Organizations

Since ancient times, people have formed groups to achieve goals that they were unable to achieve on their own. Whether it was for protection, shelter, food, or profit, organizing gave people the means to achieve more than they could by acting alone. With the advent of the Industrial Revolution in the late eighteenth century, organizations grew larger and more complex as the goals to be achieved became more complex. As the production of goods moved from a single worker creating an entire product to multiple workers completing pieces of a single product, the need for control over the production process became greater. The modern organization evolved to coordinate the many different activities that are needed to produce the goods or services necessary to achieve its goals.

Businesses in the United States are organized in one of four basic structures: sole proprietorships, partnerships, corporations, or limited liability companies.

Sole Proprietorships

This business structure is the most basic and easy to organize. The owner is a single (sole) person who is the final authority for all decisions in the business. Any profits earned by the business belong to the owner, and the owner has unlimited, personal liability for all business decisions and activities.

Partnerships

A partnership is owned by two or more people who share final authority for all business decisions and are jointly liable for the actions of the business. Partners are liable not only for their own individual actions, but for the actions taken by their other partner(s) as well. The profits of the business are split according to the ownership share established at the beginning of the partnership (most often equal shares, but ownership can be any arrangement agreed upon by the partners). There are several types of partnership arrangements:

In a general partnership (GP), the partners share responsibility for managing the business based on the partnership agreement.

In a limited partnership (LP), or a limited liability partnership (LLP), most of the partners are involved only as investors and have little input into daily operations of the business.

These forms are commonly used for medical clinics, accounting practices, law firms, and other service businesses.

A **joint venture (JV)**, is similar to a GP but is formed to manage a specific project or for a limited time frame.

Corporations

Corporations are entities defined by four characteristics:

1. Liability is limited to assets owned by the corporation.
2. The life of the corporation can extend beyond the life of its original owner/founder.
3. There is a central management structure.
4. Ownership may be transferred freely by selling stock.

Corporations sell stock to raise the funds necessary to operate the business. Owners of the stock, known as stockholders or shareholders, are free to sell the stock they own to other investors at any time. These stockholders can be individuals or other entities, and for the most part are not involved in the daily operation of the business. They elect a Board of Directors to represent their interests with the senior management team in making decisions about the strategic direction of the company. Because corporate liability is limited to the assets owned by the corporation, stockholder/owner liability is generally limited to the amount of stock owned by individual investors; there are exceptions for corporate officers who may be held personally liable for any wrongdoing or negligence.

Corporations are legal entities and may incur debts, sign contracts, and be sued in the same way that individuals may be. This is the most common form of business for large enterprises in the United States.

Limited Liability Company

A limited liability company (LLC) is a cross between a general partnership and a corporation and provides its owners with the liability protection of a corporation with fewer operating restrictions. An LLC exists for a finite period of time defined at the time it is organized, and it can be extended by a vote of the owner/members when it expires. An LLC may have only two of the four characteristics of a corporation; otherwise, the entity must become a corporation.

Regardless of an organization's legal form, there are three aspects of organizations that must be considered by HR professionals in developing plans and programs: structures, functions, and life cycles. Chapter 2 discussed various structures. The next section describes organization functions and life cycles.

Organization Functions

Every business has some common components: production and operations, sales and marketing, research and development, finance and accounting, information technology and, of course, the people who make everything happen. Whether the business is simple or complex, or has one employee or hundreds of thousands, these components are all necessary for success.

Production and Operations

The terms "production" and "operations" are, in many cases, used interchangeably. When used separately, *production* generally refers to the process by which businesses create the product or service they offer to customers. Traditionally, this meant manufactured goods, but with the growth of service and information businesses, it has come to include services as well.

The *operations* function encompasses all of the activities necessary to produce the goods or services of the business. These can include such activities as:

Capacity   Determining how much of a product or service is able to be produced with the available materials, labor, and equipment (known as inputs) as well as what changes in inputs are required by fluctuating customer demands.

Production layout   The way in which the goods or service will be produced, for example, the design of an assembly line or, in the case of a service, the process to be used in providing it, such as a model plan or protocol for a financial audit.

Scheduling   Scheduling activities make sure that the products or services are available at times of peak customer demand.

Quality management   Quality assurance (QA) ensures that the product or service meets acceptable standards.

Inventory management   Operations managers must balance two conflicting needs related to inventory: the cost of maintaining a large inventory and the need to satisfy customers by filling orders promptly. *Just-in-time (JIT) inventory* management systems attempt to do this by purchasing smaller amounts of supplies more frequently to reduce inventories and ensure a steady supply of products for distribution.

Technology   Increasing the use of technology can improve product quality and the amounts that are produced.

Facility location   Evaluating the best places to locate production facilities involves many considerations: the cost of labor, distribution systems, and government regulations, to name a few.

Cost control   As with all business functions, operations must provide products or services that meet the quality standards set by the organization at the lowest possible cost.

Sales and Marketing

Sales and marketing are closely related activities involved with creating a demand for the company's products and moving them from the company to the customer.

The *sales* function includes all the activities involved in transferring the product or service from the business to the customer.

Marketing incorporates all the functions necessary to promote and distribute products in the marketplace, provides support for the sales staff, conducts research to design products that customers will be interested in purchasing, and determines the appropriate pricing for the product. Marketing begins with an identification of the target market for the organization's product or service. Once that has been identified, decisions about the 4 P's of marketing (product, price, place, and promotion) can be made:

Product   This can be a physical product or a service or, in some cases, both. Product development includes making decisions about what the product will do, how it will look, what kind of customer service is needed, whether a warranty or guarantee is appropriate, and how the product will be packaged to attract customers.

Price   Setting the correct price point for a product is an important marketing function. The price must attract the customer, compete with other similar products, and return a profit. Pricing looks not only at the "list price" but at any discounts or allowances that will be offered.

Placement   Also referred to as distribution, this is where decisions are made about where the customer will find the product. Having an in-depth description of the target customer is helpful in this step: how does the customer shop? Is it on the Internet? At the mall? By phone? These and similar questions must be answered to appropriately place the product.

Promotion   Products are promoted in many different ways including advertising, public relations, personal selling, and providing incentives for customers to buy. Incentives such as discounts, rebates, or contests are techniques commonly used to market products and services.

Research and Development

The research and development (R&D) function is charged with designing new product offerings and testing them to make sure they do what they are designed to do before they are offered to the public. R&D develops new products and redesigns old ones to meet changing market demands, often developing products to create demand where none previously existed. R&D works closely with marketing and production in this process. Marketing provides information it gathers from customers about their needs while production provides input on the ability of the production process to create the product, or the need for new processes.

Depending on the nature of the organization and industry, for example, automobile manufacturing and pharmaceuticals, research and development (R&D) is a separate function. In other organizations it may be shared by the marketing and operations functions.

Finance and Accounting

Finance and accounting are closely related functions and include all the activities related to the movement of money into and out of the organization.

The *finance* function is responsible for obtaining credit to meet the organization's needs, granting credit to customers, investing and managing cash for maximum return on investment, and establishing banking relationships for the organization. The finance function also provides technical expertise for the analysis of current operations or proposals for new business directions and the projection of future financial needs.

Financial analysts work with all functions of the organization in a variety of ways. For the operations function, an analyst can provide models to predict the number of employees needed at different production levels, along with the budget impact of those different levels. Working with personnel in the operations and marketing functions, analysts compile cost data, profit margins, and pricing information to provide accurate profitability forecasts at different sales volumes and pricing levels. HR practitioners may work with analysts to project needed staffing levels or benefit costs for budget planning purposes.

The *accounting* function is responsible for activities that record financial transactions within an organization. Transactions related to product sales and the costs related to creating the product are known as cost accounting; this information is critical for the operations function to manage production costs. Other accounting activities include the processing of various transactions such as payroll, expense reimbursements, accounts receivable and payable, and the establishment of internal controls to ensure compliance with government regulations, FASB standards, and GAAP. The accounting function is also responsible for preparing the budget reports managers use to maintain control of operating costs.

Under the Securities Exchange Act of 1934, Congress gave statutory authority for establishing reporting standards for publicly held companies to the Securities and Exchange Commission (SEC). In 1939, the American Institute of Certified Public Accountants (AICPA) established a committee to develop accounting standards and reports for the private sector. This committee developed generally accepted accounting principles (GAAP) for use by accounting professionals. In 1972, an independent body, the *Financial Accounting Standards Board (FASB)*, was created by the AICPA to take over responsibility for setting accounting standards. FASB standards are officially recognized by the SEC as the authority for accounting practices. These standards are essential to the efficient functioning of the economy because they enable investors, creditors, auditors, and others to rely on credible, transparent, and comparable financial information.

Information Technology

Information technology (IT) is the area of the business responsible for managing systems such as voice mail, computer networks, software, websites, and the Internet as well as the data collected by these systems.

As technology has become more prevalent and sophisticated, the use of IT systems has expanded from the original data storage and retrieval function. For example, the ability of new systems to increase the accuracy of scheduling requirements for operations managers by providing real-time sales and inventory tracking makes the IT function a strategic advantage in organizations. As a result, IT plays a growing role in the strategic management of organizations.

People/Employees

Whether it is a one-person operation or a company with hundreds of thousands of employees throughout the world, the people who do the work *are* the business. With appropriate and effective human resource strategies, employees are satisfied, productive good-will ambassadors for the company. Conversely, low productivity, higher costs, and poor customer service are by-products of ineffective HR strategies. The connection between these differing results and the level of employee engagement in an organization was made by the Gallup Organization in research conducted over a period of years and presented in the book, *First, Break all the Rules* by Marcus Buckingham and Curt Coffman (Simon and Schuster, 1999). Buckingham and Coffman identified four factors that contribute to an engaged workforce:

- Identify the best fit for employees
- Concentrate on individual employee strengths

- Clearly establish desired results
- Look for talent as well as KSAs when selecting employees

So what does it take to build employee engagement in a workforce? To an extent, the specifics of an engaged workforce are unique in each organization, but generally speaking, employees who see a connection between their daily responsibilities or tasks and the organization's goals are more engaged in its success. Three themes have emerged in research on engagement: leadership, professional development, and employee recognition.

Leadership   The most important connection for employees is the one they have with their direct manager or supervisor, and how this relationship is managed directly affects their level of engagement. Chapter 5 includes a discussion of the importance of emotional intelligence, the ability for managers to create personal connections with their direct reports. This personal connection, combined with a manager's enthusiastic support for the organization and its goals, is necessary for employees to develop a level of trust. Trust is reinforced by managers who do what they say they will do by following through on their commitments to employees. Leadership is also demonstrated when managers communicate about organizational goals and the workgroup's role in achieving those goals. Further, clearly communicating individual employee expectations within the context of organizational goals helps to keep them focused on what is important for the organization. Making this an interactive communication by listening to employees and acting on suggestions whenever possible is also key to engaging employees.

Professional Development   Professional development begins with the selection process when employers hire talented candidates who demonstrate potential for, and interest in, professional growth opportunities. Employees are engaged by managers who not only talk about development, but also "walk the talk" and actively groom subordinates for higher-level responsibilities.

Chapter 5, "Human Resource Development," goes into more detail on professional development.

Employee Recognition   It is human nature for employees to respond positively to recognition for achievements or for performing "above and beyond" normal expectations. Recognition can take many forms, and knowing what form appeals most to a particular individual is crucial. It is also important that the recognition, whatever form it takes, be genuine and gratefully expressed.

Organization Life Cycles

As organizations are established and grow, they move through four distinct phases: startup, growth, maturity, and decline. Organizations approach each of these stages with different expectations and needs.

Startup   During the startup phase, organization leaders struggle to obtain funding so the organization can survive. Because employees hired during this phase must wear many different hats, there is little time for training, so they are usually fully qualified for their positions, and base pay is very often below the market rate. At this stage, outsourcing can be a cost-effective alternative for specialized functions that do not require full-time employees. There are generally few layers of management, which allows employees to work closely with the founders and leaders.

Growth   In the growth phase, the founder is not able to manage the organization alone and additional management personnel are brought into the company. This can lead to morale issues as employees who once had access to organization leaders lose the daily contact common in the startup phase. As the organization becomes more successful, funds are available to provide competitive compensation and benefits to attract and retain qualified employees. From an operation standpoint, the growth phase presents challenges when it exceeds the ability of the infrastructure to handle it, sometimes necessitating the outsourcing of some functions to meet needs.

Not all organizations are able to make it through the growth phase and collapse under the weight of their good fortune or are acquired by larger entities with the infrastructure to support operations.

Maturity   At the maturity phase, the organization has enough resources to provide planning and standardize policies and procedures. In this stage, it is possible to become bureaucratic and unwieldy, making it difficult for the company to change direction as rapidly as may be necessary to remain competitive. From an HR standpoint, the relative stability of this phase means that it is possible to hire less experienced personnel and provide them with training and development so that they are able to take on additional responsibilities. The compensation and benefits for executives are often enhanced during this stage.

Decline   A declining organization is characterized by inefficiency and bureaucracy. In order to remain viable, leaders may implement workforce reductions, close facilities, and take other cost-cutting measures. The organization's products may be outdated and unable to compete, resulting in a downward sales trend.

Organizations in the declining phase of the life cycle will need to reinvigorate themselves in order to survive. This may happen with the development of new product lines or with the redesign of existing products to bring them up to current competitive standards. When this does not occur, the organization may be acquired by a competitor or may cease to exist altogether.

From this discussion, you know that all organizations are made up of similar components. Why, then, do some organizations succeed while others either stumble along at a mediocre level or fail completely? The difference lies in how well the organization is able to position itself to take advantage of market opportunities and avoid the pitfalls present in the business environment. The strategic planning process provides a framework within which organizations are able to do this.

Strategic Planning

Global competition requires business leaders to use tools that give them an advantage in the marketplace. One such tool is known as *strategic planning*. Broadly defined, strategic planning is a systematic way of setting the direction for an organization and developing strategies, tactics, and operational plans to ensure its success. Strategic planning is a dynamic process— it's not something an organization does one time to produce an attractively bound booklet that sits on the shelf gathering dust. By its very nature, strategic planning requires that organizations constantly revisit the plan to make sure it is still viable in the face of changes within the organization and in the marketplace. The strategic planning process answers four essential questions:

- Where are we now?

- Where do we want to be?
- How will we get there?
- How will we know when we arrive?

Because strategic planning has been a popular topic for business writers, consultants, and academicians during the past decade, there are a number of planning models from which to choose.

The specific model selected for use in an organization will depend upon the structure and culture of that organization (both of which are discussed in this chapter). The elements of all the models fall into four very broad categories: environmental scanning, strategy formulation, strategy implementation, and strategy evaluation.

For purposes of the PHR/SPHR exam, candidates should be aware of how all of these elements contribute to the strategic planning process. Figure 3.1 illustrates a typical strategic planning process.

> The steps are described here in a logical sequence. In real life, the process may not occur in a straight-line progression; if new information that will affect results is uncovered at any stage, previous steps may be revisited so the information can be incorporated into the plans and goals.

Planning to Plan

Very often, a strategic planning initiative is led by a consultant experienced in the process. This is helpful for many reasons, not least of which is that during the course of determining the future of the organization, disagreements about the long-term direction of the company may surface, and these are more readily resolved with a neutral third party who is better able to facilitate a resolution and move the process forward than someone with a vested interest in the outcome. When a consultant is used, the preplanning process is generally part of the service they provide.

The "preplan" includes decisions about who will be invited to participate and at what stages in the process, a time frame for completing the plan, and determination of the tools to be utilized in collecting data for the plan. Spending this additional time at the beginning of the process could prevent costly errors or omissions from being made and can assist in making the resulting strategic plan more accurate and meaningful.

The result of this stage should be an agreement about the process to be followed, a list of those who will be involved at various stages in the process and the type of information they will be asked to provide, the time line for completing the plan, and a list of the planning tools to be utilized in gathering information to be used in the planning process.

Let's begin by defining the terms that will be used to discuss the strategic planning process.

A *strategy* uses the strengths of a business to its competitive advantage in the marketplace. A *goal* describes the direction the business will take and what it will achieve. Goals are set at the corporate and business unit level of the organization.

FIGURE 3.1   Elements of the strategic planning process

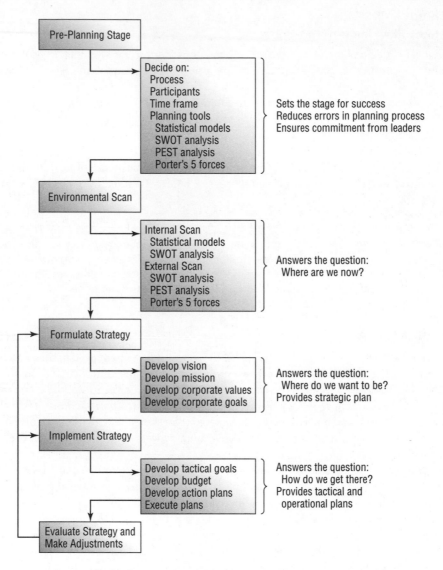

An *objective* is a specific description of the practical steps that will be taken to achieve the business goals. Objectives are set at the functional level of the organization.

In order to effectively determine the future direction of a company, it's necessary to know what is going on within the organization, in the industry, and the marketplace and what technology developments will mean for operations. Beginning the strategic planning process with this information can help to focus management on a plan that will avoid pitfalls and take advantage of existing opportunities.

Environmental Scanning

As discussed more fully in Chapter 2, an environmental scan is the framework for collecting information to create a successful plan for future growth. Information gathered during the scan is used to forecast future business circumstances so that the organization can take advantage of the strengths and opportunities presented by the marketplace while reducing the negative impact of its weaknesses and external threats. The forecasting process is particularly crucial when organizations are in the midst of rapid change. For example, the forecast allows management to be proactive by redesigning products that will comply with regulations being proposed by federal or state governments so that they are available when the regulations take effect.

During the forecasting process, management must consider the impact of changes that are anticipated to take place over the long-term, mid-term, and short-term. *Long-range plans* set the organization's direction for three to five years, *mid-range plans* can be accomplished in one to three years, and *short-range plans* will be achieved within six to twelve months. Plans that incorporate the information gathered during the environmental scan are developed during the next planning phase, strategy formulation.

Strategy Formulation

Having scanned both the internal and external environments and gathered data relevant to the strategic planning process, the executive team is ready to create the vision, mission, and core value statements, which guide the organization over the long term. Once these long-term guidelines have been established, corporate goals are developed to provide direction during the implementation phase.

Vision statement   A vision statement should inspire the organization, describing what will carry it into the future and what it will accomplish. In a very concise way, it should communicate what the company does, for whom they do it, and what long-range success will look like.

Mission statement   The mission statement gets a bit more specific, describing how the organization will achieve the vision. Effective mission statements describe the company, what it does, where it is going, and how it is different from other organizations. The message of the mission statement should be directed at employees in the organization, and it should tell them where the company is headed in the mid- to long-range.

Core competencies   During the formulation of a strategic plan, organizations often identify their core competencies, that is, what parts of their operations they do best and set them apart from the competition. Many organizations believe that focusing on these core competencies makes it possible to expand their revenue streams. Competencies can be related to the technology utilized in operations, customer relationship management, product characteristics, manufacturing processes, knowledge management, organization culture, or combinations of these or other organizational aspects that work together synergistically and are difficult to replicate by others. When core competencies are identified, organizations can focus their strategy on ways to build related products or services instead of moving into unrelated areas.

Corporate values statement   A statement of corporate values is a way for the executive team to communicate their standards for how the organization will conduct business. The values chosen for this purpose should be those that will be true regardless of changes in product lines or business processes. A question to ask in selecting an organization's values is whether or not the value would hold true if the organization changed its focus entirely and began doing business in a completely different way. Values such as integrity, excellence, teamwork, customer service, and mutual respect are some of those that remain constant regardless of changes in business operations.

These beliefs about the organization are usually reflected in its culture. When identifying corporate values, it is important to look not only at what the management team would like to see in the way of behaviors in the organization, but also to look at the values being demonstrated in the course of business each day. When there are discrepancies between the stated, formal values and the informal values demonstrated by the workforce, the strategic plan can include goals designed to align the two.

Once the vision and mission statements have defined why the organization exists, corporate goals are needed to describe how the organization will get there in the mid- to long-range. Effective corporate goals follow the SMART model:

Specific   The goal should be descriptive enough to guide business unit managers in developing action plans that will accomplish the goal.

Measurable   A goal must include a method for determining when it has been met.

Action-oriented   Goals must describe the actions that will be taken.

Realistic   The goal must be high enough to challenge the organization or individual but not so high that it is unachievable.

Time-based   Goals must include a time frame for completion.

Strategy Implementation

The strategy implementation phase further defines the corporate goals for implementation at the business unit and functional levels of the organization. It is at this stage that most of the short-range goals are developed.

Develop tactical goals   While the strategic goal broadly defines direction, the tactical goal describes what will be accomplished to achieve the strategy.

Develop action plans   The action plan breaks the tactical goal down into steps to be taken by an individual, team, or operating group to accomplish the tactical goal.

Develop budget   When the action plans are complete, it is possible to determine how many and what kind of resources will be required to implement the plan. Whether the plan requires additional employees, funds to outsource elements of the plan, new technology, or new equipment, these elements determine how much cash is required to achieve the goal.

Real World Scenario

Wright Sisters, Inc. Strategic Plan

As you recall from Chapter 2, Wright Sisters, Inc. (WSI) is a fictional company with 3,000 employees that has been recently challenged by the appearance of a new manufacturing plant in the small Midwestern city where they are located. The unexpected impact of this seemingly small change in the external environment has made senior management and the board of directors realize how unprepared they are to respond rapidly to changes in their business sector. They've decided to be proactive and implement a strategic planning process to discover what other unexpected changes could be lurking in the future.

Over the years, there have been many changes in the market for their products, both technological and demographic. Because WSI has always maintained strong relationships with the hardware stores who distribute their products, they've been able to meet the changing needs of their customer base.

As a result of the strategic planning process, the WSI board has settled on the following statement of their vision for the company:

"Bringing the joy of gardening to new generations of gardeners."

In order to accomplish this vision, WSI has developed a mission to guide its operations over the next five years:

"We are the home-gardening source. The quality of our products allows busy families to enjoy gardening together. Our gardening education programs grow 'gardeners for life' by teaching adults and children to make gardening easier and more enjoyable."

Based on its history and its vision and mission statements, the board created a corporate value statement to set expectations for how employees and managers interact:

"WSI values integrity and excellence in its products and its people. We treat ourselves, our customers, and our suppliers with dignity and respect. We believe in and encourage new ideas to make our products better and help our business grow, and we acknowledge and reward those who present these ideas. We are accountable for our actions and, when mistakes occur, we focus on preventing future errors and moving forward. We are passionate about achieving our goals, and we are passionate about gardening."

As a result of the environmental scan, the WSI board learned that one of its underutilized strengths is the popularity of "Ask Lydia," a gardening column written by one of its founders, Lydia Wright. Because of this, they have decided to capitalize on Lydia Wright's knowledge of and passion for gardening. To do this, they have developed the following corporate goal:

"Within three years, create a nationally recognized gardening education program based on the 'Ask Lydia' columns."

In order to accomplish this mid-range goal, the marketing department has developed a short-range tactical goal and action plan:

Tactical goal: "Increase the number of newspapers in which 'Ask Lydia' appears by 25 by the end of the fiscal year."

Action plan:

1. Identify newspapers to target.

2. Create sales pitch.

3. Contact editors.

4. Draw up contracts.

5. Submit weekly columns.

With the goals in place, the marketing department is now able to develop a budget and implement the plan.

Develop budget

When the action plans are developed, it is possible to determine how many and what kind of resources will be required to implement the plan. Whether the plan requires additional employees, funds to outsource elements of the plan, new technology, or new equipment, these elements determine how much cash is required to achieve the goal. Refer to Chapter 2 for a discussion of the budget development process.

Strategy Evaluation

Evaluating the strategy tells you how well you are doing toward achieving your goals. This stage is important because if the action plans are not working or if conditions in the marketplace change, the organization must be prepared to respond immediately and adjust the tactical goals and action plans. In some cases, the corporate goal may need to be revisited and adjusted to adapt to the change in conditions. One method of evaluation is the balanced scorecard discussed later in this chapter.

Organizational Structure and Design

One possible result of a strategic planning process can be structural changes to an organization. While intellectually many people understand the need for these changes, how they are personally affected has a direct impact on employee morale and productivity. Because the change process involves structural changes (covered in this chapter) and individual behavior (covered in Chapter 5), I struggled with where to discuss the details of change and how structuring an organization can ease the change process. The discussion of methods and how they can be used to effect organizational change occurs in Chapter 5, along with the discussion of the impact of changes on individuals in the organization. This section provides a brief look at the structural changes that significantly affect workforce populations today.

Reengineering   Reengineering involves looking at the entire organization to simplify or eliminate unnecessary processes with the goal of increasing customer satisfaction through improvements in efficiency.

Corporate restructuring   Corporate restructuring looks at individual units in the organization to reduce or eliminate redundancy or bureaucratic processes in order to reduce costs and increase production.

Workforce expansion   Workforce expansions create their own type of stress in an organization. When a large number of employees enter an organization within a short period of time, it can be difficult for them to assimilate into the existing culture and climate. The resulting clashes of operating styles (face-to-face versus email communication, team orientation versus individual contributors, or authoritarian versus laissez-faire management styles, for example) can create mistrust and reduce productivity.

Workforce reduction   Workforce reductions, also known as reductions in force (RIFs), downsizing, or rightsizing, are used to decrease expenses by reducing the size of the workforce. One way RIFs are used is to lower expenses for short-term improvements in net profits in order to meet previously stated earnings targets for stock market analysts.

Mergers and acquisitions   Mergers and acquisitions (M&A) have similar results—the combining of two organizations into one, but they happen for different reasons and in somewhat different ways. A merger occurs when two or more organizations are combined into a single entity with the goal of leveraging the assets of both into a more successful entity. One of the best-known recent mergers is that between AOL and Time-Warner in 2001.

An acquisition occurs when one organization, generally a corporation, purchases or trades stock to gain controlling interest in another. Acquisitions can be hostile, when the management and board of directors of the company being acquired object to the takeover. Hostile takeovers are usually antagonistic, with the acquiring company purchasing shares on the open stock market. This type of acquisition can negatively affect employee morale as rumors about mass layoffs circulate among the staff of the target organization.

In a friendly takeover, the management and board of the targeted company agree to terms offered by the acquiring organization, generally a cash purchase of stock or a predetermined number of shares in the acquiring company. An example of an acquisition is the purchase of Siebel Systems in 2005 by its competitor, Oracle Software.

HR professionals participate in the due diligence process prior to a merger or acquisition. There are many aspects to review in order to obtain a complete picture of the employment practices of the target company. The types of information to be collected as part of the due diligence process include the following:

- Documents
  - Names of all employees and their locations
  - Offer letters
  - Employment contracts
  - I-9 forms and visa documentation

- Compensation
  - Hourly wage rates by job
  - Salary schedules
  - Number of employees in each position
- Policies and procedures
  - Employee handbook
  - Supervisor/manager handbook
- Equal opportunity compliance
  - EEO-1 reports
  - Affirmative Action Plans (if required)
  - Government notices of compliance activity
- Legal compliance
  - COBRA notices and participants
  - Active FMLA leaves
  - WARN compliance
  - OSHA compliance
- Labor relations
  - Collective bargaining agreements
  - Ongoing negotiations
  - Union activity
  - Grievance history and outstanding grievances
- Legal exposure
  - Pending or resolved sexual harassment claims
  - Termination disputes
  - Violations of state or federal laws

HR professionals also work to facilitate successful integration of the two workforces in a merger or acquisition. To begin with, an analysis of the workforce of the two organizations provides information on how to best utilize people in the new entity. This may result in transferring employees into different positions or reducing the workforce as redundant operations are identified and streamlined. Development of strategies to retain key employees is an important task particularly during the initial period of uncertainty. In the longer term, one of the most difficult transitions is the combining of two cultures into a cohesive environment that enhances productivity.

Divestitures   In a divestiture, a company asset such as a product line, division, or other part of an organization is sold or somehow disposed of. This may occur as the result of a strategic decision to focus on core competencies or because the asset has greater value as a standalone operation than as part of the original organization. In some cases, there will be little change to day-to-day operations for employees since the organization remains intact with a new ownership structure.

Offshoring and outsourcing decisions and management   Offshoring is the process of moving production or service processes to other countries to realize cost savings. India has become a popular offshore site for service processes, such as customer support call centers.

Outsourcing contracts internal business services to outside organizations that specialize in the specific process, such as payroll processing, IT, or janitorial services.

Either decision generally results in a reduction in staff for employees who previously did the work which will now be done externally. In some cases, an outsource firm may hire those employees who will continue to do the same work as members of the new organization.

No matter the cause, even employees who remain in the company after a change occurs are affected by it. A key contribution to be made by HR during change is to be sure that the decision makers understand the difficulties that employees will face during and after the change and how those difficulties affect productivity. HR can put programs into place that mitigate the negative effects of the change as much as possible. Some steps that can help to reduce employee anxiety include the following:

- Keep employees in the loop about the actual situation.

- If there are actions employees can take to remedy the situation, tell them what they can do.

- When talking to employees, be honest and truthful. Don't hide the facts.

Good or bad, the way companies handle change will be remembered long after employees have adjusted to the new way of doing business. The long-term impact of including employees in the change process through open and honest communication is to increase loyalty and productivity. If the organization has a habit of being brutal in its change processes, long-term productivity suffers and it will be more difficult to attract and retain the quality of employees needed for future success.

Strategic HR Planning

During the strategic planning process, HR, along with all other business functions, must develop tactical goals and action plans designed to meet the needs of the organization. HR professionals must base their planning on corporate strategy and goals and work with managers of other functional areas to ensure that recruiting and hiring goals meet the needs created by the tactical goals and action plans of those functional areas.

For example, planning for future staffing needs requires an analysis of many factors: prospects for future product sales, new product development, anticipated customer demand, competition (both global and local), changes in government regulations, economic conditions, and other factors discovered during the environmental scanning process discussed in Chapter 2. Reviewing these plans with line managers provides HR with the information needed to conduct a staffing needs assessment to ensure that individuals with the appropriate knowledge, skills, and abilities (KSAs) are available when the business needs them.

Strategic HR planning also involves scrutiny of current HR practices with an eye toward streamlining them to provide better service to internal customers. The accuracy of information and speed of access can be improved by providing employees and managers with direct access to information they need. For employees, this could mean the ability to access and update personal information such as address and dependent status changes (referred to as employee self-service).

For managers, this could take the form of access to performance management or training records. Even candidates can benefit through the ability to input their resumes or applications directly into the applicant tracking system. All of these process changes reduce HR department costs and free professionals to spend more time on other organization issues.

Building Strategic Partnerships

The role of human resources in organizations is characterized by change. Not long ago, HR practitioners were expected to contribute to the organization in an advisory capacity, provide services to employees and others, and control employment policies and procedures in their organizations. As advisors, we were asked to provide information and guidance for managers to deal with employee issues. As service providers, HR professionals were required to answer questions and provide information for a wide range of constituents, from government agencies to candidates for employment and senior management. In the control role, HR was expected to enforce policies and ensure compliance with federal, state, and local employment regulations and laws.

Today, while the roles are still in flux, they have begun to evolve into strategic, administrative, and operational roles.

Strategically, HR professionals contribute to decisions that build on employee strengths to meet corporate goals. Establishing recruiting and retention plans to attract the best-qualified employees and keep them in the organization is a key contribution that HR is uniquely qualified to make. Developing performance management systems to motivate employees and providing continuous development opportunities are other areas that provide strategic advantage to organizations. Managing change and leading or participating in reengineering or restructuring programs to ensure the retention of key employees furthers the organization's ability to meet its goals.

Administratively, HR manages compliance issues related to government regulations, maintains employee and benefit records, and ensures the confidentiality of employee information.

Operationally, HR professionals manage the employee relations and recruiting functions that require daily attention to maintain a productive work environment.

Management

As organizations developed and continue to grow ever larger, the need for controlling large numbers of workers in geographically diverse locations presented a challenge for business owners, who responded by creating bureaucracies to ensure that operations were conducted in accordance with the direction set by senior management. These bureaucracies, developed by American businessmen in the mid-nineteenth century, enabled the dominance of American products throughout the world for 100 years and were emulated by businesses in other countries. As long as the demand for products was greater than the number of products available, this model, in which business dictated what it would produce to the customer, worked extremely well.

When business conditions changed and customers became more demanding, this "one size fits all" approach was not as successful. Japanese manufacturers gave customers an alternative, and the customers responded by purchasing their products. American businesses, due to their large bureaucratic methods, were slow to respond. The need for constant innovation to satisfy changing customer needs was a difficult transition, and continues to affect American business.

It is up to management to ensure that "the strategies and plans developed to meet changing" customer needs are "also" implemented and accomplished. To do this, managers utilize four basic management functions: planning, organizing, directing, and controlling. These functions ensure that organization resources are utilized in the best way to achieve corporate goals. The planning function has been covered extensively; let's talk briefly now about the other functions.

Organizing   Managers are responsible for providing a structure within which employees are able to complete their work. Many factors must be considered, including what work needs to be done, how employees interact and with whom, the decision-making process in the organization, and how work is delegated. Issues to be considered in developing an organization structure are whether the management is centralized or decentralized, the nature of the functions, and the span of control for each manager.

A *centralized organization* is one in which the decision-making authority is concentrated at higher levels in the organization; while in a *decentralized organization*, the decision-making authority is delegated to lower levels.

Business functions are classified as either *line functions*, such as operations and sales, which make decisions about operating needs, and *staff functions*, such as human resources and finance, which do not make operating decisions but do advise line managers.

Finally, *span of control* refers to the number of employees that one manager can directly supervise. Depending on the nature and complexity of the task, this number varies, with managers responsible for very complex tasks requiring closer supervision able to supervise fewer employees than managers responsible for less complex tasks.

The five basic organization structures: functional, product-based, geographical, divisional, and matrix are described in Chapter 2, as is the emerging seamless organization. Each is appropriate for different situations as described in that chapter.

Directing   Managers must establish relationships with the employees they supervise to encourage and support them in accomplishing their goals. Management style contributes to the development of these relationships. Chapter 2 discussed different management styles in detail in the section "Leadership Styles."

Controlling   The control function is used by managers to ensure that the strategies, tactics, and plans developed during the planning process are implemented. As discussed earlier in "Strategy Evaluation," this is an ongoing process. In addition to the evaluations of individual goals and action plans described in that section, management must have a "big picture" view of overall progress.

One way of getting the big picture is by utilizing the *balanced scorecard*, a strategic management system developed by Robert Kaplan, PhD and David Norton, PhD. Their concept was that because traditional business measurements focused only on financial results, other key elements that impacted business success were not included in strategic management decisions. To address this shortcoming, the balanced scorecard concept tracks information in four key areas: financial results, customer results, key internal processes, and how people are hired and trained to achieve organization goals.

The balanced scorecard accomplishes this by tying objectives to specific measures of performance and setting targets for meeting the objectives. The purpose of the scorecard process is to tie all business functions into specific plans for achieving goals and to provide a means of measuring how each objective contributed or failed to contribute to organization-wide goals.

The Balanced Scorecard Institute provides a complete discussion of the concept at `www.balancedscorecard.org/basics/bsc1.html`.

There are other methods for controlling operations, such as Six Sigma, Total Quality Management, and Management by Objectives. These are also used as organizational development strategies and are discussed in Chapter 5.

Another management responsibility is managing risk to protect the organization's assets and ensure continuity of operations in extreme conditions.

Enterprise Risk Management

Enterprise risk management (ERM) is a practice of forecasting possible risks to the organization and taking steps to mitigate their impact on operations. The first step in ERM is to identify the risks; for HR, that means conducting an audit of HR practices to identify areas of potential loss. An audit identifies areas that may be out of compliance with legal requirements or are in need of updating due to strategic changes within the organization and defines elements that are working well. Once possible risks are identified and analyzed, steps to mitigate the risks are identified, and recommendations for handling the risk are made. Depending on the level of risk and its possible impact on operations, decisions about how to handle each risk can be made. For some risks, the purchase of an insurance policy will adequately protect the organization. In cases where the risk is low, a plan for self-insuring—that is, to pay out of pocket should the risk occur—may make sense. It may be possible to reduce the level of risk for some practices, such as unsigned I-9 forms, by implementing checklists or review procedures. The potential exposure from other risks may be so high that eliminating the practice would provide the best protection for the organization.

An experienced HR professional is capable of identifying the elements that should be audited and monitoring the process. A complete audit will include a review of policies and practices in all of the functional areas of HR, including hiring, compensation, benefits, training and development programs, records management, and compliance with changing legal requirements. HR audits can use a variety of methods to obtain the information needed for an assessment, including checklists or questionnaires, surveys of employees and managers, and interviews.

Legislative and Regulatory Processes

The human resource profession can play a key role in the development of legislation and regulations affecting the employment relationship between an organization and its employees. HR professionals should be aware of the ways in which they, as individual citizens and as business leaders, can affect these processes. Because the PHR/SPHR exam is based on federal laws, this section will discuss how proposed legislation or regulation is handled by the federal government. A similar process is followed by state and local governments, and involvement at any level of government can benefit business organizations.

Legislative Process

The federal legislative process begins when someone has an idea. This idea can come from a senator or congressman, an individual, business, church, or professional association. If the idea comes from someone other than a member of congress (MOC), it must be presented to a member of the House or Senate to begin the process of becoming a law.

1. When an MOC agrees to sponsor a bill and presents it to the full body of the House or the Senate, it is assigned to a committee for study.

2. The committee first determines the likelihood that the bill will be able to pass a vote in the full body; if the determination is made that it is not likely to pass, no further action is taken and the bill effectively dies in the committee.

3. Bills that are deemed likely to pass a vote of the full body are studied by a subcommittee, and hearings are conducted to hear from government representatives, subject matter experts, and citizens with points of view for or against the bill.

4. Once the bill has been studied, the subcommittee may make changes in a process known as "marking up" the bill. The subcommittee then votes on whether or not to return the bill to the full committee with a recommendation for further action. A bill that is not reported back to the committee dies in the subcommittee.

5. Bills that are returned to the full committee may be subjected to further study, or the committee may vote to accept the subcommittee recommendations and "order the bill reported" to the full body.

6. When the committee votes to report a bill to the full body, a written report of the findings and recommendations of the committee is prepared, including dissenting views of members who voted against the bill.

7. Bills that are reported out of committee are placed on the "legislative calendar" and scheduled for a vote by the full body.

8. Members of the full body are able to present their views about passage of the bill prior to a vote. During the debate period, members may offer amendments that will take effect if the bill is passed.

9. When debate is completed, a vote is conducted.

10. If the full body passes the bill, it must go to the other body and usually begin the process again; in some cases the other body may vote to pass the bill as it was presented. During the review process, the second body may vote it down, table it, or change the bill. Bills that are rejected or tabled at this stage are considered dead and will not become laws.

11. If the bill passes the second body, any major differences between the two bills are reconciled in a conference committee. If the conference committee cannot agree on the form of the bill, it will die and not become a law. If the committee recommends a conference report incorporating the changes, both houses of Congress must vote to approve the conference report before the bill is forwarded to the president for signature.

12. When the president receives the bill, he has three choices: he may sign it into law, veto it, or fail to sign it. If the bill is vetoed, Congress may override the veto by a two-thirds vote of a quorum in each house, in which case the bill will become a law in spite of the veto.

If the president simply fails to sign a bill, one of two things will happen. When Congress is in session, a bill that remains unsigned for 10 days will become law without the president's signature. When Congress adjourns before the 10-day period is up, the bill will not become law. This is known as a pocket veto.

Administrative Law

In addition to the laws passed by Congress and signed by the president, HR professionals should be aware of the process by which administrative law is developed. There are three types of administrative law that impact employment relationships: agency rules and regulations, agency orders, and executive orders.

Much of the legislation passed by Congress empowers and requires federal agencies to develop enforcement regulations. An example of this is the Occupational Safety and Health Act of 1970, in which Congress established the Occupational Safety and Health Administration and required that it develop regulations to improve the safety of American workplaces. In developing these regulations, the agencies follow an established process.

First, they develop rules or regulations and publish them in the *Federal Register* (which is the official daily publication for rules, proposals, and notices of federal agencies and the Office of the President) and give the public an opportunity to comment on the proposals. Once the comment period has been completed, the agency publishes final rules that take effect no less than 30 days after the date of public notice.

Some federal agencies, such as the National Labor Relations Board (NLRB) and the Equal Employment Opportunity Commission (EEOC) have the power to order compliance with federal laws in courts known as Administrative Law Courts. The orders issued by an Administrative Law Judge (ALJ) in these cases have the effect of law and many of these decisions are published in the *Federal Register* as well.

The final type of administrative law with which HR professionals should be familiar is the executive order (EO). EOs are issued by the President of the United States and become law after they have been published in the *Federal Register* for 30 days.

Lobbying

Lobbying is an activity in which anyone can participate when they wish to influence new laws and regulations. HR professionals can contribute as individuals or as part of the HR profession. The Society for Human Resource Management (SHRM) has legislative affairs committees (LAC) on the national and local levels that monitor and provide information on proposed changes to employment-related legislation and regulation in addition to coordinating lobbying efforts.

HR professionals who wish to influence the legislative or regulatory processes should first make sure they fully understand the topic and are able to provide sound justifications for the position they take. It is also important to gather as much support as possible—legislators are more likely to be responsive when there are a large number of voters who feel the same way. To be an effective lobbyist, it is also important to find a senator or congressman who will guide you through the process and introduce you to other legislators.

There are many avenues for contacting elected officials or regulators. The House of Representatives has a website, `www.house.gov`, which provides information about contacting congressmen; the Senate has a similar site at `www.senate.gov`.

HR professionals who wish to stay abreast of legislative activity can find information on pending legislation in many places. In addition to the LACs mentioned previously, information about pending legislation is available at the House and Senate sites just mentioned and on the SHRM website at `www.shrm.org`.

Corporate Governance

Corporate governance refers to the various influences and processes that impact the way corporations are managed and the relationship between its stakeholders, principally the shareholders, board of directors, and management. Other groups, including employees, vendors, customers, lenders, and members of the general public are affected by the way decisions are made in the process of governance. Let's look at the roles of each of the key stakeholders.

Shareholders Shareholders are the owners of the corporation.

Board of directors Members of the board of directors (BOD) are elected by the shareholders to represent their interests with management. There are two types of directors: inside and outside. An *inside director* is a person with operational responsibilities who is employed by the organization, such as the CEO, CFO, or another officer of the corporation. An *outside director* is someone who is not employed by the corporation and does not have operational responsibilities.

Management Management includes the officers of the corporation, such as the CEO, CFO, COO, and other executives who make day-to-day decisions about company operations.

As discussed at the beginning of this chapter, a corporation is a legal entity that has rights and obligations. While a corporation itself cannot make decisions, those at top levels in the organization must make decisions on behalf of its owners. They have a *fiduciary responsibility* or obligation to act in the best interests of the shareholders by making decisions that benefit the organization over decisions that benefit them personally. Recent events have demonstrated that this responsibility is sometimes ignored by those at the highest corporate levels. The failures of corporate executives at Enron, WorldCom, Tyco, and other public corporations to appropriately perform their fiduciary responsibilities led to enactment of the Sarbanes-Oxley Act (SOX) in 2002.

One of the major factors that determine how a corporation is run is the values and ethics of those who have fiduciary responsibility.

Organization Values and Ethics

Since the Enron scandal erupted in December 2001, the issue of business ethics has come to the forefront of discussions about the behavior of corporate executives, auditors, attorneys, and board members. Subsequent revelations about possible accounting irregularities at other multinational corporations such as AOL, WorldCom, and Global Crossing make it clear that this was not simply a case of one company that ran amok, but it was a pervasive problem at top levels of major corporations. SOX made many of the practices that occurred in these companies illegal and provided penalties for violations. Some of the changes made by Sarbanes-Oxley include:

- Established the Public Company Accounting Oversight Board and required all public accounting firms to register with the board, which will conduct periodic inspections to ensure their compliance with audit standards.

- Established new standards to ensure the independence of auditors relative to the businesses they audit, including restrictions on nonaudit-related services such as bookkeeping, management, human resource consulting, or other similar services; rotation of audit partner assignments at least every five years; and a requirement that the audit report and recommendations to the management team be delivered directly to the audit committee of the board of directors.

- Established standards for corporate responsibility, holding the chief executive of a public company accountable for the fairness and accuracy of financial reports filed with the Securities and Exchange Commission (SEC).

- Required CEOs and CFOs to reimburse the company for incentive- or equity-based compensation in the event of a material restatement of financial reports to the SEC caused by misconduct.

- Prohibited insider trading of stock during pension fund blackout periods when employees are not able to trade the stock in their pension accounts.

- Established ethical requirements for senior financial officers.

- Took steps to ensure the fairness, accuracy, and independence of stock analysis.

- Established criminal penalties for management officials who defraud shareholders, destroy documents, or obstruct justice.

Ethical behavior begins at top levels in the organization. The board of directors must demand it of the executive team, and the executive team must model it for all others in the organization. It would seem that this should be a pretty simple thing to do; after all, at the end of the day, ethical behavior occurs when, as Spike Lee said, people "do the right thing." Because the values people hold are different depending on the culture they grew up in, their family background, and their personal experiences, the right thing can mean different things to different people. That is why the executive team must set the standard of behavior, communicate it, model it, and enforce it if they are serious about maintaining an ethical workplace.

Code of Ethics

A corporate values statement can begin to set the stage for ethical behavior, but a code of conduct or code of ethics is really necessary to inform people in the organization about what behavior is expected and what is unacceptable. A code of ethics should cover topics such as those discussed in the following sections.

Confidentiality

In most companies, confidential information can be found in every department: marketing plans, new product development, financial statements, personal employee information, and email accounts can all contain highly confidential information. HR professionals work every day with confidential employee information and are sometimes pressured to share this information for one reason or another. The inappropriate use of information collected during the employment process, information about an employee's age, medical condition, or credit history may not be used in making employment decisions. HR professionals and other employees with access to confidential information have a duty to maintain its confidentiality.

Conflicts of Interest

As mentioned at the beginning of this section, employees must put the interests of the organization before their own. Any time an employee stands to gain personally from an action taken by the employer, there is a conflict of interest (except, of course, for payment of the employee's salary). At a minimum, these situations must be disclosed to the employer, or the employee should remove themselves from the situation. The ethics statement should make it clear that even the appearance or perception of a conflict of interest is damaging to the company and should be avoided.

Fairness

Actions taken by employers have the ability to significantly impact the lives of their employees. Whether decisions are being made about hiring or layoffs, or accusations of malfeasance or inappropriate behavior are being made, employers have an obligation to treat employees fairly in all their actions. Employees who have the power to make decisions such as selecting suppliers or evaluating employee performance have an equal responsibility to handle these decisions fairly.

Real World Scenario

Whistle-Blowing in the Wake of the Enron Scandal

In the wake of the Enron scandal, and particularly during the month when congressional hearings into the bankrupt corporation's activities were televised each day, the Securities and Exchange Commission saw a marked increase in complaints, from an average of 365 per day in 2001 to 525 per day for the month of January 2002. On February 27, 2002, Katie Fairbank of the *Dallas Morning News* also reported an increase in whistle-blower complaints at the Department of Justice, from 33 in 1987 to 483 in 1999.

Sherron Watkins, who is credited with blowing the whistle on the Enron accounting practices that eventually led to its bankruptcy in December 2001, may have inspired the increased reports. Ms. Watkins followed a path typical of whistle-blowers by meeting with Enron CEO Ken Lay long before she went to the regulators. Her desire was to advise him of the wrongdoing so he could put an end to it. That unfortunately did not happen, and the company filed for bankruptcy a few months after their meeting.

While some whistle-blowers have statutory protection from retaliation, courts are divided on just what whistle-blowing activity is protected; those who go to regulators are often unable to work in their chosen profession after taking the action.

One whistle-blower who paid the price for his actions is Dr. Jeffrey Wigand, a former tobacco executive who was fired by Brown & Williamson Tobacco Corporation in 1993 after the company refused to remove a known carcinogen from their cigarette products. After his termination, Dr. Wigand testified against tobacco companies in civil lawsuits and appeared in an interview on the television show *60 Minutes*; his former employers launched a campaign to discredit him. Dr. Wigand was a key witness in the lawsuit brought by 46 states against tobacco companies that was settled when they agreed to pay $206 billion to reimburse the states for medical expenses that were related to smoking.

A real test of an organization's fairness occurs when an employee makes a complaint to a federal agency, claiming that illegal activity has occurred. A person who does this is known as a whistle-blower. Some federal statutes, such as the Occupational Safety and Health Act, Railroad Safety Act, Safe Drinking Water Act, and Toxic Substances Control Act provide protection for employees who "blow the whistle" on their employers. Even so, it is a true ethical test to see how the whistle-blower who continues to work for the company is treated in the workplace once the complaint has been made.

Codes of Conduct

Corporations are citizens of the communities in which they live and as such have responsibilities to their fellow citizens. This social responsibility ranges from making appropriate decisions about pollutants that are released into the environment to working with and training disadvantaged individuals to become productive members of society. In this section, we will explore some of the issues in both of these areas.

Gifts

An ethics policy should address the issue of gift exchanges with customers, vendors, and employees. It should describe under what circumstances gifts are acceptable and define limitations on the amounts if they are to be allowed. When the receipt of a gift unfairly influences a business decision, it becomes unethical and should be refused.

For companies operating outside the United States, this can be a difficult issue because in some cultures exchanging business gifts is a standard and expected practice, and the failure to do so can be seen as an insult. The Foreign Corrupt Practices Act of 1977 was enacted by Congress in response to revelations by multinational corporations of the bribes that were paid to obtain business in some foreign countries. The act prohibits the payment of bribes and requires accounting practices that preclude the use of covert bank accounts that could be used to make these payments.

Honesty

The code of ethics should set an expectation of honesty in the workplace. As with all other aspects of an ethics code, the executive team must model honesty in the representations they make to employees, customers, suppliers, and all other stakeholders in order for the message to be taken seriously within the company.

Insider Information

While insider information is most commonly associated with trading securities on the stock exchange, it can also apply to other areas. Inside information is any information that an employee has access to or comes into contact with that is not available to the general public. Using this information in the stock exchanges is illegal and can result in criminal prosecution and civil penalties.

The prohibitions against using inside information apply to an employee who overhears the information as much as they apply to decision makers in the organization. Federal law requires that those with access to inside information may not act on it until the information is made public.

Integrity

Integrity is defined as a firm adherence to a code of moral values. Integrity is demonstrated when an individual does the right thing, even when that "thing" is unpopular.

Personal Use of Company Assets

A code of ethics should clearly state what the employer considers to be an appropriate and acceptable use of company assets. In some organizations, the receipt of any personal telephone calls or emails is considered inappropriate, while in other companies a limited number is acceptable. Copying and distributing copyright material from newspapers, books, magazines, CDs, or other company assets may also violate patents or copyrights and employees should be made aware of the consequences if they use any of these assets inappropriately.

Workplace Privacy

Some employers feel the need to install surveillance cameras in work areas. This happens for a variety of reasons. For a retail store open late at night, it provides a measure of security for employees. Concerns about productivity or pilferage can spur an employer to install a surveillance camera in a distribution warehouse, for example. Whatever the reason, the employer must balance the need to manage the workforce with the employee's expectation of privacy.

Advances in technology have also made it possible for employers to monitor Internet, email, and voice mail usage, and this is seen as an invasion of privacy by some employees. Employers who plan to monitor employee communication and Internet usage should develop and distribute a policy clearly stating what information is subject to monitoring and under what conditions.

The code of ethics should include a statement about the use of surveillance and monitoring to reduce the risk for claims of invasion of privacy.

As important as a code of ethics is, it is equally important to be aware of situations where conflicting needs and desires make doing the right thing less clear-cut. As those responsible for maintaining the confidentiality of personal employee information, HR professionals make ethical decisions on a regular basis and are in a position to model ethical behavior in the way they respond to inappropriate requests for information.

Ethics Officers

Businesses serious about establishing meaningful ethics programs have appointed ethics officers or facilitators charged with the responsibility to ensure that the organization adheres to the ethical standards set by the executive team. Ethics officers advise employees at all levels in an organization on ethical issues and manage programs designed to allow confidential reporting of ethical concerns by employees, customers, shareholders, or others and investigate allegations of wrongdoing. Ethics officers provide periodic reports for the executive team to keep them apprised of ethical issues in the organization.

HR Metrics—Measuring Results

Chapter 2 includes a discussion of two of the best measures of HR results: return on investment (ROI) and cost-benefit analysis (CBA). Other useful metrics for the Strategic Management functional area of the BOK include:

Business impact measures   The business impact of HR plans created to support the organization's strategic plans and goals can be difficult to measure because it is difficult to isolate the effect of the HR support from the other factors. However, it is easier to measure whether or not HR achieved its specific goals, for example, if the marketing department staffing plan was to hire three marketing analysts and three were hired, HR met its target for that objective. The impact of HR initiatives designed to improve productivity, such as an engagement initiative, can be measured with the use of metrics such as revenue per employee or units produced per employee.

There are other ways to measure how HR is adding value, such as how well risk is being managed, measured by the presence or absence of employee complaints or lawsuits. If functions such as benefit administration or payroll are outsourced, an analysis of employee satisfaction with service levels and cost savings realized from outsourcing versus performing the service in-house can be used to measure business impact.

Tactical accountability measures   Meaningful measures of tactical accountability for Strategic Management include:

HR expenses as a percent of operating expenses   This metric is calculated by totaling all the direct and indirect HR costs and dividing them by the total operating expenses.

Ratio of total employees to HR staff   The total number of HR staff is divided by total employees in the organization to calculate this ratio.

HR department expenses per employee   As the organization grows, this metric can help HR maintain costs in line with other expenses. Total direct and indirect HR department expenses are divided by the total number of employees to obtain the ratio.

The data collected from these measures can be examined over a period of time to identify and measure trends that indicate problems on the horizon and allow HR to be proactive in addressing those issues. This information is important not only as part of the internal scanning process, but it also provides ongoing controls for HR during the strategy evaluation phase of the strategic planning process.

Global Considerations

The decision to open a facility in a new country requires thought be given to a variety of issues from employment laws unique to each country, to the business culture in the region, and the legal form of the entity. Some of the more common issues include:

- Determining the rate of pay for the new hire
- Offer letters or employment contracts that comply with foreign and U.S. laws
- The impact of foreign tax structures on the corporate income statement
- Details of starting operations in a new country for the first time, such as compliance with payroll processing regulations, understanding foreign stock option rules, and intercompany agreements
- Decisions about how day-to-day support will be delivered
- Corporate tax filings

In addition, there are very real cultural and practical differences in the ways business is done in the United States and other countries. For example, the US is a *low-context culture*, in that we take our cues from what others say to us. In a country with a *high-context culture* like Japan, the opposite is true: people rely more on nonverbal clues and relationships to discern what is meant. Acclimating to this difference presents unique challenges to operating globally.

Summary

Strategic management occurs as the result of a planning process that reviews internal and external factors affecting the ability of an organization to successfully achieve its goals. This process requires that all business functions provide their expertise in both the planning and implementation of goals, objectives, and action plans.

The strategic planning process begins by gathering information from internal and external sources using the SWOT technique to identify internal strengths and weaknesses and external opportunities and threats. As a result of the scanning, long-range, mid-range and short-range forecasts can be made to provide the information necessary for developing the vision, mission, and goals for the organization, which are needed by functional area managers to set tactical goals and action plans for their business units.

As HR moves into the twenty-first century, its role is changing into one that is more strategic and involved with planning the future direction of the organization. As a result, it is crucial for HR professionals to have a working knowledge of other functional areas of the business in order to provide the operational and administrative support necessary to attract and retain qualified employees in each area.

As change becomes increasingly prevalent in business, HR plays a role in advising management and counseling employees to reduce the stress of the change process in the organization.

HR professionals are expected to act ethically and handle their organizational responsibilities with care and respect. Employees rely on HR practitioners to carry out their responsibilities in a professional manner, assuming a moral responsibility to preserve the integrity and personal nature of employee information they handle. The organization relies on HR to protect its best interests by maintaining a high standard and adhering to a professional code of ethics.

Through active involvement in the development of legislation at the federal, state, and local levels, HR professionals can influence the course of proposed laws and regulations thus providing a benefit to their employers, their employees, and the profession.

Exam Essentials

Understand different business functions.   HR professionals must understand the purpose of different business functions and how they interact with each other and with HR. Understanding the unique needs of production and operations, sales and marketing, finance, accounting, and information technology and how each contributes to the organization's success allows HR to be more effective in providing services to the organization.

Understand the strategic planning process.   The strategic planning process consists of four broad elements: scanning the environment; formulating the corporate strategy with the vision, mission, values, and corporate goals; implementing the strategy with tactical goals, action plans, and budgets to accomplish organization goals; and evaluating the strategy to ensure that it can be adjusted to accommodate changes in the organization or the external environment.

Be able to describe the environmental scanning process.   An environmental scan uses a SWOT analysis to assess the strengths, weaknesses, opportunities, and threats that must be considered in the strategic plan. A PEST analysis is a way of looking at the external environment to assess the political, economic, social, and technological factors that will affect the organization. Porter's 5 Factors (new competitors, suppliers, customers, availability of replacement products, and level of market competition) provide additional insight into the external environment and how it will affect the organization's goals.

Understand the importance of change management and HR's role in managing change. Change is a fact of life in organizations; reengineering, restructuring, and downsizing occur often as a result of strategic decisions and changes in the marketplace. HR can develop programs that provide a means for communication, both top-down and bottom-up, to ease the process and reduce stress in the work environment.

Understand HR's role in the organization.   The role of HR is evolving into one that provides strategic, administrative, and operational services for the organization.

Be able to describe the steps involved in the legislative process.   A bill can originate in the House of Representatives or in the Senate. A bill is referred to a committee for consideration and then, if it's reported out of committee, is ready for full floor consideration. After all debate is concluded, the bill is ready for final passage. It must pass both bodies in the same form before it can be presented to the president for signature. The president may sign the bill; veto it, and return it to Congress; let it become law without signature; or at the end of a session, pocket veto it.

Key Terms

Before you take the exam, be certain you are familiar with the following terms:

accounting	long-range plans
balanced scorecard	marketing
centralized organization	mid-range plans
decentralized organization	objective
fiduciary responsibility	operations
finance	outside director
goal	production
high-context culture	sales
information technology (IT)	short-range plans
inside director	span of control
just-in-time (JIT) inventory	staff functions
knowledge, skills, and abilities (KSAs)	strategic planning
line functions	strategy
lobbying	
low-context culture	

Review Questions

1. HR participates in the strategic planning process by
   A. Formulating the strategy
   B. Scanning the environment
   C. Providing expertise
   D. Identifying strategic goals

2. Restructuring is used to:
   A. Remove redundant operations
   B. Assimilate employees into the organization
   C. Simplify processes to increase customer satisfaction
   D. Purchase stock to gain controlling interest in a competitor

3. A statement that describes what an organization does that is different from others is a:
   A. Values statement
   B. Corporate goal
   C. Vision statement
   D. Mission statement

4. One characteristic of an organization during the growth phase is:
   A. Executive benefit packages are upgraded.
   B. New hires may have less experience.
   C. The compensation package is competitive.
   D. Employees work closely with founders.

5. Improvements in technology have had their greatest effect on
   A. Employee morale
   B. Productivity
   C. Cost of living
   D. Management's span of control

6. The balanced scorecard concept does *not*:
   A. Tie objectives to specific performance measures
   B. Eliminate unnecessary processes to increase customer satisfaction
   C. Measure how objectives contribute to organization goals
   D. Set targets for meeting objectives

7. Which of the following is an appropriate use for an HR audit?

    A. To determine which employees no longer have the skills needed by the organization

    B. To determine the employee productivity and turnover rates

    C. To determine whether the employee handbook is in compliance with current government regulations

    D. To determine the timeline for changes that are necessary in the HR department

8. The four P's summarize the marketing function. Which of the following is not one of the P's?

    A. Perception

    B. Price

    C. Placement

    D. Promotion

9. Which of the following is one of the elements of a SMART goal?

    A. Action-oriented

    B. Strength

    C. Technology

    D. Threat

10. What is a pocket veto?

    A. The president vetoes a bill from Congress. Congress holds a vote but the bill does not pass.

    B. Congress submits a bill to the president and then adjourns. The president does not sign the bill within ten days.

    C. The president vetoes a bill from Congress. Congress holds a vote but does not have a quorum.

    D. Congress submits a bill to the president but the president does not sign the bill within ten days.

Answers to Review Questions

1. C. HR participates in the strategic planning process by providing expertise on attracting, retaining, and managing a qualified workforce. Organization strategies (A) are formulated by the executive team. Each business function participates in the environmental scanning process (B), gathering information about its area of responsibility. Strategic goals (D) are identified by the executive team during the strategy formulation phase.

2. A. Corporate restructuring examines individual business units to eliminate redundancy, reduce costs, and increase production. Employee assimilation (B) is accomplished with new hire orientation and similar programs. Reengineering looks at the entire organization to improve efficiency and increase customer satisfaction (C). In an acquisition, one corporation purchases or trades stock to gain controlling interest in another (D).

3. D. The mission statement describes who the organization is, what it does, where it is going, and how it is different from others. The corporate values statement (A) communicates the executive team's expectations for the way the organization conducts business. Corporate goals (B) describe what the organization plans to achieve in the future. The vision statement (C) is a short, inspirational statement of what the organization will accomplish in the future.

4. C. As an organization becomes more successful during the growth phase, it can afford to provide competitive compensation and benefits for employees. Executive benefit packages (A) are often enhanced during the maturity stage of organizational growth. During the maturity stage, the organization is able to hire new employees with less experience (B) and train them to grow into positions requiring additional experience. Employees work the closest with organization founders (D) during the startup phase.

5. B. The greatest effect of technology is increased worker productivity. Employee morale (A) may be affected positively or negatively by technological improvements but is not the main impact. The cost of living (C) is a function of the cost of consumer goods and is a factor in an environmental scan. Span of control (D) may also be affected by technological improvements, allowing managers to directly supervise a larger number of employees, but is not the main effect.

6. B. The balanced scorecard ties objectives to performance measurements (A), sets targets (D), and measures how the objectives contribute to organization goals (C). The elimination of unnecessary processes to increase customer satisfaction (B) is the purpose of reengineering.

7. C. An HR audit examines HR policies and procedures for compliance and to determine whether or not the department is successfully meeting the organization needs. Evaluating employee skills (A) is part of a SWOT analysis during the strategic planning process. Employee productivity and turnover rates (B) are metrics used to diagnose potential workforce problems. A timeline for changes in the HR department (D) would be included in an HR plan.

8. A. The four P's of marketing are product, price, placement, and promotion, which summarize the responsibilities of the marketing team.

9. A. A SMART goal is specific, measurable, action-oriented, realistic, and time-based.

10. B. Once Congress forwards a bill, the president has ten days to sign it. A pocket veto occurs when Congress adjourns before the ten days are up and the president does not sign it. When the president vetoes a bill (A), Congress may try to override it with a two-thirds vote of a quorum in each house. If the bill does not pass, the veto stands. If Congress cannot raise a quorum to override a veto (C), the veto stands. If Congress submits a bill to the president and stays in session (D), the bill becomes law if the president does not sign it within ten days.

Chapter

4

Workforce Planning and Employment

THE HRCI TEST SPECIFICATIONS FROM THE WORKFORCE PLANNING AND EMPLOYMENT FUNCTIONAL AREA COVERED IN THIS CHAPTER INCLUDE:

✓ **Ensure that workforce planning and employment activities are compliant with applicable federal, state, and local laws and regulations.**

✓ **Identify workforce requirements to achieve the organization's short- and long-term goals and objectives (for example, corporate restructuring, M&A activity, workforce expansion or reduction).**

✓ **Conduct job analyses to create job descriptions and identify job competencies.**

✓ **Identify and document essential job functions for positions.**

✓ **Establish hiring criteria based on job descriptions and required competencies.**

✓ **Analyze labor market for trends that impact the ability to meet workforce requirements (for example, SWOT analysis, environmental scan, demographic scan). SPHR** ONLY

✓ **Assess skill sets of internal workforce and external labor market to determine the availability of qualified candidates, utilizing third-party vendors or agencies as appropriate.**

✓ **Identify internal and external recruitment sources (for example, employee referrals, online job boards, resume banks) and implement selected recruitment methods.**

✓ **Evaluate recruitment methods and sources for effectiveness (for example, return on investment (ROI), cost per hire, time to fill).**

- ✓ Develop strategies to brand/market the organization to potential qualified applicants.

- ✓ Develop and implement selection procedures, including applicant tracking, interviewing, testing, reference and background checking, and drug screening.

- ✓ Develop and extend employment offers and conduct negotiations as necessary.

- ✓ Administer post-offer employment activities (for example, execute employment agreements, complete I-9 verification forms, coordinate relocations, schedule physical exams).

- ✓ Implement and/or administer the process for non-U.S. citizens to legally work in the United States.

- ✓ Develop, implement, and evaluate orientation processes for new hires, rehires, and transfers.

- ✓ Develop, implement, and evaluate retention strategies and practices.

- ✓ Develop, implement, and evaluate succession planning process.

- ✓ Develop and implement the organizational exit process for both voluntary and involuntary terminations, including planning for reductions in force (RIF).

- ✓ Develop, implement, and evaluate an AAP, as required.

In today's fast-paced business environment, HR professionals must be able to "turn on a dime," adjusting workforce plans and employment activities to meet the changing needs of their organizations. Workforce Planning and Employment (WFP) is the functional area of the Human Resource BOK that tests your knowledge of workforce planning and the associated employment activities of staffing, retaining, and exiting employees from the organization. The workforce planning process identifies skills and timelines for acquiring the employees needed to achieve organization goals; staffing is the process by which HR professionals work with line management to locate, hire/transfer, and integrate new employees into existing workgroups. Once employees are hired, activities include ensuring that talented individuals in the organization are identified, developed, and retained so that they are available to move into positions of greater responsibility as organization needs evolve. The fourth function of Workforce Planning and Employment, organizational exits, includes voluntary exits (those due to resignations or retirements) and involuntary exits (those occurring due to mergers, outsourcing, terminations for cause, and so on). This chapter reviews the PHR and SPHR responsibility and knowledge requirements for Workforce Planning and Employment, including the impact of federal legislation, regulation, and case law on these activities.

Let's begin with the federal laws and regulations that govern employment relationships.

As you begin this chapter, be sure to refer to the knowledge requirements for WFP in the *HRCI Certification Guide* described in the introduction to this book. In addition, several sections in Chapter 2, "Core Knowledge Requirements for HR Professionals," have particular relevance here: a review of the discussions on needs assessment, communication strategies, development of RFPs, quantitative and qualitative analysis tools, job analysis and description methods, organizational documentation requirements, and employee records management will enhance your review of the material in this chapter.

Federal Employment Legislation

Over the years, all three branches of the federal government have participated in regulating the ways employers interact with their employees. Congress has enacted legislation, the Executive Branch has promulgated regulations, and the courts have adjudicated cases to clarify the legislation and regulation created by the other two branches. As shown in Table 4.1, no employment activity is free from some type of regulation. Understanding these various laws, regulations, and cases is a key element in the development and implementation of compliant workforce plans and activities

TABLE 4.1   Federal Legislation Governing WFP Activities

Type	Enforcement Agency	Chapter Reference
Civil rights	EEOC and/or OFCCP	4
Executive Orders	OFCCP	4
Fair Credit	Federal Trade Commission	4
Immigration	USCIS	4
Mass layoffs	Department of Labor	4
Polygraph	Department of Labor	4
Privacy	Department of Justice	4

This section describes the civil rights legislation and executive orders that affect employment activities. Other government requirements listed are reviewed in the section where they are most used by HR practitioners.

Civil Rights Legislation

While several pieces of civil rights legislation were enacted between 1866 and 1963, the Civil Rights Act of 1964 is regarded as the milestone for modern equal employment opportunity. This sweeping legislation impacted many areas of American life, and Title VII of the act was dedicated to providing equal employment opportunities for all Americans. Title VII has been amended several times to expand coverage to areas not covered in the original act of 1964.

Title VII of the Civil Rights Act of 1964

Title VII of the Civil Rights Act of 1964 (Title VII) introduced the concepts of *protected classes* and *unlawful employment practices* to American business. Unlawful employment practices are those which have an adverse impact on members of a protected class. Some practices, known as *disparate treatment*, treat some candidates or employees differently, such as requiring women to take a driving test when they apply for a job, but not requiring men to take the test when they apply for the same job. Practices that have a *disparate impact* on members of protected classes seem fair on their face, but result in adverse impact on members of protected classes. Title VII created the Equal Employment Opportunity Commission (EEOC) with a mandate to promote equal employment opportunity, educate employers, provide technical assistance, and study and report on its activities to Congress and the American people. The EEOC is the enforcement agency for Title VII and other discrimination legislation. The act identified five protected classes: race, color, religion, national origin, and sex, and defined unlawful employment practices including:

- Discriminatory recruiting, selection, or hiring actions

- Discriminatory compensation or benefit practices

- Discriminatory access to training or apprenticeship programs

- Discriminatory practices in any other terms or conditions of employment

Legitimate seniority, merit, and piece-rate payment systems are allowable under Title VII as long as they do not intentionally discriminate against protected classes.

Title VII allowed for limited exceptions to its requirements, some of which are listed below:

- *Bona fide occupational qualifications (BFOQ)* occur when religion, sex, or national origin is "reasonably necessary to the normal operation" of the business.

- Educational institutions were not originally subject to Title VII.

- Religious organizations may give preference to members of that religion.

- A potential employee who is unable to obtain, or loses, a national security clearance required for the position is not protected.

- Indian reservations may give preference to Indian applicants and employees living on or near the reservation.

 You can review the full text of Title VII at www.eeoc.gov/policy/vii.html.

Amendments to Title VII

Title VII was amended in 1972, 1978, and 1991 to clarify and expand its coverage.

Equal Employment Opportunity Act of 1972

Created in 1972, the Equal Employment Opportunity Act (EEOA) provides litigation authority to the EEOC in the event that an acceptable conciliation agreement cannot be reached. In those cases, the EEOC is empowered to sue nongovernmental entities, including employers, unions, and employment agencies.

The EEOA extended coverage of Title VII to entities that had been excluded in 1964, including:

- Educational institutions

- State and local governments

- The federal government

In addition, the EEOA reduced the number of employees needed to subject an employer to coverage by Title VII from 25 to 15 and required employers to keep records of the discovery of any unlawful employment practices and provide those records to the EEOC upon request.

The EEOA also provided administrative guidance for the processing of complaints by providing that employers be notified within 10 days of receipt of a charge by the EEOC and that findings be issued within 120 days of the charge being filed. The EEOC was empowered to sue employers, unions, and employment agencies in the event that an acceptable conciliation agreement could not be reached within 30 days of notice to the employer. The EEOA also provided protection from retaliatory employment actions for whistle-blowers.

NOTE   The full text of the EEOA of 1972 can be viewed at www.eeoc.gov/abouteeoc/35th/thelaw/eeo_1972.html.

Pregnancy Discrimination Act of 1978

Congress amended Title VII with the Pregnancy Discrimination Act of 1978 to clarify that discrimination against women on the basis of pregnancy, childbirth, or any related medical condition is an unlawful employment practice. The act specified that pregnant employees receive the same treatment and benefits as employees with any other short-term disability.

NOTE   To read the text of the PDA, go to www.eeoc.gov/abouteeoc/35th/thelaw/pregnancy_discrimination-1978.html.

Civil Rights Act of 1991

The Civil Rights Act (CRA) of 1991 contained amendments that affected Title VII, the Age Discrimination in Employment Act (ADEA), and the Americans with Disabilities Act (ADA) in response to issues raised by the courts in several cases that were brought by employees based on Title VII. The CRA is discussed later in this chapter, as are the cases that led to this legislation.

Age Discrimination in Employment Act of 1967

According to the preamble, the purpose of the Age Discrimination in Employment Act (ADEA) is to "promote employment of older persons based on their ability rather than age; to prohibit arbitrary age discrimination in employment; to help employers and workers find ways of meeting problems arising from the impact of age on employment."

The ADEA prohibits discrimination against persons 40 years of age or older in employment activities including hiring, job assignments, training, promotion, compensation, benefits, terminating, or any other privileges, terms, or conditions of employment. The act applies to private businesses, unions, employment agencies, and state and local governments with more than 20 employees. As with Title VII, the ADEA provides for exceptions to the act such as:

- BFOQs that are reasonably necessary to business operations
- The hiring of firefighters or police officers by state or local governments
- Retirement of employees age 65 or older who have been in executive positions for at least two years and are eligible for retirement benefits of at least $44,000 per year
- Retirement of tenured employees of institutions of higher education at age 70
- Discharge or discipline for just cause

The act also provides that any waiver of rights must be written in an understandable manner and refer specifically to the waiver requirements contained in the ADEA. Any waiver of rights is valid only if valuable consideration, usually some form of payment, is exchanged and must include the following elements:

- Advice to consult with an attorney before signing the agreement
- A period of not less than 21 days to review and consider the agreement
- A period of no less than 7 days during which the agreement may be revoked

Additional requirements are needed for waivers made in connection with exit incentives or other termination programs, such as a reduction in force or layoff that involves more than one employee. In addition to the preceding requirements, the waiver must provide protected individuals with no less than 45 days to consider the agreement and:

- A list of the eligibility factors for the group or individuals affected by the employment action
- A list of the job titles and ages of all individuals participating in the program as well as those who were not selected for the program

Individuals who feel they have been subjected to an unlawful employment practice must file charges with the EEOC, which has federal enforcement responsibility for the ADEA, or with the state equal employment agency (if one exists for the location in which the incident occurred). Timely filing of charges is essential for complainants, since the EEOC will not investigate charges that are not made according to the guidelines described in this chapter.

 Real World Scenario

Discrimination Claim Filing Requirements

One of the changes made by the EEOA was increasing the period of time individuals have to file discrimination complaints. These time limits apply to all laws enforced by the EEOC except the Equal Pay Act (discussed in Chapter 6, "Total Rewards").

- In states without their own EEO enforcement agencies, an individual must file a charge with the EEOC within 180 days of the incident.

- In states with EEO enforcement agencies, a charge must be filed within 300 days of the incident or, if the charge was initially filed with the state enforcement agency, within 30 days after receiving written notice from the state that the investigation was terminated. (For ADEA complaints, only state laws extend the filing limit to 300 days.)

- If the EEOC does not file a civil suit or enter into a conciliation agreement within 180 days of the initial charge, the complaining individual is notified and may file a civil suit within 90 days of receiving that notification.

- Once an individual has filed a charge with the EEOC, there is a 60-day waiting period before the individual may request a right-to-sue letter. This request ends the EEOC investigation and requires the individual to file a civil action within 90 days or lose the right to pursue this claim in the future.

Visit www.eeoc.gov/policy/adea.html to view the full text of the ADEA.

Americans with Disabilities Act of 1990

The Americans with Disabilities Act (ADA) of 1990 was based in large part on the Rehabilitation Act of 1973 (discussed in the section, "Federal Contractors, Subcontractors, and Agencies" later in this chapter), and it extended protected class status to qualified persons with disabilities. Employment discrimination is covered by Title I of the act and identifies entities covered by the act as employment agencies, labor unions, joint labor-management committees, and employers with 15 or more employees for each working day in each of 20 weeks in the current or previous calendar year. Excluded from coverage are the federal government and 501(c) private membership clubs. The act prohibits discrimination in job application procedures; the hiring, advancement, or discharge of employees; employee compensation; job training; and other terms, conditions, and privileges of employment.

The ADA requires covered entities to make *reasonable accommodation* to develop employment opportunities for qualified persons with disabilities in two areas:

1. Facilities should be accessible to persons with disabilities.

2. Position requirements may be adjusted to accommodate qualified persons with disabilities.

The ADA allows that accommodations constituting an *undue hardship* to the business are not required and defines undue hardships as those which place an excessive burden on the employer. The act identifies the factors to be considered in determining whether an accommodation is an undue hardship by looking at the cost, the financial resources of the organization, the size of the organization, and other similar factors.

The text of the ADA can be read at www.eeoc.gov/policy/ada.html.

Civil Rights Act of 1991

The purpose of the Civil Rights Act (CRA) of 1991, as described in the act itself, is fourfold:

1. To provide appropriate remedies for intentional discrimination and unlawful harassment in the workplace;

2. To codify the concepts of "business necessity" and "job related" articulated by the Supreme Court in *Griggs v. Duke Power Co.* and in other Supreme Court decisions prior to *Wards Cove Packing Co. v. Atonio*;

3. To confirm statutory authority and provide statutory guidelines for the adjudication of disparate impact suits under Title VII of the Civil Rights Act of 1964; and

4. To respond to recent decisions of the Supreme Court by expanding the scope of relevant civil rights statutes in order to provide adequate protection to victims of discrimination.

Amendments contained in the CRA affected Title VII, the Age Discrimination in Employment Act (ADEA), and the Americans with Disabilities Act (ADA). One of the issues addressed is that of disparate impact, first introduced by the *Griggs v. Duke Power* case in 1971. Disparate impact occurs when an employment practice, which appears on its face to be fair, unintentionally discriminates against members of a protected class. The CRA places the burden of proof for discrimination complaints on the complainant when there is a job-related business necessity for employment actions. When an individual alleges multiple discriminatory acts, each practice in itself must be discriminatory unless the employer's decision-making process cannot be separated, in which case the individual may challenge the decision-making process itself. The CRA also provides additional relief for victims of intentional discrimination and harassment, codifies the concept of disparate impact, and addresses Supreme Court rulings over the previous few years that had weakened equal employment opportunity laws.

The CRA made the following changes to Title VII:

- Allowed for compensatory and punitive damages on a sliding scale based on company size as shown in Table 4.2

- Provided that any party to a civil suit in which punitive or compensatory damages are sought may demand a jury trial

- Expanded Title VII to include congressional employees and some senior political appointees

- Required that the individual alleging an unlawful employment practice is in use prove that it results in disparate impact to members of a protected class

- Provided that job-relatedness and reasonable business necessity are defenses to disparate impact, and that if a business can show that the practice does not result in disparate impact, it need not show the practice to be a business necessity

- Provided that business necessity is not a defense against an intentional discriminatory employment practice

- Established that if discrimination was a motivating factor in an employment practice it was unlawful, even if other factors contributed to the practice

- Allowed that if the business would have made the same employment decision whether or not an impermissible motivating factor was present, that there would be no damages awarded

- Expanded coverage to include foreign operations of American businesses unless compliance would constitute violation of the laws of the host country

TABLE 4.2   CRA Limits for Total Punitive and Compensatory Damages

Number of Employees*	Maximum Damage Award
15–100	$50,000
101–200	$100,000

TABLE 4.2   CRA Limits for Total Punitive and Compensatory Damages   *(continued)*

Number of Employees*	Maximum Damage Award
201–500	$200,000
501 +	$300,000

*Number of employees in each of 20 or more weeks in the current or preceding calendar year.

Visit http://thomas.loc.gov/cgi-bin/query/z?c102:S.1745.ENR: to view the full text of the CRA.

Federal Contractors, Subcontractors, and Agencies

The employment legislation described in previous sections does not always apply to agencies of the federal government, but discrimination in these entities is prohibited by executive orders and other legislation.

Rehabilitation Act of 1973, Sections 501, 503, and 505

The Rehabilitation Act of 1973 was enacted to expand the opportunities available for persons with physical or mental disabilities. The employment clauses of the act apply to agencies of the federal government and federal contractors with contracts of $10,000 or more during a 12-month period. Section 501 addresses employment discrimination, while section 505 details the remedies available for those who have been subjected to unlawful employment practices. The EEOC has enforcement responsibility for section 501. Under section 503, individuals with disabilities who feel a federal contractor has violated the requirements of the Rehabilitation Act may also file complaints with the Department of Labor through the Office of Federal Contract Compliance Programs (OFCCP).

The text of the Rehabilitation Act can be viewed at www.eeoc.gov/policy/rehab.html.

Vietnam Era Veterans' Readjustment Assistance Act of 1974

Equal employment opportunity and affirmative action protection for veterans who served during the Vietnam War are provided by the Vietnam Era Veterans' Readjustment Assistance Act (VEVRA), which applies to federal contractors or subcontractors with contracts of $25,000 or more. The act requires that contractors list all openings with state employment agencies unless they are for senior-level management positions, positions that will be filled from within, or positions lasting three days or less. State employment agencies are required to give priority to Vietnam-era veterans when providing referrals to these openings.

A Vietnam-era veteran is one who meets specific criteria related to having served on active duty between August 5, 1964 and May 7, 1975. The act provides additional protections for special disabled veterans who have disabilities rated at 10, 20, 30 percent or more who are entitled to compensation from the Department of Veterans Affairs.

You can view the DOL compliance requirements for additional details at www.dol.gov/esa/regs/compliance/ofccp/ca_vevraa.htm.

Executive Orders

Executive orders (EOs) are presidential proclamations which, when published in the Federal Register, become law after 30 days. Executive orders have been used to ensure equal employment opportunities are afforded by federal agencies and private businesses that contract or subcontract with those agencies. Executive orders relating to equal employment issues are enforced by the OFCCP.

Executive Order 11246 This executive order, established in 1965, prohibits employment discrimination on the basis of race, creed, color, or national origin and requires affirmative steps be taken in advertising jobs, recruiting, employing, training, promotion, compensation, and terminating employees.

Executive Order 11375 Created in 1967, EO 11375 amended 11246 and expanded coverage for protected classes to include discrimination on the basis of sex.

Executive Order 11478 This order, written in 1969, again expanded the scope of EO 11246 by adding handicapped individuals and those over age 40 to the list of protected classes.

Executive Order 12138 In 1979, with the passing of EO 12138, the National Women's Business Enterprise policy was created. This EO also required federal contractors and subcontractors to take affirmative steps to promote and support women's business enterprises.

Executive Order 13087 This EO from 1998 expanded coverage to include sexual orientation.

Executive Order 13152 Added "status as a parent" to the list of protected classes first identified in EO 11246. This EO, written in 2000, protects those who must care for an "individual who is under the age of 18 or who is 18 or older but is incapable of self-care because of a physical or mental disability" from employment discrimination. The order broadly defines a parent as a biological, adoptive, foster or step-parent, legal custodian, one who is acting as a parent, or one actively seeking legal custody or adoption of a child.

Executive Order 13279 This EO limited the impact of EO 11246 on faith-based and community organizations providing social services as federal contractors or subcontractors.

The National Archives provides a list of all executive orders searchable by president, number, and year at www.archives.gov/federal-register/executive-orders/disposition.html.

There are two levels of compliance required by executive orders. The first level, which prohibits employment discrimination and requires contractors to take affirmative action in employment actions, applies to contracts totaling $10,000 or more in a 12-month period.

The second level of compliance, for contractors with 50 or more employees who have contracts of $50,000 or more, requires that a written Affirmative Action Plan (AAP) be developed within 120 days from the origination of the contract with the OFCCP, the agency charged with enforcing EOs.

Annual EEO Survey

Working together, the EEOC and the OFCCP developed a reporting format designed to meet statistical reporting requirements for both agencies. This form, known as the EEO-1, must be filed on or before September 30 of each year using employment data from any pay period during July, August, or September of that year. All employers who meet the following criteria must complete the report:

- Private employers subject to Title VII with 100 or more employees, EXCEPT
  - State and local governments
  - Primary and secondary school systems
  - Institutions of higher education
  - Indian tribes
  - Tax-exempt private membership clubs (other than labor organizations)
- All federal contractors or subcontractors with more than 50 but less than 100 employees, which
  - Have contracts, subcontracts, or purchase orders of $50,000 or more OR
  - Are depositories of government funds in any amount OR
  - Are financial institutions issuing and paying U.S. savings bonds and notes

Report Types

EEO-1 reports may be submitted electronically or on paper. Employers with operations at a single location or establishment complete a single form, but for those who operate multiple locations employment data is reported on multiple forms:

Headquarters Report   Employment data for the principal office of the organization is reported on the Headquarters Report.

Locations with 50 or more employees   A separate Establishment Report is required for each of these locations.

Locations with fewer than 50 employees   Locations with fewer than 50 employees may be reported on an Establishment Report or on an Establishment List. The Establishment List provides the name, address, and total number of employees for each location with fewer than 50 employees along with an employment data grid combining this data by race, sex, and job category.

Consolidated Report   Data from all the individual location reports is combined on the Consolidated Report. The total number of employees on this report must be equal to data submitted on the individual reports.

Parent corporations that own majority interest in another corporation report data for employees at all locations, including those of the subsidiary establishments.

Race and Ethnicity Categories

Revisions to the race and ethnicity reporting categories are effective with the reports due September 30, 2007. Prior reports required employees to be reported in one of five categories; the revision expanded this to seven:

- Hispanic or Latino
- White (not Hispanic or Latino)
- Black or African-American (not Hispanic or Latino)
- Native Hawaiian or Other Pacific Islander (not Hispanic or Latino)
- Asian (not Hispanic or Latino)
- American Indian or Alaska Native (not Hispanic or Latino)
- Two or More Races (not Hispanic or Latino)

The OFCCP prefers that whenever possible, employees should be encouraged to self-identify their race and ethnicity. If employees choose to not self-identify, the employer is allowed to make a good-faith selection.

Job Categories

The EEO-1 report requires employers to group jobs into job categories based on the average skill level, knowledge, and responsibility of positions within their organizations. These categories have also been revised for the 2007 reporting period.

- Executive/Senior Level Officials and Managers
- First/Mid-Level Officials and Managers
- Professionals
- Technicians
- Sales Workers
- Administrative Support Workers
- Craft Workers
- Operatives
- Laborers and Helpers
- Service Workers

Data Reporting

To assist employers in categorizing their employees for the report, the EEOC provides descriptions for each of the race/ethnicity and job categories, available in the instructions posted on their website at www.eeoc.gov/eeo1/instruction_rev_2006.html. For each job category, employers report the total number of male and female employees according to their ethnicity and race. A sample of the revised EEO-1 form is shown in Figure 4.1.

Section D – EMPLOYMENT DATA

Employment at this establishment—report all permanent full- and part-time employees including apprentices and on-the-job trainees unless specifically excluded as set forth in the instructions. Enter the appropriate figures on all lines and in all columns. Blank spaces will be considered as zeros.

Number of Employees
(Report employees in only one category)

Job Categories		Hispanic or Latino		Race/Ethnicity Not-Hispanic or Latino												Total Col A - N
				Male							Female					
		Male	Female	White	Black or African-American	Native Hawaiian or Other Pacific Islander	Asian	American Indian or Alaska Native	Two or more races	White	Black or African American	Native Hawaiian or Other Pacific Islander	Asian	American Indian or Alaska Native	Two or more races	
		A	B	C	D	E	F	G	H	I	J	K	L	M	N	O
Executive/Senior Level Officials and Managers	1.1															
First/Mid-Level Officials and Managers	1.2															
Professionals	2															
Technicians	3															
Sales Workers	4															
Administrative Support Workers	5															
Craft Workers	6															
Operatives	7															
Laborers and Helpers	8															
Service Workers	9															
TOTAL	10															
PREVIOUS YEAR TOTAL	11															

1. Date(s) of payroll period used: _____ (Omit on the Consolidated Report.)   O.M.B. No. 3046-0007 Revised 01/2006 Revised 01/2006 Approval Expires 1/2009

FIGURE 4.1 EEO-1 Report revised for 2007

As previously mentioned, information collected on the EEO-1 report is the result of collaboration between the EEOC and OFCCP. The race/ethnicity and job categories are not only used for statistical analysis by the EEOC, but also as the basis for the collection of information in Affirmative Action Plans submitted to the OFCCP.

Affirmative Action Plans

The components of an AAP are determined by the OFCCP, and in a revision effective on December 13, 2000, include the items stated in Table 4.3.

TABLE 4.3   Components of an Affirmative Action Plan

AAP Component	Description
Organizational profile	Organizational display (traditional organization chart) or workforce analysis (listing of job titles from lowest to highest paid)
Job group analysis	Places job titles with similar duties and responsibilities into groups for analysis
Placement of incumbents in job groups	Percentages of minorities and women in each job group
Determination of availability	Reports demographic data on the labor pool for each job group
Comparison of incumbency to availability	Compares protected classes employed in each job group with availability of protected classes in the labor pool
Placement goals	Sets reasonable goals to address under-representation of protected classes in the workforce
Designation of the person responsible for implementation within the business	Assigns responsibility for achieving placement goals in the AAP to a person with access to the executive team in the business
Identification of problem areas	Requires analysis of employment processes to determine where barriers to equal opportunity exist
Action-oriented programs	Requires modification of current employment practices to remove barriers to opportunity
Periodic internal audits	Requires periodic review of employment activity with management and reports to executives on actions taken to improve results

The OFCCP has posted a "Sample Affirmative Action Program" on its website at www.dol.gov/esa/regs/compliance/ofccp/pdf/sampleaap.pdf. The sample depicts one way of presenting the information required by an Affirmative Action Plan, but the OFCCP points out that an AAP should be customized to reflect the organizational structure of individual employers.

It may be helpful to refer to the sample while reading the following explanations of the various components.

Organizational profile   The organizational profile looks at how employees are placed in specific job titles and may be presented as a traditional organization chart or as a workforce analysis. The workforce analysis lists job titles from the lowest to the highest paid within each department or work unit. For each title, the wage rate or salary grade is identified, along with the EEO-1 category, job group, and total number of employees holding that title. The analysis also breaks down the total number of employees into the number of males and females of the seven EEO-1 racial/ethnic descriptions (Hispanic, White, Black or African-American, Native Hawaiian or Other Pacific Islander, Asian, American Indian or Alaska Native, and Two or More Races).

Job group analysis   The job group analysis organizes jobs into groups established for the EEO-1 report. For this report, employers list all of their job titles that fall into each job group, as well as the number of employees in the job group, and identify the associated EEO-1 category.

Placement of incumbents in job groups   This report lists each job group with the total number of incumbents in each group. The total is broken down into the number and percentage of females and the number and percentage of minorities in each group.

Determination of availability   For each job group, the AAP shows how many minorities or women with the required skills are available externally (within a "reasonable recruiting area") and the percentage of minorities or women available internally for promotion, transfer, or training into the job group. This report identifies the source used to gather the information (most often the most recent Census data for external hires and the internal source for promotable employees), the weight placed on the source, reason for the weighting, and the statistics adjusted based on the weight assigned.

Comparison of incumbency to availability   This information is most easily presented as a chart showing each job group with the percentage of female and minority incumbents compared to the availability.

Placement goals   Placement goals are required if the comparison of incumbency to availability indicates that women and/or minorities are under-represented in a job group. Under-representation is determined by the 80 percent rule, described in the section "Uniform Guidelines on Employee Selection Procedures" later in this chapter.

Designation of responsibility for implementation   This section of the AAP provides the titles of employees with affirmative action responsibility and details the scope of responsibility for each title.

Action-oriented programs   Problem areas are identified and corrective actions planned by the employer are described as part of the Action Oriented Program section of the AAP. The action plans include specific steps to be taken along with timelines to correct the identified problem areas.

Periodic internal audits   The last section of the AAP describes how the responsibilities detailed in the Designation of Responsibility for Implementation section will be monitored within the organization.

Strategic Workforce Planning

The goal of strategic workforce planning is to ensure the availability of qualified employees when they are needed to achieve organization goals. An effective workforce planning process is based on:

- Workforce goals and objectives that forecast the organization's future workforce needs
- Job analysis and description that identifies the knowledge, skills, and abilities needed to meet the future needs
- Identification of qualified employees beginning with the organization's current workforce demographics
- Translating the goals and objectives into tactical staffing plans to build the future workforce

The workforce plan resulting from this process provides the framework for targeting and prioritizing future staffing requirements, remaining flexible enough to allow HR to respond rapidly to changing business needs.

Workforce Goals and Objectives

During the strategic planning process discussed in Chapter 3, "Strategic Management," organization leaders make decisions about how to achieve business goals and objectives that attain a competitive advantage, improve the level of business performance, and add value to stockholders. Chapter 3 discussed organizational design decisions that occur as part of the strategic planning process. Depending on the goals established by the plan, these decisions affect workforce planning in different ways.

Reengineering   The goal of reengineering is to realign operations in a way that adds value to customers. For workforce planning, this may mean eliminating jobs in some areas and adding jobs in others.

Corporate restructuring   Corporate restructuring looks at individual units in the organization to reduce or eliminate redundancy or bureaucratic processes in order to reduce costs and increase production. For workforce planning, this means a reduction in the workforce or reassignment of employees to new jobs.

Mergers and acquisitions   In some cases, business leaders make a decision to acquire products and market share by purchasing other companies instead of building them internally. One result of a merger or acquisition is a reduction in labor costs as economies of scale allow jobs to be combined or eliminated.

Divestitures   When the strategic plan includes a decision to divest an operating unit, this can mean the elimination of jobs or transferring employees to a new operating entity. The effect on workforce planning can be twofold: reducing the workforce in one organization and, in some cases, performing due diligence to transfer employees to the new entity.

Offshoring/outsourcing   In most cases, offshoring or outsourcing decisions result in a workforce reduction or transfer of employees to other jobs. When employees are acquired by an outsource provider, they are terminated from the organization and hired by the new company.

Workforce expansion   An organization may decide to expand its workforce in order to accomplish any of the business objectives described above. For example, if the strategic plan calls for increasing sales by 15 percent, leaders may determine that achieving that goal requires increasing the sales force.

Workforce reduction   Whether necessitated by a restructuring, merger, or acquisition or in response to falling sales, reducing labor costs is a painful result of some business decisions. There are many examples of workforce reductions in the business environment, including the job losses that occurred during the dot-com bust of 2000–2001.

One thing is certain: human resource professionals must be ready to respond rapidly to changes in business workforce requirements with a road map that produces employees who possess the talent needed by the business to achieve its goals. This road map is built on the jobs that need to be performed and the individuals who will perform those jobs.

Job Analysis and Description

As described in detail in Chapter 2, job analysis provides the foundation for identifying the knowledge, skills, and abilities (KSAs) needed to achieve specific results in an organization. Historically, this information has been compiled into job descriptions used to locate individuals who possess the needed KSAs.

In the staffing process, more information is always better. Hiring managers and potential candidates can make more effective decisions when all the particulars about a job are known. In addition to the information in Chapter 2, the following criteria have particular relevance for the staffing process.

Job competencies   Job competencies guide interviewers in formulating questions that elicit information beyond specific tasks and responsibilities assigned to a specific job. This information helps determine how well a candidate will fit into a particular work group and contribute to organization goals. Core competencies may be developed for traits the organization values and would like to see in all its employees, such as teamwork, communication, or customer focus. Job-specific competencies are related to a specific role in the organization. For example, a job with management responsibilities may include competencies for developing subordinates, leadership, and strategic thinking.

Essential job functions   Well-defined essential job functions are important in the recruiting process to ensure that the organization complies with equal employment opportunities for all candidates, particularly those with disabilities.

Job specifications   Job specifications are another tool for interviewers, helping to further define expectations for performance. Candidates can use them to evaluate their interest in the position and how well they will be able to perform if hired.

Qualified Employees

Organizations have three options for locating the talent they need to achieve business goals: internal transfers or promotion, external hires, and alternative staffing methods. Are there sufficient skills within the organization that can be redirected to the new requirements through transfers or promotions? Is it best to bring in full-time employees or better to use temps or some other staffing alternative? Let's take a brief look at these alternatives and discuss the strategic implications of each source.

Internal Talent

The first place to look for qualified employees to fill future needs is among those who already work for the organization. There are a number of advantages to filling jobs internally or "promoting from within." Management has an opportunity to evaluate candidates and determine their suitability for advancement over an extended period of time as they perform current duties, and the possibility of future promotion can encourage employees to maintain a high level of performance. Providing advancement opportunities for employees communicates to them that the organization values and rewards their contributions. When promotion from within is an organization policy, most external hiring is done at the entry level, which allows employees to become acclimated to the organization culture and operating procedures early in their careers, leading to greater success when they move into positions with greater responsibility.

Of course, there are disadvantages associated with relying solely on promotion from within to fill positions of increasing responsibility. First, there is the danger that employees with little experience outside the organization will have a myopic view of the industry. Second, while the morale of those promoted will be high, employees who have been passed over or lost out on promotions may have lower morale and be less motivated in performing their jobs. When several people are being groomed for promotion, the competition can lead to a breakdown in teamwork and jockeying for political position. If the organization lacks diversity in its workforce, over-reliance on promoting from within can perpetuate the imbalance. Finally, reduced recruiting costs will be offset by an increase in training costs to prepare employees for supervisory or management positions.

External Talent

At some point organizations need to look outside for new employees. Even if there is a policy of promotion from within, entry-level positions will need to be filled as employees are promoted or transferred. There are, of course, advantages and disadvantages to bringing new people into the organization.

One advantage is that experienced professionals bring new ideas with them and can revitalize operations. Another is that it is usually easier and more cost-effective to hire individuals with highly specialized skills than it is to develop them within the organization. In addition to those reasons, if there is an urgent need for someone with particular skills, it is usually faster to hire those skills than to provide on-the-job training. Looking outside the organization to fill positions provides opportunities to increase the diversity of the workforce as well.

There are several disadvantages to looking outside the organization. First, current employees who have been passed over for promotion will very likely have lower morale. Second, it is always difficult to know how someone from outside the organization will fit into an existing team once they start working. Finally, the new hire is an unknown—until the person actually starts doing the job, it's very difficult to know what their performance level will be.

Alternative Staffing Methods

To expand the pool of available candidates with the desired skills, it's often wise to consider alternative staffing methods. There are a wide range of alternatives that can provide varying levels of flexibility to the organization. Particularly when staffing needs require specialized skills or when the labor is market tight, these methods can provide access to highly qualified candidates who might otherwise be unavailable to the organization.

Due to advances in technology, *telecommuting*, which allows employees to work at home and connect to the office electronically, has become a viable solution for individuals who do not wish to commute or who have other reasons to work at home. Aside from the benefits telecommuting employees enjoy, reducing the number of employees required to be at the office each day can allow employers to reduce overhead costs as well as contribute to reductions in commute traffic congestion.

Job sharing is an alternative that allows two people with complementary skills to share the duties and responsibilities of a full-time position.

Part-time employees are those who work less than a regular work week. They can be a cost-effective solution for organizations needing particular skills on an ongoing but not full-time basis.

Internship programs are usually designed to give students opportunities to gain experience in their chosen fields prior to graduation. Successful programs provide meaningful work and learning experiences for the students, including opportunities to meet with senior executives. The student gains a valuable learning experience, and the organization benefits by developing low-cost access to employees and the chance to observe the intern's performance prior to making an offer for full-time employment.

The temporary worker category covers a wide range of flexible staffing options. The traditional "temp" is employed by an agency that screens and tests candidates prior to sending them to a work site for variable periods of time, from short, one-day assignments to assignments lasting for long periods of time. Temp-to-perm arrangements allow organizations to observe and evaluate a worker's performance prior to making an offer of full-time employment. *On-call workers* are employed by the organization, available on short notice, and called to work only when they are needed. *Payrolling* allows the organization to refer individuals they want to hire to an agency. The agency hires them to work for the organization and provides payroll and tax services for either a fixed fee or percentage of the salary, which is generally less than a traditional temp agency fee. *Seasonal workers* are hired only at times of the year when the workload increases, such as the Christmas shopping season, or when it is time to harvest agricultural products.

Contract workers provide another solution for acquiring talent. There are two types of contract workers. Independent contractors are self-employed individuals who work on a project or fee basis with multiple customers or clients. Both federal and state governments have guidelines to determine the difference between an independent contractor and an employee. Misclassifying an employee as an independent contractor can result in substantial penalties to the employer, so it is important to ensure that the guidelines are followed. *Contract workers* are employed by brokers or agencies that act as the employer of record, providing payroll, marketing, and other services to the worker, including negotiating the contract with the client on the worker's behalf.

A *professional employer organization (PEO)* operates as the organization's HR department. The PEO becomes the employer of record and then leases the employees back to the organization. PEOs provide full service HR, payroll, and benefit services and can provide a cost-effective solution that enables smaller companies to offer benefits comparable to those offered by much larger organizations.

 Real World Scenario

Employee or Independent Contractor?

The Internal Revenue Service (IRS) has established guidelines for determining whether an individual can be considered an independent contractor or an employee. Recently, the IRS clarified the factors it uses to determine the appropriate status for an individual. These standards fall into three categories: behavioral controls, financial controls, and type of relationship of the parties.

- Behavioral controls establish whether or not the organization has the right to direct and control tasks completed by the worker, including:

  - Instructions given by the organization to the worker as to when and where the work is done, the tools or equipment that are used, whether or not the worker must perform the task or may hire others to assist, the order or sequence of tasks, and who must perform specific tasks.

  - Organizations train employees to perform services in a particular manner while independent contractors determine their own methods.

- Financial controls establish whether the organization controls the business aspects of the individual, including:

  - The extent to which the business expenses are *not* reimbursed

  - The extent of investment

  - The extent to which the worker makes services available to the relevant market

  - How the worker is paid

  - The extent to which the worker can realize a profit or loss

- The type of relationship that exists between the parties is demonstrated by:

  - The existence of a written contract

  - The existence of benefits such as insurance, pension, and vacation and sick pay

  - The permanency of the relationship, that is, an indefinite period of time (employee) or a specific project or period of time (contractor)

  - The extent to which the services performed are a key aspect of the regular business of the organization

Additional information about the IRS guidelines is available at www.irs.gov/pub/irs-pdf/p15a.pdf.

Many states have established their own rules for determining the appropriate status for workers. As with all employment laws and regulations, the highest standard is the one with which employers must comply, so be sure to familiarize yourself with the standards for the state(s) you practice in.

Outsourcing moves an entire function out of the organization to be handled by a company specializing in the function. This solution can be beneficial by allowing the organization to focus on its basic business operations.

Translating Organization Goals into Staffing Plans

Translating strategic workforce goals and objectives into a tactical action plan is accomplished with the use of a *staffing needs analysis*. This tool is used to determine the numbers and types of jobs forecasted in the organization's strategic plan. Figure 4.2 depicts a typical staffing needs assessment.

Staffing Needs Analysis

The strategic plan identifies two key pieces of information for HR: the work that needs to be done and how many people are needed to do it. That information forms the objective for the staffing needs analysis and identifies the information to be collected.

Collect data   Workforce planning provides an opportunity for HR professionals to build key relationships within their organizations, demonstrating the value they can add to the business. As business unit managers identify the goals and objectives that form the basis of their contribution to the achievement of organization goals, HR should meet with those managers to identify the KSAs that will be needed to execute on those objectives and the number and timing of people required.

During these meetings, HR also collects information about current employees who may be ready to assume new tasks and responsibilities and any training needed to prepare them for new roles. Organizations fortunate enough to have a robust Human Resource Information System (HRIS) can utilize that tool to further analyze the current workforce.

FIGURE 4.1   Staffing Needs Analysis

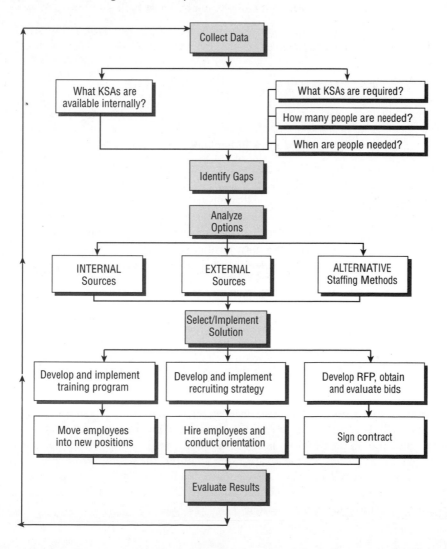

Identify gaps   Building on the data collected from individual business unit managers, HR develops a comprehensive list of the KSAs required to meet future needs for the organization. Factored into this list should be contingencies for retirements or unexpected resignations of current employees based on prior history of turnover, transfers, and promotions. Comparing the answers to these questions identifies the gaps that will need to be filled and allows for analysis of the best way to fill those needs, whether internally or externally or by utilizing alternative staffing methods.

Analyze options   Once the list of numbers, types, and timing of future openings is available, HR identifies options for filling the positions, whether from internal transfers or promotions, external hires, or the use of alternative staffing methods.

Select/implement solutions   Conducting a cost/benefit analysis of the options identified in the previous step provides a means for comparison between the available options.

Evaluate results   After the solution has been implemented, an evaluation of its success is conducted to ensure that it meets the needs of the organization.

Labor Market Analysis

Conditions in the labor market affect the ability of an organization to hire the qualified individuals it needs. A labor market analysis looks at various economic indicators and other factors that impact the availability of those individuals.

Economic indicators   A variety of economic measures are used in labor market analysis. The Bureau of Labor Statistics (BLS) collects data from employers throughout the United States and makes this information available on its website. Some of the measures useful in analyzing the labor market include the unemployment rate, occupational outlook, demographics, and wages by area and occupation. In 2001, BLS introduced the Job Openings and Labor Turnover Survey (JOLTS), which analyzes open positions, hiring statistics, and terminations.

Industry activity   Another important factor to consider in a labor market analysis is the situation in your industry. Are there new competitors entering the market? Is an existing competitor ramping up to produce a new product? Is a competitor losing market share and laying off employees? Activity within an industry affects an organization's ability to obtain qualified individuals to fill job openings.

Labor market categories   Depending upon specific job requirements, the labor market most often falls into one of three broad categories: geographic, technical or professional skills, and level of education.

> **Geographic**   This labor market can be local, regional, national, or international and contains individuals with a wide variety of technical and professional skills and levels of education. Selection of the geographic labor market depends on the availability of candidates with the necessary skills for the position. For example, the pool of candidates for an entry-level customer service representative opening could be quite large in the local labor market, while obtaining a sufficient pool of candidates to fill an open CEO position could require looking at the national or international labor market.

Technical/professional skills   This labor market contains individuals with expertise in a specific skill or discipline, such as accounting or information technology. These skills are often transferable between industries and can expand the available pool of candidates for openings.

Education   This labor market includes individuals with similar levels of education. In some professions, such as teaching, medicine, or science, an advanced degree may be required to fill a position.

A useful labor market analysis for a particular organization includes data that is relevant to the needs of the organization and the types of employees and skills it is seeking to hire.

Staffing Programs

The workforce plan and staffing needs analysis have identified the jobs to be filled, when they are needed, where they are located, and the KSAs and competencies needed for successful performance. The job descriptions and specifications for successfully recruiting qualified candidates are in place. A review of internal demographics indicates if past recruiting efforts have resulted in a diverse workforce or whether it is necessary to explore alternative ways to promote diversity within the organization. Armed with this information, the process of finding qualified candidates for open positions can begin. The question now becomes where to find the appropriate people to fill the gaps.

Sourcing and Recruiting Candidates

The sourcing and recruiting of qualified candidates to fill open positions is critical to the success of any organization. Sourcing and recruiting functions may be combined into one position or, in large organizations or during periods of intense hiring, may be split. *Sourcing* provides names and contact information for potential candidates in the active and passive markets. Active job seekers are seeking work and often attracted through traditional advertising methods (see the section "External Recruiting"). Passive candidates are those who are not currently looking for work so locating them requires additional research, such as identifying professional associations or organizations that are likely to employ individuals with similar skills. *Recruiting* is the process of creating interest about open positions in an organization and seeking candidates who possess the necessary qualifications to successfully fill them.

Recruiting Strategies

An effective recruiting strategy is ongoing. Even during times when few positions are open, continuing to communicate with potential candidates, educational institutions, search firms, and other sources can help to shorten the time needed to fill positions when they do occur and result in better service to internal customers.

Employer Brands

Defining the employer's brand identity sets the stage for many aspects of the recruiting process. Each organization has a brand identity in the marketplace, whether or not it has been consciously developed. The reputation established with employees, current and former, along with the way the organization presents itself in the general marketplace, contribute to the brand. Because the information is out there, HR can take a leading role in defining the brand so that it is an accurate reflection of where the company wants to be and can be utilized in the recruiting process.

Simply developing a catchy PR campaign is not enough to make an effective employer brand. For a brand to be useful in attracting high-quality employees to the organization, it must first match the reality of working in the organization and describe what is unique about it. When that happens, every employee becomes an ambassador for the organization, creating interest among others in working for the organization.

Building an employer brand begins with identifying unique elements of the organization culture. What values are important to the company? How are employees treated? Is the company on the leading edge in its industry? Is risk-taking encouraged or frowned upon? Are employees involved in the decision-making process? Is the performance management process perceived to be fair? Do employees receive regular feedback? How does the company respond to economic downturns? These are some of the considerations that become part of the brand. An accurate brand message gives candidates an idea of what it would be like to work in the organization and positively impacts retention. If the employer has differentiated its organization as an employer of choice with a clearly defined message about the benefits of working there, then attracting the quality of candidates desired by the organization becomes less difficult. It is critical, however, that the "official" brand message is an accurate reflection of the organization. To ensure that this is the case, an employee survey can be conducted to find out if current employees perceive the organization the way the brand portrays it. If there is a discrepancy, the organization can choose whether to adjust the brand message or make operational changes that address the differences between employee perceptions and the branding message.

An effective employer brand that accurately portrays the organization culture benefits the organization in any economic climate. During times of economic growth when high-quality employees are in great demand, the brand both attracts and retains them. In an economic downturn, the brand becomes a vehicle for fostering communication and improving morale.

Total Reward Packages

An organization's total rewards philosophy impacts its ability to attract qualified candidates. This strategy is a key element in the organization's recruiting strategy because it directly affects how well it will be able to attract and retain employees with the KSAs it needs. Chapter 6 discusses the philosophies in greater detail, but in general terms, organizations interested in acquiring the "best and brightest" candidates, or candidates with unique and highly desirable skills, employ a philosophy of leading the market, paying a premium to attract candidates. This philosophy, of course, requires the financial ability to pay at a premium. Organizations that may not be financially able to pay a premium but want to hire qualified employees compete with a philosophy of meeting the market, meaning that they pay the average market rate. There are organizations that decide to lag the market by paying below the market rate. This may be a financial necessity or a conscious decision on the part of management, if, for example, jobs require little or no skill or training and employees are easily replaced.

Recruiting Methods

During the process of creating job competencies, descriptions, and specifications, HR works with line managers to ensure that the job requirements are accurately presented. In the recruiting process, HR works with line managers to create a candidate profile so that applicants who go through the selection process fit the requirements of the position. In developing this profile, line managers often want to describe an "ideal candidate" who possibly even exceeds the requirements of the position. It's up to HR to work with line managers in developing candidate profiles that are realistic, given the working conditions and salary range offered for the position At the same time, it's also effective to work with line managers to develop alternatives to the candidate profile, possibly substituting years of experience for education requirements, or lowering experience requirements if the experience is in the same industry. This expands the pool of available candidates and increases the chances of success in the recruiting process.

With the job description and candidate profile in hand, HR is able to determine the best sources for qualified candidates. Choosing appropriate sources for candidates depends upon how available the specific KSAs are in various labor markets, along with workforce diversity issues that need to be addressed in the hiring process. In general terms, where you recruit for candidates depends in large part upon the scarcity of the KSAs you need to hire—the scarcer the KSAs, the larger the labor market to reach and the greater the recruiting budget.

Internal Recruiting

Once the organization has decided to fill positions internally, there are several methods for communicating information about the openings to employees. A *skills inventory* is an HR management tool used to collect and store a wealth of information that would otherwise be obtained only after many hours of research by HR staff. An effective skills inventory collects information on special skills or knowledge, performance appraisals, fluency in foreign languages, educational qualifications, previous experience in or outside of the company, credentials or licenses that may be required, and any continuing education employees have obtained through training classes, seminars, or educational institutions. When made a part of an automated HRIS system, obtaining a report with detailed information about the internal talent pool can be accomplished in minutes. When replacement and succession plans are in place, conversations with potential candidates can take place over a period of time, often during performance reviews and goal setting sessions.

Once possible internal candidates for openings are identified using the skills inventory or a replacement or succession plan, there are two methods used to publicize current openings throughout an organization.

The first method, *job posting*, is an internal job announcement that provides basic information about the opening, including the title; a brief description of the competencies, duties, responsibilities, and specifications; the salary range; and the application procedure.

The second method is known as *job bidding* and provides a means by which interested employees express interest in a position before it is available. This gives the supervisor and HR department an opportunity to review the job qualifications with the employee, provide training opportunities, let the employee gain additional experience if needed to meet the position requirements, and add the employee's name to the replacement or succession plan as appropriate.

Succession Planning

A well thought-out *succession plan* identifies individuals within the organization who have the talent and ability to move into management and executive positions in one to five years. Once these individuals are identified, development plans are created to ensure that they are mentored and have opportunities to obtain education, training, and experience in areas that will enhance their ability to move into senior positions when the organization needs them.

Organizations might also choose to develop, implement, and utilize a *replacement chart*. This tool is useful at all levels of the organization and helps HR and line managers identify staffing needs by categorizing current employees in one of four categories:

Ready for promotion   Employees in this category demonstrate the KSAs to assume additional responsibilities and are ready to move forward in the organization.

Develop for future promotion   This group includes employees who are proficient in their current positions and, with additional training opportunities and experience, will be ready to move forward in the organization.

Satisfactory in current position   These employees are proficient in their current positions but do not demonstrate the KSAs or interest to assume greater responsibility in the organization.

Replace   Employees are placed in this category for a variety of reasons, such as transfer or promotion, impending retirement, short-term disability, or unsatisfactory performance.

External Recruiting

Once it's been decided that the appropriate method for filling positions is to hire from outside, a number of factors must be considered. Particularly when the skills needed by the organization are in short supply in the labor market, the organization must find ways to effectively publicize its openings to appropriate candidates.

There are a variety of recruiting methods to be considered for finding new employees. The appropriate method depends upon the type of employee needed by the organization in a particular situation. This means that a number of methods may be utilized in a single organization at any given time:

Media sources   Up until the advent of Internet job boards, the most prevalent means for recruiting was newspaper advertising; for many jobs it is still the preferred method. Advertising jobs on the radio is used quite less often than newspaper ads, but it can be effective if a company is trying to fill a large number of positions in a short period of time. Television advertising is rarely used to advertise individual positions; when used it is most often by agencies who accomplish a dual purpose with the ads—attracting candidates and soliciting clients.

Internet job boards   Advertising open positions on the Internet has become quite prevalent in recent years, particularly for positions in high technology companies. Its popularity as a recruiting source is growing because it is often more cost-effective than traditional media advertising. A downside for employers who use this method is that some job seekers are indiscriminate when responding to posted jobs, which results in a large number of resumes from unqualified applicants that must be sorted through to find appropriate candidates.

Company websites   Most companies with a web presence have a "career" or "opportunities" page on their websites where current openings are posted. When combined with recruiting software that requires applicants to enter their own information into the recruiting database, this recruiting method can greatly reduce the time spent wading through resumes from applicants who do not qualify for positions.

Colleges and universities   Colleges and universities are a good source for entry-level hires in areas such as accounting, engineering, or human resources. An effective college recruiting program capitalizes on school ties by sending alumni to the campus as recruiters. Recruiters are carefully chosen for their enthusiasm about the students as well as for the company. Key factors for recruiting success are delivering informative presentations about the organization and being honest about the job opportunities currently available in the organization.

College recruiting has become a reliable source for locating minority applicants in recent years.

Job fairs   Job fairs are events designed to bring employers and job seekers together in a single location. This format gives employers a chance to meet many potential job applicants in a short period of time. Including line managers and other employees with HR reps in the booth staff gives job seekers an opportunity to find out about the organization without going through an interview process.

Alumni employees   Building and maintaining professional relationships with former employees who left in good standing and on good terms can be a cost-effective, worthwhile source for re-recruiting. Particularly if they enjoyed their experience in the organization, they may be enticed to return if an appropriate opportunity presents itself, and they can be good sources for referrals.

Previous applicants   Often during the recruiting process, a recruiter may remember a candidate who was not the best fit for one position but left an impression as someone who would be good elsewhere in the organization. Maintaining professional contact with such individuals can pay off when an appropriate position becomes available.

Vendors and suppliers   Individuals who provide goods or services to the company are often aware of potential candidates for openings. Particularly when there has been a long-term relationship, the vendor is aware of the organization's culture and needs and may prove to be a good source for applicants.

Labor unions   In union environments, the union hiring hall can be a good source for qualified employees.

Professional associations   Relationships developed in connection with attendance at professional association functions or conferences often provide leads for qualified applicants. In addition, many associations provide job posting opportunities on websites or sell job advertisements in their publications.

Employment agencies   Each state has an agency dedicated to providing services to job seekers, including job counseling and training opportunities. There is no charge for employers to list job openings with the agency, which then screens, tests, and refers appropriate candidates.

Contingent employment agencies generally focus on jobs in a specific profession or job category, such as accounting professionals or administrative employees. Fees, paid by the employer only when a candidate is hired, are usually based on a percentage of the first year's salary and vary widely with different agencies. The fee is often negotiable.

Retained employment agencies are often referred to as headhunting firms or executive search firms. When these agencies are engaged by an organization, a fee for recruiting services is paid whether or not any of the candidates are hired. Retained firms are generally used for executive-level positions and specialize in sourcing candidates from the passive labor market.

Walk-in candidates   Candidates may come into the business in person to fill out applications and apply for jobs.

Where you search for candidates depends upon your analysis of the availability of the specific KSAs in the various labor markets. Where you look for candidates also impacts the cost of the recruiting effort as well as how much you must pay to attract the right candidate.

Uniform Guidelines on Employee Selection Procedures

The Uniform Guidelines on Employee Selection Procedures (UGESP) were jointly developed by the EEOC, the Civil Service Commission (CSC), the OFCCP, and the Department of Justice (DOJ) to assist employers in complying with requirements of Title VII, EO 11246 (as amended), and other federal equal employment opportunity legislation. Specifically exempted from the UGESP are requirements under the ADEA and the Rehabilitation Act. The UGESP states that any selection tool that has an adverse impact against a protected class is discriminatory unless the employer can show that the tool is both job-related and a valid predictor of success in the position. The UGESP directs that if employers have access to more than one selection tool, the tool that has the least adverse impact is the one to be used. Records are to be kept by sex, race, and ethnic group, using categories consistent with the EEO-1 report (Hispanic, White, Black or African-American, Native Hawaiian or Other Pacific Islander, Asian, American Indian or Alaska Native, and Two or More Races) and EEO reporting purposes.

One report required by the UGESP is a determination of whether or not selection procedures have an adverse impact on one or more protected groups. An *adverse impact* occurs when the selection rate for a protected class is less than 4/5ths or 80 percent of the selection rate for the group with the highest selection rate. Table 4.4 illustrates an adverse impact calculation.

TABLE 4.4   Calculating Adverse Impact

Group	Applicants	Hired	Selection Rate	4/5 of highest rate
Males	255	48	19%	15%
Females	395	52	13%	
Totals	650	100		

In this example, the company advertised 100 openings. Applications were received from 255 males and 395 females for the position. Adverse impact is calculated as follows:

1. For each group, divide the number of applicants hired by the total number of applicants:

    Males: 48/255 = 19%

    Females: 52/395 = 13%

2. Multiply the highest selection rate by 80%:

    Males: 19% × 80% = 15%

3. Compare the selection for the other group(s) to determine if adverse impact has occurred:

    Females: 13%

    Males: 15%

In this example, female applicants were adversely impacted by the selection process.

Applicant Tracking

The UGESP requires employers to keep records of individuals who apply for open positions based on their sex and race/ethnicity as previously described for the EEO-1 report. In 1974, the UGESP defined an applicant as "…a person who has indicated an interest in being considered for hiring, promotion, or other employment opportunities. This interest might be expressed by completing an application form or might be expressed orally, depending on the employer's practice."

As the Internet grew into an increasingly important factor in the recruitment and selection of new employees, it became clear that an additional definition was needed. In October 2005, the UGESP were amended to include the definition of an Internet applicant as meeting these criteria:

1. The employer has acted to fill a particular position;

2. The individual has followed the employer's standard procedures for submitting applications; and

3. The individual has indicated an interest in the particular position.

Candidate Selection Tools

The result of the recruiting phase of the employment process should be resumes and application forms from job seekers hoping to be selected for the position. Screening these hopeful candidates to find those who best meet the needs of the position begins with establishing procedures that ensure equal employment opportunities.

Communicating with Applicants

HR departments are often criticized for ignoring job applicants. While a large volume of applications makes it difficult to personally contact each person who expresses interest in a position, many companies use an "auto respond" email to acknowledge receipt of electronic resumes and applications and let candidates know that they will be contacted if selected for the interview process. Mail or in-person applications can be similarly acknowledged with pre-printed post cards carrying the same message.

Recruiters need to stay in contact with candidates who move forward in the process until they have been removed from consideration and then a final, respectful communication that they are no longer being considered is appropriate. These communications can be made in writing, but candidates who have made it to the final round of interviews deserve a personal call. This allows job seekers to move forward in their job searches and leaves them with a favorable impression of the HR department and the organization.

Screening Tools

The goal of the assessment process is to narrow down the candidate pool into a manageable group including those candidates most qualified for a position. There are a variety of tools used to assess candidate qualifications.

Resumes

Many organizations rely on candidate resumes as a first step in the assessment process. While they generally contain relevant information, it can be difficult to compare qualifications of different candidates due to the lack of uniformity of style and content. Resumes generally present information about the applicant in the most favorable light and do not always contain all of the information necessary to determine if the applicant is qualified for the position. For those reasons, having all applicants complete an employment application is a good practice.

Employment Applications

Because application forms are considered employment tests by the EEOC, employers must be certain that the information requested on them is both job related and a valid predictor of success in the position. A key benefit to using a standard application form is the inclusion of a statement to be signed by the applicant stating that the information contained in the document is true and complete. This statement can be useful in the event that an employer becomes aware of misstatements or discrepancies subsequent to hiring a candidate.

There are four basic types of application forms to consider using; one will suit the needs of the specific position or organization:

Short form employment application   As its name implies, the short form application is less extensive than other application forms; the term "short" is relative—it describes application forms that range from one to five pages. Short form applications are often used by employees who are applying for transfers or promotions and are useful for prescreening candidates or for positions with minimal skill requirements.

Long form employment application   The long form application provides space for additional information related to the job requirements, such as advanced degrees and longer employment histories.

Job-specific employment application   If the organization hires a substantial number of employees for positions with similar requirements, the application form can be designed to gather specific information related to the position or profession. This type of form would be appropriate for teaching, scientific, or similar professions.

Weighted employment application   The weighted application form was developed to assist recruiters in evaluating candidate qualifications. The form is developed using the job description; aspects of the job that are more important for success are given higher weights than other, less critical requirements. Weighted applications tend to reduce bias in the screening process, but they are expensive to maintain as they must be redesigned whenever job requirements change.

Screening Interviews

After reviewing the application forms and choosing those that meet the job specifications and candidate profile, the recruiter conducts screening interviews to decide which candidates will be forwarded to the hiring manager. The purpose of these interviews is to both discover facts about the candidate and provide information about the position. The recruiter can assess the candidate's interest in the position and begin the process of determining which candidates are the best fit for the requirements. Screening interviews are relatively short, lasting from 15 to 30 minutes.

Selection Tools

Once HR has screened the applicants for a position and narrowed the candidate pool to those who meet the job requirements and fit the candidate profile, the process of selecting the best candidate for the position begins. The most common selection tool is the in-depth interview conducted by hiring managers and others who know what the successful candidate will need to do in the position. The selection process may include other elements, such as a realistic job preview, an in-box test, or participation in an assessment center process (all discussed later in this chapter). In-depth interviews, however, are the cornerstone of the selection process, used in virtually all hiring decisions.

Types of Interviews

There are several types of interviews that can be conducted. Not all of them are appropriate for every situation, and it is up to HR to counsel the hiring manager on what will work best in each situation.

Behavioral interviews   These interviews are based on the premise that past behavior predicts future behavior and ask candidates to describe how they have handled specific situations in previous jobs. Candidates are expected to be able to describe a situation or problem, the actions they took to resolve it, and what outcome resulted. Interviewers skilled in this type of questioning are able to drill down into the answers to determine the depth of experience the candidate has.

Directive interviews   As the name implies, a directive interview is very much controlled and guided by the interviewer with a predetermined set of questions asked of all candidates.

Nondirective interviews   In this interview style, the interviewer asks broad questions and allows the candidate to guide the conversation. This style may produce a great deal of information relating to the candidate's qualifications, but it is difficult to ensure consistency in questions for all candidates, and that can become a problem when evaluating them.

Patterned interviews   A patterned interview is structured to cover specific areas related to the job requirements. The interviewer will cover each area with all candidates but may ask different questions of them.

Panel interviews   In a panel interview, several interviewers interview the candidate at the same time.

Structured interviews   A structured interview is similar to a directed interview: a list of questions is prepared in advance and used for all candidates.

Stress interviews   There are some positions in which employees encounter highly stressful situations on a regular basis, such as airline pilots, law enforcement officers, or astronauts. A stress interview subjects candidates to an intimidating situation to determine how the candidate will handle stress in the position.

Question Guidelines

Equal opportunity legislation and regulations described earlier in this chapter require that questions asked of candidates during the selection process be constructed to obtain only job-related information. There are some topics that may never be a consideration in a selection decision, such as race. Others, such as age, are BFOQs that may be asked in a nondiscriminatory manner (for example, state laws may require that a bartender be at least 21 to serve alcoholic beverages). Table 4.5 illustrates appropriate and inappropriate ways to obtain job-related information in an interview.

TABLE 4.5   Appropriate Job-Related Questions

Inappropriate Interview Questions	Appropriate Interview Questions
Affiliations	
What clubs or social organizations do you belong to?	Do you belong to any professional or trade associations or other organizations you think are relevant to this job?
Do you go to chuch?	
Age	
How old are you?	Are you over the age of 18?
When did you graduate from high school?	Can you, after employment, provide proof of age?
Arrest Record	
Have you ever been arrested?	Have you ever been convicted of _____? (Name a crime that is plausibly related to the job in question.)

TABLE 4.5   Appropriate Job-Related Questions *(continued)*

Inappropriate Interview Questions	Appropriate Interview Questions
Disabilities	
Do you have any disabilities?	After reviewing the job description, are you able to perform all the essential functions of the job?
Have you had any recent or past illnesses or operations? If you, list them and give dates when these occurred.	After reviewing the job description, are you able to perform all the essential functions of the job?
How's your family's health?	
When did you lose your vision/arm/hearing? How did it happen?	Any job offer will be made contingent upon a medical exam. Are you willing to undergo one if we offer you a job?
Marital/Family Status	
What is your marital status?	Are you willing to relocate?*
With whom do you live?	This job requires frequent travel. Are you willing and able to travel when needed?*
What was your maiden name?	Is there anything that will prevent you from meeting work schedules?*
Do you plan to have a family? When? How many children will you have?	
What are your child-care arrangements?	
Military	
Were you honorably discharged?	In what branch of the armed services did you serve?
What type of discharge did you receive?	What type of training or education did you receive in the military?

TABLE 4.5   Appropriate Job-Related Questions *(continued)*

Inappropriate Interview Questions	Appropriate Interview Questions
National Origin/Citizenship	
Are you a U.S. citizen?	Are you authorized to work in the United States?
Where were you/your parents born?	
What is your race?	What language(s) do you read/speak/write fluently? (Acceptable if related to essential functions.)
What language did you speak in your home when you were growing up?	
Personal	
How tall are you?	This job requires the ability to lift a 50-pound weight and carry it 100 yards. Are you able to do that?
How much do you weigh?	
Would working on weekends conflict with your religious beliefs?	This job will require work on the weekends. Are you able to do so?

*Acceptable if asked of every candidate.

Interviewer Bias

Any interviewer may bring preconceived ideas or biases into an interview situation; these can have an unintended impact on the hiring decision. The following list includes some of the different types of interview bias that can occur. Once interviewers are aware of these, it is possible to reduce the impact on the selection process.

Average/central tendency   The *average bias* becomes apparent when the interviewer has difficulty deciding which candidate is best and rates them all about the same.

Contrast   The *contrast bias* occurs when an interviewer compares candidates to each other or compares all candidates to a single candidate. For example, if one candidate is particularly weak, others may appear to be more qualified than they really are.

Cultural noise   *Cultural noise bias* occurs when candidates answer questions based on information they think will get them the job—what they think the interviewer wants to hear. For example, a candidate who has been an individual contributor may tell an interviewer that they prefer working as part of a team.

First impression   This bias can work either for or against a candidate, depending on the interviewer's *first impression*. A candidate who is very nervous and stutters during the first few minutes of the interview may be viewed as less qualified even if during the remainder of the interview they are poised and well spoken.

Gut feeling The *gut feeling bias* occurs when the interviewer relies on an intuitive feeling that the candidate is a good (or bad) fit for the position without looking at whether or not the individual's qualifications meet the criteria established by the job specifications and candidate profile.

Halo effect The *halo effect bias* occurs when the interviewer evaluates a candidate positively based on a single characteristic. For example, a candidate's self-confident attitude may overshadow a lack of experience in a particular requirement.

Harshness/horn effect *Harshness bias*, or the *horn effect*, occurs when the interviewer evaluates a candidate negatively based on a single characteristic.

Knowledge-of-predictor *Knowledge-of-predictor bias* occurs when the interviewer is aware that a candidate scored particularly high (or low) on an assessment test that has been shown to be a valid predictor of performance.

Leniency *Leniency bias* occurs when an interviewer tends to go easy on a candidate and give a higher rating than is warranted, justifying it with an explanation.

Negative emphasis The *negative emphasis bias* occurs when the interviewer allows a small amount of negative information to outweigh positive information.

Nonverbal bias *Nonverbal bias* occurs when an interviewer is influenced by body language. For example, a candidate who frowns when answering questions could be rated negatively even though the answers were correct.

Question inconsistency *Question inconsistency* occurs when an interviewer asks different questions of each candidate. While this is acceptable to a certain extent in order to delve more deeply into each candidate's qualifications, there is no baseline for comparison if there are no questions that were asked of all candidates.

Recency The *recency bias* occurs when the interviewer recalls the most recently interviewed candidate more clearly than earlier candidates.

Similar-to-me The *similar-to-me bias* occurs when the candidate has interests or other characteristics that are the same as those of the interviewer and cause the interviewer to overlook negative aspects about the candidate. For example, an interviewer who played college football may select a candidate who did so even though the candidate's qualifications are not the best for the position.

Stereotyping The *stereotyping bias* occurs when the interviewer assumes a candidate has specific traits because they are a member of a group. For example, an interviewer may assume that a woman would not be able to successfully perform in a job that requires frequent lifting of packages weighing 50 pounds.

Conducting Effective Interviews

Job interviews are stressful situations for interviewers and candidates alike. The interviewer has a very short period of time to determine whether or not the candidate is the best choice for the position, and the candidate wants to make a good impression with the ultimate goal of obtaining a job offer. To reduce the stress and improve the chances of obtaining the information needed to make the best hiring decision, preparing for the interview is essential. HR can assist interviewers in this process by providing advice on structuring an effective interview.

Selecting the interview team   HR's role in selecting the interview team is to work with the line manager to ensure that everyone who needs to be involved in the interview process is involved. In a team environment, it may be appropriate for all members of the team to participate in the interview process; in other situations, employees from other business units who have frequent contact with the person in the position may be invited to participate in the process, along with employees who are knowledgeable about the work to be done.

Pre-interview strategy meeting   Conducting a pre-interview strategy meeting with the interview team provides an opportunity for the hiring manager to share what will be required of the successful candidate and to ensure that all interviewers are on the same page for the interviews. Topics for discussion can include the job description, specifications, and competencies. At this time, a discussion of the type of interview to be conducted and of common interview biases is also appropriate. This is a good opportunity for HR to share best interview practices with interviewers, such as not making notes on the application form or resume, and a review of appropriate interview questions.

Candidate evaluation forms   During the pre-interview strategy discussion, HR can review the candidate evaluation form with the interview team. This form provides consistency in the interview process by providing interviewers with a list of topics to be covered during the interview. The form is useful in rating candidates on job requirements and acts as a reminder of what to discuss during the candidate evaluation phase of the selection process.

The interview   Interviewers should prepare to meet the candidates by reading the application forms or resumes and making notes of any items that need explanation. During the interview, the candidate should be treated with dignity and respect, beginning with starting the interview on time and giving full attention to the candidate during the course of the interview. Setting the candidate at ease in the first few minutes will set the stage for a productive and informative interview. Providing a clear explanation of the organization's mission, values, and culture; the position; and what will be expected of the successful candidate early in the interview gives prospective employees a context in which to answer questions. Listening carefully to the candidate's answers, taking notes as appropriate, and following up on points that need clarification indicate a genuine interest in what is being said and encourage an open and honest exchange. Be honest with the candidate about the workplace environment, and give them time to ask their own questions. End the interview with an explanation of the next steps in the process.

Post-interview evaluation   When everyone on the interview team has met with all of the candidates, a final meeting takes place. During this meeting, the interviewers review the candidate evaluation forms and share their thoughts on each candidate.

Realistic Job Preview

A *realistic job preview (RJP)*, designed to give candidates an accurate picture of a typical day on the job, provides an opportunity for them to self-select out if the job is not what they expected it would be. This increases the chances for success on the job, thereby reducing turnover. Depending on the type of job, the RJP can take many forms, including observing a current employee doing the job (as in a call center environment, for example), a simulated experience of the job, or a video presentation about the organization, work environment, and coworkers. A tour of the workplace is another way to provide candidates with an idea of what it would be like to work in the organization. These techniques, either singly or in some combination, can provide candidates with realistic expectations of the job and the organization.

In-Box Test

An in-box test provides candidates with a number of documents describing problems that would typically be handled by an employee in the position, with instructions to prioritize the problems and/or decide how the problems should be handled. Candidates are evaluated on the appropriateness of their decisions as well as on the length of time it takes for them to complete the test.

Assessment Centers

Assessment centers are characterized by multiple tests designed to measure different aspects of the job. Generally used to assess candidates for management potential and decision-making skills, they have been demonstrated to be valid predictors of success on the job. Used extensively by state and local governments and large organizations for assessing internal candidates for promotion, their use is limited due to the high cost of conducting them. Typical assessments include interviews, testing and problem-solving skills, in-basket tests, leaderless group discussions, and role-playing exercises.

The purpose of an interview strategy is twofold: First, it ensures that everyone on the interview team is aware of the position requirements and candidate profile. Second, when several interviewers will be interviewing the candidates for a position, it ensures that everyone is using the same criteria to evaluate candidates. During the strategy development phase, you must decide the appropriate type of interview for the position.

Candidate Testing Programs

The use of pre-employment tests has become more prevalent in recent years. These tests take many forms and have a variety of purposes. The key issue to keep in mind with regard to employment tests is the requirement that they must be job-related and, should they be challenged by an EEOC complaint, defensible as valid predictors of success in the position.

Types of Selection Tests

Aptitude tests   These tests are designed to measure an individual's knowledge and ability to apply skills in various areas, such as mathematics, typing, language, and reasoning. Properly constructed aptitude tests have been shown to be valid predictors of job success.

Cognitive Ability Test (CAT)   CATs measure an individual's ability to analyze and solve problems and draw conclusions from a set of facts. They also measure an individual's potential for learning, thinking, and remembering.

Personality test   Personality or psychometric tests assess how a candidate will "fit" into a specific job. If, for example, an employer uses a personality test that has shown particular characteristics to be valid predictors of success in sales positions and an applicant does not reflect those characteristics when tested, the test would indicate an area to be explored with the candidate prior to making the hiring decision.

Real World Scenario

The Courts Address Employment Tests

Once Title VII was enacted, employees who felt they had been subjected to unlawful employment discrimination were able to initiate lawsuits to resolve their grievances. Pre-employment testing practices were the subject of a number of cases, the most prominent of which are described here.

1971: *Griggs v. Duke Power Co.* Duke Power Company, located in North Carolina, employed 95 workers in its Dan River Steam Station in 1964. There were five departments at the plant: Labor, Coal Handling, Operations, Maintenance, and Laboratory and Test. The Labor Department was the lowest paid department in the company; in fact, the highest paying job in the department paid less than the lowest paying job in the other four. In 1955, the company began to require that employees in all departments except Labor have a high school diploma, but prior to that time employees could be hired into any of the departments without one. On July 2, 1965, the effective date of Title VII, Duke added a requirement that all new employees must pass two aptitude tests, and that an employee wishing to transfer from Labor to another department needed a high school diploma.

Willie Griggs was one of 14 black employees working in the Labor Department at the plant. There were no black employees in any of the other departments. Mr. Griggs filed a class action lawsuit on behalf of himself and 12 of the black employees, alleging that the requirement for a high school diploma and satisfactory scores on the aptitude tests discriminated against them. The district court that first heard the case dismissed it. The court of appeals found that Griggs had not shown that there was a discriminatory purpose to the requirements and that a discriminatory purpose was required to show discrimination. The Supreme Court granted *certiorari* (agreed to review the case) and heard oral arguments in December 1970. Because a number of the white employees who did not have high school diplomas had been hired prior to the requirements for the diploma or the aptitude tests, and those employees performed well on the job, it was clear that the requirements did not predict job performance, and Duke Power did not dispute this fact. The Supreme Court found that "good intent or absence of discriminatory intent" in the face of a job requirement that adversely impacts a protected class is not a sufficient defense against discrimination. The job requirement must be shown to be job related in order to be lawful, and it is up to the employer to prove this. The HR significance of *Griggs v. Duke Power Co.* is that discrimination does not need to be intentional to exist. It is up to employers to prove that job requirements are related to the job.

1975: *Albemarle Paper v. Moody* In 1966, a group of current and former black employees at Albemarle Paper's mill in Roanoke Rapids, North Carolina, filed a lawsuit against both their employer, Albemarle Paper, and the union representing them with the company. The group asked the court for an injunction against "any policy, practice, custom, or usage" at the mill that was in violation of Title VII. When the case dragged on for several years, a demand for back pay was added to the injunction request in 1970. One of the policies in question was the employment testing practice used by Albemarle Paper. The district court denied the claim for back pay and refused to consider the testing procedure, saying that the tests had been validated.

The court of appeals reversed the ruling, finding that the absence of bad faith was not sufficient grounds to deny back pay, and that the validation process had four serious flaws:

1. It had not been used consistently.

2. It had compared test scores to the subjective rankings of supervisors, which could not be tied to job-related performance criteria.

3. The tests were validated against the most senior jobs and not entry-level positions.

4. The validation study used only experienced white employees, not the new job applicants, who were mostly nonwhite.

The HR significance of *Albemarle Paper v. Moody* is that test validation must be in accordance with the Uniform Guidelines on Employee Selection Procedures. Subjective supervisor rankings are not sufficient for criterion validation; the criteria must be able to be tied to the job requirements.

1975: *Washington v. Davis* In 1970, two applicants for the police department in Washington, D.C., filed suit against the city, claiming that the written personnel test given to applicants had an adverse impact on black applicants. The Supreme Court upheld the district court's finding that the test was a valid predictor of successful performance in the police training program. The HR significance of *Washington v. Davis* is that tests that have an adverse impact on a protected class are lawful if they are valid predictors of success on the job.

Integrity tests Also known as honesty tests, integrity tests assess a candidate's work ethic, attitudes toward theft and drug and alcohol use, and similar traits. According to the EEOC, professionally developed integrity tests do not create an adverse impact for protected classes as long as the tests are administered equally to all candidates.

Psychomotor assessment tests A psychomotor assessment tests an individual's coordination and manual dexterity.

Physical assessment tests Physical assessment tests are used to determine whether or not candidates are physically capable of performing specific job duties. The tests generally require that tasks be completed within a predetermined period of time and most often simulate activities that regularly occur on the job. A common physical assessment test is one that is given to potential firefighters to ensure that they are capable of lifting and carrying heavy weights for predetermined periods of time in a variety of circumstances.

As previously discussed, a key requirement for selection tools is that they be both related to specific job requirements and valid predictors of successful job performance. To determine whether or not a specific employment test meets those criteria, employers must ensure that tests are both reliable and valid.

Reliability and Validity

The UGESP require that selection tests be reliable and valid predictors of success on the job.

Reliability

Reliability measures whether or not a test or other measurement produces consistent results so that, over time, the scores will not vary greatly. Test reliability is enhanced by several factors, including wording instructions and test questions clearly. Providing optimal conditions for administering the test contributes to its reliability, as does making sure it is long enough to accurately test the candidate's knowledge.

Validity

Validity considers the characteristics being measured by a test and whether or not the test is measuring the characteristic accurately.

Content validity   *Content validity* is the simplest of the three validation measures. Job analysis is a key element of the content validity process, which confirms that a selection procedure samples significant parts of the job being tested. For example, a driving test given to a delivery person who would drive a truck 80 percent of the time if hired for the job is a test with content validity.

Construct validity   *Construct validity* determines whether a test measures the connection between candidate characteristics and successful performance on the job. According to the DOL, construct validity is not only a more complex validation technique, it has not been widely used in employment testing. While it is an acceptable method for validation, its use in employment testing is still the subject of research and, therefore, care should be taken to ensure that its use meets DOL validation standards.

Criterion validity   A criterion is a trait or work behavior that is predicted by a test. *Criterion validity* is established when the test or measure either predicts or correlates the behavior.

   Predictive validity   *Predictive validity* compares the test scores of a test given at the beginning of a job before new employees have experience. When the employees have had some experience (for example, six months or one year) with the job, the manager evaluates their performance. The original test scores are then measured against the criterion (the evaluation ratings) and the test is validated if they are similar.

   Concurrent validity   The process for determining *concurrent validity* is similar to that of determining predictive validity. The difference is that the criterion measurement occurs at the same time the test is given and not at a later time.

Real World Scenario

Validity in Action

What does all this validity stuff have to do with HR? Federal courts look to validation studies to determine whether or not specific job requirements discriminate against protected classes. A professionally developed validation test serves as proof in court that the employment requirement is a valid predictor of successful performance on the job. Following are some ways that companies can use forms of validity in various situations.

Imagine a company needs to hire business analysts who will spend 95 percent of their time analyzing sales trends and predicting future sales. The company would want to administer a test that measures a candidate's ability to reason. In this case, a test that measures a candidate's ability to reason would have *construct validity*.

In another example, an accounting firm that has had significant turnover in its entry-level accounting positions in the last few years wants to put some measures in place that will result in new hires with a better chance of success in their positions. As a result, the HR director commissioned a test to measure analytical ability to use in the hiring process. The firm recently hired 100 recent college graduates with accounting degrees as entry-level accountants, none of whom has ever worked in the accounting field. On their first day of work, all 100 accountants took the new test. Six months later, the accountants were evaluated by their supervisors, and the results of the evaluation ratings (the criterion) were compared to the test results. The accountants who were highly rated by their supervisors had high scores on the test, and those who scored poorly on the test had lower evaluation ratings. The test has *predictive validity*.

Here's an example to illustrate the use of concurrent validity. The owner of CADServ, a computer aided design service bureau, recently won a large contract for design work with a nationally known real estate developer. The project will require that CADServ hire at least 20 more CAD operators within a few months. The owner would like to bring in some entry-level operators but needs to be sure they will be successful on the job. The owner contracts with a testing firm to administer an abstract reasoning test to the candidates but wants to be sure it will be accurate. The owner decides to have the 30 CAD operators who already work at CADServ take the test. The test is given around the same time as the annual review cycle, and when the test results come in, they are very similar to the ratings received by the employees—those who received high test scores also received high performance ratings. The test has *concurrent validity*, and CADServ will use it in the hiring process for the new operators.

NOTE   To read an excellent (and easy-to-understand) explanation of testing, assessment, reliability, and validation, go to www.uniformguidelines.com/testassess.pdf.

Pre-Employment Inquiries

Pre-employment inquiries or background checks cover a range of activities designed to ensure that candidates who receive employment offers are who they represent themselves to be during the selection process. Information collected during these processes should be protected from inappropriate dissemination, and at the appropriate time, disposed of in a way that ensures its security. Pre-employment inquiries verify information collected from candidate resumes and/or interviews during the selection process. Some of the information is relatively easy to verify, such as educational degrees and previous employment, and provides insight into previous educational and employment experiences. Pre-employment inquiries may also include a check of the candidate's financial records, driving record, and any previous criminal behavior, depending on the type of job. Any background or reference check conducted by a third party is considered a consumer investigative report and subject to requirements of the Fair Credit Reporting Act (FCRA). When employers conduct their own reference checks, those requirements do not apply.

Reference Checks

An organization may ask for several types of references from potential employees. Some kinds of references include the following:

Employment references   To make an informed decision about a potential employee, employers should obtain all the information they can from previous employers. Information collected during the reference checking process includes previous employment history, dates, job titles, and type of work performed. Many employers are reluctant to provide more information than this for privacy reasons, but as long as the information is factual and given in good faith, most states consider it "qualifiedly privileged," which protects the employer from legal action. It is desirable to obtain additional information about the employee's work habits and interpersonal skills and find out if the employee is eligible for rehire.

Educational references   Depending upon the position applied for and the length of time since graduation, some employers request high school, college, and post-graduate transcripts to verify the accuracy of information presented during the selection process.

Financial references   Financial references are generally only used when candidates will be handling large sums of cash. As with all other selection tools, a financial reference must be shown to be job related and a valid predictor of success in the position. When required, financial references, generally provided by credit reporting agencies, are subject to requirements of the federal Fair Credit Reporting Act (FCRA).

Criminal Record Checks

Criminal record checks can uncover information about substance abuse, violent behavior, and property crimes such as theft or embezzlement. Because private employers do not have access to a central database that collects information from every level of government (federal, state, county, and local), it can be difficult to do a comprehensive check. When applicants have lived or worked in several states, counties or municipalities, records in each jurisdiction must be checked to ensure completeness.

The Fair Credit Reporting Act of 1970

The FCRA was first enacted in 1970 and has been amended several times since then. Enforced by the Federal Trade Commission (FTC), the FCRA requires certain actions be taken by employers prior to the use of a consumer report or an investigative consumer report in employment decisions.

First, a clear and conspicuous disclosure that a consumer report may be obtained for employment purposes must be made in writing to the candidate before the report is acquired.

Second, the candidate must provide written authorization to the employer to obtain the report.

Third, before taking an adverse action based in whole or in part on the credit report, the employer must either provide the candidate with a copy of the report and a copy of the FTC notice, "A Summary of Your Rights Under the Fair Credit Reporting Act," or, if the application was made by mail, telephone, computer, or similar means, the employer must notify the candidate within three business days that adverse action has been taken based in whole or in part on the credit report; provide the name, address, and telephone number of the reporting agency; and indicate that the agency did not take the adverse action and cannot provide the reasons for the action to the consumer. The employer must provide the candidate with a copy of the report within three days of a request from the candidate for a copy of the report, along with a copy of the FTC notice just described.

The FCRA may be viewed in its entirety at www.ftc.gov/os/statutes/fcra.htm#603.

Negative information obtained through criminal record checks should be carefully reviewed on a case-by-case basis, considering all of the relevant information:

- How does the type of crime relate to the position applied for?
- How recent was the conviction?
- How old was the applicant when the conviction occurred?
- What is the level of risk to customers, coworkers and others in the workplace if the applicant is hired?

Criminal record checks are considered consumer investigations and must comply with related FCRA requirements.

When an employer considers making an adverse hiring decision based on negative information received in an investigative consumer report, the applicant must be notified in writing and given a chance to respond. Should the negative information be the result of a mistake, the applicant can provide information to clear the record. If the employer decides to proceed with the adverse action, the applicant must receive a second written notice stating that the adverse action has been taken.

The Privacy Act of 1974

The Privacy Act of 1974 was an attempt by Congress to regulate the amount and type of information collected by federal agencies and the methods by which it was stored in an effort to protect the personal privacy of individuals about whom the information had been collected. The act requires written authorization from an individual prior to releasing information to another person. The act does not currently apply to private employers.

First, the act provides individuals with the right to know what kind of information is being collected about them, how it is used and maintained, and whether it is disseminated. The act prevents this information from being used for purposes other than that for which it was collected, and it allows individuals to obtain copies of the information, review it, and request amendments to inaccurate information. The act requires the government to ensure that information collected is not misused. Except under specific circumstances covered by the Privacy Act, such as law enforcement or national security needs, the information collected by one agency may not be shared with another. Damages for violation of these requirements may be sought in federal district court, and if found by the judge to be warranted, are subject to reimbursement of attorney's fees and litigation costs, as well as a fine for actual damages incurred by the individual of up to $1,000 paid by the federal government.

Negligent Hiring

Negligent hiring occurs when an employer knew or should have known about an applicant's prior history that endangered customers, employees, vendors, or others with whom the employee comes in contact. Employers can prevent negligent hiring lawsuits by carefully checking references and running background checks for all candidates. Once an employer finds out about such a history, the employer is obligated to safeguard others who come in contact with the individual during the work day by taking whatever action is necessary to maintain a safe work environment.

To defend themselves against claims of negligent hiring, employers can demonstrate that they exercised due diligence in the hiring process by taking the following steps:

- Conducting reference checks with previous employers
- Obtaining reports from the Departments of Motor Vehicles in the states where the applicant has lived or worked
- Verifying the validity of the applicant's social security number
- Conducting criminal record checks
- Verifying the validity of any government-issued licenses, such as a medical or engineering license issued by a state
- Conducting drug screening tests

Polygraph Tests

The use of polygraph tests in the employment process is limited by the Employee Polygraph Protection Act (EPPA).

The Employee Polygraph Protection Act of 1988

The EPPA prohibits private employers from using polygraph tests in making employment decisions except under very limited conditions. The act applies to private employers but not federal, state, or local governments and is administered by the Wage and Hour Division of the Department of Labor. Violations of its provisions may result in fines of up to $10,000 against an employer.

The EPPA allows polygraph tests to be administered to employees of federal contractors or subcontractors with national defense, national security, or FBI contracts; to prospective employees of armored car or security services; and to prospective employees who would have access to the manufacture, storage, distribution, or sale of pharmaceutical products. The act also allows the use of polygraph tests during an ongoing investigation of an economic loss to the employer if an employee had access to the property in question. Under these limited circumstances, polygraph tests may be administered by individuals licensed by the state in which the test takes place.

See http://www4.law.cornell.edu/uscode/29/2006.html to view the complete text of the Employee Polygraph Protection Act.

Medical Examinations

As with all other assessment tools, medical examinations are allowable if their purpose is job related and they are required of all candidates. These exams are used to ensure that the employee will be fully capable of performing the requirements of the job, and in some cases, may be part of an employer's health and safety program. Under the ADA, employers may make a job offer conditional on a medical examination before the candidate begins working as long as all applicants for positions in the same job category must undergo the exam. If the offer is rescinded as a result of the medical exam, the employer must be able to demonstrate that the job requirement eliminating the candidate from consideration is related to a business necessity.

Drug Screening Tests

Studies conducted by the Occupational Safety and Health Administration (OSHA) indicate that drug screening programs reduce job-related accidents. Substance abuse is also linked to reduced productivity.

Drug screening tests are specifically excluded from the ADA's medical examination requirement and may be required prior to extending an offer.

Employment Offers

The post-interview strategy meeting has been concluded, the references have been checked, and results of the pre-employment tests are in. It's been a difficult decision for the hiring manager, but the decision has been made and it is time to extend an offer. After discussion with

HR, the hiring manager contacts the successful candidate and extends a verbal offer, or in some organizations, HR may be responsible for extending verbal offers. When the verbal offer is accepted, a written offer agreement is prepared.

Employment Agreements and Contracts

Employment relationships in many states are subject to the common law concept of "employment at-will" meaning that the relationship can be ended at any time by either party with or without a reason (more about employment at-will and other common law concepts in Chapter 7, "Employee and Labor Relations"). As a result, few employees today work under employment contracts. In most cases, the relationship is defined in an offer letter that is composed after negotiations are complete.

Making and Negotiating Offers

One of the goals of the selection process is to collect information from candidates about their expectations for cash compensation, benefits, and other terms and conditions of employment that may be appropriate to the position. When it is time to make an offer, these expectations are incorporated into the decision-making process of crafting the offer. Prior to making the offer, any required approvals are obtained, along with approval for any "wiggle room" should the candidate come back with a request for a higher salary or increased benefits. Once the verbal negotiations are complete, the written agreement can be completed.

Offer Letters

The offer letter should be prepared immediately upon acceptance of the verbal offer by the candidate. The standard offer letter should be reviewed by the corporate attorney to ensure that its provisions do not compromise the organization and that it contains the terms of the offer as well as any contingencies that apply, such as a medical exam. The salary offer should be stated in an hourly or monthly amount. The offer should state clearly that the organization is an at-will employer and that only the terms and conditions of the offer contained in the offer letter are valid. Finally, there should be a reasonable time frame for returning a signed acceptance of the offer.

Care should be taken to ensure that any promises of benefits or special conditions agreed upon by the hiring manager are included in the offer letter so that there is no ambiguity about the complete offer.

Employment Contracts

An employment contract binds both parties to the agreements contained in the contract. Contracts are generally reserved for senior-level managers and can cover a wide range of topics. Any areas of the employment relationship not specifically covered in the contract are subject to common law. Some standard clauses seen in employment contracts can include the following:

Terms and conditions of employment   This clause covers the start date and duration of the contract and, if the contract is for a set period of time, includes any automatic extension agreements.

Scope of duties   The general and specific duties and responsibilities are covered by this clause. The duties can be part of the contract or the job description may be incorporated into the agreement as an addendum. Expectations for performance are included here as well.

Compensation   The compensation package is described in this clause, which includes the base salary, any bonus and incentive agreements, auto allowance, company car, or other agreements.

Benefits and expense reimbursements   Items covered by this clause include disability and health insurance benefits and retirement plans. The extent and conditions for expense reimbursements are also described here.

Nondisclosure of proprietary information   Requirements for the maintenance of confidentiality with regard to proprietary information are included here, along with noncompete language and requirements for the return of company property when the employment relationship ends.

Nonsolicitation agreement   This clause sets forth agreements that limit the employee's ability to solicit customers, vendors, and employees during the course of the contract and for an agreed-upon period of time after the contract ends.

Advice of counsel   A clause advising the employee to seek legal counsel prior to signing the contract is often included.

Disability or death   The employer can include a clause that states what happens to the agreement in the event of the disability or death of the employee.

Termination clause   The termination clause sets forth conditions that would lead to a termination for cause, such as inability to perform, neglecting the duties of the position, misconduct, violations of company policy, or other egregious acts.

Change of control   A change of control clause protects the employee's job and compensation in the event of a reorganization, acquisition, or merger, for a specified period of time.

Post-Offer Employment Activities

When the offer has been accepted, the transition from candidate to employee begins. At this stage employees form their first impressions about what it will be like to work in the organization. During this time, employers can take steps to begin the relationship positively by including employees in special events that may be scheduled prior to their first day, providing them with information that will help them become productive more quickly and begin assimilating into the work group.

Relocation Practices

In some circumstances, employers may be willing to pay the costs of relocating an employee or an applicant. When that occurs, HR may manage the process. Elements of relocation packages that can be negotiated include a company-paid trip for the spouse and family to see the area and look for a new home, assistance with selling the old and/or purchasing the new home, payment of moving expenses, assisting the spouse in a job search in the new area, and guaranteeing the sale price of the old house if it doesn't sell.

Relocation is an activity that lends itself to outsourcing, and there are many professionals who will manage the entire process for the organization and the family. This can be a cost-effective solution that saves time for in-house staff.

Immigration Processes

In 2003, enforcement responsibility for the Immigration and Nationality Act (INA) of 1952 and its amendments was transferred to the U.S. Citizenship and Immigration Services (USCIS), an agency of the Department of Homeland Security.

Immigration and Nationality Act (INA) of 1952 and Amendments of 1965   The purpose of the INA was to simplify the multiple laws that previously governed U.S. immigration policy. Immigration quotas continued to be set on the basis of national origin.

Following the trend of equal opportunity established by the Civil Rights Act of 1964, the 1965 amendment eliminated national origin, race, and ancestry as bars to immigration and changed the allocation of immigrant visas to a first-come, first served basis. The amendment also established seven immigration categories with the goals of reunifying families and giving preference to those with specialty skills that were needed in the U.S.

Immigration Reform and Control Act (IRCA) of 1986   The Immigration Reform and Control Act (IRCA) was enacted in 1986 to address illegal immigration into the United States. The law applied to businesses with four or more employees and made it illegal to knowingly hire or continue to employ individuals who were not legally authorized to work in the United States. Unfair immigration-related employment practices were defined as discrimination on the basis of national origin or citizenship status.

Employers were required to complete Form I-9 for all new hires within the first three days of employment and to review documents provided by the employee that establish identity or employment authorization or both from lists of acceptable documents on the I-9 form. IRCA requires employers to maintain I-9 files for three years from the date of hire or one year after the date of termination, whichever is later, and allows, but does not require, employers to copy documents presented for employment eligibility for purposes of complying with these requirements. The act also provides that employers complying in good faith with these requirements have an affirmative defense to inadvertently hiring an unauthorized alien. Substantial fines for violations of both the hiring and recordkeeping requirements were provided in the law. Failure to maintain acceptable records of I-9s is subject to fines of not less than $100 nor more than $1,000 for each employee without a completed form available upon request to an authorized agent of the USCIS. The following table outlines the fines for hiring violations under IRCA.

Violation	Amount of Fine
First	Not less than $250 or more than $2,000 for each unauthorized employee
Second	Not less than $2,000 or more than $5,000 for each unauthorized employee
Third	Not less than $5,000 or more than $10,000 for each unauthorized employee

In addition to the fines listed, employers who knowingly hire unauthorized workers are subject to fines of $3,000 per employee and/or six months imprisonment.

Until 2005, IRCA required employers to store I-9 forms on one of three types of media: paper, microfilm, or microfiche. Passage of HR 4306, which was signed into law by President Bush, allows employers to store I-9 forms n PDF files or other electronic formats.

Immigration Act of 1990   The Immigration Act of 1990 made several changes to IRCA, including adding the requirement that a prevailing wage be paid to H-1B immigrants to ensure that U.S. citizens did not lose jobs to lower-paid immigrant workers. The act also restricted to 65,000 annually the number of immigrants allowed under the II-1B category and created additional categories for employment visas as shown next. In 1996, the number and types of documents to prove identity and eligibility to work were reduced.

VISA	CLASSIFICATION
	Visas for Temporary Workers
H-1B	Specialty occupations, DOD workers, fashion models
H-1C	Nurses going to work for up to three years in health professional shortage areas
H-2A	Temporary agricultural worker
H-2B	Temporary worker: skilled and unskilled
H-3	Trainee
J-1	Visas for exchange visitors
	Visas for Intracompany transfers
L-1A	Executive, managerial
L-1B	Specialized knowledge
L-2	Spouse or child of L-1
	Visas for Workers with Extraordinary Abilities
O-1	Extraordinary ability in sciences, arts, education, business, or athletics
	Visas for Athletes and Entertainers
P-1	Individual or team athletes
P-1	Entertainment groups
P-2	Artists and entertainers in reciprocal exchange programs

P-3	Artists and entertainers in culturally unique programs
Visas for Religious Workers	
R-1	Religious workers
Visas for NAFTA Workers	
TN	Trade visas for Canadians and Mexicans

Illegal Immigration Reform and Immigrant Responsibility Act (IIRIRA) of 1996   This act reduced the number and types of documents allowable to prove identity, employment eligibility, or both in the hiring process and established pilot programs for verification of employment eligibility.

 Visit www.uscis.gov/graphics/lawsregs/INA.HTM to view the full text of INA and its amendments.

Employee Orientation Programs

Orientation or on-boarding programs exist to reduce the length of time it takes for new employees to become productive team members. The first day on a new job is exciting and stressful, and new employees are frequently subjected to information overload—a situation which reduces their ability to retain all of the information thrown at them. From benefit selections and application forms to the names of their new coworkers and other contacts, it can be an overwhelming introduction to a new organization. This situation can be alleviated by stretching the orientation over a longer period of time, beginning as soon as the written offer letter is sent. Many organizations provide benefit information and application forms with the written offer so that the employee has time to review them and make appropriate selections and include their spouses in those decisions.

Prior to the first day of work, all the tools that will be needed should be set up, from a desk or other work area to a working telephone and computer and whatever other job-specific tools are needed. This helps the employee to feel welcome and important to the organization.

Formal orientation programs are composed of two elements: a general introduction to the organization as a whole and a job-specific orientation. HR often has responsibility to provide the organization orientation, providing information about the mission, goals, and values, and answering general questions. The job-specific orientation is conducted or overseen by the hiring manager and provides information specific to the department and position, sets performance expectations, and ensures the new hire knows where to go for assistance when it is needed. The most effective orientations take place over an extended period of time with regularly scheduled follow-ups that provide opportunities to check in with the employee and provide support as needed.

Buddy programs are sometimes used to provide additional, informal support to new employees. Buddies are employees in good standing with enough time on the job to be familiar with how things work in the organization and can answer questions or direct the new employee to a person with the answers.

Orientation programs are an important part of a new hire's introduction to the organization. In many organizations, daily events move so quickly that they are sometimes left to fend for themselves without understanding what it is they are supposed to do or how to get help when they need it. The orientation program helps to ensure that new employees have the support they need to be successful.

Employee Retention Programs

Retaining key employees is crucial to a successful organization. Many organizational factors contribute to an organization's ability to retain those employees, including compensation, culture, opportunities for growth, and the ability of direct supervisors to manage employees fairly with dignity and respect. Each of these factors will be discussed in the chapter of the most relevance.

Organization Exit Processes

Organization exits happen in one of two ways: the employee either chooses to leave of their own volition (resignations and retirements), or they are asked to leave in one way or another (termination, downsizing, or layoff). Organization exits are stressful. Even when the employee has chosen to leave and is going on good terms, issues arise for the organization in replacing the employee or allocating duties to remaining coworkers. Coworkers can be affected by the change as well, so developing an exit process that reduces the stress and builds a smooth transition will pay off in many ways. Most significant for HR is the positive message a smooth transition sends to employees who remain in the organization.

Voluntary Exit Processes

Employees voluntarily exit the organization by either resigning or retiring. Resignations occur when an employee decides to leave the organization and pursue other opportunities. For HR, resignations present few legal issues, but they do require decisions about replacement or reassignment of work that may lead to promotions or transfers of other employees, all of which affect the workforce planning process. Resignations require HR to ensure that any outstanding loans or advances are repaid to the organization or arrangements are made for that to happen. In addition, COBRA and HIPAA notices must be provided for departing employees. (COBRA and HIPAA requirements are covered in detail in Chapter 6.)

Planned retirements occur when an employee decides to stop working full time and pursue other interests. HR can provide preretirement counseling to prepare employees for the transition from the structure provided by full-time work to unstructured time for pursuing other activities in leading a full and rewarding life. Employee Assistance Programs (EAPs) are excellent sources for this type of counseling and assistance. (EAPs are covered in detail in Chapter 6.)

Before an employee leaves the company, the HR department should conduct an *exit interview*. An effective exit interview provides an opportunity for employees to communicate information to the organization about why they decided to leave, what improvements the organization could make to enhance the employment experience, and any specific issues that need to be addressed. If the employee is one who has been a significant contributor and whom the organization would consider rehiring in the future, this would be the time to leave the door open for that possibility. Ideally, exit interviews are conducted by a third party so that employees feel free to be candid. There are a number of organizations that provide this service, most often as a telephone or online interview.

Involuntary Exit Processes

Involuntary exits occur as the result of either performance problems or changing business needs. Performance problems and terminations resulting from those issues are discussed in Chapter 7. This chapter discusses issues related to downsizing, which occurs as businesses change strategic direction or react to economic situations. There are a number of issues to consider in this process, beginning with legal notice requirements.

Worker Adjustment and Retraining Notification (WARN) Act of 1988

The WARN Act was passed by Congress in 1988 to provide some protection for workers in the event of mass layoffs or plant closings. The act requires 60 days advance notice be given to either the individual workers or their union representatives. The intent of Congress was to provide time for workers to obtain new employment or training before the loss of their jobs. The WARN Act is administered by the Department of Labor and enforced through the federal courts.

Employers with 100 or more full-time employees or those with 100 or more full- and part-time employees who work in the aggregate 4000 hours or more per week are subject to the provisions of the WARN Act. The employee count includes those who are on temporary leave or layoff with a reasonable expectation of recall.

The WARN Act established that a *mass layoff* occurs when either 500 employees are laid off or 33 percent of the workforce and at least 50 employees are laid off. A *plant closing* occurs when 50 or more full-time employees lose their jobs because a single facility shuts down, either permanently or temporarily. In cases where the employer staggers the workforce reduction over a period of time, care must be taken that appropriate notice is given if the total reductions within a 90-day period trigger the notice requirement.

The WARN Act also established rules on notice. For instance, notice is required to be given to all affected employees or their representatives, the chief elected official of the local government, and the state dislocated worker unit. Notice requirements vary according to which group they are being sent to, but they must contain specific information about the reasons for the closure, whether the action is permanent or temporary, the address of the affected business unit, the name of a company official to contact for further information, the expected date of closure or layoff, and whether or not bumping rights exist.

The WARN Act provides for three situations in which the 60-day notice is not required, but the burden is on the employer to show that the reasons are legitimate and not an attempt to thwart the intent of the act.

1. The "faltering company" exception applies only to plant closures in situations where the company is actively seeking additional funding and has a reasonable expectation that it will be forthcoming in an amount sufficient to preclude the layoff or closure, and that giving the notice would negatively impact the ability of the company to obtain the funding.

2. The "unforeseeable business circumstance" exception applies to plant closings and mass layoffs and occurs when circumstances take a sudden and unexpected negative change that could not have reasonably been predicted.

3. The "natural disaster" exception applies to both plant closings and mass layoffs occurring as the result of a natural disaster.

Once the organization has determined whether or not compliance with WARN Act requirements is necessary, decisions regarding a reduction in force (RIF) can be made. Also commonly referred to as a layoff, planning and conducting a RIF is stressful for managers, who must decide which employees will be asked to leave the organization, and even more so for employees, who usually figure out that layoffs are coming long before the management announcement. Maintaining productivity in a workforce that is waiting to find out whether or not they will have jobs is a challenging prospect. During these times, honest communication with employees is essential, and management should provide as much information as possible before actual layoff decisions are complete. Once the layoff has occurred, open and honest communication is still essential, as remaining employees struggle with feelings of anger that their coworkers had to leave the company, "survivor guilt" because they are still employed, and dissatisfaction if they are now asked to take on the work of the employees who left the company.

 Some states have enacted WARN acts with more stringent requirements than the federal WARN act. Be sure to know the difference between state and federal requirements when you take the exam.

Making Layoff Decisions

As managers struggle with decisions about who will go and who will stay, the focus of those decisions must be on what is necessary for the business. Documenting the business reason for the decision with clear and unambiguous reasoning is essential in case the decision is challenged on the basis of disparate impact or other equal opportunity requirements.

Managers often look to layoffs as a way to remove low performers. If this is the route taken, documentation of the method used to determine who these employees are is necessary. Performance appraisals are often utilized for this purpose.

Severance   Offering a severance package to departing employees helps to ease the shock of unemployment. Severance packages must be consistent, based on a rationale that ensures equity to all departing employees. Severance amounts can be based on seniority or employee classes, or some combination of the two.

Real World Scenario

Taxman v. Board of Education of Piscataway (1993)

In 1989, the Piscataway Board of Education found it necessary for budgetary reasons to reduce the faculty. According to state law, the board was required to conduct the layoffs based on seniority. There were two teachers with the least seniority, Sharon Taxman and Debra Williams. Both had been hired on the same day in 1980, had equivalent educational qualifications and had received equally outstanding evaluations. In essence, the board felt they were both equally qualified to be retained. In making previous layoff decisions in similar cases when there were no differences in qualifications, the board had drawn lots to determine which teacher to lay off. In this case, however, there was one difference between the teachers that the board considered: Taxman was white and Williams was black. The board decided that it was in the interest of the school to demonstrate the importance of diversity in the workplace and decided to retain Williams because she was black.

There was no evidence of past discrimination that needed to be rectified based on the Affirmative Action Plan; in fact, blacks were employed in the school district at about twice the rate of the applicable labor pool. Sharon Taxman sued the school board for racial discrimination in violation of Title VII. The federal district court that heard the case found in favor of Taxman, and the school board appealed to the Third Circuit Court of Appeals, which also found in favor of Taxman. The school board then appealed to the U.S. Supreme Court, but agreed to settle the case before the Supreme Court hearing.

Outplacement   *Outplacement* services are utilized to transition employees who are leaving the company, most often as the result of a downsizing or layoff. These services assist employees with updating resumes, preparing for interviews, and in searching for a new job. They are often provided in a group seminar setting for individuals who have been terminated as part of a mass layoff. Your local unemployment office may provide outplacement assistance as well, including on-site meetings with impacted employees.

Executive outplacements may occur as the result of a merger or acquisition and may include additional benefits, such as headhunting services and one-on-one counseling.

Providing this service for employees can be a great assistance in finding new jobs or in coping with the change in circumstances. Continuing the EAP for a finite period of time for laid off workers is another way to assist them in coming to terms with a job loss.

Unemployment insurance   If the RIF or layoff meets WARN notice thresholds, the state unemployment office will be aware of the pending layoff. Whether or not that is the case, HR should ensure that employees are clear about their eligibility for unemployment benefits and how to apply for them. Most states provide pamphlets explaining the requirements that are distributed at the time of the layoff.

Conducting the Layoff Meeting

During the layoff meeting, managers should communicate the message unambiguously and with compassion. If the layoff decision is a permanent one, employees should be advised that they will not be called back to work; if there is a possibility for rehire, they should be advised of the time frame in which that will occur. Employees should be given adequate time to gather personal items prior to leaving but should not be allowed to hang around indefinitely, as this negatively impacts productivity and is hard on the morale of employees who will be staying with the organization. Once the termination meetings have been conducted, it is important that management meet with the remaining employees to answer questions and provide reassurance.

Metrics—Measuring Results

Workforce Planning and Employment is a function that lends itself more readily to measurement than some other areas of HR.

Business impact measures   In addition to ROI measures discussed in Chapter 2, employee productivity is a key measures for business impact in the WFP function. Productivity metrics are calculated by dividing "total output" (expressed in revenue dollars or [in manufacturing industries] by a measure of inventory output) by the number of employees. This metric can be calculated for the whole organization or by work groups, depending on specific information needs.

Tactical accountability measures   There are a number of established metrics used to measure HR's tactical accountability in WFP. Some of the more common include:

Accession rate   The accession rate measures the number of new employees against the total number of employees. This measurement is useful for determining the types of HR programs needed to manage and support the workforce. Accession rate is calculated by dividing the total number of new employees by the number of employees at the end of the previous measurement period.

Quality of hire   In order to calculate a quality of hire metric, HR must first develop criteria to identify what constitutes a quality hire. This information includes accurate job descriptions, assessment tools that accurately identify the best-qualified candidates, clear communication of expectations to new hires, and pre-established criteria to measure performance against. The measurement is often based on performance ratings made by hiring managers after observing employees on the job.

Cost per hire   Cost per hire is a common metric but is often calculated without including all the costs associated with a hire. For example, a meaningful cost-per-hire calculation includes costs for advertising, in-house recruiter time to review resumes, screen candidates, and/or recruiter fees, HR staff salary, salaries for hiring managers and other members of the interview team, assessment tests, pre-employment inquiries, administrative costs, and any other costs involved in hiring a new employee. The metric is calculated by dividing the total costs by the number of hires for the measurement period.

Time to hire   The time to hire metric is calculated from the date a job is posted to the date a job is accepted by the new employee.

Replacement cost   Replacement cost per employee can be an eye-opener for managers and executives. In addition to the costs calculated for the cost-per-hire metric, this measurement also includes costs for training, lost productivity, temporary replacements, overtime for employees who fill in while the position is vacant, and others. These costs can easily reach 300 percent of annual salary for the position.

Turnover   One of the most commonly used metrics, turnover is calculated by dividing the average number of total employees for the measurement period by the number of employees who exited the organization. This measurement can be calculated in a variety of ways to meet specific organization needs. Some variations include calculating on a monthly or annual basis, calculating turnover for voluntary separations only, or for different business units within the organization.

SPHR ONLY

Global Considerations

As businesses of all sizes becoming increasingly global, American companies find themselves employing all or part of their workforce in positions overseas. In addition to the planning steps discussed previously, there are a number of additional factors to consider for an international workforce, beginning with determining in what labor market the company will recruit its employees. There are three possible areas:

- The home or parent country is the domicile of the company, where its corporate headquarters are located. Employees who originate from the home country are known as *expatriates*, or *parent-country nationals (PCNs)*.

- The host country is the country wherein the corporation is operating, or is planning to operate, a business unit. Employees originating from the host country are known as *host-country nationals (HCNs)*. While this may seem to be a solution with few problems, there can be many unexpected issues to resolve, including those related to compensation and cultural differences.

- Employees from any country other than the home or host country are known as *third-country nationals (TCNs)*. Experienced third-country nationals who are familiar with the organization culture and business practices are most often utilized to set up a new business unit in a neighboring country. This can be an advantageous situation for the business because it is less expensive than relocating an expatriate.

It is important to understand the international staffing strategies that can be used in building the global workforce. There are four basic strategies used by multinational corporations in making these decisions.

The *ethnocentric* approach is one in which all of the key management positions are filled by expatriates. The benefits of an ethnocentric approach include the ability of the organization to maintain control of its business units and ensure that business is conducted in accordance with corporate mandates. Communication with the home office is made easier because the expatriate is familiar with the organization's culture and business practices. International assignments also provide opportunities to develop individuals who are part of the succession plans for senior management roles. This approach is often taken during the startup phase of a business unit to ensure that organization standards are maintained, or when there is a real or perceived lack of management talent available in the host country labor market. While this approach encourages a cohesive culture throughout the organization, it focuses on the home country/parent organization and doesn't take into consideration local customs and business practices. This can lead to misunderstandings and create ill will between the local government and the company.

A *polycentric* approach fills corporate positions in the home country with expatriates, while management positions in the host country are filled by home country nationals. This approach can have a positive impact by showing commitment to the host country and generating good will for the business, but it does not afford upward mobility for top managers in the host country. The business benefits, because it is less expensive to hire local employees— even at top dollar—than it is to fill international positions with expatriates. However, it can also limit communication between business units in the different locations and result in animosity between the home and host country business units due to differences in cultural practices and compensation levels between countries.

A *regiocentric* approach takes a somewhat larger operational view than does the polycentric, covering a trade region such as the European Union and having managers move between business units in different countries in the region.

The *geocentric* approach seeks to place the best-qualified person into each position, regardless of their country of origin. As a result, the business builds an international management team whose members are able to move into and address issues in any geographic area.

Once the company has decided which approach best suits its strategic goals and culture, there are many complex issues to be addressed by HR. There are a myriad of laws, customs, and local practices to be dealt with that often conflict with home-country practices, and it is important to understand the impact of these issues when evaluating international workforce needs.

Expatriate issues in workforce planning fall into three main categories.

Cost   The cost of sending an employee to work in a foreign country can be substantial, up to twice the annual salary after you factor in family moving costs, costs required to minimize the cultural adjustment of the employee and their family, and adjustments in pay (to keep the employee's salary "whole" and retain their equity within the company, it is often necessary to subsidize schooling costs, taxes, and housing costs).

Foreign business practices   The way business is done in foreign countries can be significantly different from the way business is done in the United States. Candidates for expatriate jobs must receive training on the culture and practices of the country to which they will be assigned to be successful in their positions and to avoid unintentionally insulting those with whom they are working, thereby straining business relationships. It is important as well to provide training on laws governing U.S. business practices in foreign countries, particularly the Foreign Corrupt

Practices Act (FCPA), which prohibits American businesses from proffering bribes in order to obtain contracts or encourage foreign bureaucrats to get things done in a timely fashion.

Cultural acclimation   Cultural acclimation can be difficult not only for the employee, but also for the employee's spouse and children, and often results in the resignation of the employee or insistence on transfer back to the home country. Another issue is that, while women are accepted in business leadership positions in this country, cultural difficulties can be encountered in other countries with fewer women in the workforce. This issue alone can become a huge conflict, with equal employment opportunity requirements to provide equal access to training and upward mobility at odds with the ability to do business in a country unaccustomed to dealing with women in powerful positions.

Finally, *inpatriates* may be brought to the home office for a period of time for training and to become accustomed to the culture and practices of the organization before returning to their countries of origin for work assignments as host-country nationals.

In evidence of the increasing significance of human resource expertise in global work environments, HRCI has developed a certification specifically for professionals who manage global HR needs on a regular basis. The Global Professional in Human Resources (GPHR) certifies professionals with expertise in this area in greater detail than the SPHR exam. SPHR candidates can expect to be tested on their general knowledge of international HR practices and the impact of a global workforce on organization needs.

Summary

When strategically tied to the organization's vision, mission, and goals, planning for workforce needs is a key element for success. HR professionals must provide expertise for management in deciding whether to aggressively develop current employees for future growth in the organization, hire candidates from the outside, or use alternative staffing methods to accomplish the work that needs to be done. Understanding the implications of each approach allows HR to guide management in making decisions that best suit the organization's needs, culture, and values.

Identifying candidates who have not only the best KSAs for the job, but whose personal goals, ambitions, and qualities complement the needs of the organization requires HR professionals to be keenly aware of its strategic direction. Providing opportunities to all qualified candidates opens up the labor pool available to the organization and includes candidates with a great deal to offer who might not have been considered in the past.

An effective hiring process begins with using sources that produce a pool of candidates with diverse backgrounds who have the required KSAs, continues with screening the candidates with a fair and equitable process designed to find the best match for the organization, and concludes by welcoming them with orientation programs that assist them to be productive members of the team. Having an effective organizational exit process in place eases the transition for the employees who remain with the company as well as for those who are leaving. When downsizing decisions are made fairly and equitably, voluntary exits are treated with respect, and terminations for poor performance are handled with due process, remaining employees respond with greater loyalty and commitment to organization goals.

HR professionals can show that they understand the fundamental needs of business by making recommendations and decisions based on quantifiable measures. Being able to show, for example, how much a bad hiring decision costs the organization in terms of the direct and indirect costs of hiring, training, and replacing employees demonstrates to management that effective HR management has a positive effect on the bottom line.

Exam Essentials

Be able to develop and implement a strategic workforce plan.   A strategic workforce plan provides a framework for HR professionals to ensure that the right people with the right qualifications are available at the right time to achieve the organization's goals.

Be able to conduct a staffing needs assessment.   A staffing needs assessment is used to determine which KSAs are needed to meet future strategic goals and where training efforts (if filling jobs internally) or recruiting efforts (if hiring from the outside) should be focused.

Be able to develop a succession plan.   A succession plan identifies high-performing individuals within the company who have the capability to take on positions at the senior and executive management levels. Once the individuals have been identified, they are coached, mentored, and provided with training opportunities to prepare them for greater responsibility.

Understand the Affirmative Action Plan process.   An AAP is required to be filed by companies with federal contracts of $50,000 or more per year and 50 employees. The plan identifies how many incumbents in different job classifications are members of protected classes and compares that information to the availability of protected classes in the labor market.

Be able to develop job requirements from a job analysis.   Job analysis provides the information necessary to develop the job competencies, job descriptions, and test specifications necessary to both identify what needs to be done on a daily basis and recruit effectively for the best candidate to fill the position.

Be able to identify recruitment methods.   Depending on the level of experience and skill being sought, there are a variety of methods to consider in the recruiting process. HR professionals must understand which methods will produce the candidates who are most appropriate to fill positions at different levels.

Be able to establish and implement selection procedures.   Effective selection procedures help ensure that candidates selected for the organization meet all the job requirements and are the best fit for the position. Interviewing, testing, realistic job previews, and assessment centers help organizations determine if the candidate is the right fit for the job. Reference checks ensure that the candidate has performed successfully in previous positions.

Understand the implications of federal immigration policy.   Immigration laws were designed to protect American workers while encouraging the immigration of highly educated and skilled workers for jobs requiring high-level KSAs. Employers may only hire noncitizens when they can demonstrate that no American citizens with the necessary qualifications are available. When noncitizens are hired, they must be paid the prevailing wage for the position.

Be able to conduct post-hire activities.   HR activities conducted during the post-hire phase have implications for the long-term success of new hires. It is important to understand the ramifications of employment offers and ensure that the new employee has all the necessary information to be successful. An effective orientation will make new employees feel welcome, introduce them to the company and provide information on company policies.

Be able to create the organization exit process.   HR professionals must develop fair and equitable processes for downsizing and laying off employees and be aware of legal notice requirements that must be followed when applicable. Resignations and retirements require that HR conduct exit interviews and create processes that provide for timely replacement of exiting employees.

Key Terms

Before you take the exam, be certain you are familiar with the following terms:

adverse impact	executive orders
average bias	exit interview
bona fide occupational qualifications (BFOQ)	expatriates
certiorari	first impression bias
concurrent validity	geocentric
content validity	gut feeling bias
construct validity	halo effect bias
contract workers	harshness bias
contrast bias	horn effect bias
criterion validity	host-country nationals (HCNs)
cultural noise bias	inpatriates
disparate impact	internship programs
downsizing	job bidding
disparate treatment	job posting
ethnocentric	job sharing

knowledge-of-predictor bias

layoff

leniency bias

mass layoff

negative emphasis bias

negligent hiring

nonverbal bias

on-call workers

orientation

outplacement

outsourcing

parent-country nationals (PCNs)

payrolling

polycentric

predictive validity

professional employer organization (PEO)

protected classes

question inconsistency bias

realistic job preview (RJP)

reasonable accommodation

recency bias

recruiting

regiocentric

reliability

replacement chart

seasonal workers

similar-to-me bias

skills inventory

sourcing

staffing needs analysis

stereotyping bias

succession plan

telecommuting

third-country nationals (TCNs)

undue hardship

unlawful employment practices

validity

corporate restructuring

Review Questions

1. The marketing director needs to hire a replacement for the marketing coordinator, who is being promoted. The position has changed quite a bit since the last time the job was advertised, and the director is looking to HR to assist in redefining the job requirements so that the recruiting process can begin. Which of the following would *not* be used in determining the job requirements?

    A. Job competencies

    B. Job description

    C. Job specifications

    D. Candidate profile

2. Which of the following is *not* a BFOQ?

    A. A synagogue hiring a new rabbi requires that the rabbi be Jewish.

    B. A lingerie catalog hires only female models.

    C. A retail store in a predominantly Asian neighborhood advertises for Asian clerks.

    D. A swimming club requires that the men's changing room attendant be male.

3. The court case that identified adverse impact as an unlawful employment practice was

    A. *Griggs v. Duke Power Co*

    B. *Albemarle Paper v. Moody*

    C. *Washington v. Davis*

    D. *Taxman v. School Board of Piscataway*

4. To determine the numbers and types of jobs necessary to realize business goals, HR must assess the KSAs available within the organization during a staffing needs analysis. What other factor is necessary to complete the assessment?

    A. The KSAs needed to achieve future goals

    B. The tasks, duties, and responsibilities for the work

    C. The KSAs available in the local labor market

    D. The organization's core competencies

5. Your New Orleans plant has an opening for a controller and four candidates have been selected for interviews. Jack, the son of a plant employee, worked as an accountant for two years to put himself through the Wharton Business School and recently earned his MBA. Richard is a CPA with eight years of experience in a public accounting firm. Susan also has a CPA and has worked as an accounting manager in the corporate office of a large corporation in the same industry. Jane does not have a CPA or MBA but has worked as controller of a smaller local competitor for eight years. After interviewing all four candidates, the general manager told you that he wants to hire Jack because he shows promise. You know from previous conversation with the GM that he also worked his way through college. Which of the following biases could be influencing the GM's decision:?

A. Knowledge of-predictor

B. Halo effect

C. Similar to me

D. Gut feeling

6. Please refer to the following table for this question. A company advertised for 100 sales representative positions. They received 650 applications and hired the 100 employees as follows:

Group	Applicants	Hired
Black	140	23
Asian	120	21
Hispanic	145	19
Caucasian	230	35
Native American	15	2
Total	650	100

Which group has the highest selection rate?

A. Black

B. Asian

C. Caucasian

D. Native American

7. Please refer to the following table for this question. A company advertised for 100 sales representative positions. They received 650 applications and hired the 100 employees as follows:

Group	Applicants	Hired	Selection Rate	4/5 of Highest Rate
Black	140	23	16%	
Asian	120	21	18%	14%
Hispanic	145	19	13%	
Caucasian	230	35	15%	
Native American	15	2	13%	
Total	650	100		

In which groups has adverse impact occurred?

A. Hispanic and Caucasian

B. Caucasian and Black

C. Hispanic and Native American

D. Native American and Black

8. An Affirmative Action Plan must be completed by employers who meet which criteria?

A. Private employers with 25 or more employees

B. Government contractors and subcontractors with contracts of $10,000 or more in a 12-month period

C. Government contractors with contracts of $2500 or more in a 12-month period

D. Government contractors with 50 or more employees and contracts of $50,000 or more each year

9. When a reduction in force occurs, the ADEA allows that protected employees may waive their rights under some circumstances. In order for the waiver to be valid, the protected employee must be allowed how long to review and consider the agreement?

A. 7 days

B. 21 days

C. 45 days

D. 180 days

10. Which of the following is *not* required by IRCA?

A. That an I-9 form be completed for all new hires within five days of hire

B. That employers comply with IRCA in good faith

C. That I-9 forms be maintained for all employees

D. That copies of documents presented for employment eligibility be maintained

Answers to Review Questions

1. D. The candidate profile is developed after the job requirements have been determined, beginning with the job description and developing the competencies (broad requirements of the position) and the specifications necessary for successful performance. Job competencies (A) identify skills and qualities beyond tasks and responsibilities specific to the position that help determine how well a candidate will fit into the work group, such as team orientation vs. individual contribution or ability to learn new skills quickly. The job description (B) provides the tasks and responsibilities that must be accomplished. Job specifications (C) define the job-specific KSAs that will be needed for success in the position.

2. C. According to the EEOC, there are no circumstances where race or color are a BFOQ. (A) is incorrect because Title VII specifically allows religious organizations to give preference to members of the religion. (B) and (D) are incorrect because Title VII specifically allows sex as a BFOQ if it is "reasonably necessary" for business operations.

3. A. *Griggs* identified adverse impact, that discrimination need not be intentional to exist; *Albemarle Paper* (B) extended the concept to require that tests must be validated in accordance with the EEOC Uniform Guidelines for Employee Selection Procedures. *Washington* (C) determined that employment tests resulting in adverse impact are acceptable if they predict future success on the job. *Taxman* (D) found that employment decisions made on the basis of race are discriminatory.

4. A. A staffing needs analysis begins with an assessment of the KSAs needed to achieve future goals along with those that are currently available within the organization. While the tasks, duties, and responsibilities (B) are used to determine what the KSAs are, it is possible for individuals with the same or similar KSAs to perform different jobs so (B) is not used in a needs analysis. KSAs available in the local labor market (C) will be used to develop the recruiting strategy and plan but are not relevant to the staffing needs analysis. The organization's core competencies (D) are factors that make the organization unique but are not generally part of the staffing needs analysis.

5. C. The GM could be influenced by his similar experience working his way through college. Knowledge-of-predictor bias (A) is a factor when the interviewer knows that a candidate scored particularly high or low on an assessment test. The halo effect (B) occurs when interviewers allow one positive characteristic to overshadow other, less positive attributes. The gut feeling bias (D) occurs when interviewers rely on intuition to make hiring decisions.

6. B. To calculate the selection rate, divide the number of applicants hired by the total number of applicants in each group:

Black	23/140 = 16%
Asian	21/120 = 18%
Hispanic	19/145 = 13%
Caucasian	35/230 = 15%
Native American	2/15 = 13%

7. C. To determine whether adverse impact has occurred, multiply the highest selection rate, which is Asian, at 18%, by 4/5 or 80%. (18% × .80 = 14%) Only two groups fall below 14%, Hispanic and Native American, both at 13%.

Group	Applicants	Hired	Selection Rate	4/5 of Highest Rate
Black	140	23	16%	
Asian	120	21	18%	14%
Hispanic	145	19	13%	
Caucasian	230	35	15%	
Native American	15	2	13%	
Total	650	100		

8. D. Government contractors with 50 or more employees and $50,000 or more each year must complete Affirmative Action Plans. (A) was the original compliance requirement for Title VII and was changed to 15 employees by the EEOA of 1972. The criteria in (B) applies to employers who must comply with the Rehabilitation Act and federal contractors who must take affirmative action for all terms and conditions of employment based on EOs. (C) is not a compliance requirement.

9. C. ADEA waivers are valid *during a reduction in force* only if the employee has 45 days to consider the agreement. Once employees sign a RIF-related waiver, the ADEA requires that they have 7 days (A) to revoke it. Terminations that are not part of a reduction in force require only 21 days (B) for consideration. An employee has 180 days (D) to file a charge with the EEOC in states that do not have their own EEO enforcement agency.

10. D. The IRCA allows, but does not require, employers to make copies of documents presented for employment eligibility. The employee section of the I-9 must be completed by the end of the first day of employment (A). The employer section must be completed and documents checked by the end of the third day of employment. Employers who make a good faith effort to comply with IRCA (B) have an affirmative defense to inadvertently hiring an unauthorized alien. IRCA requires that I-9 forms be maintained and available for audit (C) by the USCIS for three years from date of hire or one year after the date of termination.

Chapter

5

Human Resource Development

THE HRCI TEST SPECIFICATIONS FROM THE HUMAN RESOURCE DEVELOPMENT FUNCTIONAL AREA COVERED IN THIS CHAPTER INCLUDE:

- ✓ Ensure that human resource development programs are compliant with all applicable federal, state, and local laws and regulations.

- ✓ Conduct a needs assessment to identify and establish priorities regarding human resource development activities. **SPHR** ONLY

- ✓ Develop/select and implement employee training programs (for example, leadership skills, harassment prevention, computer skills) to increase individual and organizational effectiveness.

- ✓ Evaluate effectiveness of employee training programs through the use of metrics (for example, participant surveys, pre- and post-testing). **SPHR** ONLY

- ✓ Develop, implement, and evaluate talent management programs that include assessing, developing, and placing high-potential employees. **SPHR** ONLY

- ✓ Develop/select and evaluate performance appraisal process (for example, instruments, ranking and rating scales, relationship to compensation, frequency).

- ✓ Implement training programs for performance evaluators. **PHR** ONLY

- ✓ Develop, implement, and evaluate performance management programs and procedures (for example, goal-setting, job rotations, promotions).

- ✓ Develop/select, implement, and evaluate programs (for example, flexible work arrangements, diversity initiatives, repatriation) to meet the unique needs of employees. **SPHR** ONLY

Human resource development (HRD) is the functional area of human resources that seeks to affect the behavior of employees so the organization can achieve its goals. This chapter explores organization development (OD), employee development, training, and performance management.

Chapter 3, "Strategic Management," examined the structural, procedural, and technological aspects of an organization's systems and discussed the vision, mission, and value statements that result from the strategic planning process. Building on that information, this chapter looks at ways organizations implement the changes necessary to accomplish their missions and the strategies they use to align employees with the vision, mission, and goals developed by their leaders.

This chapter begins with a review of federal legislation that impacts HRD activities. It then examines several different approaches to organization development and the ways these approaches positively impact organizational culture and climate. That discussion is followed by a review of techniques for developing employees, managers, and leaders and a systems model for use in developing training programs.

HRD does not occur in a vacuum; it occurs within the context of how the organization sees itself, how it conducts business, and how it views its employees. Every organization makes determinations about these issues, whether consciously, as part of an OD process, or unconsciously, as a result of the way its leaders operate on a day-to-day basis. Effective organizations are those in which values and beliefs are shared at all levels and reflected in the behavior of individuals throughout the organization.

Be sure to review the HRCI knowledge requirements for HRD as you begin this chapter. Several sections in Chapter 2, "Core Knowledge Requirements for HR Professionals," have particular relevance here: a review of the discussions on needs assessment, adult learning processes, training techniques, communication, leadership, change management, job descriptions, motivation, and employee attitude assessment will enhance your review of the material in this chapter.

Federal Employment Legislation

Candidates for the PHR/SPHR certifications should understand the effects of federal civil rights legislation and executive orders on HRD activities. These legal requirements were reviewed in Chapter 4, "Workforce Planning and Employment." Civil rights legislation covers all the terms and conditions of employment, which means that members of protected groups must be provided with equal opportunity to participate in workplace training and development programs.

In addition, the use of original works created by others, whether they are authors, composers, inventors, or other individuals, is protected by copyright and patent laws. Table 5.1 summarizes federal legislation for HRD activities.

TABLE 5.1   Federal Legislation Governing HRD Activities

Type	Enforcement Agency	Chapter Reference
Civil rights	EEOC and/or OFCCP	4
Executive Orders	OFCCP	4
Copyright	Civil litigation	5
Patent	Civil litigation	5

Copyright Act of 1976

The use of musical, literary, and other original works without permission of the owner of the copyright is prohibited under most circumstances. The copyright owner is, for the most part, the author of the work. There are two exceptions to this. The first is that an employer who hires employees to create original works as part of their normal job duties is the owner of the copyright because the employer paid for the work to be done. The second exception is that the copyright for work created by a freelance author, artist, or musician who has been commissioned to create the work by someone else is owned by the person who commissioned the work. These exceptions are known as work-for-hire exceptions.

For trainers who want to use the work of others during training sessions, there are two circumstances that do not require permission. The first is related to works that are in the *public domain*. Copyrights protect original works for the life of the author plus 70 years; after that, the works may be used without permission. Works-for-hire are protected for the shorter of 95 years from the first year of publication or 120 years from the year of creation.

Other works in the public domain include those produced as part of the job duties of federal officials and those for which copyright protection has expired. Some works published without notice of copyright before January 1, 1978, or those published between then and March 1, 1989, are also considered to be in the public domain.

The second circumstance for use of published works without permission is known as fair use. The act specifies that use of a work for the purposes of criticism, commentary, news reporting, teaching (including multiple copies for classroom use, scholarship, or research) is not an infringement depending upon four factors:

1.   The purpose and character of the use: is it to be used for a profit or nonprofit educational purpose?

2.   The nature of the work itself.

3. How much of the work (1 copy or 50?) or what portion (one paragraph or an entire chapter?) of the work will be used?

4. What effect will the use of the material have on the potential market value of the copyrighted work?

Permission for the use of copyright-protected material that is outside the fair use exceptions can generally be obtained by contacting the author or publisher of the work.

U. S. Patent Act

A *patent* allows inventors exclusive rights to the benefits of an invention for a defined period of time. Patent laws in the United States define three types of patents:

Design patents   *Design patents* protect new, original, and ornamental designs of manufactured items. Design patents are limited to 14 years.

Utility patents   *Utility patents* protect the invention of new and useful processes, machines, manufacture or composition of matter, and new and useful improvements to the same. Utility patents are limited to 20 years.

Plant patents   *Plant patents* protect the invention or discovery of asexually reproduced varieties of plants for 20 years.

Organization Development

Organization development (OD) is a systematic method of examining an organization's technology, processes, structure, and human resources, and developing action strategies to improve the way it achieves its goals. These action strategies are known as *OD interventions* and may be directed toward structures, processes, technology, individuals, groups of individuals, or entire organizations. This section focuses on organization-wide changes to structure, process, and technology.

This sharing of values and beliefs and the behavior related to them is known as the organization culture. The culture of an organization, combined with leadership and management styles and the level of bureaucracy, creates a work environment or climate that will either inspire and motivate employees to achieve the corporate mission, or inhibit employee motivation and enthusiasm for their jobs, thereby limiting the success of the organization. Organizational culture and climate determine the level of employee involvement in the decision-making process and provide the unwritten ground rules upon which decisions can be based in the absence of relevant policies. More information on organizational culture and climate can be found in Chapter 7, "Employee and Labor Relations."

While it is possible for businesses to earn a profit without considering the needs of their employees (and some do), the results of job satisfaction surveys consistently show that employees are motivated to perform at a high level of productivity by a variety of factors that can be influenced by culture and climate. Challenging work and respect are very often of equal or greater importance to employees than the amount of money they earn in determining their level of satisfaction, commitment, and productivity. While it is important to keep in mind that businesses exist to earn a profit, not to merely provide a satisfying work experience for employees, organizations that are able to create atmospheres including trust, respect, and challenging work are generally rewarded with higher rates of productivity than are organizations focused only on cost reduction and efficiency. The OD process provides a method for developing strategies to accomplish this.

When the culture and climate tend to inhibit goal achievement instead, an OD intervention can be implemented to correct the problem. In their text *Organization Development and Change* (South-Western College Pub, 7th edition, January 2001), Thomas Cummings and Christopher Worley identify four categories of interventions: strategic, techno structural, human process, and human resource management. As is evident by the category names, interventions can remove obstacles in strategy, technology, structure, process, and management. This section concentrates on interventions and strategies in each category that relate to human resource development and the ways they can influence the organization culture and climate.

Strategic Interventions

Strategic OD interventions are often utilized to implement changes made to the vision, mission, and values of the organization during a strategic planning process as discussed in Chapter 3. These interventions are designed to align various elements within the organization with the new direction or focus established by the leaders. Some examples of strategic OD interventions are change management, knowledge management, and learning organizations.

Change Management

The result of any OD process is a change in the way things are done in an organization. Whether it is new technology, a more efficient process, or a different reporting structure, the resulting change will have to be implemented by people—and no matter how difficult it is to create the new operating plans, implementing them successfully will be even more difficult because the people in the organization must be motivated and committed to making the changes work.

Change Process Theory

An early model of *change process theory*, developed by a social psychologist named Kurt Lewin, described three stages for change:

Unfreezing   This stage creates the motivation for change by identifying and communicating the need for the change. In this stage it is important to create a vision for the outcome of the change and a sense of urgency for getting to the new outcome.

Moving   During this stage, resistance is examined and managed and the organization is aligned with the change. Communication remains an integral part of the process.

Refreezing   In the final stage of the theory, the change becomes the new norm for the organization, the outcome is evaluated, and additional changes occur to adjust the actual outcomes to those that are desired.

Human resource professionals can use change process theory to aid employees through a stressful work change. Let's take a look at some other ways HR can help employees deal with change.

Tools for Successful Change

People dislike change for a variety of reasons: change moves them out of the "comfort zone" to which they have become accustomed and they may be fearful of the unknown. The politics of the organization may make change undesirable in one group or another, and employees may perceive that they will lose status or control. Changes fail most often because the people who are expected to implement them are not prepared to do so. Organizations can take steps to ensure the success of change initiatives, including the following:

Prepare for change   The only constant in the current business environment is change. Organizations must be aware of situations developing within the industry or geographic areas in which they operate so that they can be ahead of the curve in developing strategies that will effectively handle changes in the environment.

Communicate   To enhance the likelihood of a successful implementation, leaders must communicate with employees well in advance of any planned implementation. Soliciting ideas from those who are closest to operations may provide insight into better solutions and increase buy-in when it is time to implement the change. Communication at every stage of the process will enable employees to get used to the idea of the change gradually, increase the level of acceptance, and build commitment for the process.

Develop a plan   A comprehensive plan that clearly defines the goals of the change, addresses all of its implications, and includes tools for evaluating its success is essential. Scheduling training for employees who may need to upgrade skills, integrating processes from different areas of the organization, upgrading equipment, and developing a plan to address resistance to the change and reduce stress will increase the chances for successful implementation.

Have a sponsor   The CEO or another senior executive who is committed to and enthusiastic about the change must be able to inspire employees to commit to the implementation.

Motivate direct supervisors   Employees want to know how their supervisors feel about changes and will be influenced by what the supervisors say about the change. When direct supervisors and managers are motivated to implement a change, employees will be more likely to accept it.

Recruit unofficial leaders   Every organization has unofficial leaders who are able to influence coworkers; obtaining their commitment to the change will influence others.

Implement   Put the change into action. Ensure that employees have the tools needed to successfully implement the change, whether that is new equipment, facilities, training, or support.

Evaluate   Compare results to the evaluation criteria developed during the planning stage to determine whether or not the change was successfully implemented.

HR professionals are in a unique position to act as change agents during this process. A *change agent* must be able to balance the needs of various stakeholders in the process, listen to their concerns, and move them toward acceptance of and commitment to the change.

Knowledge Management

Increasingly, organizations are realizing how important it is to manage the knowledge acquired by individual employees. Given the increasing mobility of the workforce, much of the knowledge that an individual acquires over time in an organization disappears when that person leaves the organization. Finding a way to retain that knowledge in a database that is accessible by others turns information into useful knowledge needed for improving processes and increasing profits.

An application of knowledge management (KM) is exemplified by the intelligence services of the United States. As has been well-reported since September 11, 2001, the Federal Bureau of Investigation (FBI), National Security Agency (NSA), and Central Intelligence Agency (CIA) all had pieces of information about the hijackers. Even within the FBI, field offices in different parts of the country had bits of information that, taken together, could have provided some warning of what was being planned. Had a knowledge management process to collect and collate these different pieces of information been in place, it may have been possible to prevent the attacks.

An example of an effective knowledge management program with which many people have had some experience is customer relationship management (CRM). For example, you may have experienced the frustration of calling a customer support or help line and having to repeat all the details of a problem with a product to each new customer service representative (CSR) who comes on the line. An effective KM process has each CSR enter facts about customer problems into a database so that, when the customer calls back, the next CSR to answer the call knows everything that has already transpired between the customer and the company. The customer does not need to repeat information, and the CSR can avoid going back to step one in the problem solving process.

Learning Organizations

Learning organizations are innovative environments in which knowledge is originated, obtained, and freely shared in response to environmental changes that affect the ability of the organization to compete. The atmosphere in a learning organization is one in which employees are able to solve problems by experimenting with new methods that have been observed outside the organization or that have been experienced in other parts of the organization.

Peter Senge, author of *The Fifth Discipline* (Doubleday/Currency, 1990), identifies five disciplines, or guiding principles, that enable organizations to increase their ability to realize desired results, cultivate new ways of thinking, expand on individual ideas, and encourage continuous lifelong learning within the organization. These disciplines include the following:

Systems thinking   *Systems thinking* describes the ability of individuals and organizations to recognize patterns and project how changes will impact them.

Personal mastery   *Personal mastery* describes a high level of expertise in an individual's chosen field and a commitment to lifelong learning.

Mental models   *Mental models* refer to the deep-seated beliefs that color perceptions and affect how individuals see the world around them and react to it.

Building a shared vision   Stretching beyond the corporate vision statement and building a *shared vision* encourages the organization to plan for a future that inspires commitment on the part of all individuals in the organization.

Team learning   *Team learning*, as defined by Senge, refers to the ability of a team to share and build upon their ideas without holding anything back.

Techno-Structural Interventions

OD interventions that fall into the techno-structural category address issues of how work gets done in the organization by examining the level of employee involvement and redesigning work processes. *Total quality management (TQM)*, a process that focuses all resources within the organization on providing value for customers, is an example of a techno-structural intervention, as is Six Sigma. Another intervention that is used in this category is known as a high involvement organization.

Total Quality Management

TQM is a long-term intervention requiring employees at all levels within an organization to focus on providing products that meet customer needs. A successful TQM implementation requires the commitment of top management to lead the process. Because TQM is focused on customer needs, market research and product development are key components of the system. Processes are reviewed to eliminate wasted time as well as materials that either do not contribute or are obstacles to producing the end product. Teamwork is an essential function in a TQM environment; all members involved in the product or service, from front-line workers to suppliers and sales managers, must work together to solve problems for customers.

There have been a number of leaders in the quality movement; four who have made significant contributions are briefly introduced here:

W. Edwards Deming   The quality movement originated in the 1940s with the work of W. Edwards Deming, who proposed that quality is defined by the consumer. Deming developed a 14-point plan that placed the burden for quality on management because they are able to control the systems within the organization. While American business was initially cool to the quality concept, Deming's theories were warmly received in Japan during the 1950s. In 1951, the Japanese named their quality award, the Deming Prize, after him.

Joseph M. Juran   Another early proponent of the quality movement was Joseph M. Juran who, like Deming, believed that quality begins with defining customer needs. Unlike Deming, Juran proposed that once customer needs were identified, they would be translated into the "language" of the business in order to deliver a product or service that met the needs of both customers and the business. He developed the Juran Trilogy, which identified three phases in the process: quality planning, quality control, and quality improvements. *Quality planning* initiates programs by addressing quality concerns during the product or service development process. *Quality control* ensures conformance to the parameters established in the planning phase during the operations phase. *Quality improvements* are used to continually improve operations and reduce waste.

Dr. Kaoru Ishikawa   Dr. Kaoru Ishikawa made significant contributions to the quality movement. He provided a collection of analytical tools to use in the workplace and developed the cause and effect diagram that bears his name. The following list explains some of these tools and provides examples.

Check sheets   *Check sheets* are the simplest analysis tools, requiring only a list of items that might be expected to occur. In an HR setting, a check sheet might be used to keep track of the reasons people resign from their positions. Figure 5.1 is an example of a check sheet used for that purpose. When an item occurs, a check or tick mark is placed next to it on the list. The data collected with a check sheet may be graphically represented in a histogram to facilitate analysis.

FIGURE 5.1   Sample check sheet

Reason	Number of Occurrences	Total
Lack of advancement	ʼʼʼʼ	5
Lack of recognition	ʼʼʼʼ ʼʼʼʼ ‖‖‖‖	14
Long commute	‖	1
Low pay	‖‖	2
Poor supervision	ʼʼʼʼ ʼʼʼʼ ʼʼʼʼ ‖	16
		38

Histograms   *Histograms* provide a way of looking at random occurrences to find out if there is a pattern. Using the data from the previous check sheet, a histogram provides a visual image of the reasons for resignations as illustrated by Figure 5.2.

FIGURE 5.2   Histogram

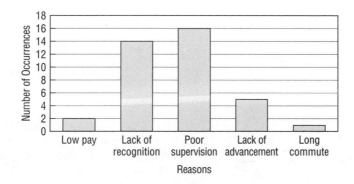

Pareto chart   The *Pareto chart* provides a graphical representation of the 80/20 rule: 80 percent of the problems are caused by 20 percent of the reasons, a principle established by an Italian economist named Vilfredo Pareto. The Pareto chart points out which areas of concern will provide the greatest return when corrected. The difference between a Pareto chart and a histogram is that the Pareto chart arranges the data in descending order and includes a cumulative percentage on the right side of the chart. Figure 5.3 uses the Pareto chart to identify the most significant causes of resignations. In this case, poor supervision and a lack of recognition cause 80 percent of the resignations.

Cause and effect diagram   A *cause and effect diagram* aids in organizing information during brainstorming sessions. This quality analysis tool is also known as the Ishikawa diagram or fishbone diagram. In Figure 5.4, I use it to analyze what PHR/SPHR candidates can do to maximize their chances for success on the exam.

Stratification   *Stratification charts* show the individual components of a problem in addition to the total or summary. This aids in identifying possible strategies for correcting problems. Figure 5.5 is an example of a stratification chart. In the resignation example, the shorter bars represent components of each category, the taller bar is the total amount. For example, the poor supervision reasons could be broken down into categories for poor management skills and the inability to delegate. This kind of chart aids in the development of appropriate programs to solve the individual problems that make up a whole.

Scatter charts   Also known as an xy chart, a scatter chart provides a graphical representation for the relationship between two sets of numbers. Information presented on a scatter chart is used for various forms of statistical analysis. Chapter 2 provides more information about data analysis and the concept of correlation.

FIGURE 5.3   Pareto chart

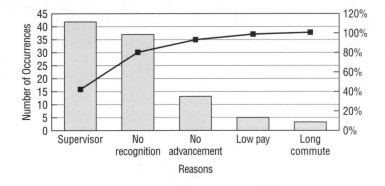

FIGURE 5.4   Cause and effect diagram

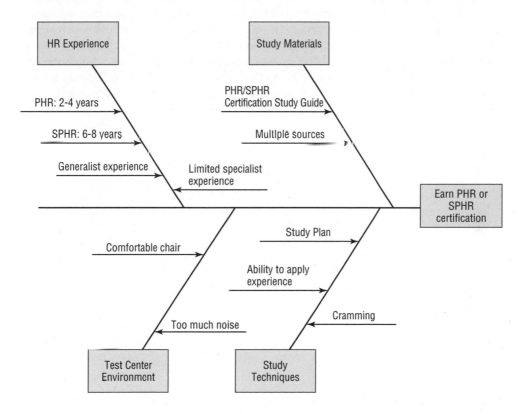

FIGURE 5.5   Stratification chart

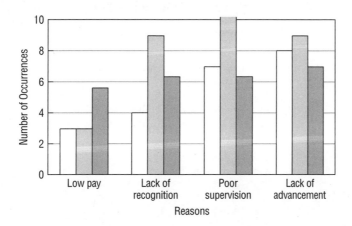

Process control charts *Process control charts* provide a graphical representation of elements that are out of the acceptable range by setting parameters above and below the range. This tool is most effective for determining variances in production processes over time. While this tool is generally used in a production context, to help you understand how it works, let's look at how it could be applied in an HR context. Let's say your department has established that open positions will be filled within 30 days from the date of notification to the HR department with a five-day grace period. The sample process control chart in Figure 5.6 shows you that two positions were out of the normal range: one took less than 25 days and the other took more than 35 days. Both of these are considered to be "out of control" and warrant investigation to determine what caused the variance.

FIGURE 5.6 Process control chart

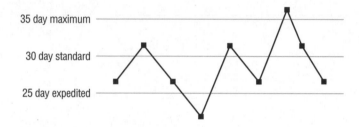

Philip B. Crosby Philip B. Crosby's approach to quality, unlike that of Deming and Juran, focused on management as the key factor. His approach is based on strategic planning as the means to accomplish a high level of quality. Crosby advanced four absolutes of quality:

Conformance to requirements Crosby believed that once management clearly described what was required, quality could be determined by whether or not the product met the standard.

Prevention "Do it right the first time" is a phrase Crosby associated with this absolute.

Performance standards "Zero defects" is another term Crosby came up with to describe the quality standard that should be met.

Measurement In Crosby's view, quality should be measured by the additional cost of not producing zero-defect products the first time.

Although TQM originated in manufacturing environments, its concepts translate easily to service and other industries. For example, a public accounting firm can establish standards and then develop checklists and templates for accountants to follow when providing client services. By emphasizing the importance of accuracy and measuring how many corrections must be made, the firm can quantify the work of its accountants to ensure that it is up to the standards it established.

Six Sigma

Six Sigma is a quality philosophy developed by engineers at Motorola during the 1980s, when they were looking for a more precise way to measure process defects. The Six Sigma quality standard is measured on a "defects per million" basis unlike previous standards measured on a "defects per thousand" basis. The Six Sigma methodology is referred to as DMAIC: Define, Measure, Analyze, Improve, and Control.

Define   The first step is to define the customer and issues of importance to them, along with the process and project parameters.

Measure   Once the process is defined, data about defects and other measures is collected and then compared to the original parameters to identify underperformance.

Analyze   An analysis of the data is made to identify gaps between the goal and actual performance, explain why the gaps occurred, and rank possible improvements.

Improve   Based on the analysis, solutions are created and implemented.

Control   During the control phase, systems are revised to incorporate the improvements and employees are trained in the new processes. The goal of this phase is to prevent backsliding into the previous process by ongoing monitoring.

A significant component of Six Sigma is the quality team structure used to develop, implement, and manage initiatives. In these organizations, employees who are trained and certified in the Six Sigma methodology work full time on quality initiatives. There are requirements for certification at each level in the structure, including a specific curriculum and requirements for demonstrating effectiveness by working on quality initiatives. In addition, candidates must pass a written test prior to certification.

Quality leader/manager   The quality leader in an organization generally reports to the CEO or president in order to remain objective. This role represents customer requirements and focuses on continually improving operations.

Master black belt   Master black belts generally work with a single function, such as marketing or accounting. They work closely with process owners to implement the DMAIC methodology and ensure that projects stay on track.

Process owner   Process owners are individuals responsible for a specific process in the organization; for example, the highest level HR employee in the organization would be the process leader for HR initiatives.

Black belt   Black belt employees work full time on quality initiatives, coaching green belts to improve their quality skills.

Green belt   Green belts have received Six Sigma Training and participate on project teams part time while continuing to work in another role for the balance of their time.

High-Involvement Organizations

In *high involvement organizations (HIOs)*, employees are involved in designing their own work processes, empowered to take the actions necessary to complete their work, and accountable for the results. HIOs are characterized by broadly defined jobs in flat hierarchies in which continuous feedback is provided and information flows between and among self-directed work teams.

Edward E. Lawler III, founder of the Center for Organizational Effectiveness at the University of Southern California and author of numerous books on organizational effectiveness, identified four elements needed to create an HIO:

Power   Traditional organization structures are built on a "command and control" model in which decisions are made at the top with little or no input from lower levels in the hierarchy. HIOs grant decision-making power down to the employees assigned to carry out the decision and hold them accountable for the results.

Information   "Information is power," and in traditional organizations that often means individuals hold on to information that could be used to improve results and don't share it with the individuals who could use it to make improvements. In an HIO, a variety of information (production statistics, sales, expenses, profits, customer feedback, and so on) is disseminated so that everyone can use it to direct their efforts toward improving results.

Knowledge   Increasing the KSAs available within the organization enhances the ability of all employees to contribute to bottom-line success. Providing training and development opportunities increases the organization's capability for making decisions and taking actions that improve operating effectiveness.

Rewards   Tying pay to performance compensates employees according to the level of effort they expend to accomplish their goals and objectives and contribute to organizational success. When employees know that their contributions will be recognized, they are encouraged to go "above and beyond" normal job requirements. These rewards can be based on individual or team contributions and are discussed in more detail in Chapter 6, "Total Rewards."

One example of an HIO is the Saturn Corporation. From its inception in 1985, Saturn focused on building an organization in which employees at all levels were involved in making decisions about operations and production. As a result, Saturn customers consistently rank among the most-satisfied with their purchases based on surveys conducted by J. D. Power and Associates, an organization that conducts independent customer surveys for a variety of industries.

Human Process Interventions

Human process interventions are directed at developing competencies at the individual level within the organization. Common interventions in this area include teambuilding activities, conflict resolution, management by objective programs, leadership and management development (discussed later in this chapter), supervisory training (also discussed later in this chapter), and developing an understanding of the impact emotional intelligence has on organizational success.

Teambuilding Activities

In order for a team to function effectively, the members must know the goals they are working toward and what is expected of them as team members. Teambuilding exercises build relationships within the team to communicate expectations and to involve team members in developing creative and effective ways of accomplishing their goals. Teambuilding activities run the gamut from expensive events staged by consultants, such as wilderness adventures, to games devised by managers in their individual work groups. The goal of any teambuilding activity is to put team members in unusual situations which require them to rely on each other to solve a problem. These activities can be fun and effective methods for starting the process, but to be fully effective the team spirit built or lessons learned must be reinforced when team members are back in the normal routine.

 Real World Scenario

Process Council and Facilitators

When organizations get employees involved with team building, leadership, and process improvement, the result can improve organizational processes as well as morale.

One San Francisco Bay Area organization has given the responsibility of process updating and building to a Process Council. Process Council members are specifically chosen for their leadership abilities, experience at the organization, and knowledge of how the organization operates as a whole. When a process issue is identified, the Process Council decides whether a team is needed to tackle the problem. With the help of upper management, the Process Council recommends team members and a team leader and facilitator and provides the leader with a charter outlining the council's expectations for the team. The Process Council meets quarterly to discuss process issues, appoint new teams, and discuss teams in progress.

The organization appoints several facilitators to help the Process Council teams meet their goals. Facilitators are chosen for their leadership abilities, their work with various employees across the organization, and their energetic personalities. Facilitators are specifically trained to provide a safe, objective environment in which team members can discuss the process issue at hand without judgment or criticism. Facilitators guide team members by asking pointed questions, politely interrupting "time robbers" (those who talk incessantly with no relevance to the team goal), and keep members on track to solve the issue in a timely manner.

The Process Council and facilitators have tackled several cross-departmental problems and have even been involved with two reorganizations that occurred as a result of Process Council team decisions. Because facilitators and Process Council members are also employees organization who will be affected by Process Council results, they have a vested interest in team success. They are also trained to tackle day-to-day problems that may not need a team discussion.

Conflict Resolution

Conflict occurs whenever people work together; it can affect relationships between individuals or groups and cover a wide range of intensity levels. *Conflict resolution* is a process of developing strategies for resolving issues and maintaining or rebuilding effective working relationships. These interventions can be conducted by a direct supervisor or manager, an HR professional, or in some cases, a consultant who specializes in this process. The nature and intensity of the conflict will determine which solution will be most effective in a specific case.

Management by Objectives

A *management by objectives (MBO)* intervention aligns individuals with organization goals and measures the successful attainment of objectives as well as the quality and/or quantity of performance. Because it is an effective way of tying results to goals, MBO is often used as a performance appraisal tool. Its application and acceptance results, at least in part, from its philosophy that rewarding people for what they accomplish is important. The MBO process is built on the concepts of mutual involvement in setting performance goals, ongoing communication during the performance period (usually one year), measurement, and reward for accomplishments at the end of the period. The process identifies and clarifies expectations and provides for a broad assessment of individual performance. It usually begins in the first quarter of each fiscal year when the supervisor and the employee agree upon a few significant business objectives, such as sales volume, new business development, completion of specific projects, or achievement of other specific goals. You'll recall from Chapter 3 that utilizing the SMART goal process will result in goals that clearly communicate what is expected.

The use of an MBO process to tie individual goals to corporate goals and objectives has value but must consider the rapid pace of change in the current business environment and use goals that are broad enough to be meaningful for the entire review period or that allow for revision as business objectives change.

Emotional Intelligence

Emotional intelligence (EI or EQ) describes how people deal with their feelings and how they perceive and interact with others. On an individual level, understanding yourself and why you react to others in the way you do increases your ability to work well with others in general. In an organizational setting, individuals who understand how their feelings impact their thought processes can increase their ability to collaborate with coworkers and influence relationships within the organization.

An EI intervention seeks to improve individual interactions and increase individual effectiveness. Individuals who are able to influence and motivate others are able to move the organization more rapidly toward successful accomplishment of its goals. While EI is not particularly necessary in organizations characterized by strictly authoritarian management methods, it is a necessary component for business environments seeking to manage with more facilitative models. EI competencies, while not a substitute for technical expertise, are essential in growing and developing successful organizations.

Human Resource Management Interventions

Human resource management (HRM) interventions focus on individuals within the organization. Some examples of these types of interventions include:

- Developing hiring and selection procedures that attract people with the KSAs needed by the organization (as discussed in Chapter 4).
- Designing jobs that increase employee satisfaction.
- Developing performance management systems that develop individuals for future needs in the organization.
- Developing diversity programs that blend employees from various backgrounds into cohesive work units for the organization.
- Developing reward systems (discussed in Chapter 6) that provide incentives for employees to exceed expectations.

Whether a strategic, techno-structural, human process, or HRM intervention is the appropriate choice for any particular organization or situation depends on the needs and goals required to achieve results that enable the organization to move forward.

Employee Development

As you recall from Chapter 2, talent management brings together activities in those HR functions that attract and retain employees with the skills needed by the organization to move forward in the marketplace. One of the key elements of a talent management program is development: of employees, managers, leaders, and the high-potential employees being groomed to lead the organization into the future.

Organizations which use a staffing strategy of promotion from within will need to develop employees to equip them with the KSAs they need to move forward and take on additional responsibilities. Development opportunities come in many forms.

Job design One of the factors to consider as part of the job analysis process described in Chapter 2 is how the tasks, duties, and responsibilities that are needed by the organization can be combined for use as a development tool. When an employee shows potential and is interested in growth opportunities, employers can assign new responsibilities or tasks that challenge the employee to use existing skills and abilities in new ways or to develop new ones as they tackle new assignments.

Skills training Skills training provides employees with specific information that is needed to do their jobs. In some cases, skills training will be job-specific, for example, to teach accounting staff how to use new accounting software, or provide a software engineer with training in a new language that will be needed to develop a product. Training in soft skills is often used to assist employees, for example, training on meeting management might be provided to reduce the amount of time spent in meetings and make them more productive. Training for communication and time management skills are other examples of soft skills training. Another type of skills training is provided for employees who are moving into supervisory or management positions for the first time.

Supervisory training   When the organization is successful in advancing employees, very often they end up in positions with supervisory responsibility. Some organizations make the mistake of assuming that a person who excels in a technical area will automatically be able to supervise employees in that area, but that is rarely the case. Providing training for new supervisors gives them the tools they need to succeed at their new responsibilities.

Supervisory training usually involves topics related to interactions with employees, such as performance management, progressive discipline, performance appraisals, workplace safety, interviewing, and training. New supervisors also benefit from training on topics such as legal requirements for employers (such as exemption status, leave policies, EEO, ADA, FMLA, and so on), and policies and procedures specific to the organization. Other topics that help supervisors accomplish more through others include:

- Effective management skills
- Conflict management
- Team building
- Influencing and negotiation
- Communication skills
- Time management
- Interview skills
- Delegation
- Planning
- Motivation skills

Supervisors must understand that different employees are motivated by different approaches and be able to adjust their techniques to encourage each individual to excel.

High-potential employees   The workforce planning process identifies the skills, knowledge, individuals, and positions which are critical to organization success. Some of the individuals identified as future organization leaders in this process are known as high-potential employees (HiPos) and are provided with extensive training opportunities to prepare them for future roles. Identifying HiPos can be difficult, because future performance cannot always be predicted from current performance (as described in *The Peter Principle*, a book written in 1968 by Dr. Lawrence Peter that describes how organizations tend to promote people until they rise to their level of incompetence and leave them in that position). Many of the selection procedures described in Chapter 4 are used to screen candidates for the HiPo track, including assessment centers, behavioral interviews, and observation. In addition, personality inventories such as Meyers-Briggs, the Keirsey Temperament Sorter, and others can be useful in evaluating individuals for a HiPo development program.

The results of these types of assessments highlight the characteristics representative of HiPo performers such as having a capacity to learn and incorporate new ideas and concepts into daily performance, using feedback to improve skills and performance, and a commitment to continuing career development. Potential HiPos are also able to assess and take risks. These individuals demonstrate a high EQ, understanding how to inspire and motivate others, qualities that are essential in effective leaders.

Once identified, HiPos receive assignments that challenge their abilities and allow them to take risks. Organizations that create succession plans as part of the workforce planning process factor HiPos into the plan. Very often they are paired with senior-level executive mentors to guide them as they take on assignments with increasing levels of difficulty. Job rotation, which moves HiPos through various divisions, departments, and functions, provides them with a broad view of the organization's needs that will be necessary at the most senior levels.

Mentoring programs   In a business context, a mentor is generally an experienced individual who acts as a teacher, guide, counselor, or facilitator and provides personalized feedback and guidance to a more junior colleague. In many cases, a mentor is someone who takes an interest in an employee's career and acts as a sponsor for them, providing a sounding board for issues and decisions. Traditionally, the mentor relationship is based more on an informal personal interest than on a formal program. *Mentoring programs* formalize this concept and ensure that the benefits of mentoring are available to a diverse group of employees who demonstrate leadership potential.

Formal mentors are those approved by an organization to take on protégés after being screened to ensure that only those who are best suited for mentor relationships enter the program. Mentors in formal programs receive training to develop skills in mentoring, and both mentors and mentees receive training to ensure everyone understands what to expect from the relationship.

A relatively new feature of mentoring is the *reverse mentor*. These are young individuals who help older coworkers understand technology and the culture of the "younger generation."

Coaching programs   A coach is typically a specialist who becomes involved, often at the organization's expense, to develop an employee in a particular area; for example, to hone leadership skills, or to improve communication skills. Some coaches can offer guidance in many areas. However, ultimately, they differ from mentors in that they focus on skills rather than development.

Management Development

A *management development* program seeks to upgrade skills for managers who are accountable for achieving results through others. The skills and abilities required for successfully managing people were described previously with regard to supervisory skills training. In addition, management development programs include exposure to financial and technology management, internal controls, and the basic management skills described in Chapter 2. Chapter 2 described the various styles of management in some detail, from the authoritarian Theory X to the opposite participative management styles.

While formal training can be useful in providing information for managers, one of the best ways to develop them is by assigning a mentor or coach.

Management skills are different from leadership skills. While managers must keep people on track, leaders must inspire; while managers must implement plans, leaders must innovate and set the direction for others to follow.

Leadership Development

Chapter 2 reviewed various leadership theories used to explain how a leader becomes a leader. However that happens, effective leaders are crucial to the success of organizations. They are responsible for inspiring everyone in the organization to achieve the goals they set, and leaders who do this well are rewarded with a motivated and committed workforce. Leaders must be creative individuals who are able to project future needs and aim the organization in a direction that will be successful for the long term. They must be able to inspire trust and confidence and challenge others to put forth their best efforts.

Leaders must also be able to balance the needs of the various constituencies in the organization from the Board of Directors, who represent the owners; to the management team, who are responsible for implementing the goals; to employees, who are on the front line of the organization working with customers to achieve organization goals.

A *leadership development* program seeks out employees who show promise as potential leaders. Leadership development programs can be a combination of classroom training in specific areas, sponsorship of an advanced degree program such as an MBA, and hands-on training with a mentor or coach. It may mean time spent in company operations outside the country, in different divisions within the country, or in different functional areas. Leaders who are exposed to multiple facets of the organization are better able to understand the various needs and challenges of these areas and thus are more effective in the leadership role.

Employee Training Programs

Training is an effective tool for improving productivity and increasing operational efficiency, but it is not the answer to every organizational problem. Training can solve problems related to employee skills or knowledge about a specific process, but it cannot solve problems caused by structural or system issues. Before developing a training program, it's important to find out what is causing the problem and if training is the appropriate solution.

For example, if customer service representatives (CSRs) are expected to handle an average of 20 calls per hour and they are handling an average of 12, it is important to find out why. One possibility is that the CSRs are not familiar enough with the products to answer the questions easily, so they must look up answers in a manual. Another possibility is that the call volume has tripled since the call center phone system was installed and it can no longer handle the load so it is frequently offline. The first possibility can be resolved with training, but the second cannot.

Training may take place at one of three levels: organizational, task, or individual.

Organizational *Organizational level training* may encompass the entire organization or a single division or department. At this level, training is focused on preparing for future needs.

An analysis of organizational effectiveness can indicate the need for a training intervention. For example, a high number of accidents, a change in strategic direction, or addition of a new product line, as well as employee satisfaction and productivity measures, are all indicators that training is needed at this level.

Task   *Task level training* involves processes performed in a single job category. The need for training at this level may be indicated by low productivity for a single process or poor quality results.

Individual   *Individual level training* involves a review of performance by individual employees and can be indicated by poor performance reviews or requests for assistance by the employee.

While development programs address long-term organizational needs, training programs are designed to address short-term needs. Training activities are more technical in nature and include such topics as new-hire orientation, safety, and skill development, among others. The design and development of training programs follows an instructional design model known as the *ADDIE model.* ADDIE is an acronym that describes the five elements of instructional design:

- Analysis
- Design
- Development
- Implementation
- Evaluation

The ADDIE model is discussed here in the context of training at the task level, but the principles of the model can be used to develop training programs at the organizational or individual levels as well.

Training needs are often identified by managers who notice a problem in their departments and determine that training is needed to correct it. This determination may be based on a drop in the production rate, installation of new machinery or equipment, or the addition of a new line of business. Once the need for training has been identified, a needs assessment determines whether or not training will solve the problem and, if it will, proposes possible solutions.

Analysis

The generic needs assessment process described in Chapter 2 provides the basis for analyzing the need for training assessment. Figure 5.7 demonstrates how the generic needs assessment model is modified for use in assessing training needs.Using the model, the following process will provide the information to determine what type of training is necessary to solve the problem.

1.   Identify goal.

The needs assessment begins by identifying the desired outcome. In the preceding example, the customer service manager determined that the CSRs should handle an average of

20 calls per hour, which is the desired outcome. The desired outcome forms the basis for several other steps in the analysis process, including what data is collected, the identification of instructional goals, and development of solutions.

2. Gather and analyze data.

   Once you know the desired outcome, you can begin to collect relevant information that will be used to determine the cause of the problem. Information may be gathered in a number of ways from a variety of sources:

   Review documents   There are many types of documents that can be used to gather information about training needs. These include measures of organizational effectiveness such as production records and records of customer complaints, a review of the human resource succession plan to determine what training is needed to prepare individuals for future needs based on skills inventories and performance appraisal forms, and an analysis of the organizational climate based on HR metrics such as turnover rates and the results of exit interviews.

   Ask people   There are many methods for gathering information from people, including observations; interviews with employees, supervisors, or subject matter experts (SMEs); attitude surveys; questionnaires; focus groups; or advisory committees. See Chapter 2 for more information on these techniques.

   Test employees   Some options for testing employee knowledge to determine if training is needed include assessment centers, knowledge tests to measure what people know, and practical tests to determine if they know how to apply what they know.

   Analyze jobs   In some cases, it may be necessary to conduct a full job analysis as described in Chapter 2 to determine where training is needed.

   When the data has been gathered and analyzed, a determination can be made as to whether or not training is the appropriate solution. If it is, the needs analysis continues; if not, HRD can report the results of the analysis to the requesting manager with a recommendation for an appropriate solution.

3. Identify the performance gap.

   Once all the data has been gathered, it is possible to compare where the organization is to where it wants to be. At this stage, the HRD professional begins to have a sense of the type of training that will be required.

4. Identify instructional goals.

   The performance gap is the starting point for identifying the corrections that need to be put into place.

5. Propose solutions.

   At this stage in the needs assessment, all possible means for filling the gap should be identified and considered to find the solution that best meets the organization's needs.

6. Evaluate options and estimate budget impact and training time line.

Once a comprehensive list of possible solutions is available, it is possible to conduct a cost-benefit analysis (described in Chapter 2) to estimate the cost of implementing each of them and the benefits that will result from the training. It is important to include both direct and indirect costs associated with the program in the estimated budget. This includes the cost of the trainer, facility, preparation of materials, use of equipment, transportation, meals and lodging costs, wages and salaries of the participants for the time they spend training and in traveling to the training, and the cost of lost production time due to the training and incidental office support costs. It is also important to consider potential savings, increased productivity, reduced errors, better quality, and other similar gains that will result from the training and, finally, what it will cost the organization if the training does not occur.

At the same time, an estimate of the time required to implement the solution can be made.

FIGURE 5.7   Training Needs Assessment Model

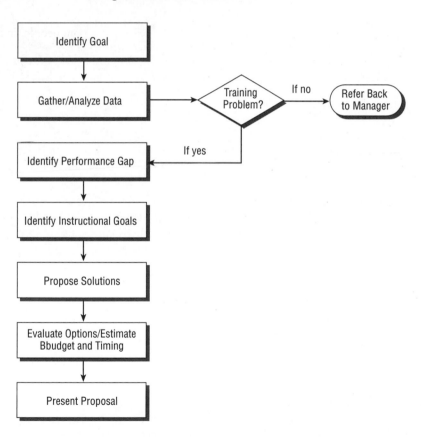

The result of the needs assessment should be a proposal that describes the desired outcome, the current situation, and the gap between the two. The proposal should include as many alternative solutions as is feasible, with an estimate of the cost and time needed to implement each of them and HRD's recommended solution.

During the assessment phase, a key consideration will be whether the program will be created internally, if a prepackaged program will be used, or whether the process will be outsourced. These decisions are based on a variety of factors unique to every organization and include the size of the organization, training expertise and availability of in-house staff, the uniqueness of the subject matter, and availability of prepackaged programs on the topic. For example, sexual harassment training may be best conducted by a trainer specializing in the subject matter who is able to answer in-depth legal questions and "what-if" scenarios. Conversely, a training program that is specific to a proprietary manufacturing process may be better developed in house.

Design

When the appropriate decision maker(s) concur that training is the appropriate solution for the problem, the design phase begins. During this phase of a training project, the program begins to take shape. The data gathered during the needs analysis phase will be useful in this stage as well.

1. Compile a task inventory.

   To complete the design process, the trainer must know what tasks are required for the job in question. A task inventory lists all tasks included in the job. Each task description should contain an action verb, an object, and a function, for example, "Answer phone to assist customers."

   The inventory can be compiled from information collected during the needs assessment process, or additional information can be acquired during the design phase. The inventory may also be gleaned from a job description if it was written as a result of a job analysis.

2. Identify the target audience.

   Knowing who will be attending the training will be of great use in designing a program that will keep the audience interested. Preparing a training program about proper completion of expense reports for a group of middle managers from the accounting department will look very different from the same presentation to the sales force.

   In identifying the audience, it is important to keep in mind the three learning styles that impact an individual's ability to learn: visual, auditory, or kinesthetic.

   Visual learners retain information better when they can see or read it.

   Auditory learners retain information more easily when they hear it.

   Kinesthetic learners retain information best when they are able to have a hands-on experience during training.

   Incorporating elements of all three learning styles in a training program helps to ensure that all individuals attending the program will benefit from the information presented.

3. Develop training objectives.

Training objectives are statements that describe a measurable outcome of the training and are developed based on the target audience and task inventory. Objectives help the HRD professional during the development process and during implementation let employees know what they will learn. They are also useful during the evaluation phase to determine whether or not the training was successful.

A useful training objective is a precise description of what is to be accomplished in normal job circumstances. For example, a training program for carpenters may include a session on building walls that are straight. The objective begins with a description of a normal job situation, uses an action verb to describe a measurable behavior, describes the conditions under which the behavior will occur, and finally describes the criteria that will be used to measure the results. An objective that includes all these elements could be something like this:

"Given the necessary materials and tools, build a wall that is perfectly plumb."

This objective leaves no doubt about what is to be accomplished and includes the basis for determining whether or not the training was successful.

4. Develop the course content.

Based on the training objectives, the trainer can begin to design the course, identifying what material should be included to best prepare the attendees to take the information back to their jobs and begin using it immediately.

An important consideration for this aspect of training design is the learning curve associated with various subjects. A *learning curve* is a graphical representation of the rate of learning over time. Let's look at some examples of various learning curves:

Negatively accelerating learning curve A *negatively accelerating learning curve* is characterized by rapid increases in learning at the beginning that taper off as the learner becomes more familiar with the process or task. Negative learning curves are representative of routine tasks, for example, operating a cash register. Figure 5.8 provides an example of this learning curve.

FIGURE 5.8 Negatively accelerating learning curve

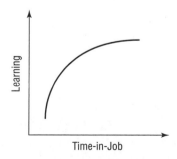

Positively accelerating learning curve   A *positively accelerating learning curve* is characterized by a slow start in learning that increases as the learner masters different aspects of the process or task. Positive learning curves are representative of tasks that are complex, such as a junior accountant learning to use an accounting software program. The accountant must first know basic accounting practices in order to become proficient in using the program. Figure 5.9 shows a positive learning curve.

FIGURE 5.9   Positively accelerating learning curve

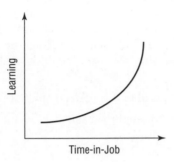

S-shaped learning curve   The *S-shaped learning curve* is a combination of positive and negative learning curves. It begins with a slow learning process that accelerates over time and then slows down again. This learning pattern can be found in software conversion projects. The system users must understand how the new system works before they are able to become as proficient at it as they were with the older system. Figure 5.10 is an example of an S-shaped learning curve.

FIGURE 5.10   S-shaped learning curve

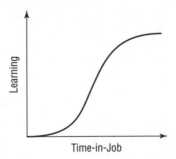

Plateau curve   A *plateau learning curve* begins with a rapid increase in knowledge that levels off after a period of time, and no additional progress occurs for an extended period of time. A plateau curve might occur when an employee performs a task irregularly, not often enough to become proficient. Figure 5.11 shows a plateau learning curve.

FIGURE 5.11   Plateau learning curve

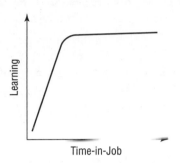

5. Develop evaluation criteria.

Now is the time to develop the evaluation criteria for the program. The initial evaluation will be based on whether or not the trainees are able to perform the task described by the objective within the parameters that it sets forth. The real evaluation of training effectiveness is whether or not the trainees are able to maintain the level of proficiency that was developed during the training and improve operating results.

Development

During the training development phase, the program design is translated into the presentation format. Keeping in mind the characteristics of adult learners described in Chapter 2, the program developer creates a strategy for the presentation, deciding on the materials, instructional techniques, and program delivery methods that will be used. The trainer may conduct a pilot presentation during this phase to "work out the kinks" and, if necessary, will revise the program based on the results of the pilot.

Training Materials

One of the activities occurring during the development phase of the training process is the collection of appropriate training materials. It is often tempting to use work created by others, particularly if the material is perfectly suited to the topic of the training. The two federal laws protecting the rights of writers, artists, and inventors with regard to unauthorized use of their original works, the Copyright Act of 1976 and the U.S. Patent Act, are discussed at the beginning of this chapter.

Aside from considerations related to the use of copyrighted material, training materials created in the development phase should be appropriate to the subject matter and the needs of the participants. Some types of materials to consider include:

Leader guide   When more than one trainer will be presenting the training sessions, a leader guide is developed to ensure consistency in the presentations. These guides may provide notes to assist the trainer in presenting the material, timing information, and questions for use in facilitating discussion during the session. The guide provides a basic road map for the presentation.

Manuals   Manuals can provide a reference to assist in reinforcing the information covered during the training session when participants return to their jobs. In addition to an agenda or schedule, they can contain handouts and copies of slides for note-taking purposes as participants follow along during the presentation.

Handouts   Handouts may be used in place of a manual or included with the manual. For presentations that do not require a manual because they are relatively straightforward, a handout can help keep participants focused and provide a place to take notes. In addition, handouts can provide additional information that is not covered during the presentation but is related to the topic. When the material being covered is technical in nature, a handout can make it easier for participants to follow along and may also be used as a handy reference when employees return to their jobs.

Instructional Methods

There are a variety of instructional methods to choose from when designing a training program, and selecting the appropriate one for a given situation can add to the success of the training.

Passive training methods   *Passive training methods* are those in which the learner listens to and absorbs information. These methods are instructor focused and require little or no active participation from the learner.

> **Lecture**   *Lectures* are used to inform and to answer questions, often in combination with other training methods such as demonstrations.

> **Presentation**   A *presentation* provides the same information to a group of people at one time.

> **Conference**   *Conferences* are generally a combination of lecture or presentation with question-and-answer sessions involving the participants.

Active training methods   *Active training methods* are those in which the learning experience is focused on the learner.

> **Facilitation**   Facilitation is a moderated learning situation led by a facilitator who leads a group to share ideas and solve problems. Facilitators generally have skills in moderating group discussions and may be experts in the subject of discussion.

> **Case studies**   A *case study* reproduces a realistic situation that provides learners with the opportunity to analyze the circumstances as though it was encountered in the course of business. Case studies provide learners with the opportunity to investigate, study, and analyze the situation and then discuss possible solutions with the group. Solutions are developed and presented to fellow learners.

Simulation   *Simulation training* is an interactive training method that provides the learner with opportunities to try out new skills or practice procedures in a setting that does not endanger the inexperienced trainee, coworkers, or the public.

Vestibule   *Vestibule training* is a form of the simulation method. It allows inexperienced workers to become familiar with and gain experience using equipment that is either hazardous or requires a level of speed that can only be attained with practice. Vestibule training is commonly used to train equipment operators in the construction industry and to help retail clerks gain speed at the checkout counter.

Socratic seminar   Socratic seminars are based on the method of instruction used by the Greek philosopher Socrates in which ideas are examined in a question-and-answer format. A question may be posed by the seminar leader at the beginning of the seminar and discussed by participants to gain a full understanding of the topic.

Experiential Training Methods   *Experiential training methods* provide experience in real-time situations.

Demonstration   The *demonstration* method of training can be used as part of an on-the-job training program or combined with a lecture program. The method involves the trainer explaining the process or operation, demonstrating it on the equipment, and then having the learner perform it under the guidance of the trainer.

One-on-one   In *one-on-one training*, an inexperienced worker is paired with an experienced supervisor or coworker who utilizes a variety of techniques to provide the worker with the information and hands-on experience necessary to do the job.

Performance   *Performance-based training (PBT)* is most often utilized to correct performance problems in highly technical or hazardous professions. The trainee is provided with opportunities to practice and demonstrate the necessary skill or knowledge until the required level of proficiency is mastered.

Program Delivery Mechanisms

Devising suitable delivery methods for training programs is subject to a number of factors, including what information is to be covered, who will be attending the training, the experience level of the participants, availability of technology, and so on.

Classroom   Classroom training provides the same content to a group of employees in a classroom setting. It is effective for small groups when providing the same information to everyone in the group.

Self-study   A program of self-study is directed entirely by the learner, who determines what, when, and where learning will occur. It may be based on a defined program and involve a trainer or mentor, but it is controlled by the learner.

Programmed instruction   *Programmed instruction*, also referred to as self-paced training, is the forerunner of CBT. In this method, the learner progresses from lesson to lesson in a pre-designed course of instruction as mastery of the objectives is attained. This method allows learners to progress at their own rate. Programmed instruction is effective for disseminating facts and concepts, refreshing previously learned skills, or expanding a learner's knowledge in a field that is already familiar.

e-learning   E-learning encompasses several types of electronically based training delivery systems that are generally cost-effective, self-directed methods for training employees.

> **Electronic performance support systems**   An electronic performance support system (EPSS) is a training tool integrated in the computer system used by employees on the job. It allows instant access to information that helps them complete tasks more effectively.

> **Computer-based training (CBT)**   *Computer-based training* is an interactive training method that combines elements of the lecture, demonstration, one-on-one, and simulation methods, thus allowing the learner to have a real-world learning experience. Well-designed CBT programs ensure consistency of training across a company that is geographically dispersed. CBT is based on the programmed instruction method.

> **Distance learning**   Sometimes referred to as a virtual classroom, *distance learning* is similar to lectures and allows simultaneous training to occur in geographically dispersed multiple locations. Distance learning provides participants with the ability to communicate with presenters and participants in other locations.

> **Blended learning**   Blended learning uses multiple delivery methods to enhance the learning experience. The term is currently used to describe different ways of combining delivery methods, such as multiple web-based learning methods, a combination of instructor-led delivery with some form of technology, or combining learning technology with the performance of actual job tasks.

> **Online bulletin boards**   Online bulletin boards allow trainees to post questions and share information with each other. They may be supervised or facilitated by a leader who is knowledgeable in the subject matter and acts as a resource for the participants.

Implementation

Implementation is the phase of training where all the preceding work comes together for the presentation. The process begins with selection of the facility and trainers or facilitators. The trainer or facilitator sets up a program schedule, creates the agenda, and notifies participants of the training. At this time, it may be necessary to conduct "train the trainer" sessions to ensure that those who will implement the trainings are themselves fully trained to proceed.

Facility   The facility selected for the training will depend on the type of training to be conducted, the number of participants attending, and the amount budgeted for the program. While individual level training may best be conducted at the employee's work station, training for larger groups of people is best conducted away from the distractions of the workstation. A conference room at the work site may provide an adequate training facility if the size of the group is small (or the room large enough). It may be necessary for a variety of reasons to conduct the training offsite. While the cost will be greater to rent a facility, the reduction of distractions may result in a more effective training experience with longer lasting results.

The amount of space needed for the training depends largely on what training activities will take place. Passive training that requires little more of participants than listening requires the least amount of space. More space is required for situations in which participants will be taking notes or practicing work activities. Figures 5.12 through 5.17 depict some of the more common seating styles for trainings and the types of training for which each is most appropriate.

FIGURE 5.12 Theater-style seating

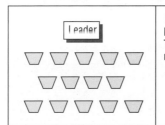

Theater-style seating is best for training when lectures, films, or video presentations are used. This seating style accommodates the largest number of people in any space.

FIGURE 5.13 Classroom-style seating

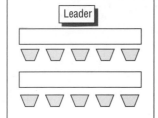

Classroom-style seating is best for training situations when participants will be listening to presentations, using manuals or handouts, and taking notes.

FIGURE 5.14 Banquet-style seating

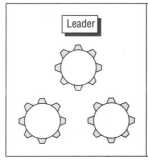

Banquet-style seating is best for training situations in which participants will be taking part in small group discussions and interacting with each other in addition to participating in activities as a single group.

FIGURE 5.15   Chevron-style seating

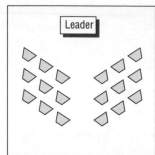

The chevron arrangement is appropriate for training situations in which participants will be interacting with the instructor and each other. This seating style is able to accommodate larger groups than some other seating styles. Useful for situations in which participants will be engaged in several activities: lectures, films, or video presentations, in addition to interacting with others in the room. Chevron-style seating can be used with tables or without, depending on the particular training and space available.

FIGURE 5.16   Conference-style seating

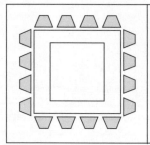

Conference-style seating is used when participants are of equal status and the training is led by a facilitator instead of an instructor. This arrangement provides for maximum interaction between individuals, but is not conducive to the use of visual aids.

FIGURE 5.17   U-shaped-style seating

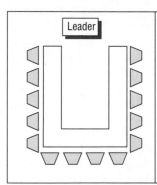

U-shaped-style seating is an effective seating style for collaborative training situations when presentations and discussions will take place. The center area may be used for additional seating or for role-playing.

Another very important step in preparing the facility is to ensure that the physical environment is conducive to learning. For example, that the room temperature will be comfortable for most people, sufficient restroom facilities are available to accommodate the number of participants, and that beverages and/or food are available as appropriate.

Trainers   Trainers may be selected based on their mastery of the subject matter or for their ability and skill in training. This decision will be based largely on the nature of the training being conducted.

Schedule   The training schedule is affected by many factors, including the feasibility of shutting down operations entirely for the length of the training session so that all employees are trained at the same time, or whether it is more cost effective to conduct multiple sessions in order to maintain operations. Sessions may need to be broken into segments and scheduled over a period of days or weeks to accommodate operational needs.

The selection of program delivery mechanisms and instructional methods for various types of training needs are related to the size of the group, type of training needed, and geographic location of the participants.

Evaluation

Training evaluation occurs after the training takes place and is based on criteria established in the assessment phase. The ultimate goal of the training is to improve performance on the job. This is known as *transfer of training*, and takes place when learning occurs away from the regular work environment and must then be applied to the real job situation. It is obviously important that the investment made in training employees provide a return in increased productivity, quality, or safety (whatever the subject of the training) on the job. A failure of training to transfer to the job can occur when the new skill is not applied in the work environment so that it is reinforced. A technique that can overcome this problem is the development of an action plan to be implemented after training. This approach requires trainees to visualize and describe how they plan to apply the training when they are back on the job so they are more likely to use their new skills. An effective evaluation will include provisions for measuring job performance for a period of time after the training has been completed to ensure that the new skills have been transferred to the job.

A common model for training evaluation was developed by Donald Kirkpatrick. He proposed four levels of evaluation for training programs: reaction, learning, behavior, and results. Measurements at each level are based on the objectives developed during the design phase.

Reaction   The *reaction evaluation method* measures the initial reaction of the participants. This is most commonly determined by a survey completed by participants at the end of the training. While this level of evaluation does not measure the organization impact, it does provide feedback for the trainer in terms of the presentation of the information.

Learning   The *learning evaluation method* uses a test to measure whether or not the participants learned the information that was presented. While this level of evaluation provides more information about the effectiveness of the training, it still does not provide feedback about the application of the information on the job.

In some cases, learning evaluation uses an experimental design known as the pretest/posttest comparison.

- A group of employees is selected for training.
- The employees are randomly assigned to two different groups.
- An identical pretest is administered to both groups of employees.
- One group receives the training, also known as a treatment.
- An identical posttest is administered to both groups of employees.
- The results are compared to see if the training resulted in improved performance.

The pretest/posttest comparison is appropriate when an organization wants to isolate the impact of training on productivity. In order to make a legitimate comparison, all other factors that could affect performance must be equalized. For example, all employees in the group should have similar KSAs, be using similar equipment, and have access to similar resources. If other factors are dissimilar, it is not possible to isolate the training impact on performance.

Experimental design evaluation requires three criteria:

- More than one group created for the purpose of the comparison,
- A measurable outcome common to both groups, and
- Random assignment of group members.

For any number of reasons, it is not always possible to satisfy these criteria. In those cases, a quasi-experimental design may be used. The evaluation may be made between two groups with dissimilar backgrounds, a posttest only may be used, or a time-series evaluation (in which several tests are administered over a period of time) may take place.

Behavior   The *behavior evaluation method* measures job performance between six weeks and six months after the training. This follow-up evaluation can be based on observations, interviews, tests, or surveys and tells the trainer if the new skills were successfully transferred to the job.

Results   The *results evaluation method* provides the feedback most meaningful to the business: did the training have an impact on business results? The measurement compares an objective statement, such as, "This training will reduce product defects by 20 percent in 12 months," to the actual product results at the end of the 12-month period to determine its success.

Performance Management Programs

Performance management is an ongoing process of providing feedback for employees about their performance to develop them into increasingly productive contributors to the organization. This process ensures that employees are on the right track for completion of their goals, that individual goals are aligned with organization goals, and that employees receive the support they need to be successful. The performance management process provides for an employee's professional development within the context of organizational needs.

Effective performance management must be based on an agreement between the manager or supervisor and the employee about what the job requires. This information comes from the organization's strategic plan, the manager's goals and objectives, and the employee's essential job functions as contained in an accurate job description. With these elements, the parties can develop individual goals and objectives and agree upon the standards of performance to be used in measuring results.

Meaningful feedback that can be used to improve performance is specific, describing the behavior so the employee is clear about what is being done correctly or incorrectly. For example, instead of saying "Good job," telling an employee, "The way you handled Bob Kent's complaint yesterday was professional and effective. I was impressed with how quickly you were able to calm him down by remaining calm yourself and solving his problem." Feedback should also focus on behaviors, not personal attributes. Telling an employee, "You have a bad attitude," is open to interpretation and doesn't help them to see where they need to improve. Instead, use a comment like, "Sally, I noticed that you were scowling at your desk this morning and when Joe asked you a question you told him to find the manual himself. That is not an appropriate way to respond to questions. Part of our job is to assist our coworkers in finding the reference materials we maintain." This response provides actionable information for the employee. It is also important for the feedback to be as timely as possible, and at least within the same day as the observed behavior.

Corrective feedback should be given privately to avoid embarrassing the employee—the point of feedback is to improve behavior, not to alienate the employee. The employee should also be able to respond, explain, or ask for clarification.

On the other hand, positive feedback given more publicly can motivate the recipient and observers to repeat the positive behavior and receive additional recognition.

Performance management is not a once-a-year proposition—for maximum effectiveness, it must be an ongoing process that enables a manager to intervene in the early stages if an employee is getting off track.

Performance Appraisal

One important aspect of performance management is the *performance appraisal*, *performance evaluation*, or *performance review* process. These three terms are used interchangeably to describe the process of reviewing how well employees perform their duties during a specified period of time. The appraisal process has the potential to be a powerful tool for building the important relationship between supervisors and their direct reports.

When used well, appraisals provide a structured means for communication, helping to build working relationships. This structure provides for positive performance feedback, recognition of accomplishments during the review period, honest discussion of areas for improvement, and development opportunities for the future. More detail on this is provided in the section "Training Performance Evaluators" later in this chapter.

Another important function of the performance appraisal process is the documentation it provides for employment decisions—positive or negative. For example, appraisals that document a history of achievement and positive contribution provide the basis for promotion decisions or inclusion in a HiPo development program. Conversely, appraisals that document a history of mediocre or below-average performance are crucial when making adverse employment decisions. Contemporaneous performance documentation can be essential in defending employment actions at either end of the spectrum if challenged by disgruntled employees.

There are three factors in the appraisal process that are important to understand: the elements included in an appraisal process, the timing of review cycles, and the methods used.

Elements of Performance Appraisal

There are several elements that should be included as part of an effective annual review.

Supervisor assessment   The supervisor's assessment begins with a review of the goals and objectives set at the beginning of the review cycle and whether or not the anticipated results were achieved. The supervisor must then evaluate whether any deficiencies were due to inadequate performance by the employee or whether they were the result of circumstances outside the employee's control, such as a change in the organization's direction. The supervisor must then develop a plan to address the discrepancies.

Employee self-assessment   Because this process is meant to be a two-way conversation, employees should be asked to assess their own performance as part of the appraisal. Giving employees advance notice of the scheduled review meeting allows time for reflection about their past performance as well as goals they may have for the future and areas of professional development that are of interest to them.

Assessment from others   It is important for supervisors to obtain feedback from those with whom the employee has contact each day to find out if there are areas of concern or outstanding performance about which the supervisor may not be aware. When this is part of the formal review process, it is known as a 360° review and includes feedback from coworkers, internal and external customers, vendors, and subordinates.

Goal setting   A key component of the review is planning for the future using changes to the strategic plan and the supervisor's goals and objectives to help plan the employee's goals. It is important for employees to participate in the setting of their own goals to facilitate their commitment to achieving them.

Development goals   As part of the review, supervisors can provide training opportunities for employees to address any areas of deficiency or to prepare them for the next level.

Timing Performance Appraisals

Performance appraisals can be conducted either on employee anniversary dates or during an organization-wide focal review period. In organizations that time reviews to coincide with employee anniversary dates, managers conduct individual reviews throughout the year. The advantage to this process is that there are fewer reviews to conduct at one time; disadvantages occur when awarding salary increases and when utilizing comparative appraisal methods.

Managers who do not plan adequately for salary increases may find that increases for high performers toward the end of the year are lower than increases awarded to average performers earlier in the year. It is also difficult to use comparative appraisal methods when appraisals occur on individual employee anniversary dates because the manager will need to consider the performance of employees not up for review at the same time.

During a *focal review period*, all employees in the organization are reviewed at the same time. This is more difficult for managers, as well as for HR, due to the sheer volume of reviews that must be completed. On the other hand, the focal process provides managers with an opportunity to allocate salary increases to appropriately reflect individual performance levels. Comparative appraisal methods are more easily conducted during a focal review as well.

Performance Appraisal Methods

Employee performance appraisal may be based on quantitative data, such as whether or not specific goals were accomplished, or on more qualitative factors. There is currently much discussion in the HR field about the effectiveness of traditional performance appraisal processes. Some HR texts suggest that appraisal systems be abolished and replaced with more effective methods of providing feedback and developing employees.

There are a number of methods that have been developed for use in evaluating employee performance; all of them can be placed in one of four basic categories: comparison, rating, essay, and behavioral.

Comparison Methods

Comparison appraisal methods compare the performance of individuals or employees to each other. The most common methods of comparison are ranking, paired comparison, and forced ranking.

Ranking   In the *ranking* method, employees are listed in order from the highest to the lowest performer. This method works well for small groups of employees but becomes increasingly difficult as the size of the group increases.

Paired comparison   In the paired comparison method, all employees in the group are compared to one employee at a time. For example, if there are three employees in the work group, Susan, Jack, and Rachel, Susan's performance is compared to Jack's and Rachel's, Jack's performance is compared to Susan's and Rachel's, and finally, Rachel's performance is compared to Susan's and Jack's.

Forced ranking   Also known as forced distribution or forced choice, *forced ranking* requires managers to rank employees according to the bell curve, rating a small group of employees at the high end, a small group at the low end, and the bulk of the employees in the average range. This appraisal tool can be utilized as part of any of the appraisal methods to reduce the effects of the leniency or harshness biases discussed in detail in Chapter 4.

Rating Methods

Common rating methods for performance appraisal include the use of rating scales and checklists.

Rating scales   Rating scales may be numeric, with scales of from 3 to 10 ratings to differentiate levels of performance, or may use phrases such as "exceeds expectations," "meets expectations," or "does not meet expectations." Rating scales attempt to quantify what is a very subjective process, but because of the different ways in which the descriptors are interpreted by raters, these scales are not as objective as they may appear at first glance.

Checklists   A performance checklist is a list of statements, phrases, or words that describe levels of performance, such as, "always finishes work on time." The reviewer checks off those that best describe the employee. The various descriptions may be weighted and used to calculate a rating score.

Narrative Methods

Narrative methods of appraisal require managers to describe the employee's performance. These include critical incident, essay, and field reviews.

Critical incident   The *critical incident review* process requires that during the review period supervisors make notes of successful and unsuccessful performance issues for each employee. At the time of the review, the supervisor is able to review these critical incidents and present them to employees in a written narrative.

Essay   An *essay review* requires the reviewer to write a short description of each employee's performance during the year. This format provides maximum flexibility for managers to cover areas they see as those most important to improving employee performance.

Field review   A *field review appraisal* may be conducted by someone other than the supervisor. This can be an HR practitioner or someone from outside the organization.

Behavioral Methods

The best-known behavioral review method is the *behaviorally anchored rating scale (BARS)*. The BARS method uses the job description to create dimensions that represent the most important requirements of the job. For each dimension, anchor statements are created to represent varying levels of performance behaviors that describe rating numbers on a scale. For example, a job dimension for a receptionist might be greeting customers. The anchors that could be used to measure the behaviors associated with this job dimension are shown in Table 5.2.

Continuous feedback   The most effective review process is a *continuous feedback program* that addresses basic employee/employer needs on an ongoing basis throughout the review period. This provides employees with the support they need to be successful in their work, eliminates surprises when projects are completed and submitted, and reduces the stress related to providing feedback only once a year, or only when things go wrong.

TABLE 5.2   Sample BARS Anchor Statements

Rating	Anchor Statement
5	Greets customers warmly and makes them feel welcome.
4	Pleasant to customers and answers their questions.
3	Courteous to the customer.
2	Finishes other work before greeting customers.
1	Rude to customers when they approach the desk.

Regardless of the review method utilized in an organization, raters should be aware of the various biases that can impact the fairness of a review. It is also important to keep in mind that the same bias and errors described in Chapter 4's discussion of interviewer bias, such as the halo/horn effect, leniency, harshness, and similar-to-me errors, can influence a review. Supervisors should be cognizant of this when preparing the review. When bias is a concern, organizations can use a process known as *inter-rater reliability*, which uses multiple raters to reduce the possibility of rating errors due to bias. The scores of all raters are averaged, with the goal of providing a review that is as free from bias as possible.

Training Performance Evaluators

It is unfortunate that the performance appraisal process is disliked by so many supervisors and employees, because when well-used it provides a structure for building positive, productive working relationships. One of the concerns many employees have about the appraisal process is their perception of its fairness, or lack of fairness. Some employees may feel that their boss is much tougher than other managers, and some managers have developed reputations for being "easy graders." Those perceptions may never go away entirely, but providing training for those who conduct appraisals will at least ensure that everyone is beginning from the same place. Evaluators should be made aware of biases that can affect the appraisal process (as discussed in Chapter 4), and of course, learn how to utilize the organization's appraisal process.

The training should provide information for activities before, during, and after the actual appraisal meeting.

Before the Meeting

Preparation prior to meeting with employees helps to alleviate some of the stress and discomfort that many evaluators feel, particularly when they are new to providing feedback. The goal of the process is to make sure employees know they are valued team members and to motivate them to continue positive performance and improve any areas in which they may be deficient.

- Schedule the meeting for a mutually convenient time and allow sufficient time for an open conversation. Give the employee advance notice—ideally one week. Don't schedule the meeting for a time when other pressures, such as deadlines or other commitments, will be a distraction.

- Provide the employee with a self-appraisal form to complete prior to the meeting; at least two days before the meeting, provide employees with a copy of the completed appraisal and have them submit the self-appraisal to the evaluator.

- If reviewing multiple employees in the same job category, use the same appraisal criteria for all of them.

- Prepare for the meeting by reviewing the job description, performance standards, goals set during previous appraisals, and the critical incident log or other notes about specific performance issues (positive and negative) that occurred during the review period.

- Complete the review form using specific, job-related comments to describe positive and negative performance issues. This helps the employee to see what to do more of and how to improve when needed.

- Make sure the appraisal is balanced. Keep in mind that few employees are all good or all bad; in most cases, even those with serious performance deficiencies are usually doing some things right, and outstanding performers can improve in some area.

- Whenever possible, use quantitative measurements, such as on-time project completions, missed deadlines, production data, and so on. Describe how the behaviors impacted the organization.

- If improvements are needed in some areas, provide specific information on what is expected from the employee and how feedback will be given. Don't sugar coat problems—appraisals that neglect to document performance problems make future adverse employment actions difficult and expose the organization to litigation.

- Arrange a private area to conduct the meeting; even if the evaluator has an office, the use of a conference room may be advisable to eliminate interruptions.

During the Meeting

Adequate preparation is essential and demonstrates that the supervisor values the employee. It is equally important for evaluators to make full use of that preparation during the meeting. This is an opportunity to communicate about things that are important to both participants—feedback, expectations, goals, and, in some cases, rewards.

Most employees enter an appraisal meeting wanting to know how they are doing, what the supervisor expects from them, and what their reward for previous performance will be. Some will approach the meeting as though it were a guillotine, while others see it as an opportunity to learn the positive and negative information provided to continue developing their careers.

The evaluator's goal during the meeting is to acknowledge the employee's value to the organization and provide them with constructive feedback to enhance their productivity. Training for evaluators should include the following information:

- Set a tone of mutual respect. It is up to evaluators to ease anxiety by creating an open atmosphere and providing employees with their full attention.

- Discuss the appraisal forms that were exchanged prior to the meeting. If there are areas of disagreement, seek to understand the employee's perspective; be willing to revise the appraisal if warranted due to misunderstanding of the facts. Don't, however, change an appraisal to avoid confrontation on accurate facts.

- Discuss training options and development needs. Find out what career direction the employee wants to take and provide realistic guidance on how that may be achieved.

- Set goals for the next review period. Make sure to include the employee in developing the goals instead of merely assigning them. Keep in mind that the goal of the appraisal is to enhance performance; giving employees a voice in setting their goals helps them to feel invested in the outcome.

- Communicate expectations clearly. If attendance or tardiness is an issue, say so flat out—don't leave anything up to interpretation.

- Give employees an opportunity to ask questions about the appraisal, expectations, or goals so that when they leave the meeting they are clear about any next steps.

- Once the appraisal part of the meeting is completed, in many organizations the discussion turns to rewards, whether that is a salary increase, bonus, promotion, or other reward.

- Have the employee sign any necessary paperwork required for the appraisal or reward.

After the Meeting

Provide information to supervisors about how to complete the appraisal process. In most cases, this will include submitting paperwork to HR for retention and processing salary changes. In addition, encourage supervisors to make continuous feedback part of their daily interaction with employees. This reduces the level of stress involved in annual appraisals because the feedback becomes a regular part of the daily routine instead of an annual review of what should have been done differently during the year. An appraisal with no surprises is easier on supervisors and their employees.

Training those individuals who conduct appraisals is one way to make the experience, if not pleasant, at least more effective.

Nonsupervisory Evaluators

Evaluators are generally supervisors or managers, but in the case of 360° appraisal systems, coworkers may be asked to provide feedback as well. These evaluators should receive training on the organization's appraisal process and the importance of keeping the feedback related to job activities. They should also be made aware of the biases that can affect the appraisal process.

Unique Employee Needs

Employees are people with needs and concerns about other areas of their lives than just work. While some employers would like to think what happens outside the workplace doesn't affect performance, there are times when even the best performers may be hindered by personal situations or points of view. In order to maintain productivity levels and retain otherwise high performers, organizations sometimes find it necessary to provide programs that deal with unique situations. Three common activities in this category include diversity initiatives, flexible work arrangements, and repatriation of global employees.

Diversity Initiatives

Discussed in more detail in Chapter 2, diversity programs are designed to ensure that all members of the organization are treated equitably and to facilitate understanding between employees with widely divergent cultural backgrounds. Diversity programs can be used as a human resource management intervention to help individuals feel more connected within the company and promote understanding and tolerance among employees.

Flexible Work Arrangements

The need for employers to consider the impact of family issues on an employee's performance has been increasing in the United States, due to pressure from dual-income families, an aging population, and government regulations. Employers respond to this in different ways. At one end of the spectrum are employers who comply with legal requirements but do not provide any additional leeway for employees who must deal with family issues. At the other end of the spectrum are companies like SAS, a software company in North Carolina that provides onsite childcare, an eldercare information and referral program, wellness programs, recreation and fitness facilities, and other benefits designed to assist employees in managing the balance between their work and the rest of their lives. These types of programs provide resources for employees so that they are able to stay focused on work instead of taking time off to deal with family or other personal needs.

Repatriation

As businesses become more globally oriented, issues of expatriating and repatriating employees will continue to grow. Issues of expatriate training were discussed in Chapter 4, but of equal concern to employees returning from expatriate assignments is how their careers will be impacted after having been away from the home office for an extended period.

As with all issues related to employee relations, it is crucial that appropriate expectations be set before employees begin their expatriate assignments, including the issue of what types of assignments will be available to them when they return to the home office. As business conditions at the home office change, the expatriate should be kept advised of any possible changes to the expectations for return assignments. Employees who expect to return to a position of equal or greater authority, responsibility, and pay but find themselves in a position they see as a demotion are understandably demotivated and provide a negative report to their coworkers of their experience. A formal repatriation program that includes a component of career planning services can assist employees in making the transition back to the home office. Returning expatriates can be a valuable resource for others entering expatriate assignments and ensuring that the experience is a positive one will add value to the organization. For many companies, repatriation management and career planning are keys to developing global leadership in the long term.

Managing the repatriation process effectively includes time to debrief the repatriate personally, to assist in managing the transition back to the home country and professionally, to add to the knowledge base for the organization and increase its effectiveness in the global marketplace. The manager responsible for the repatriate plays a key role in the integration process by reacquainting the repatriate with corporate policies and politics.

With formal repatriation management and career planning strategies in place, companies will more effectively manage assignees' career expectations upon repatriation, retain their valuable international experience, and, as a result, maximize the return on investment for both the individual assignee and the organization as a whole.

Metrics—Measuring Results

The most important measure for human resource development is how (or whether) an intervention affected business results. For example, if a training program was implemented to improve call center response times, did that occur? If so, was the result immediate, or did improvement occur more slowly as CSRs gained confidence from experience implementing the training?

Business impact measures   Metrics that validate the impact of training programs on results are the ones that provide useful information to management. Depending on the situation, some of these metrics may be appropriate:

Production measures   Metrics that provide measures taken prior to training and several months after training takes place demonstrate how well the program solved the business issue. There are many applications of this for production issues, such as increased speed, number of rejected items, or increased output. A similar measure can be used for other types of training. For example, measuring the number of incidents of sexual harassment prior to training and then again six months to one year after training occurs demonstrates whether or not the training was effective.

Return on investment   As discussed in Chapter 2, ROI is a key measurement for any HR function. Measuring the ROI of HRD programs provides objective information about how they are increasing productivity or providing other benefits to the organization that justifies investing in them.

Tactical Accountability Measures There are a number of established metrics used to measure HR's tactical accountability in HRD. Some of the more common include:

Training cost per employee Training cost per employee is calculated by collecting all costs related to training, including design and development, materials, equipment rentals, time spent by HR staff and managers or others who aided in development, cost of participant time to attend the training, facilities, beverages, food, and so on. The total cost is then divided by the number of full-time equivalent employees.

Employee satisfaction surveys Employee satisfaction surveys can provide general information about the effectiveness of HRD programs, such as whether or not employees are satisfied with the amount and types of training and development provided. This question can be tailored to individual organizations by making it specific with regard to programs provided.

Global Considerations

Operating in a global marketplace presents unique challenges for the HRD function. Some of these challenges are logistical, such as scheduling the delivery of an organization-wide OD intervention so that all employees have access to the same information as close to simultaneously as possible and that employees are able to hear it in their native languages. Other challenges in an OD context, for example, necessitate presenting business initiatives in a way that is sensitive to the cultures of the different regions and nations in which the organization has facilities. In putting together presentations that will be delivered globally, HRD must keep in mind societal norms that will affect how the presentations are interpreted.

Teamwork in a global organization presents another challenge, although in some ways it is similar to working with virtual teams within the United States. Adding to the inherent possibilities for misunderstandings when the majority of team communication occurs via email is the additional possibility for misinterpretation when this informal communication tool is read from the perspective of different cultural experiences.

Understanding cultural differences is equally important to motivating employees. Specifically, the motivation techniques that work in Western cultures may have little or no meaning for employees in other regions of the world. In order to motivate employees in different cultures, it is important to first understand the cultural norms and values that are meaningful to those employees. At the same time, the techniques used should meet some common organization requirements.

Summary

Human resource development (HRD) is tied closely to organization development (OD). HRD is more often tied to organizational "software" issues of change management, leadership and management development, and performance management, while OD is generally utilized to address the "hardware" issues of the organization: developing its strategy, technology, and structure.

HRD/OD interventions address organizational challenges with such programs as learning organizations, total quality management, and management by objectives that are designed to align the workforce with the leaders and the organization strategy. These programs must be selected to fit in with the culture and strategy of the organization to be successful.

Development programs prepare talented individuals to accept positions of greater responsibility and authority in the organization and aid the retention of individuals who are key to its long-term success.

Training is an important aspect of HRD. The ADDIE model is used to develop training programs that address the needs of the organization and of individuals within the organization.

The continuous feedback provided by effective performance management programs encourages and assists employees. Ongoing feedback helps to maintain the positive aspects of daily performance and to address areas that need improvement. The performance appraisal process provides documentation for employment decisions such as promotions and terminations.

Finally, HRD programs that address the unique needs of some employees can be implemented to increase goodwill and attract and retain quality employees.

Exam Essentials

Understand and be able to describe the ADDIE model.   The ADDIE model is an instruction design tool used in creating training programs and stands for Analysis, Design, Development, Implementation, and Evaluation.

Be able to conduct a training needs analysis.   A training needs analysis begins with an identification of the goal, the current level of training, and the performance gap. The analysis then identifies instructional goals, proposes solutions, estimates their budget impact, and recommends the preferred solution.

Understand the connection between change management and OD.   OD *is* change management. It seeks to address issues that prevent organizations from becoming fully effective and introduces interventions to align the workforce with the organization strategy.

Be able to identify the five characteristics of a learning organization.   The following five characteristics of a learning organization distinguish it from other organizations: systems thinking, personal mastery, mental models, building a shared vision, and team learning.

Be able to identify the four types of training evaluation.   The four types of evaluation are reaction, which measures immediate feedback; learning, which measures what was learned through testing; behavior, which measures job performance six months or more after training; and results, which measures whether or not the training had a positive impact on the bottom line.

Key Terms

ADDIE model

Auditory learners

behavior evaluation method

behaviorally anchored rating scale (BARS)

cause and effect diagram

change agent

change process theory

check sheets

conflict resolution

continuous feedback program

design patents

emotional intelligence (EI or EQ)

essay review

field review appraisal

focal review period

forced ranking

high involvement organizations (HIOs)

histograms

Individual level training

inter-rater reliability

kinesthetic learners

leadership development

learning curve

learning evaluation method

learning organizations

management by objectives (MBO)

management development

mental models

mentoring programs

negatively accelerating learning curve

OD interventions

organization development (OD)

organizational level training

Pareto chart

patent

performance appraisal

performance evaluation

performance management

performance review

personal mastery

plant patents

plateau learning curve

positively accelerating learning curve

process control charts

public domain

ranking

reaction evaluation method

results evaluation method

reverse mentor

shared vision

S-shaped learning curve

stratification charts

supervisory training

systems thinking

task level training

team learning

total quality management (TQM)

transfer of training

utility patents

visual learners

Review Questions

1. _____ is one of several learning organization characteristics.
   A. An assessment center
   B. Massed practice
   C. Systems thinking
   D. Programmed instruction

2. Which of the following should be included in a supervisory training program?
   A. Conflict resolution skills
   B. Budgeting
   C. Rotation through various divisions
   D. Internal controls

3. In the evaluation phase, the _____ evaluation method focuses on how well the training resulted in learning new skills and competencies.
   A. Reaction
   B. Learning
   C. Behavior
   D. Results

4. Which of the following factors can adversely affect transfer of training?
   A. The trainer's expertise
   B. A lack of job reinforcement
   C. The subject of the training
   D. None of the above

5. A _____ learning curve begins slowly, with smaller learning increments, but increases in pace and with larger increments as learning continues.
   A. positively accelerating
   B. negatively accelerating
   C. S-shaped
   D. plateau

6. The most common reason for the failure of organizational change initiatives is that
   A. The strategic plan was not communicated to employees.
   B. Organization leaders did not support the change.
   C. There was no training system in place.
   D. Employees were not prepared for the change.

7. The best quality tool to use for gathering information about a specific problem is:

    A. A Pareto chart

    B. An Ishikawa diagram

    C. A stratification chart

    D. A histogram

8. Which employee growth and assessment program is characterized by performance objectives?

    A. Behavioral-based performance assessment

    B. Skills-based performance assessment

    C. Management by objectives (MBO)

    D. Continuous feedback program

9. Which performance appraisal method would be used most effectively in a large, geographically dispersed organization with many similar jobs?

    A. Critical incident

    B. Forced ranking

    C. Behaviorally anchored rating system

    D. Field review

10. Mentoring involves someone

    A. Who monitors an employee's performance in doing their job.

    B. Whose goal is to develop an employee in a particular area.

    C. Who takes a personal interest in an individual's career and who guides and sponsors the individual.

    D. Who provides training in areas of interest to an employee.

Answers to Review Questions

1. C. Systems thinking refers to the characteristic of a learning organization that uses a variety of information-gathering techniques to acquire knowledge of new technology, determine its value, and convert this knowledge into new and improved practices and procedures. Assessment centers (A) are used to determine what kind of training an individual needs. Massed practice (B) is a form of practicing job tasks during training in which all tasks are practiced at the same time. Programmed instruction (D) is a type of self-instruction that requires trainees to complete each step in the training before moving on to the next step.

2. A. Supervisory training programs concentrate on topics related to interactions with employees, such as conflict resolution skills. Budgeting skills (B) and internal control training (D) are included in management development programs. Rotation through various divisions (C) is part of a leadership development program.

3. B. The learning evaluation method focuses on how well the training resulted in learning new skills. The reaction evaluation method (A) focuses on participant reactions. The behavior evaluation method (C) measures on-the-job behavior changes as a result of training, and the results evaluation method (D) measures organizational results. Of the four methods, the results evaluation method is considered the most valuable for the organization.

4. B. A lack of job reinforcement can adversely affect transfer of training. Other adverse impacts are the result of interference from the immediate work environment and a nonsupportive organizational climate. The trainer's expertise (A) could affect how well trainees learn information but does not specifically affect transfer of training. The subject of the training (C) affects how receptive trainees are to the information but not necessarily how the information transfers to the job.

5. A. The positively accelerating learning curve begins with smaller increments but increases in pace and size as learning continues. The negatively accelerating curve (B) begins with larger increments that decrease as learning continues. The S-shaped learning curve (C) is a combination of the positively and negatively accelerating learning curves, while a plateau (D) occurs when no learning seems to take place.

6. D. The most common reason for the failure of change initiatives is that people were not prepared for the change and given time to assimilate the reasons for the change. Failing to communicate a change in strategic direction (A) as the basis for organization changes in and of itself will not lead to failure of a change initiative. Leaders who do not support change (B) do have an influence on employees, but that factor alone is not the most common reason for failure. The absence of a training system (C) may negatively impact the change process, but it is not the most common reason for failure.

7. B. An Ishikawa diagram is an effective tool for organizing information about a problem when brainstorming with a group. A Pareto chart (A) graphically represents the 80/20 rule. A stratification chart (C) shows the individual components of a problem in addition to the total or summary. A histogram (D) provides a way of looking at random occurrences to find out if there is a pattern.

8. C. The first three choices are all employee growth and assessment programs. Behavioral-based performance assessment (A) focuses on behaviors, while skills-based performance assessment (B) focuses on skills. MBO programs measure the successful attainment of objectives. The continuous feedback program (D) is a performance management program.

9. C. The BARS system is used most effectively in organizations when a number of jobs have similar duties. Because it is expensive and time-consuming to implement, an organization must have enough resources available to develop the program. Critical incident appraisal tools (A) are most effectively used by managers who have daily interaction with subordinates. Forced ranking (B) is best for use in organizations with fewer than 100 employees as it becomes unwieldy for large groups. Field reviews (D) are conducted by someone other than a director supervisor.

10. C. A mentor is someone who takes a personal interest in an employee's career and who guides and sponsors them. While a supervisor may be a mentor, mentors are usually individuals who are outside the chain of command and may even be someone outside the organization. The functions in A, B & D are not generally performed by mentors.

Total Rewards

THE HRCI TEST SPECIFICATIONS FROM THE TOTAL REWARDS FUNCTIONAL AREA COVERED IN THIS CHAPTER INCLUDE:

✓ Ensure that compensation and benefits programs are compliant with applicable federal, state, and local laws and regulations.

✓ Develop, implement, and evaluate compensation policies/ programs and pay structures based upon internal equity and external market conditions that support the organization's strategic goals, objectives, and values.

✓ Administer payroll functions (for example, new hires, deductions, adjustments, terminations).

✓ Conduct benefits programs needs assessments (for example, benchmarking, employee survey).

✓ Develop/select, implement, and evaluate benefits program that support the organization's strategic goals, objectives, and values (for example, health and welfare, retirement, wellness, employee assistance programs [EAP], time off).

✓ Communicate and train the workforce in the compensation and benefits programs and policies (for example, self-service technologies).

✓ Develop/select, implement/administer, and evaluate executive compensation programs (for example, stock purchase, stock options, incentive, bonus, supplemental retirement plans. **SPHR** **ONLY**

✓ Develop, implement/administer, and evaluate expatriate and foreign national compensation and benefits programs. **SPHR** **ONLY**

Understanding total rewards (TR) programs and their impact on the strategic objectives of an organization is a basic component of human resource management. For those taking the PHR/SPHR exams, knowledge of federal employment laws governing both aspects of TR—compensation and benefits—is essential. It is important to keep in mind that these federal laws and regulations may differ from state and local requirements, so be certain you understand the differences between them for the exams. Table 6.1 summarizes federal legislation that governs employment activities in the total reward functional area.

Because this area of human resources is closely tied to the accounting function, understanding accounting practices as they relate to payroll, compensation calculations, and benefit reporting is required. Exam candidates must understand how to develop and implement fair pay practices utilizing job evaluation methods to price jobs and set pay structures for the organization. HR professionals must also be conversant with executive compensation needs and programs and understand noncash compensation methods.

The HRCI core knowledge requirements that will be particularly helpful in understanding this functional area include needs assessment and analysis, third-party contract negotiation and management, project management, communication skills, HR technology, employee surveys, and basic budgeting concepts. PHR/SPHR candidates should also understand how TR programs relate to and affect HR programs in other functional areas.

Finally, with the continuing globalization of business organizations, PHR/SPHR candidates need a basic understanding of international compensation and benefit laws as they apply to expatriates, host-country nationals, and third-country nationals, including mandated benefit programs.

TABLE 6.1 Federal Legislation Governing Total Rewards Activities

Type	Enforcement Agency	Chapter Reference
Civil rights	EEOC and/or OFCCP	4
Compensation	DOL, Employment Standards Administration	6
Family Medical Leave	DOL, Employment Standards Administration	6

TABLE 6.1 Federal Legislation Governing Total Rewards Activities *(continued)*

Type	Enforcement Agency	Chapter Reference
Health and Welfare	DOL, Employee Benefits Security Administration; EEOC (older worker benefits)	6
Payroll	Internal Revenue Service, DOL, Wage and Hour Division	6
Pensions	DOL, Employment Standards Administration; Internal Revenue Service	6

Total Rewards Defined

At the broadest level, total rewards can be described as an exchange of payment from an employer for the services provided by its employees. Also referred to as total compensation or the compensation package, in today's competitive economy a competitive TR program is vital to attracting, retaining, and motivating employees. In many organizations, TR costs are the single largest operating expense and therefore an extremely important component of the human resource program. A TR package includes all forms of rewards, which are generally categorized into one of two components: monetary and nonmonetary compensation. Let's look now at what goes into each of these components.

Monetary compensation   Monetary compensation includes any costs the organization incurs for the benefit of employees, such as all forms of cash compensation, 401(k) matching, medical care premiums, pension plans, and paid time off. Other kinds of rewards include benefits that support the organization's culture such as stock options, Employee Stock Ownership Programs (ESOPs), and incentive plans.

Nonmonetary compensation   It is important to recognize that just as monetary rewards are critical to offering a competitive TR program, so are nonmonetary rewards. This chapter focuses primarily on tangible rewards, but providing an environment that supports intrinsic and extrinsic nonmonetary rewards is a very important part of the total compensation package.

An *intrinsic reward* is one that encourages individual employee self esteem, such as satisfaction from challenging and exciting assignments. An *extrinsic reward* is one in which esteem is achieved from others, such as fulfillment from working with a talented team of peers. The relationship employees have with their supervisors, recognition of accomplishments, and teamwork are a few examples of nonmonetary rewards. Nonmonetary rewards also include nontraditional benefits such as telecommuting, employee training, on-site child care, and flex time. The motivational theories discussed in Chapter 2, "Core Knowledge Requirements for HR Professionals," help explain how these nonmonetary rewards can be used effectively in organizations. Theories such as Maslow's hierarchy of needs and McClelland's acquired needs theory help clarify how the individual's drive to achieve nonmonetary rewards such as belonging, esteem, and self actualization can be impacted with these reward systems.

Other terms that will be used throughout this chapter are direct and indirect compensation.

Direct compensation   *Direct compensation* includes payments made to employees that are associated with wages and salaries. This includes base pay, variable compensation, and pay for performance.

Indirect compensation   *Indirect compensation* is comprised of any employee payments not associated with wages and salaries. This includes fringe benefits such as vacation, sick, and holiday pay; insurance premiums paid on behalf of employees; leaves of absence; 401(k) or other pension plans; and government-mandated benefits such as social security or FMLA and other benefits.

The mix of components included in a total rewards package is unique to the TR philosophy, strategic direction, and culture of each organization. Ultimately, the goal of a total rewards package is to maximize the ROI of resources spent on employee rewards.

Total Rewards Philosophy

The *total rewards philosophy* is a high-level mission statement used to guide the development and implementation of compensation and benefit programs that attract, motivate, and retain employees. Typically, HR works closely with the executive management team to develop and implement the organization's TR philosophy.

During the development or revision of a TR philosophy, the HR management team facilitates the process by gathering input from and building consensus with key stakeholders such as members of the executive team and, in organizations governed by a board of directors, may involve board members in the process as well. Creating a TR philosophy in this way provides an opportunity to look at the whole package offered to employees and analyze which combination of programs will best achieve the organization's hiring and retention objectives. In smaller organizations or new startups that may not take the time to proactively define a TR philosophy, one may develop over time as a result of compensation programs implemented to meet specific needs and decisions made for individual employees. The danger in relying on this type of de facto philosophy in the long term is that it is not likely to provide a framework that supports organization-wide goals and objectives as it grows. Instead, business units may develop TR practices designed to satisfy their individual needs but conflict with programs implemented by other units.

The challenge in developing a compensation philosophy comes from balancing the diverse conditions faced by the organization as a whole in a way that is consistent with the organizational culture. These conditions can be split into two categories: internal and external.

Internal Conditions

Internal conditions affect an organization's willingness and ability to pay. In some cases, financial constraints prevent an organization from following through with a generous bonus program, for example. Products and services that are cost-sensitive to industry competition and competing priorities within an organization impact its ability to introduce new rewards programs and maintain existing ones.

Another internal consideration with impact on the TR philosophy is how the organizational culture combines with the types of products and services offered by the organization. This combination determines the "pecking order" for certain positions—and is different in every organization. Consciously or unconsciously, organizations identify the jobs that are the most valuable for achieving their goals and objectives. Differentiating jobs is an important aspect of the TR philosophy. For example, implementing an organization-wide incentive program may not be feasible due to cost. In that case, the organization might choose to include jobs with the highest impact on the organization's success in an incentive program while jobs with less impact would be ineligible.

Another internal condition that impacts TR philosophy is organizational structure. Organizations that answer to a parent company or corporate headquarters have additional constraints to consider when making TR decisions, such as the need to conform to the TR philosophy of the parent corporation.

External Conditions

The executive team must decide if the organization's TR programs will lead, meet, or lag the market. If the organization's TR philosophy is to lead the market, it will provide compensation and benefit programs above the market rate. If an organization wants (or finds it necessary for financial reasons) to lag the market, its TR programs will be below the market rate. If an organization wants to compete at a level equivalent to its competitors, it will meet the average market rate. This strategy is a key element in the organization's TR philosophy because it determines the development of salary structures, merit budgets, bonus programs, benefit offerings, and other compensation programs.

Organizational Culture

Organizational culture (discussed in Chapter 7, "Employee and Labor Relations), is rooted in the values and beliefs advocated by an organization's leadership and the ways in which members of the organization behave. It is important that the TR philosophy reflect these values and beliefs to reinforce the culture. The TR philosophy determines whether pay is based on merit/performance (a performance-based culture) or on seniority (an entitlement culture) and how the total compensation package is divided among base salary, variable pay, equity pay, and benefits. To a certain degree, the culture of an organization dictates how the components are allocated in the TR package.

Performance-based philosophy   Organizations with a *performance-based philosophy* use compensation to shape a key component of the corporate culture, employee behavior, by rewarding performance or behavior that moves the organization closer to achievement of the goals established by its leaders.

In a performance-based culture, compensation programs have what is known as line of sight. *Line of sight* occurs when employees know that their performance, good or bad, impacts their pay. This provides an increased consciousness for associating behavior with a reward. If employees have the awareness that their performance impacts their rewards, both monetary and nonmonetary, a high performance culture can be created.

Entitlement philosophy   An *entitlement philosophy* rewards seniority or employee longevity. When pay is based on seniority, performance will be secondary to time with the company or time in a particular job. Rewarding seniority creates loyalty to the company and, ideally, benefits such as pension plans, stock options, and vacation accrual can reinforce the importance of seniority.

An effective TR philosophy complements the organizational culture, provides rewards for those who contribute to the achievement of organizational goals, and addresses internal and external conditions.

Total Rewards Strategy

Most organization leaders have to make choices about how to best use limited resources. A *total rewards strategy* is used to determine how the resources available for rewards programs can be used to best advantage in attracting, motivating, and retaining employees. As organizations grow, the TR strategy can be modified to reflect changing needs. Table 6.2 provides a look at how strategy could change in a growing organization. As sales generate the resources necessary to fund compensation and benefit programs, the strategy evolves to meet the changing needs of the organization. In the early years when cash is tight, the organization lags the competition in compensation and benefits, then meets the competition and adds medical insurance for employees when sales increase. In Year 3 when sales have increased and staffing has doubled, stock options are provided to reward employees while conserving cash. In Year 4, salary increases are possible and additional benefits are added. Sales slow in Year 5, so a low-cost benefit is added. When the company is acquired in Year 6, all employees receive large cash payouts for their options. In Year 7, the new parent company implements a long-term incentive bonus to retain employees and provides a discount for employee stock purchases.

TABLE 6.2   Evolving TR Strategies

Phase	Sales	Employees	TR Strategy
Year 1 (start-up)	$750,000	2	Base salaries lag competition
Year 2	$6,800,000	32	Base salaries meet competition Add medical insurance
Year 3	$10,800,000	63	Add stock options for all employees

TABLE 6.2   Evolving TR Strategies *(continued)*

Phase	Sales	Employees	TR Strategy
Year 4	$18,360,000	70	Salary increases for all employees Add 401(k) Add dental and vision insurance Add bonus opportunity for some employees
Year 5	$20,000,000	70	Add on-site massage therapy
Year 6	$21,300,000	90	Company acquired—all employees receive cash payouts for options
Year 7	$28,700,000	90	Long-term incentive bonuses for all employees based on earnings targets for next two years Stock purchase in parent company at 15 percent discount

These TR strategy changes attract, motivate, and retain employees who are able to achieve organizational goals and objectives.

Chapter 4, "Workforce Planning and Employment," discussed the importance of an employer brand in attracting and retaining employees, and TR strategy is a key element of the brand. Based on the TR philosophy, a carefully crafted TR strategy reinforces the brand. For example, if the brand tells prospective employees that the organization places a high value on teamwork but actually rewards employees for individual contributions, the practice will eventually undermine the teamwork element of the brand.

Let's look now at the compensation options available for TR packages.

Compensation

Deciding how best to compensate employees for the work they do is based on various factors including internal value (the importance of jobs relative to each other), external value (economic factors, such as supply and demand) and the knowledge, skills, and abilities (KSAs) individual employees demonstrate on the job.

Organizations must be aware of a variety of external factors when developing programs and administering compensation including economics, the labor market, competition in the marketplace, and other pressures such as those related to tax and accounting requirements and government legislation and regulations.

Economic factors   The ability of an organization to find qualified employees is affected by a number of economic factors at the local, national, and global levels including economic growth, inflation, interest rates, unemployment, and the comparative cost of living. These factors impact the *cost of labor*, or the cost to attract and retain individuals with the skills needed by the organization to achieve its goals. Organizations recruiting employees with a particular skill set create a competitive environment for individuals with those skills, resulting in an increase in the cost of labor. For example, when two large companies in a metropolitan area are hiring large numbers of experienced manufacturing technicians, the supply of individuals with this skill set is in demand and the availability of qualified individuals decreases. This combination of increased demand and decreased availability raises the competitive compensation rate for this skill set, thereby increasing the cost of labor.

With the increasingly competitive global economy, many industries are constantly assessing how to increase quality, accelerate time to market, and improve productivity. This increased intensity has resulted in a creative approach to organizing and redesigning work which, in turn, affects the skill sets needed by the organization and the cost to employ individuals with those skills.

Labor market   Organizations may need to revise their compensation programs to meet the demands of changing labor markets. The *labor market* is comprised of any sources from which an organization recruits new employees; a single organization may find itself recruiting from several different labor markets depending on the availability of skills for different positions. Ultimately, the combination of supply and demand for a certain skill set in the labor market impacts what the employers competing for those skills must pay to individuals who possess them. For example, during the unprecedented growth of the late 1990s, intense competition for software engineering skills led to upwardly spiraling levels of compensation for individuals who possessed those skills. Because the U.S. labor market was not producing enough college graduates to meet the demand for qualified candidates, the labor market expanded to include candidates from other countries. This resulted in an increase in the annual immigration quota for the year 2000 to meet the demand of U.S.-based companies for employees with these technical skills.

Labor markets vary by region and industry. In urban areas, there is a greater pool of candidates with a wider set of skills from which to select. Because there are more businesses in urban areas competing for this pool of candidates, urban environments may be more competitive, leading to an increase in the cost of labor. As a result, the cost of labor for a single skill set may vary widely between the areas in which an organization operates. To offset these differences, many companies utilize regional pay structures to reflect the market conditions of the different areas in which they have business locations. For example, a company that is headquartered in the southeast may have a different pay structure for their regional offices in New York City and the Silicon Valley in California to reflect the higher cost of labor in those areas.

Over the years, the way people look at pay has changed because of the increased mobility of the workforce, the shift from a manufacturing economy to a knowledge-based economy, and fluctuating economic conditions. During the technology boom of the late '90s, job hopping and generous compensation packages were prevalent. Organizations recruited at a national level and were willing to relocate candidates because the labor market was so competitive. When the technology bubble burst and the unemployment rate increased, organizations were able to recruit for many positions locally, reducing the cost of labor. As the economy heats up again, competition for talented employees will once again lead to increased labor costs. HR professionals must be aware of changing labor market conditions to ensure compensation programs in their organizations achieve the desired objective of maintaining a competitive edge in the labor market.

Market competition   Competition in the marketplace places financial pressure on an organization and challenges its ability to attract and retain qualified employees. Increased competition creates pressure to do everything faster, better, and cheaper. These added pressures place a strain on the employee population. In a climate epitomized by strong competition between organizations accompanied by a decrease in demand, issues related to the financial health of an organization will likely surface. Some of the repercussions of these pressures for employees can include wage freezes, which may result in skipping a merit review process, eliminating promotions, and/or not paying incentives. In a strong economy, increased competition can mean growth for the organization due to increasing demand resulting in increased financial rewards for employees. HR professionals must be aware of the implications of changes in the competitive environment to ensure that the programs they propose are in line with these pressures.

Tax and accounting   The Internal Revenue Service (IRS) affects compensation and benefits issues through its enforcement of federal tax legislation, such as social security and Medicare taxes, pension regulation, and enforcement of rules about some benefit programs (these will be discussed later in this chapter in the "Benefits" section). When an organization wants to make changes to compensation or benefit programs it may want to find out how the IRS will view the changes for tax purposes before it makes them. In that situation, it may be beneficial to request a *private letter ruling* from the IRS before the changes are made. These rulings apply only to the specific taxpayer and circumstances included in the request and are used to find out what the tax implications of a complex or unusual financial transaction will be.

 You can find additional information about IRS requirements, FASB and its requirements, and the SEC at www.irs.gov, www.fasb.org, and www.sec.gov, respectively.

Of course, the major government impact on the TR function comes from legislation that regulates pay and benefit practices. Compensation legislation is discussed in the next section. Benefits legislation is discussed later in the chapter.

Federal Employment Legislation

The federal government first began regulating compensation practices during the Great Depression. Initially, legislation impacted only those private employers who did business with the government, but a few years later the Fair Labor Standards Act expanded coverage to include virtually all employers in the United States. These laws were designed to protect workers from unfair pay practices and other abuses by employers and are administered by the Wage and Hour Division of the Department of Labor, Employment Standards Administration.

Davis Bacon Act (1931)   The Davis Bacon Act was the first federal legislation to regulate minimum wages. This act required that construction contractors and their subcontractors pay at least the prevailing wage for the local area in which they are operating if they receive federal funds. Employers with federal construction contracts of $2,000 or more must adhere to the Davis Bacon Act.

More information and a link to the full text of the Davis-Bacon Act is available at www.dol.gov/esa/programs/dbra.

Walsh Healy Public Contracts Act (1936)   The Walsh Healy Public Contracts Act requires government contractors with contracts exceeding $10,000 (for other than construction work) to pay their employees the prevailing wage for their local area as established by the Secretary of Labor.

More information and a link to the full text of the Walsh-Healey Act is available at. www.dol.gov/compliance/laws/comp-pca.htm.

Service Contract Act (1965)   The Service Contract Act of 1965 requires any federal service contractor with a contract exceeding $2,500 to pay its employees the prevailing wage and fringe benefits for the geographic area in which it operates, provide safe and sanitary working conditions, and notify employees of the minimum allowable wage for each job classification, as well as the equivalent federal employee classification and wage rate for similar jobs.

The Service Contract Act expands the requirements of the Davis Bacon and Walsh Healy Acts to contractors providing services to the federal government, such as garbage removal, custodial services, food and lodging, and the maintenance and operation of electronic equipment. Federal contractors already subject to the requirements of Davis Bacon, Walsh Healy, or laws covering other federal contracts, such as public utility services or transportation of people or freight, are exempt from the Service Contract Act.

More information and a link to the full text of the Service Contract Act is available at www.dol.gov/compliance/laws/comp-sca.htm.

Fair Labor Standards Act (1938)

Enacted in 1938, the Fair Labor Standards Act (FLSA) today remains a major influence on basic compensation issues for businesses in the United States. FLSA regulations apply to workers who are not already covered by another law. For example, railroad and airline employers are subject to wage and hour requirements of the Railway Labor Act so the FLSA does not apply to their employers.

There are two categories of employers subject to the requirements of the FLSA: enterprise and individual. *Enterprise coverage* applies to businesses employing at least two employees with at least $500,000 in annual sales or to hospitals, schools, or government agencies. *Individual coverage* applies to organizations whose daily work involves interstate commerce. The FLSA defines interstate commerce so broadly that it includes those who have regular contact by telephone with out-of-state customers, vendors, or suppliers; on that basis, it covers virtually all employers in the United States.

The FLSA established requirements in five areas relevant to the PHR/SPHR exams:

1. It introduced a minimum wage for all covered employees.

2. It identified the circumstances in which overtime payments are required and set the overtime rate at one and one half times the regular hourly wage.

3. It identified the criteria for determining what jobs are exempt from FLSA requirements.

4. It placed limitations on working conditions for children to protect them from exploitation.

5. It identified the information employers must keep about employees and related payroll transactions.

Minimum Wage

The FLSA sets the federal minimum wage, which at the time of this writing is $5.15 per hour. Some states have set the minimum wage at a higher rate than the federal government; when this is the case, the state requirement supersedes the federal minimum wage. The DOL provides a useful map showing current minimum wage requirements by state at www.dol.gov/esa/minwage/america.htm. Nonexempt employees must be paid at least the minimum wage for all *compensable time*. The FLSA defines compensable time as the time employees work that is "suffered or permitted" by the employer. For example, a nonexempt employee who continues to work on an assignment after the end of the business day to finish a project or make corrections must be paid for that time.

In July 2006, legislation that would have raised the minimum wage to $7.25 per hour over a three-year period was introduced in both houses of Congress. The bills were ultimately defeated because they were tied to a reduction in the estate tax. It is possible that the legislation will be reintroduced, so be sure to check the DOL website for the current minimum wage.

Maximum Hours

The FLSA established 40 hours per week as the maximum for nonexempt employees and requires overtime to be paid for any compensable hours worked in excess of 40.

Overtime

Regulations established by the FLSA require nonexempt employees to be paid *overtime*, defined as one and one half times their regular wage rate, for all compensable time worked that exceeds 40 hours in a work week (also commonly known as *time-and-a-half*).

While double-time, or two times regular pay, is not required by the FLSA, it may be required by some states or may be part of a labor agreement. Candidates for the PHR/SPHR exams must be aware of the difference between the federal requirements that will appear on the test and state requirements or other practices that are more stringent.

While the FLSA does not require payment of overtime for exempt employees, it also does not prohibit overtime payments for them. Employers who choose to compensate exempt employees for hours worked above the regular work week are free to do so without risking the loss of exemption status. As long as overtime payments are in addition to the regular salary, exemption status is not affected. Exempt overtime can be paid at straight time, time and a half, or as a bonus.

Public employers may compensate employees with what is known as compensatory time off, or *comp time*, instead of cash payment for overtime worked. For example, a road maintenance worker employed by a city government may work 20 hours of overtime during a snow storm. Instead of being paid time and a half for the overtime hours, the employee may receive 30 hours of additional paid time off (1.5 times 20 hours) to be used just as paid vacation or sick leave. From time to time, initiatives to expand comp time to private employers are presented in Congress, but at this time, the FLSA does not permit private employers to use comp time.

Overtime calculations are based on time actually worked during the week. For example, in a week with a paid holiday, full time nonexempt employees will actually work 32 hours even though they are paid for 40 hours. If some employees then work 6 hours on Saturday, for a total of 38 actual hours worked during the week, those hours are paid at straight time, not time and a half (unless, of course, a state law or union contract requires otherwise). This requirement also applies when employees use paid vacation or sick leave or some other form of paid time off (PTO).

In order to accurately calculate overtime payments, it is necessary to understand the difference between compensable time—hours that must be paid to nonexempt employees—and noncompensable time. The FLSA defines several situations for which nonexempt employees must be paid, such as the time spent in preparing for or cleaning up after a shift by dressing in or removing protective clothing. Other types of compensable time include the following:

Waiting time   Time spent by nonexempt employees waiting for work is compensable if it meets the FLSA definition of *engaged to wait*, which means that employees have been asked to wait for an assignment. For example, a marketing director may ask an assistant to wait for the conclusion of a meeting in order to prepare a PowerPoint presentation needed for a client meeting early the next morning. If the assistant reads a book while waiting for the meeting to end, that time is still compensable.

Time that is spent by an employee who is *waiting to be engaged* is not compensable. For example, time spent by an employee who arrives at work 15 minutes early and reads the newspaper until the beginning of a shift is not considered to be compensable.

On-call time   Employees who are required to remain at the worksite while waiting for an assignment are entitled to on-call pay. For example, medical interns required to remain at the hospital are entitled to payment for all hours spent at the hospital waiting for patients to arrive. The FLSA does not require employees who are on call away from the worksite to be paid for time they spend waiting to be called. These employees may be required to provide the employer with contact information. If, however, the employer places other constraints on the employee's activities, the time could be considered compensable.

Rest and meal periods   While rest and meal periods are not required by the FLSA, if they are provided, that time is subject to its requirements. Commonly referred to as "breaks," short periods of rest lasting less than 20 minutes are considered compensable time. Meal periods lasting 30 minutes or longer are not compensable time unless the employee is required to continue working while eating. For example, a receptionist who is required to remain at the desk during lunch to answer the telephone must be paid for that time.

Lectures, meetings, and training programs   Nonexempt employees are not required to be paid to attend training events when all four of the following conditions are met: the event must be outside normal work hours, it must be voluntary, it may not be job related, and no other work is performed during the event.

Travel time   There are some situations in which the FLSA requires payment for travel time. Regular commute time is not compensable, but when nonexempt employees are given a one-day assignment at a different location than their regular worksite, the travel time is considered compensable. Nonexempt employees (such as plumbers or electricians) who are required to drive to different worksites to perform their regular duties must also be paid for the driving time between worksites.

When nonexempt employees travel away from their home community for several days, the FLSA considers the travel time during regular work hours as compensable time. The DOL excludes the time spent as a passenger on an airplane, train, boat, bus, or automobile from compensable time calculations.

Exemption Status

The FLSA covers all employees except those identified in the law as *exempt* from the regulations. All other employees are considered *nonexempt* and must be paid in accordance with FLSA requirements.

Positions may be exempt from one or all of the FLSA requirements (minimum wage, overtime, or child labor). For example, police officers and firefighters employed by small departments of less than five employees are exempt from overtime requirements, but not exempt from the minimum wage requirement. On the other hand, newspaper delivery jobs are exempt from the minimum wage, overtime, and child labor requirements.

The determination of exemption status is often misunderstood by both employers and employees. Employers often think that they will save money by designating jobs as exempt and paying incumbent employees a salary. Employees often see the designation of a job as exempt as a measure of status within the company. Neither of these perceptions is accurate, and jobs that do not meet the legal exemption requirements can have costly consequences for employers.

For purposes of the PHR/SPHR exams, candidates should be familiar with exemption requirements for the more commonly used exemptions—those for white collar jobs (executive, administrative, professional, and outside sales) and computer professionals.

In 2004, the DOL revised exemption requirements that had been in effect for decades with the goal of simplifying classification for employers. To assist employers in properly classifying positions, the DOL regulations include exemption tests to determine if a job meets those requirements and is therefore exempt from FLSA regulations.

Salary basis requirement   The DOL defines a salary as a regular, predetermined rate of pay for a weekly or less frequent basis (e.g. biweekly, semimonthly, monthly, and so on). With the exception of outside sales employees, teachers, practicing attorneys, and medical doctors, employees must be paid a minimum salary of $455 per week or $23,660 per year to be classified as exempt. Employees who otherwise qualify for exemption as computer professionals may be paid $455 per week on a salary basis or at an hourly rate of $27.63.

Salary deductions   A key element of the new regulations is the definition of permissible deductions for exempt employees that do not affect exemption status. The DOL defines permissible deductions as:

- Absence for one or more full days for personal reasons other than sickness or disability
- Absence for one or more full days due to sickness or disability if the deduction is made in accordance with a bona fide plan, policy, or practice of providing compensation for salary lost due to illness
- To offset amounts employees receive for jury or witness fees or military pay
- For good-faith penalties imposed for safety rule infractions of major significance
- Good faith, unpaid disciplinary suspensions of one or more full days for infractions of work place conduct rules
- During the initial or terminal weeks of employment when employees work less than a full week
- Unpaid leave under the Family and Medical Leave Act

Employers who have an "actual practice" of improper deductions risk the loss of exemption status for all employees in the same job classification, not just for the affected employee. The loss of exemption status will be effective for the time during which the improper deductions were made.

Actual practice   The DOL looks at a variety of factors to determine whether or not employers have an actual practice of improper deductions from exempt pay. These factors include:

- The number of improper deductions compared to the number of employee infractions warranting deductions
- The time period during which the improper deductions were made
- The number of employees affected
- The geographic location of the affected employees and managers responsible for the deductions

Safe harbor   The DOL provides a safe harbor provision for payroll errors that could affect exemption status. The safe harbor applies if:

1. There is a clearly communicated policy prohibiting improper deductions that includes a complaint mechanism for employees to use.

2. The employer reimburses employees for improper deductions.

3. The employer makes a good faith commitment to comply in the future.

Employers who meet these criteria will not lose exemption status for the affected employees unless they willfully violate the policy by continuing to make improper deductions after receiving employee complaints.

Executive exemption   Employees who meet the salary basis requirement may be exempt as executives if they meet all of the following requirements:

-   They have as their primary duty managing the organization or a business unit.

-   They customarily and regularly direct the work of at least two other full-time employees.

-   They have the authority to hire, fire, promote, and evaluate employees or to provide input regarding those actions that carries particular weight.

Administrative exemption   Employees who meet the salary basis requirement may qualify for the administrative exemption if they meet all of the following requirements:

-   The primary duty is to perform office work directly related to management or general business operations.

-   The primary duty requires discretion and independent judgment on significant matters.

Professional exemption   The DOL identifies two types of professionals who may qualify for exemption.

Learned professional exemption   Employees who meet the salary basis requirement may qualify for exemption as learned professionals if they also meet all of the following criteria:

-   They have advanced knowledge in a field of science or learning acquired through a prolonged course of intellectual instruction.

-   The primary duty requires the use of this advanced knowledge for work that requires the consistent use of discretion and judgment.

Creative professional exemption   Employees who meet the salary basis requirement may qualify for exemption as creative professionals if they also meet all of the following criteria:

-   The primary duty requires invention, imagination, originality, or talent in a recognized field of artistic or creative endeavor.

Computer employee exemption   Employees who meet either the weekly or hourly salary basis requirement may qualify for the computer employee exemption if they perform one of the following jobs:

-   Computer systems analyst
-   Computer programmer

- Software engineer
- Other similarly skilled jobs in the computer field

and if they perform one or more of the following primary duties as part of the job:

1. Apply systems analysis techniques and procedures, including consulting with users, to determine hardware, software or system functional specifications;

2. Design, develop, document, analyze, create, test or modify computer systems or programs, including prototypes, based on and related to user or system design specifications;

3. Design, document, test, create or modify computer programs related to machine operating systems; or

4. A combination of the previously described duties, at a level requiring the same skill.

Outside sales exemption   Unlike the other white collar exemptions, there is no salary requirement for outsides sales personnel. To qualify for this exemption, employees must meet both of the following requirements:

- The primary duty of the position must be making sales or obtaining orders or contracts for services or for the use of facilities for which a consideration will be paid by the client or customer; and
- The employee must be customarily and regularly engaged away from the employer's place of business.

Child Labor

The FLSA states that a child must be at least 16 years old to work in most nonfarm jobs and 18 to work in nonfarm jobs that have been identified as hazardous either in the law or by the Secretary of Labor.

Children 14 and 15 years of age can work in nonfarming, nonmining, and nonhazardous jobs outside of school hours if they work the following hours:

- No more than 3 hours a day or 18 hours in a work week
- No more than 8 hours on a nonschool day or 40 hours in a nonschool work week

During the school year, youths can work between 7:00 AM and 7:00 PM. During the summer months, June 1 through Labor Day, the work day can be extended to 9:00 PM.

Record Keeping

There are two common methods for reporting time worked: *positive time reporting*, in which employees record the actual hours they are at work along with vacation, sick, or other time off, and *exception reporting*, in which only changes to the regular work schedule are recorded, such as vacation, sick, or personal time. While the DOL regulations accept either method, in general, the positive time method is best for nonexempt employees because it leaves no doubt as to actual hours worked by the employee and protects both the employee and the employer if there is ever a question about overtime payments due. Exception reporting is more appropriate for exempt employees because their pay is not based on hours worked.

The FLSA does not prevent employers from tracking the work time of exempt employees. These records may be used for billing customers, reviewing performance, or for other administrative purposes, but they may not be used to reduce pay based on the quality or quantity of work produced. Reducing the salary invalidates the exemption status and subjects the employee to all requirements of the FLSA.

The FLSA requires the maintenance of accurate records by all employers. The information that must be maintained includes:

- Personal information including name, home address, occupation, sex, and date of birth if under 19 years old;
- The hour and day when the work week begins;
- The total hours worked each work day and each work week;
- The total daily straight-time earnings;
- The regular hourly pay rate for any week including overtime;
- Total overtime pay for the work week;
- Deductions and additions to wages;
- Total wages paid each pay period; and
- The pay period dates and payment date.

These FLSA records are usually maintained by the payroll department.

Penalties and Recovery of Back Wages

It is not uncommon for an employer to make an inadvertent error in calculating employee pay. In most cases when that happens, the employer corrects the error as soon as the employee points it out or the employer catches the error in some other way. While distressing for employees, employers who make a good faith effort to rectify the error in a timely manner remain within FLSA requirements.

In other cases, employers intentionally violate FLSA regulations by either paying employees less than the minimum wage, not paying overtime, or misclassifying employees as exempt to avoid overtime costs. These and other employee complaints about wage payments are investigated by state or federal agencies. If the complaints are justified, the employers are required to pay retroactive overtime pay and penalties to the affected employees. The investigation of a complaint by a single employee at an organization can trigger a government audit of the employer's general pay practices and exemption classification of its other employees and may result in additional overtime payments and penalties to other employees if they are found to be misclassified.

Employees whose complaints are verified can recover back wages using one of the four methods the FLSA provides. The least expensive cost to the employer requires payment of the back wages.

1. The Wage and Hour Division of the DOL can supervise the payment of back wages.
2. The DOL can file a lawsuit for the amount of back wages and liquidated damages equal to the back wages.

3. Employees can file private law suits to recover the wages, plus an equal amount of liquidated damages, attorney fees, and court costs.

4. The DOL can file an injunction preventing an employer from unlawfully withholding minimum wage and overtime payments.

There is a two-year statute of limitations for back pay recovery unless the employer willfully violated the FLSA. In those cases, the statute extends to three years. Employers may not terminate or retaliate against employees who file FLSA complaints. Willful violators of the FLSA may face criminal prosecution and be fined up to $10,000; if convicted a second time, the violator may face imprisonment. A civil penalty of up to $1,100 per each violation may be assessed against willful or repeat violators.

More information about FLSA exemption requirements can be viewed at www.dol.gov/esa/regs/compliance/whd/fairpay.

FLSA Amendments

The FLSA has been amended numerous times since 1938, most often to raise the minimum wage to a level consistent with changes in economic conditions.

There are two significant federal amendments that have been added to the FLSA since 1938, the Portal to Portal Act and the Equal Pay Act.

Portal to Portal Act (1947)   The Portal to Portal Act clarified what was considered to be compensable work time and established that employers are not required to pay for employee commute time. This act requires employers to pay nonexempt employees who perform regular work duties before or after their regular hours or for working during their lunch period.

Equal Pay Act (EPA) (1963)   The Equal Pay Act, the first antidiscrimination act to protect women, prohibits discrimination on the basis of sex. Equal pay for equal work applies to jobs with similar working conditions, skill, effort, and responsibilities. The Equal Pay Act applies to employers and employees covered by FLSA and is administered and enforced by the Equal Employment Opportunity Commission (EEOC). The EPA allows differences in pay when they are based on a bona fide seniority system, a merit system, a system that measures quantity or quality of production, or any other system that fairly measures factors other than sex. Prior to the EPA, the comparable worth standard was used by the U.S. government to make compensation decisions. When Congress passed the EPA, it deliberately rejected the comparable worth standard in favor of the equal pay standard.

You can view the text of the EPA at http://www.eeoc.gov/policy/epa.html.

FLSA can be complicated, and compliance is critical to protecting both the organization and the employee population.

Types of Compensation

Compensation comes in many forms. The topic of this section is all forms of direct compensation, from base pay to differentials, variable pay plans, and other types of special incentives. The backbone of a compensation program is base pay, the salary or hourly wage paid to employees for the work they do.

Base Pay

Whether paid as a salary or as an hourly wage, *base pay* is the amount of compensation that the employer and the employee agree will be paid for the performance of particular job duties. Base pay is closely correlated to the company's compensation philosophy as it reflects the internal value of jobs while striving to recognize their external market value.

HR professionals take a variety of factors into consideration when making base pay determinations: the KSAs employees bring to the job, previous earnings, and internal equity are all part of the decision-making process. Once an employee is hired, changes in base pay may be based on various factors, including performance in the job, seniority, or increased skills.

Base pay is typically evaluated on an annual basis, through a merit- or seniority-based process, discussed in more detail later in this section. When employees take on new roles and responsibilities, base pay can increase through the promotion process. Other changes in base pay can occur as result of demotions or changes in job duties.

When determining a new hire's base pay, the length and type of previous experience are key factors to consider. Years of experience in a certain profession, a certain industry, or total experience may be relevant to the job. Type of experience may also be relevant to a certain position. How well the new hire will perform in the job is an unknown variable and will be taken into account once the employee begins work.

The company's compensation philosophy drives the type of compensation program that is used. These are categorized as either performance-based or seniority-based programs.

Performance-based Compensation

Performance-based pay programs, which may include merit increases or promotions, are based on how well individual employees perform against the company's process for measuring performance (as discussed in Chapter 5, "Human Resource Development"). The performance ratings earned by employees determine the eligible range of increase for the review period. Differentiating pay based on performance means that the base salaries of employees in the same classification or salary range may vary from one another. When utilizing a performance-based compensation system, it is important to ensure that accurate records are kept with regard to the reasons for disparity in salaries between employees in the same positions. This documentation will be useful in defending against claims of unfair pay practices should they occur.

Seniority-based Compensation

Organizations that utilize *seniority-based compensation* systems make pay decisions based on the length of time employees have been in a position and on years of related experience. A seniority-based compensation system is representative of an entitlement compensation philosophy, discussed earlier in this chapter.

A good example of seniority-based compensation is an organization with a union representing its workers. In a union context, long-term and short-term compensation decisions are the result of negotiations between the union and the employer. Because of this, they are not necessarily driven by an organization's compensation philosophy. In a union environment, annual increases are typically determined by seniority.

Pay Differentials

Some organizations use pay differentials to encourage employees to perform work that is uncomfortable, out of the ordinary, inconvenient, or hazardous. Pay differentials serve as incentives for employees to work on tough assignments or to be available to respond at inconvenient times. A *pay differential* provides additional pay for work that is considered beyond the minimum requirements of the job. For example, multinational employers who require employees to travel and work in potentially dangerous parts of the world may utilize hazard pay to make those jobs more attractive to employees.

Examples of pay differentials include overtime, shift pay, on-call pay, call-back pay, reporting pay, hazard pay, and geographic pay.

Overtime

While the FLSA only requires payment for overtime exceeding 40 hours in a week, some states have overtime laws that exceed federal requirements, and employees are paid at the more generous state rate. Federal law allows employers to require unlimited overtime as long as employees are paid at the required wage rate. It is not common practice to pay overtime to exempt employees, but doing so is not prohibited by the FLSA; however, doing so by definition requires employees to keep track of their hours. As discussed previously, requiring exempt employees to keep track of their time is not prohibited by the FLSA as long as it does not result in a reduction of their pay based on the quality or quantity of work produced.

It is important for employers to take a leadership position in managing overtime costs. To prevent abuse, it is ideal for overtime work to be approved in advance. Employers may also want to develop a process or policy when scheduling overtime work for large groups of employees, scheduling employees for overtime based on their skill sets, seniority, or shift, depending on the needs of the employer. Overtime is an area that is commonly cut when employers face financial and/or economic challenges.

Shift Pay

The days and hours of a typical work week vary by industry—the most common work schedule is one in which employees work Monday through Friday. A *shift* is any scheduled block of time during the work week when employees perform job-related duties. Shifts have a specific start and end time and are most applicable to nonexempt employees but can also affect exempt employees. There are three commonly recognized shifts: the day shift, with hours from 8 AM to 4 PM; the evening or *swing shift*, with hours from 4 PM to 12 AM; and the *graveyard shift*, with hours from 12 AM to 8 AM. Shift work is necessary in industries with 24-hour operations, such as hospitals, airlines, law enforcement, and some manufacturing operations.

In some cases, employers pay more than what is required by the state or federal government for shifts or other time spent at work, such as paying employees for rest or meal periods.

Compensating employees in excess of FLSA requirements typically reflects common practice in an industry or market segment. Employers may decide to pay for these items in order to maintain a competitive advantage to more effectively attract, motivate, and retain employees.

A *shift premium* is additional compensation provided for employees who work other than the day shift. Shift premiums may be paid as a percentage of base pay or may be factored into the hourly rate. For example, in high-tech manufacturing, it is common to pay a 10 percent shift premium for shifts that overlap 6 PM to midnight and 15 percent for shifts that overlap the midnight to 6 AM time period. While it is most common for nonexempt employees to be paid shift premiums, they may also be paid to exempt employees.

Shift premium calculations can be a little bit tricky. Here's an example: Laura works as a nonexempt manufacturing technician at MonoCorp, working an 8-hour shift, 5 days a week, resulting in a 40-hour work week, making $10 an hour. Laura also works some hours on the second shift, from 4 PM to midnight, Monday through Friday. The second shift at MonoCorp pays a 10 percent shift premium. Table 6.3 illustrates the base pay and overtime costs for Laura's work.

TABLE 6.3   Laura's Schedule—Hours Worked

Day	Shift/Scheduled Hours	Overtime
Monday	8	0
Tuesday	8	2
Wednesday	8	0
Thursday	8	2
Friday	8	2
Total Hours Worked	40	6

As you can see, Laura worked a full 40-hour week and put in 6 hours of overtime. Table 6.4 illustrates Laura's pay based on her $10/hour salary and her 10 percent shift premium.

TABLE 6.4   Laura's Pay Schedule

Category	Hours	Pay
Regular	40	$400
Overtime	6	$90 (1$\frac{1}{2}$ time)

TABLE 6.4   Laura's Pay Schedule   *(continued)*

Category	Hours	Pay
Subtotal	46	$490
Shift Premium @ 10 percent		$9
Total		$499

On-call Pay

While the FLSA establishes minimum requirements for on-call time, employers may decide to provide *on-call pay* that is more generous. Employees who are required to respond to work-related issues on short notice, typically emergencies, and who must be available via pager, telephone, or e-mail, may be paid an hourly or daily premium. In certain professions, being on call is part of the job and on-call premiums are not paid.

Call-back Pay

Some companies may provide *call-back pay* to employees who are called to work before or after their scheduled work week. Nonexempt employees who are called into the facility or who work from home are paid their regular rate of pay and any other applicable premiums.

Reporting Pay

When an employee is called into work and there is no work available, the employer may be required by state law or employment agreements to pay for a minimum number of hours of work. This is called a *reporting premium* and ensures the employee receives compensation for showing up for their regular shift or when called to the worksite.

Hazard Pay

Hazard pay is additional pay for dangerous and/or extremely uncomfortable working conditions. Hazard pay may be needed to attract candidates to jobs that require contact with hazardous elements such as radiation, chemicals, or extreme conditions. Firefighters commonly receive hazard pay, as they deal with extreme conditions and physically demanding duties. Examples of other professions that may receive hazard pay include medical positions that work with infectious diseases, police officers, and federal employees who are posted to assignments in countries that are considered dangerous due to wars and/or active hostilities. Although certain jobs may have risks, they may not provide a hazard pay premium and their compensation is instead reflective of the labor market. The Fair Labor Standards Act does not require hazard pay, but it does require employers who provide hazard pay to factor it into overtime calculations.

Geographic Pay

Organizations utilize *geographic pay* to ensure that employees in different locations are paid at rates competitive in the labor market for specific jobs and locations. Geographic structures are put into place to make sure the employees are paid competitively and aligned with the organization's compensation philosophy. It is common to find nonexempt pay structures that vary by city and/or state due to the local cost of labor.

Exempt structures may be adjusted by region to reflect regional labor markets. Having an exempt salary structure specific to the Northeast, Pacific Northwest, or Southeast may be appropriate for some labor markets. As an example, if a manufacturing organization is headquartered in the Silicon Valley in Northern California and has manufacturing plants in San Francisco, St. Louis, and Boston, it would be appropriate to have a salary structure specific to each location.

Variable Compensation

Increasingly, organizations are designing compensation programs that include individual or group incentives as a significant component of the total compensation package. According to several salary surveys, almost two-thirds of U.S. companies include some sort of variable compensation in the pay packages offered to employees. Known as *variable compensation, incentive pay*, or *pay for performance*, these programs reward employees for individual and/or organizational results. When aligned with the organization's compensation philosophy, this form of compensation can help to shape or change employee behavior or organizational culture by rewarding behaviors that are valued by the organization. An effective variable pay program motivates employees to achieve the objectives by providing line of sight between desired performance and the reward.

Another reason that incentive pay has become a key component of compensation packages is that the broad spreading of merit dollars may not always reinforce performance. Merit budgets have become smaller, on average, which can make it difficult to provide meaningful rewards that differentiate between levels of performance. Providing meaningful rewards to employees through the merit process, given the average merit budget, requires many employees to be passed over for annual merit increases so the dollars can be spent on top performers.

Once an organization determines the type of employee performance or behavior it wants to encourage, an appropriate incentive plan can be selected. Whether the incentive plan is based on individual or group performance, or on some type of special incentive depends on the organization's specific needs.

Individual Incentives

Individual incentives reward employees who achieve set goals and objectives and can be powerful tools for motivating individual performance. Incentives are prospective in that they state specific objectives that need to be achieved over designated periods of time and include payout targets stated either as a percentage of base pay or a flat dollar amount.

There are three critical phases to successful incentive plan programs: the plan design, review process, and communication and implementation.

Plan design   Plan design should be kept simple and make it as easy and convenient as possible for employees to understand and recall performance goals (for instance, an employee or group needs to increase production by 10 percent or decrease defective parts by 5 percent). Complicated incentive plans tend to create confusion and distrust and may not produce the desired results.

Research on incentive programs has found that a minimum bonus target of 10 percent is required to influence and change behavior. Bonus targets of less than 10 percent of base pay may not provide sufficient motivation for employees to put forward the effort or spend the additional time to achieve the plan objectives and as a result may not produce the desired results.

Review process   Typically, bonus review and payment corresponds to the end of the organization's fiscal year. In some cases, incentives may be paid more frequently if employees have a direct influence on revenue generation. As with most compensation programs, the *ability to pay* (the company affordability factor) is critical to any incentive program. Many bonus-based incentive programs define desired financial metrics that must be achieved before incentives are paid.

Communication and implementation   Individual incentive plan objectives are ideally communicated before or at the beginning of the review period. For example, annual, calendar-based plans are usually communicated in January. Targets for incentive plans are commonly part of an offer package but can be modified as needed. When bonus targets are modified, whether they are increased or decreased, great care should be taken in communicating the rationale. Legal counsel and/or local HR representatives should be involved in making these changes to ensure legal compliance with state and local law, particularly in global environments when modifying bonus targets may require new employment contracts.

Communication of an incentive plan program is key to ensuring employees understand the metrics of the plan. As part of a communication strategy, some organizations may choose to create and publish a plan document that describes the incentive program in detail.

Organization or Group Incentives

Organization incentives or *group incentives* have many of the same characteristics as individual incentives. A sure step to a successful organization or group incentive plan is that the plan objectives align with the organization's compensation philosophy. Organization or group incentives are commonly used to increase productivity, foster teamwork, and share financial rewards with employees. There are several types of group incentives, including gainsharing, Improshare, the Scanlon Plan, profit sharing, and employee stock ownership plans (ESOPs). Benefits that are common to all group incentives include increased awareness and commitment to company goals. As the name implies, group incentives are not used to reward individual performance.

Gainsharing   *Gainsharing* programs involve employees and managers in improving the organization's productivity and sharing the benefits of success.

The key components of gainsharing include:

- Employees and management work together to review organizational performance.
- When measurable improvements are achieved, employees and managers share the success.
- The organization and the employees share the financial gains.

Some of the organizational benefits derived from gainsharing include:

- Teamwork, sharing knowledge, and cooperation
- Increased motivation

- Employee focus and commitment to organizational goals
- Greater employee acceptance of new methods, technology, and market changes
- Perceived fairness of pay results in increased productivity at all levels

Improshare   *Improshare* was developed in the 1970s by Mitchell Fein. It is differentiated from other group incentive plans because a key part of the program is the establishment of a baseline for organization productivity and a baseline for productivity costs. The difference between the baseline productivity and the new output is used to calculate the group or organization's performance.

Scanlon Plan   The *Scanlon Plan* is one of the earliest pay for performance plans. In the 1930s, Joseph Scanlon created his plan to increase productivity and decrease costs through employee involvement. Employees receive a portion of cost savings achieved through productivity gains and cost savings. This type of group incentive requires the disclosure of financial information and productivity metrics to employees. Scanlon Plans are administered by committees that are representative of the employee population.

Profit sharing   Very similar to the Scanlon Plan, profit sharing is an incentive-based program that shares company profits. Profit sharing plans are typically qualified plans found across many industries and available to employees at all levels, from individual contributors to senior management. Profit sharing plans distribute pretax dollars to eligible employees, typically based on a percentage of an employee's base salary. Distribution of profit sharing dollars typically occurs annually, after the close of the fiscal year. The set formula for a profit sharing plan defines individual contributions and distributions. It is typical for the plan to have a vesting schedule, described in the plan document. The document details when and how distributions occur and what happens at milestone events, such as employee termination, leave of absence, death, retirement, and so on. Because most profit sharing plans are a form of defined contribution plan, they are covered by regulations required by the Employee Retirement Income Security Act (ERISA). Additional information on those requirements is provided in the "Defined Contribution Plans" section of this chapter.

Employee Stock Ownership Plans   An Employee Stock Ownership Plan (ESOP) is a defined contribution plan that allows employees to own company stock. An employer sets up a tax-deductible trust that accepts tax-deductible contributions made by the company. Employee eligibility can be based on a formula that may include base salary, length of service, or other factors. At the time of termination, retirement, or death, employees are able to receive the vested portion of their ESOP which becomes taxable at the time funds are distributed. Additional information is also provided in the "Defined Contribution Plans" section of this chapter.

Special Incentives

In some cases an organization may decide to provide incentive plans to address specific circumstances. For example, as part of an acquisition, the acquiring company may want to make sure specific executives or other key employees from the company being acquired stay with the new organization long enough to ensure a smooth transition. A financial incentive, often referred to as a retention bonus, is one way to do this. Retention bonuses are generally structured so that the full bonus is paid if the employee remains with the company through a date certain, but the entire amount is forfeited if the employee leaves before that date. Retention bonuses are also used in situations when an organization is closing its doors. Some employees, such as an accounting manager, will be needed to complete final tasks, and a retention bonus can be used to make sure those employees don't accept new jobs until the necessary tasks are completed.

Special incentive plans can also be included as part of executive compensation packages to reward top executives for achieving established financial goals, such as a percentage of increased sales, a predetermined stock price increase, and other performance goals established by a board of directors.

Commissions and Sales Bonuses

Commissions provide incentives to sales employees by paying them a percentage of the sale price for products and services sold to a customer. Commissions may serve as the entire cash compensation package, or they may be used in combination with a base salary. When sales employees receive a base salary, it is usually a portion of their target cash compensation. The incentive or variable component is intended to drive sales objectives. Compensation for sales employees paid on a commission-only basis must meet at least the minimum wage.

An alternative to a commission plan is a sales bonus plan, in which a percentage of base pay compensates the employee for sales targets achieved. The difference between commission and bonus plans is the method of calculation, and this has many implications for the design of sales compensation programs. For example, Joaquim sells new cars and has an annual quota of 100 cars. For every car Joaquim sells over 100, he receives a bonus of 1 percent of his base salary.

When performance targets are clearly communicated, commissions and bonuses are an excellent way to motivate sales employees to perform desired behaviors and achieve desired results.

Bonus Plans

A bonus is additional compensation for performance above and beyond what was expected and is paid in addition to an employee's base salary or hourly rate. Most bonuses are considered discretionary, meaning the bonus is optionally offered and is not based on established objectives. An example of a *bonus plan* is a holiday bonus program that some organizations distribute at the end of the year. Individual bonus amounts and eligibility of employees are discretionary. Another example is a "spot bonus" plan, which provides an immediate reward for outstanding performance. Bonus plans are different from incentive plans because incentives are communicated prior to the start of the project. Bonuses also take the form of performance and referral bonuses, patent awards, employee of the month rewards, and so on.

Traditional Pay Structures

Traditional pay programs have existed relatively unchanged for over 50 years. The way an organization develops pay structures and uses them to administer pay on a day-to-day basis is known as salary administration, compensation administration, or pay administration. Figure 6.1 represents the steps in this process.

FIGURE 6.1   Salary administration

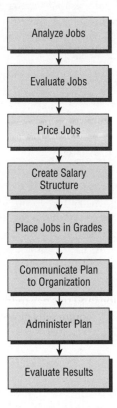

Each step in this process is aligned with the organization's compensation philosophy and a description of the process may be kept in its policy manual. The first step in salary administration is the job analysis process described in Chapter 2. As you recall from that discussion, job analysis is the process used to collect information about jobs and create job descriptions. Accurate job descriptions are an essential element of the job evaluation process.

Compensation administration includes concepts and tools that are used on a regular basis to manage compensation decisions. These include job evaluation, job pricing, comparable worth, designing a pay structure that supports organizational goals, salary surveys, and salary administration.

Job Evaluation

Job evaluation is the process used traditionally to determine the value of jobs relative to each other within the organization. It is an inexact science that attempts to remove subjectivity from the process as much as possible by replacing opinions and preconceived ideas with more objective criteria. Job evaluations are normally conducted when a job is developed, the job duties change, or as part of a routine job evaluation process. HR professionals partner with line management when conducting job evaluations; defined job evaluation methods allow for a repeatable process for this key component of the compensation system.

Job evaluation methods identify and define the compensable factors of each job that are most relevant for the organization. *Compensable factors* are characteristics that define and distinguish jobs from one another. For instance, a junior-level engineer's compensable factors might include:

- Bachelor's Degree in Electrical Engineering
- Two years of industry-related experience
- Two years of experience testing products for quality and reliability

The two methods discussed in this chapter for job evaluation include the ranking method and classification method. Let's discuss each of these in greater detail.

Ranking Method

The *ranking method* requires evaluators to compare the value of jobs to one another. Since this is a subjective method for evaluating jobs, evaluators can be influenced by any preconceptions they may have about different positions or job duties, and this impacts the way in which jobs are ranked. While ranking is a simple and cost-effective method for use in small organizations, it can become a very complicated process in a complex organization with many positions to be evaluated. In this method, it is also difficult to compare unrelated jobs.

Here is an example of the ranking method in action: SkyLine Healthcare uses the ranking method to compare Judy, an administrative assistant, to Leonard, a file clerk. Both Judy and Leonard are administrative-level employees. Judy's job requires higher or more advanced qualifications and experience than Leonard's, therefore Judy's position is ranked higher than Leonard's.

Classification Method

The *classification method* involves identifying key *benchmark positions*. Benchmark positions are jobs that are commonly found across organizations regardless of size or industry, such as accountants or administrative assistants. Once a job is matched to a benchmark position, it may be classified according to value on a vertical scale. Benchmark positions are then associated with a grade on a hierarchical salary structure. Positions with similar characteristics are slotted into the same grade or level, which are identified by a similar level of knowledge, skills, and abilities.

In order to utilize the classification method, companies must determine *internal equity*, or the value of jobs to each other relative to their value to the organization. There are several ways to measure and assess internal equity, including broadbanding (discussed in the section "Nontraditional Pay Structures" later in this chapter), the point factor method, and the HAY system.

Point factor   The *point factor* methodology provides organizations with a system of points that are assigned to the position being evaluated. Based on the total number of points a position receives, a pay grade/range is assigned to the position. Each company that uses this complicated method for evaluating jobs may have abstract or very specific factors that broadly fall under five categories: education, skill, effort, responsibility, and working conditions.

HAY system   In 1943, Edward Hay, founder of The Hay Group, a professional services organization and consulting agency, developed the *HAY system*, a classification method that utilizes a complex point factor system. Jobs are evaluated using three factors: knowledge, problem solving, and accountability. Using the points from the evaluation, the job(s) are matched to a profile.

Job Pricing

Job pricing occurs when a new job is created or an existing job has undergone changes and is a common practice when administering compensation. Many organizations, especially those going through high growth periods, use job pricing to ensure pay is competitive. A four-step process is used to determine the appropriate pay level for a position.

1. Review the job description and understand the level and scope of the job and its required responsibilities and skills.

2. Select a salary survey (salary surveys are discussed in the next section). When selecting a salary survey, it is important to consider the type and number of survey participants. For example, if pricing a job in Austin, Texas, it may not be appropriate to use data from a salary survey if most of the participants are located in Silicon Valley. Most compensation managers like to see several competitors or other premier employers as part of the survey so the data is perceived as valid.

3. Review compensation components, such as base pay, variable pay, equity pay, and so on. At this time it is also important to review a number of matches for a certain position. The more matches, the better, as the data will be more reliable and less likely to be skewed by outliers (jobs that are paid significantly above or below the average).

4. Recommend a salary range. The recommendation should be in alignment with your organization's compensation philosophy of leading, matching, or lagging the market. In addition to a salary range, it may be appropriate to recommend incentive pay or special pay programs.

It is important for HR professionals to review job pricing results with management to validate that the survey positions and data match the job. Once a job is priced, it is appropriate to slot the job into the appropriate pay range and grade.

Salary Surveys

Salary surveys allow organizations to gather compensation and benefits data that reflects current trends in the labor market. Surveys are often provided by professional services vendors or compensation consulting firms. The vendor provides a confidential data collection process by administering the survey and compiling data into a usable, aggregated format. Salary surveys identify trends in labor costs and are integral in ensuring that compensation and benefits programs continue to attract, retain, and motivate employees. There are different types of salary surveys for an organization to consider; these include government, industry, and commissioned surveys.

Government Surveys

A great source for compensation data is the Bureau of Labor Statistics (BLS), an independent national statistical agency whose mission is to collect, analyze, and distribute statistical data. The BLS is a statistical resource to the Department of Labor as well as a source for salary survey data.

Industry Surveys

For certain jobs, it may be important to consider industry-specific salary surveys for greater validity. For example, the high-tech and hospitality industries are two that provide specific surveys for companies in their sectors.

Commissioned Surveys

Many organizations operate in industries with very specific skill requirements that may be difficult to match in readily available surveys, or they may want to find out how their compensation practices stack up against several specific competitors. This information can sometimes be collected by commissioning a third party to conduct a survey, aggregate the data, and supply the results to participating organizations. Commissioning a survey can be very costly and time consuming but may provide the best data for building a competitive salary structure. An alternative way to collect some of this data is to use an informal process where HR professionals exchange information on pay practices with their counterparts in other organizations. Another informal option is to work with a local/regional HR or compensation association and have the group facilitate the collection of pay practice data from participating members.

When conducting or participating in a salary survey, one of the first decisions to be made is which jobs will be priced in the survey. The most accurate data would be obtained by including all of the organization's jobs, but this may not be practical. Generally, including 65 to 70 percent of organization jobs in a survey provides a solid base for use in the creation of a salary structure.

It is very important for HR professionals and employees to keep salary survey data confidential in order to comply with legislative mandates. Over the years, there have been a number of lawsuits against organizations and individuals who share salary data inappropriately.

Salary Structure Development

A salary structure provides an organized, systematic way of identifying base pay for employees in different jobs throughout the organization. The structure is made up of a specified number of salary grades with a range of compensation attached to each. Developing a salary structure requires an analysis of both internal equity and external labor market conditions obtained through the job pricing process. Jobs are grouped using the data collected during job evaluation and pricing. During the pricing process, job descriptions are matched to comparable benchmark positions which provide a market range for each.

In most cases, the market median or 50th percentile is used as the data comparison point for each job. There may be times when an organization decides to use a higher point of comparison for some jobs (highly skilled positions that are in short supply in the labor market, for example) or for all jobs (if the compensation philosophy is to lead the market). Jobs are grouped according to the data points established by the survey. These groups of jobs with similar market levels provide the basis for determining the number of job grades to include in the structure.

Using the grouped jobs as a starting point, midpoints are established for each job grade. The *midpoint progression*, or difference between the midpoints of consecutive grades, is generally narrower for lower grades, increasing for higher grades. Typically, the midpoint progression ranges from 12–15 percent at lower grades to 25 percent at higher grades. Once grades are established, a pay range is developed for each grade.

A *pay range* (also known as a salary range) is the spread between the minimum and maximum pay for the job grade. Ranges can be stated as an hourly amount for workers paid on an hourly basis or a monthly, semimonthly, biweekly or annual amount for salaried workers. The spread of traditional pay ranges is typically narrow and varies depending on level. At entry-level grades, ranges are the narrowest based on the assumption that employees in those grades will gain KSAs and progress to higher job grades. At the highest grades, the spread is quite wide to provide salary progression for highly valued employees who remain in positions for longer periods of time. The spread for entry-level job grades usually begins at 15 percent and can go as high as 25–30 percent for the highest job grades. The spread is calculated based on the midpoint established by the market.

For example, the pay grade for a group of midlevel professional positions might have an 18 percent spread. At a midpoint of $50,000, the minimum would be 82 percent of the midpoint, or $41,000 and the maximum would be 118 percent of the midpoint, or $59,000.

Placing Jobs in Grades

Initially, jobs are placed in pay grades based on the grouping done to develop the grades. If market data was only collected for benchmark positions, the rest of the jobs will need to be placed in the ranges based on internal equity with the benchmark positions. At this point, the placements are reviewed with senior management to make sure that they make sense in the context of the organization's strategic direction. By providing a chart or spreadsheet that shows the jobs in each job grade by business unit, executives can determine if changes are necessary. Once agreement is reached, the structure is finalized and communicated to employees.

 Real World Scenario

Comparable Worth

Comparable worth, or *pay equity*, describes the concept of minimizing pay disparities between jobs traditionally held by women, such as teachers, with higher-paying jobs traditionally held by men, such as carpenters. This concept suggests that jobs with similar duties and responsibilities requiring similar levels of knowledge, skill, and ability should be paid similarly. Comparable worth does not reflect supply and demand in the labor market because it is about the inherent value of the job's content to society. The issue is complex because value is a subjective measure and how jobs are valued often depends on who is valuing them. Those opposed to this concept argue that the price of a particular job in the labor market is based on the supply and demand for its skills, and that social engineering is not an appropriate role for business.

Communicating the Structure

The goal of the communication plan is to have buy-in at all levels of the organization so that the salary structure accomplishes what it needs to do: provide a fair and equitable structure for making pay decisions. To do this, communication about the pay structure takes place at two levels: employee and manager. Employees need to understand how the structure was developed so that they feel fairly compensated for their work and have line of sight from their performance to their compensation. Explaining how the structure was created should alleviate any concerns about political influence or favoritism in the decision-making process.

Managers need to understand how the salary structure can be used to influence behavior in a way that encourages employees to accomplish their goals and objectives. They need to be well versed in how the structure works so that they can effectively explain pay decisions to employees.

Administering the Compensation Plan

Once a pay structure is created, managers must have the tools they need to administer pay for their work units. Compiling a salary administration handbook helps managers throughout the organization apply the system consistently. A typical handbook contains information about the organization's compensation philosophy, the roles played by HR, line managers, and executives in salary administration, basic information about pay increases, and how to determine salaries or wages for new hires. If variable compensation is part of the compensation mix, information about bonus and other incentives is included as well.

Range Placement

Up to this point, the pay structure discussion has concentrated on jobs, not on the employees in the jobs. The focus now turns to using the pay structure to make decisions for individual employees. One of the key factors to consider when making individual pay decisions is the employee's place in the pay range. Table 6.5 illustrates how ranges are used to make individual pay decisions.

TABLE 6.5   Using Ranges in Pay Decisions

Placement	Use For:
Minimum	Entry-level employees Employees new to the organization or the position Employees performing below standard
Midpoint	Fully proficient employees
Maximum	Employees highly valued by the organization based on: • technical skill level • company-specific experience • consistently outstanding level of performance

When changes are made to an existing salary structure, pay for some employees may fall outside the new range. Pay that falls below the minimum of the salary range is referred to as a *green circle* rate of pay. Employees may also be green circled because their experience and/or skills do not meet the requirements of the position or as a result of performance issues. Conversely, *red circle* pay refers to employees whose pay falls above the maximum of the salary range. This may occur when an employee is demoted without a corresponding decrease to base pay, due to a transfer, or for some other unusual circumstance.

Wage Compression

Wage compression occurs when new employees are hired at a rate of pay greater than that earned by incumbent employees for similar skills, education, and experience. These situations are usually the most challenging during high-growth economic times or when there is high demand for certain skill sets. Compression may also occur if the organization's pay practices, merit increases, and promotional budgets are not in line with the market. One way to reduce compression is to provide salary adjustments for the incumbent population.

Compa-ratios

A *compa-ratio* is a simple calculation that compares an employee's base pay to the midpoint of the pay range. This measure is commonly used for comparison against a group of employees and is especially useful when providing recommendations for pay increases for promotions, merit increases, and so on.

Here's the formula for finding the compa-ratio:

Base Salary ÷ Midpoint of Salary Range × 100

An example of a compa-ratio in action is:

120,000 base salary ÷ 100,000 midpoint × 100 = 120 percent

A compa-ratio of 100 percent indicates that the base pay equals the midpoint of the salary range; for example, an HR manager, Elena, is evaluating the new base pay for Joseph, an executive who is about to be promoted to the next pay grade. Elena determines that incumbents in the new position have an average compa-ratio of about 110 percent. Because Joseph is entering this level for the first time, a compa-ratio of less than 100 percent may be most appropriate for him.

Increases to Base Pay

Base pay can be increased for a variety of reasons: cost-of-living adjustments, annual reviews, and promotions are some of the most common.

Cost of Living Adjustments (COLAs)

Cost of living adjustments are generally used during periods of high inflation to reduce the effects of wage compression. These adjustments are used more often in public sector jobs than in the private sector, which generally relies on survey data to maintain compensation at a level that is competitive with the appropriate labor market, whether at the local or national level.

Annual Reviews

Calculating increases for annual reviews can be simple or complex. In a seniority-based compensation system where increases are based on time in the job, the calculation is relatively simple—a fixed dollar amount or percentage of base pay are the most common methods used. In a performance-based system, where *merit increases* are based on demonstrated performance, the calculation is usually more complex.

Merit programs are often aligned with a performance management system. When this is the case, an annual performance rating is the key determining factor for the amount of a merit increase. Reviews may be conducted on an employee's anniversary date or during a *focal review* period when all employees are reviewed at the same time.

A merit matrix is commonly developed by HR as a tool for managers to use in planning increases for their work units. A merit matrix combines a performance rating with the employee's position in the salary range to recommend the amount of increase. The matrix shown in Table 6.6 demonstrates that in addition to differentiating employees based on performance, it is important to also differentiate based on their positions in the salary range. For example, employees at the midpoint of the salary range are considered to be fully trained and able to perform all job duties. Employees on the low end of the salary range who are moving up the learning curve quickly may warrant a higher merit increase than an employee at the midpoint or maximum of the salary range.

TABLE 6.6   Merit Increase Matrix, Assuming 5 Percent Annual Merit Budget

Performance/ Position in Range	Minimum	Midpoint	Maximum
Exceed Expectations	Merit 8–10 percent	Merit 6–8 percent	Merit 3–6 percent
Meet Expectations	Merit 5–7 percent	Merit 4–6 percent	Merit 0 percent
Does Not Meet Expectations	Merit 0 percent	Merit 0 percent	Merit 0 percent

There are several things to consider before giving a merit-based salary increase, including an employee's current standing in the salary range, tenure in the position, and the work of the employee compared to other employees in the same position.

Employee's position in the salary range   Before providing a merit increase, consider the employee's current salary and where it fits into the range for the job title. For example, Tanya and Maurice are both customer service representatives. They perform the same job equally well. Tanya is at the high end of the salary range and Maurice is on the low end. In order to keep Tanya and Maurice within the same range, Maurice, with his salary on the low end, should receive a higher merit increase than Tanya. Typically, the midpoint of the salary range is the ideal place in the salary range for a fully trained, solidly performing employee.

Tenure in position (hire date/date of last promotion)   It is important to consider how long an employee has held a job, the amount of time since the employee's last promotion, and the date of the last increase. For example, an employee who was recently promoted may still be learning a position and not performing all job requirements at a fully qualified level. The impact of this situation on the amount of increase would be to reduce the amount of the award so that the employee's salary is between the low and midpoints of the salary range. This would reflect the level of performance being delivered.

Skill set and performance compared to peer group   Human resource managers and supervisors should be aware of the marketable skills and current compensation of an employee relative to the employee's peers. Employees have access to market data via the Internet and many are very aware of their worth in the marketplace. From the employer's perspective, this places them at risk for recruitment by competitors if they believe their pay is substandard.

In addition to merit matrices, some organizations require managers to use some sort of forced distribution calculation when awarding merit increases. This helps to manage the salary increase budget and forces managers to differentiate between varying levels of performance by employees in their work units. In order to reward outstanding performers with a meaningful increase, increases for poor performers are minimal or nonexistent. This approach is designed to send a message to employees in both categories.

Managers should understand how to connect merit increases to performance and explain it to employees. When the connection between the two is unclear, employees can begin to view merit increases as cost of living adjustments. Connecting the two will help managers to avoid an atmosphere of entitlement in their work units.

Promotions

Promotions occur when employees are moved into new positions with different duties and greater responsibilities, or when they develop a level of experience and skill enabling them to assume added responsibilities in their current positions. Typically, a promotion is accompanied by a change in title and salary level. In organizations with traditional pay structures, this also means an increase in salary grade.

When determining how much of an increase to provide for a promotion, several factors are considered, including how long the employee has been in the current position, how recently a merit increase was awarded, whether the new position is in the same area of the organization or a different one, and where the new salary will place the employee in the new salary range. Generally speaking, an increase of 10–15 percent is provided for promotions.

Nontraditional Pay Structures

In the more than 50 years that traditional pay structures have been utilized, significant changes in the way businesses operate have taken place, and many compensation professionals feel that traditional, job-based systems do not serve current employer needs. Some organizations may strongly consider skill sets as determining factors for pay decisions, awarding increases to employees who possess skills that are critical to the organization's success. Other organizations may provide additional compensation for the development and acquisition of new skills. An example of this can commonly be found in manufacturing environments, where an entry-level operator who acquires additional skills for the position receives additional compensation for these skills. One method for doing this is competency-based compensation.

While traditional pay programs focus on job requirements, a *competency-based compensation* program focuses on employee KSAs, tying individual pay to increased ability. Competency-based pay programs place responsibility for advancement on each employee: the greater the level of competence, the higher level of pay is available. The underlying concept for organizations is that as employees gain competence in their jobs, fewer employees are needed to achieve organizational goals and employers can afford to pay them more.

As the information and knowledge economy replaced the industrial economy, many organizations found the bureaucracy of traditional pay programs an impediment to the rapid changes necessary for responding to changing market conditions. Instead of conducting a job analysis and evaluation so that a new job description can be created each time an employee's duties change, competency-based programs encourage employees to hone their current KSAs and develop new ones, rewarding them for their increased abilities instead of for specific job duties that may change over time.

Competency profiles replace job descriptions in these programs. A competency profile consists of 10–12 key competencies identified by those who know the job requirements best—in most cases that is job incumbents who are performing at a high level. A career ladder then identifies specific levels of competency required at various stages (usually three or four, beginning at entry level and advancing to a senior, highly skilled level). The profile describes the level of fully functional competence expected from employees at each stage and the corresponding pay for each level. Competency profiles include technical skills specific to individual jobs and softer skills identified as valuable to the organization, such as communication skills, teamwork, or adaptability. Since competency-based compensation does not reward performance in the way traditional programs do, they are often combined with cash incentive programs to reward desired performance.

Competency-based compensation is used most effectively with broadband salary ranges to maximize flexibility as employees attain greater levels of competence in current KSAs or add new ones. Range levels are generally tied to the different stages of the competency profile.

This type of pay program communicates organizational focus to employees by selecting competencies that support strategic goals, for example, creating competencies that reward teamwork will help to change the culture from highly competitive to one that is more team based by rewarding those employees who work effectively in teams. Clearly defined competencies help employees to see that increased competence results in higher compensation and places responsibility for advancement on individual employees.

Traditional salary structures do not support the needs of competency-based pay, so some organizations have utilized broadbanding in conjunction with this pay program. *Broadbanding* splits positions in the company into just a few specific pay ranges. Each range includes a variety of jobs. For example, a broadband classification structure may have four levels, such as individual contributor, manager, director, and VP. All jobs in the company fit into one of the four classifications. Broadbanding helps organizations remain flat and facilitates lateral career movement. In contrast, narrow banding or traditional pay classifications have many levels and are organized in a hierarchical and vertical fashion. These structures may not facilitate lateral movement and may create an employee focus on level. One benefit of broadbanding is that it can lead to greater collaboration by limiting employee focus on hierarchical differences between jobs.

Benefits

Employee benefit programs are an integral part of a company's total compensation plan and represent a significant cost to employers. Of equal importance to compensation in the total rewards mix, employee benefit programs are varied and designed to meet specific employee needs. There are two basic types of benefit programs: those that are legally mandated and those that are voluntary. The purpose of this section is to explore how HR professionals, working with senior management, can determine the mix of benefits that will attract and retain the type of employees needed by the organization to achieve its goals.

When most employees think about their benefit packages, they think of medical and dental insurance, vacation and sick leave, and the retirement plan, but employers provide many other benefits that employees often overlook. These include such things as the location of their facilities and the length of the daily commute for employees, "dress down" days, and salaries that are competitive with the industry and profession. These are all factors taken into consideration by candidates when considering whether or not to accept an offer. However, without specific effort on the part of employers, employees are often unaware of the value of the benefits provided for them because they rarely consider these costs when they think about their total income. Decisions about these facets of the employment relationship in each company can either help or hurt the efforts of the organization to attract and retain employees.

There are two main categories of benefits that may be offered, those that are legally mandated and those that are voluntary. Legally mandated benefits are easy. They include social security, Medicare, unemployment insurance, family and medical leave, workers compensation, and COBRA benefit continuation.

The kinds of benefits that organizations may voluntarily provide are significantly more complicated. Table 6.7 provides some examples of the voluntary benefits.

TABLE 6.7   Voluntary Employee Benefits

Types of Benefits	Benefit Details
Deferred compensation	Qualified pension plans
	Nonqualified pension plans
Health and welfare benefits	Medical insurance
	Dental insurance
	Vision insurance
	Life insurance
	AD&D insurance

TABLE 6.7 Voluntary Employee Benefits *(continued)*

Types of Benefits	Benefit Details
	Short-/long-term disability insurance
	Prescription coverage
Work-life balance	Vacation leave
	Sick leave
	Paid time off
	Paid holidays
	Child care
	Fitness
	Elder care
Other voluntary benefits	Employee assistance plans
	Relocation assistance
	Tuition reimbursement
	Flexible spending accounts
	Cafeteria plan
	Adoption assistance
	Section 529 plans
	Commute assistance

Let's begin our discussion with a brief review of the benefits that are mandated by the federal government. Once again, keep in mind that legal requirements in your state may differ in some respects from the federal requirements. For purposes of the PHR/SPHR examinations, you must be familiar with the federal requirements.

Involuntary Benefits

The first involuntary, or legally mandated, employee benefits were introduced as part of President Franklin Delano Roosevelt's (FDR) New Deal programs during the mid-1930s to aid the millions of Americans who lost their jobs and were unable to find work during the Great Depression. Unemployment reached 25 percent at the low point of the Depression in 1933, leaving many families destitute, homeless, and living in shantytowns throughout the nation. In response to this economic crisis, when FDR was elected in 1932, he set about creating protections for American workers to provide a safety net during economic downturns.

Social Security and Medicare

A key piece of the legislation introduced by FDR that has had an enduring impact on employers was the Social Security Act of 1935 (SSA). The SSA introduced *Old Age, Survivors, and Disability Insurance (OASDI)* that is to be paid to qualified workers upon retirement or disability or to their surviving dependents in the event of a worker's death. In addition to these social welfare benefits, the SSA established unemployment insurance (UI) for workers. The constitutionality of both the OASDI and UI was challenged in court, and in 1937, the U.S. Supreme Court ruled that both were valid and constitutional.

In the early 1960s, Presidents John F. Kennedy and Lyndon B. Johnson committed themselves to raising the standard of living among poor and elderly Americans, and in his State of the Union message in 1965, President Johnson presented a report to Congress recommending what became the Medicare program. This program was created by the Social Security Amendments of 1965 and provided medical and hospital insurance benefits for the elderly.

Taxes to support the OASDI and Medicare programs are paid equally by employers and employees. The original legal basis for the tax was contained in the SSA of 1935, but in 1939 Congress repealed the tax sections of the SSA and enacted the Federal Insurance Contributions Act (FICA) to replace them. The FICA transferred responsibility for collecting these taxes to the Internal Revenue Service, which remains the taxing authority for OASDI and the Medicare program. There have been many changes in both the tax rates and the wage base over the years as a result of changes in the economy. The tax rates for both programs are set by statute and reviewed as needed by Congress to ensure the fiscal viability of the programs. The wage base for social security tax is revised each year according to a formula set by statute; there is no maximum wage base for Medicare tax. Table 6.8 shows the changes in the taxable rate over several years.

TABLE 6.8   OASDI and Medicare Tax Rates for 1937–1958 and 1999–2003

Year	OASDI Rate	Maximum Wage	Medicare Rate
1937–49	1.000	$3,000	—
1950	1.500	3,000	—
1951–53	1.500	3,600	—

TABLE 6.8   OASDI and Medicare Tax Rates for 1937–1958 and 1999–2003 *(continued)*

Year	OASDI Rate	Maximum Wage	Medicare Rate
1954	2.000	3,600	—
1955–56	2.000	4,200	—
1957–58	2.250	4,200	—
		data cut	
2004	6.200	87,900	1.450
2005	6.200	90,000	1.450
2006	6.200	94,200	1.450
2007	6.200	97,500	1.450

The complete table of OASDI and Medicare tax rates is available on the DOL website at www.ssa.gov/OACT/ProgData/taxRates.html.

Employees must receive a statement of all taxes withheld from their paychecks each pay period. Depending upon the payroll system that is selected, the deduction for social security tax may be listed on paychecks as OASDI, FICA, or SSA. Deductions for the Medicare tax are listed separately and generally easier to identify as they are usually referred to as Medicare withholdings.

Another change in the OASDI program that affects employers is the change in the age at which workers may receive maximum benefits. This increase in the retirement age was necessary due to improvements in health care and the resulting increased longevity of older Americans. This, combined with the impending retirement of employees born during the Baby Boom (people in the U.S. born between 1946 and 1964 are considered part of the Baby Boom) required Congress to take action to ensure the continued viability of the fund. In 1983, amendments to the SSA gradually increased the age at which workers are eligible to receive full retirement benefits based on a worker's year of birth. Table 6.9, based on data prepared by the Social Security Administration, shows the gradual increase for workers born in different years.

These increases in the retirement age mean that Americans will be part of the work force for longer periods of time. As discussed in Chapter 4, just as employers must consider these demographic changes when forecasting their needs for employees, an aging workforce will also impact benefit programs with increased health care costs.

TABLE 6.9   Changes in Full Retirement Age

Year of Birth	Full Retirement Age
1937 or earlier	65
1938	65 and 2 months
1939	65 and 4 months
1940	65 and 6 months
1941	65 and 8 months
1942	65 and 10 months
1943–1954	66
1955	66 and 2 months
1956	66 and 4 months
1957	66 and 6 months
1958	66 and 8 months
1959	66 and 10 months
1960 and later	67

Unemployment Insurance

Recall that the SSA of 1935 established the first federal unemployment insurance program. The SSA confers upon the states the responsibility for UI administration and distributes federal unemployment insurance funds to them for that purpose. Each state develops its own UI program, so eligibility requirements for *state unemployment insurance (SUI)* vary between states, as do the SUI tax rates. The state rates vary between employers as well, since states increase or decrease the amount of tax based on the number of employees terminated during the year.

When Congress moved taxing authority for OASDI to the IRS in 1939 by creating FICA, it also created the Federal Unemployment Tax Act (FUTA), moving unemployment taxing authority to the IRS as well. The FUTA tax rate is set by statute and is currently 6.2 percent of the first $7,000 earned by each worker during the year. All employers who make their SUI payments on time receive a credit of 5.4 percent toward their FUTA taxes, which means the effective FUTA tax rate is .8 percent for them.

Although unemployment is administered by the states, FUTA mandates minimum requirements for them to follow as described next.

Employers Subject to FUTA

Amendments to FUTA have changed the definition of which employers are subject to FUTA since the law was first enacted. Currently, employers subject to FUTA include those who pay employees who are not farm workers or household workers. Those employers who paid wages of $1,500 or more in any calendar quarter in either 2002 or 2003 or employed one or more employees for a portion of a day in any 20 or more different weeks during the previous year or the current year to date are also subject to FUTA.

Employers of farm workers are subject to FUTA if they paid $20,000 or more to the workers during a calendar quarter in the previous year or the current year to date, or if 10 or more farm workers were employed during some part of a day (not necessarily at the same time) during any 20 or more different weeks during the previous year or the current year to date.

Employers of household workers are subject to FUTA tax if they pay $1,000 or more per calendar quarter to those who work in private homes, college clubs, or chapters of college sororities and fraternities.

Employee Eligibility for Unemployment Benefits

As previously mentioned, each state determines SUI eligibility requirements within its jurisdiction. With few exceptions, unemployment compensation is paid for a maximum of 26 weeks, during which the recipient must be actively pursuing employment. From time to time when the unemployment rate is very high, Congress will submit a bill to the president extending this time period. If the president signs the bill, compensation will be paid, usually for an additional 13 weeks.

Reducing Unemployment Tax Rates

As previously mentioned, employers are able to reduce the SUI tax rate by carefully managing their employment processes. There are a number of ways to do this, beginning with an effective hiring process that appropriately screens candidates to ensure that whoever is selected has all the qualifications for the position. Particularly in very large organizations, establishing a means of communicating between divisions and departments to avoid hiring new employees when employees in other areas of the organization with the necessary skills and experience are being laid off will make better use of the organization's investment in training and reduce the SUI tax rate. An effective performance management program in which employees are regularly coached and counseled about their performance so that they have an opportunity to improve will also reduce the need to terminate employees. When employees must be terminated for cause, maintaining accurate records of the reasons for termination will provide the basis for aggressively fighting claims that are not justified. Finally, the HR department must be diligent in following up with claims for unemployment to ensure that unjustified claims are challenged.

Family Medical Leave Act

In 1993, President Bill Clinton signed the Family Medical Leave Act (FMLA), which was created to assist employees in balancing the needs of their families with the demands of their jobs. In creating the FMLA, Congress intended that employees not have to choose between keeping their jobs and attending to seriously ill family members. FMLA provides three benefits for eligible employees of covered organizations:

1. 12 weeks of unpaid leave within a 12-month period
2. Continuation of health benefits
3. Reinstatement to the same position or an equivalent position at the end of the leave

FMLA applies to all public agencies and schools, regardless of their size and to private employers with 50 or more employees working within a 75-mile radius. The law provides detailed descriptions on how employers determine if these requirements apply to them:

50 or more employees Employers must comply with FMLA when they employ 50 or more employees for each working day during each of 20 or more calendar work weeks in the current or preceding year. The statute does not require the work weeks to be consecutive. Guidelines in FMLA state that the number of employees at a worksite is determined by the number of employees on the payroll.

Employers remain subject to FMLA rules until the number of employees on the payroll is less than 50 for 20 nonconsecutive weeks in the current and preceding calendar year. This means that if employers with 50 employees on the payroll for the first 20 weeks in 2006 reduce the number of employees for the rest of 2006 and remain at the reduced level throughout 2007, they must continue to comply with FMLA through the end of 2007.

Worksites within a 75-mile radius The number of employees at each worksite is based on the employees who report to work at that site, or in the case of outside sales representatives or employees who telecommute, the location from which their work is assigned.

This can either be a single place of business or a group of adjacent locations, such as a business park or campus.

A worksite may also consist of facilities that are not directly connected if they are in reasonable geographic proximity, used for the same purpose, and share the same staff and equipment.

Employees, such as construction workers or truck drivers, who regularly work at sites away from the main business office, are counted as employees at the business site to which they report, the worksite that is their home base, or from where their work is assigned, not from a worksite where they may be temporarily deployed for the duration of a project.

Employees Eligible for FMLA

FMLA also provides guidelines for determining which employees are eligible for leave. This includes employees who:

- Work for an employer who is subject to FMLA as described previously.
- Have been employed by the employer for at least 12 months, which need not be consecutive. Employees who received benefits or other compensation during any part of a week are counted as having been employed for that week.
- Have worked at least 1,250 hours during the 12 months immediately preceding the leave, based on the FLSA standards for determining compensable hours of work. If accurate

time records are not maintained, it is up to the employer to prove that the employee did not meet the requirement; if this is not possible, the law provides that the employee will be presumed to have met the requirement.

The determination of whether or not an employee meets the requirement for 1,250 hours of work within the past 12 months is counted from the date the leave begins. Within two days of notice by an employee of the intent to take an FMLA leave, the employer must confirm that the employee will meet the FMLA requirements as of the first day of the leave or advise the employee when they will become eligible for leave. Once the employer has confirmed an employee's eligibility, it may not be revoked at a later time. Similarly, if an employer neglects to inform an employee that they are ineligible for FMLA leave prior to the date the leave begins, the employee is considered eligible to take the leave and the employer may not deny it at that point.

Key Employee Exception

FMLA leave is available to all employees of covered organizations who meet the FMLA eligibility requirements. FMLA includes a provision that key employees may be denied reinstatement to the position they held or an equivalent position if the employer demonstrates that the reinstatement would cause "substantial and grievous economic injury" to its operations. A key employee is defined by FMLA as a salaried employee among the highest-paid 10 percent of employees at the worksite as defined previously. The law requires that the determination of which employees are the highest paid is calculated by dividing the employee's year-to-date earnings (base salary, premium pay, incentive pay, and bonuses) and dividing the total earnings by the number of weeks worked. Whether or not an employee meets the definition of a key employee is to be determined at the time leave is requested, and the employee must be advised of this status and its implications within a reasonable period of time.

Reasons for FMLA Leave

FMLA presents covered employers with a list of circumstances under which FMLA leave must be provided if requested by an eligible employee:

- The birth of a child and caring for the infant. FMLA leave is available to both fathers and mothers; however, if both parents work for the same employer, the combined total of the leave may not exceed the 12-week total. In addition, the leave must be completed within 12 months of the child's birth.

- Placement of an adopted or foster child with the employee. The same conditions that apply to the birth of a child apply here as well; in this case, the leave must be completed within 12 months of the child's placement.

- To provide care for the employee's spouse, son, daughter, or parent with a serious health condition. For purposes of FMLA leave, a spouse must be recognized as such by the state in which the employee resides.

  A parent can be the biological parent of the employee or one who has legal standing *in loco parentis*, a Latin term that means "in place of the parent" and applies to those who care for a child on a daily basis. In loco parentis does not require either a biological or legal relationship.

A son or daughter may be a biological child, adopted or foster child, stepchild, legal ward, or the child of someone acting in loco parentis. A child must also be under 18 years of age or, if over 18, unable to care for themselves due to a physical or mental disability.

Employers may require those employees requesting FMLA leave to provide reasonable documentation to support the family relationship with the person for whom they will be providing care.

- When an employee is unable to perform the functions of the job due to a serious health condition. According to FMLA, a serious health condition is an illness, injury, impairment, or physical or mental condition that requires:

  - Inpatient care or subsequent treatment related to inpatient care.

  - Continuing treatment by a health care provider due to a period of incapacity of more than three consecutive calendar days. Incapacity refers to an inability to work, attend school, or perform other daily activities as a result of the condition.

  - Incapacity due to pregnancy or prenatal care.

  - Treatment for a serious, chronic health condition.

Types of FMLA Leave

FMLA provides for three types of leave: continuous, reduced leave, and intermittent. A *continuous FMLA leave* is one in which the employee is absent from work for an extended period of time. A *reduced FMLA leave schedule* is one in which the employee's regular work schedule is reduced for a period of time. This can mean a reduction in the hours worked each day or in the number of days worked during the week. An *intermittent FMLA leave* is one in which the employee is absent from work for multiple periods of time due to a single illness or injury. When utilizing intermittent leave, employees must make an effort to schedule the leave to avoid disruption of regular business operations. In addition, the employer may assign an employee requesting intermittent leave to a different position with equivalent pay and benefits in order to meet the employee's needs.

Calculating the FMLA Year

FMLA provides four possible methods for employers to use in calculating the FMLA year, the 12-month period during which employees may use the 12 weeks of leave. A FMLA year can be calculated as:

1. The calendar year

2. Any fixed 12-month period (such as the fiscal year or anniversary date)

3. The 12-month period beginning when a FMLA leave begins

4. A rolling 12-month period that is measured back from the date FMLA is used by an employee

While the most difficult to administer, for many employers the rolling 12-month period is best. Other methods are more open to abuse of FMLA by some employees, resulting in the use of 24 weeks of leave by bridging two 12-month periods, including an employee being on continuous FMLA leave for 24 weeks.

If an employer does not have a stated policy, the FMLA year must be calculated in the way that provides the most benefit to employees. Whichever method is selected, it must be used to calculate FMLA for all employees. Employers who decide to change the way they calculate the FMLA year must provide written notice to employees 60 days in advance of the change and obtain written acknowledgement of the change.

Tracking Reduced and Intermittent FMLA Leave

While keeping track of the amount of FMLA used for a continuous leave is fairly straightforward, ensuring that accurate records of reduced and intermittent FMLA records are maintained can be a bit more difficult. In either case, only the amount of leave used may be deducted from the 12 weeks available to the employee. For example, an employee whose regular work schedule of 40 hours per week is reduced to 20 hours per week would be charged one-half week FMLA leave for each week that they work the reduced schedule.

For intermittent leave, employers may charge for leave in increments of not less than one hour. Employees should provide at least two days notice of the need to utilize the intermittent leave whenever possible.

 Real World Scenario

Ragsdale v. Wolverine

In 2002, the United States Supreme Court affirmed a U.S. District Court decision that affects FMLA leave designations by employers.

Wolverine Worldwide, Inc. is a global footwear manufacturer headquartered in Rockford, Michigan. In 1996, Wolverine granted 30 weeks of medical leave to Tracy Ragsdale after she was diagnosed with a serious illness but did not designate the leave as FMLA. At the end of 30 weeks, Ms. Ragsdale requested a 30-day extension of the leave, which was denied by Wolverine. When she did not return to work, Wolverine terminated her employment. Ms. Ragsdale filed a lawsuit against Wolverine claiming that they had violated a DOL regulation that if "the employer does not designate the leave as a FMLA leave, the leave taken does not count against an employee's FMLA entitlement." The lawsuit claimed that she should be eligible for an additional 12 weeks of leave.

Wolverine filed a motion for summary judgment which was granted by the District Court in a finding that the DOL regulation was invalid because it would have required Wolverine to provide more than 12 weeks of FMLA leave to Ms. Ragsdale in one 12-month period. The Supreme Court upheld the District Court in a 5-4 decision. Writing for the majority, Justice Anthony M. Kennedy stated that the DOL regulation "imposes a high price for a good-faith but erroneous characterization of an absence as non-FMLA leave, and employers like Wolverine might well conclude that the simpler, less generous route is the preferable one."

Ending FMLA Leave

FMLA leave ends when the employee has used the full 12 weeks of leave, the serious illness of the employee or family member ends, or, in some cases, when the family member or the employee dies. When one of these three circumstances occurs, the employee may return to the same or an equivalent position with no loss of benefits. If the employee wishes to continue the leave at that point, the company is under no obligation to grant it, unless there is a company policy in place to provide a longer leave.

FMLA Implications for Employers

FMLA requirements are complex and confusing, particularly when used in conjunction with worker compensation or the ADA. There are some things employers can do to ensure that they comply with its requirements. HR professionals need to ensure that supervisors throughout their organizations are aware of the requirements for FMLA leaves and the consequences for noncompliance.

To start, review current leave practices to ensure that they comply with FMLA requirements and any state laws with more stringent requirements. FMLA leave policies should be included in the employee handbook; new hires should be advised of its availability. It is important for HR professionals to work with supervisors and managers throughout the organization to ensure that they understand the implications for situations that may be subject to FMLA regulations and encourage them to talk to HR about potential FMLA leave situations. HR needs to take an active role in educating the management team about the interaction of FMLA, ADA, and worker compensation requirements. Before an FMLA situation occurs, a documentation procedure and policy should be developed and HR should take an active role in ensuring that all leaves comply with established procedures to avoid possible claims of discriminatory practices. When workers compensation and FMLA leaves occur simultaneously, make sure to advise the employee that the leaves run concurrently.

 NOTE   The complete text of the FMLA can be found online at http://www.dol.gov/esa/whd/fmla/.

Workers compensation laws require employers to assume responsibility for all employee injuries, illnesses, and deaths that are related to employment. These laws are enacted and enforced by the individual states and provide benefits for employees that cover medical and rehabilitation expenses, provide income replacement during periods of disability when employees are unable to work, and pay benefits to their survivors in the event of an employee's death.

The amount of compensation paid is based on actuarial tables that take into account the seriousness of the injury, whether the disability is permanent or temporary, whether it is a full or partial disability (such as the loss of an eye or hand) and the amount of income lost due to the injury. In most cases, employers fund workers compensation obligations by purchasing coverage through private insurance companies or state-sponsored insurance funds. The premiums for workers compensation coverage are based on a percentage of the employer's payroll in various job categories. The percentages are different and depend on previous claim activity in each category. The rate charged for a roofer, for example, is much higher than that for an office worker due to the inherent danger of the job and the number and severity of claims that result.

In some states, companies may self-fund workers compensation programs, meaning that they pay the total costs of any injuries or illnesses when they occur instead of paying insurance premiums. These are known as "nonsubscriber" plans and are rare; generally, self-funded insurance plans only make economic sense for very large organizations with the financial base to support the payment of large claims when they occur.

While increased emphasis on safety programs and training has led to a reduction in the number of nationwide workers compensation claims filed each year, the insurance rates are increasing due largely to increased medical costs. This is most evident in California, where employers saw costs double between 2000 and 2003, but it has also led to state reform of workers compensation programs in Florida, West Virginia, Washington state, and Texas.

Implementing programs aimed at reducing the cost of workers compensation coverage for their organizations is one way HR professionals can show a positive impact on the bottom line. Implementing safety training and injury prevention programs as discussed in Chapter 8, "Risk Management," is one way to reduce job-related injury and illness and prevent claims. The costs of individual claims can be reduced by ensuring the availability of jobs that meet "light duty" medical requirements so that employees are able to return to work earlier, shortening the length of their leave.

Health Benefit Continuation

Prior to 1986, employees who were laid off or resigned their jobs lost any health care benefits that were provided as part of those jobs. While no federal law requires employers to provide health benefits, organizations with 20 or more employees who provide health care benefits are required to continue the benefits for those who leave the company or for their dependents when certain qualifying events occur. An amendment to ERISA, the Consolidated Omnibus Budget Reconciliation Act (COBRA) was signed by President Ronald Reagan in 1986 and requires employers to continue health care coverage at the employee's expense. The requirements placed on employers by the law are discussed later in this chapter.

Voluntary Benefits

Making decisions about the voluntary benefit package that is most appropriate for a particular organization's workforce requires consideration of many factors: demographics, industry standards, local area practices, the financial situation of the company, and the organizational culture among them. There are many possible benefits that an employer can offer as part of a total compensation package, and finding the right mix can significantly affect its ability to attract and retain employees with the desired qualifications.

While the level of cash compensation can be varied to attract candidates at different skill levels, the mix of employee benefits can be used to attract and retain different segments of the employee population. For example, an organization interested in attracting employees who are focused on maintaining a high level of knowledge in their chosen fields may offer a generous educational reimbursement benefit and provide training opportunities as a way of attracting and retaining those employees.

There are a wide variety of benefits for companies to choose from at varying levels of cost. Determining which benefits will best suit a particular organization begins with a needs assessment, which is described in Chapter 2. Whatever benefits are offered, it is crucial that they meet the needs of the type of employees the organization is trying to attract and retain.

As previously described in Table 6.7, voluntary benefits fall into four main categories: deferred compensation, health and welfare benefits, work-life balance benefits, and other benefits. While there are no federal laws requiring employers to provide any of them, there are some federal laws that regulate pensions or benefits when employers choose to include them in total rewards package. Three of these laws have implications in both areas (pension and benefits) and are discussed here. Those laws that apply to only one area (pension or benefits) are discussed in subsequent sections.

Employee Retirement Income Security Act of 1974   ERISA was created by Congress to set standards for private pensions and some group welfare programs such as medical and life insurance. ERISA was amended in 1986 by the Consolidated Omnibus Budget Reconciliation Act (COBRA), which requires businesses with 20 or more employees to provide health plan continuation coverage under certain circumstances. The Health Insurance Portability and Accountability Act (HIPAA) of 1996 was another amendment to ERISA. HIPAA prohibits discrimination based on health status and limits restrictions that can be placed on individuals with pre-existing conditions. The requirements of these laws are discussed in detail in following sections.

Older Worker Benefit Protection Act (OWBPA) of 1990   In 1990, Congress passed the OWBPA in response to a Supreme Court decision that placed limitations on the Age Discrimination in Employment Act (ADEA) discussed in Chapter 4. The OWBPA amends the ADEA to include a prohibition on discrimination against older workers in all employee benefit plans unless any age-based reductions are justified by significant cost considerations. This amendment allows seniority systems as long as they do not require involuntary terminations of employees based on their age and extends ADEA protections to all employee benefits.

The OWBPA also defines the conditions under which employees may waive their rights to make claims under the act. To be acceptable, waivers must include the following components:

- Waiver agreements must be written in a way that can be understood by the average employee.
- Waivers must refer specifically to the rights or claims available under the ADEA.
- Employees may not waive rights or claims for actions that occur subsequent to signing the waiver.
- Employees must receive consideration in exchange for the waiver in addition to anything to which they are already entitled.
- The waiver must advise employees of their right to consult an attorney prior to signing the document.
- In individual cases, employees must be given 21 days to consider the agreement before they are required to sign; when a group of employees is involved, employees age 40 or over must be given 45 days to consider their decision.

- Once the waiver is signed, employees may revoke the agreement within seven days.

- In cases of group terminations (such as a reduction in force or early retirement program), employees must be advised of the eligibility requirements for any exit incentive programs, any time limits for the programs, and a list of the job titles and ages of employees who have been selected or who are eligible for the program.

The federal agency responsible for enforcement of the OWBPA is the EEOC.

Omnibus Budget Reconciliation Act (OBRA) of 1993   The parts of the 1993 OBRA with relevance to HR have to do with changes that were made to employee benefit programs in addition to the cap on executive pay discussed in the "Executive Compensation" section later in this chapter. These changes require that health plans honor court-issued qualified medical child support orders for dependent children of employees. Other changes in this amendment require that group health plans provide coverage for dependent adopted children when those children are placed for adoption in a covered employee's home.

Deferred Compensation

Deferred compensation refers to tax-deferred retirement plans, such as individual retirement accounts (IRAs), 401(k) programs, or traditional employer pension plans. There are some terms that will be used throughout this section with which candidates for the PHR/SPHR examinations should be familiar. The following list defines these terms to aid in your understanding of the discussion of deferred compensation.

Defined benefit   *Defined benefit* plans are traditional pension plans in which the employer provides a specific benefit upon retirement. The funds in these plans are not accounted for individually.

Defined contribution   *Defined contribution* plans are individual plans in which the amount of funds contributed is known, but the amount of the benefit that is eventually paid out is not known because it depends on the investment returns that are earned. The funds are accounted for in individual accounts for each participant.

Nonforfeitable   A *nonforfeitable* claim is one that exists due to a participant's service. Nonforfeitable claims are unconditional and legally enforceable.

Party in interest   A *party in interest* may be a fiduciary, a person or entity providing services to the plan, an employer or employee organization, a person who owns 50 percent or more of the business, relatives of any of the above, or corporations that are involved with the plan in any of these functions.

Plan administrator   The *plan administrator* is the person designated by the plan sponsor to manage the plan.

Plan sponsor   The *plan sponsor* is the entity that establishes the plan. This may be a single employer, a labor organization, or, in the case of a multi-employer plan, a group representing the parties that established the plan.

Qualified plan   A *qualified plan* meets ERISA requirements and provides tax advantages for both employees and employers. To be classified as a qualified plan, a pension plan cannot provide additional benefits for officers, shareholders, executives, supervisors, or other highly compensated employees—all employees in the organization must be eligible for all plan benefits.

Nonqualified plan   A *nonqualified retirement plan* is one in which the benefits exceed the limitations of qualified plans or do not meet other IRS requirements for favorable tax treatment. These plans are not required to include all employees, so may provide additional benefits to officers, shareholders, executives, supervisors, or other highly compensated employees.

Pension benefits for American workers were first provided in the late nineteenth century by business owners who used them to reward long-term employees. Early pension plans were defined benefit plans with all funds being provided by the employers. The payments to retirees were not set aside specifically for retirees but were made from business operating funds. As a result, a company that went out of business was no longer able to make the pension payments and employees did not receive the benefits that had been promised to them. To encourage businesses to provide pension benefits, in 1935 the SSA allowed employers who provided pension plans to deduct the full amount of the payments they made to employees, but there were no laws to govern how the plans operated or to require that the funds to pay pensions be set aside to ensure their availability for retirees. In 1958, Congress made its first attempt to exert some control over private pension plans when it passed the Welfare and Pension Disclosure Act (WPDA) requiring the administrators of health insurance, pension, and supplemental unemployment insurance plans to file descriptions of the plans and annual financial reports with the Department of Labor.

As the number of pension plans provided for employees by American businesses grew, some companies found ways to obtain tax benefits from pension plans while denying benefits to employees. There were no requirements for communicating information to plan participants, so many employees were unaware of eligibility requirements. There was also little oversight of the ways the plans were operated. Vesting schedules were inadequate and many long-term employees found themselves ineligible to receive pension benefits as a result. There were no established standards to ensure the viability of plans to pay promised benefits. The result of this was that many employees found themselves without pensions when they were ready to retire. Furthermore, some businesses set lengthy vesting schedules to obtain tax benefits but terminated long-term employees just before they became vested in the plan.

ERISA Requirements

ERISA requires organizations to file three types of reports: a summary plan description, an annual report, and reports to participants of their benefit rights.

Summary plan description (SPD)   A *summary plan description (SPD)* provides plan participants with information about the provisions, policies, and rules established by the plan and advises them on actions they can take in utilizing the plan. ERISA requires that the SPD include the name and other identifying information about plan sponsors, administrators, and trustees, along with any information related to collective bargaining agreements for the plan participants. The SPD must describe what eligibility requirements must be met for participating in the plan and for receiving benefits, as well as the circumstances under which participants would be disqualified or ineligible for participation or be denied benefits.

Real World Scenario

Retirement Before ERISA

In 1963, almost 7,000 employees of the Studebaker Corporation lost all or most of their pension benefits due to a plant closure in Indiana. More than 4,000 of these employees had served an average of more than 22 years with the company and, at the time of the plant's closure, were an average of 52 years old. The pension fund failed largely because there was no legal precedent requiring organizations to set aside adequate funds with which to pay retirement benefits; plans at that time were still being funded from current operating funds within the Studebaker Corporation.

While the failure of the Studebaker Corporation fund was not unique, the large number of workers deprived of benefits focused national attention on the problem and led eventually to the passage of the Employee Retirement Income Security Act. ERISA replaced the WPDA, increasing the reporting requirements, requiring that pension funds be separated from the operating funds of the business, establishing vesting schedules for plan participants, requiring employers to provide summary plan descriptions of the plans to employees, and setting minimum standards for fund management.

The SPD must also describe the financing source for the plan and the name of the organization providing benefits. Information on the end of the plan year and whether records are maintained on a calendar, plan, or fiscal year basis must be included in the description.

For health and welfare plans, the SPD must describe claim procedures, along with the name of the DOL office that will assist participants and beneficiaries with HIPAA claims. The SPD must also describe what remedies are available when claims are denied.

A new SPD reflecting all changes made must be prepared and distributed every five years unless no changes have occurred. Every ten years, a new SPD must be distributed to participants whether or not changes have occurred.

Annual reports   ERISA requires annual reports to be filed for all employee benefit plans. The reports must include financial statements, the number of employees in the plan, and the names and addresses of the plan fiduciaries. ERISA mandates that any persons compensated by the plan (such as an accountant, for example) during the preceding year be disclosed, along with the amount of compensation paid to each, the nature of the services rendered, and any relationship that exists between these parties and any party in interest to the plan. Information that is provided with regard to plan assets must be certified by the organization that holds the assets, whether it is the plan sponsor, an insurance company, or bank.

The annual reports must be audited by a CPA or other qualified public accountant and any actuarial reports must be prepared by an *enrolled actuary*, who has been licensed jointly by the Department of the Treasury and the Department of Labor, to provide actuarial services for U.S. pension plans.

The DOL is given authority to simplify filing and reporting requirements for plans with less than 100 participants.

Once submitted, annual reports and other documents become public record and are made available in the DOL public document room. The DOL may also use this information to conduct research and analyze data.

Participant benefit rights reports   Participants may request a report of the total benefits accrued on their behalf along with the amount of the benefit that is nonforfeitable. If there are no nonforfeitable amounts accrued at the time the report is requested, the earliest date that benefits will become nonforfeitable must be provided. Participants are entitled to receive the report no more than once per year.

ERISA records must be maintained for six years from the date they were due to be filed with the DOL. In addition to requiring the preparation of these reports, ERISA regulations stipulate that annual reports are to be filed with the DOL within 210 days of the end of the plan year. The DOL may reject reports that are incomplete or that contain qualified opinions from the CPA or actuary. Rejected plans must be resubmitted within 45 days or the DOL can retain a CPA to audit the report on behalf of the participants. ERISA authorizes the DOL to bring civil actions on behalf of plan participants if necessary to resolve any issues.

In addition to the reporting requirements it contains, ERISA sets minimum standards for employee participation, or eligibility requirements, as well as vesting requirements for qualified pension plans.

Employee participation   A *participant* is an employee who has met the eligibility requirements for the plan. The law sets minimum participation requirements as follows:

- When one year of service has been completed or the employee has reached the age of 21, whichever is later, unless the plan provides for 100 percent vesting after two years of service. In that case, the requirement changes to completion of two years of service or reaching age 21, whichever is later.

- Employees may not be excluded from the plan on the basis of age; that is, they may not be excluded because they have reached a specified age.

- When employees have met the minimum service and age requirements, they must become participants no later than the first day of the plan year after they meet the requirement, or six months after the requirements are met, whichever is earlier.

Vesting   Qualified plans must also meet minimum vesting standards. *Vesting* refers to the point at which employees own the contributions their employer has made to the pension plan whether or not they remain employed with the company. The vesting requirements established by ERISA refer only to funds that are contributed by the employer; any funds contributed by plan participants are owned by the employee. Employees are always 100 percent vested in their own money but must earn the right to be vested in the employer's contribution.

Vesting may be immediate or delayed. *Immediate vesting* occurs when employees are 100 percent, or fully, vested as soon as they meet the eligibility requirements of the plan. *Delayed vesting* occurs when participants must wait for a defined period of time prior to becoming fully vested. There are two types of delayed vesting: cliff vesting and graded vesting.

- With *cliff vesting*, participants become 100 percent invested after a specified period of time. ERISA sets the maximum period at five years for qualified plans, which means that participants vest nothing until they have completed the five years of service, after which they are fully vested.

- *Graded vesting*, which is also referred to as *graduated or gradual vesting*, establishes a vesting schedule that provides for partial vesting each year for a specified number of years. A graded vesting schedule in a qualified plan must allow for at least 20 percent vesting after three years and 20 percent per year after that, with participants achieving full vesting after seven years of service. Table 6.10 illustrates a graded vesting schedule that complies with ERISA requirements.

TABLE 6.10 ERISA Graded Vesting Schedule

Years of Service	Percent Vested
3	20 percent
4	40 percent
5	60 percent
6	80 percent
7	100 percent

Benefit accrual requirements   ERISA sets specific requirements for determining how much of an accrued benefit participants are entitled to receive if they leave the company prior to retirement. Plans must account for employee contributions to the plan separately from the funds contributed by the employer since the employees are entitled to all the funds contributed by them to the plan when they leave the company.

Form and payment of benefits   ERISA sets forth specific requirements for the payment of funds when participants either reach retirement age or leave the company. The act also provides guidance for employers to deal with *qualified domestic relations orders (QDRO)*, legal orders issued by state courts or other state agencies to require pension payments to alternate payees. An alternate payee must be a spouse, former spouse, child, or other dependent of a plan participant.

ERISA also defines funding requirements for pension plans and sets standards for those who are responsible for safeguarding the funds until they are paid to employees. Finally, ERISA provides civil and criminal penalties for organizations that violate its provisions.

Funding   An enrolled actuary determines how much money is required to fund the accrued obligations of the plan, and ERISA requires that these funds be maintained in trust accounts separate from business operating funds. These amounts must be deposited on a quarterly basis; the final contribution must be made no later than eight and a half months after the end of the plan year.

Fiduciary responsibility   A *fiduciary* is a person, corporation, or other legal entity that holds property or assets on behalf of, or in trust for the pension fund. ERISA requires fiduciaries to operate pension funds in the best interest of the participants and their beneficiaries and at the lowest possible expense to them. All actions taken with regard to the plan assets must be in accord with the *prudent person standard of care*, a common law concept that requires all actions be undertaken with "the care, skill, prudence, and diligence . . . that a prudent man acting in like capacity" would use, as defined in ERISA itself.

Fiduciaries may be held personally liable for losses to the plan resulting from any breach of fiduciary responsibility that they commit and may be required to make restitution for the losses and be subject to legal action. They are not held liable for breaches of fiduciary responsibility that occur prior to the time they became fiduciaries.

ERISA specifically prohibits transactions between pension plans and parties in interest.

Administration and enforcement   Criminal penalties for willful violations of ERISA include fines of between $5,000 and $100,000 and imprisonment for up to one year. Civil actions may be brought by plan participants or their beneficiaries, fiduciaries, or by the DOL to recover benefits or damages or to force compliance with the law.

Economic Growth and Tax Relief Reconciliation Act of 2001 (EGTRRA)

The EGTRRA made a number of changes to contribution limits, increasing many and allowing for catch-up contributions for employees over 50 years of age. The act provided a schedule of changes through the end of the year 2010, which were extended by Congress in the Pension Protection Act of 2006.

Defined Benefit Plans

As mentioned previously in this chapter, a defined benefit plan is one in which the employer provides a pension for employees based on a formula. The formula looks at two factors: salary and length of service with the company. In most traditional defined benefit plans, the retirement benefit is based on the salary earned during the last five to ten years of earnings, but it may also be based on career average earnings, a flat dollar amount for each year of service, or a unit benefit plan in which the benefit payment is based on a percentage of earnings multiplied by the years of service.

In these plans, the company is committed to pay a specified benefit amount when an employee retires. How much the company must accrue each year may fluctuate based on the return earned on the invested funds. If the funds are invested in high growth investments, the company will need to transfer less cash from its operating funds to the pension trust, but if the return earned on the investment drops, the company may have to play "catch up" with larger than anticipated transfers of cash to maintain the viability of the plan. During the stock market boom of the late 1990s, many companies did not need to transfer large sums to fund their pension accounts, but when the stock market dropped, much of the value of the pension funds was lost. This required larger transfers to be made to maintain availability of the pension funds for employees. In defined benefit plans, employers take the risk for paying out the promised benefit at retirement.

Cash Balance Plans

Cash balance plans (CBPs) have become increasingly popular since they were approved by the IRS in 1985—between 1996 and 2000, the percentage of cash balance plans nationwide grew from 4 to 23 percent. While some companies see them as a hybrid of the defined benefit and defined contribution plans, they are subject to the regulations placed on defined benefit plans. Cash balance plans are less costly for employers: in 1999, IBM revised its defined benefit plan to a CBP and projected savings of $500 billion over ten years as a result of the change.

In a CBP, benefits are determined by using a hypothetical personal pension account (PPA); each month this account is increased by a set rate, for example, 5 percent of the employee's salary. The account also accumulates interest, typically related to the interest rate on Treasury bills.

For employees, the benefit of the cash balance plan is that it is portable: when an employee resigns, the funds may be withdrawn in a lump sum payment, converted to an annuity, or remain in the employer's account and withdrawn at a later time. The downside to these plans is that they significantly reduce pension benefits for older workers when traditional defined benefit plans have been converted to CBPs. A number of lawsuits challenging these plans have been filed, alleging that the plans discriminate against older workers in violation of ERISA. Due to the controversy, the IRS suspended approval of conversions in 1999, pending resolution of the issue in the courts or by Congress. The federal district courts have been split in their rulings on this issue, but a case decided on July 31, 2003, *Cooper v. IBM Personal Pension Plan and IBM Corporation*, in which the Court found that the plan did discriminate, may be the first to reach a federal appeals court for clarification. This case did, in fact reach the 7th Circuit Court of Appeals, which reversed the district court's finding in August 2006.

Defined Contribution Plans

A defined contribution plan relies on contributions from employees and employers to fund individual retirement accounts. In these plans, the amount of the contribution is fixed, but the amount of the benefit available upon retirement can vary based on the type of investments that are made and the returns earned on them. In these plans, the employee takes the risk for having funds available at retirement. There are several types of defined contribution plans:

Profit sharing plans   Also known as *discretionary contributions*, *profit-sharing plans* allow employers to contribute deferred compensation based on a percentage of company earnings each year. A maximum contribution of 25 percent may be made for an individual employee each year. The maximum amount was indexed to inflation in increments of $1,000 beginning in 2003. For 2006, the maximum contribution is the lesser of $44,000 or 25 percent of compensation. When calculating contributions, employers may only use the first $200,000 of an employee's compensation; as of 2003 this amount was indexed to inflation and adjusted annually in increments of $5,000. The percentage of the contribution may vary from year to year, and the company may elect to make no contributions in some years. The maximum tax deduction for contributions that can be taken by the employer is 25 percent of total employee compensation. Because the contributions may vary from year to year, profit sharing plans work well for companies with erratic profit levels.

Money purchase plans   A *money purchase plan* uses a fixed percentage of employee earnings to defer compensation. This type of plan works well for organizations with relatively stable earnings from year to year because the percentage is fixed and, once established, contributions must be made every year. The contribution limits are the same as the limits for profit sharing plans.

Target benefit plans   A *target benefit plan* is a hybrid plan, with similarities to a defined benefit plan and a money purchase plan. Instead of using a fixed percentage of employee salaries to determine annual contribution amounts, the contributions are calculated using actuarial formulas to calculate the amount needed to reach a predetermined benefit amount at retirement. Because this amount takes into consideration the current age of each employee, different amounts will be contributed for employees with equal compensation packages. As with other deferred contribution plans, the amounts are distributed to individual employee accounts, and the contribution limits are the same as the limits for profit sharing plans.

401(k) plans   A common type of deferred compensation is the *401(k) plan*, established by the Revenue Act of 1978. A 401(k) plan allows for contributions from both employees and employers. Employees may defer a part of their pay before taxes up to limits established by the EGTRRA. Employers may make contributions as well; the limits for these are the same as those for profit sharing plans. Plans similar to the 401(k) are available for nonprofit workers (403(b) plans) and for public employees (457 plans). Any earnings or losses that accrue in the account impact on the funds available for retirement and employees are ultimately responsible for ensuring that the funds are properly managed and available for use when they are ready to retire.

One requirement of 401(k) plans is that they may not provide greater benefits to *highly compensated employees (HCEs)* than other employees. An HCE is defined as a plan participant who, during the current or prior year, earned $90,000 or more, owns 5 percent or more of the company and, at the company's discretion, is one of the top paid 20 percent of employees. Each year, an *actual deferral percentage (ADP) test* must be conducted to ensure that the plan is within limits set by IRS regulations. When the ADP test indicates that HCE participants are realizing greater benefits from the plan than non-HCE participants, the company must take action to correct this or lose the tax benefits of the plan. To correct the problem, a company may refund the excess contributions to HCE participants, which will increase their taxable income for the prior year, or they may increase matching contributions to non-HCE employees in order to pass the test. Another option to correct imbalances is to aggregate the plan with other plans sponsored by the employer if available.

Other Laws Impacting Deferred Compensation

Changes to different aspects of deferred compensation laws have been made at various times. They include the following:

Retirement Equity Act (REA) of 1984   The REA lowered age limits for participation and vesting in pension plans. It also required written approval from a spouse if the participant did not want to provide survivor benefits in the plan and placed restrictions on the conditions that could be placed on survivor benefits.

Unemployment Compensation Amendments of 1992   Among other provisions unrelated to pension administration, this act reduced rules for rolling over lump sum distributions of qualified retirement plans into other plans and subjected some distributions to 20 percent income tax withholding.

Small Business Job Protection Act of 1996   In order to relieve the costs of administering qualified plans for small businesses, this act simplified ADP tests for 401(k) plans and redefined highly compensated employees. In addition, it detailed minimum participation requirements and made changes to disclosure requirements for qualified plans.

Pension Protection Act (PPA) of 2006   The main focus of the Pension Protection Act of 2006 was to require employers to fully fund their pension plans to avoid future cash shortfalls in the plans as employees retire. Beginning in 2008, companies have seven years to bring their plans into compliance; for those who don't comply, the act provides a penalty in the form of a 10 percent excise tax. The act also specifies funding notices that must be provided by defined benefit plans.

One of the biggest changes to pension rules made by the PPA was to allow employers to automatically enroll employees in 401(k) plans. Employees who do not want to participate must now opt-out of the plan. Another change is that plan advisers may now provide investment advice to plan participants and their beneficiaries under certain conditions.

Largely as a result of the Enron scandal, the PPA now includes a requirement for defined contribution plans that include employer stock to provide at least three alternative investment options and allow employees to divest themselves of the employer's stock.

When the EGTRRA was enacted, Congress increased contribution limits for 401(k) plans and IRAs, and allowed catch-up contributions for taxpayers over 50 years of age. These changes were set to expire in 2010, but the PPA made them permanent. Employees over age 50 will be able to make 401(k) "catch-up" contributions of $5,000 which may be adjusted for inflation in multiples of $500 each year.

Nonqualified Deferred Compensation

Nonqualified deferred compensation plans are not protected by ERISA and are generally made available only to a limited number of employees at the executive level. Known as "top hat" plans, these benefits provide retirement funds that supplement qualified retirement benefits and are not subject to ERISA discrimination testing requirements. These plans allow highly compensated employees to defer income in excess of limits placed on qualified plans. Two types of nonqualified plans are grantor or rabbi trusts and excess deferral plans.

Grantor or rabbi trusts   Commonly known as *rabbi trusts*, *grantor trusts* are nonqualified deferred compensation plans established to provide retirement income for officers, directors, and highly compensated employees (HCEs). The funds are unsecured and therefore subject to claims made by the organization's creditors. Benefits are taxable as ordinary income at the time they are paid to beneficiaries.

Excess deferral plans   An excess deferral plan allows the organization to make contributions to a nonqualified plan in order to reduce the impact of discrimination testing on highly compensated employees. This is done by making up the difference between what the executive could have contributed to the plan and what was actually allowed due to limits required by the qualified plan.

On October 22, 2004, President George W. Bush signed into law the American Jobs Creation Act (the "Act"). The Act created Section 409A of the Internal Revenue Code of 1986 (the "Code") that provides material changes to the tax treatment of non-qualified deferred compensation plans and arrangements. For a deferral to escape current taxation, it must be subject to a substantial risk of forfeiture and must follow limited deferral and distribution rules, which apply to amounts deferred after December 31, 2004.

Health and Welfare Benefits

Health and welfare benefits have come to be expected by most American workers. The benefits that fall into this category are listed in Table 6.7 at the beginning of this section and are described here in more detail.

Medical insurance   The cost of medical insurance is substantial for employers and employees. The costs can be controlled to a certain extent by the type of plan selected. Some plans to consider include:

Health Maintenance Organizations (HMOs)   HMOs are a type of managed care plan that focuses on preventive care and controlling health costs. HMOs generally utilize a *gatekeeper*, most often the patient's primary care physician (PCP), to determine whether or not patients need to be seen by a specialist.

Preferred Provider Organizations (PPOs)   PPOs utilize a network of health care providers for patient services and do not require patients to be referred by a gatekeeper. Employees who utilize health care services within the network make copayments and must also pay the difference between the fees negotiated by the plan and those charged by the physician.

Point of service plans (POSs)   POS plans include network physicians but allow for referrals outside of the network. When a network physician refers an employee to a care provider outside of the network, payment is covered by the plan, but when the employee sees a care provider outside the POS network, a coinsurance payment is required.

Exclusive Provider Organizations (EPOs)   An EPO consists of a network and includes a hospital. Unlike physicians who participate in a PPO, EPO physicians may only see patients who are part of the EPO. Patients in an EPO may only see health care providers within the network; they receive no reimbursement for health care obtained outside of the network.

Physician Hospital Organizations (PHOs)   In a PHO, physicians join with a hospital and together rely on the PHO structure to develop and market their services and to negotiate and sign contracts. PHOs are unique in that they contract directly with employer organizations to provide services.

Fee-for-service plans (FFSs)   An FFS plan is typically the most expensive to employers and employees because it places no restrictions on the doctors or hospitals available to the patient. These plans require patients to pay for services out-of-pocket and submit claims to be reimbursed for expenses.

In managed care settings, providers often determine premiums based on the costs incurred by the group during the current coverage period. The costs are analyzed by type and premiums for the following period are adjusted based on this *experience rating*. Some organizations have implemented wellness programs to improve the experience rating and lower premiums.

Most carriers use a standard coordination of benefits (COB) process when an employee is also covered as a dependent on another plan, such as that of a spouse or parent. When this occurs, the employee's primary coverage pays according to the plan benefits. The secondary coverage will then pay up to 100 percent of the allowable expenses, including deductibles and copayments for the claim. The secondary plan will only pay up to the amount it would have paid as the primary carrier, so the total insurance payout may still be less than 100 percent of the claim.

Dental insurance   Employers may choose dental insurance plans to provide varying levels of coverage for preventive or restoration work such as fillings; major restoration work, such as bridges; and orthodontia.

Vision insurance   One of the lowest-cost benefits available, vision insurance provides employees with reduced costs for eye examinations and contact lenses or glasses.

Prescription coverage   Even though most medical plans include some form of coverage for prescription drugs, these plans are also offered separately. The cost of the plans is managed by controlling the amount of the required copayment and requiring the use of generic drugs instead of named brands.

Regardless of the health plans selected, it is crucial for HR professionals to manage the cost of the benefits by selecting the most cost-effective method for funding the benefits. There are several choices and determining the most appropriate choice for a particular organization depends upon factors such as the size of the organization and claim history.

One common funding method for smaller organizations is to purchase insurance coverage for the plan. The organization pays premiums for all participants in the plan and the insurance company manages payment to the service provider and manages claims issues. In this funding method, the insurer assumes the risk for any unusual claims that may result in claim costs exceeding premiums received. Insurers keep track of the claim history and adjust premiums in subsequent years to recover any losses.

In larger organizations, it may make sense to self-fund the insurance plan. A *self-funded plan* is one in which the employer creates a claim fund and pays all claims through it. Self-funded plans must conduct annual discrimination tests to ensure that HCEs are not utilizing the plan disproportionately to non-HCEs. In this case, the employer assumes the risk for unusual claims that may exceed the amount budgeted for the plan.

Another option is for organizations to implement a *partially self-funded plan*. These plans utilize *stop-loss insurance* to prevent a single catastrophic claim from devastating the claim fund. The employer agrees upon a preset maximum coverage amount that will be paid from the claim fund for each participant before the insurance company begins to pay the claim.

Self-funded organizations may decide to contract with an insurance company to manage and pay claims, which is known as an *administrative services only (ASO) plan*. A *third-party administrator (TPA)*, which provides claim management services only and is not part of an insurance company, may also be utilized for self-funded plans.

In order to take advantage of economies of scale, smaller employers may form *health purchasing alliances (HPA)* with other employers in the geographic area. The HPA will negotiate and contract for the plans on behalf of all members of the group.

Life insurance   Many insurance companies bundle basic life insurance with medical or dental insurance for a very low rate and offer supplemental insurance for employees who are willing to pay an additional premium for the coverage.

It is important to keep in mind that the IRS views group life insurance in excess of $50,000 as *imputed income* (any indirect compensation paid on behalf of employees) when the premiums are paid by employers. The calculation of imputed income for group life insurance is based on a table provided by the IRS. The table assigns a small amount per month for each $1,000 of coverage that exceeds $50,000 based on an employee's age. The amounts range from $.05 for employees who are 25 years old to $2.06 per month for employees age 70 and older.

A complete discussion of imputed income can be found at www.cpadvantage.com/ articles/imputedincomesection79.aspx?LNC=_4_5.

Accidental Death and Dismemberment Insurance (AD&D) insurance   AD&D insurance can provide insurance for employees and their dependents in the event of an accident that results in the death of the covered person or the loss of a bodily function. AD&D does not pay benefits in the event of death due to an illness.

Short- and long-term disability insurance   Disability insurance protects employees from income loss due to disability caused by illness or accident. Disability protection generally begins with sick leave provided by employers. When employees exhaust their sick leave, they may become eligible for short-term disability insurance, which can be in effect for anywhere between three and six months. Employees who are still disabled when short-term disability ends become eligible for long-term disability coverage, which can last for anywhere from two years until age 65.

Because these benefits are so common, businesses seeking to use them as recruiting and retention tools must find some way to differentiate their plans from those of their competitors. This need must be balanced with the skyrocketing cost of medical insurance and its impact on the bottom line. Companies looking for a way to increase the attractiveness of their benefit packages may want to reduce or eliminate the employee contribution toward premiums for themselves or for their families, or include coverage for domestic partners in the package.

Flexible Spending Accounts

Flexible spending accounts (FSAs) were authorized by the Revenue Act of 1978. Also known as *Section 125 plans*, these plans allow employees to set aside pretax funds for medical expenses they plan to incur during the calendar year. Employees should be cautioned to be conservative when projecting the amounts they plan to spend during the year because any funds left in the FSA after all expenses for the year have been paid will be forfeited and may be used by the employer to pay the administrative costs of the plan. For employers, a downside to offering an FSA account is that employees may be reimbursed for expenses before the funds have been withheld from their paychecks. If they leave the company before the funds have been withheld, they are not required to reimburse the company for those expenses.

Expenses that may be included for reimbursement are the costs of any copayments and deductibles from the medical, dental, or vision care plans and other medical expenses approved by the IRS for reimbursement. Other allowable expenses include acupuncture treatments, orthodontia, psychiatric care, wheelchairs, physical therapy, Braille books and magazines, and a variety of other medical expenses. Some expenses that are not included are memberships to fitness clubs or gyms, elective cosmetic surgery, weight loss programs, and over-the-counter medications. To receive reimbursement, employees must provide receipts for expenditures.

A similar *dependent care account* is authorized by Section 129. Employees may set aside a maximum of $5,000 to be used to care for dependent children or elders. To obtain reimbursement for dependent care expenses, employees must provide an itemized statement of charges from the caregiver. Unlike the flexible spending account for medical expenses, employees may not be reimbursed for expenses in excess of the amounts that have been withheld from their paychecks.

For employees to utilize either of these accounts, they must sign up at the beginning of the year, at the time they join the company, or during an open enrollment period. Once the contribution amount has been set for the year, it may only be changed if a qualifying event occurs, such as the birth, death, or adoption of a dependent or a change in employment status for the employee or the employee's spouse.

The IRS requires employers to conduct annual discrimination tests to ensure that FSA plans are being used consistently. Two types of tests are used to determine this: eligibility tests and utilization tests such as the key employee concentration test or dependent care test. A plan that does not pass the test may lose its favorable tax treatment.

As mentioned previously, there are no federal laws requiring employers to offer any of these benefits; when they are offered, amendments to ERISA, COBRA, HIPAA, and the Mental Health Parity Act (MHPA) of 1996 have implications for administering them.

Cafeteria Plans

Large employers with diverse employee populations may offer cafeteria plans with a wide variety of benefit options in response to various needs of different employee groups. At the beginning of each plan year, employees select the benefits that best meet their needs. For example, a parent with young children may select dependent coverage as a benefit to cover day care needs. Once children no longer need day care, another benefit, such as 401(k) matching may be selected.

COBRA Requirements

As discussed previously in this chapter, COBRA requires employers with 20 or more employees during the previous year who provide group health coverage to continue this coverage for employees when specific qualifying events occur. Employers must notify employees of the availability of COBRA coverage when they enter the plan and again within 30 days of the occurrence of a qualifying event. Table 6.11 shows the qualifying events that trigger COBRA, as well as the length of time coverage must be continued for each event.

TABLE 6.11   COBRA Qualifying Events and Coverage Requirements

Qualifying Event	Length of Coverage
Employee death	36 months
Divorce or legal separation	36 months
Dependent child no longer covered	36 months
Reduction in hours	18 months

TABLE 6.11   COBRA Qualifying Events and Coverage Requirements *(continued)*

Qualifying Event	Length of Coverage
Reduction in hours when disabled*	29 months
Employee termination	18 months
Employee termination when disabled*	29 months
Eligibility for SSA benefits	18 months
Termination for gross misconduct	0 months

*An employee who is disabled within 60 days of a reduction in hours or a termination becomes eligible for an additional 11 months of COBRA coverage.

Employers may charge COBRA participants a maximum of 102 percent of the group premium for coverage and must include them in any open enrollment periods or other changes to the plans. Employers may discontinue COBRA coverage if payments are not received within 30 days of the time they are due.

Employees must notify the employer within 60 days of a divorce, separation, or the loss of a child's dependent status. Employees who fail to provide this notice risk the loss of continued coverage.

HIPAA Requirements

HIPAA prohibits discrimination on the basis of health status as evidenced by an individual's medical condition or history, claims experience, utilization of health care services, disability, or evidence of insurability. It also places limits on health insurance restrictions for *preexisting conditions,* which are defined as conditions for which treatment was given within six months of enrollment in the plan. Insurers may exclude those conditions from coverage for 12 months, or in the case of a late enrollment, for 18 months.

Insurers may only discontinue an employer's group coverage if the employer neglects to pay the premiums, obtained the policy through fraudulent or intentional misrepresentation, or does not comply with material provisions of the plan. Group coverage may also be discontinued if the insurer is no longer offering coverage in the employer's geographic area, if none of the plan participants reside in the plan's network area, or if the employer fails to renew a collective bargaining agreement or fails to comply with its provisions.

In April 2001, the Department of Health and Human Services (HHS) issued privacy regulations that were required by the act. The regulations defined *protected health information (PHI),* patient information that must be kept private, including physical or mental conditions, information about health care given, and payments that have been made. While these regulations were directed at *covered entities* that conduct business electronically, such as health plans, health care providers, and clearinghouses, they have had a significant impact on the way employers handle information related to employee health benefits. Many employers had to redesign forms for open enrollment periods and new hires and update plan documents and company benefit policies to reflect the changes. The regulations impact employers in other ways as well.

Although flexible spending accounts (FSAs) are exempt from other HIPAA requirements, they are considered group health plans for privacy reasons, so employers who sponsor FSAs must comply with the privacy requirements for them.

Employers who are self-insured or who have fully insured group health plans and receive protected health information are required to develop privacy policies that comply with the regulations, appoint a privacy official, and train employees to handle information appropriately.

While the HIPAA regulations do not prevent employees from seeking assistance from HR for claim problems or other issues with the group health plan, they do require employees to provide the insurance provider or TPA with an authorization to release information about the claim to the HR department.

The new regulations include stiff civil and criminal sanctions for violations; civil penalties of $100 per violation and up to $25,000 per person each year can be assessed. There are three levels of criminal penalties:

- A conviction for obtaining or disclosing PHI can result in a fine of up to $50,000 and one year in prison.

- Obtaining PHI under false pretenses can result in fines of up to $100,000 and five years in prison.

- Obtaining or disclosing PHI with the intent of selling, transferring, or using it to obtain commercial advantage or personal gain can be punished with a fine of up to $250,000 and ten years in prison.

Mental Health Parity Act of 1996

The Mental Health Parity Act of 1996 requires insurers to provide the same limits for mental health benefits in their plans as they provide for other health benefits.

Wellness Benefits

Some employers have developed *health and wellness programs* to prevent employee illnesses and to lower health care costs. As with any program proposal, it is essential that HR professionals show management how the company will benefit from the program, how much it will cost, and what return the company can expect on its investment. Being able to provide specific costs and savings that will be realized demonstrates HR's ability to develop programs that serve the long-term strategic goals of the business. Table 6.12 illustrates some of the benefits and costs to be considered in analyzing the advantages of a wellness program to the company.

TABLE 6.12   Costs and Benefits of Wellness Programs

Benefits	Costs
Increased productivity	Program implementation
Reduced turnover	Ongoing vendor costs

TABLE 6.12   Costs and Benefits of Wellness Programs *(continued)*

Benefits	Costs
Reduced medical costs	Administrative costs
Reduced absenteeism	Liability issues
Enhanced ability to attract top-quality employees	
Reduced worker compensation premiums	

A typical wellness program must be voluntary for employees and includes a physical screening to assess each employee's current fitness level and needs, nutrition counseling, education programs for weight control, smoking and stress reduction, and a program of physical exercise. Other programs could include education about substance abuse, back care, and prenatal care, depending on the needs of the particular employee population. Health and wellness programs can take many forms, depending on the budget of the employer, the needs of the employees, and the availability of services in the local area.

Employees like wellness programs because they provide convenient opportunities to make healthful lifestyle choices that result in more energy and less stress, both on and off the job.

The size of the budget available for a wellness program will obviously dictate how the program is offered. Some large companies provide fitness centers on site, along with employee cafeterias that serve healthful meals. Smaller organizations may engage a wellness vendor to provide the educational piece of the program and offer employees subsidies for gym memberships or develop walking or sports programs for employee participation.

An important consideration for programs that include on-site fitness centers will be to analyze the total costs, including not only the space and equipment, but fitness personnel and liability for injuries suffered while an employee is working out. Recommendations for on-site programs should therefore include an assessment of the possible risks involved as part of the cost analysis.

Employee Assistance Programs

An *employee assistance program (EAP)* is sponsored by the employer as a benefit. EAPs are often as advantageous for employers as they are for employees because they are generally a low-cost benefit that provides a resource for employees with problems that are not work related and cannot be solved within the work context. In some cases, this assistance allows people who might not otherwise be able to remain employed to stay on the job.

EAPs offer a variety of counseling services, for problems ranging from alcohol and drug abuse to legal assistance or financial counseling. Many EAPs are a source for outplacement counseling during a layoff, and some programs offer on-site smoking cessation. During times of crisis, for example, the death of an employee or an incident of workplace violence, the EAP can be a resource for employees to come to grips with their feelings so that they are able to continue with their jobs.

EAP services are most often provided through a third party to ensure the confidentiality of employee information, but some employers have in-house programs with counselors on staff. Smaller businesses may join together in a consortium and jointly contract with an EAP to lower costs.

Time-off Programs

Paid time off, like health insurance coverage, is a benefit that employees have come to expect. Over the years, businesses have developed different programs to accommodate various needs for time off, such as those described here.

Vacation pay   Vacation pay is generally earned as employees complete time in the job. Many companies require employees to work a specific period of time, usually three to six months, before they are eligible to use any accumulated vacation pay. Some companies allow employees to accumulate vacation pay year-to-year, while others may have a "use it or lose it" policy, although some state laws prohibit companies from forcing employees to forfeit time off that has been earned. In those cases, companies may decide to pay employees for the leave that would otherwise be forfeited.

Most vacation pay policies require employees to schedule time off in advance and obtain approval from their supervisors before scheduling vacations.

Sick pay   Sick pay is provided for employees to use when they are ill or when they need to care for a sick child or other family member.

Holiday pay   Many companies provide paid holidays for between 6 and 12 holidays each year. These can include New Year's Day, Presidents' Day, Martin Luther King's Birthday, Memorial Day, July 4th, Labor Day, Columbus Day, Veterans Day, Thanksgiving, and Christmas.

Paid time off   Many companies have combined all forms of time off into a single PTO bank that employees can use as they see fit to handle illnesses, personal needs, vacations, and other matters.

Sabbaticals and leaves of absence   In educational institutions, sabbaticals are a long-standing benefit provided for educators in which, after working for a specified period of time, they receive a year off with pay to pursue further education, conduct research, or write books in their field of study. Some private companies have adopted this benefit for long-term employees to encourage professional development.

Jury duty pay   Employers are required to provide time off for employees who are called to jury duty, although most states do not require employees to be paid for this time. Many employers pay the difference between the employee's regular earnings and the amount they are paid for performing jury duty.

Bereavement leave   Most companies allow employees time off with pay to attend funeral services for close relatives.

Parental leave   Some companies provide paid leave for parents of newborns or newly adopted children.

Payroll

In many organizations, payroll is administered as a function of the finance department, but there are others in which it is an HR responsibility. While an in-depth knowledge of payroll systems and administration is not required for the PHR/SPHR exams, candidates should have basic knowledge of payroll activities and how they interact with HR responsibilities.

Payroll Systems

Whether an organization employs one person or hundreds of thousands, a payroll system must meet some basic requirements:

- It must accurately calculate payments due to employees.
- It must accurately calculate statutory and voluntary deductions.
- It must track payroll tax payments owed to federal and state agencies.
- It must provide accurate reports of payroll costs to management.
- It must provide security for payroll information.

In a small organization with a few employees, all of these requirements may be met with a manual system in which a qualified bookkeeper manually calculates the payments due to employees, uses federal and state tax publications to look up withholding information, and prepares checks. This process can be streamlined with the addition of an off-the-shelf accounting software program that makes the calculations, prints the checks, and tracks tax payments owed to federal and state agencies. As organizations grow, manual systems are no longer feasible and may be replaced by a service bureau, which performs the necessary calculations, prints the checks or deposits them electronically, and submits payroll tax payments on behalf of the organization. Very large organizations may develop proprietary software designed to handle their specific needs.

Because payroll systems collect some of the same information that is entered into HRIS systems, HR managers can benefit from systems that are able to interact and share information to reduce or eliminate the double entry of information into separate systems.

Payroll Administration

Administering payroll is one of the most visible functions performed in any organization because it affects every employee from the CEO to the most junior assistant. Not only is it visible to everyone, payroll errors have the potential for profoundly affecting an employee's life, if only until the error can be corrected. Payroll administration is the function in the company that is responsible for calculating employee earnings and deductions and maintaining records of those payments.

Employee Earnings

The payroll department is responsible for preparing employee paychecks and ensuring that earnings are calculated correctly. To calculate nonexempt earnings, the payroll department must know the employee's base pay rate, shift differentials, tips, bonuses, how many hours the employee worked during the pay period, and whether or not any paid leave was used. With this information, the *gross pay*, or earnings before taxes, can be calculated.

To calculate earnings for exempt employees, payroll will need to know the base salary, bonus amounts, and any paid leave that was used during the pay period.

Statutory Deductions

As everyone knows, before you receive your paycheck, various deductions are made from your gross earnings. These deductions include:

- Social security
- Medicare
- Federal income tax
- State income tax
- Unemployment insurance (in some states)
- Disability insurance (in some states)
- Other state and local taxes

These amounts are withheld from employee earnings. As explained earlier in the "Social Security and Medicare" section, employers match the amount of social security and Medicare taxes that are withheld from employees. These amounts, along with the federal income tax withheld, are remitted to the IRS at regular intervals. Failure to remit taxes on time results in substantial penalties for employers. State and local taxes are remitted separately to the appropriate government agency according to payment schedules established by each agency.

At the end of each calendar quarter, reports of gross payroll and withheld taxes are filed with the federal, state, and local taxing authorities. These reports reconcile the amount of tax withheld to the amounts deposited during the quarter. At the end of the year, W-2 forms are prepared for each employee and submitted to federal and state tax agencies.

Voluntary Deductions

There are a number of other deductions that may be made from an employee's paycheck. These include medical, dental, and other health benefit contributions; 401(k) contributions; union dues; and, in some cases, contributions to charities designated by employees.

Involuntary Deductions

From time to time, employers may be required by a court order or tax levy to withhold additional funds from employee paychecks. These withholdings are known as *wage garnishments* and are issued to satisfy a debt owed by the employee. Garnishments may come in the form of a court order (for example an order to pay child support or another debt) or from a government agency such as the Internal Revenue Service or other taxing authority to collect unpaid back taxes. Wage garnishments are not voluntary, and employers have no discretion as to whether or not to honor them.

The Federal Wage Garnishment Law is found in Title III of the Consumer Credit Protection Act (CCPA) of 1968, and applies to all employers and employees. Employers are required to withhold funds from an employee's paycheck and send the money to an entity designated in the court order or levy document.

Title III of the CCPA protects employees in three ways:

1. Prohibits employers from terminating employees whose wages are garnished for any one debt, even if the employer receives multiple garnishment orders for the same debt.

2. Sets limits on the amount that can be garnished in any single week.

3. Defines how disposable earnings are to be calculated for garnishment withholdings.

The law does not protect employees from termination if the employer receives garnishments for more than one debt.

Disposable earnings are what is left in an employee's paycheck after all legally mandated deductions have been made, such as federal and state income tax, social security, state and local taxes, disability insurance, and so on. Title III provides a separate garnishment calculation methods for debt garnishments and child support orders.

Debt garnishment calculations   Title III defines two methods for calculating the maximum weekly garnishment. The first method allows garnishment of up to 25 percent of disposable earnings. The second method is calculated by multiplying the federal minimum wage (currently $5.15 per hour) by 30 ($154.50). The total is subtracted from the disposable earnings. Any disposable earnings that exceed that amount must be sent directly to the recipient designated in the order and not to the employee.

The maximum amount of garnishment allowed is the lesser of those two calculations.

Child support garnishment calculations   Title III allows child support garnishments of up to 50 percent of an employee's disposable earnings if the employee is currently supporting a spouse or child and up to 60 percent if not. If support payments are more than 12 weeks in arrears, wages may be garnished an additional 5 percent. There are no restrictions on child support garnishments.

Depending on the nature of a violation, employers who violate the CCPA may be required to reinstate a terminated employee, pay back wages, and refund any improper garnishments. Whenever possible, the DOL tries to resolve garnishment violations informally. If that is not possible, they may take legal action. Willful violators are subject to criminal prosecution and may be fined up to $1,000 and/or face imprisonment for up to one year.

Record Keeping

The FLSA requires employers to keep accurate records that identify employees, such as their name, address, and social security number, along with their birth date if they are under 19 years of age, their sex, and their occupation. For nonexempt employees, the employer's records must include the work week (for example, 12:00 AM Sunday through 11:59 PM Saturday). Nonexempt records must also include the hours worked each day, total hours for the week, and the basis for payment (the dollars per hour, per week, or per piece), as well as any differentials, bonuses, and other additions described previously. Finally, the records must include the pay period dates, how much straight time and overtime pay was earned for the pay period, any deductions withheld, and the date of payment.

A more recent record keeping and reporting requirement was enacted by Congress to aid state and federal welfare agencies in collecting child support from parents who neglect to pay it, and is known as the Personal Responsibility and Work Opportunity Reconciliation Act of 1996.

Personal Responsibility and Work Opportunity Reconciliation Act of 1996

This legislation requires employers to report all new hires within 20 days of their hire date to the State Department of New Hires. The law requires only that employers forward the W-4 form to the state, but some states have developed their own forms for this purpose. As a side benefit for employers, the new hire reporting database has reduced and prevented fraudulent or erroneous unemployment payments that would otherwise be charged to the employer's unemployment insurance account. The database also cross-checks against workers compensation claims, which has reduced fraud and errors in those programs as well.

As long as employee paychecks are processed accurately and delivered on time, payroll administration is often taken for granted. HR professionals contribute to a smooth payroll process by providing accurate information to those responsible for processing payroll. Working with payroll to establish a procedure that meets the needs of both can ensure employees are paid correctly and on time.

Communicating TR Programs

Taking the time to develop a compensation philosophy, participate in salary surveys, and develop new compensation programs does not help the organization unless results and objectives are clearly communicated to employees and managers.

For example, when rolling out the annual merit increase process, it is important to have timely communications geared toward both management and employee populations. Management typically receives different or additional information designed to facilitate their role as evaluator. Sharing salary survey results with management continues the dialogue about attracting, retaining, and motivating talent through existing or new programs.

Communicating compensation programs or philosophy involves a series of written communications. Updating the company intranet, the employee handbook, or plan documents are a few examples of written information that serve as a great resource for employees.

The compensation philosophy should be known by management and, in some organizations, all employees. Ultimately, communication of compensation programs should be simple, and the alignment to compensation philosophy should be visible.

Metrics—Measuring Results

As mentioned earlier in this chapter, total rewards costs are significant in virtually all organizations. Using metrics to monitor whether or not TR programs are delivering the type of qualified employees needed by the organization is therefore key to demonstrating how HR professionals add value to their organizations.

Business impact measures   One of the clearest indications that there is a problem with the total rewards package in an organization is an increase in turnover and exit interviews that indicate employees are easily able to find higher compensation and/or a richer, more appropriate benefits package with other employers.

Tactical accountability measures   Two metrics that may provide useful information about total rewards programs are:

> **Compensation as a percent of operating expenses**   This metric provides information about the cost of human capital relative to other operating expenses for an organization. The higher the compensation costs are, the more impact HR programs can have on the bottom line. To calculate this metric, divide the total compensation costs (base salary, variable pay, and any deferred compensation) by the total operating expenses.

> **Benefits as a percent of operating expenses**   This measure helps to view increased benefits costs within the context of other expenses. Tracking the cost of benefits relative to other operating expenses can help organizations make decisions about the appropriate mix of benefits to offer as costs rise and to view increasing benefits costs in the context of other expense increases. This metric is calculated by dividing the cost of benefits (health and welfare, paid time off, and so on) by the total operating expenses.

Executive Compensation

Executive compensation packages vary by industry and company culture, some having more pay at risk than others. The majority of executive compensation is in the form of short- and long-term incentives. The size of the executive bonus pool is usually related to the profitability of the company. Key elements of executive compensation are the benefits and *perquisites*. Perquisites, often referred to as "perks," are additional benefits that provide comfort and luxury to the work and/or personal environment, usually intended for senior management and executives. Perks may include generous pension plans and access to a company jet, club memberships, limousine service, and so on. These extra benefits can be very attractive to candidates for executive positions and effective in attracting, retaining, and motivating organization leaders. While these programs create loyalty, they do not pay for performance.

   Recent legislation has impacted executive pay. In 1993, the Omnibus Budget Reconciliation Act (OBRA) modified certain aspects of executive compensation by limiting tax deductions for executives to $1,000,000 annually.

Stock Options

A *stock option* is the right to purchase an employer's stock at a certain price (the strike price), at a future date, within a specified period of time. Options provide an employee with an opportunity to purchase shares, but do not require that the employee do so. The *grant price* or *strike price* of the stock is based on the market price at the time the options are issued. It is common to find stock options vesting to occur over a three- to five-year period as a retention tactic; they can be exercised for up to ten years. Stock options are only valuable if the stock price rises over time, so their value to employees depends upon the company's financial performance. While stock option plans vary between companies, all plans must be operated within parameters established by the SEC (Securities Exchange Commission) and IRS (Internal Revenue Service).

 Real World Scenario

Executive Pay Trends

In June 2003, New York Stock Exchange (NYSE) Chairman Richard Grasso was forced to resign from his position amid outrage over his $140 million pay package (which included $48 million in special benefits). Grasso's situation at the NYSE is just one example of how executive-ranked businesspeople manage to be paid extraordinary amounts of money, even during poor economic times.

According to *USA Today*, the median pay for CEOs of the 100 largest companies in America in 2005 was $17.9 million—a 25 percent increase over 2004. Several CEOs earned more than $100 million in total compensation. The American Federation of Labor-Congress of Industrial Organizations (AFL-CIO), which keeps track of U.S. executive pay trends on their Executive Paywatch website (www.aflcio.org/corporateamerica/paywatch/), calculates the ratio of executive to employee pay for 2005 at 411:1. While this ratio has dropped from the peak of 525:1 in 2000, it has increase tenfold since 1980. Even CEOs who were fired from their positions managed to exit organizations with large payouts—one executive received a payout of $52 million.

It is surprising to some that even in the face of tighter regulation from the SEC as a result of the scandals at Enron, MCI WorldCom, and other major corporations, executive pay continues to rise—this is the second year in a row in which executive pay increased by 25 percent. This trend has been difficult for many employees and shareholders to accept. The debate continues as stockholders scrutinize executive compensation packages and compensation committees of boards of directors take an active role in monitoring those packages.

There are two types of stock options: *incentive stock options (ISO)* and *nonqualified stock options*. The difference between the option types is the tax treatment for the employer and employee.

Incentive or qualified stock options   ISOs are stock options that can be offered only to employees; consultants and external members of the board of directors are not eligible. The tax treatment for ISOs is often favorable for employees because they do not face taxes at the time the stock option is exercised—they do not have income to report until the stock is sold at a later date. When an ISO is sold, however, it is likely that capital gains taxes will be due and subject to the alternative minimum tax under certain conditions. Use of ISOs is not as favorable to employers because the company receives a tax deduction only if certain conditions are met.

Nonqualified options   Nonqualified stock options can be used for consultants and external members of the board of directors as well as for employees. The organization receives a tax deduction when the options are exercised, and employees pay tax on any gain they realize from the sale. Income from the stock is treated as compensation, and when the stock is sold there are further tax implications.

Two other types of stock options employers utilize are restricted stock and phantom stock.

Restricted stock   *Restricted stock* is common stock offered to employees, typically executives or employees who demonstrate outstanding performance. Restricted stocks are actual shares, not the option to buy shares, like stock options. Restricted stock usually follows a vesting schedule designed to reward retention. Employees may be motivated to stay with the organization to realize the full benefit of their restricted stock, which is why employees perceive these as "golden handcuffs" or a financial benefit that will be lost if they leave the organization. In a broad yet creative move to motivate its employees, Microsoft Corporation gave 600 employees restricted stock plans tied to their achievement of certain performance targets.

Phantom stock   *Phantom stock* is used in privately held companies to provide the benefits of employee ownership without granting stock. Organizations use phantom stock to motivate and retain employees without granting equity or sharing ownership in the company. Phantom stock can generate the kind of payoffs that stock options or restricted stock can yield. Executives and outside members of the board of directors are the most common recipients of phantom stock. There is usually a vesting schedule based on length of service and performance (individual or company). Like common stock, phantom stock follows the company's market price movements. There is a valuation formula that determines the value of the stock. When the phantom stock yields a pay-out, the employer is eligible to receive a tax deduction for the amount paid.

Board of Directors/Outside Directors

The board of directors is elected by shareholders to oversee the management of the corporation on behalf of its stockholders. Members of the board can be executives of the organization (known as inside directors) or those who are external to the organization (known as outside directors).

Inside directors receive executive compensation packages, consisting of stock options, benefits, and base pay, to which they are entitled based on their roles as corporate executives. Outside directors commonly receive cash for meeting fees and retainers.

🌐 Real World Scenario

Stock Options and Compensation

Stock options have been a key part of employee compensation packages for decades, but they were never so popular as during the time of the dot-com boom. Employees at all levels, especially in the high-tech sector, were receiving stock options as part of their compensation packages. This was attractive for many reasons to both employers and employees. The alignment between employee, company, and market performance provided the upside opportunity for employees to profit if the company performed well in the stock market. During the dot-com boom, many average employees realized great wealth due to the performance of the stock market. Some employees believed so wholeheartedly in the value of their organizations that they declined salaries in exchange for more stock options. This outlook backfired on employees who lost their jobs and had nothing but worthless paper to show for their hard work.

While stock options are no longer the highlight of a typical offer package, they are still a key component of total compensation. Due to financial abuses committed by companies such as Enron, there is pressure from regulators and legislators to change the way that options are expensed, requiring that the expense be recorded when they are issued instead of when they are exercised. While many companies objected to this change due to concern that it would adversely affect their net profits, those companies that have voluntarily implemented this reporting change have found it has had little effect on their profits. Beginning in 2006, accounting rules require the expensing of all stock options.

Employers enjoyed this too, as there was the potential to create wealth without dipping into the company's cash flow. When the dot-com industry became unable to sustain itself in a declining economy, the opportunity for upside potential with stock options went away.

The requirement for expensing options has opened the door for companies to consider other types of equity grants which have always been expensed. For example, companies are now granting restricted stock more often and driving a close tie between employees and other shareholders by replacing time-based vesting with performance-based vesting.

Total Rewards Budgets

HR professionals work closely with line managers and finance professionals to build the total rewards budget for the organization. Compensation and benefit budgets are projected during the annual budget process and must consider increases to base salaries as well as adjustments to the salary structure to keep salary ranges competitive with current labor market trends. At this time, budgets are also projected for incentive pay programs and planned promotions. Salary surveys are particularly helpful in forecasting changes to base salaries and salary structure adjustments.

Global Considerations

Compensation practices vary widely from country to country, and are often subject to heavy regulation, particularly in Europe. A significant consideration when crafting a compensation package for a third-country national or expatriate is the effect on the tax situations for the employee and employer. In some countries that are highly unionized, unions have significantly more influence on compensation practices than employers find in the United States. Expatriate employees often receive some type of pay differential to ensure that their pay remains equitable with their peers and to equalize tax burdens and living costs unique to their specific situations. Many assignments include housing allowances and COLAs that help them maintain their standard of living while out of the country. It is not uncommon to find total expatriate compensation that exceeds three times base pay. Globally operating organizations make increasing use of home country and third-party nationals to relieve some of this financial pressure.

Summary

Total rewards packages are a key factor in virtually every organization's quest to attract and retain employees who are best qualified to achieve its goals. The total rewards package is guided by the corporate mission and goals and reflects its organization culture. The culture in particular impacts the intrinsic and extrinsic rewards that employees derive from their work. TR philosophy drives the organization's ability to attract, retain, and motivate its employees to meet strategic objectives.

TR philosophy is impacted by internal considerations such as an organization's willingness and ability to provide compensation and benefits that lead, meet, or lag the market. Whether an organization chooses a performance culture that rewards employee contributions or an entitlement culture that rewards employee service impacts the the motivation and loyalty of employees.

The first mandatory benefits, social security, Medicare, and unemployment insurance, were developed to provide a safety net for American workers. More recent benefits such as FMLA and COBRA require employers to more actively participate in and administer programs.

The mix of voluntary benefits chosen by an organization can help them to attract and retain employees with particular characteristics; for example, a generous educational reimbursement benefit will help the company attract employees who are committed to continuous learning and skill development.

Exam Essentials

Be aware of the federal laws that govern compensation and benefit programs.   The Fair Labor Standards Act in 1938 was the first to impact compensation in private businesses in America, and it continues to do so today. ERISA and its amendments, COBRA and HIPAA, require employers who offer benefits to meet minimum standards of fairness in benefit programs. IRS regulations often impact decisions on benefits that are offered.

Understand the provisions of the FLSA. The FLSA established a minimum wage, overtime requirements, laws protecting American children against labor exploitation, criteria for exempt and nonexempt employees, exemption tests to determine exemption status, and payroll record-keeping requirements.

Be aware of the components of compensation. Base pay is the foundation of an employer's compensation program because it reflects the value placed on individual jobs by the organization. Differentials such as overtime and hazard pay motivate employees to spend longer hours at work or to accept assignments that may be unpleasant or hazardous. Incentive pay motivates and rewards employees when they achieve corporate goals.

Understand the job evaluation process. Job evaluation is an objective mechanism used to determine the worth of different jobs to the company. Compensable factors distinguish jobs from each other and are used in determining their value to the organization.

Understand the purpose of salary surveys and how they are conducted. Salary surveys are used to determine current market trends and competition for different skills and knowledge and assist the employer in setting pay levels that lead, meet, or lag the market. Surveys are conducted by gathering information about specific jobs in a large number of companies in an industry, profession, or geographic area and summarizing it by job.

Understand how HR interacts with payroll systems. Whether HR interacts with or administers payroll, HR professionals are involved in ensuring that changes to employee pay and deductions are accurate.

Be able to communicate the total rewards program to employees. An effective communication program informs employees about the total rewards package so that they are able to take advantage of benefits that are offered and have an understanding of the full cost to the employer of providing the different programs.

Be aware of the wide variety of benefits that are available. With an awareness of the various and sometimes unusual benefits that are available, employers are able to develop a benefit mix that meets the needs of employees at the lowest cost to net profits.

Be aware of mandatory benefits. Mandatory employee benefits are determined by Congress and affect employers with varying minimum numbers of employees. Social security, Medicare, unemployment insurance, FMLA leave, and COBRA continuation benefits are required by statute.

Understand how voluntary benefits influence employees. Voluntary benefits fall into four categories: deferred compensation, health and welfare, work-life balance, and other benefits. Some benefits such as medical insurance and paid time off have come to be expected by employees, while others will attract and retain different types of employees with different needs.

Be aware of FMLA leave requirements. FMLA requires unpaid leave be provided by companies with 50 or more employees within 75 miles of the worksite. Employees who meet the eligibility requirements are entitled to leave for the birth or adoption of a child or a serious illness of an immediate family member or themselves.

Key Terms

Before you take the exam, be certain you are familiar with the following terms:

401(k) plan

ability to pay

actual deferral percentage test (ADP)

administrative services only (ASO) plan

base pay

benchmark positions

bonus plan

broadbanding

call-back pay

cash balance plans

classification method

cliff vesting

commissions

comp time

comparable worth

compa-ratio

compensable factors

compensable time

competency-based compensation

continuous FMLA leave

cost of labor

covered entities

defined benefit

defined contribution

delayed vesting

dependent care account

internal equity

intrinsic reward

job pricing

labor market

line of sight

midpoint progression

money purchase plan

nonexempt

nonforfeitable

nonqualified retirement plan

nonqualified stock options

Old Age, Survivors, and Disability Insurance (OASDI)

on-call pay

organization incentives

overtime

partially self-funded plan

participant

party in interest

pay differential

pay equity

pay for performance

pay range

performance-based pay

performance-based philosophy

perquisites

phantom stock

direct compensation

discretionary contributions

disposable earnings

employee assistance program (EAP)

engaged to wait

enrolled actuary

enterprise coverage

entitlement philosophy

exception reporting
experience rating

exempt

extrinsic reward

fiduciary

Financial Accounting Standards Board
(FASB)

flexible spending accounts (FSAs)

focal review

gainsharing

gatekeeper

geographic pay

graded vesting

graduated or gradual vesting

grant price

grantor trusts

graveyard shift

green circle

gross pay

group incentives

HAY system

plan administrator

plan sponsor

point factor

positive time reporting

preexisting conditions

private letter ruling

profit-sharing plans

protected health information (PHI)

prudent person standard of care

qualified domestic relations orders (QDRO)

qualified plan

rabbi trusts

ranking method

red circle

reduced FMLA leave schedule

reporting premium

restricted stock

salary surveys

Scanlon Plan

Section 125 plans

self-funded plan

seniority-based compensation

shift

shift premium

state unemployment insurance (SUI)

stock option

stop-loss insurance

hazard pay

health and wellness programs

health purchasing alliances (HPA)

highly compensated employees (HCEs)

immediate vesting

Improshare

imputed income

in loco parentis

incentive pay

incentive stock options (ISO)

merit increases

indirect compensation

individual coverage

intermittent FMLA leave

strike price

summary plan description (SPD)

swing shift

target benefit plan

third-party administrator (TPA)

time-and-a-half

total rewards philosophy

total rewards strategy

variable compensation

vesting

wage compression

wage garnishments

waiting to be engaged

Review Questions

1. The Federal Insurance Contributions Act requires employers to
   - **A.** Contribute to a defined benefit plan.
   - **B.** Contribute to a deferred compensation plan.
   - **C.** Withhold social security tax from pay.
   - **D.** Provide health insurance for all employees.

2. Employers are required to provide a portable retirement plan to employees based on
   - **A.** Employee Retirement Income Security Act
   - **B.** Omnibus Budget Reconciliation Act
   - **C.** Older Worker Benefit Protection Act
   - **D.** Retirement benefits are not required by federal law

3. An example of an intrinsic reward is
   - **A.** Recognition of accomplishments
   - **B.** The satisfaction of a job well done
   - **C.** A great supervisor
   - **D.** An exciting assignment

4. A total rewards philosophy can help achieve an organization's strategic goals by
   - **A.** Attracting and retaining employees with the necessary KSAs
   - **B.** Establishing a pecking order for jobs within the organization
   - **C.** Positioning the company to lead the competition for employees
   - **D.** Maintaining an entitlement culture

5. An entitlement culture is appropriate for a business that needs a work force that
   - **A.** Continues to show productivity increases over time
   - **B.** Has line of sight to retirement
   - **C.** Is highly competitive in completing daily assignments
   - **D.** Has a skill set in high demand

6. A company that wants to reduce the cost of its unemployment insurance should
   - **A.** Aggressively fight unjustified claims for unemployment
   - **B.** Establish an effective performance management program
   - **C.** Terminate employees who violate company policy
   - **D.** All of the above

7. A reduced FMLA leave schedule is one in which

    A. The employee is absent from work multiple times for the same illness or injury.

    B. The employee works fewer hours each day or week.

    C. The employee's leave schedule is disruptive to the work schedule.

    D. Accurate records of time off are maintained.

8. The Older Worker Benefit Protection Act requires that an employee age 40 or over who is asked to waive their rights under the act must be given

    A. 7 days to consider the agreement before signing it

    B. 21 days to consider the agreement before signing it

    C. 45 days to consider the agreement before signing it

    D. 60 days to consider the agreement before signing it

9. The Omnibus Budget Reconciliation Act of 1993 does *not* require that

    A. Group health coverage be offered for children placed for adoption before the adoption is final

    B. Group health plans honor qualified medical child support orders

    C. Tax deductions for executive pay be capped at $1,000,000 per year

    D. Income tax be withheld from some distributions to rollover accounts

10. A summary plan description is required for all of the following *except*

    A. Defined contribution plans

    B. Defined benefit plans

    C. Flexible spending accounts

    D. AD&D insurance

Answers to Review Questions

1. C. FICA requires employers to pay social security and Medicare for employees and to withhold an equal amount from employee paychecks. There is no federal law requiring employers to provide pension plans (A) and (B). No federal law requires employers to provide health insurance (D).

2. D. No federal law requires employers to provide a retirement plan to employees. If employers do provide retirement benefits, ERISA (A) regulates how the plans are offered and administered. OBRA (B) capped executive pay, required health plans to honor qualified medical child support orders, and that group health plans provide coverage for dependent adopted children of employees. The OWBPA (C) amended the ADEA to prohibit discriminating against older workers in benefit plans and defined requirements for employee waivers of their rights under the act.

3. B. Intrinsic rewards are those in which esteem is achieved from within oneself. A, C, and D are examples of extrinsic rewards which come from external sources.

4. A. A total rewards philosophy helps determine what kind of employees will be attracted to the organization. Developing a philosophy to target employees with the KSAs needed by the organization can help to advance the organization's mission. The pecking order for jobs (B) is based on the value of those jobs to the organization. The philosophy defines leading the competition as a strategy; positioning the company to do so (C) is a result of creating the compensation structure. An entitlement culture is maintained (D) by continuing to pay employees for time on the job instead of for performance.

5. A. An entitlement culture rewards longevity in the job. If increased productivity is a function of time in the job, an entitlement culture will encourage employees to stay with the company. Line of sight (B) occurs when employees know that their performance impacts their pay. A highly competitive work force (C) is more likely to exist in a pay for performance culture. A work force with a highly desired skill set (D) would be better served by a pay for performance culture.

6. D. A and B are both obviously correct. While C may seem counterintuitive to some because many employers are hesitant to terminate employees for policy violations, those terminated for cause are generally not eligible for unemployment insurance. Since retaining an employee who is not contributing to the organization is a poor business decision, maintaining adequate records to demonstrate the reasons for termination provides the tools to fight claims that are unjustified.

7. B. A reduced FMLA leave is one in which the employee's regular work schedule is reduced by some number of hours per day or days per week. An intermittent FMLA leave (A) is one in which an employee is absent from work multiple times for the same illness or injury. Disruption to the work schedule (C) is not a factor in the type of FMLA leave. While accurate records of time off (D) should be maintained for all FMLA leaves, they are most critical for intermittent leaves.

8. B. Workers age 40 or over who are asked to sign a waiver of their rights must be given 21 days to consider the agreement before signing it, unless they are part of a group termination or layoff. In that case, they must be given 45 days to sign the agreement (C). In both instances, they may revoke the agreement within 7 days (A). The OWBPA does not require 60 days to consider the agreement (D).

9. D. The Unemployment Compensation Amendments of 1992 required 20 percent withholding from some distributions. OBRA capped executive pay (C), required that group health coverage be offered when children are placed for adoption before it is finalized (A), and required health plans to honor qualified medical child support orders (B).

10. D. Summary plan descriptions are required only for group health plans.

Chapter

7

Employee and Labor Relations

THE HRCI TEST SPECIFICATIONS FROM THE EMPLOYEE AND LABOR RELATIONS FUNCTIONAL AREA COVERED IN THIS CHAPTER INCLUDE:

✓ Ensure that employee and labor relations activities are compliant with applicable federal, state, and local laws and regulations.

✓ Assess organizational climate by obtaining employee input (for example, focus groups, employee surveys, staff meetings).

✓ Implement organizational change activities as appropriate in response to employee feedback.

✓ Develop employee relations programs (for example, awards, recognition, discounts, special events) that promote a positive organizational culture.

✓ Implement employee relations programs that promote a positive organizational culture.

✓ Evaluate effectiveness of employee relations programs through the use of metrics (for example, exit interviews, employee surveys).

✓ Establish workplace policies and procedures (for example, dress code, attendance, computer use) and monitor their application and enforcement to ensure consistency.

✓ Develop, administer, and evaluate grievance/dispute resolution and performance improvement policies and procedures.

✓ Resolve employee complaints filed with federal, state, and local agencies involving employment practices, utilizing professional resources as necessary (for example, legal counsel, mediation/arbitration specialists, and investigators).

✓ Develop and direct proactive employee relations strategies for remaining union-free in nonorganized locations.

The Employee and Labor Relations (ELR) function includes the tasks and responsibilities necessary to sustain effective employment relationships in both union and nonunion environments. This chapter reviews the rights and responsibilities of both employers and employees in this relationship and HR's role in those processes.

In order to be fully prepared for the PHR/SPHR exam, candidates must be well versed in the basic knowledge for this functional area as well as the core knowledge requirements covered in Chapter 2, "Core Knowledge Requirements for HR Professionals," that pertain to ELR. The *PHR & SPHR Certification Handbook* described in the introduction to this book provides the detailed list of ELR knowledge requirements and should be reviewed prior to studying this area of the BOK.

 The HRCI core knowledge requirements that will be particularly helpful in understanding this functional area include communication skills, motivation and leadership concepts, the ways in which interpersonal and organizational behavior affect employee relations programs, the impact of diversity on employee relations programs, methods to measure and analyze employee satisfaction, types of organizational structures, and, finally, the implications of employee relations programs on HR programs in other functional areas.

Federal Employment Legislation

The federal employment legislation covered in detail in Chapter 4, "Workforce Planning and Employment", is equally applicable for this functional area of the BOK. In addition, Congress has enacted labor legislation that significantly impacts employment relationships. Table 7.1 summarizes the legislation that impacts ELR activities.

TABLE 7.1 Federal Legislation Governing ELR Activities

Type	Enforcement Agency	Chapter Reference
Civil rights	EEOC and/or OFCCP	4
Labor relations	NLRB	7

TABLE 7.1   Federal Legislation Governing ELR Activities *(continued)*

Type	Enforcement Agency	Chapter Reference
Executive orders	OFCCP	4
Mass layoffs	DOL	4
Polygraph	DOL	7
Privacy	Department of Justice	7
Veterans' Rights	DOL, Veterans Employment and Training Service	7

Also included in this chapter is a discussion of the common law doctrines that impact employment relationships.

Employee Relations

The employment relationship has broad implications for both employers and employees. Employers rely on those they hire to produce the goods and services that bring money into the organization to operate the company, compensate employees, and produce a profit for the owners. Employees, particularly in the United States, spend the majority of their waking hours at work, which means that the effects of the employment relationship, good or bad, can spill over into other areas of the employee's life. An effective employee relations (ER) program can positively affect the bottom line through its impact on employee morale, retention, and the maintenance of union-free status.

Both employers and employees have rights that have either been granted through the legislative process or developed over time as the result of court decisions and common law practices. Along with these rights come associated responsibilities to act in a lawful and equitable manner within the relationship.

Employer Rights and Responsibilities

Employment relationships are affected both by common law doctrines and statutory requirements that protect employers and employees and require certain actions and behaviors. Employers (be they individuals or stockholders represented by a board of directors) have the right to structure organizations in the most cost-effective way necessary to fulfill the vision, strategy, mission, and goals developed to earn a profit. They also have the right to determine how to run their organizations to achieve that outcome and to develop the policies, procedures, and work rules necessary to make it happen. With those rights comes the responsibility to provide safe working conditions, pay wages for all work done by employees, and reimburse employees for expenses incurred on behalf of the employer.

Employment relationships are generally covered either by the common law doctrine of employment at-will or by employment contracts that were discussed in Chapter 4. Employment disagreements may result in legal action on the basis of a breach of the terms of a contract, or on a tort action. A *tort* is a civil action based on a duty or obligation that has been breached by one party, causing an injury of some kind to the other.

In the absence of an employment contract, common law doctrines apply to employment relationships.

Common Law Doctrines

Common law doctrines are the result of legal decisions made by judges in cases that were adjudicated over a period of centuries. There are a number of doctrines with implications for employment relationships, the most common of which is the concept of employment at-will. Other common law issues that affect employment relationships are respondeat superior, constructive discharge, and defamation.

Employment At-Will

In *Payne v. The Western & Atlantic Railroad Company* in 1884, Justice Ingersoll of the Tennessee Supreme Court defined employment at-will in this way: "... either party may terminate the service, for any cause, good or bad, or without cause, and the other cannot complain in law." This definition allowed employers to change employment conditions, whether it was to hire, transfer, promote, or terminate an employee, at their sole discretion. It also allowed employees to leave a job at any time, with or without notice. In the absence of an employment contract that could be legally enforced, this definition was unaltered for over 70 years.

While there have always been exceptions to at-will employment based on employment contracts, beginning in 1959, the doctrine began to be eroded by both court decisions and statutes. This erosion resulted in several exceptions to the at-will concept, including public policy exceptions, the application of the doctrine of good faith and fair dealing to employment relationships, and the concepts of promissory estoppel and fraudulent misrepresentation.

Contract exceptions   Employment at-will intentions may be abrogated by contracts, either express or implied. An *express contract* can be a verbal or written agreement in which the parties state exactly what they agree to do. Employers have been known to express their gratitude for a job well done with promises of continued employment, such as, "Keep doing that kind of work and you have a job for life," or, "You'll have a job as long as we're in business." Statements such as these can invalidate the at-will doctrine.

An *implied contract* can be created by an employer's conduct and need not be specifically stated. For example, an employer's consistent application of a progressive discipline policy can create an implied contract that an employee will not be terminated without first going through the steps set forth by the policy. A disclaimer can offset the effects of an implied contract; however, there is little agreement in the courts as to what and how the disclaimer must be presented in order to maintain at-will status.

Statutory exceptions   The at-will doctrine has been further eroded by legislation. At-will employment may not be used as a pretext for terminating employees for discriminatory reasons as set forth in equal opportunity legislation or other legislation designed to protect employee rights.

Public policy exceptions   Erosion of the doctrine of at-will employment began in 1959 when the California Court of Appeals heard *Petermann v. International Brotherhood of Teamsters* in which Mr. Petermann, a business agent for the union, alleged that he was terminated for refusing to commit perjury on behalf of the union at a legislative hearing. The court held that it is "...obnoxious to the interest of state and contrary to public policy and sound morality to allow an employer to discharge any employee, whether the employment be for a designated or unspecified duration, on the ground that the employee declined to commit perjury, an act specifically enjoined by statute."

The public policy exception to employment at-will was initially applied conservatively by the courts, but over time, its application has been expanded. There are generally four areas in which the public policy exception has been applied. The first is exemplified by the *Petermann* case—an employee who refuses to break the law on behalf of the employer can claim a public policy exception. The second application covers employees who report illegal acts of their employers (whistle-blowers); the third covers employees who participate in activities supported by public policy, such as cooperating in a government investigation of wrong-doing by the employer. Finally, the public policy exception covers employees who are acting in accordance with legal statute, such as attending jury duty or filing a worker's compensation claim.

While the public policy exception to at-will employment originated in California, it has been adopted by many, although not all, states.

Duty of good faith and fair dealing   This tenet of common law provides that parties to a contract have an obligation to act in a fair and honest manner with each other to ensure that benefits of the contract may be realized. The application of this doctrine to at-will employment issues varies widely from state to state. The Texas Supreme Court, for example, has determined that there is no duty for good faith and fair dealing in employment contracts. On the other hand, the Alaska Supreme Court has determined that it is implied in at-will employment situations.

Promissory estoppel   Promissory estoppel occurs when an employer entices an employee (or prospective employee) to take an action by promising a reward. The employee takes the action, but the employer does not follow through on the reward. For example, an employer promises a job to a candidate who resigns another position to accept the new one and then finds the offered position has been withdrawn. If a promise is clear, specific, and reasonable, and an employee acts on the promise, the employer may be required to follow through on the promised reward or pay equivalent damages.

Fraudulent misrepresentation   Similar to promissory estoppel, fraudulent misrepresentation relates to promises or claims made by employers to entice candidates to join the company. An example of this might be a company that decides to close one of its locations in six months, but in the meantime, needs to hire a general manager to run the operation. If, when asked about the future of the company during the recruiting process, the company tells candidates that the plant will be expanded in the future and withholds its intention to close the plant, they would be fraudulently misrepresenting the facts about the position.

In addition to employment at-will, the common law doctrines of respondeat superior, constructive discharge, and defamation can have serious and costly implications for employers.

Respondeat Superior

The Latin meaning of *respondeat superior* is "let the master answer." What this means is that an employer can be held liable for actions of its employees that occur within the scope of assigned duties or responsibilities in the course of their employment. This concept has implications for many employment situations; one is sexual harassment and will be discussed later in this chapter. Respondeat superior could also come into play if a manager promised additional vacation time to a candidate and the candidate accepted the position based on the promise. Even if the promise was not in writing and was outside the employer's normal vacation policy, and the manager made the promise without prior approval, the employer could be required to provide the benefit based on this doctrine.

Constructive Discharge

Constructive discharge occurs when an employer makes the workplace so hostile and inhospitable that an employee resigns. In many states, this gives the employee a cause of action against the employer. The legal standard that must be met varies widely between the states, with some requiring the employee to show that the employer intended to force the resignation, while others require the employee only to show the conditions were intolerable.

Defamation

Accusations of defamation in employment relationships most often occur during or after termination. *Defamation* is a communication that damages an individual's reputation in the community, preventing them from obtaining employment or other benefits. When an employer, out of spite or with a vengeful intent, sets out to deliberately damage a former employee, the result is malicious defamation.

Concerns about defamation have caused many employers to stop giving meaningful references for former employees. Employers are generally protected by the concept of "qualified privilege" if the information provided is job-related, truthful, clear, and unequivocal. Obtaining written authorization prior to providing references and limiting responses to the information being requested without volunteering additional information can reduce the risks of being accused of defamation.

Legal Statutes

Legal statutes are laws that have been enacted by the legislature, as with the Civil Rights Act of 1964, or pronounced by the president in the form of executive orders. In Chapter 4, I discussed extensively the requirements of equal employment opportunity legislation as it relates to hiring and terminations. Those legal statutes govern the employment relationship as well; in this section, I will cover those aspects that apply more specifically to existing employment relationships.

Sexual Harassment

Title VII of the Civil Rights Act of 1964 (covered in depth in Chapter 4), and its subsequent amendments require employers to furnish a workplace that is free from sexual harassment. There are two forms of sexual harassment that must be prevented: quid pro quo and hostile work environment.

Quid pro quo is a legal term that means, in Latin, "this for that." Quid pro quo harassment, therefore, occurs when a supervisor or manager asks for sexual favors in return for some type of favorable employment action. "Sexual favors" is a broad term that covers actions ranging from unwanted touching to more explicit requests.

A *hostile work environment* has been defined by the EEOC as one in which an individual or individuals are subjected to unwelcome verbal or physical conduct "when submission to or rejection of this conduct explicitly or implicitly affects an individual's employment, unreasonably interferes with an individual's work performance, or creates an intimidating, hostile, or offensive work environment." When investigating these charges, the EEOC looks at many factors. In most cases, a single incidence of inappropriate and unwelcome behavior does not rise to the level of a hostile work environment, but in some cases when the actions or behavior are particularly offensive or intimidating, the EEOC may find that harassment has occurred. A hostile work environment can also be found to exist for victims who have been affected by unwelcome offensive conduct toward someone other than themselves.

Unlike the quid pro quo form of harassment, a hostile work environment can be created by coworkers, suppliers, customers, or other visitors to the workplace.

Courts have held employers responsible for the harassing actions of their employees, whether or not the employer was aware of the harassment. Beginning in 1986, the Supreme Court issued a number of rulings to clarify employer responsibilities in the prevention of sexual harassment. The most commonly cited of these for HR purposes are *Meritor Savings Bank v. Vinson* (1986), *Harris v. Forklift Systems* (1993), and two cases decided at the same time in 1998, *Burlington Industries v. Ellerth* and *Faragher v. City of Boca Raton.*

Meritor Savings Bank v. Vinson **(1986)**   Mechelle Vinson applied for a job at a branch of Meritor Savings Bank in 1974 when Sidney Taylor was a vice president and manager of the branch. Taylor hired Vinson, who worked at the branch for four years starting as a teller trainee and working her way up to assistant branch manager, based on her performance in the jobs she held. Once she passed her probationary period as a trainee, Vinson claims that Taylor began to harass her, requesting that they go to a motel to have sexual relations. Although Vinson refused Taylor's advances initially, she gave in eventually because she believed she would lose her job if she did not. Vinson claims that Taylor's harassment escalated to the point that she was fondled in front of other employees and expected to engage in sexual relations at the branch both during and after work. In September 1978, Vinson took an indefinite medical leave and the bank terminated her in November 1978.

The Supreme Court issued its opinion in June 1986, finding that a claim of "hostile environment" sex discrimination is actionable under Title VII. The Court rejected the idea that the "mere existence of a grievance procedure and a policy against discrimination" is enough to protect an employer from the acts of its supervisors. The opinion indicated that a policy designed to encourage victims of harassment to come forward would provide greater protection.

Harris v. Forklift Systems (1993)   In April 1985, Teresa Harris was employed by Forklift Systems, Inc. as a manager, reporting to the company president, Charles Hardy. Hardy insulted Harris frequently in front of customers and other employees and made sexually suggestive remarks. When Harris complained in August 1987, Hardy apologized and said he would stop the conduct. But in September of that year, Hardy once again began the verbal harassment, and Harris quit on October 1.

Harris then filed a lawsuit against Forklift, claiming that Hardy had created a hostile work environment on the basis of her gender. The District Court found that although Hardy's conduct was offensive, it did not meet the required standard of severity to seriously affect her psychological well being.

The Supreme Court agreed to hear the case in order to resolve conflicts in the lower courts on what conduct was actionable for a hostile work environment. The Court found that the appropriate standard is one that falls between that which is merely offensive and that which results in tangible psychological injury. While this is not a precise guideline, it does allow courts to take into consideration a number of factors about the work environment, the frequency and severity of the conduct, the level of threat or humiliation that the victim is subjected to, and whether the conduct interferes unreasonably with performance of the employee's job.

Faragher v. City of Boca Raton (1998)   Beth Faragher and Nancy Ewanchew were two of about six females out of more than 40 lifeguards for the City of Boca Raton in Florida from 1985 to 1990. During their tenure, they were verbally and physically harassed by two supervisors, Bill Terry and David Silverman. They both complained to a third supervisor, Robert Gordon, about the harassment but did not file a formal complaint, and no corrective action was taken. Ewanchew resigned in 1989 and wrote to the city manager in 1990 to complain about the harassment. The city investigated and (when it found that both Terry and Silverman had acted inappropriately) reprimanded and disciplined both supervisors.

The Supreme Court found that employers are responsible for actions of those they employ and have a responsibility to control them. Going further, the Court determined that a supervisor need not make an explicit threat of an adverse *tangible employment action (TEA)*, which the Court defined as "a significant change in employment status, such as hiring, firing, failing to promote, reassignment with significantly different responsibilities, or a decision causing a significant change in benefits" in order for harassment to be actionable. The Court determined that subordinates know that the possibility of adverse supervisory actions exists whenever requests are made, even if the adverse actions are not stated.

Burlington Industries v. Ellerth (1998)   Kimberly Ellerth worked for Burlington Industries in Chicago as a salesperson from March 1993 to May 1994. During that time, Ellerth claims that she was subjected to ongoing sexual harassment by Ted Slowick, who was not her direct supervisor but did have the power to approve or deny a TEA with regard to her employment. While Ellerth was aware of Burlington's policy prohibiting sexual harassment during her employment, she did not complain about the harassment until after she resigned. After resigning, she filed a complaint with the EEOC and, when she received a right-to-sue letter in October 1994, filed suit against Burlington.

A key issue in this case was that of *vicarious liability* (an element of the legal concept of respondeat superior) which, in this context, means that an employer may be held accountable for the harmful actions of its employees, whether or not the employer is aware of those actions. The Supreme Court decided in part that, "An employer is subject to vicarious liability to a victimized employee for an actionable hostile environment created by a supervisor with immediate (or successively higher) authority over the employee."

The costs to employers for sexual harassment can be substantial, as a partial list of recent cases illustrates:

$34,000,000   In June 1998, Mitsubishi agreed to a consent decree and the largest sexual harassment settlement in the history of the EEOC to date. This case was brought on behalf of women on the assembly line in the Illinois factory who were subjected to a hostile work environment by coworkers and supervisors.

$9,850,000   In February 1998, Astra USA agreed to a settlement and consent decree with the EEOC on behalf of female employees who were subjected to both quid pro quo and hostile work environment harassment. Astra fired the president, who had been aware of the activities, and took action against other employees and customers who had taken part in the harassment.

$7,750,000   In 1999, Ford Motor Company agreed to settle a case regarding harassment of women in two plants in the Chicago area. The women were subjected to crude remarks, groping, and sexually explicit graffiti. As part of the settlement, Ford also agreed to conduct sensitivity training in its plants nationwide, promote more women into management positions, and hold supervisors accountable by making them ineligible for promotion and bonuses when they fail to take action against harassment they observe but allow to continue.

 Real World Scenario

Oncale v. Sundowner Offshore Services, Inc.

In late October 1991, Joseph Oncale was a roustabout employed by Sundowner Offshore Services on an oil rig in the Gulf of Mexico. During the time he worked on the rig, three of his coworkers, including two who had supervisory authority over him, humiliated him in front of other employees on the rig using sexually explicit words and actions. At one point, Oncale was physically assaulted and threatened with rape. When Oncale complained to other supervisors about the harassment, no corrective action was taken, and one of them, the company's safety compliance clerk, told him that he too was subjected to similar treatment by the three. When Mr. Oncale quit his job, he gave his reason for leaving as being "due to sexual harassment and verbal abuse."

Mr. Oncale filed a complaint against Sundowner, alleging discrimination on the basis of his sex. The district court denied the complaint, and on appeal, the Fifth Circuit Court of Appeals upheld the district court. Oncale then appealed to the U.S. Supreme Court. The Court heard oral arguments in the case in December 1997, and comments of the justices during the arguments gave a rare early indication of the way they were leaning: Chief Justice Rehnquist commented, "I don't see how we can possibly sustain the holding."

In March 1998, Justice Scalia wrote the majority opinion, referencing in part the Court's opinion in an earlier sexual harassment case that, "When the workplace is permeated with discriminatory intimidation, ridicule, and insult that is sufficiently severe or pervasive to alter the conditions of the victim's employment and create an abusive working environment, Title VII is violated." (*Harris v. Forklift Systems, Inc.*)

Scalia went on to say that even though the intent of Title VII was to protect harassment of women in the workplace, "sexual harassment of any kind that meets the statutory requirements" must be covered as well.

The courts have been divided on the question of same-sex harassment. Since sexual orientation does not constitute a protected class under federal law, some courts have been reluctant to classify cases of same-sex harassment as unlawful. In 1997, the first case of same-sex harassment reached the U.S. Supreme Court. In the majority opinion issued for *Oncale v. Sundowner Offshore Services, Inc.* (see sidebar), Justice Antonin Scalia observed that ". . . male on male sexual harassment was assuredly not the principal evil Congress was concerned with when it enacted Title VII. But statutory prohibitions often go beyond the principal evil to cover reasonably comparable evils . . ." A number of cases following Oncale resulted in substantial awards or settlements in cases of same-sex harassment:

$1,900,000   In 1999, the EEOC reached a settlement with the Long Prairie Packing Company in Minnesota in the amount of $1.9 million dollars, along with a consent decree that required the company to establish a zero-tolerance policy for sexual or disability harassment and to conduct mandatory sexual harassment training for all employees in the company.

$1,050,000   In 2000, $1.7 million dollars was awarded to the plaintiff in *Jones v. Yellow Freight Systems, Inc.* in a civil law suit.

$500,000   The EEOC obtained a $500,000 settlement in August 2000 on behalf of a complainant who was harassed at a Chevrolet dealership in Denver, Colorado. As part of the settlement agreement, the dealership also agreed to provide mandatory sexual harassment training to its employees.

EEOC Guidelines for the Prevention of Sexual Harassment

The EEOC has developed detailed guidelines entitled "Enforcement Guidance: Vicarious Employer Liability for Unlawful Harassment by Supervisors" to assist employers in developing policies that clearly express the employer's prohibition against harassment and conducting investigations that meet EEOC standards. These guidelines are fully described at www.eeoc.gov/policy/docs/harassment.html.

Medina Rene v. MGM Grand Hotel, Inc.

Even though federal law does not prohibit discrimination based on sexual orientation, the courts have applied Title VII protections to complainants in these cases.

For two and a half years, Medina Rene worked as one of a group of male butlers for high-profile guests of the MGM Grand Hotel in Las Vegas. He alleged that he was subjected to a hostile work environment by his supervisor and coworkers and provided extensive documentation of inappropriate behavior over a two-year period. According to the evidence he provided to the court, the behavior included inappropriate touching, caressing, and being forced to look at sexually explicit photographs. At one point, Mr. Rene was asked why he thought his coworkers were behaving that way toward him, and his answer was that it was because he was gay.

Attorneys for the MGM Grand argued that this case was different from Oncale because Mr. Rene was openly gay and Title VII did not provide protection for sexual orientation. The District Court granted summary judgment for the hotel, and Mr. Rene appealed to the Ninth Circuit Court of Appeals. The appellate court found that sexual orientation was not a pertinent fact in this case and remanded the case because Mr. Rene was singled out and subjected to offensive sexual conduct , the conduct was sexual in nature and discriminatory, and he was treated differently based on his sex.

As described previously in the discussions of the *Ellerth* and *Faragher* cases, the Supreme Court found that employers always have vicarious liability for unlawful harassment by supervisors when it results in a TEA, but when there is no TEA, liability may be avoided with an affirmative defense including two elements:

1. The employer exercised reasonable care to prevent and correct promptly any harassing behavior, and
2. The employee unreasonably failed to take advantage of any preventive or corrective opportunities provided by the employer or to avoid harm otherwise.

To summarize the guidelines, employers are encouraged to develop antiharassment policies, along with complaint procedures for those who feel they have been harassed. The policy should clearly explain unacceptable conduct and reassure employees who complain that they will be protected against retaliation. The complaint process should describe multiple avenues for reporting harassment and provide assurances of confidentiality to the extent it is possible. Investigations of allegations should be prompt and impartial and, should the investigation find that harassment did indeed occur, the policy should provide for immediate corrective action.

Glass Ceiling Act

In 1991, Senator Robert Dole included the Glass Ceiling Act as part of Title II of the Civil Rights Act of 1991. An article in the *Wall Street Journal* in 1986 had coined the term *glass ceiling* to describe the limitations faced by women and minorities when it came to advancing into the senior ranks of corporate management. The act established a commission whose purpose was to determine whether or not a glass ceiling existed and, if it did, to identify the barriers to placing more women and minorities in senior management positions. The commission found that although CEOs understood the need to include women and minorities in the ranks of senior management, this belief was not shared at all levels in the organization. The study went on to identify three barriers that prevented women and minorities from advancing to senior levels:

Societal barriers   Result from limited access to educational opportunities and biases related to gender, race, and ethnicity.

Internal structural barriers   Encompass a wide range of corporate practices and shortcomings over which management has some control, including outreach and recruiting programs that do not try to find qualified women and minorities, and organizational cultures that exclude women and minorities from participation in activities that will lead to advancement, such as mentoring, management training, or career development assignments.

Governmental barriers   Related to inconsistent enforcement of equal opportunity legislation and poor collection and dissemination of statistics that illustrate the problem.

The commission also studied organizations that have successfully integrated glass ceiling initiatives into their operations and found some common traits that can be adopted by other organizations. These successful initiatives begin with full support of the CEO, who ensures that the initiative becomes part of strategic planning in the organization and holds management accountable for achieving goals by tracking and reporting on progress. These comprehensive programs do not exclude white men but do include a diverse workforce population. Organizations implementing programs to increase diversity benefit with improved productivity and bottom-line results for shareholders.

As a result of the study, the EEOC conducts glass ceiling audits to monitor the progress of including women and minorities at all levels in business organizations.

Uniformed Services Employment and Reemployment Rights Act (USERRA) of 1994

Congress enacted the Uniformed Services Employment and Reemployment Rights Act (USERRA) in 1994 to protect the rights of reservists called to active duty in the armed forces. The act provides reemployment and benefits rights and is administered through the Veterans Employment and Training Service (VETS) of the Department of Labor. USERRA applies to all public and private employers in the United States, including the federal government. Some of its stipulations include:

- In most circumstances, employees must give verbal or written notice to the employer that they have been called to active service.

- The employer must grant a leave of absence for up to five years, although there are several exceptions that extend coverage beyond five years.

- The employer must reinstate employees to positions that the employees would have earned had they remained on the job, referred to as an "escalator position."

- Employees continue to accrue seniority and other benefits as though they are continuously employed.

- The employer must make reasonable accommodation to provide training or retraining to reemploy a returning service member disabled as a result of service; if reasonable accommodation creates an undue hardship, reemployment can be made to a position "nearest approximate" in terms of status and pay and with full seniority to which the person is entitled.

- The employer is required to grant pension plan benefits accrued during military service.

- For leave greater than 30 days duration, the employer must offer COBRA-like health coverage upon request of the employee; for service less than 30 days, and at the employee's request, the employer must continue health coverage at the regular employee cost.

- Reemployment rights are forfeited if the employee has been discharged dishonorably or other than honorably from the service, has been expelled as a result of a court martial, or has been AWOL (absent without leave) for 90 days.

To be eligible for reemployment rights, the service member must report back to work within time frames that vary according to the length of service. Table 7.2 shows the reporting time requirements established by USERRA.

Visit www.dol.gov/vets/whatsnew/uguide.pdf to view the full text of USERRA.

TABLE 7.2   USERRA Reemployment Reporting Times

Length of Service	Reporting Time
1 to 30 days *or* absence for "fitness for service" exam	The first regularly scheduled work day that falls 8 hours after the end of the calendar day.
31 to 180 days	Submit application for reemployment no later than 14 days after the end of service, or on the next business day after that.
181 or more days	Submit application for reemployment no later than 90 days after the end of service, or on the next business day after that.
Disability incurred or aggravated	Reporting or application deadline is extended for up to two years.

Employee Rights and Responsibilities

As discussed in the previous section, employment rights developed over time from common law doctrines as well as from statutes. In essence, statutory law provides employees with the right to expect equal opportunity in a workplace free from harassment. The common law doctrine of employment at-will provides employees with the right to leave a job at any time, with or without notice.

Due process, while not a legal requirement for private employers, is a practice that is in the best interest of the employer. *Due process* in the employment context means that employment actions are taken in accordance with established procedures, including notifying employees of pending actions and providing the opportunity to respond to any allegations prior to making a final adverse employment decision.

Employees have responsibilities in the employment relationship as well. The *duty of diligence* requires an employee to act "with reasonable care and skill" in the course of performing work for the employer. The *duty of obedience* requires employees to act within the authority granted by the employer and to follow the employer's reasonable and legal policies, procedures, and rules. The *duty of loyalty* requires that employees act in the best interest of the employer and not solicit work away from the employer to benefit themselves.

Organization Climate and Culture

For many, the terms organization climate and culture are used interchangeably. Researchers trying to identify and describe how organizations work and what influences productivity and other organizational behaviors define the difference as one between a quantitative description (climate) and a qualitative one (culture).

The *organizational climate* describes how people feel about an organization based on a number of factors, including observable practices and employee perceptions. Climate is strongly influenced by organization structure as reflected in the organization chart—is it hierarchical and bureaucratic or flat and open? The management style of organization leaders also has significant influence over its climate. Are employees encouraged to take risks or punished for doing so? How are employees held accountable for their successes and failures? Are there opportunities for growth? The climate is built on the way leaders manage and interact with employees.

If climate is reflected by *how* people feel, culture reflects *why* they feel the way they do. *Organizational culture* is based on the values and beliefs shared at all levels and reflected by interactions between employees within the organization as well as with customers and vendors. Culture includes the workplace atmosphere and the way newcomers are integrated into "how we do things around here."

The level of employee involvement and communication in an organization influences and can play a part in changing the culture that is created.

Employee Involvement Strategies

A significant factor in effective employee relations is the extent to which employees are involved in making decisions that affect them on a day-to-day basis. This requires a commitment from senior management to both ask for and listen to what employees have to say and, whenever possible, implement changes suggested by employees. It's also important that management communicate to employees that the changes were implemented. Employee involvement can be very simple, such as a suggestion box, or more complex, such as a self-directed work team. The previous section discussed a number of communication strategies that are a key aspect of effective employee involvement programs. Other strategies for involving employees include the following:

Suggestion boxes   A suggestion box provides an anonymous means by which employees can provide management with ideas for improvements. As with any method of soliciting information from employees, it is important that suggestions be acted upon in a timely manner, or the concept of the suggestion system loses its credibility.

Delegating authority   Management demonstrates respect for its employees by trusting them to make the decisions necessary to do their jobs. To do this effectively, management needs to delegate a sufficient level of authority to employees for making decisions or incurring expenses so that they are free to act without waiting for approval to take necessary action.

Task force   A task force is brought together to research and recommend solutions for a significant undertaking or problem; once the solution has been determined, the task force disbands. A task force might be created to analyze technological improvements in a manufacturing plant and recommend improvements that will meet the long-term strategic objectives of the organization.

Committees   Committees are often formed to address ongoing issues in the organization and may be permanent, such as a safety committee, or ad hoc, such as a group appointed to plan a company function.

Work team   A work team is made up of employees who work together each day to accomplish their assignments. The team can be composed of members within a single functional area, or it can have members from several functions that are needed to accomplish the goal. A functional work team might be made up of employees in the marketing department who develop collateral pieces for company products. A cross-functional work team might be made up of employees from the research and development, manufacturing, marketing, operations, and accounting departments who are responsible for developing, launching, and marketing a specific product.

Virtual work team   A virtual work team operates in much the same way as a work team, with one major exception: team members are not located in the same building but may work anywhere in the world and connect through the Internet to accomplish team assignments.

Employee-management committees   Employee-management committees are used to solve problems in a variety of areas, such as production schedules, safety, or employee social events. The inclusion of employees on these committees helps to bring all the information to the table for making decisions and provides employees with input into how they do their jobs. From this point of view, they make positive contributions to operations.

Employers should use care when creating committees to address issues related to any terms and conditions of employment such as wages, safety, training, scheduling, and overtime, because they can by viewed as "employer-dominated unions" by the National Labor Relations Act (NLRA). The NLRA prohibits employers from creating mock unions with no real power to bargain on behalf of employees. In 1992, the National Labor Relations Board (NLRB) found that committees established by Electromation were employer-dominated unions. More information about the Electromation case can be found in Appendix B, "Federal Employment Legislation and Case Law."

Self-directed work team   A self-directed work team is a group of employees who are jointly responsible for accomplishing ongoing assignments. Team members set the work schedules, determine who will do which jobs, and hold each other accountable for accomplishing goals.

Communicating with Employees

Because communication is a large element of an ER program, it's important to know the most effective ways of providing information to employees. Depending on the size of the organization, communication may be as simple as an "all-hands meeting," in which the owner talks to the whole company about issues, or it may be as complex as a simultaneous web broadcast for a multinational corporation. The most effective communication methods are those that occur between employees and their direct supervisors because these provide the best opportunities for a meaningful exchange of information.

Open-door policy   Open-door policies are an effective means for managers to keep their fingers on the pulse of operations and stay in touch with employee concerns. Giving employees access to the decision makers who can provide support, answer questions, or address concerns also shows a commitment from management to the needs of employees.

Management by walking around   Publicized in the 1980s by Tom Peters in his book *In Search of Excellence*, management by walking around (MBWA) is a practice first used at Hewlett-Packard in which management provided employees with goals and then spent time with them observing their progress and listening to their concerns or ideas.

Department staff meetings   Regularly scheduled meetings, in which direct supervisors meet with their staff for updates and coordination of activities, as well as to disseminate information about organization policies and changes, provide a vehicle for employees to voice their questions and concerns and have input into their schedules.

All-hands staff meetings/town hall meetings   From time to time, employees like to hear from senior management to find out what's really going on with the company. The all-hands meeting is a means by which executives can update employees on the "state of the company" and answer questions about its future direction, new products, or stock prices. Depending on the size of the company, these meetings can occur in person, via video teleconferencing, or as a web broadcast.

Brown-bag lunches   A brown-bag lunch program provides an informal setting for a small group of employees to meet with a senior manager to learn more about the company or a specific goal and ask questions. These informal meetings get their name from the fact that they occur over a lunch period on company premises, with employees bringing their own lunches.

Newsletters   Newsletters can provide employees with regular updates on company projects, profits, and goals. They are an effective means for introducing employees to other areas of the organization, reporting on financial issues, and soliciting input for changes in the employment relationship.

Intranet   An employee intranet can be an effective, easily updated source for information to employees. In many organizations, the employee handbook is available on the intranet, as are the company newsletter and updates on company goals.

Word of mouth   In many organizations, word of mouth is the main means by which employees obtain information. This, of course, has drawbacks. While word-of-mouth communications based on accurate information from management can be an effective way to "get the message out," the information tends to be distorted by the employee grapevine.

Email   Email provides a virtually instantaneous means of communicating information to large groups of employees at the same time. However, email, by its very nature, can be the source of problems, for example, when an executive inadvertently sends a confidential communication about pending layoffs to all staff instead of to the executive team. Particularly with regard to human resource issues, email should be used cautiously to avoid embarrassment and legal complications because it is discoverable in the event of legal action.

Employee Relations Programs

The employee relations (ER) function is, by definition, concerned with relationships in the workplace: how employees interact with each other and with management, how they feel about the work they do, and whether they feel that they are treated fairly. While employee relations as a concept is difficult to quantify, the impact it has on the organization can be considerable. During times of organizational downsizing, if employees are unsure of the future of the organization and of their continued employment, they spend work time worrying about the future instead of doing their jobs, which reduces productivity. When employees feel supported and fairly treated, they are able to concentrate fully on their work and productivity increases.

While some aspects of employee relations are governed by the law, as previously discussed, the fact is that employers who wish to have a profitable organization will increase the chances of doing so by treating their employees with dignity and respect. Senior and executive management may not always recognize the connection between fair treatment and profitability, and it is up to the HR professional to build the business case for implementing effective ER programs by showing the connection.

Positive Employee Relations Strategies

An effective employee relations program is based on mutual respect, open and honest communication, fair and equitable treatment, and mutual trust. These characteristics begin at the top. If the executive team behaves autocratically, expecting adherence to strict and restrictive policies, procedures, and work rules, this demonstrates a lack of trust in the ability of employees to do competent work. When the executive team supports employees in making decisions and taking risks, it demonstrates trust in the competence of its employees. Employees who are empowered to take ownership of the work they do, accepting the rewards of good work and consequences of errors, are more productive.

An organization characterized by mutual respect is one in which management listens to employee ideas and concerns and acts on them, and in which employees feel that they are partners with management in the workplace. Management can demonstrate respect for the workforce by actions such as promoting from within, providing training for employees to prepare them for increased responsibility, and providing opportunities for employees to demonstrate their capabilities. Employees demonstrate respect for management and each other by listening to differing points of view and supporting decisions that are made.

The role of open and honest communication in the organization cannot be underestimated. Communication must be both top-down and bottom-up; management must be willing to hear and act on information that may be contrary to its decisions. To be effective, management needs to solicit information from those employees closest to the issue being discussed in order to make fully informed decisions. Employees must feel comfortable in approaching management with relevant information when they are aware it has not been included in the decision-making process.

The concept of fair and equitable treatment goes beyond that which is required by legal statute and common law doctrine. An effective ER program is one in which favoritism does not exist and where employees can see that employment decisions, even the ones they may not agree with, are based on objective criteria and equitable treatment. When disputes occur, an effective ER program has a nondiscriminatory process for adjudicating them, and it provides a means for employees to appeal unfavorable decisions to an impartial party.

Finally, none of the preceding concepts work effectively in the absence of an atmosphere of mutual trust within the organization. Trust is built over time, when management continuously demonstrates that its actions are based on fairness and equity and gives employees input into decisions that affect them. A key element of building trust occurs when management communicates not only the "rosy scenario" but an honest evaluation of problems and challenges being faced by the organization. This accomplishes two goals: it encourages employees to come up with creative solutions to the problem or challenge, and it demonstrates that management both respects and values employees and trusts them to handle the information appropriately. The role of the HR professional in employee relations is to provide expertise in developing programs containing these elements and develop methods for measuring the impact of ER programs on the bottom line.

Workplace Policies and Procedures

Employers need a consistent and understandable means to communicate important information about how the company operates and what is expected of employees. This is best done through *policies*, which are broad guidelines developed by the employer to guide organizational decisions. *Procedures* provide further explanation and more details on how the policy is to be applied, and work rules state what employees may or may not do to be in compliance with the policy. For example:

Policy   Employees will conduct business in a manner consistent with the highest standards of business ethics.

Procedure   Employees should avoid situations in which the best interest of the company conflicts with the employee's self-interest.

Work rule   Employees may not own, in whole or in part, any venture that seeks to do business with, or is a competitor of, this organization.

Some employment policies are required by law, such as the sexual harassment policy previously discussed. Other policies help to ensure the consistent application of employment practices throughout the organization, and still others serve to motivate employees, such as education reimbursement, recognition, or telecommuting policies. The number and type of policies in each organization should be reflective of the mission, values, and culture of the organization and seek to further successful employment relationships. Regardless of how policies are utilized in any organization, it is important that they be reviewed and updated periodically to ensure that they are still relevant for the organization.

HR policies, procedures, and work rules are developed in conjunction with line management. The role of HR in this process is to advise management on current best practices and legal requirements and work with management to develop policies that are consistent with organization goals, easily communicated, and viewed by employees as equitable. Once developed, HR is responsible to advise management on appropriate ways to administer the policies, procedures, and work rules, and provide training as needed.

Employee handbooks can be useful as a way of communicating policies, procedures, and work rules to employees in an organized fashion and providing a reference. However, poorly worded handbooks have, in some cases, been found by the courts to create implied contracts. When this happens, courts have required employers to abide by the contract implied in the handbook. If the organization wishes to maintain status as an at-will employer, it is important to clearly state this in the handbook, and more importantly, to have the handbook reviewed by legal counsel to ensure that it accomplishes the purpose intended without a negative impact.

Handbooks generally begin with a welcoming statement from senior management and a statement of the organization's employee relations philosophy. Some handbooks provide a history of the organization to give new employees a feel for the type of organization they have joined. Handbooks also contain legally required policies, such as statements of the organization's compliance with equal employment opportunities, prohibitions against unlawful harassment, and information about federally mandated leaves such as the FMLA (Family and Medical Leave Act). The employer then has the opportunity to describe the terms and conditions of employment in the organization, including such things as work hours, safety, ethics, employment status, eligibility for benefits, and benefit programs. The handbook is a good place to inform employees of workplace privacy considerations; if the organization has a policy of monitoring the workplace or places restrictions on Internet usage, clear descriptions of those policies can prevent future problems.

It is advisable to include a tear-out acknowledgment form for employees to sign, or, if the employer utilizes an online handbook, an electronic acknowledgment. The acknowledgment should include statements that employment is at-will, that the employer has the right to unilaterally change the terms and conditions described in the handbook, and that the employee has received, read, and understands the contents of the handbook. While some of this language may be viewed negatively by employees, it provides documentation for the employer in any future disciplinary or legal actions that may occur.

Employee Feedback

A key component of effective employee relations programs is staying in touch with how well ER programs are meeting the needs of employees. Some of the communication techniques previously described gather this information in an informal way; there are also several more structured methods to do this:

Employee surveys   As you recall from Chapter 2, employee surveys can be used to gather information on any number of issues and are often the most effective means for obtaining information from large numbers of employees.

Employee focus groups   As discussed in Chapter 2, an employee focus group consisting of a cross-section of employees from various departments and levels in the organization can be used to involve employees in decisions.

Skip-level interviews   A *skip-level interview* process in which employees are interviewed by their manager's manager provides insight into employee goals and job satisfaction, as well as an opportunity for career counseling.

Analyzing and Reporting Feedback Results

> You can prove anything with statistics.
>
> —*Carl Jung*

When an organization undertakes a feedback initiative, it is critical that the results be reported back to both management and employees. The HR professional should carefully review the data to ensure that it is accurate. If the results are quantified, they should be viewed critically to make sure they make sense and accurately reflect what is truly happening in the organization. Any quantitative analyses should be carefully reviewed for data entry errors or inadvertent misrepresentations of the information. For example, if only a representative sample of the employee population was surveyed, are the results skewed because the members of the group were not truly representative of the entire population? If the entire workforce was surveyed, did the phrasing of the questions influence the results? There are many ways in which statistical data can be misinterpreted, intentionally or unintentionally. Before reporting any survey results, it is important to ensure that they are accurate. Chapter 2 discusses quantitative and qualitative data collection methods in more detail.

Retention Strategies

One goal of effective employee relations programs is to retain employees. An effective employee relations program that includes the components discussed in this chapter contains the building blocks for retention. In addition, "employee-friendly" policies and programs provide flexibility and recognize that employees have obligations outside the workplace and can enhance the employer's ability to retain employees. Advances in technology have made nontraditional work arrangements feasible that were not possible in the past:

Telecommuting   Employees who telecommute connect to the company network via the Internet and communicate with coworkers and managers via email, fax, and telephone, all from their homes. The telecommuting solution for organizations that are willing to embrace it has many benefits for the organization, the employee, and the community. The organization is able to hold on to employees who might otherwise choose to leave, maintaining the KSAs and training that have been invested in the individual. The employee is able to continue working while remiaing available to handle personal needs, such as caring for an ill child or parent. The community benefits from reduced rush-hour traffic congestion.

Flextime   Flextime allows employees to work the hours that enable them to take care of personal business, such as taking children to school, attending classes, or avoiding heavy commute traffic. Many organizations set "core hours" during which all employees are required to be at work, but other than that allow employees to determine what hours meet their needs.

Compressed work weeks   Some organizations allow employees to work four 10-hour days or a 9/80 schedule in which the employee works nine 9-hour days in each two-week period and has a day off every other week. There are a number of variations to these schedules; employers must be aware of FLSA overtime requirements for nonexempt employees and ensure that the compressed work week does not violate those requirements.

Part-time work   Occasionally, employees may wish to reduce their hours for a variety of reasons such as attending school or caring for parents or young children. Employers who agree to a regular part-time schedule will retain qualified employees who would otherwise need to leave the organization.

Job sharing   Job sharing is a situation where two part-time employees share one job. The employer can benefit from this practice in several ways. First, it allows accommodation of an employee's request for a part-time schedule yet maintains full-time coverage for the job. Second, it can allow the employer to hire two people with complementary skills that enhance results.

Performance Improvement

As in any relationship, there are times when disagreements occur; in the employment relationship, these disagreements are usually related to some form of performance issue and can result in a disciplinary action. Much has been written about this topic, as it can become a source of legal action if the employer does not act appropriately. HR's role in the disciplinary process is to provide the expertise needed to set up a fair and equitable process that is applied consistently throughout the organization.

Organizations with effective employee relations programs work to prevent the need for disciplinary action. The establishment and publication of clear policies, procedures, and work rules combined with clearly communicated expectations for individual employees are the cornerstones of prevention. With regular feedback, both positive and negative, employees are better able to improve performance issues when they are easily remedied. If a performance problem cannot be resolved at this level, the supervisor moves into a formal progressive disciplinary process. You can find a full discussion of the steps in a disciplinary process in Chapter 2.

Weingarten Rights

Leura Collins was employed by J. Weingarten, Inc., a company that operated a chain of retail stores. Collins worked at the lunch counter at store #2 for about 9 years and was then transferred to store #98. After working at the second store for about two years, an undercover member of Weingarten's security department investigated a complaint that Collins was stealing money by observing her at work for two hours during which he found nothing to substantiate the complaint. He met with the store manager who told the investigator that a coworker reported that Collins had just underpaid for a box of chicken. Collins was called to the office and interrogated by the investigator and the store manager. Collins asked several times that her union representative be included in the meeting but each time her request was denied. Collins explained what had happened. The investigator confirmed her story with the coworker, found that the complaints were caused by a misunderstanding, and determined that Collins had not violated any company rules. Collins informed the shop steward of the incident and the union filed an unfair labor practice complaint with the NLRB.

The NLRB found that employees are entitled to have a union representative present at any investigatory interview which the employee believes could result in disciplinary action. Employers are not required to inform employees of this right, but if an employee requests that a coworker be present, the employer has three options:

- Discontinue the interview until the coworker arrives.

- Decide not to conduct the interview at all and make any disciplinary decision based on other facts.

- Give the employee the choice of voluntarily waiving the Weingarten rights and continuing the interview or having the employer make disciplinary decisions without an interview.

Weingarten appealed the finding and the case was eventually heard by the Supreme Court. In 1975, the Court upheld the NLRB's decision.

The NLRB has extended and withdrawn Weingarten rights to *non*union workers several times since then. The rights were first extended in 1982 and withdrawn in 1985. In July 2000, the NLRB reinstated Weingarten rights to nonunion employees based on a case involving the Epilepsy Foundation of Northeast Ohio. In its decision, the Board determined that nonunion employees invoking Weingarten rights are entitled to the presence of another coworker but are not entitled to have a family member or attorney present. In a case involving IBM Corp. in June 2004, the board reversed its Epilepsy Foundation decision, once again denying Weingarten rights to nonunion employees.

So what should nonunion employers do? First, understand that employees still have the right to *ask* for a coworker's presence, so employers should not take disciplinary action based on such a request. While employers currently have no obligation to allow coworkers into these meetings, it may be prudent to act cautiously in this area given the unsettled nature of the law.

Disciplinary Terminations

If informal coaching and the initial stages of the disciplinary process does not remedy the performance problem, it is time to move to the termination stage. When this becomes necessary, the manager should work with HR to ensure that, to the extent possible, all necessary steps to prevent legal action as a result of the termination have been taken. As discussed earlier in this chapter, due process is not required in employment actions taken by private employers, but ensuring that employees are informed of the issues and given the opportunity to tell their side of the story demonstrates that the employer treats them in a fair and equitable manner.

In cases where employee actions create a dangerous situation for the employer, as in theft of company property or violence in the workplace, the employer should move immediately to the termination phase of the disciplinary process. When this occurs, the best course of action is to suspend the employee pending an investigation, conduct the investigation in a fair and expeditious manner, and, should the results of the investigation support termination, terminate the employee. Terminations are always difficult situations, and HR professionals need to be able to provide support for managers who must take this action. There are two areas in which HR's expertise is critical: the termination meeting and providing information so that managers avoid wrongful termination claims.

The Termination Meeting

Termination meetings are among the most difficult duties any supervisor has to perform. When termination becomes necessary, HR should meet with the supervisor to ensure that there is sufficient documentation to support the action and to coach the supervisor on how to appropriately conduct the meeting. By this stage in the process, the employee should not be surprised by the termination, since it should have been referred to as a consequence if improvement did not occur. The meeting should be long enough to clearly articulate the reasons for the termination and provide any final papers or documentation. Managers should be counseled to be professional, avoid debating the action with the employee, and conclude the meeting as quickly as possible. The timing of termination meetings is a subject of disagreement as to the "best" day and time. Taking steps to ensure that the termination occurs with as little embarrassment for the employee as possible should be the guiding factor in making this decision. Once completed, and, of course, depending on corporate policy and the circumstances surrounding the termination, the employee should be escorted from the building. Company policies differ on this part of the process: some companies have a security officer escort the employee from the building; others allow the employee to pack up personal items from the desk with a supervisor or security officer present. While the supervisor is conducting the termination meeting, facilities and IT personnel are often simultaneously taking steps to prevent the employee from accessing the company network or facilities once the termination has been completed.

In any situation with the possibility of the employee becoming violent, HR should arrange for security personnel to be nearby, or, in extreme cases, ensure that the local police department is advised of the situation.

Wrongful Termination

Wrongful terminations occur when an employer terminates someone for a reason that is prohibited by statute or breaches a contract. For example, an employee may not be terminated because they are a member of a protected class. If an employer gives a different reason for the termination, but the employee can prove that the real reason was based on a discriminatory act, the termination would be wrongful. Similarly, an employee may not be terminated as retaliation for whistle-blowing activity or for filing a worker's compensation claim.

Workplace Behavior Issues

Employees are human beings whose behavior at work is influenced by many factors, including experiences and situations which exist outside the context of the workplace. Regardless of the source, these factors influence the way employees behave while they are at work. Employee behavior and management's response (or in some cases, lack of response) affects the productivity and morale of the entire workgroup and, in some cases, spills into other parts of the organization.

Absenteeism   Employees call in sick for many different reasons—sometimes they themselves are ill or perhaps a child or parent needs care. Some employees have been known to call in sick to go surfing, hang out with friends, go shopping, or have a "mental health" day. Regardless of the reasons employees give for absences, more often than not the absence causes problems for the work group. At the very least, another employee usually must take on additional tasks or responsibilities for the duration of the absence. When one employee has an excessive number of absences, an absentee policy provides the basis for disciplinary action. An effective policy includes a clear statement of how much sick leave is provided, whether each day off work is counted as one absence or several days off in a row for the same illness is considered one absence. The policy should also tell employees if the absences are counted on a fiscal, calendar, or rolling year basis, and when a doctor's note is required before sick leave may be used.

Dress code   Dress code policies let employees know how formal or informal their clothes need to be in the workplace. Some types of clothing may not be appropriate for safety reasons (such as to prevent a piece of clothing from getting caught in a machine) or to ensure a professional appearance throughout the organization. A policy should describe what type of clothing is appropriate for different jobs, give examples to clarify, and let employees know the consequences for inappropriate attire. If appropriate, the policy may also describe functions or situations in which employees are expected to dress more formally than normal.

Insubordination   Insubordinate behavior can be as blatant as employees refusing to perform a legitimate task or responsibility when requested by their managers. It can also be more subtle, such as employees who roll their eyes whenever a manager gives them direction. It is not only disrespectful to the manager or supervisor on the receiving end of the behavior; it can also create morale problems with other members of the work group. While few organizations have specific policies for insubordination, a code of conduct that describes the organization's expectations for appropriate behavior, such as treating all employees with dignity and respect, provides managers with the tools they need to correct unacceptable behavior.

When discussing performance issues with employees, managers should be encouraged to focus on describing the unacceptable behavior as specifically as possible instead of using general terms such as "bad attitude," or "poor performance." The more specific the description, the easier it will be for the employee to understand and improve. Specific descriptions of performance issues make any adverse actions easier to defend if an employee decides to take legal action.

Dispute Resolution

Most employment disputes are resolved within the organization, but on some occasions that is not possible. In the worst case, employment disputes are resolved in court—a very long and expensive process for all parties. *Alternative dispute resolution (ADR)* covers a range of methods used to solve disagreements without litigation. These alternatives are often able to resolve problems with less animosity than occurs when a lawsuit is filed, and at far less cost to the parties.

ADR Methods

There are several different methods to use in resolving disputes before they reach the level of court action. Initially, the parties involved in a dispute may attempt a cooperative problem-solving meeting, where they work together to find a solution to the problem. Another internal ADR technique is known as a *peer review panel*, which consists of management and nonmanagement employees who are trained in company policies, procedures, and work rules. The panel hears disputes and makes decisions which, depending upon the individual program, can be final and binding on both parties to the dispute. Some companies establish an *ombudsman* or ombuds, an impartial person not involved in the dispute, who speaks with both parties and suggests alternative solutions. An ombudsman can be someone within the company or an outsider.

Arbitration

Arbitration is a means of resolving conflicts without the expense of a lawsuit. *Voluntary arbitration* occurs when both parties to a disagreement agree to submit the conflict to an arbitrator for resolution. *Compulsory arbitration* can be a contract requirement or may be mandated by a court system as a means of reducing the backlog of civil lawsuits or by legal statute, as with public employee unions, which are prohibited from striking.

Arbitration decisions may either be binding or nonbinding. In *binding arbitration*, the parties agree to accept the arbitrator's decision as final. In *nonbinding arbitration*, either party may reject the decision and continue the dispute by filing a lawsuit.

There are a number of organizations offering arbitration services throughout the country; most of them have a roster of individuals with expertise in a variety of business and legal disciplines so that the arbitrator assigned to a particular case will be knowledgeable in its requirements and common practices. These organizations develop standards for those selected as arbitrators to ensure that they have the qualifications necessary to make fair and impartial decisions in the matters they hear. For example, the oldest of these organizations, the American Arbitration Association (AAA), requires that its arbitrators have a minimum of 10 years senior-level experience and educational degrees and/or professional licenses in their area of expertise as well as training in arbitration or dispute resolution. In addition, the AAA wants their arbitrators to demonstrate professional recognition for excellence in their field and memberships in professional associations.

Arbitration proceedings begin with the selection of the arbitrator. The arbitration service provides a list of individuals with relevant expertise, and each party to the arbitration has an opportunity to eliminate those who may have a conflict of interest in the proceedings.

There are three types of arbitrators: ad hoc, permanent, and a tripartite panel. An *ad hoc arbitrator* is one who is selected to hear only a single case. A *permanent arbitrator* is one who both parties agree is fair and impartial to resolve any disputes arising between them. A *tripartite arbitration panel* consists of three arbitrators who hear the issues and reach a joint decision in the matter.

In an arbitration proceeding, each party makes an opening statement describing their case for the arbitrator. The parties then present evidence, in the form of documents or witnesses, to support their case. The arbitrator asks questions of both sides to obtain additional information, and then each side makes a closing statement to sum up the evidence that was presented. The arbitrator then weighs the evidence and renders a decision, notifying the parties by mail.

Mediation

Mediating a grievance involves having the parties work together with the aid of a mediator to devise a solution for a problem. The decisions of a mediator are not binding on the parties, and if the process fails, the parties may continue to the arbitration process. Mediation is an informal undertaking without evidentiary rules, and no formal record of the proceedings is retained. Mediators assist the parties by using a variety of problem-solving skills to move the disagreement to a resolution.

There are several steps in the mediation process, described in the following list:

Structure   Before the parties meet, the mediator develops a structure for the mediation, deciding on the time, place, and attendees for the session.

Introductions   The mediator makes introductions, explains the mediation process, and sets expectations and goals for the mediation.

Fact-finding   During the mediation, each party presents its side of the issue in a joint session and, generally, the mediator meets with each party individually as well, to ask questions and ensure that everyone has the same facts and that the issues are clearly identified.

Options   As the parties present their facts and listen to those of the other side, alternative solutions may become clear; the mediator may guide the parties to this as well.

Negotiating   Once the possible alternatives are on the table, the mediator facilitates negotiations during which the parties come to an agreement.

Writing the agreement   The mediator or the parties write the agreement that has been reached and the parties sign it.

Mediation is a cost-effective solution that successfully resolves many employment disagreements. In mediation, the parties are in control of the decision-making process and resolving the conflict; the mediator facilitates the process that allows this to occur.

In either mediation or arbitration (unless it is a binding arbitration), either party may choose to continue the dispute by taking the matter to court if they are dissatisfied with the decision. In most cases, the use of either of these methods results in an agreement that is acceptable to both sides.

The implications of arbitration and mediation in a union environment are discussed in the section entitled "Contract Enforcement."

Constructive Confrontation

Constructive confrontation is a form of mediation developed by Guy Burgess, PhD and Heidi Burgess, PhD to resolve long-standing, deep-rooted conflicts about difficult, significant issues in organizations. This method is based on the idea that conflict can be healthy and is designed to move those in conflict from a focus on solving a large problem to removing the nonessential elements from the conflict until only the core issue remains.

Constructive confrontation begins with identifying the fundamental issue causing the conflict, the stakeholders, and their positions about the issue. The process then looks at other conflicts that arise as a result of the fundamental disagreement and how interactions between the parties, including their beliefs about the problem and how to handle it, limit their ability to resolve the conflict. These ancillary issues usually serve to increase the level of hostility surrounding the conflict without adding any benefit. The ancillary issues, when separated from the core issue, can be more easily resolved when treated as single issues. Once the ancillary issues are resolved, the core issue can be seen objectively and resolved more easily. Sometimes, the way the core problem or the way facts about the problem are stated causes one party to react harshly, further limiting resolution of the conflict. One party to the conflict may not like the process being used; others may believe that their points of view are being ignored. These and other issues can cause misunderstandings between the parties, escalating hostility, or force participants to take sides, making it increasingly difficult to have meaningful discussions about the core issues. Constructive confrontation identifies ways in which the parties are exacerbating the problem and provides tools to help the parties work through the conflict such as training, mediation, or facilitation.

Once the ancillary issues have been resolved, the parties can move on to the core issue. At this stage, the core issue can be seen more clearly, and the parties can seek alternative solutions that were not readily apparent earlier in the process. The goal of constructive confrontation is not necessarily to have the parties agree, but to find a way to work together.

Labor Relations

The history of American labor relations begins with the formation of the Knights of Labor in 1869. This organization was an advocate of the 8-hour work day when 12 or 14 hours per day was the norm. Labor unions grew in importance for the next century, but in recent years have lost some of their appeal to working people. By the end of the nineteenth century, unions became powerful enough to threaten business profitability and federal anti-trust laws were used to hinder their growth. In reaction, Congress enacted labor legislation that supported union growth. The pendulum swung back and forth until the 1960s when the political focus turned to civil rights legislation. Let's take a look next at the various labor laws that were enacted and their impact on business-labor relations in the United States.

Labor Laws and Organizations

The first piece of legislation to impact the labor movement was the Sherman Anti-Trust Act, passed in 1890. This legislation was originally intended to control business monopolies that conspired to restrain trade in the United States. The act allowed *injunctions*, court orders that either require or forbid an action by one party against another, to be issued against any person or group that conspired to restrain trade. It was first used against a labor union to obtain an injunction against the American Railway Union in 1894 to end its strike against the Pullman Palace Car Company.

The Clayton Act, passed in 1914, limited the use of injunctions to break strikes and exempted unions from the Sherman Act.

In 1926, Congress enacted the Railway Labor Act, the intention of which was to avoid interruptions due to strikes, protect the rights of employees to join a union, and allow for a cooling off period of up to 90 days if the president deemed a strike to be a national emergency. Originally intended to cover the railroad companies, today this act applies to airlines as well.

The Norris-La Guardia Act was passed in 1932 and protected the rights of workers to organize and strike without the interference of federal injunctions. It also outlawed *yellow dog contracts*, which employers had used to prevent employees from joining unions by requiring them to sign an agreement that the employee was not a member of a union, would not become one in the future, and that joining a union would be sufficient grounds for dismissal.

In 1935, the National Labor Relations Act (NLRA), or Wagner Act, was passed as part of President Franklin Roosevelt's New Deal. At the time, it was referred to as "labor's bill of rights" and represented a marked change in government attitudes toward unions. The NLRA allowed employees to organize, bargain collectively, and engage in "concerted activities for the purpose of collective bargaining or other mutual aid or protection." The right to engage in concerted activities applies not only to union employees, but to nonunion employees as well. The NLRA went on to identify five employer unfair labor practices and created the *National Labor Relations Board (NLRB)*. The NLRB was established by the NLRA to enforce provisions of the act. It is charged with conducting elections and preventing and remedying unfair labor practices. The NLRB does not instigate actions on its own; it only responds to charges of unfair labor practices or petitions for representation elections filed in one of its offices.

In 1947, when a Republican majority was elected to Congress, the Taft-Hartley Act, or Labor-Management Relations Act (LMRA) was passed in response to employer complaints about union abuse. Not surprisingly, union leaders decried the act as a "slave labor" law. The LMRA prohibits closed shops and allows union shops only with the consent of a majority of employees. It also provides that states have the right to outlaw closed and union shops by passing "right to work" laws. Jurisdictional strikes and secondary boycotts were also prohibited. When employers bring replacement workers in during an economic strike, they may permanently replace union workers; however, if the strike is in response to unfair labor practices committed by the employer, the union members will be reinstated when the strike ends. The LMRA established the Federal Mediation and Conciliation Service to "prevent or minimize interruptions of the free flow of commerce growing out of labor disputes" by providing mediation and conciliation services.

An important feature of Taft-Hartley is the power granted to the president to obtain an injunction ending a strike or lockout for an 80-day "cooling off" period if, in the president's estimation, the continuation of the strike could "imperil the national health or safety." This power is rarely invoked since its record of leading to successful long-term agreements is mixed.

The Labor-Management Reporting and Disclosure Act (LMRDA) of 1959, also known as the Landrum-Griffith Act, placed controls on internal union operations. Congress felt this was necessary due to "a number of instances of breach of trust, corruption, disregard of the rights of individual employees, and other failures to observe high standards of responsibility and ethical conduct" on the part of union leadership. The act provided a bill of rights for union members which required equal rights for all members to participate in the union, granted freedom of speech and assembly for union members to gather and discuss union issues, and restricted increases in dues and assessments to those that were approved by majority vote of the union. Landrum-Griffith gave employees the right to sue the union and provided safeguards against retaliatory disciplinary actions by the union. The act also prohibited "extortionate picketing" by unions and required that union leadership elections be conducted no less often than every three years for local unions and every five years for national or international officers.

Employee Rights

The NLRA grants employees the right to organize, join unions, bargain collectively, and engage in other "concerted activities" for mutual aid or protection, as well as the right to refrain from doing so.

The NLRA also protects the right of employees to strike and identifies lawful versus unlawful strikes:

Lawful strikes   One type of lawful strike is an economic strike in which the union stops working in an effort to obtain better pay, hours, or working conditions from the employer. In an economic strike, employers may hire permanent replacements for striking employees and are not required to rehire the strikers if doing so means the replacement workers would be fired. If employees make an unconditional request to return to work, they may be recalled at a later time when openings occur.

The other type of lawful strike is one that occurs when the employer has committed an unfair labor practice and employees strike in protest. In this case, strikers may not be discharged or permanently replaced.

Unlawful strikes   Strikes can be characterized as unlawful for several reasons, such as:

- Strikes in support of union unfair labor practices;
- Strikes in violation of a no-strike clause in the contract; or
- Lawful strikes can become unlawful if the strikers engage in serious misconduct.

Unfair Labor Practices

An *unfair labor practice (ULP)* is an action by an employer or a union that restrains or coerces employees from exercising their rights to organize and bargain collectively or to refrain from doing so. As discussed previously in this chapter, Congress has identified ULPs for both employers and unions.

Employer Unfair Labor Practices

Employers who attempt to restrain or otherwise interfere with the right of employees to organize and bargain collectively can, in a worst-case scenario, be ordered by the NLRB to bargain with a union even if an election did not take place or if the union loses an election. For that reason, it is extremely important for employers to be certain that all supervisory personnel are aware of what constitutes an unfair labor practice. An acronym that is helpful in avoiding prohibited activity is *TIPS*: employers may not threaten, interrogate, promise, or spy on employees. Employer ULPs defined by the NLRA are as follows:

Interfere with, restrain, or coerce unionization efforts   Employers may not interfere in any way with attempts to unionize the workplace, including organizing activity, collective bargaining, or "concerted activity" engaged in by employees for mutual aid or protection. Interfering also includes inhibiting free speech of employees who advocate unionization.

Dominate or assist a labor organization   Employers are precluded from forming company unions that are controlled by management and, therefore, do not allow employees an independent representative. Employers are also prohibited from showing favoritism to one union over another.

Discriminate against employees   Employers may not discriminate against union members in any of the terms and conditions of employment. This includes taking disciplinary action against employees for participating in union activities.

Discriminate against NLRB activity   Employers may not retaliate against employees who have filed charges or participated in an investigation conducted by the NLRB.

Refuse to bargain in good faith   Employers must bargain with a union once it has been designated by a majority of the employees and the union has made a demand to bargain.

Enter into a hot cargo agreement   It is unlawful for employers and unions to enter into a *hot cargo agreement* in which, at the union's request, employers stop doing business with another employer.

Union Unfair Labor Practices

The LMRA identified the following union actions that were considered ULPs:

Restrain and coerce employees   Union conduct that interferes with an employee's right to choose a representative or to refrain from participating in organizing or collective bargaining activity is a ULP. The act identifies some of the coercive behavior that is unlawful, including assaults, threats of violence, and threats to interfere with continued employment. Unions are also held responsible for coercive acts committed by union members in the presence of union representatives if the representatives do not renounce the actions.

Restrain or coerce employers   Unions may not refuse to bargain with representatives chosen by the employer to negotiate with the union or fine or expel from the union a supervisor based on the way the supervisor applies the contract during the course of business. Unions may not insist that employers accept contract terms the union has negotiated with other bargaining units.

Require employers to discriminate   Unions may not require the employer to terminate an employee for working to decertify the union or require employers to hire only union members or others of whom the union approves.

Refuse to bargain in good faith   Unions must meet and confer with employer representatives at reasonable times to negotiate the terms and conditions of the contract.

Engage in prohibited strikes and boycotts   Unions may not engage in hot cargo actions or secondary boycotts.

Charge excessive or discriminatory membership fees   Membership fees must be reasonable and in line with the members' wages and industry standards.

Featherbedding   Unions may not require employers to pay for services that are not rendered. For example, unions may not require employers to continue to pay employees to do jobs that have been rendered obsolete by changes in technology. An example of this is the fireman on a train who fed coal into the fire on a steam engine to keep the water hot enough to run the train. When diesel trains came along, the fireman was no longer needed to run the train. If a union insisted on keeping the firemen on the trains even though they were not necessary, this was known as "featherbedding."

Organizational and recognitional picketing   Picketing is discussed later in this chapter in the "Union Organizing Tactics" section.

Consequences of Unfair Labor Practices

If, as the result of an investigation, an employer or a union has been found to have committed a ULP, the NLRB can order remedial actions to be taken. The NLRB goal is to eliminate the ULP and to undo the effects of the illegal action to the extent possible. One of the requirements is that the offending party post notices in the workplace advising employees that the ULP will be discontinued and describing the actions to be taken to correct the offense.

Employer remedies   The NLRB may require that the employer disband an employer-dominated union, reinstate employees to positions they held prior to the ULP, or engage in the collective bargaining process and sign a written agreement with the union.

Union remedies   Unions may be required to agree to reinstatement of employees it caused to be terminated or rejected for employment, refund excessive dues with interest to members, or engage in the collective bargaining process and sign a written agreement with the employer.

Filing an Unfair Labor Practice Charge

ULP charges can be filed by an employee, an employer, or a union representative (the charging party) on a form available from the NLRB. Charges may be filed in person, by fax, or by mail at the regional office of the NLRB where the alleged violation occurred. The statute of limitations for ULPs requires that they be filed within six months of the incident.

Once the case has been received by the NLRB, the charged party is notified, invited to submit a written statement of the facts and circumstances about the case, and advised that they have the right to counsel. The case is then assigned to a board agent for investigation.

The board agent conducts interviews with all parties to the action, as well as with any witnesses, and makes a recommendation to the regional director for disposition of the case. At this stage, the charges may be dismissed if unwarranted or result in a complaint if valid. Depending on the nature and severity of the offense, the complaint may result in an informal or formal settlement agreement. An informal settlement agreement requires that the charged party will take specified actions to remedy the ULP and does not involve a board order or court decree. A formal settlement involves a complaint issued by the NLRB against the charged party and results in a board order or court hearing.

Charges that are not settled are heard by an administrative law judge (ALJ), who conducts a hearing on the evidence, reviews the record, and issues a "decision and order." If a party is not satisfied with the order of the ALJ, they have 28 days to file an exception with the NLRB office in Washington, D.C., which will issue a final order concurring with or amending the finding of the ALJ.

If the charged party is not satisfied with the NLRB findings, an appeal can be filed with the U.S. Court of Appeals in the appropriate jurisdiction.

Union Organization

By the time management notices signs of union activity, the organizing process may already be well underway. One early indication that an organizing campaign has begun is a noticeable change in employee behavior. For example, employees may begin to challenge management decisions using union terminology related to benefits or employee rights.

What Can an Employer Do?

To begin with, employers can make truthful statements about the consequences of unionization in response to union claims—as long as the TIPS guideline is followed. Just as union organizers work to convince employees to join the union, management may communicate their reasons for opposing unionization. During any organizing campaign, an experienced labor attorney should review management statements about the union before they are disseminated. All members of the management team should be coached on ULPs and how to avoid them, particularly first line supervisors since they interact most frequently with rank-and-file employees. First line supervisors also have more influence with their direct reports than any other member of management, and employers should make use of this relationship by providing them with the information they will need to effectively represent the management view to employees.

Finally, unions understand that the enthusiasm and support for the union peaks at a certain point and then support begins to dwindle. For that reason, unions like to schedule elections to coincide with the peak of interest, and they gear their organizing activities to that goal. If an employer can delay the election, the chances of prevailing against the union are improved.

The Organizing Process

There are seven basic elements in the recognition process, but not all of them occur in every situation. The process consists of authorization cards, a demand for recognition, a petition to the NLRB, an NLRB conference, a pre-election hearing, a campaign, and finally, the election.

Authorization Cards

The goal of the union during the organizing process is to obtain signed authorization cards from employees. An *authorization card* is the means by which the NLRB determines that there is sufficient support for a union to hold an election. The NLRB will hold an election if 30 percent of the eligible employees in the anticipated bargaining unit sign the authorization cards. In practice, the union would like to have far more signed cards before submitting a petition for an election—generally they would like to have signed cards from at least 50 percent of the eligible employees.

Demand for Recognition

When the union has a sufficient number of signed authorization cards, they are ready to approach the employer with a demand for recognition. This usually comes in the form of a letter to the employer in which the union claims to represent a majority of workers and demands to be recognized by the employer as the exclusive bargaining agent for employees. The demand may also be made in person when a union representative approaches any member of the management team, including a first line supervisor, offering proof that a majority of employees want the union to represent them. It is crucial that whoever is approached does not respond in a way that could be construed as recognition by the union, politely referring the union to the HR department or a senior member of the management team.

Union representatives may also approach employers requesting a neutrality agreement or a card-check election. In a neutrality agreement, an employer agrees not to say or do anything in opposition to the union. A card-check election means that the employer agrees to recognize the union based on signed authorization cards. At a minimum, agreeing to either situation limits the employer's ability to resist unionization efforts. Agreeing to one of these alternatives may be interpreted as voluntary recognition of the union.

An employer may choose to recognize a union voluntarily under some circumstances, but this should only be done after conferring with legal counsel. One way unions may seek voluntary recognition is to approach management with signed authorization cards to have management witness its majority status by accepting the cards. There are a number of NLRB cases involving union claims that management has witnessed majority status by counting the authorization cards, so supervisors and management should be made aware of the consequences of handling the cards.

Petitioning the NLRB

If management refuses to grant voluntary recognition, the union files a petition for an election with the NLRB, along with evidence of employee interest in union representation. The NLRB reviews the petition to determine that it represents an appropriate level of interest in union representation and that signatures on the petition or authorization cards are valid.

NLRB Conference/Pre-election Hearing Issues

When the NLRB is satisfied with the legitimacy of the petition, it schedules a conference with the employer and employee representatives. During the conference, an NLRB representative reviews any jurisdictional issues, the makeup of the bargaining unit, eligibility of voters in the proposed unit, and the time and place of the election. If either party disputes issues related to the bargaining unit, legitimacy of the authorization cards, or timing of the election, a formal hearing is held by the NLRB to resolve those issues.

Bargaining Units

The makeup of the bargaining unit is a critical factor to both union and employer points of view. The union wants the unit to be as large as possible and include a majority of employees who are in favor of the union. Management, of course, wants to limit the size of the unit and include a majority of employees who choose to remain union-free.

The NLRA grants broad discretion for bargaining unit determinations to the NLRB. Guidance in the act is that ". . . the unit appropriate for the purposes of collective bargaining shall be the employer unit, craft unit, plant unit, or subdivision thereof." Aside from that, the only specifics provided are that a bargaining unit may not consist of both professional and non-professional employees unless the professional employees vote to be included in the unit, and that individuals hired as guards to protect the employer's premises or property may not be included in a unit with other employees. The NLRB looks at several objective criteria to devise a bargaining unit that is appropriate for the individual situation, beginning with determining if there is a "community of interest" within the unit; that is, that the interests of members of the unit are sufficiently similar to preclude disagreements during the bargaining process. The NLRB looks as well at factors such as how the employer administers its business (whether it's with standard policies across the entire company or diverse policies in different locations), geography (how far apart the locations are in the proposed unit), whether the unit is comprised of employees involved in a major process of the company, whether employees are cross-trained or frequently transfer between locations, what unit the employees want to be part of, and any relevant collective bargaining history. Finally, the NLRB considers the extent to which employees are already organized, although the act makes it clear that this may not be the determining factor.

Bargaining units may be comprised of two or more employees in one employer location, or employees in two or more locations of a single employer. If there is an employer industry association, the bargaining unit may include employees of two or more employers in several locations.

Some employees are not eligible for inclusion in a bargaining unit. These consist of confidential employees, supervisors, and management personnel. The act also excludes independent contractors and some agricultural laborers from bargaining units.

Temporary Workers

In August 2000, the NLRB made a significant change to its previous rulings on the inclusion of temporary workers in an employer's bargaining unit in a case involving M. B. Sturgis, Inc. Sturgis is a gas hose manufacturer in Missouri that was the target of an organizing campaign. When the union petitioned for an election, Sturgis wanted to include the temp workers on its site in the bargaining unit, but the union did not want them included. The NLRB reversed two long-standing positions in this case by deciding that the determining factor in this decision is whether or not a community of interest in wages, scheduling, and working conditions exists between the regular employees and the temp workers, and that a unit including temp workers is not considered a multi-employer unit needing consent of both employers.

Union Campaign Tactics

At their peak in 1953, unions represented 35.7 percent of the private sector workforce. Numbers released by the Bureau of Labor Statistics in January 2006 revealed that unions represented only 7.8 percent of the private sector workforce in 2005. However, unions are far more prevalent in today's public sector: 36.5 percent of public sector employers are unionized. As unions struggle to maintain membership levels, they have had to re-examine their strategies for attracting new members.

As the economy in the United States moved from a manufacturing to an informational base, the workforce changed from predominantly blue-collar workers, traditional union members, to white-collar workers who have not traditionally been attracted by union membership. While the strategies vary with each union, the general trend is to find ways of attracting white-collar workers to union membership. Once potential members indicate interest in unionizing their place of work, there are a number of methods used to organize the employees:

Internet   Many unions have sophisticated websites that provide information for employees who are interested in forming a union. The sites contain information on labor laws, unfair labor practices, advice on beginning a campaign, and opportunities for interested workers to contact union personnel.

Home visits   This tactic is most often used when the union is trying to gain initial supporters in the company. It provides an opportunity for organizers to have private conversations with potential inside organizers. Because home visits are expensive for the union and can be viewed as an unwanted invasion of privacy, they are not widely used.

Inside organizing   The most effective organizing process occurs when one or more employees work from within the organization to build support for the union. Insiders can use their influence on coworkers, identify those most likely to respond to the effort, and encourage participation.

Salting   *Salting* occurs when a union hires a person to apply for a job at an organization they have targeted. Once hired, the employee acts in much the same way as an inside organizer who was already employed by the company.

Meetings   Union organizing meetings bring together experienced organizers, inside organizers from the company, and employees who are undecided about supporting the organizing process. Meetings provide opportunities to communicate the benefits of membership and exert peer pressure on potential members.

Leafleting   The goal of union leaflets is to point out the advantages the union will bring to the workforce and to counter information that management provides to employees about the benefits of remaining union-free. Leaflets are generally utilized when the organizing campaign is well under way.

Media   Unions have developed expertise in getting their message out. When management commits an unfair labor practice or takes any action the union perceives as unfavorable, the union will issue a press release that interprets the action in the most favorable way for the union. For example, in 1999, the Union of Needletrades, Industrial, and Textile Employees (UNITE) was conducting an organizing campaign at Loehmann's Department Store in New York City. Just over a month before the scheduled NLRB election, the store fired one of the leaders of the organizing campaign. UNITE issued a press release that concentrated on the fact that the employee had an exemplary work record at the store and was a single mother. The union went on to allege that the store had spied on the employee during her lunch break in order to find a reason to fire her. The union used this as the basis for encouraging the public to boycott the store.

Picketing   *Picketing* occurs when a group of employees patrols the entrance to a business in order to inform customers and the public about disputes, or to prevent deliveries to a business that the union is trying to influence in some way. It can also occur to advise the public about unfair labor practices the union believes the employer has committed. The NLRB recognizes three types of picketing:

> **Organizational picketing**   *Organizational picketing* occurs when the union wants to attract employees to become members and authorize the union to represent them with the employer.

> **Recognitional picketing**   *Recognitional picketing* occurs when the union wants the employer to recognize the union as the employee's representative for collective bargaining purposes. The NLRA places a limit of 30 days on recognitional picketing, after which a petition for an election must be filed.

> **Informational or publicity picketing**   *Informational or publicity picketing* is done to truthfully advise the public that an employer is a union-free workplace.

There are three instances when picketing is prohibited. First, when another union has been lawfully recognized as the bargaining representative for the organization; second, when a representation election has been held within the previous 12 months; and third, when a representation petition is not filed within 30 days of the start of the picketing.

NLRB Elections

The purpose of an NLRB election is to determine whether or not a majority of employees in the unit desire to be represented by the union. If issues between the parties are resolved during a conference, the NLRB schedules a *consent election* to take place within 30 days. A *directed election* occurs when a pre-election hearing is required to resolve those issues prior to scheduling the election. Within 7 days of the consent to or direction of an election, the employer must provide an *Excelsior list* containing the names and addresses of all employees in the bargaining unit to the union.

During the time between the NLRB decision and election day, both management and union present the case for their point of view to employees in the bargaining unit. The employer is required to post notices of the election in prominent locations frequented by employees in the bargaining unit. In the 24 hours immediately preceding the campaign, the NLRB prohibits the employer from holding company meetings for the purpose of influencing the vote.

On the day of the election, neither the employer nor the union may conduct campaign activities in or around the polling area.

To be eligible to vote in the election, an employee must have worked during the pay period prior to the election and must be employed by the business on the day of the election. Employees who are sick, on vacation, on military leave, or have been temporarily laid off may vote subject to rules established by the NLRA. Economic strikers who have been replaced by bona fide permanent employees may vote in any election that takes place within 12 months of the beginning of the strike.

During the election, representatives of the employer and the union may challenge the eligibility of any vote before it is placed in the ballot box. These votes are set aside and, if it is possible that the challenged votes would change the result of the election, the NLRB will determine whether or not they are valid after the election ends.

The NLRB representative counts the votes at the end of the voting period and provides the vote count to the parties at that time. If the union receives 50 percent plus one vote, the union is certified as the bargaining representative for the unit. In the event of a tie vote, the union is not certified.

After a vote, the party that lost the election may file charges that the prevailing party interfered with the election results by committing ULPs. The NLRB will investigate the charges in accordance with its administrative procedures and, should they be justified, will take remedial action against the offending party.

For those unfamiliar with the organizing process, the 1979 movie *Norma Rae* provides dramatic insight into the unionization of a garment factory in the South. Based on a true story, the movie follows the efforts of a union organizer from New York to build support for a union in a textile factory in a small southern town. The organizer begins by visiting the homes of some of the workers, distributing leaflets at the front gate of the factory, and enlisting the support of one of the workers who becomes the "inside" organizer. This insider lends credibility to the union representative by introducing him to coworkers, sponsoring organizing meetings, and obtaining signed union authorization cards. In the course of the campaign, management commits several unfair labor practices. One of the final scenes dramatizes the vote count: as the NLRB official observes, representatives for management and the union count each vote.

Bars to Elections

The NLRA will not allow elections in some circumstances; these are known as election bars:

Contract bar   Except in very limited circumstances, the NLRB will not direct an election while a bargaining unit is covered by a valid collective bargaining agreement.

Statutory bar   The NLRA prohibits an election in a bargaining unit that had a valid election during the preceding 12-month period.

Certification-year bar   When the NLRB has certified a bargaining representative, an election will not be ordered for at least one year.

Blocking-charge bar   An election petition will be barred when there is a pending unfair labor practice charge.

Voluntary-recognition bar   If an employer has voluntarily recognized a union as the representative for a bargaining unit, an election will be barred for a reasonable period of time to allow the parties to negotiate a contract.

Prior-petition bar   When a union petitioning for an election withdraws the petition prior to the election, then no elections will be approved for six months.

Union Decertification

Employees may petition the NLRB for *decertification* if they are dissatisfied with the union's performance. A decertification petition requires signatures of at least 30 percent of the employees before the NLRB will act upon it. Employees may want to decertify the union for a variety of reasons, including poor performance by the union in its representation of the employees or the desire of the employees to be represented by a different union. Decertification may also occur because the employee relationship with management is a good one, and employees no longer feel the need for union representation. It is critical for HR professionals and management to understand that the employer may not encourage or support employees in the decertification process. Doing so constitutes an unfair labor practice and may well result in employees being compelled to continue to be represented by the union.

Union Deauthorization

Employees may wish to maintain the union but remove a union security clause, such as union-shop, dues check-off, or maintenance of membership clause (discussed in the next section). The NLRB will approve *deauthorization* based on a petition by 30 percent or more of the members of the bargaining unit. As with decertification, employers must not participate in the effort to deauthorize the union as doing so is considered to be an unfair labor practice.

Collective Bargaining

The NLRA imposes a duty to bargain on employers and unions. Mandatory subjects for the bargaining process include wages, hours, terms and conditions of employment, the agreement itself, and any questions that arise from the agreement. Bad faith in the bargaining process can be evidenced by a lack of concessions on issues, refusing to advance proposals or to bargain, stalling tactics, or withholding information that is important to the process. Evidence of bad faith by management in the bargaining process can also be evidenced by attempts to circumvent the union representative by going directly to employees with proposals before they have been presented to the union. Another indicator of bad faith bargaining by management occurs when unilateral changes are made to working conditions. An indication of bad faith by the union would be failing to notify management of the intent to renegotiate the contract within 60–90 days before it expires.

Collective Bargaining Positions

Before discussing the components of collective bargaining, it is important to understand the different bargaining positions that can be taken and how each position impacts the bargaining process. There are two basic approaches to negotiating: positional bargaining and principled bargaining.

Positional bargaining   *Positional bargaining* is a strategy represented by demands made by each side. During positional negotiations, each side views the object of the negotiation as something finite that must be shared, stakes out the position they believe is in their own interest, and concentrates on "winning" that position for their side. This makes the process an adversarial, competitive one. Also known as *hard bargaining* or *distributive bargaining*, positional bargaining is a zero-sum game: in order for one side to gain something, the other side must lose something.

Principled bargaining   *Principled bargaining* as a negotiating strategy is characterized by parties who are more interested in solving a problem than they are in winning a position. In doing so, the parties remain open to looking at the problem in new ways, brainstorming for ideas, and often coming up with an agreement that solves the original problem in a way that was not originally contemplated by either side. The most common forms of principled bargaining are integrative bargaining and interest-based bargaining.

> **Integrative bargaining**   *Integrative bargaining* is a form of principled bargaining in which the parties look at all the issues on the table and are able to make mutually agreeable trade-offs between those issues.

> **Interest-based bargaining (IBB)**   *Interest-based bargaining (IBB)*, another form of principled bargaining, is based on the concept that both sides in the negotiation have harmonious interests. In labor-management negotiations, for example, both labor and management have an equal interest in the continuing viability of the business—for management to earn profits and for labor to have continued employment.

Collective Bargaining Strategies

In addition to collective bargaining positions, HR professionals should be aware of the four basic negotiating strategies used in union environments:

Single-unit bargaining   The most common strategy, single-unit bargaining occurs when one union meets with one employer to bargain.

Parallel bargaining   In *parallel bargaining*, also known as *pattern bargaining*, *whipsawing*, or *leapfrogging*, the union negotiates with one employer at a time. Once a contract has been reached with this employer, the union uses the gains made during the negotiation as a base for negotiating with the next employer.

Multi-employer bargaining   In *multi-employer bargaining*, the union negotiates with more than one employer in an industry or region at a time. This situation can occur when temporary workers are part of a client employer's bargaining unit and the union negotiates with both the temp agency and the client employer on employment issues.

Multi-unit bargaining   *Multi-unit bargaining*, or *coordinated bargaining*, occurs when several unions represent different bargaining units in the company. An example of this occurs in the airline industry, when the employer negotiates with the unions representing pilots, flight attendants, and mechanics or other employee classes. This allows the employer to coordinate negotiations on mandatory and permissive bargaining subjects while allowing the unions to cooperate on issues that have similar meaning to their various members.

Collective Bargaining Subjects

The subjects open for negotiation during the collective bargaining process fall into four areas.

Mandatory subjects   The NLRA defines the subjects that are mandatory in the collective bargaining process. These are wages, hours, other terms and conditions of employment, and the negotiation of the agreement and bargaining related to questions that arise from the agreement. Both parties must bargain on mandatory subjects, and unresolved issues on them are the only ones that may be the subject of a strike or lockout.

Illegal subjects   The NLRA also identifies topics that are unlawful for inclusion in a collective bargaining agreement, including topics such as hot cargo clauses or closed shop security agreements.

Voluntary subjects   Voluntary or permissible subjects for negotiation would be any lawful topic other than those identified as mandatory by the NLRA. These generally include management rights, such as production scheduling, operations, or selecting supervisors.

Reserved rights doctrine   Management generally includes a clause in the contract that states that any rights not covered specifically in the agreement are the sole responsibility of management.

Collective Bargaining Agreement (CBA)

The *collective bargaining agreement* is a contract governing the employment relationship for a specified period of time. The clauses contained in the CBA will, of course, be reflective of the bargaining topics in individual companies; some of the clauses found in many contracts include the following:

Wages, hours, terms, and conditions of employment   The clauses that describe the wages, medical and other benefits, overtime, hours, and other conditions of employment are the backbone of the collective bargaining agreement.

Union security clauses   The union security clause requires members of the union to provide financial support to the union. A security clause helps to ensure that the union will be financially able to carry out its bargaining obligations.

A *union shop* clause requires that all employees join the union within a grace period specified by the contract, but no fewer than 30 days, or, in the construction industry, 7 days.

An *agency shop* clause specifies that all employees must either join the union or pay union dues if they choose not to join the union.

A *closed shop* clause requires that all new hires be members of the union before they are hired. The closed shop is illegal except in the construction industry.

A *maintenance of membership* clause allows employees to choose whether or not to join the union, but once they join, they must remain members until the expiration of the contract. The employee must notify the union to discontinue membership within 30 days of the contract expiration.

No strike/no lockout clause   These clauses are considered very important to both unions and management because they provide economic protection from work stoppages on both sides. Strikes and lockouts are discussed more fully in the "Lockouts and Boycotts and Strikes...Oh My!" section of this chapter.

Contract administration   This clause covers the nuts and bolts of how the contract will be administered over its duration. Procedures for disciplinary actions, grievance resolution, and arbitration, as well as agreements on how clauses may be modified during the contract term, can be included in this clause.

Dues check-off   Most unions prefer to have employees agree to automatic deduction of their union dues. To be enforceable, employees must give written authorization for the deductions.

Zipper clause   A *zipper clause* or *totality of agreement* clause is an agreement between the parties that the CBA is the entire agreement between them and that anything not in the agreement is not part of the agreement. The purpose of this clause is to prevent reopening of negotiations during the term of the contract.

Contract Enforcement

Disagreements that arise during the course of the contract may take many forms; some are easily resolved through the grievance process established in the CBA, others may go to arbitration before they are resolved.

Grievance Procedure

When disagreements occur in a union environment, the grievance process described in the CBA provides the framework for resolving them. The framework describes the steps to be taken and the time frames within which actions must be implemented to either resolve or reply to the grievance. Many grievances can be resolved at the first step in the process with the immediate supervisor, grievant, and union steward working together. If resolution is not possible at that level, a union official takes the dispute to the next level of company management, where the grievant generally does not attend but is represented by the union. If the dispute is not resolved at the second level, a member of the union grievance committee meets with the next level of management in the company. Grievances that are serious enough to be unsolved at the highest management level in the process then go to a third party for resolution. Depending on the terms of the CBA, this may involve binding arbitration, as is the case in the majority of contracts, or it may utilize mediation or another form of alternative dispute resolution.

Binding Arbitration

As discussed previously in the section entitled "Dispute Resolution," arbitration is one method of resolving disputes without litigation. In the union environment, binding arbitration is used to resolve conflicts without resorting to work stoppages. Compulsory arbitration is mandated by legal statute to resolve disputes in the public sector where labor strikes are prohibited.

Mediation

The process used to mediate disputes in a union environment is the same as it is in a nonunion environment. With the aid of the mediator, the parties to the disagreement are able to develop a solution that is acceptable to both of them.

Court Injunctions

As explained earlier in this chapter, injunctions are sought when immediate action is needed to temporarily prevent something from occurring. One example of the use of injunctions in the collective bargaining process is the national emergency strike. The Taft-Hartley act empowers the president to seek an injunction to stop a strike or lockout for an 80-day "cooling off" period.

Duty of Successor Employers

In the event that a company with collective bargaining agreements is acquired by a new company, the new management may be required to maintain the union contract. Whether or not the NLRB will consider an acquiring owner to be a successor employer is based on the following factors:

- There is substantial continuity in operations.
- The number of employees assimilated into the new company.
- Similarity of operations and products.
- The agreement with the previous employer.

While the terms and conditions may be changed by the new employer, the changes are required to be made through the collective bargaining process, and may not be made unilaterally by the employer.

Lockouts and Boycotts and Strikes. . .Oh My!

For a variety of reasons, such as when communication between union and management breaks down and tempers flare, or when workplace conditions become so hazardous that employees are afraid they will be maimed or seriously injured on the job, one party or the other may determine that the only course of action left to them is a work stoppage.

Lockouts

A *lockout* occurs when management shuts down operations to keep the union from working. This can happen for several reasons. For example, union members may be engaging in a work slowdown, and it may be costing management more to have the employees working slowly and producing a limited number of goods or services than it would cost to shut down the operation.

Boycotts

Boycotts occur when the union and the employees in the bargaining unit work together against an employer to make their dissatisfaction with the employer's actions known or to try to force the employer into recognizing the union or conceding to the demands of the union. Boycotts occur in several ways:

Ally doctrine   The *ally doctrine* states that when an employer whose workers are on strike contacts a neutral employer and asks the neutral employer to produce the work that would normally be performed by the striking workers, the neutral employer becomes an ally of the struck employer and is therefore a legitimate target of a picket line.

Alter ego doctrine   The *alter ego doctrine* developed originally as a means to protect creditors from frauds perpetrated by shareholders. Its application has been extended to labor relations to preclude employers from dodging their collective bargaining responsibilities. An alter ego employer consists of two or more businesses with substantially identical management, business purposes, operations, equipment, customers, supervision, and ownership. In 1965, the Supreme Court heard a case, *Radio Union v. Broadcast Services, Inc.*, in which it identified four criteria that determine whether or not a single employer exists: interrelation of operations, central control of labor relations, common management, and common ownership. When these four criteria are present, the NLRB may determine that employees of the alter ego employer are part of the bargaining unit.

Double breasting   Double breasting refers to a common owner of two businesses, one of which is a union shop and the other a nonunion shop. Unions would like to include both businesses in a bargaining unit due to their common ownership. Historically, as long as each business had different management, equipment, and customers and a legitimate business purpose separate and apart from the other company, the union was prohibited from striking the second business because that was considered a secondary boycott by the NLRB. More recently, the NLRB has determined that unionization of both businesses may be a legitimate topic for contract negotiation, and if the owner refuses to bargain, the union may strike.

Secondary Boycott   A secondary boycott occurs when a union tries to compel an employer who is not involved in a dispute (such as a supplier) to stop doing business with another employer who is part of a dispute with the union. For the most part, secondary boycotts are defined as ULPs by the Taft-Hartley Act.

Straight line operations   A straight line operation is one in which two businesses perform operations that complement each other's operations. If one business is struck, the other may be as well because they are engaged in a single economic enterprise.

Strikes

A *strike* occurs when the union decides to stop working. Earlier in the chapter, I discussed the difference between unlawful and lawful strikes. Whether or not a strike is lawful depends on the purpose of the strike, and the NLRA identifies several specific strikes:

- A strike in support of a ULP committed by the union is an unfair labor practice and therefore an unlawful strike.

- A strike that occurs in violation of a no-strike clause in a CBA is not a protected activity, and employees engaging in this type of activity may be terminated or disciplined.

- Strikers who engage in serious misconduct during a strike, including violence, threats of violence, physically blocking someone from entering or leaving the place of business, or attacking management personnel will cause a strike to be deemed unlawful.

- Work slowdowns are considered unlawful strikes and may result in disciplinary action, including termination.

- A *wildcat strike* is one that occurs in violation of a contract clause prohibiting strikes during the term of the contract.

- A *sit-down strike*, in which employees stop working and stay in the building, is considered an unlawful strike.

- Strikes in support of a hot cargo clause are prohibited.

Picketing

As discussed in the section "Union Campaign Tactics," picketing can be a lawful activity and a way for unions to advertise their message. Although picketing often occurs in connection with a strike or work stoppage, it is not the same thing as a strike. The difference is that picketing occurs to simply inform other parties about issues under dispute, while a strike occurs when the employees stop working. Even in the public sector where strikes are prohibited by law, picketing can be used to inform the public about the issues. The three different kinds of picketing that PHR/SPHR candidates should be familiar with are the following:

Common Situs picketing   *Common Situs picketing* happens when an employer shares a building with other employers. Because picketing a common business location can interfere with the ability of secondary businesses to operate, the union must ensure that picket signs clearly state the name of the business they are striking, and where possible, restrict picketing to an entrance that is used only by the primary employer.

Consumer picketing   *Consumer picketing* is done to advise consumers that goods have been produced by a business whose workers are on strike.

Hot cargo pickets   Hot cargo was described earlier in the chapter. Because it is an unlawful activity, picketing against hot cargo issues is prohibited.

Union Avoidance Strategies

Most employers prefer to operate in a union-free environment. An effective employee relations program and organization culture that treats employees with dignity and respect is more likely to remain union-free because employee needs are being met without a union. When employees are treated poorly, overworked, stressed about their jobs, and don't have management support, union promises of better pay and working conditions are attractive, and employees often turn to unions with the hope that the union will be able to improve their work situation. Unions also offer leadership opportunities as shop stewards and union officers for members who may otherwise not have those opportunities.

Metrics—Measuring Results

While employee relations as a concept is difficult to measure, there are two indicators of employee satisfaction that *can* be measured—absenteeism and turnover. Excessive unplanned absences can be an indication of employee stress, dissatisfaction with job requirements, supervisory conflicts, and feeling undervalued by the employer. Measuring absence rates over time can provide feedback on the success of ER programs, as well as provide indicators of supervisory issues that may be resolved through coaching or training. As discussed in Chapter 4, the turnover rate is the ultimate indicator of dissatisfaction with the supervisor, company, and/or employee relations programs.

Global Considerations

From an ELR point of view, when considering the question of whether to fill a position with an expatriate from the United States, with a host-country national, or with a third-country national, employers must weigh the answers to several questions:

- Does the host country restrict the number of expatriates allowed in the country?
- How does the legal system view an employee handbook, and is it advisable to create one?
- Does the legal system recognize at-will employment? Or is an employment contract required?

As global business operations continue to expand, these and other questions specific to particular countries must be answered. To avoid costly errors, HR must be able to provide executives with accurate, specific information about the differences in employment laws and practices that exist in the countries where the business operates.

Summary

Effective management of Employee and Labor Relations is a critical element of a successful business. Employees who are treated with dignity and respect and given the tools they need to succeed reward employers with increased production, fewer sick days, and a loyal and committed workforce. Organization culture begins with management attitudes toward employees and ranges from those that are based on an autocratic philosophy characterized by "top-down" communication and interactions to those of employee empowerment where individuals and work teams make the decisions necessary to get their jobs done.

Effective dispute resolution programs that solve employment disagreements without the need for legal action are both cost effective and more successful than lawsuits. Establishing programs in the workplace that provide opportunities for employees who feel they have been mistreated is one way for HR professionals to add value to their organizations.

Management of the employment relationship is subject to the laws prohibiting discrimination in all terms and conditions of employment, as well as to common law doctrines. HR professionals must be aware of the requirements of these statutes and doctrines in order to provide sound advice to management in making employment decisions and to ensure that the programs and policies developed by HR are in compliance with them.

Labor relations are governed by a number of laws designed to protect the rights of employees. The unionization process is strictly regulated by the NLRB, which conducts union recognition elections and adjudicates charges of unfair labor practices by both unions and employers. Unions, whose membership has steadily declined over the past 20 years, are now seeking to expand their organizing efforts by targeting nontraditional union members and developing sophisticated methods for attracting new members. The most effective way for management to avoid unionization of the workplace is to treat employees fairly and give them a voice in decisions that affect their day-to-day work.

Exam Essentials

Be aware of the requirements of equal employment opportunity legislation on the employment relationship.   EEO legislation requires employers to provide equal opportunities and a safe workplace that is free from harassment. Federal EEO legislation established protected classes for race, color, religion, sex, national origin, age, and disability. Employers must ensure that all employees are aware that the business does not tolerate harassment on the basis of any protected category, and they must create written policies that clearly state the employer's position and consequences that will occur if employees violate the policy.

Be aware of the impact of an effective employee relations program on the bottom line.   Providing a workplace environment in which employees are treated with dignity and respect, are involved in making decisions that affect them each day, and have work that is satisfying and challenging benefits employers. Employees who feel respected and valued are more productive and loyal to the company and, in the long run, have a positive impact on the bottom line.

Be aware of employer unfair labor practices.   Employers may not interfere with attempts of employees to organize unions or assist a union in organizing, nor can they discriminate against employees who advocate for the union or who engage in protected NLRB activities.

Be able to establish fair and effective disciplinary processes.   The most effective disciplinary process is one that prevents performance problems by providing clear performance expectations and regular feedback, both positive and negative, on how the employee is meeting those expectations. A fair and effective process tells employees clearly what the problem is, allows the employee to respond, and involves the employee in developing a solution to the problem.

Be able to identify various methods for alternative dispute resolution.   Lawsuits are costly and time consuming for employers and generally disruptive to operations. Establishing alternative methods of resolving employment disputes demonstrates that an employer has provided due process to employees. An effective ADR program involves successively higher levels of management in resolving disputes.

Know how to identify and respond to union organizing activity.   Union organizing activity is most effective when conducted by employees within the organization. Some signs that an organizing effort is underway include employees who begin challenging management in staff meetings, talking with employees that they haven't had contact with before, and a newly hired employee who is very vocal about perceived management abuses toward employees.

Understand the collective bargaining process.   The collective bargaining process is required by the National Labor Relations Act and provides that employers must bargain in good faith with the union representative chosen by the employees. Employers have a duty to bargain in good faith on mandatory subjects, which include wages, hours, and other terms and conditions of employment.

Key Terms

Before you take the exam, be certain you are familiar with the following terms:

ad hoc arbitrator	authorization card
agency shop	binding arbitration
ally doctrine	blocking-change bar
alter ego doctrine	certification-year bar
alternative dispute resolution (ADR)	closed shop
collective bargaining agreement	lockout
common law doctrine	maintenance of membership
Common Situs picketing	multi-employer bargaining
compulsory arbitration	multi-unit bargaining
consent election	National Labor Relations Board (NLRB)
constructive confrontation	nonbinding arbitration
constructive discharge	ombudsman
consumer picketing	organizational climate
contract bar	organizational picketing
organizational culture	parallel bargaining
coordinated bargaining	pattern bargaining

deauthorization

decertification

defamation

directed election

distributive bargaining

due process

duty of diligence

duty of loyalty

duty of obedience

Excelsior list

express contract

glass ceiling

hard bargaining

hostile work environment

hot cargo agreement

implied contract

informational picketing

injunctions

integrative bargaining

interest-based bargaining (IBB)

leapfrogging

tripartite arbitration panel

unfair labor practice (ULP)

union shop

vicarious liability

voluntary arbitration

peer review panel

permanent arbitrator

picketing

policies

positional bargaining

principled bargaining

prior-petition bar

procedures

publicity picketing

quid pro quo

recognitional picketing

salting

sit-down strike

skip-level interview

statutory bar

strike

tangible employment action (TEA)

TIPS

tort

totality of agreement

voluntary-recognition bar

whipsawing

wildcat strike

yellow dog contracts

zipper clause

Review Questions

1. A supervisor has called an employee in for an interview about an inventory shortage. When the supervisor begins asking questions, the employee invokes his Weingarten rights. The supervisor has the option to

    A. Stop the discussion while the employee calls an attorney.

    B. Stop the discussion until the shop steward is available upon return from vacation in four days.

    C. Discontinue the interview and make the determination based on other evidence and documentation.

    D. Continue the interview while waiting for a coworker to return from lunch.

2. An employee has resigned and during the exit interview tells HR that the reason for the resignation is that for the last three months the supervisor has been hostile, refused to provide instructions on work assignments, given the employee all of the most unpleasant tasks in the department, and verbally reprimanded the employee in front of coworkers and customers. The employee may have a cause of legal action based on

    A. The employer's duty of good faith and fair dealing

    B. Constructive discharge

    C. Promissory estoppel

    D. Fraudulent misrepresentation

3. All of the following statements about employment at-will are true except:

    A. The employer may terminate the employee at any time for any reason.

    B. The employee may resign at any time, with or without notice.

    C. The employer may terminate the employee for cooperating with an SEC investigation.

    D. The employer may withdraw an offer of employment after the employee has accepted the position and resigned another job.

4. During a unionizing campaign, management may do the following in response to union allegations:

    A. Point out the consequences of unionization based on past facts.

    B. Encourage nonunion employees to talk about the reasons they don't want the union.

    C. Tell employees the company will have to move the jobs to another country if the union is elected.

    D. Ask employees what the union is saying about the company.

5. As a result of the Sturgis case,

   A. Temporary employees may only form a union and bargain with the temp agency.

   B. The temporary agency must agree to bargain with a client company's union.

   C. Temporary employees who work side by side with regular employees may be part of the bargaining unit.

   D. Temporary employees may not be unionized.

6. If employees no longer want the union to represent them, they may petition the NLRB for

   A. Decertification

   B. Deauthorization

   C. Contract bar

   D. Statutory bar

7. A union security clause that requires all employees to join the union after they are hired is

   A. An agency shop clause

   B. A union shop clause

   C. A closed shop clause

   D. A maintenance of membership clause

8. Double breasting occurs when

   A. An employer has two companies that are substantially identical.

   B. A neutral employer performs work that is normally done by striking employees.

   C. An employer has two businesses, one union and one nonunion, that do substantially the same work but have different management, equipment, and customers.

   D. Two businesses perform operations that are part of the same product.

9. During a representation election, votes may be challenged

   A. By management or the union at any time

   B. By management or the union before the votes are cast

   C. By management only

   D. By the union only

10. Salting is a practice in which

   A. The union hires an individual to publicize its reasons for targeting an employer for unionization.

   B. The union hires an individual to distribute leaflets to employees as they are leaving work at the end of the day.

   C. The union hires an individual to picket the employer's business.

   D. The union hires an individual to apply for a job with an employer and begin to organize the company.

Answers to Review Questions

1. C. Weingarten rights give all employees the right to request a coworker or union representative be present during an interview if the employee believes the interview could lead to disciplinary action. The employer may decide to use other facts available without interviewing the employee. The Weingarten ruling does not entitle employees to have an attorney present (A). Employers are not required to wait for a lengthy period of time until the coworker returns (B). The interview must be discontinued while waiting for the coworker (D). As of 2004, employers are only required to honor Weingarten requests for union members.

2. B. Constructive discharge occurs when the employer forces an employee to resign by creating a work environment that is so unpleasant a reasonable person would resign. The duty of good faith and fair dealing (A) applies to contracts, requiring both parties to act in a fair and honest manner with each other to ensure that benefits of the contract are realized. Promissory estoppel (C) occurs when an employer entices an employee to take an action by promising a reward but then does not follow through on the reward. Fraudulent misrepresentation (D) occurs when an employer makes untrue promises or claims to a candidate.

3. C. The public policy exception to the at-will doctrine prevents an employer from terminating an employee who is cooperating in a government investigation of wrong-doing. (A) and (B) are elements of at-will employment. (D) would also be allowed based on the at-will doctrine, but could be affected by other common law doctrines.

4. A. The company may make truthful statements about a unionized environment during an organizing campaign, such as pointing out that employees will have to pay dues to the union. While nonunion employees are free to talk about their reasons for not wanting a union (B), it is an unfair labor practice for the employer to encourage them to do so. Telling employees the company will have to move the jobs to another country if the union is elected (C) is also a ULP, as it constitutes a threat. Employers may not threaten, interrogate, promise, or spy (TIPS) on employees during an organizing campaign (D).

5. C. Temporary employees who have a community of interest with regular employees of the client company may become part of the bargaining unit whether or not the temp agency agrees to bargain with the union.

6. A. The NLRB will conduct a decertification election if the employees present a petition signed by 30 percent of the employees in the bargaining unit. Management may not participate in or encourage employees to circulate the petition or provide any support in the process. Doing so is considered an unfair labor practice. A union can be deauthorized (B) if employees want to remove a union security clause, such as dues check-off. If there is a valid CBA in place (C), the NLRB will not direct an election. The NLRA prohibits an election if one took place during the preceding 12 months (D).

7. B. A union shop clause requires all new employees to join the union within a grace period specified by the contract, no less than 30 days, except in the construction industry, where the grace period must be 7 days. An agency shop clause (A) requires all employees to pay union dues whether they join the union or not. A closed shop clause (C) requires all new hires to be members of the union before they are hired. Closed shops are illegal except in the construction industry. A maintenance of membership clause (D) allows employees to choose whether or not to join the union, but once they join, they must remain members until the expiration of the contract.

8. C. Double breasting occurs when an employer has two companies that are separate and distinct from each other but do the same type of work, and one company is union while the other is nonunion. This occurs most often in the construction industry when contractors have two different crews for bidding on union and nonunion jobs. An alter ego employer has two substantially identical businesses (A). The ally doctrine describes work that is done by a neutral employer while another business is shut down by a strike (B). A straight line operation is one in which two businesses perform operations that complement each other's operations (D). If one business is struck, the other may be as well because they are engaged in a single economic enterprise.

9. B. Votes may be challenged by the union representative or by management only before the vote goes into the ballot box.

10. D. Salting occurs when a union hires an individual experienced at organizing tactics to apply for a job with a company that has been targeted for an organizing campaign. A, B, and C are tactics used by unions during organizing campaigns.

Chapter

8

Risk Management

THE HRCI TEST SPECIFICATIONS FROM THE RISK MANAGEMENT FUNCTIONAL AREA COVERED IN THIS CHAPTER INCLUDE:

✓ Ensure that workplace health and safety, security, and privacy activities are compliant with applicable federal, state, and local laws and regulations.

✓ Identify the organization's safety program needs.

✓ Develop/select and implement/administer occupational injury and illness prevention, safety incentives, and training programs. **PHR** ⓞⓝⓛⓨ

✓ Develop/select, implement, and evaluate security plans and policies to protect employees and other individuals, and to minimize the organization's loss and liability (for example, emergency response, evacuation, workplace violence, substance abuse).

✓ Communicate and train the workforce on the security plans and policies.

✓ Develop and monitor business continuity and disaster recovery plans.

✓ Communicate and train the workforce on the business continuity and disaster recovery plans.

✓ Develop internal and external privacy policies (for example, identity theft, data protection, HIPAA compliance, workplace monitoring).

✓ Administer internal and external privacy policies.

One of the changes made to the HR BOK as a result of the most recent practice analysis study was the renaming of this functional area from "Occupational Health, Safety, and Security" to "Risk Management." This reflects the move of the profession in general from a focus that is process-driven to one that is based more on anticipating risks and mitigating their impact on the organization. Even with this change in focus, legal compliance still drives many risk management activities.

For over a hundred years beginning in 1867, sporadic legislation was enacted by different states and the federal government to address specific safety concerns, usually in regard to mine safety or factory conditions, but there was no comprehensive legislation requiring employers to protect workers from injury or illness. That changed with the Occupational Safety and Health Act of 1970 (the OSH Act), a comprehensive piece of federal legislation that continues to impact employers in virtually every company in America. While normally this law is referred to as OSHA, this chapter talks at length about the act and the agency that is known by the same initials. For the sake of clarity, the law is referred to as the OSH act throughout the chapter.

In order to be fully prepared for the PHR/SPHR exam, candidates must have the basic knowledge needed to fully understand, develop, implement, and evaluate programs related to the activities detailed in the test specifications for Risk Management. Knowledge of the OSH Act and other federal laws in this area is key to understanding these requirements. Candidates should understand safety and security risks for the company and its employees, be aware of potentially violent behaviors and conditions in the workplace, and understand processes for preventing or reducing the impact of violence in the workplace. The exams require a thorough knowledge of health and safety practices and the ability to develop and implement response plans. Questions on the exams will also require knowledge of internal investigation and surveillance techniques, as well as employee privacy practices. PHR/SPHR candidates will need to be able to recognize the signs of substance abuse and dependency and be aware of the legally appropriate ways to respond to situations involving illegal drug use.

The HRCI core knowledge requirements that will be particularly helpful in understanding this functional area include needs assessment and analysis, communication strategies, documentation requirements, adult learning concepts, motivation, liability, and risk management techniques.

Federal Employment Legislation

In the years prior to passage of the OSH Act, there was a growing recognition that employers were largely unwilling to take preventive steps to reduce the occurrence of injuries, illnesses, and fatalities in the workplace. On December 6, 1907, 362 miners died in an explosion at the

Monongah coal mine in West Virginia—the single worst mining disaster in American history. In that year alone, a total of 3,242 coal miners lost their lives. As a result, in 1910 Congress established the Bureau of Mines to investigate mining accidents.

Annual fatalities in the railroad industry also peaked in 1907 when there were 4,218 work-related deaths. Railroad safety technology began developing at the end of the nineteenth century, but most railroad owners did not implement these preventive measures until much later, partially as a result of federal legislation requiring safety improvements.

The connection between work and health was first studied in sixteenth-century Europe when two traveling physicians, Philippus Aureolus (writing under the name Paracelsus) and Georgius Agricola wrote about mine conditions and advocated changes to protect workers. One treatise by Paracelsus, entitled "On the Miner's Sickness and Other Mine Diseases," investigated the relationship between mining and an illness identified as the "Miner's Sickness," which today we know as silicosis, a disabling and often fatal disease that still takes the lives of more than 250 American workers each year. Between that time and the advent of the Industrial Revolution, however, work done for hire was largely agrarian, and the potential for large-scale injury or illness did not exist in the way it does today.

When steam-powered machinery and equipment took the place of animals and hand tools in the workplace and workers moved from agricultural to industrial jobs, lung diseases were the first to be noticed and addressed by government regulation. Early safety legislation in the United States was enacted by state governments and focused on conditions in factories and mines, often spurred as the result of a tragic accident. In 1869, the federal government established the Bureau of Labor to study and report on job-related accidents, but it had no ability to require changes in safety practices.

There was a long period of time in America when it was cheaper for employers to fight lawsuits filed on behalf of workers killed or injured on the job than it was to implement safety programs. Because the courts rarely held employers accountable for worker injuries, many chose this approach. Employer attitudes in this regard did not change until the shortage of skilled workers during World War II gave employees plentiful options for places to work—and they opted to work for employers who provided safe environments over those who did not.

The tragic nature of large accidents in the railroad and mining industries captured public attention and created pressure on the federal government to take action. This led Congress to enact legislation requiring safety improvements in the coal mining and railroad industries, but these measures were specifically targeted to those industries. Little attention was paid to equally dangerous workplace safety and illness issues that did not produce the spectacular accidents prevalent in mines or on railroads. By the late 1960s, 14,000 American workers lost their lives each year due to injuries or illnesses suffered while on the job. The federal government had been working on solutions, but was mired in bureaucratic turf battles over which agency should have control of the process. The Department of Health, Education, and Welfare wanted legislation that applied only to federal contractors, and the Department of Labor, spurred by Secretary Willard Wirtz's personal interest in the subject, wanted to protect *all* American workers. After several years of this infighting, the proposal by the Department of Labor was sent to the Congress and enacted as the Occupational Safety and Health Act of 1970. A key component of this legislation was the creation of the *Occupational Safety and Health Administration (OSHA)*, which now sets safety standards for all industries. OSHA enforces those standards with the use of fines, and in the case of criminal actions, can call on the Department of Justice to file charges against offenders. Table 8.1 summarizes the federal legislation that impacts risk management activities.

TABLE 8.1   Federal Legislation Governing Risk Management Activities

Type	Enforcement Agency	Chapter Reference
Civil rights	EEOC and/or OFCCP	4
Health and safety	OSHA, MSHA	8
Privacy	Civil litigation	8
Security	SEC	8
Substance abuse	Contracting government agency	8

Let's begin with a review of the OSH Act and other legislation that protects workers.

Occupational Safety and Health Act of 1970

The major piece of federal legislation applicable to the Risk Management functional area is the Occupational Safety and Health Act of 1970, as amended. The intent of Congress, as stated in the preamble to the OSH Act, is to ensure safe and healthful working conditions for American workers. To accomplish this purpose, the act establishes three simple duties:

1. Employers must provide every employee a place to work that is "free from recognized hazards that are causing or are likely to cause death or serious physical harm."

2. Employers must comply with all safety and health standards disseminated in accordance with the act.

3. Employees are required to comply with occupational safety and health standards, rules, and regulations that impact their individual actions and behavior.

As mentioned previously, the OSH Act created OSHA and gave it the authority to develop and enforce mandatory standards applicable to all businesses engaged in interstate commerce. The definition of interstate commerce is sufficiently broad to cover most businesses, excepting only those sole proprietors without employees, family farms employing only family members, and mining operations, which are covered by the Mine Safety and Health Act (to be discussed later in this section). The act encouraged OSHA to work with industry associations and safety committees to build on standards already developed by specific industries, and it authorized enforcement action to ensure that employers comply with the standards. OSHA was charged with developing reporting procedures to track trends in workplace safety and health so that the development of preventive measures would be an ongoing process that changed with the development of new processes and technologies.

The OSH Act also created the *National Institute of Occupational Safety and Health (NIOSH)* as part of the Department of Health and Human Services. NIOSH is charged with researching and evaluating workplace hazards and recommending ways to reduce the effect of those hazards on workers. NIOSH also supports education and training in the field of occupational safety and health by developing and providing educational materials and training aids and sponsoring conferences on workplace safety and health issues.

The NIOSH website (`www.cdc.gov/niosh/homepage.html`) provides a wealth of information that may be of assistance to PHR and SPHR candidates looking for additional study resources.

Finally, the OSH Act encourages the states to take the lead in developing and enforcing safety and health programs for businesses within their jurisdictions by providing grants to help states identify specific issues and to develop programs for enforcement and prevention.

Employer Responsibilities

As discussed earlier in this chapter, the OSH Act has three requirements, two of which pertain to employers. Not only must employers provide a workplace that is safe and healthful for employees, they must also comply with established standards. OSHA has established other requirements for employers as required by the law:

- Employers are expected to take steps to minimize or reduce hazards and ensure that employees have and use safe tools, equipment, and personal protective equipment (PPE) and ensure that they are properly maintained.

- Employers are responsible to inform all employees about OSHA, posting the OSHA poster in a prominent location and making them aware of the standards that apply in the worksite. If employees request copies of a standard, the employer must provide it to them.

- Appropriate warning signs that conform to the OSHA standards for color coding, posting, or labels must be posted where needed to make employees aware of potential hazards.

- Compliance with OSHA standards also means that employers must educate employees about safe operating procedures and train them to follow the procedures.

- Businesses with 11 or more employees must maintain records of all workplace injuries and illnesses and post them from February 1 through April 30 each year.

- Within eight hours of a fatal accident, or one resulting in hospitalization for three or more employees, a report must be filed with the nearest OSHA office.

- An accident report log must be made available to employees, former employees, or employee representatives when reasonably requested.

- When employees report unsafe conditions to OSHA, the employer may not retaliate or discriminate against them.

Employer Rights

Employers have some rights as well, including the right to seek advice and consultation from OSHA and to be active in industry activities involved in health and safety issues. Employers may also participate in the OSHA Standard Advisory Committee process in writing or by giving testimony at hearings. Finally, employers may contact NIOSH for information about substances used in work processes to determine whether or not they are toxic.

At times, employers may be unable to comply with OSHA standards due to the nature of specific operations. When this happens, they may apply to OSHA for temporary or permanent waivers to the standards along with proof that the protections developed by the organization meet or exceed those of the OSHA standard.

Employee Rights and Responsibilities

When the OSH Act was passed in 1970, employees were granted the basic right to a workplace with safe and healthful working conditions. The act intended to encourage employers and employees to collaborate in reducing workplace hazards. Employees have the responsibility to comply with all OSHA standards and with the safety and health procedures implemented by their employers. The act gave employees the following specific rights to:

- Seek safety and health on the job without fear of punishment.

- Know what hazards exist on the job by reviewing the OSHA standards, rules, and regulations that the employer has available at the workplace.

- Be provided with the hazard communication plan containing information about hazards in the workplace and preventive measures employees should take to avoid illness or injury, and to be trained in those measures.

- Access the exposure and medical records employers are required to keep relative to safety and health issues.

- Request an OSHA inspection, speak privately with the inspector, accompany the inspector during the inspection, and respond to the inspector's questions during the inspection.

- Observe steps taken by the employer to monitor and measure hazardous materials in the workplace, and access records resulting from those steps.

- Request information from NIOSH regarding the potential toxic effects of substances used in the workplace.

- File a complaint about workplace safety or health hazards with OSHA and remain anonymous to the employer.

OSHA Enforcement

OSHA's success is the result of strong enforcement of the standards it has developed. As demonstrated in the nineteenth and twentieth centuries, without the threat of financial penalty, some business owners would choose to ignore injury and illness prevention requirements. That being the case, OSHA established fines and penalties that can be assessed against businesses when violations occur. Table 8.2 describes the violation levels and associated penalties for noncompliance.

During fiscal year 2004, OSHA conducted 39,167 inspections. Tables 8.3 and 8.4 provide a breakdown of the numbers and reasons for inspections, as well as the costs of violations identified during the inspections.

TABLE 8.2   Categories of OSHA Violations

Violation	Description	Fine
Willful	Assessed when there is evidence of an intentional violation of the OSH Act or "plain indifference" to its requirements.	$5,000 to $70,000 per violation
Serious	Assessed when there is substantial probability of death or serious physical harm as a result of the hazard.	Up to $7,000
Other-than-Serious	The hazard could have a direct and immediate effect on the safety and health of employees.	Up to $7,000
Repeat	OSHA has previously issued citations for substantially similar conditions.	Up to $70,000 per violation
Failure to Abate	The employer failed to abate a prior violation.	Up to $7,000 per day past the abatement date
de-minimus	Assessed for violations with no direct or immediate relationship to safety or health.	$0

Source: OSHA Facts, www.osha.gov/as/opa/oshafacts.html

TABLE 8.3   OSHA Inspections During Fiscal Year 2004

Number	Percent	Reason for Inspection
9,176	23.4%	Complaint/accident related
21,576	55.1%	High hazard targeted
8,415	21.5%	Referrals, follow-ups, etc.

Number	Percent	Industry Sector
22,360	57.1%	Construction
8,755	22.4%	Manufacturing
378	1%	Maritime
7,674	19.6%	Other industries

Source: OSHA Facts, www.osha.gov/as/opa/oshafacts.html

TABLE 8.4   Violations and Penalties from 2004 Inspections

Violations	Percent	Type	Current Penalties
462	0.5%	Willful	$14,553,171
61,666	71.1%	Serious	$54,526,440
2,360	2.7%	Repeat	$9,755,960
301	0.3%	Failure to Abate	$1,611,943
21,705	25%	Other	$1,960,084
214	0.2%	Unclassified	$2,785,342
86,708	TOTAL		$85,192,940

Source: OSHA Facts, www.osha.gov/as/opa/oshafacts.html

OSHA Record Keeping Requirements

OSHA requires employers to record health and safety incidents that occur each year and to document steps they take to comply with regulations. Records of specific injuries and illnesses are compiled, allowing OSHA and NIOSH to identify emerging hazards for research and, if warranted, create new standards designed to reduce the possibility of similar injury or illness in the future. These records include up-to-date files for exposures to hazardous substances and related medical records, records of safety training meetings, and OSHA logs that record work-related injuries and illnesses.

As of January 1, 2002, OSHA revised the requirements for maintaining records of workplace injuries and illnesses in order to collect better information for use in prevention activities, simplify the information collection process, and make use of advances in technology. Three new forms were developed:

1. OSHA Form 300, Log of Work-Related Injuries and Illnesses
2. OSHA Form 300A, Summary of Work-Related Injuries and Illnesses
3. OSHA Form 301, Injury and Illness Incident Report

Completion of the forms does not constitute proof of fault on the part of either the employer or the employee and does not indicate that any OSHA violations have occurred. Recording an injury or illness on the OSHA forms does not mean that an employee is eligible for worker compensation benefits. Detailed guidance about completing the forms is available at www.osha.gov/recordkeeping/detailedfaq.html#1904.0.

The following list covers the basic requirements for OSHA record keeping, including who should file OSHA reports, which employers are exempt from filing, and what injuries are considered work related:

Who must complete and file OSHA forms?   All employers with 11 or more employees are required to complete and file the OSHA forms just discussed.

Are there any exemptions?   Employers with 10 or fewer employees are not required to file the forms. In addition, OSHA has identified industries with low injury and illness rates and exempted them from filing reports. These include the retail, service, finance, insurance, and real estate industries. Unless OSHA has notified a business in writing that reports must be filed, they are exempt from the requirement.

What must be recorded?   There are three considerations taken into account in determining whether an injury or illness should be recorded. First, is the employee covered by OSHA? Second, is the employee covered by OSHA regulations? And finally, is it a new case?

Injury or illness to any employee on the employer's payroll must be recorded, regardless of how the employee is classified, full or part time, regular or temporary, hourly or salary. Injuries to employees of temp agencies, if under the employer's direct supervision on a daily basis, must also be recorded. The owners and partners in sole proprietorships and partnerships are not considered employees for OSHA reporting purposes.

Privacy concern cases are new protections developed by OSHA to protect employee privacy by substituting a case number for the employee name on the OSHA 300 log. Cases where this is appropriate include injury or illness that involved an intimate body part or resulted from a sexual assault; HIV infection, hepatitis or tuberculosis; needlestick injuries involving contaminated needles; or other illnesses when employees request that their names not be included on the log.

An injury or illness is generally considered to be work related if it occurred in the workplace. Table 8.5 is provided in the regulations to provide guidance in determining when an injury or illness is not considered to be work related.

Once the employer has determined whether or not the injury or illness is work related, it must determine whether this is a new case or a continuation of a previously recorded case. To a certain extent, this decision is left to the employer's common sense and best judgment. OSHA considers a new case to have occurred when an employee has not had a previous injury or illness that is the same as the current occurrence, or when the employee had recovered completely from a previous injury or illness of the same type.

TABLE 8.5   Injuries and Illnesses Not Considered Work Related

1904.5(b)(2)	You are not required to record injuries and illnesses if
(i)	At the time of the injury or illness, the employee was present in the work environment as a member of the general public rather than as an employee.
(ii)	The injury or illness involves signs or symptoms that surface at work but result solely from a non-work-related event or exposure that occurs outside the work environment.
(iii)	The injury or illness results solely from voluntary participation in a wellness program or in a medical, fitness, or recreational activity such as blood donation, physical examination, flu shot, exercise class, racquetball, or baseball.

TABLE 8.5   Injuries and Illnesses Not Considered Work Related *(continued)*

1904.5(b)(2)	You are not required to record injuries and illnesses if
(iv)	The injury or illness is solely the result of an employee eating, drinking, or preparing food or drink for personal consumption (whether bought on the employer's premises or brought in). For example, if the employee is injured by choking on a sandwich while in the employer's establishment, the case would not be considered work related. **Note:** If the employee is made ill by ingesting food contaminated by workplace contaminants (such as lead), or gets food poisoning from food supplied by the employer, the case would be considered work related.
(v)	The injury or illness is solely the result of an employee doing personal tasks (unrelated to their employment) at the establishment outside of the employee's assigned working hours.
(vi)	The injury or illness is solely the result of personal grooming, self medication for a non-work-related condition, or is intentionally self-inflicted.
(vii)	The injury or illness is caused by a motor vehicle accident and occurs on a company parking lot or company access road while the employee is commuting to or from work.
(viii)	The illness is the common cold or flu. **Note:** Contagious diseases such as tuberculosis, brucellosis, hepatitis A, or plague are considered work-related if the employee is infected at work.
(ix)	The illness is a mental illness. Mental illness will not be considered work related unless the employee voluntarily provides the employer with an opinion from a physician or other licensed health care professional with appropriate training and experience (psychiatrist, psychologist, psychiatric nurse practitioner, etc.) stating that the employee has a mental illness that is work related.

Source: OSHA Regulations Section 1904.5

Annual summary   At the end of each year, employers must review the OSHA 300 log and summarize the entries on the form 300A, which must then be certified by a company executive as correct and complete, and then posted as previously mentioned in February of the following year.

Retention   The OSHA 300 log and annual summary, privacy case list, and 301 Incident Report forms must be retained for five years following the end of the calendar year that they cover.

Employee involvement   Employers are required to provide employees and employee representatives, former employees, or a personal representative of an employee with information on how to properly report an injury or illness, and they are also required to allow limited access to employees or their representatives to the records of injury and illness.

The OSHA 300 log must be provided to these requestors by the end of the following business day.

The OSHA 301 Incident Report must be provided by the end of the next business day when the employee who is the subject of the report requests a copy. When an employee representative requests copies, they must be provided within seven calendar days, and all information except that contained in the "Tell Us About the Case" section must be removed.

OSHA Inspections

OSHA is empowered by the OSH Act to inspect workplaces. Most inspections are conducted without notice by a Compliance Safety and Health Officer (CSHO) who has been trained on OSHA standards and how to recognize safety and health hazards in the workplace. OSHA has established a hierarchy of situations to give priority to inspection of the most dangerous workplace environments. Table 8.6 describes the priorities OSHA uses in allocating time for inspections.

TABLE 8.6   OSHA Inspection Priorities

Priority	Hazard	Description
First	Imminent Danger	A reasonable certainty that immediate death or serious injury from existing workplace hazards will occur before normal enforcement procedures can take place.
Second	Catastrophes and Fatal Accidents	Employers must report fatal accidents or serious injuries resulting in the hospitalization of 3 or more employees within 8 hours. OSHA will inspect to determine if any safety violations contributed to the accident.
Third	Employee Complaints	Employees may request inspections when they feel violations exist that threaten physical harm.
Fourth	Programmed High-Hazard Inspections	Based on statistical analysis, OSHA conducts planned inspections of industries or jobs that have high incident rates for death, injury, and illness.
Fifth	Follow-up Inspections	CSHOs follow up on previously issued citations to ensure that the employer has taken action to correct the violation.

During an inspection, OSHA follows a distinct procedure. In advance of the inspection, the CSHO prepares by reviewing records related to any previous incidents or inspections or employee complaints. The inspector also determines what, if any, special testing equipment will be necessary for the inspection. Upon arrival at the worksite, the inspection commences with an opening conference, proceeds to a workplace tour, and ends with a closing conference.

1. First, the CSHO arrives at the worksite and presents his credentials. If the credentials are not presented, the employer should insist upon seeing them before the inspection begins. It is critical that any employee who may be the first person approached at the worksite be

instructed as to who should be contacted when a CSHO arrives. Employers have the right to require the inspector to have a security clearance before entering secure areas. Any observation of trade secrets during the inspection remains confidential; CSHOs who breach this confidentiality are subject to fines and imprisonment.

2. Next, the CSHO holds an *opening conference*, during which the inspector will explain why the site was selected, the purpose of the visit, the scope of the inspection, and discuss the standards that apply to the worksite. The CSHO will request an employee representative to accompany the CSHO on the inspection along with the management representative. If no employee accompanies the inspector on the tour, the CSHO will talk to as many employees as necessary to understand the safety and health issues in the workplace.

3. The next step is a tour of the facilities. During the tour, the inspector will determine what route to take, where to look, and to which employees the CSHO will talk. During this part of the inspection, the CSHO may talk privately to employees, taking care to minimize disruptions to work processes. Activities that can occur during an inspection include the following:

   - Review of the safety and health program

   - Examination of records, including OSHA logs, records of employee exposure to toxic substances, and medical records

   - Ensuring that the OSHA workplace poster is prominently displayed

   - Evaluation of compliance with OSHA standards specific to the worksite

   - Pointing out unsafe working conditions to the employer and suggesting possible remedial actions

4. Finally, the inspector holds a *closing conference*, where the inspector, the employer, and, if requested, the employee representative discuss the observations made and corrective actions that must be taken. At this time the employer may produce records to assist in resolving any corrective actions to be taken. The CSHO will discuss any possible citations or penalties that may be issued, and the OSHA Area Director makes the final determination based on the inspector's report.

Should the OSHA Area Director determine that citations are necessary to ensure employer compliance with OSHA, the director will issue citations and determine the penalties to be assessed according to established guidelines that consider various factors, including the size of the company. The OSHA Area Director also determines the seriousness of the danger, how many employees would be impacted, and good faith efforts on the part of the employer to comply with the standards, among others. OSHA regulations allow for adjustments to penalties based on the size of the employer, the gravity of the offense, and the employer's good-faith efforts to cooperate with the inspector.

During the course of an OSHA inspection, an employer may raise an affirmative defense to any violations observed by the inspector. Possible affirmative defenses include:

- An isolated case caused by unpreventable employee misconduct. This defense may apply when the employer has established, communicated, and enforced adequate work rules that were ignored by the employee.

- Compliance is impossible based on the nature of the employer's work, and there are no viable alternative means of protection.

- Compliance with the standard would cause a greater hazard to employees, and there are no alternative means of protection.

The employer has the burden to prove an affirmative defense exists. If successfully proven, the OSHA Area Director may decide that a citation and penalty are not warranted.

Employers have specific responsibilities and rights during and after the inspection:

- Employers are required to cooperate with the CSHO by providing records and documents requested during the inspection and by allowing employees or their representatives to accompany the inspector on the worksite tour.

- Should a citation be issued during the inspection, the employer must post it at or near the worksite involved, where it must remain for three working days or until the violation has been abated, whichever is longer. It goes without saying, of course, that the employer is required to abate the violation within the time frame indicated by the citation.

- Employers may file a Notice of Contest within 15 days of a citation and proposed penalty. If there will be an unavoidable delay in abating a violation because the materials, equipment, or personnel will not be available, the employer may request a temporary variance until the violation can be corrected.

Within 15 days of receipt of a citation by an employer, employees have the right to object in writing to the abatement period set by OSHA for correcting violations. Employees who have requested an inspection also have the right to be advised by OSHA of the results of the inspection.

OSHA Assistance

OSHA provides many sources for employers and employees to obtain information about workplace health and safety issues. Chief among these is an extensive website (www.osha.gov), which provides access to the laws, regulations, and standards enforced by OSHA as well as general information on prevention. In addition to the website, OSHA publishes a number of pamphlets, brochures, and training materials that are available to employers.

OSHA Consultants

Educating employers and employees about workplace health and safety issues is key to preventing injuries and illnesses in the workplace. OSHA provides training programs for consultants who work with business owners in establishing effective health and safety programs. These free consultation services give employers an opportunity to learn which of the standards apply in their worksite, involve employees in the safety process, and correct possible violations without a citation and penalty. Once the consultant becomes involved, the employer must abate any violations or the consultant will refer the violation to an OSHA inspector.

The *Safety and Health Achievement Recognition Program (SHARP)* recognizes small, high-hazard employers who have requested a comprehensive OSHA consultation, corrected any violations, and developed an ongoing safety management program. To participate in the program, the business must agree to ask for additional consultations if work processes change.

Partnerships and Voluntary Programs

The *Strategic Partnership Program* is a means for businesses and employees to participate in solving health and safety problems with OSHA. Partnerships currently exist in 15 industries, including construction, food processing, logging, and health care to develop solutions specific to their businesses.

The *OSHA Alliance Program* provides a vehicle for collaboration with employer organizations interested in promoting workplace health and safety issues. The program is open to trade and professional organizations, businesses, labor organizations, educational institutions, and government agencies, among others.

The *Voluntary Protection Program (VPP)* is open to employers with tough, established safety programs. VPP participants must meet OSHA criteria for the program and, having done so, are removed from routine scheduled inspection lists. The program serves to motivate employees to work more safely, reduce worker compensation costs, and encourage further improvements to safety programs. Acceptance into the VPP is an official recognition of exemplary occupational safety and health practices.

Mine Safety and Health Act of 1977 (MSH Act)

The MSH Act established the *Mine Safety and Health Administration (MSHA)* to ensure the safety of workers in coal and other mines. The act establishes mandatory safety and health standards for mine operators and monitors operations throughout the United States. MSHA has developed a comprehensive website (www.msha.gov/) that is a resource for miners and mine operators, providing access to information on preventing accidents, year-to-date fatalities, and guidance on specific mine hazards. The site also contains a link to the complete text of the act.

Drug-Free Workplace Act of 1988

The Drug-Free Workplace Act applies to businesses with federal contracts of $100,000 or more each year. Contractors subject to the act must take the following steps to be in compliance:

Develop and publish a written policy   Contractors must develop a written policy clearly stating that they provide a drug-free workplace and that illegal substance abuse is not an acceptable practice in the workplace. The policy must clearly state what substances are covered and clearly indicate the consequences for violation of the policy.

Establish an awareness program   The employer must develop a program to educate employees about the policy and communicate the dangers of drug abuse in the workplace, discuss the employer's policy, inform employees of the availability of counseling or other programs to reduce drug use, and notify employees of the penalties for violating the policy. The program can be delivered through a variety of media—seminars, brochures, videos, web-based training—whatever methods will most effectively communicate the information in the specific environment.

Notify employees about contract conditions   Employees must be made aware that a condition of their employment on a federal contract project is that they abide by the policy and inform the employer within five days if they are convicted of a criminal drug offense in the workplace.

Notify the contracting agency of violations   In the event that an employee is convicted of a criminal drug offense in the workplace, the employer must notify the contracting agency within ten days of being informed of the conviction by the employee.

Establish penalties for illegal drug convictions   The employer must have an established penalty for any employees convicted of relevant drug offenses. Within 30 days of notice by an employee of a conviction, the employer must take appropriate disciplinary action against the employee, or require participation in an appropriate drug rehabilitation program. Any penalties must be in accordance with requirements of the Rehabilitation Act of 1973.

Maintain a drug-free workplace   Contractors must make a good faith effort to maintain a drug-free workplace in accordance with the act, or they are subject to penalties, including suspension of payments under the contract, suspension or termination of the contract, or exclusion from consideration from future contracts for a period of up to five years.

Other Legislation Impacting Risk Management

While the OSH Act of 1970 is the major piece of federal legislation that impacts employers, other legislation has less well-known requirements related to occupational health and safety. This additional legislation includes the following:

Fair Labor Standards Act   Components of the Fair Labor Standards Act (FLSA), more fully discussed in Chapter 6, "Total Rewards," apply to children in the workforce. Minors between the ages of 16 and 18 may not be employed in jobs considered particularly hazardous to them, including those that expose them to explosives, logging operations, power-driven tools, radiation, mining operations, and other jobs that require the use of equipment that poses a significant danger to the child.

Electronic Communications Privacy Act of 1986 (ECPA)   The ECPA updated Title 18 of the United States Code, to bring an older law current with technology, by adding electronic communication to the list of prohibited interceptions. Although the original law was enacted to control law enforcement wiretaps, the ECPA amendment added civil penalties that affect an employer's ability to monitor employee communication. The law permits employers to monitor communication that occurs within their normal course of business and when employees give consent.

Needlestick Safety and Prevention Act of 2000   This law was enacted in response to the ongoing public health issue of exposure to blood-borne pathogens by health care workers subjected to accidental needlestick or sharps injuries. The act mandates that all needlestick and sharps injuries be recorded, requires involvement of front-line employees in finding safer devices to replace needles and sharps, and protects employees who have endured needlestick injuries.

Risk Assessment

Risk assessment is the process used to determine the likelihood that an organization will be affected by some type of loss, such as those that occur when employees are injured as the result of unsafe working conditions, or contract illnesses caused by something in the work environment. An assessment also estimates the cost of the loss if one should happen and the impact it would have on the ability of the organization to continue operations. With this knowledge, it is possible to identify which losses are most likely to occur and what controls must be in place to prevent them. Identifying and ranking risks provides organizations with the opportunity to be proactive and implement controls to prevent losses.

Safety and Health Risks

Any discussion of safety and health risks must begin with OSHA, because it exerts overwhelming influence on those issues in the workplace. OSHA statistics, developed through the record-keeping requirements of the OSH Act, show significant improvements in workplace safety and health since 1971: fatalities have been reduced by 62 percent, and injury and illness rates have been reduced by 42 percent, even though the workforce has more than doubled during the same time period. These improvements in working conditions are a result of many factors—the change from a manufacturing to a service economy and improvements in technology among them—but underlying them all has been OSHA, with its unwavering focus on establishing standards to improve health and safety in the American workplace. In May 2003, OSHA unveiled its new five-year strategic management plan to further reduce workplace fatalities by an additional 15 percent and workplace injuries and illnesses by 20 percent by the year 2008.

OSHA estimates business costs for occupational illness and injury to be $170 billion a year. The purpose of assessing risk for environmental health and safety issues is to prevent those illnesses and injuries from occurring in the first place, to protect workers and, in the long run, to reduce the costs of turnover and worker compensation, as well as to increase productivity and eliminate OSHA fines and penalties.

Environmental Health Hazards

Environmental health hazards in the modern workplace come in many forms, from physical hazards such as noise and extreme temperatures to chemicals used for everything from making copies to manufacturing products to biological hazards from viruses and bacteria. The effects of these various hazards differ between individual employees—some are more affected than others—so employers must take steps to prevent serious health consequences in the workplace. Table 8.7 provides a list of some of the more common environmental health hazards.

Chemical Health Hazards

Many of the OSHA standards deal with specific *chemical health hazards* in the workplace. Every chemical present in the workplace should have a *material safety data sheet (MSDS)* provided by the chemical manufacturer to provide information on how to both prevent and treat

TABLE 8.7   Examples of Environmental Health Hazards

Chemical	Physical	Biological
Asbestos	Ergonomic design	Bacteria
Battery acid	Stress	Contaminated water
Corrosives	Extreme temperatures	Dusts
Gas fumes	Light, noise	Fungi
Pesticides	Electrical currents	Molds
Polyurethane foam	Radiation	Plants
Solvents	Vibrations	Viruses

an injury. The MSDS identifies the ingredients in the substance, how the substance reacts to changes in the atmosphere such as at what temperature it will boil or become a vapor, and information about its explosive and flammable qualities. The MSDS tells employees whether it is stable or unstable, what materials it must not be in contact with, and what additional hazards are present when the substance decomposes or degrades.

Most importantly for safety programs, the MSDS provides information about how the chemical may be absorbed by the body; whether it can be inhaled, ingested, or enter through the skin; whether it is carcinogenic; and what protective equipment is required to prevent illness when handling the substance.

There are some chemicals, known as *teratogens*, which have no effect on a pregnant woman but do affect an unborn child. Some employers, concerned about the health of the employee and her child as well as about potential liability, have developed policies to protect the fetus. These policies, while well-intentioned, violate the Pregnancy Discrimination Act, which prohibits sex-specific fetal protection policies.

 Real World Scenario

Automobile Workers v. Johnson Controls, Inc.

Johnson Controls, Inc. manufactures batteries, a process in which lead is a primary ingredient. Occupational exposure to lead can have serious health consequences, including posing a risk to the health of an unborn child. Prior to 1964, Johnson Controls did not employ women in any of the battery manufacturing jobs in its plant. After passage of the Civil Rights Act in 1964, women were given the opportunity to work in those jobs.

In June 1977, Johnson developed its first fetal protection policy, which stated, "(P)rotection of the health of the unborn child is the immediate and direct responsibility of the prospective parents. While the medical profession and the company can support them in the exercise of this responsibility, it cannot assume it for them without simultaneously infringing their rights as persons." Although this policy did not exclude women from the manufacturing jobs, the company discouraged women who wished to have children from taking these jobs and required them to sign a statement that they had been advised of the risks of lead exposure to a fetus.

In 1982, after eight women became pregnant while maintaining high levels of lead in their blood, the policy changed: "...women who are pregnant or who are capable of bearing children will not be placed into jobs involving lead exposure or which could expose them to lead through the exercise of job bidding, bumping, transfer, or promotion rights." The policy went on to define lead levels that would make a job inaccessible to women and required that women who wished to work in those positions supply medical proof of their inability to bear children.

In 1984, a class action petition challenging the fetal-protection policy was filed. Among the individuals in the class were Mary Craig, who had chosen to be sterilized so that she could keep her job; Elsie Nason, a 50-year-old divorcee who had been transferred out of a job where she was exposed to lead to a job that paid less; and Donald Penney, who had requested and been denied a leave of absence so that the lead level in his blood could be lowered in order for him to become a father.

Johnson Controls argued that its policy was a business necessity.

Both the District Court and the Federal Court of Appeals found for Johnson Controls. The case was then appealed to the U. S. Supreme Court in 1990, where the lower court decisions were reversed. The Supreme Court found that there was clear bias because the policy required only female employees to prove that they were not capable of conceiving children, and it was therefore in violation of the PDA.

The Supreme Court ruled that "Decisions about the welfare of the next generation must be left to the parents who conceive, bear, support, and raise them, rather than to the employers who hire those parents."

Physical Health Hazards

There are many *physical health hazards* that are easy to identify and remedy. One such hazard would be an open hole without any warning signs or barriers to prevent someone from accidentally falling. Another would be an electrical or telephone cord crossing a walkway that is not covered or secured to prevent someone from tripping. Another physical hazard would be a walk-in freezer storage unit that could not be opened from inside the unit. Other physical hazards occurring in the workplace are less obvious, such as ergonomics and stress.

Ergonomics   In 1700, Bernardino Ramazzini published his "Discourse on Diseases of Workers," which sought to connect illnesses with environmental conditions in the workplace. One of the connections he made was to identify "irregular" or "unnatural" body movements that affect the safety and health of workers. We know this concept today as *ergonomics*—the science that addresses the way a physical environment is designed and how efficient and safe that design is for the people in the environment.

Poor ergonomic designs can cause *musculoskeletal disorders* or MSDs. An MSD is the result of repeated stress to various parts of the body (including the back, arms, shoulders, and other areas) that is caused by the way tasks are performed. MSDs are referred to by several other names as well, including *repetitive stress injuries (RSI)* and *cumulative trauma injuries (CTI)*. MSD injuries that can result from poor ergonomics in the workplace include tendonitis, bursitis, and carpal tunnel syndrome. According to BLS statistics, these and other MSD injuries account for one-third of workplace injuries and illnesses each year, which makes them the largest job-related health and safety problem in the United States. Factors that contribute to MSDs include awkward postures; forceful lifting, pushing, or pulling; prolonged repetitive motions; contact stress; and vibration, such as that which occurs while using power tools for an extended period of time.

Development of an ergonomics program provides a means by which employers can determine whether or not MSDs are a problem in their workplaces. An effective ergonomics program requires management support and involves employees in the process. After a review of OSHA logs and worker compensation claims for injury patterns, an analysis of job tasks, beginning with an observation of the work area while work is being done, is needed to determine if the risk factors for potential injury exist. Jobs with poor ergonomics may be redesigned to make them less hazardous and reduce injuries.

OSHA has developed tools to assist employers in reducing potential ergonomic hazards. The tools are provided in a checklist format for various activities that are statistically prone to ergonomic injury, including handling baggage, sewing, and working at a computer workstation. The checklists provide guidance in the form of basic principles that can be used to reduce ergonomic injuries. For example, the computer workstation checklist provides guidelines for placement of the monitor, keyboard, mouse, desk, chair, and telephone along with a discussion of some common problems that can occur. The checklists may be viewed online at `www.osha.gov/dts/osta/oshasoft/index.html#eTools`. In addition to those currently available, OSHA is in the process of developing similar checklists for specific industries and jobs.

Job-related stress   In 1999, NIOSH published the results of a study entitled *Stress at Work*, which defined job *stress* as "harmful physical and emotional responses that occur when the requirements of the job do not match the capabilities, resources, or needs of the worker." When job stress is added to personal factors in an employee's life, such as a sick child or financial concerns, the effect on job performance can be magnified. Dr. Hans Selye, an endocrinologist, is generally credited with identifying stress as an influencer of health and well being. He identified three stages of stress: arousal, resistance, and exhaustion. Table 8.8 describes the three stages of stress and some of the related symptoms.

TABLE 8.8   Stages and Symptoms of Stress

Stage	Physical	Emotional	Mental
Arousal	Teeth grinding Insomnia	Irritability Anxiety	Forgetfulness Inability to concentrate
Resistance	Fatigue without a cause	Mood swings Social withdrawal Resentment Indifference Defiance	Procrastination Indecision
Exhaustion	Headaches Chronic fatigue Indigestion Intestinal problems	Chronic depression Hostility Isolation	Disorganization Poor judgment Disillusionment

Stress-related illnesses such as allergies, heart disease, panic attacks, and other diseases affect productivity, as does burnout, which can be the result of long-term, unrelenting job stress.

High levels of job stress can result in increased turnover, low morale, increased tardiness and absenteeism, reduced productivity, poor product quality, and increased accidents on the job. All of these negatively impact the bottom line.

The NIOSH study identified six circumstances that can lead to job stress. Table 8.9 explains these circumstances:

TABLE 8.9   Job Stressors Identified by NIOSH

Stressor	Characteristics
Task design	Heavy workloads and infrequent rest breaks Long, hectic hours Shift work Routine tasks with little inherent meaning Tasks that do not utilize employee skills Little or no control over daily work
Management style	Lack of participation in decisions that affect them Poor organizational communication Lack of family-friendly policies
Interpersonal relationships	Poor social environment Lack of support or help from coworkers and supervisors
Work roles	Conflicting or uncertain job expectations Too much responsibility Too many "hats to wear"

TABLE 8.9   Job Stressors Identified by NIOSH *(continued)*

Stressor	Characteristics
Career concerns	Job insecurity Lack of opportunity for growth, advancement, or promotion Lack of preparation for rapid changes
Environmental conditions	Unpleasant or dangerous physical conditions such as crowding, noise, air pollution Ergonomic problems

Source: NIOSH "Stress . . . At Work" booklet

The NIOSH study recommends a two-pronged approach to reducing job stress: organizational change and stress management. Organizational changes can take the form of employee recognition programs, career development, a culture that values individual employees, and employer actions consistent with the organization's stated values. Stress management programs are, to a certain extent, dependent upon the needs of individual employees as people react differently to job stressors. These programs include training for employees about the sources of stress and how it affects health and teaching stress-reduction skills. Managers can encourage employees to reduce the effects of stress by balancing their work with private activities, maintaining an exercise program, and building a support network at work and at home.

The full NIOSH study mentioned earlier is available free of charge at www.cdc.gov/niosh/stresswk.html.

Biological Health Hazards

Biological health hazards come in many forms, from unsanitary conditions in a food preparation area to serious diseases contracted through needlestick injuries. Infectious diseases are spread by different means to employees, but the resulting impact on the health of the workforce or the community can be substantial. Although the health care and food preparation industries are at greater risk than other industries, HR professionals should understand the implications of infectious disease in all workplaces.

HIV/AIDS   Human immunodeficiency virus (HIV) and acquired immune deficiency syndrome (AIDS) are blood-borne pathogens transmitted through blood or other bodily fluids. For this reason, transmission to coworkers in workplaces other than in the health care industry is relatively unlikely. Persons with HIV/AIDS are protected by the ADA; as long as they are able to perform their essential job functions, they are entitled to remain employed.

HBV   The hepatitis B virus (HBV) is another blood-borne pathogen posing risks to health care workers. Because transmission chiefly occurs as the result of an accidental needlestick, health care workers are at the greatest risk of infection in the workplace. The CDC recommends that health care workers at high risk of infection be vaccinated to prevent them from contracting the disease.

Tuberculosis   Tuberculosis is a lung disease that is spread through the air. Exposure occurs when someone with TB coughs or sneezes, expelling pathogens. Those at higher risk for contracting TB in the workplace are people who share the same breathing space, such as coworkers or health care workers, particularly in nursing homes.

Severe Acute Respiratory Syndrome (SARS)   According to the CDC, there have been no outbreaks of SARS since 2004. Between the initial outbreak in November 2002 and the last known outbreak in April 2004, it affected business travel and had a negative effect on some industries, particularly the travel industry. SARS appears to be transmitted by close person-to-person contact when an infected person coughs or sneezes. Preventing the spread of SARS in the workplace requires frequent hand washing and the use of common household cleaners to frequently clean surfaces.

Avian influenza   Avian influenza (H5N1) is currently a global health concern. At this time, H5N1 mainly affects wild and domesticated birds in parts of Asia, Europe, the Near East, and Africa, with only a small number of cases of human infection. A few cases in Asia have been the result of human-to-human transmission, and health care practitioners are concerned that if this type of transmission increases, a global pandemic will ensue. The CDC advises travelers to avoid contact with live birds, wash their hands often with soap and water, and cover their noses and mouths when coughing or sneezing.

Preparing for a pandemic   HR professionals can play a role in preparing their organizations to cope with a pandemic by establishing plans to maintain essential functions if a large number of employees are absent from work. The CDC encourages employers to prepare guidelines for minimizing face-to-face contact; secure vaccines for employees to prevent outbreaks; modify sick-leave policies to allow ill employees time to recover so that they do not spread the disease; utilize telecommuting, flexible work hours, and work shifts to minimize contact; and establish knowledge management programs to ensure business continuity during a health crisis. Additional information on preparing for a pandemic is available at www.pandemicflu.gov/.

Employees with infectious diseases who do not pose a threat to coworker health and safety are protected by ADA requirements for reasonable accommodation and may not be subjected to adverse employment actions because of their disease.

Environmental Safety Hazards

Although the OSH Act did not clearly define workplace hazards, it did empower OSHA to define *occupational safety and health standards* that would result in improved workplace safety and health as quickly as possible. Wherever possible the act encouraged OSHA to use previously existing federal standards or industry standards that already had substantial agreement within the industry. The resulting standards range from those that are job and industry specific, such as standards for handling toxic chemicals used in manufacturing processes, to those that apply to businesses in many different industries.

Let's review some of the more generally applicable standards now. Each standard is identified here with the OSHA title and the number assigned to it in the Code of Federal Regulations (CFR).

The General Duty Standard, Section 5   The *general duty standard* requires employers to provide jobs and a workplace environment that are free from recognized safety and health hazards that could potentially cause death or serious physical harm. This standard also requires employers to comply with all OSHA rules, regulations, and standards.

Employees are required to comply with OSHA standards and rules that apply to their own conduct in the course of performing their duties.

Emergency Action Plans, 1910.38   Employers are required to have *emergency action plans* in place to inform employees of appropriate procedures to follow during a fire or evacuation. The plan must designate employees who will remain behind during an evacuation to maintain or shut down critical operations. Employers must also develop a process to account for all employees after an evacuation and identify those employees who are responsible to carry out rescue and medical duties in the event of an emergency. Employers must provide training for employees when the plan is first developed, when new employees are hired, and when an employee is assigned new responsibilities for execution of the plan.

The plan must also identify the person responsible for maintaining it who can be contacted by employees when they have questions about the plan.

Fire Prevention Plans, 1910.39   An OSHA-required fire prevention plan must describe the major fire hazards and appropriate procedures for handling and storing hazardous materials to prevent fires. The employer must develop and implement procedures to control the accumulation of flammable or combustible refuse and ensure that devices on heat-producing machinery designed to prevent ignition of fires are adequately maintained.

The fire prevention plan must also inform employees about any fire hazards they will face when first assigned to a new job and what actions they should take to protect themselves in the event of a fire.

Occupational Noise Exposure, 1910.95   This standard establishes permissible noise levels for the workplace, establishes measurement procedures, requires implementation of hearing conservation programs when average noise levels reach 85 decibels or greater, and requires audiometric testing for employees who work in environments with noise at those levels. Audiometric test results indicating a hearing loss of 10 decibels must be reported on OSHA form 300.

Personal Protective Equipment, 1910.132   OSHA established standards for personal protective equipment (PPE) to be used for jobs in which employees come in contact with hazardous materials, compressed gases, explosives and blasting agents, liquid petroleum, and ammonia. The standard requires PPE to protect the eyes and face, respiration, head, feet, and hands. It also requires that gear be provided to protect employees from electrical shocks or other injuries. The standard requires that PPE be provided, used, and maintained in working condition. Employers are required to train employees in the appropriate use of PPE and are responsible for ensuring that employee-owned equipment is adequately maintained for use in hazardous situations.

Sanitation, 1910.141   This standard requires that the workplace be clean to the extent the type of work allows and sets forth specific guidelines for maintaining sanitary conditions.

Specifications for Accident Prevention Signs and Tags, 1910.145   OSHA has developed specifications for hazard signs and tags and requires that all workplace signs conform to the OSHA specifications. These specifications describe the colors to be used for different levels of warning, and in some cases, such as biohazard and slow-moving vehicle signs (among others) provide specifications for size, color, and design of the sign.

In general, OSHA defines red as the background color for danger, yellow for caution, orange for warning, and fluorescent orange or orange-red for biological hazards. Lettering or symbols on the signs is specified as being of a contrasting color for the background.

Permit-Required Confined Spaces, 1910.146   OSHA requires permits for employees to enter spaces that may become filled with a hazardous atmosphere that is immediately dangerous to life or health. The atmosphere in confined spaces must be tested prior to an employee's entrance into them and other personnel are required to be in close proximity to the entrance to render assistance if needed. Employees who will be entering the space have the opportunity to observe the testing process if they desire to do so.

The Control of Hazardous Energy (Lockout/Tagout), 1910.147   The lockout/tagout standard applies to machinery that may start unexpectedly when a guard or other safety device must be removed to perform a service or maintenance process and any part of an employee's body may be subjected to injury in the course of the process.

Medical Services and First Aid, 1910.151   OHSA requires that employers provide adequate first aid supplies and either have medical personnel available, or ensure that one or more workers are trained in first aid to assist injured employees in an emergency.

General Requirements for All Machines (Machine Guarding), 1910.212   OSHA requires that woodworking machines; cooperage machinery; abrasive wheel machinery; mills; power presses; forging machines; portable power tools; welding, cutting, and brazing tools; and tools for specific industries such as paper, textile, bakery, and sawmill, among others, use guards to protect employees from injury. These guards can be barrier-type guards, two-hand tripping devices, electronic safety devices, or other guards or devices that effectively prevent injuries.

Selection and Use of Electrical Work Practices, 1910.333   Employers must ensure that employees who work on or around electrical equipment or circuits are protected from injury that could result from direct or indirect contact with electrical currents.

Blood-Borne Pathogens, 1910.1030   Blood-borne pathogens are pathogenic microorganisms in human blood that can cause disease in humans. The hepatitis B virus (HBV) and human immunodeficiency virus (HIV) are examples of blood-borne pathogens but are not by any means the only ones. Workers in the health care industry are those most at risk for exposure to blood-borne pathogens, and OSHA regulations require employers to take steps to prevent exposure, including a written exposure control plan that informs employees of preventive steps, post-exposure evaluation and follow-up, record keeping, and incident evaluation procedures.

Hazard Communication Standard (HCS), 1910.1200   The HCS requires employers to provide employees with information about physical and health hazards related to the use of any chemicals in the workplace. Employers must develop and maintain an ongoing written HCS plan that is to be updated as changes occur in the materials used in the workplace. The material safety data sheets (MSDS) provided by chemical manufacturers provide sufficient information for communication and training of employees.

The comprehensive list of OSHA standards can be accessed at www.osha.gov/pls/oshaweb/owastand.display_standard_group?p_toc_level=1&p_part_number=1910&p_text_version=FALSE.

Security Risks

Security in the workplace covers a broad spectrum of topics related to protecting the company from threats of one kind or another, including fires, earthquakes, hurricanes, tornadoes, and other natural disasters and manmade threats such as terrorist attacks, computer hackers, workplace violence and theft, or unintentional release of trade secrets or confidential information. Many of these topics are not ultimately the responsibility of HR professionals, but a working knowledge of the impact they have on the workforce is essential to understanding the ways HR interacts with other functional areas in the company. HR professionals must be able to provide the expertise required to appropriately handle suspected inappropriate conduct by employees in order to protect the company from liability.

Workplace security measures are those taken by employers to ensure the safety of the people and assets of the business and begin with assessing the possible risks. When the potential risks have been identified, plans for protection of the people and the assets of the organization can be made and implemented. In this section, we will briefly review security issues with which HR professionals may become involved.

As you will recall from an earlier description in this chapter, risk assessment is the process used to identify and evaluate the likelihood that losses will occur. Security risks are assessed following a similar process. Before an employer can put plans in place to reduce security risks, the threats (external forces) and vulnerabilities (internal weaknesses) must be identified. With this knowledge, it is possible to identify what controls must be in place to protect the company and which emergencies are most likely to occur so that preventive measures can be taken to protect it.

A security risk assessment is most often a collaborative effort between internal managers and outside consultants with expertise in security issues. Depending on the nature of the business, consultants with different types of expertise would be required; for example, a software company developing a new product will have significantly different needs than a manufacturing plant whose employees may go on strike. Risk assessments are most frequently accomplished using a qualitative analysis, where all the possible emergencies are listed along with the potential financial costs and impact on operations. The emergencies can then be prioritized to address those with the greatest possible impact on the business first.

Identifying and ranking the risks provides management with the opportunity to be proactive and implement controls to prevent damage to the assets of the business. There are four basic types of company assets: financial assets, such as cash, securities, and accounts receivable; physical assets, such as buildings, machinery, and equipment; information assets; and human assets, including the effects of workplace violence and substance abuse.

Financial Assets

Financial assets, including cash, inventory, accounts receivable, and securities, are vulnerable to theft and embezzlement. Implementing policies and procedures to protect financial assets is generally the responsibility of a company's chief financial officer (CFO). CFOs are responsible for implementing *internal controls* to ensure that cash and negotiable securities are not mishandled, along with inventory controls to reduce employee pilferage or customer theft. In most organizations, CFOs implement processes to ensure that purchase commitments at certain dollar levels are reviewed and approved by higher level management to prevent mismanagement. One common control used to ensure the security of financial assets is to define accounting jobs so that more than one person handles different aspects of transactions. For example, the job with responsibility for preparing customer invoices would not also be responsible for opening the mail or making bank deposits. Separating these duties makes it more difficult for an employee to embezzle money. Sarbanes-Oxley (SOX) compliance requirements are having a major impact, not just on Finance but also HR. HR plays a major role in helping companies manage a cultural transformation to higher levels of transparency and financial accountability. HR business processes must be more consistent, reliable, and efficient, especially in the context of SOX Section 404 requirements for sound internal controls.

Physical Assets

When we think of security, often what comes most readily to mind are building security measures such as guards, security cameras, keys or card-key lock systems, and entry barriers such as fences or security gates. The size, nature, and budget of each business will determine which systems are most appropriate.

Information Assets

The most effective way to protect confidential information is to ensure that employees know what the company considers confidential before they are hired. An *Intellectual Property Agreement (IPA)* and/or *Non-Disclosure Agreement (NDA)* is used for this purpose. Because the types of confidential information vary widely between different organizations, it's important that an attorney develop an agreement to meet specific needs. An IPA should identify what the company considers to be confidential information (such as customer lists, financial information, or trade secrets) and how its use is limited by the agreement, as well as how long the information must remain confidential after the agreement expires. The agreement may contain a "nonsolicitation" clause limiting the ability of employees who leave the organization to hire coworkers. IPAs should contain clauses that require employees to describe any discoveries or inventions they may have made prior to entering into the agreement and require that they don't share confidential information from other companies with the new employer or disclose who owns the inventions or discoveries made during the course of employment. Finally, the agreement should state that materials containing confidential information are the property of the company and may not be removed from a given location.

These agreements help to prevent employees from sharing confidential proprietary information with other companies or individuals. For these documents to be effective, the organization must advise employees on a regular basis that even inadvertently sharing this information can cause damage.

While this discussion has been limited to the use of IPAs and NDAs in employment relationships, these documents are equally important when sharing proprietary information with others outside the organization. This can include business partners or others with whom the company shares the information in the course of doing business, such as candidates for jobs during the interview process.

Human Assets

Providing protection for employees takes many forms. Many of the security measures that protect physical assets also protect employees; in addition an ongoing safety training program can include information on ways in which employees can protect themselves in different situations. Protecting employees working outside of the United States presents different issues for employers. Issues of political stability and animosity toward American companies and citizens require programs and vendors that specialize in protecting them abroad. Large corporations must often take special security precautions to prevent executives from kidnapping, particularly when they travel overseas. Executive security may take several forms, including bodyguards and vendors who specialize in corporate protection.

Employees must also be protected from the effects of workplace violence and substance abuse in the workplace.

Workplace Violence

Workplace violence occurs when an employee with poor behavior control becomes highly stressed. The stress may or may not be work related, but it is often set off by an incident in the workplace. Under OSHA's General Duty Clause, employers are required to be aware of employees exhibiting the signs of possible violent behavior and take steps to prevent its occurrence. Employees who commit acts of violence in the workplace frequently show recognizable signs of stress before they commit the acts. It is up to employers to train managers and supervisors to identify these signs so that employees who are having difficulty can be referred to an Employee Assistance Program (EAP) for counseling or directed to social services if needed. Training managers to recognize and prevent workplace violence is becoming a more common topic for inclusion in management training curricula, along with supervisory skills, sexual harassment prevention, and other issues.

Some of the more common signs of stress include a change in work habits, a decline in productivity, conflicts with coworkers, depression, and refusing to take responsibility for individual actions.

Even though not everyone who exhibits signs of stress is likely to become violent, any employee who exhibits these signs should be counseled and referred to appropriate professional assistance. As part of the emergency action plan described in the next section, a plan for responding to an incident of workplace violence should be developed and communicated to employees. This plan, in addition to other requirements, can include code words to be used when employees feel threatened so they can alert coworkers to call for help, along with a resource book for managers and supervisors that contains referral agencies for different types of issues to assist employees who are troubled.

Substance Abuse

Government statistics indicate that more than 70 percent of substance abusers have jobs. They are all working in someone's business—some of them might work in your organization. Substance abusers increase costs for employers with tardiness and absenteeism, increased errors, accidents, and increases in health care costs and worker compensation claims. When a substance abuser's job is to drive a semitrailer or operate heavy equipment, an employer faces increased costs for injuries or damages that occur as a result of an accident. If the employer is a federal contractor subject to the Drug-Free Workplace Act, continued substance abuse at the workplace could result in the loss of the contract.

There are six components for an effective substance abuse program in the workplace:

- Support for the substance abuse policy from top management. (As with any policy, this is the most important component.)

- A written policy clearly stating that substance abuse will not be tolerated in the workplace.

- Training for managers and supervisors to ensure that they understand and can explain the policy, are able to recognize the signs of substance abuse, understand the importance of documenting poor performance, and know what steps to take when they become aware of a substance abuser.

- Education programs for new hires and employees to inform them of the policy and explain the consequences for violations. If the organization has a drug testing program, it should be explained prior to employment and during orientation. Employees should be made aware of resources in the community or through the EAP, as well as the effects of substance abuse on themselves, their families, and the costs to the employer.

- An EAP that provides confidential counseling for substance abusers as needed.

- An ongoing, fair, and consistent drug testing program that complies with federal, state, and local laws and union contracts. The program should identify who will be tested, when tests will occur, which drugs will be tested for, and what happens if the test is positive.

Drug Testing Programs

There are several decisions to make when a company decides to implement a drug testing program. First, the program must be implemented in a fair and consistent manner to avoid charges of discrimination. Next, the company must decide what type of testing will be done:

Pre-employment testing   Lawful only after an offer of employment has been made. Before beginning a testing program, the employer must decide which applicants will be tested. This decision may be based on the type of work done in different jobs; for example, a company may decide to test all employees who operate machinery. The test must be conducted fairly and consistently on all applicants for the designated jobs.

Random drug testing   Done on an arbitrary, unscheduled basis. To make the testing truly random and reduce the risk of legal challenges, employers may want to make use of a computer program that randomly selects employees.

Scheduled drug testing   Can be useful when monitoring rehabilitation progress of employees but has limited value because employees who may be currently using drugs are generally able to stop long enough before the test to clear their systems of the drugs.

Reasonable suspicion drug testing   Can be used any time there has been an accident in the workplace or when a supervisor suspects, based on behavior, that an employee is under the influence of drugs.

Regardless of the substance abuse testing schedule that is used, it is important to keep in mind that implementation must be fair and equitable to avoid charges of discrimination. If employers choose to test specific job categories, then all employees in those categories must be subjected to the testing process. If random testing is used, all employees in the selected category must be included in the selection group.

HR professionals must also keep in mind that, under the ADA, abusers of alcohol and drugs are considered disabled as long as they are in recovery. Employees who are current abusers do not have protection under the ADA.

Loss Prevention

Much of the first part of this chapter was spent in describing the various laws, regulations, and standards that govern workplace safety. So what exactly is workplace safety? In a word (or two): accident prevention. *Safety* is about identifying possible hazards in the workplace and reducing the likelihood that an accident will happen by correcting the hazard. Management and employees are partners in this process. Because employees are close to the possible hazards, they should feel empowered to take the steps necessary to reduce hazards that are within their control, whether that means correcting the hazard themselves or reporting the hazard to management with suggestions on how to correct it.

Workplace accidents impact the bottom line in many ways. They reduce productivity because an injured employee must be given time to recover from an injury. A high accident/injury rate increases insurance costs and, when employees sense that management is unconcerned about their safety, lowers morale and increases turnover. Employees who are not satisfied with their work care less about what kind of job they do, which has a negative impact on quality. Poor quality products tarnish the company's reputation, which makes it more difficult for the company to compete against other products. All of these consequences of poor safety policies reduce the company's ability to earn a profit, which reduces the value of the company to its owners. All of this can happen when employers don't think safety matters!

Accident prevention begins with a commitment from the top that safety does matter and that the health and well being of employees is important to the company. Employers need to provide safe operating procedures, train workers to use those procedures, and then enforce the procedures by rewarding positive safety actions and disciplining employees who fail to comply with procedures.

Because the employees doing the job know best what is safe and what is unsafe, they must be involved in developing safe operating procedures. Working in partnership, management and employees can identify the hazards present in the workplace and develop strategies to reduce or eliminate them. An added benefit of including employees in this process is that they will have a greater stake in maintaining safe operations that they were a part of creating. As safe operating procedures are identified, they become part of a safety and health management plan.

Employers who have developed effective safety management programs have safer work environments for their employees. Over the last 30 years, through workplace investigation and analysis of injury and illness statistics, OSHA has determined that effective safety and health management plans have four common characteristics:

1. Senior management is committed to a safe work environment, and employees are involved in the decisions and activities to make it happen.

2. The company is engaged in an ongoing worksite analysis to identify potential safety and health hazards.

3. The company has active hazard prevention and control programs in place to correct hazards before injury or illness occurs.

4. Safety and health training is an ongoing process in the company.

An effective plan identifies the person who is responsible for its overall implementation and creates a safety committee with representatives from both management and labor to address safety concerns and develop workable solutions to safety problems. An effective plan identifies hazards that exist in the work environment, whether they are physical, chemical, or biological, and provides guidance, in the form of OSHA safety standards, on the appropriate way to work with each hazard. The plan provides a mechanism for employee complaints so that they reach the appropriate management level for speedy resolution to prevent injuries. If the work environment requires the use of machinery, equipment, tools, or PPE, the plan spells out the appropriate methods for using and maintaining them and includes consequences for failing to comply with the standards.

The plan describes how to report accidents, who must be notified, and the time frames in which the notifications must occur and provides an accident investigation procedure, identifying who will conduct the investigation, what records must be kept, and how and where they are filed. When an investigation takes place, the plan should include a process that ensures all employees are advised of the accident circumstances and what steps should be taken to avoid similar accidents in the future.

Part of an effective plan is ongoing training for employees that addresses accidents that have occurred and ways to prevent similar occurrences in the future.

Injury and Illness Prevention Programs

Injury and illness prevention plans (IIPP) are required by OSHA and designed to protect employees from preventable workplace injuries and illnesses. OSHA describes several plans with different purposes. This section describes each of these plans. Some elements are present in all of the plans, and others are related only to individual plans. OSHA requires the following plans:

- Safety and health management plan (also known as an injury and illness prevention plan)

- Emergency action plan (also referred to as an emergency response plan)

- Fire prevention plan

Generally, employers with ten or fewer employees are not required to provide written plans unless they have been notified by OSHA to do so.

To ensure the safety of employees and business assets, an emergency action plan, combined with ongoing employee training, is essential. By developing a plan and having regular drills to reinforce the steps to be taken, employers can improve the chances that all employees will be safe in an emergency.

The OSHA emergency action plan standard requires, at a minimum, that the employer define the preferred method for reporting fires and other emergencies, an evacuation policy and procedure, and floor plans or maps that define escape procedures and assign evacuation routes. The plan must have contact information for individuals who can provide additional information during an emergency and provide procedures for employees who will remain behind to perform essential services during the emergency. Employees who will perform rescue and medical duties are to be included in the plan as well. The plan requires alarm systems to notify all employees, including those who are disabled, of the need to evacuate.

 **Real World Scenario**

Sample Emergency Action Plan

Section 1: Responsibilities   In this section is a description of everyone who has a role to play during an emergency. Who will make the decision to evacuate the building? If critical machinery must be shut down, who will do that? Who is responsible to "take roll" and ensure that all employees have been safely evacuated from the building? Which employees are certified to perform first aid until medical personnel arrive on the scene? How will the emergency be reported to authorities, and who is responsible for doing that? Finally, this section should include the names of those who have been designated to answer questions and explain duties required by the plan.

Section 2: Emergency Escape Procedures   This section of the plan identifies the emergency escape procedures that employees are to follow and provides a diagram of the building showing escape routes from each floor and each area. In this section, special procedures for evacuating persons with disabilities, visitors to the building, and others with special needs should be spelled out. A safe meeting area should be designated so that all employees know where they should go in the event of an evacuation.

Section 3: Critical Plant Operations   Particularly in manufacturing operations, there are processes that must be shut down according to specific protocols. In this section, these processes should be identified, along with instructions for employees on recognizing when they must evacuate themselves, even if the operation is not yet complete.

Section 4: Accounting for Employees   In the event of an evacuation, it is critical that rescue personnel know whether or not people are trapped in the building. Equally important is that rescue personnel not endanger themselves if everyone has been successfully evacuated. In this section of the plan, the procedures to be followed should be described, including where employees will meet, and who will account for employees and visitors to the area.

Section 5: Reporting Emergencies   This section describes how emergencies are to be reported to the appropriate authorities.

Section 6: Identifying Emergency Contacts   In this section, the plan should identify who should be contacted for specific information. This may be a single person, or it may be several individuals who are responsible for different sections of the plan.

Section 7: Alarm System   This section of the plan should describe how employees will be notified of an emergency, where alarms are located, if there are different alarms for different emergencies, what they sound like, and whether or not the alarm system automatically notifies emergency personnel.

Section 8: Types of Evacuations   If the building is located in an area in which the potential for different types of emergencies exist, such as fires, tornadoes, and floods, this section of the plan describes the evacuation plan for each type of emergency.

Section 9: Training Requirements   In this section, the plan should describe how employees will be trained in emergency procedures and how often. The person responsible for training employees should be identified, along with a schedule for emergency drills.

Section 10: Record Keeping   In this section, the plan should include documents that might be required in an emergency. This could include information on MSDSs for chemicals in the worksite, maintenance records for safety equipment, equipment inspection records, building plans and OSHA forms.

Elements Common to All Plans

Some elements are important enough for inclusion in each of the plans. They include:

- A clear statement of the company policy regarding the program
- The commitment and full support of senior management
- A process for including employees in the process, whether through the establishment of a safety committee or some other means
- Identification of those with responsibilities under the plan, including employees, vendors, and public health and safety officials, and contact information for those individuals
- A clear, unambiguous process for reporting hazards or concerns to the responsible parties
- A description of the process to be used in training employees
- Procedures for maintaining records required by OSHA

Safety and Health Management Plan

In addition to the elements common to all plans, a safety and health management plan will also include:

- A process to ensure two-way communication between management and labor
- An assessment of known hazards
- Procedures to correct known hazards

- A procedure to ensure that the company engages in an ongoing analysis of workplace hazards and conducts updated training on changes
- Maintenance procedures for any equipment, machinery, tools, or personal protective equipment used in the workplace
- An accident investigation procedure
- An accident reporting procedure

Emergency Action Plan

The emergency action plan begins with the common elements described previously and also includes:

- Emergency escape procedures, including a floor plan or diagram for employees to follow
- Procedures for shutting down critical plant operations
- Process to account for employees after an evacuation
- A description of the alarm system that will notify employees of an emergency, including how persons with disabilities, visitors, and temporary employees will be notified
- Procedures to follow for different types of emergencies, such as fires, tornadoes, earthquakes, or terrorist attacks

Fire Prevention Plan

The fire prevention plan may be included as part of the emergency action plan. Whether the plan is included with it or separate, it must provide information about the following:

- All major fire hazards, how they should be handled and stored, a description of possible causes of igniting them and how to prevent that from happening, and a description of the appropriate equipment to suppress each hazard
- The location of fire extinguishing systems or portable fire extinguishers
- The procedure describing how waste materials that are flammable or combustible will be stored before disposal

Injury and Illness Compensation Programs

As long as there have been workers and employers, there has been a debate about financial responsibility for injuries suffered on the job. The first written record of this is in the Hammurabic Code, written some 4,000 years ago. Of course, at that time, the workers were slaves, and compensation for injuries was paid to their masters, but, nonetheless, there was a recognition of financial liability when injuries occurred.

Over time, three common law doctrines developed that were applied to workers who were injured on the job: the fellow servant rule, the doctrine of contributory negligence, and voluntary assumption of risk.

1. The *fellow servant rule* absolved employers of responsibility if a coworker's actions caused the injury.

2. The *doctrine of contributory negligence* was used to mitigate the employer's responsibility if the worker's actions contributed in any way to the injury.

3. *Voluntary assumption of risk* said that workers who knew the dangers of the job when they took it assumed the associated risks, and the level of pay they accepted reflected the amount of danger involved so the employer had no responsibility when death or injury occurred.

For workers, these doctrines presented many problems. First, they assumed that the employer and the worker were equals in the labor market so the law treated employment relationships the same as it did contracts between business owners. They also assumed that if the terms and conditions of employment were not agreeable to the worker, the worker could simply seek other employment.

Second, these doctrines required workers injured on the job to seek recompense through the court system. Employers for the most part could afford the best attorneys to represent them while few employees could afford a lengthy legal battle.

These common law doctrines became known as the "unholy trinity" because the results were almost always in favor of the employer: only 50 percent of cases brought on behalf of workers killed or injured on the job resulted in any kind of compensation; of those that did receive compensation, it was rarely more than a few months' pay. As governments recognized the blatant unfairness of the lopsided way these doctrines were applied, states began enacting worker compensation laws to level the playing field for workers. Wisconsin was the first state to pass a Worker Compensation Act in 1911, and New Jersey followed in the same year.

Worker compensation laws for private employers are in most cases the purview of state government; however, there are a few industries with federal legislation to protect injured workers. These include the federal government, the longshore industry, coal mines, and the Department of Energy. Legislation pertaining to these industries is covered by the following laws:

Federal Employees Compensation Act (FECA) of 1916   FECA is administered by the DOL and is the federal employee's equivalent of worker compensation, providing similar benefits for workers injured during the course of performing their jobs.

The Longshore and Harbor Workers' Compensation Act (LHWCA) of 1927   LHWCA provides worker compensation benefits for maritime workers whose injuries occur on the navigable waters of the U.S. or on piers, docks, or terminals.

Black Lung Benefits Act (BLBA) of 1969, amended in 1977   The BLBA provides benefits to coal miners who have been disabled by pneumoconiosis as a result of their work in the mines. Benefits are also paid to surviving dependents if the miner dies from the disease.

Energy Employees Occupational Illness Compensation Program Act (EEOICPA) of 2000
This act was created to provide compensation for employees and contractors of the Department of Energy who were subjected to excessive radiation while producing and testing nuclear weapons.

Business Continuity

One of the many challenges facing organization leaders is the obligation to protect the organization from unforeseen emergencies and other circumstances. These can occur as a result of a variety of natural disasters or manmade occurrences that threaten businesses, employees, customers, or whole communities. Planning for these eventualities is a process known as *business continuity planning (BCP)*, which results in a written document used to describe possible disruptions to operations and actions to be taken to minimize those disruptions and assign responsibility for executing the plan to specific individuals. A BCP is often an umbrella that includes other emergency plans, such as the emergency response plan and disaster recovery plan. In some organizations, these terms are interchangeable, while in others they each describe a specific process. For purposes of this discussion, the BCP is treated as an umbrella covering different aspects of the business continuity process.

A successful BCP begins with a commitment from the CEO so that sufficient resources are provided for the process. When the CEO is committed to the process, a planning committee that includes representatives from each business function is appointed and defines the scope of the plan. At this point, the committee assesses the risks facing the organization.

Assess and Prioritize Organizational Risks

By their very nature, emergencies occur with little or no warning and can devastate individuals, single organizations, or whole communities. There are several different types of emergencies to consider when planning response, recovery, and continuity processes. These include:

- Environmental disasters such as earthquakes, fires, tornados, hurricanes, toxic gas releases, chemical spills, and so on.

- Organized and/or deliberate disruptions such as theft, labor disputes, sabotage, terrorism, and so on.

- Loss of utilities and services caused by power failures, oil shortages, communication system failures, and so on.

- Equipment or system failure such as a breakdown in the production line, equipment failure, or internal loss of power.

- Serious information security incidents such as loss of customer data to hackers or failure of the IT system.

- Other emergency situations such as workplace violence, legal problems, public transportation strikes, violations of health or safety regulations, and so on.

The BCP planning process identifies those risks most likely to occur based on the organization's location, industry, and other considerations. The risks are then assessed for the level of disruption each would cause and the impact on different business functions, as well as an estimate of the cost to reestablish or maintain them in the event of each risk. Information systems are so integral to operating ability that most businesses will need to assess the impact of each risk on information and communication systems. Finally, each identified risk is evaluated and prioritized for its impact on operations.

Identify Vital Processes and Key Employees

Another element of the BCP is a review of each functional business area. This review identifies vital business processes, key employees necessary to maintain operations in each critical area, and records essential for the continuation of the business. If emergency plans currently exist, the planning team will review them at this time and determine what revisions are needed for different risks. At this stage, the BCP team will identify critical vendors and suppliers and how to move forward if one or more of them are incapacitated. Alternative locations and equipment resources for use in the event that the building is destroyed are also identified.

Emergency Response Plan

An important piece of the planning process is to develop an *emergency response plan (ERP)* describing how the organization will react to different emergency situations or natural disasters as they occur. The OSHA emergency action plan (previously described) will be part of the ERP, describing how employees and visitors who are onsite during an emergency will be evacuated or shelter in place. The ERP identifies a response team and responsibilities assigned to each team member and how vital records and information will be protected and establishes an emergency communication plan. Depending on the type of emergency, the communication plan can include a public relations component and identify individuals who will represent the organization to customers, vendors, suppliers, and the media.

The ERP describes how computer systems and information will be protected and accessible. Prudent business practice includes ongoing off-site storage system backups and copies of records and legal documents needed to maintain operations in an emergency.

Disaster Recovery Plan

A *disaster recovery plan (DRP)* describes activities that take place once response to the initial emergency is over.

Planning for this phase develops alternatives for property, processes, information systems, and people. If the building is unusable, what are the arrangements for temporary facilities? If the computer systems are inoperable, how and where will the off-site backups be reinstalled to continue operations? If transportation systems and roadways are damaged, how will employees get to work?

One important factor to consider in the DRP is compliance with Sarbanes-Oxley Act requirements for information safety. This requirement is discussed in Chapter 3, "Strategic Management."

Another element to include in the DRP is a list of alternative vendors, suppliers, and service providers who are able to provide materials or support when normal sources are affected by emergencies and unable, either temporarily or permanently, to continue in the aftermath. This may make the difference in an organization's ability to continue servicing customers after an emergency.

Continuity of Operations Plan

The *continuity of operations plan (COOP)* generally refers to plans created to move from the disaster recovery phase, during which critical business functions are maintained but normal operations may not be taking place, back to pre-emergency service operating levels.

Maintaining Business Continuity Plans

Too often, organizations go through the process of creating plans, and once completed, never look at them again, assuming that the plan will work when needed. A critical component of a BCP is the need to test the plan, train employees to use the plan, and revisit it annually to keep the information current. An evaluation of the test results provides information about any necessary changes so that they can be refined.

Clearly, there are a wide range of situations that require preplanning. HR professionals can play a key role in managing emergency situations by participating in planning activities and maintaining accurate employee information that will be needed during the execution of the plans

Safety Training Programs

OSHA has developed guidelines to assist employers in developing effective training programs that reduce work-related injury and illness. These guidelines can be modified to fit the specific industry and work site requirements for individual businesses.

1. Determine if training is needed. In other words, is the safety problem something that can be corrected with training, or is another correction necessary?

2. Identify the training needs. What should employees be doing that they are not doing? The program should inform them of appropriate methods for doing the job.

3. As with any other training program, objectives for the training must be developed.

4. When the learning needs and objectives have been identified, methods for delivering the training can be developed. Will classroom training be best? One-on-one training with an experienced employee? Demonstration and practice? This will depend on the specific training needs for the organization.

5. Conduct the training.

6. Evaluate how well the training worked using the methods discussed in Chapter 5, "Human Resource Development."

7. Based on the evaluation, adjust the training to improve its effectiveness.

Workplace Privacy

Many employees are surprised and angry when subjected to electronic monitoring, physical property searches, or video surveillance of their activities in the workplace. Employers use electronic surveillance to monitor email, voice mail, and telephone conversations and to access call logs, monitor Internet use, or inspect computer files. Organizations may conduct property searches in cubicles, offices, file cabinets, employee lockers, or personal employee belongings. In some cases, employers may conduct video surveillance by installing cameras in the workplace to protect employees or monitor behavior. There can be compelling reasons for employers to monitor employee activities, including concerns about theft, employee safety, improper use of equipment, loss of confidential proprietary information, productivity, and other issues. Employers may be accused of knowingly allowing employees to disseminate harassing or inappropriate communication, and implementing some form of electronic monitoring may protect them from liability. Add to this mix concerns about identity theft, and employers have legitimate reasons to take protective actions. In doing so, it is important to balance these concerns with the effect monitoring has on employee rights, morale, and productivity.

Creating this balance requires employers to communicate with employees about the need for any type of monitoring activity and to clearly explain what activities are subject to monitoring, when they will occur, and how the information will be used. Whatever type of monitoring program is established, it is important for employers to preserve employee dignity. This may not make monitoring popular with employees but should help to reduce the lack of trust that may be created by the program. To avoid legal issues, a written policy describing the employer's practices is needed.

Reasonable expectation of privacy   A key consideration for courts in cases involving workplace searches is whether or not employees had a *reasonable expectation of privacy* based on factors such as whether or not there was a privacy policy in place and how an employer handled similar situations in the past. The combination of a legitimate business reason to conduct the search and a clearly stated policy that the employer can demonstrate was communicated to employees will help to justify a search.

Privacy policies   An effective privacy policy makes an unambiguous statement that the employer reserves the right to search, describes the activities and resources the organization will monitor, and tells employees that there should be no expectation of privacy. Specific information about what could trigger a search and how the employer will proceed should be included as well. The policy should be specific about such things as:

Monitoring telephone calls   Generally, employers are not required to provide notice before monitoring business-related calls (although some states require that both parties to a call be aware of any monitoring that occurs). The monitoring must terminate as soon as the employer becomes aware that the call is personal.

Monitoring email or instant messages   When accessing employee emails or IMs, it is best to have a legitimate business reason for doing so. Policies should make it clear that the email and instant messages sent using the employer's equipment are the property of the employer and may be monitored or reviewed at any time.

Some attorneys consider an email policy important enough to be a separate policy that is signed by every employee.

Monitoring Internet and computer use   Many issues affect employee use of the Internet, including demand for bandwidth during peak hours of operation, access to inappropriate websites, and the downloading of viruses, spyware, or other potentially harmful files. The Internet use policy should include a statement of acceptable uses, reasons to restrict access or use, and whether or not the employer allows personal use. The policy should also state that the employer reserves the right to review data stored on hard drives and require that employees provide any current password information to a designated employee.

Monitoring the use of cell phone cameras   The use of personal cell phones in the workplace can be disruptive and difficult to monitor in general, and the advent of cameraphones presents even more challenges for employers. Cell phone cameras can be used surreptitiously to take inappropriate photographs of coworkers that expose the employer to harassment claims, make copies of confidential documents, or photograph proprietary work processes or new product development.

An outright ban of cell phone cameras in the workplace is difficult to enforce, but stating clearly situations the employer considers inappropriate (such as in bathrooms, on customer premises, or in sensitive work areas) can be effective.

Video surveillance   In some workplaces, installing cameras may be viewed as a necessity, for example, in small, all-night retail stores where one employee works alone late at night. In other situations, the need for video surveillance may not be as clear. Employers who determine that video surveillance is necessary for their business operation should clearly state the reasons for the surveillance, the circumstances in which tapes will be reviewed, and how the information will be used.

Video surveillance of bathrooms or locations where employees may change their clothes is not appropriate.

Searching property   As with other privacy policies, searches should be conducted for a legitimate business reason since random searches conducted for no apparent reason are difficult to justify in court. Narrowing a search to employees suspected of theft, or to those who had an opportunity to commit the theft based on other information such as video surveillance tapes, is preferable. Although some employers may be tempted to search an employee's body, this is inappropriate. If this is believed to be necessary, law enforcement should be brought in to conduct the search.

A search policy should clearly state what types of situations will trigger a search, how it will be conducted, what types of property are liable for search (for example, company property such as a desk, office, cubicle, locker, and so on, or personal property such as a purse, or car).

Table 8.10 provides some questions to consider before conducting a search.

TABLE 8.10   Questions to Ask Before Searching

Question	Yes	No
Is there a legitimate business reason to search this employee?	X	
Does the employee have a reasonable expectation of privacy?		X
Is there another way to find out if this employee engaged in an improper activity?		X

TABLE 8.10 Questions to Ask Before Searching *(continued)*

Question	Yes	No
Do you have a workplace search policy in place?	X	
Are all employees aware of the search policy?	X	
Is this a random search?		X

If the answer to any of these questions is different in a particular situation, it may be advisable to look for another way to collect the information needed.

 Real World Scenario

EMail Monitoring: *Fraser v. Nationwide Mutual Insurance Company*

Richard Fraser was employed as an independent insurance agent for Nationwide Mutual Insurance when he was terminated in September 1998. Nationwide claimed that it terminated Mr. Fraser for disloyal activities; contacting competitors and asking if they would be interested in acquiring some of Nationwide's policyholders. When they learned of the contacts, Nationwide searched Mr. Fraser's email records on its main file server and found evidence of additional disloyalty. On the basis of this information, Nationwide terminated him.

Mr. Fraser filed this action claiming the search was a violation of two restrictions of the ECPA, claiming that interception of email is prohibited by the act. The court found that since the email was not intercepted during transmission, no violation occurred. He also claimed that the search of his email violated ECPA prohibitions against access of electronically stored communication. The court found in this instance as well that, since Nationwide provided and administered the email service on which Mr. Fraser's email was stored, the search of the email was allowable.

The 3rd Circuit Court of Appeals upheld summary judgment in favor of Nationwide.

Employers must be aware of legal restrictions on workplace-monitoring policies. In addition to the federal ECPA controls (described previously in this chapter) and state laws enacted to protect individual privacy rights, common law torts for invasion of privacy must also be considered when making the decision to implement a monitoring program. These common law torts use the "reasonable person" standard to measure whether an intrusion is highly offensive and causes harm, is publicized without a legitimate reason, or knowingly puts an individual into a false light in public. The courts often support an employer's right to monitor their employees in the workplace.

Many U.S. companies employ workers globally, where data privacy regulations are much stricter than the U.S. Don't assume that if you comply with U.S. data privacy regulations that you are compliant in other countries. For example, access to certain personal employee information U.K. employees by managers in the U.S. could be a violation of U.K. data privacy laws.

As discussed in Chapter 6, HIPAA imposes requirements on some employers to protect the privacy of personal health information for employees.

Workplace Investigations

In response to management concerns about theft or other inappropriate behavior, or as a result of accusations made by coworkers, customers, or members of the public about an employee, HR professionals are sometimes called upon to conduct *workplace investigations*. These investigations must be conducted in a way that protects the organization from liability, employees who make the accusations, and the individual accused or suspected of wrongdoing. The best way to prepare for an investigation is to establish a procedure at a time when no investigation is pending so that when it is necessary, the HR professional has a guide to ensure that all necessary steps are taken. An effective workplace investigation includes the following elements.

- Begin the investigation immediately upon receiving the complaint.

- Assign an employee or third-party investigator, as appropriate.

- Develop a clear strategy before beginning to collect evidence or conduct interviews.

- Compile a list of individuals to be interviewed and documentation to be collected.

- Prepare a list of questions based on the information presented by the complainant.

- Conduct interviews, taking contemporaneous notes; ask each interviewee to provide a signed, written statement or have them review and sign your notes at the conclusion of the interview.

  - Interview the complainant first and obtain names of possible witnesses.

  - Interview witnesses.

  - Interview the accused.

- At the conclusion of each interview, make note of the interviewee's demeanor and openness, keeping the notes free from personal opinions and judgments.

- With each interviewee, stress the importance of confidentiality for the integrity of the investigation and reiterate company policy with regard to retaliation against accusers and witnesses.

- At the conclusion of the interview with the accused, clearly state that retaliation or intimidation of those interviewed during the investigation is not acceptable and that the accused should not attempt to discuss the situation with the complainant or witnesses.

- If the accused provides an alternate description of events, completely investigate the new information, re-interviewing witnesses as necessary.
- Conclude the investigation.
  - Make a finding of fact based on the evidence obtained and observations during the interviews.
  - Include any relevant documentation that supports the finding.
  - Evaluate possible reasons for false accusations and the credibility of those involved.
  - Notify the complainant and the accused of the results of the investigation.
- As appropriate, take disciplinary action consistent with organization policy.
- In some cases, there will be no clear finding; when that occurs, explain this to the complainant and accused and document the finding.
- Compile and close the investigation file, including your handwritten notes; signed statements from witnesses, complainant and accused; relevant documentation; and transcribed copies of your notes.
- Communicate resolution only to those who have a need to know the information and maintain the investigation file in a secure location.
- If necessary, and without violating confidentiality of those involved, take appropriate action to subdue rumors about the situation.

Workplace investigations, properly conducted, document the actions by the employer to respond to accusations of wrongdoing. Particularly in sexual harassment investigations, this can make the difference in whether or not the employer will be held liable if a lawsuit is filed.

Taking clear, relevant notes in investigations is crucial, but it is essential that those notes be free from any comments or observations that could be construed as prejudicial. It is important to keep in mind that investigatory notes are discoverable in lawsuits unless they involve communication with legal counsel.

Metrics—Measuring Results

Measuring the effectiveness of risk management activities can be challenging. The key, as with measurement in all other HR functional areas, is to determine what kind of meaningful information can be provided to management in order to improve the effectiveness of risk management programs.

Evaluating health, safety, and security programs is a relatively simple matter: compile statistics on a regular basis and compare them over time. If the trend is downward, great! Your programs are working to prevent injury and illness to employees. If the trend is up, well, it's time to identify what injuries or illnesses caused the increase, review the plan to determine what changes are necessary to correct the problems, and implement the changes.

As with any HR program, it is important to provide a quantitative measurement of the results. With an ergonomics program, for example, this can be accomplished by using OSHA's recordable case rate formula to calculate the incidence rate of ergonomic injuries before the program is implemented and taking periodic measures as the program progresses to determine the reduction in injuries. The recordable case rate formula uses a base of 100 full-time employees working 40 hours per week, 50 weeks per year, or 200,000 hours. Figure 8.1 illustrates the formula for calculating the ergonomic injury rate before implementation of the program, when 53 injuries occurred, and after implementation, when the injuries were reduced to 35. The example assumes that an individual employee works 2000 hours per year (40 hours per week times 50 weeks per year).

FIGURE 8.1   Quantitative analysis of ergonomic injury program

$$\text{Ergonomic Injury Rate} = \frac{\text{Number of Ergonomic Injuries} \times 200,000}{\text{Total hours worked by all employees during the period}}$$

Total number of employees: 350 FTE
Number of Ergonomic injuries = 53

$$\text{EIR} = \frac{53 \times 200,000}{350 \times 2,000} = \frac{10,600,000}{700,000} = 15.15\%$$

Total number of employees: 350 FTE
Number of Ergonomic injuries = 35

$$\text{EIR} = \frac{35 \times 200,000}{350 \times 2,000} = \frac{7,000,000}{700,000} = 10\%$$

Global Considerations

Organizations operating in a global environment must be aware of risks that face their operations in locations outside the United States and comply with occupational safety and health laws that may differ significantly from the OSH Act and other federal requirements. While those laws are country-specific, there is a movement to improve working conditions on a global level, and several organizations focus on the issues. Two of them, the World Health Organization (WHO) and the International Labour Organization (ILO), have established programs with this goal in mind.

The WHO uses a global collaboration network to promote its strategy for improved occupational safety and health throughout the world. The strategy provides evidence of the extent of occupational illness and injury and related costs to governments and businesses, supports the development of infrastructure to improve workplace safety and health, and supports labor organizations in the quest to improve worker health. More information is available on the WHO website at www.who.int/occupational_health/en/.

The ILO is an agency of the United Nations with a broad mandate to promote social justice and human rights in addition to establishing internationally recognized standards for labor rights, including occupational safety and health. The ILO issues policy conventions that set standards for safe practices in this area. In addition, the agency collects and disseminates statistics used to promote safe workplace conditions. Information about ILO programs is available at www.ilo.org.

Managing global risks requires an understanding of what risks are endemic to the regions and countries in which organizations operate, as well as the risks that occur without regard to national boundaries, such as information security, terrorism, and the spread of contagious diseases. The OSHA website provides links to several international agreements the federal government has made with other countries at www.osha.gov/international/index.html.

In addition to the differences in health and safety compliance requirements, American corporations employing workers around the globe must also be aware of differences in data privacy management. Data privacy regulations are much stricter in other countries than they are in the U.S. Employers should not assume that if they are in compliance with U.S. data privacy regulations that they are compliant in other countries. For example, managers of American organizations who access certain personal information about employees in the United Kingdom could find themselves in violation of UK data privacy laws.

Summary

As a functional area of the HR BOK, Risk Management encompasses programs and activities designed to protect organizations in the areas of health, safety, security, and privacy.

Occupational health and safety has been a source of concern to workers and physicians for centuries, but until relatively recently, employers were not required to protect workers from dangerous environments and were rarely held accountable when death, injury, or illness occurred as a result of hazards in the businesses they managed. The OSH Act of 1970 was the first comprehensive, effective legislation that required employers to provide safe and healthful workplaces for their employees and provided an enforcement process that penalized employers who did not comply with safety standards. OSHA has been successful where other attempts to do the same thing have failed because Congress provided strong enforcement powers to the agency.

In the past, employers were also not willing to compensate workers who were injured during the course of their jobs and made full use of the "unholy trinity" of common law doctrines to avoid financial responsibility for injured workers. In 1911, Wisconsin was the first state to provide workers with a more equitable process for determining compensation due to them for injuries suffered during the course of their work by passing the first worker compensation law. This enabled workers to receive compensation for injuries and illnesses without having to utilize the court system, which was, at that time, heavily weighted in favor of employers.

OSHA has been a key proponent and motivator in identifying workplace health and safety hazards and in developing processes designed to protect workers in a variety of situations. Once employers realized the financial benefits of creating safer working environments, they developed employee benefits designed to enhance health and safety programs, such as employee assistance and wellness programs that serve employee needs as well as add value to the business bottom line.

Security—of information, individuals, and organizations—becomes more complex and challenging each day as new technologies are developed. HR professionals must be able to provide employers with the tools needed to protect them without infringing upon employee privacy rights. In the aftermath of devastating natural disasters and acts of terror, preparing to continue business operations is an essential responsibility of leadership teams in every organization. HR professionals contribute to this process through their awareness of the issues involved and participate by providing information necessary to respond, recover, and return to normal operations.

Exam Essentials

Be familiar with federal legislation and regulations for workplace health and safety.   The major federal legislation for this functional area is the Occupational Safety and Health Act of 1970. This law created OSHA, which develops and enforces workplace health and safety standards.

Understand the safety needs of organizations and be able to design, implement, and evaluate a safety program, train employees, and evaluate program effectiveness.   Employers are responsible for ensuring that those who work for them have a workplace that is free from danger. To provide this, employers must be committed to a safe workplace, involve employees in meeting safety standards by giving them the information they need to be safe in the workplace, and provide training for the equipment and materials employees will use to perform their jobs.

Understand business continuity plans and be able to contribute HR's perspective when creating a plan.   Being prepared to protect organizational assets during natural or manmade disasters can mean the difference between an organization's survival or demise when an emergency occurs. One of the key assets to be protected during an emergency is the workforce. HR can contribute valuable input with regard to employee communication plans and develop training programs that will help to keep the workforce intact in an emergency.

Understand the purpose of an emergency response plan and be able to design and implement one and evaluate its effectiveness.   The emergency response plan is created in advance of an emergency. It describes what roles are to be played in the emergency and who will play them, communicates to all employees a place to meet in the event of an evacuation, and assigns some responsibility for implementing the plan in the event of an emergency.

Understand organizational and workforce security needs and be able to develop, implement, and evaluate workplace security plans.   Organizations and employees must both feel secure in the work environment. Employees must be safe in order to work productively; employers must feel secure that the assets of the business will continue to be available for use in the business.

Key Terms

Before you take the exam, be certain you are familiar with the following terms:

biological health hazards

business continuity planning (BCP)

chemical health hazards

closing conference

continuity of operations plan (COOP)

cumulative trauma injuries (CTI)

de-minimus

disaster recovery plan (DRP)

doctrine of contributory negligence

emergency action plans

emergency response plan (ERP)

environmental health hazards

ergonomics

fellow servant rule

general duty standard

Intellectual Property Agreement (IPA)

internal controls

material safety data sheets (MSDS)

Mine Safety and Health Administration (MSHA)

musculoskeletal disorders

National Institute of Occupational Safety and Health (NIOSH)

Non-Disclosure Agreement (NDA)

Occupational Safety and Health Administration (OSHA)

occupational safety and health standards

opening conference

OSHA Alliance Program

physical health hazards

pre-employment testing

privacy concern cases

random drug testing

reasonable expectation of privacy

reasonable suspicion drug testing

repetitive stress injuries (RSI)

risk assessment

safety

Safety and Health Achievement Recognition Program (SHARP)

scheduled drug testing

security

Strategic Partnership Program

stress

teratogens

voluntary assumption of risk

Voluntary Protection Program (VPP)

workplace investigation

workplace violence

Review Questions

1. An OSHA violation with substantial probability of death or serious physical harm as the result of a workplace hazard is
   - **A.** Willful
   - **B.** Serious
   - **C.** Repeat
   - **D.** De-minimus

2. Under OSHA regulations, employers do *not* have the right to
   - **A.** Refuse to allow an OSHA inspector on the premises.
   - **B.** Request a variance to an OSHA standard while waiting for repairs.
   - **C.** Consult with OSHA to correct hazards without fear of a citation and penalty.
   - **D.** File a Notice of Contest within 30 days of the citation.

3. What is the *best* way to ensure that employees comply with the Drug-Free Workplace Act?
   - **A.** Develop and publish a written policy.
   - **B.** Notify employees about contract conditions.
   - **C.** Establish penalties for drug arrests.
   - **D.** Establish an awareness program.

4. The 16-year-old son of one of your friends is looking for a summer job and has been offered a job at a coal mine. Which of the following makes this illegal?
   - **A.** Mine Safety and Health Act
   - **B.** Occupational Safety and Health Act
   - **C.** Fair Labor Standards Acts
   - **D.** Hazard Communication

5. The company receptionist has always been cheerful and warm when greeting customers and has taken the initiative to do what needed to be done without waiting to be told. She's always kept the front desk tidy and presentable for visitors. Over the last few weeks, the receptionist has become moody and called in sick several times complaining of headaches, and the reception area looks disorganized all the time. This receptionist is showing classic signs of
   - **A.** Stress
   - **B.** Job dissatisfaction
   - **C.** Substance abuse
   - **D.** SARS

6. The union rep has requested copies of all the incident reports filed during the last year. You are required to

   A. Furnish the copies by the end of the day.

   B. Furnish copies within 15 calendar days, but only of the "Tell Us About the Case" section.

   C. Furnish the copies by the end of the next business day.

   D. Furnish copies of the "Tell Us About the Case" section within 7 calendar days.

7. An employee assistance plan does *not*

   A. Provide outplacement counseling for employees

   B. Counsel employees with substance abuse problems

   C. Counsel managers on employee relations problems

   D. Counsel employees with gambling problems

8. Which of the following injuries or illnesses is considered work-related?

   A. An employee has twisted an ankle at an aerobics class the company sponsored.

   B. An employee fell while taking a shower in the dressing room after the work shift.

   C. An employee is hit by a car in the parking lot while walking toward the building.

   D. An employee disregards the safety procedures and is cut by a table saw.

9. An effective safety and health management plan does *not* include:

   A. Senior management support

   B. Ongoing worksite analysis

   C. Regular OSHA inspections

   D. Active hazard prevention program

10. How can an employer determine if a job creates an ergonomic hazard for an employee?

    A. Review and analyze the OSHA logs.

    B. Review and analyze the worker compensation records.

    C. Review the MSDS.

    D. Observe the incumbent performing the job duties.

Answers to Review Questions

1. B. A serious violation is the second level of violation. Willful violations (A) are, in addition to having the potential for serious harm or injury, done intentionally or with "plain indifference" to the requirements. Repeat violations (C) are violations for which an employer has been previously cited and have recurred. De-minimus violations (D) are unlikely to cause serious harm or injury.

2. D. A Notice of Contest must be filed within 15 days of the citation. The OSH Act requires employers to allow the CSHO to inspect the workplace (A). Employers may request variances until repairs are made (B) or for processes that provide equal or greater safety for workers. Employers may consult with OSHA to identify possible hazards without fear of a citation or penalty (C), but once a consultant becomes involved, the employer must abate any violations or the consultant will refer the violation to an OSHA inspector.

3. A. While all of these are steps in the process, the *best* way to ensure that employees will comply with the Drug-Free Workplace Act is to develop and publish a written policy.

4. C. The FLSA defines a list of jobs not suitable for children between the ages of 16 and 18. The Mine Safety and Health Act establishes mandatory safety and health standards for mine operators and monitors operations throughout the United States (A). OSHA ensures safe and healthful working conditions for American workers, but does not address child labor (B). The Hazard Communication Standard requires employers to provide employees with information about physical and health hazards related to the use of any chemicals in the workplace (D).

5. A. The receptionist is exhibiting symptoms of all three types of stress: physical, emotional, and mental.

6. D. The employee representative is entitled to receive copies of incident reports with the identifying information covered up. Employers have 7 calendar days to provide the information to an employee representative. Copies of the OSHA 300 log must be provided by the end of the following business day (C) when requested by employees or their representatives. A and B do not apply to OSHA requirements.

7. C. EAPs provide a source of referrals for managers and employers to use when employees are having personal or other problems but do not counsel managers through employee relations issues. EAPs provide counseling for a variety of employee needs, including compulsive gambling (D), substance abuse (B), and help to quit smoking. Outplacement counseling (A) is often, but not always, included in an EAP.

8. D. Injuries that occur while performing the job are reportable, whether or not the employee was at fault. OSHA regulations exempt injuries that occur as a result of voluntary participation in fitness activities (A), from personal grooming activities (B), or those caused by motor vehicles in a company parking lot (C).

9. C. OSHA inspections are only conducted at the request of an employee based on a safety violation, as a preprogrammed high-hazard inspection, or on a random basis. The four characteristics of a safety and health management plan are senior management support (A), ongoing worksite analysis (B), active hazard prevention and control programs (C), and on-going safety and health training.

10. D. While a review and analysis of OSHA logs (A) or worker compensation records (B) can be used to determine any injury patterns occurring in the workplace, observation of the incumbent performing the work is necessary to determine whether or not there is an ergonomic hazard in the job. An MSDS (C) describes chemical hazards unrelated to ergonomics.

Appendix A

Case Study

A case study provides learners with a way to draw on information from multiple functional areas to solve problems typical to business situations. The scenario for this case study involves a fictional company, Wright Sisters, Inc., which has grown over the years from a small, family-run storefront to a global enterprise. The specific situations are drawn from real-life experiences, but the names have been changed to protect the innocent (or guilty).

The Scenario

In 1973, Lydia, Rachel, and Susannah Wright opened the Wright Sisters Garden Shoppe in Portsmouth, Rhode Island. At the time, Lydia and Susannah were young mothers and split the hours in the shop so each worked part time and could spend time with their growing families. Lydia's strength was her love of gardening—she had the proverbial green thumb and was a gifted, though not formally trained, landscape designer. Susannah's strength was her easy rapport with strangers—this made her a natural at building strong customer relationships. Rachel was a CPA at one of the Big 8 (now Big 4) accounting firms, and although she did not generally work in the shop, she contributed all the bookkeeping, accounting, and financial planning.

While not an overnight success, the shop grew steadily to the point where it was able to provide a small income for the three sisters. As Lydia and Susannah's children grew, they spent time working in the shop, either helping Lydia with gardening projects or serving customers. Over the years, the Wright Sisters Garden Shoppe built a reputation for high-quality, unique merchandise, individualized customer service, and Lydia's ability to solve virtually any gardening problem that a customer asked her about. In 1980, the local newspaper asked Lydia to write a weekly gardening column, which was called *Ask Lydia*. Eighteen months later, the column was syndicated to regional newspapers, and seven months after that, the sisters had to find a larger storefront to accommodate the increased business.

By this time, the sisters could no longer handle all the work themselves and had several part-time employees working in the shop in addition to their children. Lydia's column turned out to be a boon for business, and customers who lived too far away to get to the store began to request products mentioned in the column by mail. As the volume of the requests increased, the sisters put together a small catalog that readers of Lydia's column could request. As a result of the mail-order catalog success, they needed to add three full-time positions to keep up with the orders they received. In 1988, the sisters formed a privately held corporation, Wright

Sisters, Inc. Rachel left her job at the Big 8 firm to become president of the new business and focus on business strategy and growth. Lydia became the Vice President of Product Development, and Susannah took the role of Vice President of Sales and Marketing. The three sisters, along with their brother Michael, an attorney, formed the Board of Directors.

Once the corporation was formed, the sisters began developing their own product lines for garden supplies and equipment based on Lydia's expertise and requests from readers of her column and customers.

Today, while the original shop and two others are open in the northeast, the main focus of Wright Sisters, Inc. (WSI) is the manufacture and distribution of garden equipment and supplies that are sold through the catalog, online, and in hardware stores and home improvement centers throughout the country. Recently, the company learned that one of its key suppliers was for sale and acquired the company to ensure the availability and quality of their products. This acquisition will triple their workforce to about 1,500 people, most of whom will work on the production line. WSI will assume operational control in 60 days.

As a result of the acquisition and other anticipated changes—Susannah and Lydia in particular would like to reduce their roles at WSI over the next few years—the Board brought in a consultant who helped them develop a strategic plan. As you recall from Chapter 3, the board created the following vision, mission, and values statements:

Corporate vision   "Bringing the joy of gardening to new generations of gardeners."

Corporate mission   "We are the home-gardening source. The quality of our products allows busy families to enjoy gardening together. Our gardening education programs grow 'gardeners for life' by teaching adults and children to make gardening easier and more enjoyable."

Corporate values statement   "WSI values integrity and excellence in its products and its people. We treat ourselves, our customers, and our suppliers with dignity and respect. We believe in and encourage new ideas to make our products better and help our business grow, and we acknowledge and reward those who present these ideas. We are accountable for our actions and, when mistakes occur, we focus on preventing future errors and moving forward. We are passionate about achieving our goals, and we are passionate about gardening."

WSI prides itself on the quality of its products and the loyalty and dedication of its workforce. The personalities of Susannah and Lydia and the way the company grew naturally created an informal culture. Employees are empowered to do what is needed to satisfy customers and the atmosphere allows for a free and open exchange of ideas. The sisters are concerned about the impact of such a large acquisition on the culture and want to make sure it is not lost.

Up to this point, the company's HR team has been focused on tactical and administrative tasks under the direction of an HR manager who reported to Susannah. With the new acquisition, industry changes, and the need to plan for WSI's future leadership, the executive team recognized the need for a higher level of participation from the HR function and conducted a national search for a Vice President of Human Resources who will become a member of the executive team and report to Rachel.

The Challenge: Create an HR Plan

You have been selected for the new VP of HR position. During the interview process, you realized that the executive team is very open to ideas that will maintain the culture in light of the acquisition and create a smooth transition as the sisters begin to step back from daily operations. You have already discussed with Rachel the concept of an HR plan and she is very interested in seeing how your proposals will help WSI achieve their mission.

You are looking forward to getting started tomorrow morning—your first day on the job. During the interview process, you met with all members of the executive and HR teams, and Rachel has arranged an informal breakfast meeting to introduce you to the rest of the managers. She also provided you with a copy of the complete business plan, including goals and objectives for each business function. The HR manager has scheduled a brown-bag lunch for next week so you can meet some of the employees.

As you think about the challenges ahead, you start to make a few notes about how to proceed.

1.   What is your strategy for leading the HR function?
2.   What issues need to be addressed in the HR plan?

CFO Perspective: HR's Role in Business Planning

By Vikram Jog, CFO

Execution happens with the best people—everything else is almost a commodity. HR is the business function with the expertise and ability to ensure that the right people are in place to execute the business plan. In order to participate at this level, HR must first establish credibility throughout the organization and be able to communicate at all levels. Credibility with the management team is the foundation for equal participation in the planning process.

HR should be completely aware of the business plan providing an analysis of the plan from the practical standpoint of acquiring the people needed to execute the strategies. For example, by saying, "Fellow members of the executive team, my analysis of the business plan is that we will need people with XYZ skills to achieve the goals established. Those skills are currently in high demand in the labor market, which means that we may not be able to hire them as quickly and in the numbers we need based on our current compensation plan. Our options are to change the compensation plan to accommodate the labor market, scale back the growth targets, or develop some of our existing employees with similar skills, replacing them with new employees who have skills that are more available in the labor market."

One key role of the HR function is in building the organization culture. HR is the business function to lead the discussion by asking two questions: "What kind of place do we want this to be?" and "What kind of people do we want to attract?" Gathering this information from organization leaders is the first step in establishing an environment that is attractive to people with the skills, attitudes, and abilities the organization desires.

HR is uniquely qualified to provide key needs for organizations, including:

- Retaining the existing workforce

- Increasing productivity

- Proposing a compensation philosophy that meets specific organization needs

- Providing a reality check on business plan targets and goals

- Keeping an up-to-date skill inventory for current employees, knowing what skills can be upgraded to achieve the strategy

- Building the employment brand

In order to establish the credibility necessary to participate as a full member of the executive team, HR must fully understand the business. With credibility established, HR plays several vital roles: getting the right systems in place so the employer can function, calling management on the mat to deal with performance issues, and building a compelling case for action on differentiation in the workforce to provide a competitive edge.

About the contributor: Vikram Jog is the CFO of a rapidly growing biotech company. As a CPA with more than 25 years of finance experience in biotech, chemical, and public accounting companies, he provides a valuable perspective on HR's role as an organizational contributor.

Case Study Answer Key

1. What is your strategy for leading the HR function?   As the "new kid on the block" four important tasks must be accomplished:

1. Gather information. Talk to as many people as possible. This includes your peers, all decision-makers, and as many employees as possible, as well as vendors, customers, and members of the community who have an interest in WSI.

2. Build relationships with the HR team. Determine the strengths and weaknesses of the department, identify service gaps and development needs, and create a staffing plan to accommodate the increased workforce.

3. Build relationships with your peers.

4. Conduct an HR audit to find out what is currently being accomplished and how well the HR team has been serving the needs of the company and identify service gaps and areas for improvement.

2. What issues need to be addressed in the HR plan?   To a certain extent, the specific issues addressed in the HR plan will depend upon information gathered from the specific goals, objectives, and action plans contained in the business plan, the HR audit, and conversations with the management team and employees.

Based on the information provided, the initial plan will need to address the following issues:

- Creation of a succession plan.

- Integration of the employees being acquired, including policies, procedures, benefit plans, compensation structures, and organizational roles.

- Establishment of a communication plan for the larger organization.

- Review of the current organization structure and recommendations for changes based on the acquisition, including a plan to eliminate redundant jobs if needed and how to reassign or terminate employees.

It is important to keep the plan goals realistic and achievable by prioritizing the organization's many needs. In addition to the "must have" issues above, other plans could include some of the following:

- Review of the compensation plan, including compensation philosophy, salary structure, and incentive plans.

- Review of the recruiting process.

- Changes to the training and development process.

- Establishment of a retention plan and re-recruit key employees.

Depending on the priority of these and other issues that may need to be addressed, some can be placed on the HR plan for future years.

Appendix B

Federal Employment Legislation and Case Law

This appendix provides a brief overview of federal employment legislation and case law that is required knowledge for HR professionals. All of the legislation has been covered in detail in the appropriate chapters, as have most of the cases. I have included some additional cases in this table that exam candidates may find useful during their review. This information is not presented as or intended to replace legal advice. Please consult your employment attorney for advice on specific employment situations.

The abbreviation "USSC" refers to decisions made by the United States Supreme Court.

Year	Name	Key Requirements	Chapter
1884	*Payne v. The Western & Atlantic Railroad Company*	Defined employment at-will.	7
1869	Bureau of Labor Statistics	Established to study industrial accidents and maintain accident records.	8
1890	Sherman Anti-Trust Act	Controlled business monopolies; allowed court injunctions to prevent restraint of trade. Used to restrict unionization efforts.	7
1914	Clayton Act	Limited the use of injunctions to break strikes; exempted unions from the Sherman Act.	7
1916	Federal Employees Compensation Act	Provided benefits similar to worker compensation for federal employees injured on the job.	8
1927	Longshore and Harbor Workers' Compensation Act	Provided workers' compensation benefits for maritime workers injured on navigable waters of the U.S. or on piers, docks, and terminals.	8

Year	Name	Key Requirements	Chapter
1926	Railway Labor Act	Protected unionization rights; allowed for 90-day cooling off period to prevent strikes in national emergencies. Covers railroads and unions.	7
1932	Norris-La Guardia Act	Protected right to organize; outlawed yellow dog contracts.	7
1935	National Labor Relations Act (Wagner Act)	Protected the right of workers to organize and bargain collectively; identified unfair labor practices; established the NLRB.	7
1935	Federal Insurance Contributions Act/Social Security Act	Required employers and employees to pay social security taxes.	6
1936	Federal Unemployment Tax Act	Required employers to contribute a percentage of payroll to an unemployment insurance fund.	6
1936	Public Contracts Act (Walsh-Healey Act)	Required contractors to pay prevailing wage rates.	6
1938	Fair Labor Standards Act	Defined exempt and nonexempt employees; required and set the minimum wage to be paid to nonexempt workers; required time and-a-half to be paid for nonexempt overtime hours; limited hours and type of work for children; established recordkeeping requirements.	6
1947	Labor-Management Relations Act (Taft-Hartley)	Prohibited closed shops; restricted union shops; allowed states to pass "right to work" laws; prohibited jurisdictional strikes and secondary boycotts; allowed employers to permanently replace economic strikers; established the Federal Mediation and Conciliation Service; allowed 80-day cooling off period for national emergency strikes.	7
1947	Portal-to-Portal Act	Clarified definition of "hours worked" for the FLSA.	6

Year	Name	Key Requirements	Chapter
1952	Patent Act	Established U.S. Patent and Trademark Office.	5
1959	Labor-Management Reporting and Disclosure Act (Landrum-Griffin)	Controlled internal union operations; provided bill of rights for union members; required majority vote of members to increase dues; allowed members to sue the union; set term limits for union leaders.	7
1963	Equal Pay Act	Required that employees performing substantially similar or identical work be paid the same wage or salary rate.	6
1964	Title VII of the Civil Rights Act of 1964	Established EEOC; prohibited employment discrimination on the basis of race, color, religion, national origin, or sex.	4
1965	EO (Executive Order) 11246	Prohibited employment discrimination on the basis of race, creed, color, or national origin; required affirmative steps for all terms and conditions of employment; required a written AAP for contractors with 50 employees.	4
1965	Immigration and Nationality Act	Eliminated national origin, race, and ancestry as bars to immigration; set immigration goals for reunifying families and preference for specialized skills.	4
1965	Service Contract Act	Required government contractors to pay prevailing wages and benefits.	6
1967	Age Discrimination in Employment Act	Prohibited discrimination against persons 40 years of age or older; established conditions for BFOQ (Bona Fide Occupational Qualification) exceptions.	4
1967	EO 11375	Added sex to protected classes in EO 11246.	4
1968	Consumer Credit Protection Act	Limited garnishment amounts on employee wages; prohibited discharge of employees for a single garnishment order.	6

Year	Name	Key Requirements	Chapter
1969	EO 11478	Included disabled individuals and those over 40 years of age in protected classes established by EO 11246.	4
1969	Black Lung Benefits Act	Provided benefits for coal miners suffering from pneumoconiosis due to mine work.	8
1970	Occupational Safety and Health Act	Required employers to provide a safe workplace and comply with safety and health standards; established OSHA to enforce safety regulations; established NIOSH to research, evaluate, and recommend hazard reduction measures.	8
1970	Fair Credit Reporting Act	Required employers to notify candidates that credit reports may be obtained; required written authorization by the candidate and that the employer provide a copy of the report to the candidate before taking an adverse action.	4
1971	*Griggs v. Duke Power*	USSC: Required employers to show that job requirements are related to the job; established that lack of intention to discriminate is not a defense against claims of discrimination.	4
1972	Equal Employment Opportunity Act	Established that complainants have burden of proof for disparate impact; provided litigation authority for EEOC; extended time to file complaints.	4
1973	Rehabilitation Act	Expanded opportunities for individuals with physical or mental disabilities and provided remedies for victims of discrimination.	4
1974	Privacy Act	Prohibited federal agencies from sharing information collected about individuals.	4
1974	Vietnam Era Veterans Readjustment Assistance Act	Provided equal opportunity and affirmative action for Vietnam veterans.	4

Year	Name	Key Requirements	Chapter
1974	Employee Retirement Income Security Act	Established requirements for pension, retirement, and welfare benefit plans including medical, hospital, AD&D, and unemployment benefits.	6
1975	*Albemarle Paper v. Moody*	USSC: Required that employment tests be validated; subjective supervisor rankings are not sufficient validation; criteria must be tied to job requirements.	4
1975	*NLRB v. J. Weingarten, Inc.*	USSC: Established that union employees have the right to request union representation during any investigatory interview that could result in disciplinary action.	5
1976	*Washington v. Davis*	USSC: Established that employment selection tools that adversely impact protected classes are lawful if they have been validated to show future success on the job.	4
1976	Copyright Act	Defined "fair use" of copyrighted work; set term of copyright effectiveness.	5
1977	Mine Safety and Health Act	Established mandatory mine safety and health standards and created MSHA.	8
1977	*Automobile Workers v. Johnson Controls, Inc.*	USSC: "Decisions about the welfare of the next generation must be left to the parents who conceive, bear, support and raise them, rather than to the employers who hire those parents."	8
1978	Uniform Guidelines on Employee Selection Procedures	Established guidelines to ensure that selection procedures be both job related and valid predictors of job success.	4
1978	Pregnancy Discrimination Act	Required that pregnancy be treated the same as any other short-term disability.	4
1978	Civil Service Reform Act	Created Senior Executive Service, Merit Systems Protection Board, Office of Personnel Management, and the Federal Labor Relations Authority.	6

Year	Name	Key Requirements	Chapter
1978	Revenue Act	Established Section 125 and 401(k) plans for employees.	6
1979	EO 12138	Created National Women's Business Enterprise Policy; required affirmative steps to promote and support women's business enterprises.	4
1980	Guidelines on Sexual Harassment	Assisted employers to develop antiharassment policies, establish complaint procedures, and investigate complaints promptly and impartially.	4
1984	Retirement Equity Act	Lowered age limits on participation and vesting in pension benefits; required written spousal consent to not provide survivor benefits; restricted conditions placed on survivor benefits.	6
1986	Consolidated Omnibus Budget Reconciliation Act	Provided continuation of group health coverage upon a qualifying event.	6
1986	Tax Reform Act	Reduced income tax rates and brackets.	6
1986	Immigration Reform and Control Act	Prohibited employment of individuals who are not legally authorized to work in the U.S.; required I-9s for all employees.	4
1988	Drug-Free Workplace Act	Required federal contractors to develop and implement drug-free workplace policies.	4
1988	Employee Polygraph Protection Act	Prohibited use of lie detector tests except under limited circumstances.	4
1988	Worker Adjustment and Retraining Notification Act	Required 60 days' notice for mass layoffs or plant closings; defined mass layoffs and plant closings; identified exceptions to the requirements.	4
1990	Americans with Disabilities Act	Required reasonable accommodation for qualified individuals with disabilities.	4

Year	Name	Key Requirements	Chapter
1990	Older Worker Benefit Protection Act	Amended ADEA to prevent discrimination in benefits for workers over 40; added requirements for waivers.	6
1990	Immigration Act	Required prevailing wage for holders of H1(b) visas; set H1(b) quotas.	4
1991	Civil Rights Act	Allowed compensatory and punitive damages; provided for jury trials; established defenses to disparate impact claims.	4
1991	Glass Ceiling Act	Established commission to determine whether or not a glass ceiling exists and identify barriers for women and minorities. As a result, the OFCCP conducts audits of the representation of women and minorities at all corporate levels.	4
1992	Unemployment Compensation Amendments	Reduced rollover rules for lump-sum distributions of qualified retirement plans; required 20 percent withholding for some distributions.	6
1992	National Energy Efficiency Act of 1992	Set maximum transit subsidy at $60 per month for employees; limited tax-free parking benefits to $155 per month.	6
1993	Family and Medical Leave Act	Required qualifying employers to provide 12 weeks of unpaid leave to eligible employees for the birth or adoption of a child or to provide care for defined relatives with serious health conditions; or to employees unable to perform job duties due to a serious health condition.	6
1993	*Taxman v. Board of Education of Piscataway*	Found that in the absence of past discrimination or under-representation of protected classes, preference may not be given to protected classes in making layoff decisions.	4

Year	Name	Key Requirements	Chapter
1993	*Harris v. Forklift Systems*	USSC: Defined actionable hostile work environment as that which falls between merely offensive and that which results in tangible psychological injury.	7
1993	Omnibus Budget Reconciliation Act	Revised rules for employee benefits, set maximum deduction for executive pay at $1,000,000; mandated some benefits for medical plans.	6
1994	Uniformed Services Employment and Reemployment Rights Act	Protected the re-employment and benefit rights of reservists called to active duty.	7
1995	Congressional Accountability Act	Required all federal employment legislation passed by Congress to apply to congressional employees.	4
1996	Illegal Immigration Reform and Immigrant Responsibility Act	Reduced number and types of documents to prove identity.	4
1996	Mental Health Parity Act	Required insurers to provide the same limits for mental health benefits that are provided for other types of health benefits.	6
1996	Health Insurance Portability and Accountability Act	Prohibited discrimination based on health status; limited health insurance restrictions for pre-existing conditions; required a Certificate of Group Health Plan Coverage upon plan termination.	6
1996	Personal Responsibility and Work Opportunity Reconciliation Act of 1996	Required employers to provide information about all new or rehired employees to state agencies to enforce child support orders.	6
1996	Small Business Job Protection Act	Redefined highly compensated individuals; detailed minimum participation requirements; simplified 401(k) tests; corrected qualified plan and disclosure requirements.	6
1996	Small Business Regulatory Enforcement Fairness Act	Provided that an SBA ombudsman act as an advocate for small business owners in the regulatory process.	8

Year	Name	Key Requirements	Chapter
1998	EO 13087	Expanded coverage of protected classes in EO 11246 to include sexual orientation.	4
1998	*Burlington Industries v. Ellerth*	USSC: Established that employers have vicarious liability for employees victimized by supervisors with immediate or higher authority over them who create an actionable hostile work environment.	7
1998	*Faragher v. City of Boca Raton*	USSC: Established that employers are responsible for employee actions and have a responsibility to control them.	7
1998	*Oncale v. Sundowner Offshore Services, Inc.*	USSC: Extended the definition of sexual harassment to include same-sex harassment.	7
2000	NLRB: Epilepsy Foundation of Northeast Ohio	NLRB extended Weingarten rights to nonunion employees by allowing employees to request a coworker to be present during an investigatory interview that could result in disciplinary action.	7
2000	NLRB: M. B. Sturgis, Inc.	Established that temporary employees may be included in the client company's bargaining unit and that consent of the employer and temp agency are not required to bargain jointly.	7
2000	Needlestick Safety and Prevention Act	Mandated recordkeeping for all needlestick and sharps injuries; required employee involvement in developing safer devices.	8
2000	Energy Employees Occupational Illness Compensation Program Act	Provided compensation for employees and contractors subjected to excessive radiation during production and testing of nuclear weapons.	8
2000	EO 13152	Added "status as a parent" to protected classes in EO 11246.	4

Year	Name	Key Requirements	Chapter
2002	Sarbanes-Oxley Act	To improve quality and transparency in financial reporting; to increase corporate responsibility and the usefulness of corporate financial disclosure; to establish and maintain an adequate internal control structure and procedures for financial reporting.	7
2004	NLRB: IBM Corp	NLRB reversed its 2000 decision in Epilepsy, withdrawing Weingarten rights from nonunion employees.	7
2006	Pension Protection Act of 2006	Amends ERISA financial obligations for multi-employer pension plans; changes plan administration for deferred contribution plans.	6
2006	*Burlington Northern Santa Fe Railway Co. vs. White*	USSC: All retaliation against employees who file discrimination claims is unlawful under Title VII, even if no economic damage results.	7

Additional Cases

There is a great deal of case law that impacts human resource management. I have included many of those significant cases in the chapters where they have the most impact, but there are many more that impact HR practice on a daily basis. You should be prepared to see some of these included in questions on the exam.

1968: *Rosenfeld v. Southern Pacific*

Leah Rosenfeld began working for Southern Pacific (SP) in 1944 and was a member of the Transportation Communication Employees Union, which represented employees at that location. As part of its Collective Bargaining Agreement (CBA) with SP, the union had negotiated a clause that stated, "Employees shall be regarded as in line for promotion, advancement depending upon faithful discharge of duties and capacity for increased responsibility. Where ability is sufficient, seniority shall govern."

In 1966, Ms. Rosenfeld applied for the position of agent-telegrapher at the SP office in Thermal, CA, and was the most senior employee bidding for the opening. She was fully qualified for the position based on all the standards established by the CBA and was fully qualified to perform the services of the position, including required overtime and the physical duties required by the position. The company did not perform any tests or evaluation of her abilities for requirements of the job.

A male employee with less seniority was selected for the position.

SP gave two reasons for refusing the job to her:

1. The California Labor Code limited the number of hours of work per day that could be performed by women and placed a limit of 25 pounds on the weight that could be lifted by a woman.

2. Hiring Ms. Rosenfeld was contrary to SP's discretion as an employer.

Rosenfeld filed suit, claiming that the labor code sections were discriminatory on the basis of sex based on Title VII and that the requirements were not BFOQ (Bona Fide Occupational Qualification).

The Ninth Circuit Court of Appeal determined that the labor code did not create a BFOQ and was, in fact, discriminatory, that SP did violate Title VII, and that the refusal of SP to assign her to the position was not a lawful exercise of SP's discretion as an employer. SP was ordered to consider her for future openings.

1969: *Weeks v. Southern Bell Telephone Co.*

In 1947, Lorena Weeks began working for Southern Bell (Bell) in Georgia and was a member of the union that represented the workers. The union had a CBA with the company including a clause that seniority would be the deciding factor in determining which job bidders were placed in positions if they otherwise met all the requirements for an opening.

In 1966, Ms. Weeks and one other employee applied for an opening as a switchman. Bell refused her application, telling her they had decided not to place women in this position. The other applicant, a man, had less seniority than Ms. Weeks.

Ms. Weeks filed a complaint with the EEOC, claiming that the company had discriminated against her on the basis of her sex and later filed suit against the company on the same basis. Bell admitted a prima facie violation of Title VII but claimed that sex was a BFOQ for the position, basing this claim on the Georgia Commissioner of Labor's Rule 59, which prohibited women and minors from lifting over 30 pounds. Ms. Weeks argued that the limit was unreasonably low, arbitrary, and that it both violated the Equal Protection Clause of the Fourteenth Amendment and was contrary to Title VII.

In 1969, the Fifth Circuit Court of Appeal ruled that Bell had not proven that sex was a BFOQ for this position. The fact that by then Georgia had repealed Rule 59, replacing the specific weight limit with a requirement that the weight of loads be limited to avoid strains or undue fatigue, was noted by the court in its decision.

1973: *McDonnell Douglas Corp. v. Green*

Mr. Green was an African-American man working as a mechanic for McDonnell Douglas Corp. in St. Louis, MO, from 1956 until he was laid off at the end of August 1964 as part of a general reduction in the company's work force. Mr. Green claimed that his termination and the company's hiring practices in general were racially motivated. To protest this alleged discrimination, Mr. Green, a member of the Congress for Racial Equality (CRE), participated in a "stall-in" with other members of the group that was designed to block access to the company's plant during the morning rush hour. Mr. Green was arrested for his part in the action and pled guilty to obstructing traffic. Some time later, the CRE conducted a "lock-in" at the plant that prevented some McDonnell Douglas employees from leaving the building.

When McDonnell Douglas advertised for mechanics a few weeks after the lock-in, Mr. Green applied and was turned down based on his participation in the stall-in and lock-in. He filed a complaint with the EEOC, claiming that he was turned down because of his race and his participation in the civil rights movement. Mr. Green sued McDonnell Douglas in 1968 for violations of Title VII, and the case was heard by the U.S. Supreme Court in 1973.

In issuing its findings in 1973, the Supreme Court defined the requirements for a finding of a prima facie case of discrimination as follows: "The complainant in a Title VII trial must carry the initial burden under the statute of establishing a prima facie case of racial discrimination. This may be done by showing (i) that he belongs to a racial minority; (ii) that he applied and was qualified for a job for which the employer was seeking applicants; (iii) that, despite his qualifications, he was rejected; and (iv) that, after his rejection, the position remained open and the employer continued to seek applicants from persons of complainant's qualifications."

1978: *Regents of California v. Bakke*

While the Bakke case was based on a college admissions program, its results impacted the use of affirmative action programs in general.

The Medical School at the University of California Davis utilized two admissions programs to qualify students for the medical program. Both the regular and the special admissions programs evaluated applicants based on a number of criteria and ranked them with a "benchmark score" based on the results. Applicants for both programs were rated on similar criteria, but those in the special admissions program were not rated against those in the regular admission program when decisions were made as to which applicants would be offered admission. In addition, there were a specific number of spots allotted to applicants from the special admissions program.

In 1973 and 1974, Mr. Bakke's applications for admission to the medical program through the regular admission process were rejected, while applicants from the special admissions program, who ranked lower than he did on the admission criteria, were accepted. Mr. Bakke filed suit, claiming that the special admissions program was in violation of the Equal Protection Clause of the Fourteenth Amendment to the Constitution, as well as Title VI of the Civil Rights Act of 1964 and a provision of the California constitution. The Supreme Court handed down its decision in 1978, finding that Mr. Bakke's rights had indeed been violated by the special admissions program, which operated as a quota for admitting minorities to the medical program.

The Court's decision acknowledged the need to consider race in admission decisions when it was necessary to correct prior discriminatory practices but ruled that quotas were not an acceptable method to accomplish this.

1979: *United Steelworkers v. Weber*

This case began with an Affirmative Action Plan (AAP) that had been negotiated by the United Steelworkers of America (USWA) and Kaiser Aluminum & Chemical Corp. (Kaiser) as part of a collective bargaining agreement. The AAP had been negotiated to "eliminate conspicuous racial imbalances" in skilled craft positions at 15 Kaiser plants by reserving 50 percent of openings in the in-plant training programs for black employees until the percentage of black craftworkers in each plant corresponded with the percentage of blacks in the local labor force. Employees were selected for the program based on their seniority, as long as 50 percent of the trainees were black.

Mr. Weber filed suit against Kaiser and the USWA when he was rejected for a spot in the training program in favor of black employees who had less seniority than he did. Mr. Weber claimed that this was a violation of Title VII of the Civil Rights Act of 1964. The Supreme Court found that the AAP was permissible because it allowed that half of the participants would be white, that it had been designed to remedy prior discrimination, and that it was a temporary measure designed to eliminate a racial imbalance.

1981: *Texas Department of Community Affairs v. Burdine*

In 1972, Ms. Burdine was hired by the Texas Department of Community Affairs (TDCA) as an accounting clerk in the Public Service Careers Division (PSC) whose mission was to train unskilled workers for public sector jobs. Six months later, Ms. Burdine, who had previous training experience, was promoted to the position of field service coordinator. The project director (her supervisor) resigned a few months later and Ms. Burdine applied for the position, but it was not filled and remained open for another six months. At that point, the U.S. Department of Labor, which funded the PSC and was concerned about the quality of its operations, decided to cease funding in 30 days. Based on the efforts of the TDCA, with input from Ms. Burdine, the DOL was convinced to continue funding for the PSC if it was reorganized and a permanent director was hired.

The TDCA reassigned a male from another division to the project director position. He terminated three employees, including Ms. Burdine, retaining one male employee. Shortly after the termination, Ms. Burdine was rehired by the TDCA in another division at the same salary as was paid to the project director of the PSC.

Ms. Burdine filed this suit, claiming gender discrimination had motivated both the refusal of TDCA to promote her and her subsequent termination from PSC. The District Court determined that gender had not been a factor in either decision. The Fifth Circuit Court of Appeals found that the male hired for the project director position may have been better qualified than Ms. Burdine for the position, but that the TDCA had not proved that there were legitimate, nondiscriminatory reasons for Ms. Burdine's termination.

The Supreme Court held that employers are not required to prove the nondiscriminatory reasons for an employment action but are required only to explain the nondiscriminatory reasons for the action.

1987: *Johnson v. Santa Clara County Transportation Agency*

Paul Johnson, a male employee of the Santa Clara County Transportation Agency (SCCTA) was passed over for a promotion in favor of a female employee, Diane Joyce. Both candidates were deemed to be well qualified for the position of road dispatcher, a job classified as a Skilled Craft Worker by the EEOC. The director of the agency made the final decision based on a number of factors, including the qualifications of both candidates, the selection committee recommendation, and affirmative action issues, among others.

The affirmative action issues included the fact that the agency had established a voluntary affirmative action plan in 1978 that had as one of its goals to increase the participation of women in the Skilled Craft Worker category. At the time Ms. Joyce applied for this position, none of the 238 SCCTA positions classified as such was held by a woman.

Mr. Johnson filed a complaint with the EEOC, received a right-to-sue letter in 1981, and filed suit against the agency for violating Title VII. The Supreme Court handed down its decision in 1987.

The Supreme Court held that the SCCTA acted appropriately in promoting Ms. Joyce into the position. The Court stated that the plaintiff has the burden to prove a prima facie case of discrimination. Once that occurs, the employer has the burden to prove that there is a nondiscriminatory rationale for the decision (that is, the AAP). At that point, the burden is once again on the plaintiff to show that the AAP is invalid.

The agency's AAP was determined to be "a moderate, flexible, case-by-case approach" consistent with Title VII requirements. Key elements in this finding were that the AAP was flexible and temporary, designed only to correct an existing workforce imbalance. That being the case, it is acceptable for an employer to place a less qualified member of a protected class in a job.

1987: *School Board of Nassau v. Arline*

Gene Arline contracted tuberculosis in 1957 and was hospitalized until the disease went into remission. In 1966, Ms. Arline became an elementary school teacher in Nassau County, FL, where she taught for 13 years. In 1977, the TB became active again off and on through the 1978–79 school year. The school board suspended her with pay twice to accommodate her recovery, but in 1979 decided to terminate her employment due to the contagious nature of her ongoing illness.

Ms. Arline sued the district, alleging that her dismissal was a violation of Section 504 of the Rehabilitation Act of 1973 because its terms qualified her as a handicapped person based on her illness.

Section 504 is based on Title VI of the Civil Rights Act of 1964 and defines a handicapped individual as "any person who (i) has a physical or mental impairment which substantially limits one or more of such person's major life activities, (ii) has a record of such an impairment, or (iii) is regarded as having such an impairment." Regulations formulated by the Department of Health and Human Services define "major life activities" as "functions such as caring for one's self, performing manual tasks, walking, seeing, hearing, speaking, breathing, learning, and working."

The case centered around whether or not a person with a contagious disease could be considered a handicapped individual under Section 504 of the Rehabilitation Act.

In 1987, the Supreme Court handed down its decision that a person afflicted with tuberculosis can be a handicapped person as defined by Section 504.

Justice Brennan, writing for the majority, stated, "The fact that some persons who have contagious diseases may pose a serious health threat to others under certain circumstances does not justify excluding from the coverage of the act all persons with actual or perceived contagious diseases." The decision also stated that the determination of whether or not someone with a contagious disease poses a serious health threat to others should be left to the medical judgments of public health officials.

1989: *Martin v. Wilks*

The basic issue in this case was whether an employee can sue for reverse discrimination when hiring and promotion decisions are made pursuant to a consent decree.

The city of Birmingham, AL, and the Jefferson County Personnel Board were sued by Martin and six other black individuals in 1974, alleging that the city and the board had unlawfully discriminated against blacks when making hiring and promoting decisions for public service jobs. The case was resolved when the parties entered into consent decrees that established AAPs intended to increase the hiring and promotion of black firefighters.

At a public fairness hearing and in other subsequent actions, objections and a request for injunctive relief to prevent enforcement of the decrees by the Birmingham Firefighters Association (BFA) and white firefighters were denied by the District Court.

A third group of firefighters (including Wilks) then filed suit against the city and the board, alleging that they were being denied promotions in favor of less-qualified blacks, and that this was a violation of Title VII. Martin and the other black individuals sought to have the Wilks suit dismissed, claiming that the consent decree precluded any claims of reverse discrimination.

The Supreme Court held that, because the white firefighters were not involved in the original litigation that resulted in the consent decrees, they could not be held to employment decisions based on them and were entitled to challenge the validity of the consent decrees.

1992: *Electromation, Inc. v. NLRB*

This case resulted from an unfair labor practice charge filed against Electromation by the Teamsters union.

Electromation is a small company with 200 employees that was having financial problems in late 1988. As a result, management decided to eliminate the employee attendance bonus policy and the wage increase for 1989. Instead, they made lump-sum payments to employees based on an individual's length of service. Shortly after this decision was made, the president received a petition signed by 68 employees objecting to the change in policy. The president first met with supervisory personnel to discuss the complaints, then decided to meet directly with a group of employees to discuss their concerns. After meeting with the employees, the president realized that the employee issues were unlikely to be resolved without employee participation. The company decided to create five action committees, one for each area of concern:

1. Absenteeism/infractions
2. No smoking policy
3. Communication network
4. Pay progression for premium positions
5. Attendance bonus program

The committees met weekly, beginning in late January 1989, and included management personnel as well as employees as members. While employees were allowed to sign up for the committees, management determined how many were allowed and limited employees to serving on one committee. Management communicated to the committee members that they were expected to talk with their coworkers for ideas that could be incorporated into the work of the committees. Management also expected committee members to inform coworkers about "what was going on."

On February 13, 1989, the Teamsters union made a demand for recognition to Electromation; at that point management advised the committees that management was no longer able to participate but that the committees could continue their work if they wished to do so.

The NLRB Administrative Law Judge determined that the action committees were unlawful, employer-dominated labor organizations because:

1. They included employees, supervisors, and management as members, and management personnel had the ability to reject recommendations.
2. Management expected committee members to represent coworkers by soliciting ideas from them to be presented to the committee.
3. They included discussions about conditions of employment. Formation of the committees was a direct result of the company's unilateral change to the attendance bonus policy.
4. Management organized them by establishing their goals, determining what each committee would work on, deciding how many employees would be allowed on each committee and how they would operate, and determining their functions.
5. The company provided support in the form of a place to meet, supplies, materials, and payment for time spent on committee work.

In its decision, the NLRB indicated that not all employee-participation committees are employer-dominated organizations and that they can serve a useful purpose if they are not. It also determined that paying employees who participate in committees at work does not in and of itself violate the NLRA.

1993: *E. I. DuPont & Co. v. NLRB*

This case was initiated by the Chemical Workers Union, which represents clerical workers, production personnel, and maintenance employees at DuPont's plant located in Deepwater, NJ. The union claimed that six safety committees and a fitness committee established by DuPont were company-dominated labor organizations and that the company was bypassing the union by dealing with the committees on bargainable issues. DuPont claimed that the committees were "a management vehicle to enhance the safety of employees through labor-management communication or to carry out similar management functions."

The NLRA sets three conditions that must be met in order for a labor organization to exist:

1. Employees participate in the organization.

2. A function of the organization is dealing with the employer.

3. The function of the organization is concerned with some form of "conditions of work," including grievances, labor disputes, wages, rates of pay, or hours of employment.

The purpose of this case was to determine whether or not DuPont was using these committees to bypass the union in dealing with the employees, since clearly employees were participating in them and they dealt with safety issues, which are a mandatory subject for collective bargaining.

Some of the reasons the NLRB found these to be employer-dominated labor organizations include the following:

▪   Each committee included at least one member of management who set the weekly agenda and had veto power over any decisions or recommendations made by committee members.

▪   DuPont controlled the number of members on each committee.

▪   DuPont determined how many and which employees served on each committee.

▪   DuPont could unilaterally restructure the committees.

The board also found that DuPont was using the committees to circumvent the union. For example, the union had repeatedly requested that changes be made to the ventilation system in the welding shop. Until one of the committees made the suggestion, DuPont took no action, but once the committee suggestion was acted upon, DuPont constructed a new shop. In another instance, DuPont had consistently refused the union's request for employee fitness facilities, but when the committee made the suggestions, management acted upon them.

DuPont was required to disband the action committees and to post a notice at the plant that read, in part:

"We will not deal with these committees or their successors. We will not bypass the Chemical Workers Association as your bargaining agent. We will not unilaterally implement these committees' proposals concerning safety awards and fitness facilities without affording the union an opportunity to bargain."

1993: *St. Mary's Honor Center v. Hicks*

St. Mary's Honor Center is a halfway-house run by the Missouri Department of Corrections and Human Resources (MDCHR), which hired Melvin Hicks as a correctional officer in 1978 and, in 1980, promoted him to one of the six shift commander positions at St. Mary's. Mr. Hicks' work performance during this time was deemed to be satisfactory by his supervisors. As the result of an investigation by MDCHR, the supervisory structure of St. Mary's was reorganized in January 1984, at which time Mr. Hicks' immediate supervisor was replaced, as was the superintendent of the facility. Shortly after this change, his new supervisors singled out Mr. Hicks for disciplinary actions that his peers were not subjected to. In fact, they were more lenient with his peers even with regard to more serious violations, in some cases disregarding them entirely. At one point Mr. Hicks was suspended, and he was later demoted from his supervisory position. In June he was terminated for threatening his supervisor during a heated argument.

At this point, Mr. Hicks filed suit, alleging discrimination on the basis of his race in violation of Title VII of the Civil Rights Act of 1964. Mr. Hicks was able to convince the District Court that a prima facie case of discrimination existed. St. Mary's then provided evidence of legitimate, nondiscriminatory reasons for its actions (the rules infractions for which Hicks had been disciplined). Once that occurred, the burden fell once again to Mr. Hicks to show that those reasons were actually a pretext, designed to hide the racial motivation of St. Mary's. The District Court found that, although the court did not believe the reasons given by St. Mary's, Mr. Hicks had not proved that his termination was racially motivated. Based on the evidence offered, there was no way to determine whether the termination had been racially motivated (unlawful) or based on personal dislike for Mr. Hicks (lawful).

The Eighth Circuit Court of Appeals determined that since the Mr. Hicks had proved the reasons were a pretext, he was entitled to a judgment in his favor.

When the case reached the Supreme Court, it relied on two prior cases in making its decision: *McDonnell Douglas Corp. v. Green*, and *Texas Dept. of Community Affairs v. Burdine*. Based on *Green*, Mr. Hicks was required to establish that a prima facie case of discrimination existed. (He did.) Once that happened, according to *Burdine*, St. Mary's needed to provide a lawful explanation for the adverse employment actions taken against Mr. Hicks. (They did.) Once St. Mary's provided a nondiscriminatory reason for the employment actions, it was once again up to Mr. Hicks to prove that those reasons were racially motivated and not based on some other, lawful motivation.

1995: *McKennon v. Nashville Banner Publishing Co.*

Christine McKennon was employed by Nashville Banner Publishing Company (Banner) for 30 years. At age 62, Ms. McKennon's employment was terminated as part of a workforce reduction that was needed to reduce costs. Ms. McKennon believed that the termination was in fact unlawfully based upon her age and filed suit claiming that this violated the Age Discrimination in Employment Act of 1967 (ADEA). During a deposition, she admitted copying confidential documents that she had access to in the course of her employment. Within a few days of the deposition, Banner notified her that removal of the documents was in violation of her job responsibilities and once again terminated her employment. Banner claimed in the letter that, had Banner known of this wrongdoing, her employment would have been terminated immediately based on this fact alone. The District Court then granted summary judgment for Banner, finding that her misconduct was grounds for her termination and that she was not entitled to any remedy in light of her actions.

The Supreme Court agreed to hear the case in order to resolve the question of whether or not all relief must be denied when an employer has violated the ADEA in its discharge of an employee but later discovers employee conduct that would have justified a lawful termination. The Court ruled that after-acquired evidence of employee misconduct that would have resulted in a termination does not relieve the employer for liability in discharging the employee for an unlawful, discriminatory reason.

2001: *Circuit City Stores v. Adams*

In 1995, Saint Clair Adams applied for and was hired as a sales counselor at a Circuit City store in Santa Rosa, CA, after signing an employment application that contained a condition requiring that all employment disputes be settled through binding arbitration based on the Federal Arbitration Act of 1925 (FAA). In 1997, Mr. Adams filed a discrimination claim against Circuit City in state court, and the store responded with a federal suit seeking to stop the state action and force Mr. Adams to arbitration per the agreement he had signed. The District Court agreed with Circuit City, and Mr. Adams appealed the decision to the Ninth Circuit Court of Appeals, which ruled that the FAA does not apply to employment contracts. Because this ruling conflicted with all other circuits of the Federal Court of Appeals, the Supreme Court granted certiorari in 2000.

The Supreme Court reversed the Ninth Circuit, finding that mandatory arbitration agreements in employment contracts are enforceable under the FAA except for transportation workers, which are specifically exempted from the FAA.

Appendix
C

Resources

There are literally thousands of references available for every aspect of human resources, so it's just not possible to include every great resource here. The resources included are those that add dimension or different perspectives to the information presented in this book. While the best preparation for both the PHR and SPHR examinations is diverse generalist experience, these resources will provide a more in-depth "refresher" than is possible in this guide.

A word about the Internet   There is a wealth of information available on the Internet that is current and easily accessible. The best way to access this information is through a search engine such as Google (www.google.com) or Ask Jeeves (www.ask.com). If you haven't used a search engine before, you can get instructions on how to search by clicking the Help button on each search page. When you type in the phrase you want to research, you will get a list of websites to check out.

Information about the test   For information about eligibility requirements and test dates, the best source is the Human Resource Certification Institute (HRCI). There are two sources for information from HRCI. The first is the *PHR/SPHR/GPHR Certification Handbook* (described in the Introduction of this book), which is free of charge and published annually. The handbook provides all the information necessary to apply for the exams and includes pricing, deadlines, and general information. The second source is the HRCI website (www.hrci.org). The website contains a great deal of information about the exams and also allows you to view the handbook online, download a copy, or request that a hard copy be mailed to you. Another helpful information source is the *HRCI Certification Guide*, published by the Society for Human Resource Management. This inexpensive guide explains the testing process, discusses various study methods, and contains sample questions and answers; it can be purchased from several national online booksellers.

Professional associations   Professional associations are often a great source of information about current trends in a particular practice area. Some of these are member-only sites, but even those very often have useful information available to nonmembers.

As mentioned earlier, there are many sources of HR information available. The inclusion of these resources is not an endorsement of the information contained in them. They are provided only as suggestions for further reading should you feel the need for more detail in one of these areas. For ease of use, the list is organized according to functional area.

At the time of publication, the URLs included in the following sections were operational; given the changing nature of the World Wide Web, some of them may have been changed or no longer exist.

Strategic Management

Resources included with Strategic Management cover general human resource books and resources for other business disciplines with which HR professionals interact on a daily basis.

Books

Chase, Richard B., F. Robert Jacobs, and Nicholas J. Aquilano, *Operations Management for Competitive Advantage*, 11th ed., New York City, NY: McGraw-Hill/Irwin, 2005.

Fitz-Enz, Jac. *How to Measure Human Resources Management*, 3rd ed., New York City, NY: McGraw-Hill Trade, 2001.

Gardner, Christopher. *The Valuation of Information Technology: A Guide for Development, Valuation, and Financial Planning*, New York City, NY: John Wiley & Sons, Inc., 2000.

Hiam, Alexander. *Marketing for Dummies*, 2nd ed., Hoboken, NJ: John Wiley & Sons, Inc., 2004.

Kaplan, Robert S., and David P. Norton. *The Balanced Scorecard: Translating Strategy into Action*, Boston, MA: Harvard Business School Press, 1996.

Mathis, Robert L., and John H. Jackson. *Human Resource Management*, 11th ed., Cincinnati, OH: South-Western College Publishing, 2004.

Philips, Jack. Accountability in Human Resource Management, Burlington, MA: Gulf Professional Publishing, 1996.

Tracy, John A. *How to Read a Financial Report*, 6th ed., Hoboken, NJ: John Wiley & Sons, Inc., 2004.

Professional Associations

American Institute of Certified Public Accountants, www.aicpa.org

American Management Association, www.amanet.org

American Marketing Association, www.marketingpower.com

The Human Resource Planning Society, www.hrps.org

The Institute for Management of Information Systems, www.imis.org.uk

The Institute of Operations Management, www.iomnet.org

The International Association for Human Resource Information Management, www.ihrim.org

Society for Human Resource Management, www.shrm.org

Workforce Planning and Employment

These resources are some of the many related to planning for workforce recruiting and employment. In addition, Chapter 4, "Workforce Planning and Employment," included links to government agencies enforcing employment laws should you wish to read more about them.

Books

Ahlrichs, Nancy S. *Competing for Talent: Key Recruitment and Retention Strategies for Becoming an Employer of Choice*, Palo Alto, CA: Davies-Black Books, 2000.

Bechet, Thomas P. *Strategic Staffing*, New York City, NY: AMACOM, 2002.

McCarter, John, and Ray Schreyer. *Recruit and Retain the Best: Key Solutions for HR Professionals*, Manassas Park, VA: Impact Publications, 2000.

Phillips, Jack J., and Adele O. Connell. *Managing Employee Retention: A Strategic Accountability Approach*, Burlington, MA: Butterworth-Heinemann, 2003.

Lawson, Karen. *New Employee Orientation Training*, Alexandria, VA: American Society for Training & Development, 2003.

Steingold, Fred S., and Amy Delpo. *The Employer's Legal Handbook*, 7th ed., Berkeley, CA: Nolo Press, 2005.

Truesdell, William H. *Secrets of Affirmative Action Compliance*, 7th ed., Walnut Creek, CA: The Management Advantage, Inc., 2006.

Professional Associations

American Staffing Association, www.staffingtoday.net (look for the issue papers)

Employee Relocation Council, www.erc.org

International Labour Organization, www.ilo.org

International Public Management Association for Human Resources, www.ipma-hr.org

Human Resource Development

These resources provide additional information about developing talent within organizations.

Books

Anderson, Dean, and Linda Ackerman Anderson. *Beyond Change Management: Advanced Strategies for Today's Transformational Leaders*, San Francisco, CA: Jossey-Bass/Pfeiffer, 2001.

Becker, Brian E., Mark A. Huselid, and Dave Ulrich. *The HR Scorecard: Linking People, Strategy, and Performance*, 1st ed., Boston, MA: Harvard Business School Press, 2001.

Fitz-Enz, Jac. *The ROI of Human Capital: Measuring the Economic Value of Employee Performance*, New York City, NY: AMACOM, 2000.

Grote, Dick. *Discipline without Punishment: The Proven Strategy That Turns Problem Employees into Superior Performers*, 2nd ed., New York City, NY: AMACOM, 2006.

Knowles, Malcolm S., Elwood F. Holton, and Richard A. Swanson. *The Adult Learner: The Definitive Classic in Adult Education and Human Resource Development*, 6th ed., Burlington, MA: Butterworth Heinemann, 2005.

Philips, Jack, and Ron D. Stone. *How to Measure Training Results: A Practical Guide to Tracking the Six Key Indicators*, 1st ed., New York City, NY: McGraw-Hill Trade, 2002.

Senge, Peter M. *The Fifth Discipline*, 1st ed., New York City, NY: Currency/Doubleday, 1994.

Marquardt, Michael J. *Building the Learning Organization*, 2nd ed., Weaverville, NC: Davies-Black Publishing, 2002.

Professional Associations

American Society for Training and Development, www.astd.org

Total Rewards

Additional information about compensation and benefit issues and processes is available in the following resources.

Books

Beam, Burton T. Jr., and John J. McFadden. *Employee Benefits*, 6th ed., Chicago, IL: Dearborn Trade Publishing, 2004.

Berger, Lance A. (Editor), and Dorothy R. Berger (Editor). *The Compensation Handbook*, 4th ed., New York City, NY: McGraw-Hill Trade, 1999.

Plachy, Roger J., and Sandra J. Plachy. *Building a Fair Pay Program: A Step-by-Step Guide*, 2nd ed., New York City, NY: AMACOM, 1998.

Professional Associations

American Payroll Association, www.americanpayroll.org

Employee Benefit Research Institute, www.ebri.org

International Foundation of Employee Benefit Plans, www.ifebp.org

International Society of Certified Employee Benefits Specialists, www.iscebs.org

World at Work (formerly American Compensation Association), www.worldatwork.org

Employee and Labor Relations

These resources provide additional information on labor and employee relations.

Books

Brounstein, Marty. *Coaching and Mentoring for Dummies*, 1st ed., New York City, NY: John Wiley & Sons., 2000.

Costantino, Cathy A., and Christina Sickles Merchant. *Designing Conflict Management Systems: A Guide to Creating Productive and Healthy Organizations*, San Francisco, CA: Jossey-Bass, 1996.

Holley, William H., Kenneth M. Jennings, and Roger S. Wolters. *The Labor Relations Process*, 8th ed., Cincinnati, OH: South-Western College Publishing, 2004.

Grazier, Peter B., *Before It's Too Late: Employee Involvement...An Idea Whose Time Has Come*, Chadds Ford, PA: Teambuilding, Inc., 1989.

Kaye, Beverly, and Sharon Jordan-Evans. *Love 'Em or Lose 'Em: Getting Good People to Stay*, 3rd ed., San Francisco, CA: Berrett-Koehler Publishers, Inc., 2005.

Larkin, T.J., and Sandar Larkin (Contributor). *Communicating Change: Winning Employee Support for New Business Goals*, 2nd ed., New York City, NY: McGraw-Hill Trade, 1994.

Loughran, Charles S. *Negotiating a Labor Contract: A Management Handbook*, 3rd ed., Washington, D.C.: BNA Books, 2003.

Delpo, Amy, Lisa Guerin, and Janet Portman. *Dealing with Problem Employees: A Legal Guide*, 3rd ed., Berkeley, CA: Nolo Press, 2005.

National Labor Relations Board, Office of the General Counsel, *A Guide to Basic Law and Procedures under the National Labor Relations Act*, Washington, D.C.: U.S. Government Printing Office, 1997 (can be downloaded from www.nlrb.gov/nlrb/shared_files/brochures/basicguide.pdf).

Spitzer, Dean R., *Supermotivation: A Blueprint for Energizing Your Organization from Top to Bottom*, New York City, NY: AMACOM, 1995.

Professional Associations

Recruiting and Staffing Focus Area, www.shrm.org/ema

National Public Employer Labor Relations Association, www.npelra.org

Risk Management

These are some of the many resources available for workplace health, safety, and security issues.

Books

Blanco, James A., and Dave Evans. *Business Fraud: Know It and Prevent It,* Huntington, WV: Humanomics Publishing, 2000.

Cassily, Lisa H, and Clare Draper. *Privacy in the Workplace: A Guide for Attorneys and HR Professionals,* Silver Spring, MD: Pike & Fisher, Inc., 2002

Fay, John J. *Contemporary Security Management,* 2nd ed., St. Louis, MO: Butterworth-Heinemann, 2005.

Geller, E. Scott. *The Psychology of Safety Handbook,* 2nd ed., Boca Raton, FL: CRC Press, 2000.

Levy, Barry S., David H. Wegman, Sherry L. Baron, and Rosemary K Sokas. *Occupational Health: Recognizing and Preventing Work-Related Disease and Injury,* 5th ed., Philadelphia, PA: Lippincott Williams & Wilkins, 2005.

Mitroff, Ian I., Christine M. Pearson, and L. Katharine Harrington. *The Essential Guide to Managing Corporate Crises: A Step-by-Step Handbook for Surviving Major Catastrophes,* New York City, NY: Oxford University Press, 1996.

Professional Associations

National Association of Safety Professionals, www.naspweb.com

National Safety Council, www.nsc.org

The American Society of Safety Engineers, www.asse.org

Glossary

Numbers

401(k) plan   A common type of deferred compensation that allows contributions from both employees and employers. Employees may defer a part of their pay before taxes up to limits established by the EGTRRA.

A

ability to pay   An organization's financial resources determine the level of compensation it is able to pay its employees.

accounting   The organizational function concerned with recording financial transactions, paying bills, collecting revenue from customers, and producing financial statements.

acquired needs theory   David McClelland's theory states that people are motivated by experiences acquired throughout their lives. Overall, humans are motivated to excel in achievement, affiliation, or power.

active training methods   Learning methods in which the learning experience is focused on the learner, such as case studies, CBT, and programmed instruction.

actual deferral percentage (ADP) test   An annual test required by ERISA (Employee Retirement Income Security Act) to ensure that highly compensated employees (HCEs) do not receive greater benefits from a 401(k) plan than those received by other employees.

ad hoc arbitrator   A person who is selected to hear a single case between two parties in conflict.

ADDIE model   ADDIE is an acronym that describes the five elements of the instructional design process: analysis, design, development, implementation, and evaluation.

adverse impact   Any negative result of an employment action.

administrative services only (ASO) plan   A benefit plan utilized by some self-funded organizations. These organizations contract with an insurance company to manage and pay claims.

affirmative action plan (AAP)   An AAP analyzes a workforce to determine whether or not protected classes are underutilized in different job groups and describes how an organization will address any underutilization that exists.

agency shop clause   A clause in a labor contract that specifies that all employees must either join the union or pay union dues if they choose not to join the union.

ally doctrine   If an employer whose workers are on strike asks a neutral employer to produce the work that would normally be performed by the striking workers, the ally doctrine states that the neutral employer becomes an ally of the struck employer and is therefore a legitimate target of a picket line.

alter ego doctrine   When two businesses have interrelated operations, central control of labor relations, common management, and common ownership, they are considered alter ego employers, and the NLRB may determine that employees of the alter ego employer are part of the bargaining unit.

alternative dispute resolution (ADR)   ADR covers a range of methods used to solve disagreements without litigation. These alternatives are often able to resolve problems with less animosity than occurs when a lawsuit is filed, and at far less cost to the parties.

andragogy   The study of how adults learn; education in which the learner participates in decisions about what will be taught and how it will be delivered.

auditory learners   One of the three learning styles, auditory learners retain information best when they hear it.

authorization card   The means by which the NLRB determines that there is sufficient support for a union to hold an election. The NLRB will hold an election if 30 percent of the eligible employees in the anticipated bargaining unit sign the authorization cards.

average bias   A bias characterized by a group of candidates (in a selection process) or employees (in a performance management process) who are all rated about the same because the interviewer or reviewer has difficulty deciding which one is best.

B

balance sheet   A financial report that provides a snapshot of an organization's financial condition on a specific day, usually the last day of the accounting period. Information on the balance sheet includes the company's assets, liabilities, and equity.

balanced scorecard   A business measurement tool utilized by managers to track information in four key areas: financial results, customer results, key internal processes, and how people are hired and trained to achieve organization goals.

base pay   A preset salary or hourly rate paid to an employee for performance of job responsibilities.

behavior evaluation method   The third level of a training evaluation model developed by Donald Kirkpatrick; uses a test to measure how well participants learned the information that was presented in the training.

behavioral reinforcement   B.F. Skinner's study of behavioral reinforcement or behavior modification revealed that behavior can be changed through the use of four intervention strategies: positive reinforcement, negative reinforcement, punishment, and extinction.

behaviorally anchored rating scale (BARS)   The BARS system is a performance appraisal system that identifies key job requirements from a job description and creates dimensions and anchor statements that are used to rate employee performance.

benchmark positions   Jobs that are commonly found across organizations regardless of size or industry.

binding arbitration   A way of resolving conflicts without resorting to work stoppages. The parties to a dispute agree to accept the arbitrator's decision as final.

biological health hazard   This type of environmental health hazard spreads infectious diseases to people and is caused by many factors, including unsanitary conditions in a food preparation area or serious diseases contracted through needlestick injuries.

blocking charge bar   One of the bars to union representation elections, based on pending charges of unfair labor practices that prevent unions from petitioning the NLRB for an election.

bona fide occupational qualification (BFOQ)   A job requirement that an employee be a particular religion, sex, or national origin that is reasonably necessary to business operations. For instance, it is assumed that an opening for a Baptist minister at a local Baptist church would be filled by a minister who is actually a person who celebrates the Baptist religion and not, say, the Episcopalian religion.

bonus plan   A compensation strategy that pays employees additional compensation to encourage desired behaviors or reward results achieved. Examples of bonuses include discretionary performance bonuses, referral bonuses, patent awards, and employee-of-the-month rewards.

broadbanding   A job classification method that consolidates multiple pay grades into a few broad "bands" with a wide range between the minimum and maximum of the band.

business continuity planning   Proactive planning to protect an organization from emergencies and other circumstances that results in a written document describing possible disruptions to operations and actions to be taken to minimize those disruptions and assigns responsibility for executing the plan to specific individuals.

C

call-back pay   Compensation paid to employees when they are called to work before or after their scheduled work time.

case study   A training tool that reproduces a realistic situation providing learners with the opportunity to analyze the circumstances just as though it was one encountered in the course of business. Case studies provide learners with the opportunity to investigate, study, and analyze a situation.

cash balance plan   A plan that combines some elements of both defined benefit and defined contribution plans. These plans are regulated as deferred benefit plans but are less costly for employers.

cause and effect diagram   A quality management tool used to organize information developed by Dr. Kaoru Ishikawa for use in brainstorming sessions.

centralized organization   In a centralized organization, decision-making authority is held at senior levels or is concentrated at corporate headquarters.

certification-year bar   One of the bars to union representation elections, the NLRB will not order an election for at least one year after certifying a bargaining representative.

certiorari   A Latin term used when the Supreme Court agrees to review a case so that all lower courts are "certain" how to interpret the law.

change agent   A person who listens to various stakeholders' concerns during the change process and moves them toward acceptance of and commitment to the change.

change management   A broad term used to describe the strategies used by organizations to facilitate the acceptance of change by employees.

change process theory   Kurt Lewin's theory describes three stages for change: unfreeze, move, refreeze.

check sheet   The simplest quality management tool, often used to gather data and count items. A check sheet consists of a list of items; each time an item occurs, a check mark is placed next to it.

chemical health hazard   A type of environmental health hazard that can cause illness or injury. Manufacturers provide material safety data sheets that describe the hazards associated with chemicals used in the workplace, how they should be handled, and how employees may protect themselves from injury or illness.

classification method   A job evaluation system that identifies benchmark positions and places them in salary grades, then matches positions with similar KSAs and slots them into the same grade.

cliff vesting   A form of delayed benefit vesting in which participants become 100 percent invested after a specified period of time. ERISA (Employee Retirement Income Security Act) sets the maximum vesting period at five years for qualified plans.

closed shop clause   A clause in a collective bargaining agreement requiring all new hires to be members of the union before they are hired. The closed shop is illegal except in the construction industry.

closing conference   A conference held at the end of an OSHA inspection during which the inspector, employer, and employee representatives discuss the observations made and corrective actions that must be taken.

collective bargaining agreement   A contract between a union and an employer that governs the employment relationship for a specified period of time.

commissions   Employee compensation that allots a percentage-of-sales price for products and services sold to a customer. Commissions may serve as the entire cash compensation package or work in combination with a base salary.

common law doctrine   A doctrine developed over centuries as a result of legal decisions made by judges in individual cases.

common situs picketing   Common situs picketing occurs when an employer shares a building with other employers. Because picketing a common business location can interfere with the ability of secondary businesses to operate, unions must ensure that picket signs clearly state the name of the business they are striking, and where possible, restrict picketing to an entrance that is used only by the primary employer.

communication strategy   A communication strategy establishes a plan for disseminating business information to the organization and describes the means for doing so.

comp time   See *compensatory time off*.

comparable worth   A concept that suggests that jobs requiring similar levels of knowledge, skill, and ability should be paid similarly.

compa-ratio   A calculation tool that compares an employee's base pay to the midpoint of the base salary range; it is commonly used when making pay decisions.

compensable factors   Characteristics that define and distinguish different jobs from one another. These factors are used to evaluate jobs.

compensable time   Any time that employers "suffer or permit" employees to work.

compensatory time off   Paid time off from work in lieu of overtime pay when extra hours are worked. Only available for public employees.

competency-based compensation   A compensation program focused on employee KSAs rather than on job duties.

compulsory arbitration   Arbitration mandated by legal statute to resolve disputes in the public sector where labor strikes are prohibited.

computer-based training (CBT)   An interactive training method combining elements of the lecture, demonstration, one-on-one, and simulation methods, allowing the learner to have a real-world learning experience.

concurrent validity   Concurrent validity is a type of criterion validity that correlates a test measurement to behavior. In concurrent validity, a test is given and the behavior is measured at the same time.

conference   A passive training method that combines lecture or presentation with question-and-answer sessions involving the participants.

conflict resolution   The conflict resolution process develops strategies for resolving issues and maintaining or rebuilding effective working relationships.

consent election   A union election that is held after an NLRB conference if the employer and the union agree to jurisdictional issues, the makeup of the bargaining unit, eligibility of voters in the proposed unit, and the time and place of the election.

continuous feedback program   A form of performance management, continuous feedback programs provide ongoing communication to employees about performance during the review period.

constructive confrontation   A form of mediation developed to resolve long-standing, deep-rooted conflicts about difficult, significant issues in organizations.

constructive discharge   Occurs when an employer forces an employee to resign by creating a work environment that is so unpleasant a reasonable person would resign.

consumer picketing   An action performed to advise consumers that goods have been produced by a business whose workers are on strike.

construct validity   Measures the connection between candidate characteristics and job performance. It is not widely used due to its complexity.

continuity of operations plan   A plan created to move from disaster recovery (during which critical business functions are maintained but normal operations may not be taking place) back to pre-emergency service operating levels.

continuous FMLA leave   A continuous FMLA (Family and Medical Leave Act) leave occurs when an employee is absent from work for a single block of extended time.

contract   A legally enforceable agreement between two or more parties in which all parties benefit in some way.

contract bar   One of the bars to union representation elections, the contract bar prevents an election when a valid collective bargaining agreement is already in place.

contract workers   Workers employed by brokers or agencies who negotiate contracts for the workers and act as the employer of record, providing payroll, marketing, and other services for them.

contributory negligence   A legal doctrine used to mitigate an employer's responsibility if a worker's actions contributed in any way to an injury.

contrast bias   A form of bias that occurs when the interviewer or reviewer compares candidates to each other or compares all candidates to one candidate who may be either very weak or very strong.

coordinated bargaining   Also known as multiunit bargaining, coordinated bargaining occurs when an employer negotiates with several unions representing different bargaining units in a company.

corporate restructuring   A radical change to an organization's internal and external relationships.

correlation   A quantitative measurement tool that compares two variables to determine if there is a relationship between them. For example, if the HR department posts a quarterly reminder for employees about the referral bonus that is paid for new hires, a correlation analysis could be used to determine if there is an increase in referrals in the weeks after the reminder.

correlation coefficient   Describes the relationship between two variables and is stated as a number between −1.0 and +1.0.

cost-benefit analysis   An analysis tool that compares the costs of various possible decisions to each other, forecasts the net impact of each on the bottom line, and recommends the best alternative.

cost of labor   The cost to employers of hiring and retaining employees.

covered entities   Health plans, health care providers, and clearinghouses identified by HIPAA (Health Insurance Portability and Accountability Act) privacy rules as bearing responsibility for maintaining the confidentiality of patient information. Employers who process or have access to employee health benefit information may also be considered covered entities for purposes of HIPAA privacy requirements.

cultural noise   A form of bias that occurs when candidates answer questions based on what they think the interviewer wants to hear instead of what they believe or know about themselves.

cumulative trauma injuries (CTI)   See *musculoskeletal disorder*.

cycles   Trends characterized by a pattern of repeated performance for a period of more than one year.

D

de minimis   An OSHA violation which does not pose a direct or immediate threat to safety or health; the lowest violation level identified by OSHA.

deauthorization   The process employees use to remove a union security clause from the collective bargaining agreement.

decentralized organization   In a decentralized organization, decision-making authority is held by the managers who are closest to operating activities.

decertification   The process used by employees to remove a union as their bargaining representative if they are dissatisfied with the union's performance. A decertification petition requires signatures of at least 30 percent of the employees before the NLRB will act upon it.

defamation   A communication that damages an individual's reputation in the community, preventing them from obtaining employment or other benefits.

defined benefit   A deferred compensation plan in which the employer provides a specific benefit upon retirement. The funds are not accounted for individually.

defined contribution   An individual deferred compensation plan in which the amount of funds contributed are known, but the amount of the benefit that is eventually paid out is not known because it depends on the investment returns that are earned. The funds are accounted for in individual accounts for each participant.

Delphi technique   A qualitative analysis method in which input is obtained from a group of individuals, summarized, and resubmitted to the group for additional input until consensus is reached. The Delphi technique is unique because the group members do not meet in person but conduct the analysis in writing.

delayed vesting   A vesting plan in which participants must wait for a defined period of time prior to becoming fully vested. There are two types of delayed vesting: cliff vesting and graded vesting.

demonstration   An experiential training method in which a trainer first explains the process or operation, demonstrates it, and then observes while the learner performs it.

dependent care account   A flexible spending account authorized by Section 129 of the Internal Revenue Code in which employees may set aside a maximum of $5,000 to be used to care for dependent children or elders. To obtain reimbursement for dependent care expenses, employees must provide an itemized statement of charges from the caregiver.

design patents   A patent that protects new, original, and ornamental designs of manufactured items. Design patents are limited to 14 years.

direct compensation   Payments made to employees such as base pay, variable compensation, and pay for performance.

directed election   A union representation election that occurs after an NLRB pre-election hearing has resolved issues about jurisdiction, the bargaining unit, voter eligibility, and the time and place of the election.

disaster recovery plan (DRP)   Describes activities that take place once response to an initial emergency is over.

discretionary contributions   Also known as profit-sharing programs, discretionary contributions allow employers to contribute deferred compensation based on a percentage of company earnings each year.

disparate impact   Occurs when an employment practice that appears to be fair unintentionally discriminates against members of a protected class.

disposable earnings   The amount of employee pay left after federally mandated deductions are made, including federal and state income tax, social security, state and local taxes, disability insurance, and so on.

distance learning   A training delivery mechanism allowing simultaneous training to occur in geographically dispersed multiple locations. Distance learning provides participants with the ability to communicate with presenters and participants in other locations utilizing web technology or video conferencing.

distributive bargaining   See *positional bargaining*.

diversity   A term used to describe a multicultural, multiracial, and multiethnic workforce.

diversity initiative   A program that seeks to increase the racial, ethnic, religious, educational, personality, and economic diversity of an organization's workforce or to increase the effectiveness of an already diverse workforce.

diversity training   Training designed to educate all groups in a workforce about the cultures, needs, and attitudes of other groups in the workforce to ensure the inclusion of all groups in workplace activities.

downsizing   Actions that reduce the size of an organization's workforces as a result of a change in strategic direction or in reaction to different economic conditions.

due process   In the employment context, employment actions that are taken in accordance with established procedures. This includes notifying employees of pending actions and providing them with the opportunity to respond to any allegations prior to making a final employment decision.

duty of diligence   A common law doctrine requiring an employee to act "with reasonable care and skill" in the course of performing work for the employer.

duty of loyalty   A common law doctrine requiring employees to act in the best interest of the employer and not solicit work away from the employer to benefit themselves.

duty of obedience   A common law doctrine requiring employees to act within the authority granted by the employer and to follow the employer's reasonable and legal policies, procedures, and rules.

E

education labor market   The labor market that includes individuals with similar levels of education.

emergency action plans   A plan that informs employees of appropriate procedures to follow during a fire or evacuation.

emergency response plan (ERP)   A plan that describes how an organization will react to different emergency situations or natural disasters if they occur.

emotional intelligence (EI or EQ)   A measurement of how people deal with their feelings and how they perceive and interact with others.

employee assistance program (EAP)   A program that offers employees a variety of benefits that provide a resource for problems that cannot be solved within the work context. Some typical services available through an EAP include legal assistance, financial counseling, and alcohol and drug abuse counseling.

employee and labor relations   The functional area of the HR body of knowledge that addresses employment relationships in both union and nonunion environments.

employee stock ownership plan (ESOP)   A defined compensation plan in which employees are able to purchase stock in the organization at a reduced price.

employment practices liability insurance (EPLI)   Insurance coverage designed to protect employers against lawsuits brought by current or former employees.

engaged to wait   Time spent by nonexempt employees when the employer has asked them to wait for an assignment. The FLSA defines this time as compensable even if the employee is not working.

enrolled actuary   An actuary in charge of analyzing insurance and annuity premiums who has been licensed jointly by the Department of the Treasury and the Department of Labor to provide these services for U.S. pension plans.

enterprise coverage   The Fair Labor Standards Act (FLSA) coverage category requiring businesses employing at least two employees with at least $500,000 in annual sales or employers who are hospitals, schools, or government agencies to comply with its requirements.

entitlement philosophy   An approach to compensation based on rewarding employee longevity. This philosophy can foster a culture in which employees expect certain benefits and treatment.

environmental health hazards   These hazards come in many forms, including physical hazards such as noise and extreme temperatures, exposure to chemicals used for everything from making copies to manufacturing products, and biological hazards from viruses and bacteria.

environmental scan   A process used to collect information about an organization, industry, marketplace, and technology for use in the strategic planning process. There are two elements to the scanning process: internal assessment and external assessment.

Equal Employment Opportunity Commission (EEOC)   The federal agency responsible for enforcement of Title VII of the Civil Rights Act of 1964.

equity theory   J. Stacy Adams' equity theory states that people are constantly measuring what they put into work against what they get from work.

ergonomics   A science that addresses the way a physical environment is designed and how efficient and safe that design is for the people in the environment.

ERG theory   Clayton Alderfer's ERG theory of motivation identifies three levels of needs: existence, relatedness, and growth.

essay review   A form of performance appraisal in which the appraiser writes a short description of an employee's performance during the year.

essential job functions   Those functions of a job that are the reasons for its existence.

establishment report   The EEO-1 report required for locations with 50 or more employees.

ethnocentric   A global staffing strategy in which all key management positions are filled by expatriates.

excelsior list   A list containing the names and addresses of all employees in a bargaining unit designated by the NLRB that must be provided by the employer to the union within seven days of the consent to or direction of an election.

exception reporting   A method of reporting time worked in which only deviations from the regular work schedule are recorded, such as paid time off.

executive orders   Presidential proclamations which, when published in the Federal Register, become law after 30 days.

exempt   An exempt position is one that does not require compliance with requirements of the Fair Labor Standards Act (FLSA). Exempt positions must be paid on a salary, not an hourly basis, and must meet the requirements established by DOL exemption tests for administrative, professional, outside sales, executive, or other jobs exempted by DOL regulations.

exit interview   An interview conducted with employees when they leave the organization to determine why they are leaving, what improvements could be made to the organization, and if there are any specific issues that need to be addressed.

expatriates   Employees who originate from the corporate home country and work in another country.

expectancy theory   Victor Vroom's expectancy theory of motivation maintains that people are motivated by the expectation of the reward they will receive when they succeed, and that each individual calculates the level of effort required to receive a particular reward to determine if the reward is worth the effort that is required to attain it.

experience rating   Insurance providers sometimes calculate future premiums based on costs incurred by a group during the current coverage period.

experiential training methods   Training that uses real-time situations such as demonstrations, one-on-one training, or performance-based training to provide learners with experience.

express contract   A verbal or written agreement in which the parties state exactly what they agree to do.

extrinsic reward   A form of nonmonetary compensation in which esteem is achieved from others, such as fulfillment from working with a talented team of peers.

F

fellow servant rule   A rule that absolves employers of responsibility for worker injuries if a coworker's actions caused the injury.

fiduciary   A person, corporation, or other legal entity that holds property or assets on behalf of, or in trust for a pension fund.

fiduciary responsibility   A legal obligation placed upon executives to make decisions that benefit the organization or a pension trust fund instead of making decisions that benefit them personally.

field review appraisal   A narrative method of performance appraisal conducted by someone other than the supervisor.

finance   The organizational function responsible for obtaining credit to meet the organization's needs, granting credit to customers, investing and managing cash for maximum return on investment, and establishing banking relationships for the organization.

Financial Accounting Standards Board (FASB)   A board that establishes standards of financial accounting and reporting intended to regulate and guide financial accounting practices. Such standards are essential to the efficient functioning of the economy because investors, creditors, auditors, and others rely on credible, transparent, and comparable financial information.

first impression bias   An interview bias in which the candidate is judged based on what happens during the first few minutes of an interview.

fiscal year   An annual financial reporting period that may be different from a calendar year, such as July 1 of one calendar year to June 30 of the next calendar year.

flexible spending accounts (FSAs)   Plans authorized by the Sections 125 and 129 of the Revenue Act of 1978 that allow employees to set aside pretax funds for medical or dependent expenses they expect to incur during the calendar year.

focal review   A performance review cycle that evaluates all employees during the same period of time during the review period.

forced ranking   A comparison method of performance appraisal that requires managers to rank employees according to the bell curve, with the majority of employees receiving average ratings and fewer receiving either high or low ratings.

G

gainsharing   An organizational or group incentive plan in which employees and managers come together for the common purpose of improving the organization's productivity and sharing the benefits of success.

gap analysis   The third step of a needs assessment in which the current situation is compared to the objective, resulting in a list of people, actions, or items needed to achieve the objective. The goal of the gap analysis is to close the gap between "where we are now" and "where we want to be."

gatekeeper   One who controls the input or output of a situation or activity. For example, in a health and welfare benefits setting, a patient's primary care physician is a gatekeeper in charge of determining whether or not patients need to be seen by a specialist.

general duty standard   OSHA's general duty standard requires employers to provide jobs and a workplace environment that are free from recognized safety and health hazards that could potentially cause death or serious physical harm. This standard also requires employers to comply with all OSHA rules, regulations, and standards.

geocentric   A global staffing strategy that places the best-qualified person into a position regardless of the country of origin.

geographic labor market   The labor market that includes individuals with a wide variety of skills in a specific area, such as local, national, regional, or international.

geographic pay   A form of compensation designed to ensure that employee pay is competitive within local labor markets.

glass ceiling   A term first used by the *Wall Street Journal* to describe the limitations faced by women and minorities when it comes to advancing into the senior ranks of corporate management.

goal   A statement that describes a desired achievement that keeps employees focused on what is important to the organization.

graded vesting   Also referred to as graduated or gradual vesting, graded vesting is a delayed vesting schedule that provides for partial vesting each year for a specified number of years. A graded vesting schedule in a qualified plan must allow for at least 20 percent vesting after three years and 20 percent per year after that, with participants achieving full vesting after seven years of service.

graduated (or gradual) vesting   See *graded vesting*.

grant price   See *strike price*.

grantor trust   See *Rabbi trust*.

graveyard shift   The night to morning shift, such as midnight to 8 AM. The graveyard shift is generally thought of as an undesirable time to work.

green circle   Refers to salaries that are below the minimum of the salary range.

gross pay   Amount earned by an employee before taxes are withheld.

group incentives   Also known as organizational incentives, group incentives are benefits or bonuses shared by all employees within the organization or within a department, commonly put in place to increase productivity and foster teamwork while sharing the financial rewards with employees. Types of group incentives include gainsharing, Improshare, the Scanlon Plan, profit sharing, and employee stock ownership plans (ESOPs).

gut feeling bias   This bias occurs when the interviewer relies on intuition to determine whether or not a candidate will be a good or bad fit for the position.

H

halo effect bias   This bias occurs when an interviewer bases a positive assessment on a single characteristic and allows it to overshadow other, negative characteristics.

hard bargaining   See *positional bargaining*.

harshness bias   This bias occurs when an interviewer rates a candidate negatively based on a single characteristic, allowing it to overshadow other, positive characteristics. See also *horn effect*.

HAY system   Developed by Edward Hay of The Hay Group, the HAY system is a classification system for job evaluation that utilizes a complex point factor method. Jobs are evaluated using three factors: knowledge, problem solving, and accountability. Using the points from the evaluation, the job(s) are matched to a profile.

hazard pay   Additional pay provided for dangerous and/or extremely uncomfortable working conditions.

headquarters report   The EEO-1 report required for the principal office of an organization.

health and wellness programs   Voluntary programs that seek to prevent employee illnesses and lower health care costs.

health purchasing alliances (HPA)   An allegiance that small employers make with other employers in a geographic area to take advantage of economies of scale. The HPA will negotiate and contract for benefit plans on behalf of all members of the group.

hierarchy of needs   Abraham Maslow developed his hierarchy of needs to explain how people meet their personal needs through work. His theory describes needs that begin with the most basic requirements for life (food, shelter, and basic physical comforts) and progress through stages of growth as people strive to fill higher-level needs.

high-context culture   In a high-context culture, people rely on nonverbal clues and relationship to discern meaning.

high involvement organizations (HIO)   An HIO involves employees in designing their own work processes, taking the actions necessary to complete their work, and being accountable for the results. Jobs in these organizations are broadly defined within self-directed work teams. These organizations are characterized by flat hierarchies in which continuous feedback is provided and information flows between and among work teams.

highly compensated employees (HCEs)   The Economic Growth and Tax Relief Reconciliation Act of 2001 defines a highly compensated employee as a 401(k) plan participant who, during the current or prior year, earned $90,000 or more, owns 5 percent or more of the company, and, at the company's discretion, is one of the top-paid 20 percent of employees.

histograms   A quality management tool, often used in conjunction with a check sheet, that provides a graphical representation of the effects of changes on a process and can be used to set standards.

horn effect   Also called the harshness bias, the horn effect occurs when an interviewer rates a candidate negatively based on a single characteristic, allowing it to overshadow other, positive characteristics.

host-country nationals (HCNs)   Citizens of the country in which they work for a business that is domiciled in another country.

hostile work environment   As defined by the EEOC, an environment in which an individual or individuals are subjected to unwelcome verbal or physical conduct "when submission to or rejection of this conduct explicitly or implicitly affects an individual's employment, unreasonably interferes with an individual's work performance, or creates an intimidating, hostile, or offensive work environment."

hot cargo agreement   A ULP in which a union asks an employer to stop doing business with another employer, usually to put pressure on the second employer to recognize the union.

Human Resource Certification Institute (HRCI)   The credentialing body for the human resource profession.

human resource development   The functional area of the HR body of knowledge concerned with training, development, talent management, performance management, and performance appraisal programs to ensure that individuals with the required knowledge, skills, and abilities are available when needed to accomplish organization goals.

human resource information system (HRIS)   An electronic database that serves as a repository of information and as an aid to effective decision making, thus reducing the amount of paper that the human resource department uses and consolidating the various data needed to keep HR information stored and easily accessed.

I

immediate vesting   Vesting that occurs 100 percent, or fully, as soon as employees meet the eligibility requirements of the vesting plan.

implied contract   A contract that can be created by an employer's conduct and need not be specifically stated or written.

Improshare   Developed in the 1970s by Mitchell Fein, Improshare plans are group incentive plans that establish a baseline of productivity and reward employees with 50 percent of any gains made over the base.

imputed income   Any indirect compensation paid on behalf of employees.

in loco parentis   This Latin term means "in place of the parent" and applies to those who care for a child on a daily basis. In loco parentis does not necessarily refer to a biological or legal relationship.

incentive pay   Also known as variable compensation, incentive pay rewards employees for individual and organizational results. Individual and group incentives have become a common component of the total rewards package.

incentive stock options (ISO)   Stock options that can be offered only to employees; consultants and outside members of the board of directors are not eligible.

income statement   A financial report that describes operating results for a period of time. Also known as the profit and loss (P&L) statement, the report provides information on revenue from various sources, costs to produce the goods or services, overhead expenses, and net income for the period.

independent contractors   Self-employed individuals who work for multiple customers and clients on a project or fee basis.

indirect compensation   Payments made to employees that are not associated with wages and salaries, such as fringe benefits and government-mandated benefit programs.

individual coverage   The Fair Labor Standards Act (FLSA) coverage category requiring companies whose employees' daily work involves interstate commerce to comply with its requirements.

individual level training   Training that seeks to address the performance needs of individual employees. It can be indicated by poor performance reviews or requests for assistance by the employee.

information technology (IT)   The organizational function that is responsible for managing systems such as voice mail, computer networks, software, websites, and the Internet, and the data collected by these systems.

informational picketing   Also known as publicity picketing, informational picketing is done to truthfully advise the public that an employer is a union-free workplace.

injunction   A court order that either requires or forbids an action by one party against another. The Sherman Anti-Trust Act of 1890 allows injunctions to be issued against any person or group that conspires to restrain trade.

inpatriates   Employees brought to the home office for training to become accustomed to the corporate culture and practices before returning to their countries of origin to work as host-country nationals.

inside director   A member of an organization's board of directors with management responsibilities, such as a CEO or CFO.

integrative bargaining   A form of principled bargaining in which the parties look at all the issues on the table and make mutually agreeable trade-offs among those issues.

intellectual property agreement (IPA)   An agreement that identifies what a company considers to be confidential information (such as customer lists, financial information, or trade secrets) and how its use is limited by the agreement. In addition, the agreement may contain a nonsolicitation clause limiting the ability of former employees to hire coworkers if they leave the organization, as well as how long the agreement must remain confidential after it expires.

interest-based bargaining (IBB)   A form of principled bargaining based on the concept that both sides in the negotiation have harmonious interests.

intermittent FMLA leave   Intermittent FMLA (Family and Medical Leave Act) leave occurs when an employee is absent from work for multiple periods of time due to a single illness or injury.

internal controls   Policies and procedures designed to protect financial assets from being mishandled.

internal equity   The equitable ranking of one job relative to others within an organization.

Inter-rater reliability   The use of multiple raters to reduce the possibility of rating errors due to bias.

internship programs   Programs that give students the opportunity to gain work experience in their chosen profession prior to graduation. They are often unpaid, but the student may be given academic credit for the work done.

intrinsic reward   A noncompensatory reward that encourages individual employee self esteem, such as satisfaction from challenging work.

J

job analysis   The process used to identify the tasks, processes, or functions that make up the responsibilities of a job.

job bidding   A process that allows employees to express interest in positions before they become available.

job competencies   Broad statements of the factors needed to be successful in an organization.

job description   A document describing the tasks, processes, or functions that are part of an employee's responsibilities.

job enrichment   According to Fredrick Herzberg's research, job enrichment is the result of increasing the significance of the tasks in a job to provide challenging work and growth opportunities.

job group analysis   The component of an AAP that places job titles with similar duties and responsibilities into groups for analysis.

job posting   An internal job announcement providing basic information about an open position to current employees who may be interested in and qualified for it.

job pricing   A process used to determine the appropriate pay for a new position or one that has changed significantly. The process involves reviewing the job description, matching the job to a salary survey, reviewing the various compensation components in the survey, and recommending an appropriate salary or wage.

job sharing   An alternative staffing method that allows two part-time employees to share the duties and responsibilities of a full-time position.

job specifications   Descriptions of the KSAs necessary for successful performance of the essential functions of a position.

just-in-time (JIT) inventory   An inventory system designed to reduce inventory costs by the frequent purchase of small amounts of supplies.

K

kinesthetic learners   Learners who retain information best when they are able to have a hands-on experience during training.

knowledge-of-predictor bias   A form of bias occurring when an interviewer is aware that the candidate has scored particularly high or low on an assessment and allows this knowledge to influence the selection process.

KSAs   The knowledge, skills, and abilities required for successful job performance.

L

labor market   The sources from which an organization recruits new employees; a single organization may find itself recruiting from several different labor markets depending on the availability of skills for different positions.

layoff   Occurs when an organization eliminates jobs and terminates employees for economic reasons, a change in strategic direction, or other business reasons; also known as a reduction-in-force.

leadership development   Leadership development programs identify employees who show promise as potential leaders; provide training, mentoring, and coaching for them, and ensure that they have experience in a broad range of areas within the organization.

leapfrogging   See *parallel bargaining*.

learning curve   A graphical representation of the rate of learning over time.

learning evaluation method   The second level of Donald Kirkpatrick's training evaluation model, the learning evaluation method uses a test to measure whether or not the participants learned the information that was presented.

learning organizations   Innovative environments in which knowledge is originated, obtained, and freely shared in response to environmental changes that affect the ability of the organization to compete.

lecture   A passive training method in which speakers address an audience to inform and answer questions. Lectures are often used in combination with other training methods, such as demonstrations.

leniency bias   A bias that occurs when an interviewer or reviewer tends to go easy on a candidate and give a higher rating than is warranted.

liability   A duty or responsibility owed by one party to another, usually of a financial nature. A liability can result from an agreement or a contract or can be created through a tort.

line functions   The functions in an organization that are concerned with making decisions about operating needs, such as production and sales.

line of sight   Employees who know that their performance, good or bad, impacts their base or variable pay have line of sight.

lobbying   Activities designed to influence new laws and regulations.

lockout   Occurs when management shuts down operations to keep employees from working.

long-range plans   Business strategies, goals, or objectives projected to be achieved in three to five years.

low-context culture   A culture in which people rely on what is said to discern what is meant.

M

maintenance of membership   A clause in a union contract that allows employees to choose whether or not to join the union, but once they join, requires that they remain members until the expiration of the contract. The employee must notify the union to discontinue membership within 30 days of the contract expiration.

management by objectives (MBO)   A process that is built on the concepts of mutual involvement in setting performance goals, ongoing communications during the performance period (usually a year), and measurement and reward for accomplishments at the end of the period. MBO aligns individuals with organization goals and measures the successful attainment of objectives as well as the quality and/or quantity of performance.

management development   A program that seeks to upgrade a manager's skills so that they can better motivate employees, delegate work, manage time and productivity, set goals, plan, and communicate effectively.

marketing   An organizational function that promotes and distributes products in the marketplace, provides support for the sales staff, conducts research to design products that customers will be interested in purchasing, and determines the appropriate pricing for the product.

mass layoff As defined by the WARN Act, a mass layoff occurs when either 500 employees or 33 percent and at least 50 employees are laid off within a 90-day period.

material safety data sheets (MSDS) Documents provided by chemical manufacturers that identify the ingredients in a chemical substance, how the substance reacts to changes in the atmosphere, and its explosive and flammable qualities. An MSDS tells employees whether the material is stable or unstable, what materials it must not be in contact with, and what additional hazards are present when the substance decomposes or degrades.

mean average A quantitative measurement calculation derived from the sum of the values in a set of numbers, divided by the number of values in the set.

median A quantitative measurement derived by putting the numbers in a set in sequential order. The median is at the physical center, so half the numbers are below it and half are above it.

mental models One of Peter Senge's five disciplines of learning organizations used to describe deep-seated beliefs that color perceptions and affect how individuals see the world around them and react to it.

mentoring programs Mentoring programs assigns an experienced individual to act as a teacher, guide, counselor, sponsor, or facilitator and provide personalized feedback and guidance for a more junior colleague.

merit increase Increases to base pay earned by employee performance.

mid-point progression The difference between the midpoints of consecutive grades, generally narrower for lower grades and increasing for higher grades.

mid-range plans Business strategies, goals, or objectives projected to be achieved in one to three years.

Mine Safety and Health Administration (MSHA) Established by the Mine Safety and Health Act of 1977 to monitor the safety of mining operations.

mode In quantitative analysis, the number that occurs most frequently in a set of numbers.

money purchase plan A defined contribution plan that uses a fixed percentage of employee earnings to defer compensation; works well for organizations with relatively stable earnings from year to year because the percentage is fixed and, once established, contributions must be made every year. The contribution limits are the same as for profit sharing plans.

motivation/hygiene theory In the 1950s, Fredrick Herzberg theorized that two factors can be used to motivate people: challenging work (motivation) or the desire to avoid unpleasant experiences (hygiene); also known as the two-factor theory.

moving average Also called a rolling average, the moving average calculates an average for a specific period, for example, the average number of new hires each month for the past twelve months. As the number for the most recent month is added, the oldest number is dropped.

multi-employer bargaining Bargaining in which the union negotiates with more than one employer in an industry or region at a time.

multi-unit bargaining   Also known as coordinated bargaining, multi-unit bargaining occurs when several unions represent different bargaining units in the company and the employer negotiates with the unions for more than one bargaining unit at the same time.

multiple linear regression   A quantitative analysis tool used to measure the relationship between several variables to forecast another.

musculoskeletal disorder (MSD)   The result of repeated stress to various parts of the body, including the back, arms, shoulders, and other areas, that is caused by the way tasks are performed. MSD injuries that can result from poor ergonomics in the workplace include tendonitis, bursitis, and carpal tunnel syndrome. Also referred to as cumulative trauma injury (CTI) and repetitive stress injury (RSI).

N

National Institute of Occupational Safety and Health (NIOSH)   The OSH Act created NIOSH as part of the Department of Health and Human Services. NIOSH is charged with researching and evaluating workplace hazards and recommending ways to reduce the effects of those hazards on workers. NIOSH also supports education and training in the field of occupational safety and health by developing and providing educational materials and training aids.

National Labor Relations Board (NLRB)   Established by the National Labor Relations Act to enforce its provisions. This board is charged with conducting elections and preventing and remedying unfair labor practices. The NLRB does not instigate actions on its own, it only responds to charges of unfair labor practices or petitions for representation elections filed in one of its offices.

needs analysis   Also called needs assessment, needs analysis is used to evaluate program proposals to select those that will make the best use of organization resources. Needs analysis can be used in any area of business; in HR it is often employed in the areas of training and development, staffing projections, and benefit planning.

negative emphasis bias   This bias occurs when an interviewer or reviewer allows a small amount of negative information to outweigh positive information about the candidate or employee.

negatively accelerating learning curve   A learning curve in which learning increments are large in the beginning but become smaller as practice continues. This is the most frequent type of learning curve.

negligent hiring   Occurs when an employer knew or should have known that an applicant had a prior history of behavior that endangered customers, employees, vendors, or members of the public.

nominal group technique   A structured meeting format designed to elicit participation from all members of a group in order to arrive at the best possible solution to a problem. Participants begin by individually writing down their ideas about the issue. A facilitator then has each participant present one idea and records them for later discussion. When all of the ideas have been presented, the group prioritizes and builds consensus until a resolution is agreed upon.

nonbinding arbitration   Arbitration in which either party may reject the arbitrator's decision and continue the dispute by filing a lawsuit.

non-disclosure agreement (NDA)   A written agreement in which one party agrees to share proprietary information with another party and the other party agrees not to disseminate the information to anyone else.

nonessential job functions   A job function that is not necessary to a particular job but may be transferred to another job without adversely impacting the organization.

nonexempt   Employees who are covered by requirements of the Fair Labor Standards Act such as minimum wage and overtime pay for any hours worked in excess of 40 per week.

nonforfeitable   In deferred compensation, a nonforfeitable claim is one that exists due to a participant's service. Nonforfeitable claims are unconditional and legally enforceable.

nonqualified retirement plan   In deferred compensation, a plan in which the benefits exceed the limitations of qualified plans or do not meet other IRS requirements for favorable tax treatment.

nonqualified (NQ) stock options   Stock options offered to employees at the market or a reduced price. Employers can benefit from the possibility of an increase in stock value without risking a large amount of cash. Nonqualified stock options are the most common type of stock options and can be used for consultants and external members of the board of directors as well as employees.

nonverbal bias   Occurs when an interviewer is influenced by body language. For example, a candidate who frowns when answering questions could be rated negatively even though the answers were correct.

O

objective   A specific description of practical steps taken to achieve business goals.

Occupational Safety and Health Administration (OSHA)   Established by the Occupational Safety and Health Act of 1970, this group is charged with the responsibility of creating and enforcing safety standards.

occupational safety and health standards   The OSH Act required OSHA to develop standards to prevent illness and injury to workers. Some of the standards that have been developed include the general duty standard, noise exposure, and personal protective equipment.

Office of Federal Contract Compliance Programs (OFCCP)   The agency of the federal Department of Labor charged with enforcing equal employment opportunity laws for federal contractors and subcontractors.

Old Age, Survivors, and Disability Insurance (OASDI)   Part of the Social Security Act of 1935 (SSA), this insurance is to be paid to qualified workers upon retirement or disability or to their surviving dependents in the event of a worker's death.

ombudsman   Also called an ombuds, an ombudsman is an impartial person not involved in a dispute who can speak with the parties and suggest alternative solutions.

on-boarding programs   Programs designed to assist new hires in assimilating into the organization and accelerate attainment of full productivity; also known as orientation.

on-call pay   Extra pay provided to employees who are required to be available via pager, telephone, email, and so on to respond to work-related issues.

on-call workers   Employees available to work on short notice and called to work only when they are needed.

one-on-one training   Training in which an inexperienced worker is paired with an experienced supervisor or coworker who utilizes a variety of techniques to provide the worker with the information and hands-on experience necessary to do the job.

opening conference   The first step in an OSHA inspection, in which the inspector explains why the site was selected, the purpose of the visit, and the scope of the inspection and discusses the standards that apply to the worksite.

operations   The organizational function that encompass all of the activities necessary to produce the goods or services of the business, such as product design, capacity, production layout, schedules, quality, inventory, technology, and cost control.

organization climate   The climate created by the culture, behaviors, leadership, and management styles and the level of bureaucracy within an organization.

organization culture   The atmosphere, values, and beliefs that are shared at all levels and reflected in the behavior of individuals throughout the organization.

organization development (OD)   A systematic method used to examine an organization's technology, processes, structure, and human resources.

organization development (OD) interventions   An action strategy used to improve the way an organization achieves its goals.

organization incentives   See *group incentives*.

organizational level training   Training that focuses on preparing for future needs. It may encompass the entire organization or a single division or department.

organizational picketing   Picketing that occurs when the union wants to attract employees to become members and authorize the union to represent them to the employer.

organizational profile   The component of an AAP that describes organization structure; may be in the form of a traditional organization chart or a workforce analysis.

organizational structures   Used to coordinate activities between business functions and facilitate the flow of communication. The most common structures are functional, product-based, geographic, divisional, and matrix.

orientation   See *on-boarding programs*.

OSHA Alliance Program   A program that provides an avenue for small business owner associations to collaborate with the government in promoting workplace health and safety issues. The program is open to trade and professional organizations, businesses, labor organizations, educational institutions, and government agencies, among others.

outplacement   Outplacement helps employees who are leaving the company, most often as the result of a downsizing or layoff to transition into new positions or other opportunities. These services assist employees with updating resumes, preparing for interviews, and searching for a new job.

outside director   A member of the board of directors who is not employed by the corporation and does not have operational responsibilities.

outsourcing   Moves an entire function out of the organization to be handled by a company specializing in the function. This solution can be beneficial by allowing the organization to focus on its basic business operations.

overtime   Extra pay for extra work. Defined as one and one-half times an employee's regular wage rate for hours worked exceeding 40 hours a work week.

P

parallel bargaining   Also known as pattern bargaining, whipsawing, or leapfrogging, parallel bargaining occurs when the union negotiates with one of the employers in an industry at a time. Once a contract has been reached with the first employer, the union uses the gains made during the negotiation as a base for negotiating with the next employer.

parent-country nationals (PCNs)   A PCN originates from the organization's home country; also known as expatriates.

Pareto chart   A graphical representation of the 80/20 rule: 80 percent of the problems are caused by 20 percent of the reasons. The Pareto chart points out which areas of concern will provide the greatest return when corrected.

partially self-funded plan   A health and welfare benefit plan in which the employer utilizes stop-loss insurance and agrees upon a preset maximum coverage amount that will be paid from the claim fund for each participant before the insurance company begins to pay the claim.

participant   In reference to benefits, a participant is someone who is enrolled in a specific benefit program. A participant can also be a member of a union or work team.

part-time employees   Part-time employees work less than a regular work week. They can be a cost-effective solution for organizations needing particular skills on an ongoing but not full-time basis.

party in interest   A pension plan participant, such as a fiduciary, a person or entity providing services to the plan, an employer or employee organization, a person who owns 50 percent or more of the business, relatives of any of the above, or corporations that are involved with the plan in any of these functions.

passive training methods   Training in which the learner listens to and absorbs information. These methods are instructor-focused and require little or no active participation from the learner. Passive training methods include conferences, lectures, and distance learning.

patent   Exclusive rights granted to inventors that provide the benefits of an invention for a defined period of time.

pattern bargaining   See *parallel bargaining*.

pay differential   Additional compensation for work that is considered beyond the normal work for an organization.

pay equity   See *comparable worth*.

pay for performance   Compensation based on individual and organizational results; see also *merit increase*.

pay range   In job pricing, the span between the minimum and maximum pay rate (hourly or annual) for all jobs in a particular pay or salary range.

payrolling   Allows the organization to refer individuals they want to hire to an agency. The agency hires them to work for the organization and provides payroll and tax services for either a fixed fee or percentage of the salary, which is generally less than a traditional temp agency fee.

pay structure   The way in which pay ranges and grades are constructed in an organization.

pedagogy   The study of how children learn. Specifically, education in which a teacher decides what will be taught and how it will be delivered.

peer review panel   A form of alternative dispute resolution in which management and non-management employees trained in company policies, procedures, and work rules hear disputes and make decisions which, depending upon the individual program, can be final and binding on both parties to the dispute.

performance appraisal   Also called performance evaluation or review, the process of reviewing how well employees perform their duties during a specified period, usually one year.

performance-based pay   Merit increases or promotions, based on how an individual employee performs against the company's process for measuring performance.

performance-based philosophy   An approach to compensation that rewards employees for their accomplishments.

performance-based training (PBT)   Often utilized to correct performance problems in highly technical or hazardous professions. The trainee is provided with opportunities to practice and demonstrate the necessary skill or knowledge until the required level of proficiency is mastered.

performance evaluation   See *performance appraisal*.

performance management   An ongoing process of providing feedback to employees about their performance, developing them into increasingly productive contributors to the organization.

performance review   A process used to observe employee performance during a specified review period and provide formal feedback at the end of the period.

permanent arbitrator   A person who is viewed by the parties to an agreement as fair and impartial and able to resolve any disputes arising between them.

perquisites   Additional benefits provided for senior management and executives. Perquisites may include generous pensions plans, access to the company jet, club memberships, or limousine service.

personal mastery   One of Peter Senge's five disciplines of learning organizations, used to describe a high level of expertise in an individual's chosen field and a commitment to lifelong learning.

PEST analysis   PEST is an acronym for political, economic, social, and technological factors. Also referred to as a STEP analysis, a PEST analysis scans the external environment to identify opportunities and threats as part of the SWOT analysis.

phantom stock   A stock option plan that provides the benefits of employee ownership without granting stock. Executives and outside members of the board of directors are the most common recipients of phantom stock.

physical health hazards   A type of environmental hazard that can cause physical injury such as excessive noise, extreme temperature, chemical explosion, or poor ergonomic design.

picketing   Occurs when a group of employees demonstrate at the entrance to a business to inform customers and the public about disputes, or to prevent deliveries to a business that the union is trying to influence in some way.

plan administrator   In deferred compensation, the person designated by the plan sponsor to manage the plan.

plan sponsor   In deferred compensation, the entity that establishes the plan. This may be a single employer, a labor organization or, in the case of a multi-employer plan, a group representing the parties that established the plan.

planned retirements   Usually occurs when an employee reaches normal retirement age and decides to stop working full time and pursue other interests.

plant closing   As defined by the WARN (Worker Adjustment and Retraining Notification) Act, a plant closing occurs when 50 or more full-time employees lose their jobs because a single facility shuts down, either permanently or temporarily.

plant patent   A patent that protects the invention or discovery of asexually reproduced varieties of plants for 20 years.

plateau learning curve   A learning curve that begins with a rapid increase in knowledge and then levels off with no additional learning for an extended period of time.

point factor   A job classification method that provides companies with a system of points that are assigned to the position being evaluated. Based on the total number of points a position receives, a pay grade/range is assigned to the position.

policies   Broad guidelines developed by the employer to guide organizational decisions.

polycentric   A global staffing strategy that fills management positions in the host country with home country nationals and corporate positions in the home country with expatriates.

positional bargaining   Also known as distributive bargaining or hard bargaining, a negotiating position in which for one side to gain something, the other side must lose something.

positive time reporting   Method used to record time worked in which employees record actual hours they work and any time they were off from work, paid or unpaid.

positively accelerating learning curve   A learning curve that begins slowly with smaller learning increments but increases in pace with larger increments as learning continues. This curve occurs in situations when the material to be learned is difficult or complex.

pre-employment testing   Any testing that is done prior to employment to ascertain a candidate's ability to successfully perform a job.

predictive validity   A type of criterion validity that predicts whether a test measurement accurately predicts behavior. In predictive validity, a test is given and the behavior is measured at a later time.

pre-existing conditions   Health issues or ailments that affect a patient within six months of enrollment in a health plan. Insurers may exclude those conditions from coverage for 12 months, or in the case of a late enrollment, for 18 months.

presentation   A passive training method that provides the same information to a group of people at the same time.

primary research   Research conducted using original studies and experiments. See also *secondary research*.

principled bargaining   A negotiating strategy characterized by parties who are more interested in solving a problem than they are in winning a position. The parties remain open to looking at problems in new ways and brainstorming for ideas and often come up with an agreement that solves the original problem in a way that was not originally contemplated by either side.

prior-petition bar   One of the bars to union representation elections, no elections will be approved by the NLRB for six months after a union withdraws a petition prior to an election.

privacy concern cases   Protections designed by OSHA to protect employee privacy by substituting a case number for the employee name on the OSHA 300 log.

private letter ruling An IRS ruling requested by an organization that applies only to the specific circumstances described in the request.

procedures The details of how policies are to be applied.

process control charts A quality management tool that provides a graphical representation of elements that are out of the acceptable range by setting parameters above and below the range.

production The organizational function responsible for creation of the product or service offered to customers. Traditionally, this means manufactured goods, but with the growth of service and information businesses, it has come to include some services as well.

professional employer organization (PEO) A PEO operates as the organization's HR department. The PEO becomes the employer of record and then leases the employees back to the organization. PEOs provide full-service HR, payroll, and benefit services and can be a cost-effective solution to enable smaller companies to offer benefits comparable to those offered by much larger organizations.

profit and loss statement (P&L) See *income statement*.

profit sharing A qualified, incentive-based program, available in many industries and at all corporate levels, that shares company profits.

profit-sharing plans See *discretionary contributions*.

programmed instruction Also called self-paced training, programmed instruction is the forerunner of computer-based training. In programmed instruction, the learner progresses from lesson to lesson in a predesigned course of instruction as mastery of the objectives is attained, allowing learners to progress at their own rate.

project management The process of initiating, planning, executing, controlling, and closing an assignment that is temporary in nature.

protected classes Title VII of the Civil Rights Act of 1964 identified five protected classes: race, color, religion, national origin, and sex.

protected health information (PHI) The Department of Health and Human Services (HHS) identifies protected health information (PHI) as patient information that must be kept private, including physical or mental conditions, health care given, and payments that have been made.

prudent person standard of care In relation to fiduciary responsibility over a pension fund, a common law concept that requires all actions on behalf of the fund to be taken with care and due diligence.

public domain In the context of copyrighted material, a work in the public domain is one for which the copyright period has expired or one that was produced as part of the job duties of a federal official.

publicity picketing See *informational picketing*.

Q

qualified domestic relations orders (QDRO)   Legal orders issued by state courts or other state agencies to require pension payments to alternate payees. An alternate payee must be a spouse or former spouse or child or other dependent of a plan participant.

qualified plan   A pension plan that meets ERISA (Employee Retirement Income Security Act) requirements and that provides tax advantages for both employees and employers. Qualified plans cannot provide benefits for officers, shareholders, supervisors, or other highly compensated employees that exceed benefits for other employees.

qualified stock options   Also known as incentive stock options, qualified stock options are taxed at the capital gains rate when they are exercised, instead of at the ordinary income tax rate. They are riskier for the holder than nonqualified stock options because they must be held for a longer period of time to receive the tax advantage.

qualitative analysis   Analysis based on subjective judgments.

qualitative assessment tools   Subjective evaluations of general observations and information, including various types of judgmental forecasts. These tools can be as simple as an estimate made by a knowledgeable executive or as involved as formalized brainstorming using a Delphi or nominal group technique.

quantitative analysis   Analysis based on mathematical models that measure historical data. Some of the models used are correlation measures, regression analysis, and measures of central tendency.

quantitative assessment tools   Objective measures of historical data that are analyzed using a variety of statistical measures. These tools are used to measure trends such as turnover or absenteeism.

question inconsistency bias   This bias occurs when an interviewer asks different questions of each candidate. While this is acceptable to a certain extent in order to delve more deeply into each candidate's qualifications, there is no baseline for comparison if there are no questions asked of all candidates.

quid pro quo   A legal term which means, in Latin, "this for that." Quid pro quo harassment, therefore, occurs when a supervisor or manager asks for sexual favors in return for a favorable employment action.

R

rabbi trust   A nonqualified deferred compensation plan designed to provide retirement income for officers, directors, and highly compensated employees.

random drug testing   Drug tests conducted on an arbitrary, unscheduled basis.

ranking method   In the performance appraisal process, ranking is a comparison appraisal method in which a manager lists employees from the highest to the lowest performer. In the job evaluation process, ranking compares the value of jobs in an organization to each other.

reaction evaluation method   The first level of Donald Kirkpatrick's training evaluation model; it measures the initial reaction of the participants and is the least meaningful method of evaluation.

realistic job preview (RJP)   An accurate picture of a typical day on the job designed to give candidates an opportunity to self-select out if the job is not what they expected it would be.

reasonable accommodation   A requirement of the Americans with Disabilities Act that employers must provide workplace facilities that are accessible to persons with disabilities and to adjust the requirements of positions to accommodate qualified persons with disabilities. See also *undue hardship*.

reasonable expectation of privacy   A standard used by courts in cases involving workplace searches based on factors such as whether or not there was a privacy policy in place and how an employer handled similar situations in the past.

reasonable suspicion drug testing   A type of drug testing that can be used any time there has been an accident in the workplace or when a supervisor suspects, based on behavior, that an employee is under the influence of drugs.

recency bias   Occurs when an interviewer recalls the most recently interviewed candidate more clearly than earlier candidates or a reviewer evaluates an employee only on performance that occurred close to the review.

recognitional picketing   Occurs when a union wants an employer to recognize it as the employees' representative for collective bargaining purposes. The NLRA (National Labor Relations Act) places a limit of 30 days on recognitional picketing, after which a petition for an election must be filed.

recruiting   The process of creating interest in an organization's position to attract qualified candidates.

red circle   Refers to salaries that are above the maximum of the salary range.

reduced FMLA leave schedule   A reduced FMLA (Family and Medical Leave Act) leave is one in which the employee's regular work schedule is reduced for a period of time. This can mean a reduction in the hours worked each day or in the number of days worked during the week.

reduction in force (RIF)   See *layoff*.

regiocentric   A type of staffing strategy that fills positions within a trade region, such as the European Union, with nationals from countries within that region.

repetitive stress injuries (RSI)   See *musculoskeletal disorder (MSD)*.

replacement chart   A chart used at all levels within an organization to categorize employees as ready for promotion, to be developed for future promotion, satisfactory in current position, or to be replaced.

reporting premium   When employees arrive at work for their regularly scheduled shift but there is no work to be done, they may be paid for a minimum number of hours based on employment agreements or state laws. Reporting pay is not required by the FLSA.

request for proposal (RFP)   The process used to obtain plans and costs from vendors for a specific service or project needed by an organization. A well-constructed RFP serves as the basis on which the product or service is obtained, a means for controlling expenses, a guide to ensure that the delivery meets the organization's requirements, and a method of evaluation at the end of the project.

resignations   Occur when an employee voluntarily decides to leave the organization to accept a different position or pursue other interests.

restricted stock   Stock that is subject to special SEC regulations before it may be sold. Often awarded to insiders as the result of an acquisition or merger to prevent an adverse impact on the market price of the stock by requiring that it be held for a period of time.

results evaluation method   The fourth level of Donald Kirkpatrick's training evaluation model; provides the feedback most meaningful to the business: did the training have an impact on the business results?

return on investment (ROI)   A commonly used metric calculated by dividing the benefits realized as a result of a program by the total related direct and indirect costs.

reverse mentor   Young employees who help older coworkers understand technology and the culture of the "younger generation."

risk assessment   The process used to determine how likely it is that an emergency will occur, the cost of an emergency to the business should it occur, and the impact it would have on the ability of the business to continue operations.

risk management   1) The functional area of the HR BOK that covers programs, policies, and plans to ensure the safety and security of the workforce and reduce organizational liabilities. 2) The process of identifying risks and taking steps to ensure that those risks are minimized.

S

S-shaped learning curve   This learning curve has characteristics of both positively and negatively accelerating learning curves. Learning initially progresses slowly and then accelerates but begins to slow down again after a period of time.

safety   Workplace safety activities identify possible hazards in the workplace and reduce the likelihood that accidents will happen by correcting the hazard. Management and employees are partners in this process.

safety and health achievement recognition program (SHARP)   A program that recognizes small, high-hazard employers who have requested a comprehensive OSHA consultation, corrected any violations, and developed an ongoing safety management program.

salary surveys   A study of compensation and benefits that is collected by government agencies or private firms to assess current market trends. Salary surveys are commonly provided by a professional services vendor who is responsible for confidentially collecting and administering the salary survey data from companies and compiling this data in a format that is usable by the organization. Salary surveys are critical to ensuring the company's total compensation package continues to be aligned with the organization's compensation philosophy.

sales   The sales function is responsible for transferring the product or service from the business to the customer.

salting   A union organizing practice used to influence employees in an organization. The union hires an individual to apply for a job and, once hired, to organize employees while working for the organization.

Scanlon Plan   A type of gainsharing plan created in the 1930s by Joseph Scanlon to increase productivity and decrease costs through employee involvement. A Scanlon Plan is administered by a committee made up of employees and management and requires that the company's financial information and productivity metrics be disclosed to the employee population. See also *gainsharing*.

scheduled drug testing   Used for monitoring the rehabilitation progress of employees. Scheduled drug testing has limited value because employees who may be currently using drugs are generally able to stop long enough before the test to clear their systems of the drugs.

scientific method   A method of primary research, the scientific method has five steps that can be used to analyze and solve HR problems. identify the problem, create a hypothesis, decide a method for testing, collect data, and draw conclusions.

seasonal workers   Workers who are hired only at times of the year when the workload increases, such as the Christmas shopping season or when it is time to harvest agricultural products.

secondary research   Research based on information that has been collected or reported by others, such as books or articles by primary researchers, industry standards, or analysis of trends within an organization.

Section 125 plans   A plan authorized by the Revenue Act of 1978 that allows employees to set aside pretax funds for medical expenses they plan to incur during the calendar year. See also *flexible spending account*.

security   Workplace security protects an organization's physical, intellectual, human, financial, and other assets from threats of one kind or another, including fires, earthquakes, hurricanes, tornadoes, and other natural disasters; manmade threats such as terrorist attacks, computer hackers, workplace violence and theft; or the unintentional release of trade secrets or confidential information.

self-funded plan   An insurance plan in which the employer creates a claim fund and pays all claims through it. Self-funded plans must conduct annual discrimination tests to ensure that HCEs (highly compensated employees) are not utilizing the plan disproportionately to non-HCEs.

self-study   A type of active training directed entirely by the learner, who determines what, when, and where learning will occur. It may be based on a defined program and involve a trainer or mentor, but it is controlled by the learner.

seniority-based compensation   A system in which pay decisions are based on length of time in the position, typically found in organizations with an entitlement culture.

shared vision   One of the five elements of a learning organization, Peter Senge's shared vision goes beyond the corporate vision statement to inspire commitment of all individuals in the organization.

shift   A block of time that is scheduled for work or duty.

shift premium   Additional compensation provided for employees who work other than the day shift. It may be paid as a percentage of base pay or factored into the hourly rate.

short-range plans   Business strategies, goals, or objectives projected to be achieved in one year or less.

similar-to-me bias   A bias that occurs when the candidate has interests or other characteristics that are the same as those of the interviewer and which cause the interviewer to overlook negative aspects about the candidate's qualifications.

simple linear regression   A quantitative analysis tool used to measure the relationship between one variable (such as staffing) and another (such as production output) used to project future needs.

simulation training   An interactive training method that provides the learner with opportunities to "try out" new skills or practice procedures in a setting that simulates the work environment but does not endanger the inexperienced trainee, coworkers, or the public.

sit-down strike   An unlawful strike in which employees stop working and stay in the building.

skills inventory   A collection of information about an organization's workforce including special skills or knowledge, performance appraisals, fluency in foreign languages, educational qualifications, previous experience in or outside of the company, credentials or licenses that may be required, and any continuing education the employee has obtained through training classes, seminars, or educational institutions.

skip-level interview   A process in which employees are interviewed by their manager's manager to provide insight into employees' goals and job satisfaction, as well as an opportunity for career counseling.

Society for Human Resource Management (SHRM)   The largest organization of Human Resources professionals.

sourcing   The gathering of names and contact information for potential candidates in the active and passive labor markets.

span of control   The number of employees that one manager can directly supervise.

staff functions   Those functions not involved with making operating decisions but involved with advising line managers.

staffing needs analysis   A determination of the numbers and types of jobs needed to successfully achieve business goals; the cornerstone of the workforce planning process.

state unemployment insurance (SUI)   The SSA (Social Security Act) of 1935 mandated the states to provide unemployment insurance for displaced workers. Each state develops its own UI program, so eligibility requirements for SUI vary between states, as do the SUI tax rates. The state rates vary between employers as well because states increase or decrease the amount of tax charged to individual employers based on the number of employees who file claims for unemployment during the year.

statement of cash flows   A financial report used to show how money flows through an organization. This statement shows how much cash was a result of sales, how much was spent to produce the products that were sold, how much was borrowed or came in as a result of new capital investments, and how much was invested in assets.

statutory bar   One of the bars to union representation elections, the NLRA (National Labor Relations Act) prohibits a representation election in a bargaining unit when one has been held during the preceding 12-month period.

stereotyping bias   This bias occurs when an interviewer or reviewer assumes a candidate has specific traits because they are a member of a particular group.

stock option   The right to purchase an employer's stock at a certain price, at a future date, and at a given price for a specific period of time.

stop-loss insurance   Insurance purchased by self-funded employers to prevent a single catastrophic claim from devastating the claim fund. The employer agrees upon a preset maximum coverage amount that will be paid from the claim fund for each participant before the insurance company begins to pay the claim.

strategic management   The functional area of the HR body of knowledge area that is concerned with the "big picture" of an organization; its vision, mission, values, goals, and objectives; change management; and measuring HR's contribution to achieving organizational effectiveness.

strategic partnership program   A means for businesses and employees to participate in solving health and safety problems with OSHA. Partnerships currently exist for metal recycling, grain handling, and janitorial contractors working to develop solutions specific to their businesses.

strategic planning   A dynamic, systematic way of setting the direction for an organization and developing strategies, tactics, and operational plans that ensure its success.

strategy   A plan for generating revenue that describes how a business will use its strengths to its competitive advantage in the marketplace.

stratification chart   A quality management tool that shows problems in priority order and identifies possible strategies for correcting problems.

stress   According to NIOSH, job stress occurs when job requirements do not match the capabilities, resources, or needs of a worker, resulting in harmful physical and emotional responses.

strike   Occurs when the union decides to stop working.

strike price   Also known as the grant price, the strike price is the price at which stock options may be purchased or sold by the holder of the options when they are exercised.

subject matter experts (SME)   Professionals who possess a level of expertise gained through experience and education that qualifies them to ensure the maintenance and documentation of a particular topic or discipline.

succession plan   Identifies critical positions in an organization and how they will be filled if current incumbents leave.

summary plan description (SPD)   Provides benefit plan participants with information about the provisions, policies, and rules established by the plan and advises them on actions they can take in utilizing the plan. ERISA (Employee Retirement Income Security Act) requires that the SPD include the name and other identifying information about plan sponsors, administrators, and trustees, along with any information related to collective bargaining agreements for the plan participants.

supervisory training   Training on topics related to interactions with employees, such as progressive discipline, performance appraisals, workplace safety, interviewing, and training.

suspension   A step in the disciplinary press in which an employee is required to be absent from work (with or without pay) for varying periods of time.

swing shift   The evening shift, with hours from about 6 PM to 2 AM.

SWOT analysis   Examines the strengths, weaknesses, opportunities, and threats facing an organization. Strengths and weaknesses are internal factors that can be controlled by the organization; opportunities and threats are external factors that may impact an organization's plans.

systems thinking   One of Peter Senge's five disciplines of learning organizations, systems thinking describes the ability of individuals and organizations to recognize patterns and project how changes will impact on them.

T

tangible employment action (TEA)   As defined by the Supreme Court, "A significant change in employment status, such as hiring, firing, failing to promote, reassignment with significantly different responsibilities, or a decision causing a significant change in benefits."

task level training   Training involving processes performed in a single job category.

target benefit plan   A hybrid pension plan with similarities to both a defined benefit plan and a money purchase plan.

team learning   One of the five elements of a learning organization, Peter Senge's team learning refers to the ability of a team to share and build upon their ideas without holding anything back.

technical/professional labor market   The labor market includes individuals with expertise in specific skill or discipline such as human resources or marketing.

telecommuting   An alternative staffing method that allows employees to work at home, connecting to the office electronically. This has become a viable solution for employees who do not wish to commute or who have other reasons to work at home.

temp   A temp, or temporary employee, is employed by an agency that screens and tests candidates prior to sending them to a work site for variable periods of time, from short, one-day assignments to longer assignments.

temp-to-perm   An alternative staffing method that allows an organization to observe and evaluate a worker's performance prior to making an offer of full-time employment.

teratogens   Chemicals that do not affect a pregnant woman but can harm an unborn child.

termination   Occurs when an employee leaves an organization and can be voluntary or involuntary.

Theory X and Theory Y   The two distinct management approaches described by Douglas McGregor. Theory X managers believe employees need constant direction to complete their work and are interested in job security above all else. Theory Y managers believe that, given the opportunity, employees will seek out challenging work and additional responsibility if the work is satisfying.

third-country nationals (TCNs)   A TCN is an employee from any country other than the home country or the host country.

third-party administrator (TPA)   An entity that provides claim management services for benefit plans such as medical, dental, and vision insurance; pension plans; and Section 125/129 plans.

third-party contract   A contract in which some part of the transaction is provided by an entity other than those who have signed the contract.

time-and-a-half   The overtime rate specified by the FLSA for nonexempt employees who work more than 40 hours per week.

time series forecast   A quantitative method of analysis that can be used to measure historic staffing levels and provide a basis from which expected future needs can be calculated.

TIPS   An acronym used to remind employers of actions to avoid to prevent charges of unfair labor practices during unionizing efforts. That is, employers may not threaten, interrogate, promise, or spy on employees.

tort   A legal term used to describe an action that injures someone. Torts are not related to laws or contracts but can result in legal action: the party who has been injured can sue the wrongdoer and collect damages for the injury that has been done.

total quality management (TQM)   TQM focuses all resources within the organization on providing value for customers.

total rewards   The functional area of the HR BOK concerned with development, implementation, and evaluation of compensation and benefits programs that support an organization's strategic plan.

total rewards philosophy   A high-level mission statement used to guide the development and implementation of compensation and benefit programs that attract, motivate, and retain employees.

total rewards strategy   A TR strategy is used to determine the best way to use available resources in attracting, motivating, and retaining employees.

totality of agreement   See *zipper clause*.

transactional leadership   A form of leadership focused on getting the job done by offering rewards in exchange for the accomplishment of an organizational goal.

transfer of training   This occurs when learning that took place away from the regular work environment is applied to the real job situation.

transformational leadership   A form of leadership focused on building work group relationships to achieve organizational goals.

trend analysis   A quantitative analysis method that compares the changes in a single variable over time and, over a period of years, generally moves upward or downward.

tripartite arbitration panel   A panel consisting of three arbitrators who hear the issues and reach a joint decision regarding disputes.

two-factor theory   See *motivation/hygiene theory*.

U

undue hardship   An exception to the ADA which weighs the cost of an accommodation against the size of the organization and other similar factors.

unfair labor practice (ULP)   An action by an employer or a union that restrains or coerces employees from exercising their rights to organize and bargain collectively or to refrain from doing so.

union shop clause   A clause that requires all employees to join the union within a grace period specified by the contract, but no fewer than 30 days, or, in the construction industry, 7 days.

unlawful employment practices   As defined by Title VII of the Civil Rights Act of 1964, practices that discriminate against a member of a protected class in recruiting, selection, hiring, compensation, benefits, training, apprenticeship, or any other terms and conditions of employment.

utility patent   Patents that protect the invention of a machine, a new and useful process, or the manufacture or composition of matter or of new and useful improvements to the same. Utility patents are limited to 20 years.

V

validity   The assessment of whether or not a test is an accurate measure of the characteristics that it is supposed to measure.

variable compensation   See *incentive pay*.

verbal warning   The first step in a formal disciplinary process. The direct supervisor verbally informs an employee of the performance issue. Verbal warnings must by documented in writing.

vestibule training   A form of the simulation method, vestibule training allows inexperienced workers to become familiar with and gain experience using equipment that is either hazardous or requires a level of speed that can only be attained with practice.

vesting   The point at which employees own the contributions their employer has made to the pension plan on their behalf, whether or not they remain employed with the company. The vesting requirements established by ERISA (Employee Retirement Income Security Act) refer only to funds that are contributed by the employer. Employees are always 100 percent vested in funds they have contributed, but they must earn the right to be vested in the employer's contribution.

vicarious liability   A legal concept that holds an employer accountable for the harmful actions of its employees, whether or not the employer is aware of those actions.

visual learners   Learners who retain knowledge best when they are able to see or read information.

voluntary arbitration   Occurs when both parties to a disagreement agree to submit the conflict to an arbitrator for resolution.

voluntary assumption of risk   A common law doctrine that assumed workers who were injured on the job knew the dangers of the job when they took it and assumed the associated risks. The level of pay accepted by the worker reflected the amount of danger involved so the employer had no responsibility when death or injury occurred.

Voluntary Protection Program (VPP)   Employers with tough, established safety programs who meet OSHA criteria for the VPP program are removed from routine scheduled inspection lists.

voluntary recognition bar   One of the bars to union representation elections, n election will be barred for a reasonable period of time to allow the parties to negotiate a contract if an employer has voluntarily recognized a union as the representative for a bargaining unit.

W

wage compression   Occurs when new employees are hired at a pay rate that is greater than incumbent pay for similar skills, education, and experience. These situations occur during periods of high economic growth or when certain skill sets are in high demand.

wage garnishment   The result of a court or government order requiring a portion of an employee's earnings to be paid to another person or entity for the payment of a debt. Wage garnishments are regulated by the Federal Wage Garnishment Law and may be imposed by the IRS, a state tax collection agency, or by a court to enforce payment of child support or a debt.

waiting to be engaged   Noncompensable employee time that usually occurs before or after a shift when employees arrive early and do not begin working until the shift begins.

weighted average   In quantitative analysis, a weighted average is used to compensate for data that may be out of date; the more current data is increased because it better reflects the current situation.

weighted moving average   An average calculated for a specific period that assigns more weight to current data. See also *moving average* and *weighted average*.

whipsawing   See *parallel bargaining*.

wildcat strike   A strike that occurs in violation of a contract clause prohibiting strikes during the term of the contract.

workforce analysis   The AAP report that lists job titles from the lowest to the highest paid within each work unit.

Workforce Planning and Employment   The functional area of the HR BOK that covers sourcing, recruiting, hiring, orienting, succession planning, retention, and organizational exit activities to ensure the availability of a workforce qualified to execute the organization's strategic plan.

workplace diversity   The practice of employing individuals with diverse cultural, racial, and ethnic backgrounds and understanding the differences between people.

workplace investigation   A formal report or research into suspected illegal activity or serious violations of company policy taking place within an organization.

workplace violence   Occurs when an employee with poor behavior control becomes highly stressed. The stress may or may not be work related, but it is often set off by an incident in the workplace. Under OSHA's General Duty Clause, employers are required to be aware of employees exhibiting the signs of possible violent behavior and take steps to prevent its occurrence.

written warning   In the second and third stages of the disciplinary process, poorly performing employees receive written notices describing disciplinary steps that have already been taken, spelling out performance problems and describing the steps needed to improve the performance, as well as any agreements that have been made about performance changes.

Y

yellow dog contracts   Contracts that were used by employers to prevent employees from joining unions by requiring them to sign an agreement that the employee was not a member of a union and would not become one in the future, and that joining a union would be sufficient grounds for dismissal in the future. They were prohibited by the Norris-La Guardia Act.

Z

zero-based budget   A process that analyzes costs from the ground up without relying on previous budgets.

zipper clause   Also known as a totality of agreement clause, a zipper clause is an agreement between the parties to a collective bargaining agreement that the contract is the entire agreement between them and that anything not in it is not part of the agreement. The purpose of this clause is to prevent reopening of negotiations during the term of the contract.

Index

Note to the reader: Throughout this index **boldfaced** page numbers indicate primary discussions of a topic. *Italicized* page numbers indicate illustrations.

Numbers

80/20 rule, 204
360° review, 230
    training for, 235
401(k) plans, 303

A

AAI (ASPA Accreditation Institute), 3
absenteeism, 352
    scientific method applied to, 49
accession rate, 183
accident prevention, 409
accidental death and dismemberment
        insurance, 307
accounting, 76–77, 96
accounts payable, 76
accounts receivable, 76
accrued expense, 77
achievement, in acquired needs theory, 35
achievement leadership style, 39
acknowledgment form, for employee
        handbook, 347
acquired immune deficiency syndrome
        (AIDS), 401
acquired needs theory, 35
acquisitions, 105–106
action plans, 102
    after training, 227
active training methods, 222
actual deferral percentage (ADP) test, 303
ad hoc arbitrator, 354
ADA. *See* Americans with Disabilities Act (ADA)
Adams, J. Stacy, 36
ADDIE model of instructional design, **215–228**
    Analysis, **215–218**
    Design, **218–221**
    Development, **221–224**
    Implementation, **224–227**
    Evaluation, **227–228**
ADEA. *See* Age Discrimination in Employment
    Act (ADEA)

administrative exemption, 261
administrative law, **112**
Administrative Law Courts, 112
administrative services only (ASO) plan, 306
ADP (actual deferral percentage) test, 303
adult learning process, **32–33**
adverse impact, on protected groups, 156–157
advertising for job opening, 154
affiliation, in acquired needs theory, 35
Affirmative Action Plans (AAP), **132–143**,
        450, 451
affirmative defenses, to OSHA violations,
        392–393
Age Discrimination in Employment Act (ADEA),
        132–133, 135, 440, 455
    document retention requirements, 59, 60
agency shop, 368
Agricola, Georgius, 383
AICPA (American Institute of Certified Public
        Accountants), 96
AIDS (acquired immune deficiency syndrome), 401
Albemarle Paper v. Moody, 167, 442
Alderfer, Clayton, 35
ally doctrine, 371
alter ego doctrine, 371
alternative dispute resolution, 353–355
    arbitration, **353–354**
    constructive confrontation, **355**
    mediation, **354–355**
alumni employees, for external recruiting, 155
American Arbitration Association (AAA),
        353–354
American businesses, bureaucracy, 108–109
American Federation of Labor-Congress of
        Industrial Organizations, 318
American Institute of Certified Public
        Accountants (AICPA), 96
American Jobs Creation Act, 304
American Railway Union, 356
American Society of Personnel Administrators
        (ASPA), xx
    beginning, 2–3
Americans with Disabilities Act (ADA), 57, **134**,
        135, 443
    document retention requirements, 59
    and substance abusers in recovery, 409

analysis, in ADDIE model of instructional design, 215–218
androgogy, 32, 33
annual reporting period, 76
annual reports, ERISA requirements for, 298
annual reviews for salary adjustments, 280–281
aptitude tests, 165
arbitration, 353–354
ASPA (American Society of Personnel Administrators), xx
    ASPA Accreditation Institute (AAI), 3
    beginning, 2–3
assessment centers, 165
assessment test, xxv–xl, 14
assets, 77
Astra USA, 337
at-will employment doctrine, 174, **332–334**
    employee handbook and, 32
    public policy exception, 333
audit, of HR practices, 110
audited financial statements, 77
auditors, independence of, 114
auditory learners, 218
authoritarian leader, 40–41
authorization cards, 361
Automobile Workers v. Johnson Controls, Inc., 397–398, 442
availability of minorities and women, in AAP, 142
average, 52–53
average bias of interviewer, 162
Avian influenza (H5N1), 402

B

Baby Boom, and Social Security, 286
back wages, recovery of, 263–264
background checks on job candidates, **170–173**
bad faith bargaining, 366
balance sheet, 76
balanced scorecard, 110
banquet-style seating for training, *225*
bargaining units, **362**
base pay, **265–266**
    increases to, **279–281**
behavior evaluation method for training, 228
behavioral anchored rating scale (BARS), 232, 233
behavioral interviews, 159
behavioral methods of performance appraisal, **232–233**

behavioral reinforcement, 36
behavioral theories of leadership, **38**
benchmark positions, in job evaluation, 274
benefits programs, **283–312**. *See also* health and welfare benefits
    deferred compensation, **296–304**
    family medical leave, **288–294**
    as percent of operating expenses, 317
    Social Security and Medicare, **285–286**
    unemployment insurance, **287–288**
bereavement leave, 312
BFOQ (bona fide occupational qualifications), 131
binding arbitration, 353, 369
biological health hazards, 401–402
Black Lung Benefits Act (BLBA), 414, 441
Blake, Robert R., 39
Blake-Mouton Managerial Grid, 39
Blanchard, Kenneth, 39
blocking-charge bar to union election, 365
Blood-Borne Pathogens, 404
Board of Directors, 93, 113, 320
bona fide occupational qualifications (BFOQ), 131
book of knowledge (BOK). *See* human resource body of knowledge (BOK)
bottom-up budgeting, 78
"bottom-up" communication, 28, 29
boycotts, 370–371
brand identity of employer, 152
broadbanding, 282
Brown & Williamson Tobacco Corporation, 116
brown-bag lunch program, 344
Buckingham, Marcus, *First, Break all the Rules*, 96–97
buddy programs for new employees, 178–179
budgeting, **77–79**
    needs assessment and, 26
    in strategic planning, 102, 104
bulletin boards
    accuracy, 18
    for training program, 224
Bureau of Labor, 383
Bureau of Labor Statistics, 275, 438
    Job Openings and Labor Turnover Survey (JOLTS), 150
    union membership, 363
Bureau of Mines, 383
Burgess, Guy, 355
Burgess, Heidi, 355
Burlington Industries v. Ellerth, 336–337, 446
Burlington Northern Santa Fe Railway Co. v. White, 447

Bush, George W., 304
business case, *55*
business continuity planning (BCP), **415–417**
    maintaining, 417
business impact measures, *54*
    of human resource plans, **118–119**
    for total rewards, 317
    for Workforce Planning and Employment, 183
business planning, HR role in, 435
business strategy, 92–108

C

cafeteria plans, 308
call-back pay, 268
candidate profile, 153
capacity, *94*
capital budget, 79
card-check election, 361
Carlyle, Thomas, 38
case study, 222, 432–434
cash balance plans (CBPs), **302**
cash flows statement, 76
cause and effect diagram, 204, *205*
CBA (cost/benefit analysis), *55*
CCPA (Consumer Credit Protection Act),
    315, 440
CD with book, xxii–xxiii
cell phone cameras, monitoring use, 419
Central Intelligence Agency (CIA), 201
centralized organization, 109
certification. *See* human resource certification
certification-year bar to union election, 365
change agent, 200
change management, **55–56**, **199–200**
change process theory, 199–200
change, to organizational structure, 104–107
check sheets, as analysis tools, 203, *203*
chemical health hazards, **396–397**
chevron-style seating for training, *226*
chief executive officers (CEOs), median pay, 318
chief financial officer (CFO), 406
child labor, 262
child support, garnishment calculations, 315
Circuit City Stores v. Adams, **456**
Civil Rights Act of 1964, and sexual harassment,
    335–338
Civil Rights Act of 1964, Title VII, **130–131**, 440,
    450, 455
    document retention requirements, 59
Civil Rights Act of 1991, 132, **134–136**, 444

civil rights legislation, **130–132**
Civil Service Reform Act, 442
classification method for job evaluation,
    274–275
classroom-style seating for training, *225*
classroom training, 223
Clayton Act, 356, 438
cliff vesting, 300
Clinton, Bill, 288
closed shops, 356, 368
closing conference, by CSHO, 392
Closing phase of project life cycle, 42
coaching, 213
    and leadership, 41
COBRA. *See* Consolidated Omnibus Budget
    Reconciliation Act (COBRA)
Code of Ethical and Professional Standards
    (SHRM), 44
code of ethics, **115–116**
Code of Federal Regulations, 402
codes of conduct, **116–118**
Coffman, Curt, *First, Break all the Rules*, 96–97
cognitive ability test (CAT), 165
COLAs (cost of living adjustments), 279
collective bargaining, **366–372**
    positions, **366–367**
    strategies, **367–368**
    subjects, **368**
collective bargaining agreement (CBA), **368–369**
    enforcement, **369–370**
colleges, recruiting on, 155
"comfort zone," change and, 200
commissioned salary surveys, 276
committees, 343
    circumventing union by, 454
common law doctrines, **332–334**
Common Situs picketing, 372
communication
    in change, 200
    with employees, **344–345**
    by employees, employer monitoring of, 118
    of individual incentive plan, 270
    with job candidates, 157–158
    open and honest, 346
    professional, 30
    of salary structure, 278
communication skills and strategies, **28–30**
compa-ratios, 279
company assets, personal use of, 117
company websites, for external recruiting, 155
comparable worth, real world scenario, 277
comparison appraisal methods, 231
compensable factors, 274

compensable time, 258
compensation, 249, 253–282. *See also* payroll
   administering plan, 278–279
   base pay, **265–266**
      increases to, 279–281
   benefits, 283–312. *See also* health and welfare
      benefits
      deferred compensation, **296–304**
      family medical leave, **288–294**
      Social Security and Medicare, **285–286**
      unemployment insurance, **287–288**
   bonus plans, 272
   changing plan, real world scenario, 66–67
   commission, 272
   executive, 317–320
      Board of Directors, 320
      stock options, **318–319**
      trends, 318
   federal legislation, **256–264**
   for injury and illness, **413–414**
   nontraditional structures, **281–282**
   pay differentials, **266–269**
   as percent of operating expenses, 317
   salary
      deductions and FLSA exemption
         status, 260
      for FLSA exemption status, 260
      range, 277
      surveys, **275–276**
   salary administration, 273
   special incentives, 271–272
   traditional pay structures, **272–282**
      development, **276–278**
      job evaluation and, **273–275**
      salary surveys, **275–276**
   variable, **269–272**
compensatory time off, 258
competency-based compensation, 282
competency profiles, 282
competition
   and employee retention, 255
   "promoting from within" and, 145
Compliance Safety and Health Officer
   (CSHO), 391
compressed work week, 349
compulsory arbitration, 353, 369
computer-based testing process, xxi, 19
computer-based training, 224
computer employee exemption, 261–262
computer use, employer monitoring of, 418
concurrent validity of selection tests, 168, 169
conference-style seating for training, 226
conferences, 222

confidential information, protecting, 406
confidentiality
   code of ethics on, 115
   vs. need to know, 28
conflict resolution, 210
conflicts of interest, code of ethics on, 115
Congressional Accountability Act, 445
consent election, 364
Consolidated Omnibus Budget Reconciliation
   Act (COBRA), 294, 295, 443
   document retention requirements, 60
   requirements, **308–309**
construct validity of selection tests, 168, 169
constructive confrontation, **355**
constructive discharge, 334
consultant
   OSHA, **393**
   for strategic planning, 99
Consumer Credit Protection Act (CCPA),
   315, 440
consumer picketing, 372
contagious disease, and handicapped individual
   classification, 452
content validity, of selection tests, 168
contingency theories of leadership, **40**
contingent employment agencies, 156
continuing education courses, 10
continuity of operations plan (COOP), 416
continuous feedback, for performance
   review, 232
continuous FMLA leave, 291
contract bar to union election, 365
contract, express or implied, 332
contract management, third-party, 26–28
contract workers, 147
contractor relationship, 26
contrast bias of interviewer, 162
contributory negligence, 414
control function, 109–110
Control of Hazardous Energy standard, 404
Controlling phase of project life cycle, 42
"cooling off" period, 357
*Cooper v. IBM Personal Pension Plan and IBM
   Corporation,* 302
coordinated bargaining, 367–368
coordination of benefits (COB) process, 305
Copyright Act of 1976, **197–198**, 442
   and training materials, 221
core competencies of organization, 101, 144–145
core knowledge requirements of BOK, **6–7**, 25
Cornell University's School of Industrial
   Relations, 3
corporate governance, **113–118**

corporate restructuring, 105
    workforce planning in, 143
corporate values statement, 102
corporations, **93**
correlation, 50–51
correlation coefficient, 51
cost/benefit analysis (CBA), 55
    of training, 217
cost control, 94
cost of expatriate issues in workforce
    planning, 185
cost of goods sold, 77
cost of labor, 254
cost of living adjustments (COLAs), 279
cost per hire, 183
counseling services for employees, **311–312**
court injunctions, in union environment,
    356, 370
covered entities, 309
creative professional exemption, 261
criminal record checks, 170–171
criterion validity, of selection tests, 168
critical incident review process, 232
Crosby, Philip B., 206
CSHO (Compliance Safety and Health
    Officer), 391
cultural acclimation, 186
cultural noise bias of interviewer, 162
Cummings, Thomas, *Organization Development
    and Change*, 199
cumulative trauma injuries (CTI), 399
customer relationship management (CRM), 201
cycles, in trend analysis, 53

D

data collection
    for analysis, **50**
    for workforce planning, 149
data privacy regulations, in other countries, 421
Davis Bacon Act, 256
    document retention requirements, 60
deauthorization of unions, 366
decentralized organization, 109
decertification of unions, 366
decision-making
    authority in organization, 109
    employees involvement in, **342–344**
decision-making day for termination, 31
declining organization, 98
defamation, 334

deferred compensation, **296–304**
defined benefit plans, 296, **301**
defined contribution plans, 296, **302–303**
delayed vesting, 299
delegating authority, 343
delegating style of leadership, 40
delivery mechanism, for information, 29
delivery schedule, in proposal, 28
Delphi technique, 54
demand for recognition by union, **361**
Deming, W. Edwards, 202
democratic leader, 40–41
demonstration method of training, 223
dental insurance, 306
Department of Health, Education and
    Welfare, 383
Department of Labor, 43
department staff meetings, 344
dependent care account, 308
design, in ADDIE model of instructional design,
    218–221
design patents, 198
development, in ADDIE model of instructional
    design, **221–224**
direct compensation, 250
directed election, 364
directing function, 109
directive interviews, 159
directive leadership style, 39
disability insurance, 307
disaster recovery plan (DRP), **416**
disciplinary actions, 349
    terminations, **351–352**
    written documentation for, 31
discretionary contributions, 302
discrimination claim, filing requirements, 133
disparate impact, 130, 135
disparate treatment, 130
disposable earnings, 315
dispute resolution, **353–355**
dissatisfaction (Hygiene) factors, 34
distance learning, 224
distributed bargaining, 367
diversity, **42–43**
diversity initiative, 43, 236
diversity training, 43
divestitures, 106
    workforce planning in, 144
divisional organizational structure, 69, 70
documentation requirements, **30–32**
Dole, Robert, 339
double breasting, 371
downsizing, 105

dress code, 352
Drug-Free Workplace Act of 1988, 394–395,
    408, 443
drug screening tests, **408–409**
    for job candidates, 173
due diligence, 342
    prior to merger or acquisition, 105–106
dues check-off, for union dues, 369
DuPont & Co. v. NLRB (E.I.), **453–454**
duty of diligence, 342
duty of good faith and fair dealing, 333
duty of loyalty, 342
duty of obedience, 342
duty of successor employers, 370

E

e-learning, 224
economic concerns, 74
economic factors, impacting compensation, 254
Economic Growth and Tax Relief Reconciliation
    Act, 301
economic indicators, 150
economic strike, 357
education labor market, 151
educational references, 170
EEO-1 reports, 138–139
EEOC. *See* Equal Employment Opportunity
    Commission (EEOC)
E.I. DuPont & Co. v. NLRB, **453–454**
elected officials, contacting, 113
Electrical Work Practices, 404
Electromation, Inc. v. NLRB, **452–453**
Electronic Communications Privacy Act of
    1986, 395
electronic monitoring, 417
electronic performance support system
    (EPSS), 224
email, 345
    employer monitoring of, 418, 420
emergency action plans, 403, 413
    sample, 411–412
emergency response plan (ERP), **416**
emotional intelligence, 44, **210**
Employee and Labor Relations, 6, 330
    core knowledge requirements and, 6
    dispute resolution, 353–355
    employee relations programs, **345–349**
    employee rights, **357–360**
    employer rights and responsibilities, **331–341**
    federal legislation, 330–331
    global considerations, 373

labor laws and organizations, 356–357
    metrics, **373**
    organization climate and culture, 342–345
    performance improvement, 349–353
    resources, 462
    union organization, 360–372
        avoidance strategies, **372**
        collective bargaining, **366–372**
        employer options, **360**
        organizing process, **361–366**
    employee assistance programs (EAP), 179,
        311–312, 407
    employee attitude assessment, 75
    employee development, **211–214**
    employee handbooks, 347
    at-will employment doctrine and, 32
employee-management committees, 343
employee-participation committees, 453
Employee Polygraph Protection Act (EPPA),
        172–173, 443
    document retention requirements, 61
employee recognition, 97
employee records management, **58–64**
employee retention programs, 179
Employee Retirement Income Security Act of
        1974 (ERISA), 271, 295, 442
    document retention requirements, 61
    requirements, **297–301**
    retirement before, 298
employee rights, NLR Act and, 357
employee stock ownership plans (ESOP), 271
employee surveys, 237, 348
    for attitude assessment, 75
employees
    communication with, 28, **344–345**
    eligible for union voting, 365
    employer monitoring of communications, 118
    feedback from, **348**
    vs. independent contractor, 147–148
    rights and responsibilities, 341–342
    searches of property, 419–420
    unique needs, **236–237**
employer brands, 152
employer rights and responsibilities, **331–341**
    common law doctrines, 332–334
    Glass Ceiling Act, **339–340**
    sexual harassment, 335–339
    Uniformed Services Employment and
        Reemployment Rights Act (USERRA),
        340–341, 445
employer unfair labor practices, 358
employers
    duty of successor, 370

options during union organizing, **360**
responsibility for harassing actions of
    employees, 335
employment actions, documenting, **30**
employment agencies, 155–156
employment applications, **158–159**
employment at-will, 32, 174, **332–334**
    public policy exception, 333
employment contract, 174–175
employment discrimination, court cases,
    166–167
employment practices liability insurance
    (EPLI), 79
employment references, 170
employment relationships, 174
employment testing, legal issues, real world
    scenario, 166–167
employment visas, 177–178
Energy Employees Occupational Illness
    Compensation Program Act (EEOICPA),
    414, 446
"Enforcement Guidance: Vicarious Employer
    Liability for Unlawful Harassment by
    Supervisors" (EEOC), 338
enrolled actuary, 298, 300
Enron, 114
    and whistle-blowing, 116
enterprise coverage of FLSA, 257
enterprise risk management (ERM), **110**
entitlement philosophy of rewards, 252
environmental health hazards, **396–402**
    biological, 401–402
    chemical, **396–397**
    physical, **398–401**
environmental safety hazards, **402–404**
environmental scanning, **71–75**, 101
EPA (Equal Pay Act), 264, 440
    document retention requirements, 61
Epilepsy Foundation of Northeast Ohio (NLRB
    decision), 446
EPLI (employment practices liability
    insurance), 79
EPPA (Employee Polygraph Protection Act),
    172–173, 443
    document retention requirements, 61
EPSS (electronic performance support
    system), 224
Equal Employment Opportunity Act of 1972,
    131–132, 441
Equal Employment Opportunity Commission
    (EEOC), 112, 130
    annual survey, **138–141**
        data reporting, 139–141

job categories, 139
    race and ethnicity categories, 139
    report types, 138–139
and electronic data access, 45
Equal Pay Act (EPA), 264, 440
    document retention requirements, 61
equity, 77
equity theory (Adams), 36
ERG theory, 35
ergonomic injury rate, 423
ergonomics, 399
ERISA. *See* Employee Retirement Income
    Security Act of 1974 (ERISA)
ESOP (employee stock ownership plans), 271
essay review, 232
essential job functions, 145
esteem needs in Maslow hierarchy, 34
ethics, **44–45**
    code of, **115–116**
    of organization, **114–115**
ethics officers, **118**
ethnocentric approach to international staffing,
    184–185
evaluation
    in ADDIE model of instructional design,
        227–228
    of training, **227–228**
exam for human resource certification, **10–20**
    appearance of questions, 13
    preparing for, **14–18**
    question development, 11
    recertification by, 10
    results, 20
    retaking, 20
    taking, **18–20**
Excelsior list, 364
exception reporting, for FLSA records, 262–263
excess deferral plans, 304
exclusive provider organizations (EPOs), 305
Executing phase of project life cycle, 42
executive compensation, 317–320
    Board of Directors, **320**
    stock options, **318–319**
    trends, 318
executive exemption, 261
executive orders (EO), 112, **137–138**
    EO 11246, 440
        document retention requirements, 61
    EO 11375, 440
    EO 11478, 441
    EO 12138, 443
    EO 13087, 446
    EO 13152, 446

executive search firms, 156
executive summary, in proposal, 27
executives
    in corporate governance, 113
    security for, 407
exemption status, FLSA on, 259–262
existence in ERG theory, 35
exit interview, 179–180
exiting organization, **179–183**
    involuntary, **180–183**
    voluntary, **179–180**
expatriates, 184
    compensation, 321
expectancy theory, 36
expense, 77
experience rating, 305
experiential exam, 12
experiential training methods, 223
experimental design evaluation, 228
express contract, 332
external assessment, **73–75**
external recruiting, 154–156
external talent, **146**
extinction, 36
extrinsic reward, 249

F

facilitation, 222
facility
    locations, 94
    for training program, **224–227**
fact-finding, in mediation, 354
Fair Credit Reporting Act (FCRA), 170, 171, 441
Fair Labor Standards Act (FLSA), **257–264**,
        395, 439
    amendments, **264**
    child labor, 262
    document retention requirements, 62
    exemption status, 259–262
    and hazard pay, 268
    maximum hours, 257
    minimum wage, 257
    overtime, 258–259
    penalties and recovery of back wages,
        263–264
    record keeping, 262–263
fair use of published works, 197
Fairbank, Katie, 116
fairness, code of ethics on, 115
"faltering company" exception, 181

Family and Medical Leave Act (FMLA),
        288–294, 444
    calculating year, 291–292
    document retention requirements, 62
    employees eligible, 289–290
    ending leave, 293
    implications for employers, 293
    key employee exception, 290
    leave types, 291
    reasons for leave, 290–291
    tracking reduced and intermittent leave, 292
Faragher v. City of Boca Raton, 336, 446
farm workers, and FUTA, 288
featherbedding, 359
federal agencies, regulations, 112
Federal Bureau of Investigation (FBI), 201
federal document retention requirements, 58–64
Federal Employees Compensation Act (FECA),
        414, 438
Federal Insurance Contributions Act (FICA),
        285, 439
    document retention requirements, 63
federal legislative process, **111–112**
Federal Mediation and Conciliation Service, 357
Federal Register, 112, 137
federal requirements, and exam questions, 12
Federal Unemployment Tax Act (FUTA),
        287–288, 439
    document retention requirements, 63
Federal Wage Garnishment Law, 315
fee-for-service plans (FFSs), 305
feedback
    on employee performance, **228–229**
    from employees, 75, **348**
Fein, Mitchell, 271
fellow servant rule, 413
FICA. *See* Federal Insurance Contributions
        Act (FICA)
fiduciary, 301
fiduciary responsibility, 113–114
Fiedler, Fred E., 40
Fiedler's Contingency Theory, 40
field review appraisal, 232
The Fifth Discipline (Senge), 201–202
final written warning, 31
finance and accounting function in organizations,
        95–96
financial assets, security for, **406**
financial references, 170
fire prevention plans, 403, 413
First, Break all the Rules (Buckingham and
        Coffman), 96–97
first impression bias of interviewer, 162–163

first written warning, 31
fiscal year, 76
fishbone diagram, 204, *205*
fitness centers, 311
flexible spending accounts, **307–308**, 310
flexible work arrangements, **236**
flextime, 349
FLSA. *See* Fair Labor Standards Act (FLSA)
FMLA. *See* Family and Medical Leave Act
      (FMLA)
focal review period, 231
focus groups
      data collection from, 50
      for employee attitude assessment, 75
      of employees, 348
forced ranking method of performance
      appraisal, 231
Ford Motor Company, 337
forecasting process, in strategic planning, 101
foreign business practices, in workforce
      planning, 185
Foreign Corrupt Practices Act of 1977, 117,
      185–186
Form I-9, 176
forms, from OSHA, 388
*Fraser v. Nationwide Mutual Insurance
      Company*, 420
fraudulent misrepresentation, 333–334
friendly takeover, 105
functional organizational structure, 68, *68*
funding, for pension program, 300
FUTA (Federal Unemployment Tax Act),
      287–288, 439
      document retention requirements, 63

G

GAAP (generally accepted accounting principles),
      77, 96
gainsharing, 270–271
Gallup Organization, 96
gap analysis, 25
garnishments, 314–315
gatekeeper, for HMOs, 305
general duty standard, 402–403
general partnership (GP), 92
General Requirements for All Machines
      standard, 404
generalists, certification for, 4
Generally Accepted Accounting Principles
      (GAAP), 77

generally accepted accounting principles
      (GAAP), 96
geocentric approach to international staffing, 185
geographic labor market, 150
geographic organizational structure, 68, *70*
geographic pay, 268–269
gifts, ethics policy on, 117
Glass Ceiling Act, **339–340**, 444
global considerations
      in employee and labor relations, **373**
      in human resource development, 238
      in risk management, **423–424**
      in strategic management, **119**
      in total reward packages, **321**
      in workforce planning and employment,
            184–186
Global Professional in Human Resources
      (GPHR), 5, 186
goals
      of corporation, 102
      setting in performance appraisal, 230
      in strategic planning, 99
"golden handcuffs," 319
government salary surveys, 275
GPHR (Global Professional in Human
      Resources), 5
graded vesting, 300
gradual vesting, 300
graduated vesting, 300
grant price, 318
grantor trusts, 304
Grasso, Richard, 318
graveyard shift, 266
"great man" theory, 38
green circle rate of pay, 279
grievance procedure, in union environment, 369
Griggs v. Duke Power Co., 134, 135, 166, 441
gross profit, 77
group incentives, **270–271**
growth in ERG theory, 35
growth phase in organization life cycle, 97–98
guessing on exam, 20
Guidelines on Sexual Harassment, 443
gut feeling bias of interviewer, 163

H

halo effect bias of interviewer, 163
Hammurabic Code, 413
handouts, for training program, 222
hard bargaining, 367

Harris v. Forklift Systems, 336, 445
harshness bias of interviewer, 163
Hay, Edward, 274
HAY system, 274
Hazard Communication Standard, 404
hazard pay, 268
HCEs (highly compensated employees), 303
HCNs (host-country nationals), 184
headhunting firms, 156
health and welfare benefits, **294, 305–312**
    cafeteria plans, 308
    COBRA requirements, 308–309
    employee assistance programs (EAP), **311–312**
    flexible spending accounts, **307–308**
    HIPAA requirements, **309–310**
    life insurance, 306–307
    medical insurance, 305–306
    time-off programs, 312
    wellness benefits, **310–311**
health and wellness programs, **310–311**
health, and work, 383
Health Insurance Portability and Accountability
    Act (HIPAA), 295, 445
    requirements, **309–310**
Health Maintenance Organizations
    (HMOs), 305
health purchasing alliances (HPA), 306
Helman, Kim, *Project Management
    Jumpstart*, 41
hepatitis B virus, 401
Hersey-Blanchard theory, 39
Hersey, Paul, 39
Herzberg, Fredrick, 34
hierarchy of needs (Maslow), 33–34
high-context culture, 119
high-involvement organizations, **208**
high-potential employees, employee development
    for, 212–213
highly compensated employees (HCEs), 303
HIPAA. *See* Health Insurance Portability and
    Accountability Act (HIPAA)
hiring management systems, 48
histograms, as analysis tools, *203*, 203
historical information, budgets based on, 78
HIV (human immunodeficiency virus), 401
HMOs (Health Maintenance Organizations), 305
holiday pay, 312
home visits, by union organizers, 363
honesty, ethics policy on, 117
host country, for global company, 184
host-country nationals (HCNs), 184
hostile takeovers, 105
hostile work environment, 335

hot cargo agreement, 358
hot cargo pickets, 372
House, Robert, 39
household workers, and FUTA, 288
HPA (health purchasing alliances), 306
HR-Man website, 16
HRCI Certification Guide (Weinberg), 18, 458
HRCI (Human Resource Certification Institute),
    xx, 4, 458
    Model of Professional Excellence, 45
    website, 7
HRCP (Human Resource Certification Program), 16
HRIS. *See* human resource information
    system (HRIS)
human assets, security for, **407–409**
human immunodeficiency virus (HIV), 401
human process interventions, **208–210**
human relations, concepts, **43–44**
human resource body of knowledge (BOK), 2,
    3–10
    core knowledge requirements, **6–7**
    functional areas
        current, 4
        defining, **5–6**
        original, 3
    human resource bulletin boards, accuracy, 18
    human resource certification, xix–xxi
benefits, xx–xxi
certification process, xxi
exam, **10–20**
    appearance of questions, 13
    preparing for, **14–18**
    question development, 11
    results, 20
    retaking, 20
    taking, **18–20**
levels, **7–8**
Human Resource Certification Institute (HRCI),
    xx, 4, 458
    Model of Professional Excellence, 45
    website, 7
Human Resource Certification Program
    (HRCP), 16
human resource development (HRD), 6, 196
    core knowledge requirements and, 6
    employee development, **211–214**
    employee training programs, **214–228**
    federal legislation, **196–198**
    global considerations, 238
    metrics, **237–238**
    performance appraisal, **229–235**
    resources, 460–461
    unique employee needs, **236–237**

human resource information system (HRIS),
    45–48
  applicant tracking systems, 48
  employee self-service, 47–48
  hiring management systems, 48
  implementing, 47
  selection, 45–47
  typical access hierarchy, 46–47
human resource management interventions, **211**
human resource profession, **2–3**
human resource staff, ratio to total
    employees, 119
human resource technology, **45–48**
human resources activities, interrelationships
    among, **66**
human resources, metrics, **118–119**

I

IBM Corporation (NLRB decision), 447
Illegal Immigration Reform and Immigrant
    Responsibility Act (IIRIRA) of 1996,
    178, 445
illegal subjects of collective bargaining, 368
illnesses, decision on work related, 389–390
immediate vesting, 299
Immigration Act of 1990, 177–178, 444
Immigration and Nationality Act (INA) of 1952,
    176, 440
immigration processes, **176–178**
Immigration Reform and Control Act (IRCA) of
    1986, 176–177, 443
  document retention requirements, 63
implementation, in ADDIE model of
    instructional design, **224–227**
implied contract, 332
improshare, 271
imputed income, 306–307
in-box test, 165
In Search of Excellence (Peters), 344
incentive pay, 269
incentive stock options, 319
income statement, 76
independent contractors, 147
India, offshore operations in, 107
indirect compensation, 250
individual incentives, 269–270
individual level training, 215
industry activity, in labor market analysis, 150
industry salary surveys, 276

information
  employee access during change, 56
  in high-involvement organizations, 208
information and knowledge economy, and
    change, 282
information assets, security for, **406–407**
information technology function in
    organizations, **95–96**
informational picketing, 364
Initiation phase of project life cycle, 11–12
injunctions, in union environment, 356, 370
injuries, decision on work related, 389–390
injury and illness compensation programs,
    413–414
injury and illness prevention programs, **410–413**
inpatriates, 186
inside directors, 113
inside organizing, by unions, 363
insider information, ethics policy on, 117
insider trading of stock, 114
instant messages, employer monitoring of, 418
instructional design model (ADDIE), **215–228**
  Analysis, **215–218**
  Design, **218–221**
  Development, **221–224**
  Implementation, **224–227**
  Evaluation, **227–228**
instrumentality, in expectancy theory, 36
insubordination, 352
insurance, and risks, 79
integrative bargaining, 367
integrity
  ethics policy on, 117
  testing, 167
Intellectual Property Agreement (IPA), 406
intelligence, types, 44
inter-rating reliability, 233
interest-based bargaining (IBB), 367
intermittent FLMA leave, 291
internal assessment, **73**
internal controls, to protect financial assets, 406
internal equity, of jobs, 274
internal recruiting, 153
Internal Revenue Service, independent contractor
    guidelines, 147–148
Internal Revenue Service (IRS), 255
internal talent, **145**
International Labour Organization (ILO),
    423–424
Internet. *See also* web resources
  employer monitoring of use, 118
  information available, 458

job boards, 154
    monitoring use, 418
    union websites, 363
internship programs, 146
interpersonal intelligence, 44
interstate commerce, 384
interviews
    data collection from, 50
    for employee attitude assessment, 75
    exit, 179–180
    of job candidates, **159–160**
        conducting effective, 163–164
        interviewer bias, **162–163**
        post-interview evaluation, 164
        question guidelines, **160–162**
        team for, 164
    Intranet, 345
    intrapersonal intelligence, 44
    intrinsic reward, 249
    inventory management, 94
    involuntary benefits, **285–294**
    IRCA (Immigration Reform and Control
        Act) of 1986, 176–177, 443
    document retention requirements, 63
Ishikawa diagram, 204, *205*
Ishikawa, Kaoru, 203

J

J. Weingarten, Inc., 350
J.D. Power and Associates, 208
job analysis, **56–57**, **144–145**
job applications, **158–159**
job bidding, 153
job candidates
    applicant tracking, 157
    applicant tracking systems, 48
    communication with, 157–158
    employment offers for, **173–175**
        activities following acceptance, **175–179**
    interviews, types, 159–160
    pre-employment inquiries, **170–173**
    screening tools, **158–159**
    sourcing and recruiting, **151–157**
    testing programs, **165–168**
        legal issues, 166–167
job competencies, 144
job descriptions, **57–58**
job design, 211
job enrichment, 34
job evaluation, **273–275**

job fairs, 155
job group analysis, in AAP, 142
Job Openings and Labor Turnover Survey
    (JOLTS), 150
job posting, 153
job pricing, 275
job-related stress, 399–401
job satisfaction surveys, and productivity, 198
job sharing, 146, 349
job specifications, 145
jobs, differentiating in total rewards philosophy, 251
Johnson, Lyndon B., 285
*Johnson v. Santa Clara County Transportation
    Agency*, **451**
joint venture (JV), 93
JOLTS (Job Openings and Labor Turnover
    Survey), 150
Jones v. Yellow Freight Systems, Inc., 338
Jung, Carl, 348
Juran, Joseph M., 202
Juran Trilogy, 202
jury duty pay, 312
just-in-time (JIT) inventory, 94

K

Kaplan, Robert, 110
Kennedy, John F., 285
key employee, identifying in BCP, 416
kinesthetic learners, 218
Kirkpatrick, Donald, 227
Knights of Labor, 355
knowledge, in high-involvement
    organizations, 208
knowledge management, **201**
knowledge-of-predictor bias of interviewer, 163
knowledge requirements, 5
knowledge, skills and abilities (KSAs), 56, 153
Knowles, Malcolm, 32
KSAs (knowledge, skills and abilities), 56

L

labor laws and organizations, 356–357
Labor-Management Relations Act (LMRA),
    356–357, 439
Labor-Management Reporting and Disclosure
    Act (LMRDA), 357, 440
labor market analysis, **150–151**

labor market, impact on compensation, 254
labor relations. *See* Employee and Labor
    Relations; unions, organization
laissez-faire leader, 40–41
Landrum-Griffith Act, 357
Lawler, Edward E., 208
layoffs
    conducting meeting, 183
    decision-making, 181–182
    worker protection in, 180–181
leadership, 38–41, 97
    behavioral theories, 38
    contingency theories, 40
    development, 214
    situational theories, 39–40
    styles, 40–41
leafleting, 363
leapfrogging, 367
learned professional exemption, 261
learning curve, 219–221
learning evaluation method for training, 227–228
learning organizations, 201–202
learning process, for adults, 32–33
learning styles, 218
"least preferred coworker" scale, 40
leaves of absence, 312. *See also* Family and
    Medical Leave Act (FMLA)
lectures, 222
legislative process, 111–112
leniency bias of interviewer, 163
Lewin, Kurt, 199
liability, 77, 79
life insurance, 306–307
lifelong learning, 201–202
lifetime certification, 10
limited liability company (LLC), 93
limited liability partnership (LLP), 92
limited partnership (LP), 92
Lindeman, Eduard, 32
line functions, 109
line of sight, 251
linear regression, 53
lobbying, 113
lock-in, 449
lockout/tagout standard, 404
lockouts, 370
loco parentis, 290
Long Prairie Packing Company, 338
long-range plans, 101
long-term disability insurance, 307
longevity, rewards for, 252
Longshore and Harbor Workers' Compensation
    Act (LHWCA), 414, 438
low-context culture, 119

M

Machine Guarding standard, 404
maintenance of membership clause, 368–369
management, 108–110
    development, 213–214
    respect for workforce, 346
management by objectives, 210
management by walking around (MBWA), 344
managers, in corporate governance, 113
mandatory arbitration, 456
mandatory subjects of collective bargaining, 368
manuals, for training program, 222
market competition, and employee retention, 255
marketable skills, and compensation, 281
marketing, 94–95
"marking up" the bill, 111
Martin v. Wilks, 452
Maslow, Abraham, 33–34
material safety data sheet (MSDS), 396
matrix organizational structure, 69, 71
maturity phase in organization life cycle, 98
maximum hours, in FLSA, 257
M.B. Sturgis, Inc. (NLRB decision),
    362–363, 446
McClelland, David, 35
McDonnell Douglas Corp. v. Green,
    448–449, 455
McGregor, Douglas, 35
McKennon v. Nashville Banner Publishing Co., 455
meal periods, as compensable, 259
mean average, 52
measurement, 54–55
measures of central tendency, 52–53
media, union use of, 364
median, 53
mediation, 354–355
    in union environment, 370
medical examinations, for job candidates, 173
medical expenses, pre-tax funds for, 307–308
medical insurance, 304, 305–306
Medical Services and First Aid standard, 404
Medicare, 285–286
Medina Rene v. MGM Grand Hotel, Inc., 339
meetings
    for termination, 351
    for union organizing, 363
Mental Health Parity Act (MHPA), 308,
    310, 445
mental models, 201
mentoring, 213
mergers and acquisitions, 105–106
    workforce planning in, 144

merit increases, 265, 280
merit matrix, 280
Meritor Savings Bank v. Vinson, 335–336
metrics, 54–55
    for employee and labor relations, 373
    for human resource development, 237–238
    for workforce planning, 183–184
MHPA (Mental Health Parity Act), 308,
    310, 445
Microsoft Corporation, 319
midpoint progression, in salary structure,
    276–277
Mine Safety and Health Act of 1977
    (MSH Act), 394
Mine Safety and Health Administration, 442
minimum wage, in FLSA, 257
minorities, glass ceiling, 339–340
mission statement, 101
Mitsubishi, 337
mode (central tendency measure), 53
monetary compensation, 249
money purchase plan, 302
Monongah coal mine disaster (West
    Virginia), 383
morale, "promoting from within" and, 145
motivation concepts, 33–36
motivation/hygiene theory, 34
Motorola, 207
Mouton, Jane S., 39
moving average, 53
Moving stage of change, 199
MSDs (musculoskeletal disorders), 399
multi-employer bargaining, 367
multi-unit bargaining, 367–368
multinational corporations, international staffing
    strategies, 184
multiple linear regression, 53
musculoskeletal disorders (MSDs), 399
mutual respect, 346

N

narrative methods, of performance appraisal, 232
National Archives, website, 137
National Energy Efficiency Act of 1992, 444
National Institute of Occupational Safety and
    Health (NIOSH), 385
National Labor Relations Act (NLRA), 343,
    356, 439
    document retention requirements, 63

National Labor Relations Board (NLRB), 112, 356
    bars to election, 365–366
    conference/pre-election hearing issues,
        362–363
    elections, 364–366
    filing unfair labor practice charges, 359–360
    petitioning, 361
National Security Agency (NSA), 201
"natural disaster" exception, 181
NDA (Non-Disclosure Agreement), 406
Needlestick Safety and Prevention Act of 2000,
    395, 446
needs analysis, 25–28
needs assessment, 25–28
    in third-party contract management, 27
    for training, 215–218, *217*
needs hierarchy (Maslow), 33–34
negative correlation coefficient, *51*
negative emphasis bias of interviewer, 163
negative reinforcement, 36
negatively accelerating learning curve, 219, *219*
negligent hiring, 172
negotiating offers, 174
net profit, 77
neutrality agreement, 361
new employees
    finding, 146
    orientation programs, 178–179
new hire reporting database, 316
newsletters, 344
newspaper advertising, for job opening, 154
NLRA. *See* National Labor Relations Act
    (NLRA)
NLRB. *See* National Labor Relations Board
    (NLRB)
NLRB v. J. Weingarten, Inc., 442
no strike/no lockout clause in collective
    bargaining agreement, 369
nominal group technique, 54
Non-Disclosure Agreement (NDA), 406
nonbinding arbitration, 353
noncompensable time, 258
nondirective interviews, 159
nonforfeitable claim, 296
nonmonetary compensation, 249
nonqualified deferred compensation, 304
nonqualified retirement plan, 297
nonqualified stock options, 319
"nonsubscriber" plans, for workers
    compensation, 294
nonsupervisory evaluators, training, 235
nonunion employees, Weingarten rights and, 350

nonverbal bias of interviewer, 163
Norma Rae, 365
Norris-La Guardia Act, 356, 439
Norton, David, 110

O

OASDI (Old Age, Survivors, and Disability
    Insurance), 285
objectives
    in needs assessment, 25
    in strategic planning, 100
    of training, 219
OBRA (Omnibus Budget Reconciliation Act),
    296, 317, 445
observations, data collection from, 50
Occupational Health, Safety, and Security, 382.
    See also Risk Management
Occupational Noise Exposure standard, 403
Occupational Safety and Health Act (OSH Act),
    112, 116, 382, 383, **384–394**, 441
    document retention requirements, 63
    employee rights and responsibilities, **386**
    employer responsibilities, **385**
    employer rights, **385–386**
    enforcement, **386**
    inspections during fiscal year 2004, 387
    record keeping requirements, **388–391**
    violations categories, 387
Occupational Safety and Health Administration
    (OSHA), 112, 173, 383
    assistance, **393–394**
    inspections, **391**
OD. *See also* organization development (OD)
OFCCP (Office of Federal Contract Compliance
    Programs), 136
    and electronic data access, 45
offer letters, 174
offers of employment, **173–175**
    activities following acceptance, **175–179**
Office of Federal Contract Compliance Programs
    (OFCCP), 136
    and electronic data access, 45
offshoring, 107
    workforce planning in, 144
Old Age, Survivors, and Disability Insurance
    (OASDI), 285
Older Worker Benefit Protection Act (OWBPA),
    295, 444
ombudsman, 353

Omnibus Budget Reconciliation Act (OBRA),
    296, 317, 445
on-call pay, 268
on-call time, 259
on-call workers, 147
on-the-job experience, and recertification, 10
Oncale v. Sundowner Offshore Services, Inc.,
    337–338, 446
one-on-one training, 223
online bulletin boards, 224
online study groups, 16
open-door policy, 344
opening conference, by CSHO, 392
operant conditioning, 36
    in customer service, 37
operating expenses
    compensation as percent of, 317
    HR expenses as percent, 119
operations function in organization, **94**
opportunities, in SWOT analysis, 72
oral contract, 26
organization culture, 198
    and total rewards philosophy, **251–252**
Organization Development and Change
    (Cummings and Worley), 199
organization development (OD), **198–211**
    strategic interventions, 198, **199–202**
        change management, **199–200**
        human process interventions, **208–210**
        human resource management
            interventions, **211**
        knowledge management, **201**
        learning organizations, **201–202**
        techno-structural interventions, **202–208**
    organization exit processes, **179–183**
    involuntary exit, **180–183**
    voluntary exit, **179–180**
organization goals, translated to staffing plans,
    148–150
organization incentives, **270–271**
organizational climate, 342
organizational culture, 342
organizational level training, **214–215**
organizational picketing, 364
organizational profile, in AAP, 142
organizational risks, assessing and
    prioritizing, **415**
organizational structures, **68–69**
    strategic planning and, **104–107**
organizations, **92–93**
    functions, **93–97**
        finance and accounting, **95–96**
        information technology, **95–96**

people/employees, 96–97
  production and operations, 94
  research and development, 95
  sales and marketing, 94–95
life cycles, 97–98
values and ethics, 114–115
organizing function, 108
orientation programs, 178–179
OSH Act. *See* Occupational Safety and Health
    Act (OSH Act)
OSHA. *See* Occupational Safety and Health
    Administration (OSHA)
OSHA 301 Incident Report, 391
OSHA Alliance Program, 394
outplacement services, 182
outside directors, 113, 320
outside sales exemption, 262
outsourcing, 107, 148
  HR functions, 26
  workforce planning in, 144
overtime, 266
  in FLSA, 258–259
OWBPA (Older Worker Benefit Protection Act),
    295, 444

P

paid time off, 312
pair comparison method of performance
    appraisal, 231
pandemic, preparing for, 402
panel interviews, 160
parallel bargaining, 367
parallel budgeting, 78
parent-country nationals (PCNs), 184
parental leave, 312
Pareto chart, as analysis tool, 204, *204*
Pareto, Vilfredo, 204
part-time employees, 146, 349
partially self-funded health insurance plan, 306
participant benefit rights reports, 299
participant, in pension program, 299
Participating style of leadership, 40
participative leadership style, 39
partnership, 92–93
party in interest, 296
passive training methods, 222
  space requirements, 225
Patent Act, **198**, 440
  and training materials, 221
patents, 198

Path-goal theory, 39
patterned interviews, 159
pay. *See* compensation
pay equity, 277
pay grades, job placement in, 277
pay range, 277
  employee's place in, 278
*Payne v. The Western & Atlantic Railroad
    Company*, 332, 438
payroll, **313–316**
  deductions, **314–315**
  employee earnings, **313–314**
  record keeping, **315–316**
payrolling, 147
PCA (Walsh-Healey Public Contracts Act), 439
  document retention requirements, 65
PCNs (parent-country nationals), 184
pedagogy, 32
peer review panel, 353
pension benefits, **296–297**
Pension Protection Act of 2006, 301, 304, 447
PEO (professional employer organization), 147
people/employees function in organizations,
    96–97
performance appraisal, **229–235**
  elements of, **230**
  management by objectives in, 210
  meeting contents, 235
  methods, **231–233**
  rating methods, 232
  timing for, **230–231**
  training for evaluators, **233–235**
performance-based compensation, 265
performance-based philosophy, and
    compensation, 251
performance-based training, 223
performance evaluators, training for, **233–235**
performance improvement, **349–353**
performance issues, documenting, **30–32**
performance management, **228–229**
permanent arbitrator, 354
Permit-Required Confined Spaces standard, 404
perquisites, 317
personal mastery, 201
Personal Protective Equipment standard, 403
Personal Responsibility and Work Opportunity
    Reconciliation Act of 1996, 316, 445
"personal space," 43
personal use of company assets, 117
personality test, 165
personnel, characteristics required to establish
    profession, 3
personnel records, data collection from, 50

PES (Professional Examination Service), xx, 4
PEST analysis, 72
Peter, Lawrence, *The Peter Principle*, 212–213
*Petermann v. International Brotherhood of
    Teamsters*, 333
Peters, Tom, *In Search of Excellence*, 344
phantom stock, 319
Philippus Aureolus, 383
"PHR Only" icon, 5
PHR (Professional in Human Resources), 5
    exam, 7–8
        eligibility requirements, 9
PHR/SPHR/GPHR Certification Handbook, 8,
    9, 16, 330, 458
physical assessment tests, 167–168
physical assets, security for, **406**
physical health hazards, **398–401**
physician hospital organizations (PHOs), 305
physiological needs in Maslow hierarchy, 34
picketing, 364, *372*
placement goals, in AAP, 142
placement in marketing, *95*
plan administrator, 296
plan sponsor, 296
planning, for change, 200
Planning phase of project life cycle, 42
plant closings, worker protection in, 180–181
plant patents, 198
plateau learning curve, 220, *221*
pocket veto, 112
point factor methodology, for classifying
    jobs, 274
point of service plans (POSs), 305
policies, in workplace, **346–347**
political environment, assessment, **73**
polycentric approach to international
    staffing, 185
polygraph tests, in employment process, 172–173
Portal to Portal Act, 264, 439
Porter, Michael E., *Competitive Strategy:
    Techniques for Analyzing Industries and
    Competitors*, 72
Porter's 5 Forces analysis, 72, 74–75
positional bargaining, 367
positive correlation coefficient, 51, *52*
positive reinforcement, 36
positive time reporting, of work time, 262
positively accelerating learning curve, 220, *220*
power
    in acquired needs theory, 35
    in high-involvement organizations, 208
practice analysis study, 4
pre-employment testing for drugs, 408

predictive validity of selection tests, 168, 169
preexisting conditions, HIPAA and, 309
preferred provider organizations (PPOs), 305
Pregnancy Discrimination Act of 1978, 132, 442
prescription insurance, 306
presentation, 222
pretest/posttest comparison, 228
price in marketing, *95*
pricing information, in proposal, 28
primary research, 49
principled bargaining, 367
prior-petition bar to union election, 366
priorities, in needs assessment, 26
privacy
    of personal employee information, 30
    policies, 418–419
    in workplace, **118**, **417–421**
Privacy Act of 1974, 172, 441
privacy concern cases, OSHA and, 389
private letter ruling, from IRS, 255
procedures, in workplace, **346–347**
process control charts, *206*, 206
Process Council, 209
product-base organizational structure, 68, *69*
product in marketing, *95*
production and operations function in
    organizations, **94**
production layout, 94
production measures, for human resource
    development, 236
productivity
    employee relations and, 345
    and job satisfaction surveys, 198
    metrics, 183
professional communication, 30
professional development, 97
    for recertification, 10
professional employer organization (PEO), 147
Professional Examination Service (PES), xx, 4
professional exemption, 261
Professional in Human Resources (PHR), 5
    exam, 7–8
        eligibility requirements, **9**
professional organizations, for external
    recruiting, 155
professional standards, **44–45**
profit, 77
profit and loss statement, 76
profit sharing, 271, 302
programmed instruction, 223–224
project life cycle, 41–42
project management, **41–42**
Project Management Institute, website, 42

Project Management Jumpstart (Helman), 41
project management plan, in proposal, 27
project team, in proposal, 27
Prometric, 19
promises, in offer letter, 174
promissory estoppel, 333
"promoting from within," 145
promotion in marketing, 95
promotions, **281**
    discrimination, 447–448
protected classes, 130
protected health information (PHI), 309
prudent person standard of care, 301
psychomotor assessment tests, 167
Public Company Accounting Oversight Board, 114
Public Contracts Act, 439
    document retention requirements, 65
public domain, 197
publicity picketing, 364
Pullman Palace Car Company, 356
punishment, 36

Q

qualified domestic relations orders (QDRO), 300
qualified employees, **145–148**
qualified plan, 296–297
qualified stock options, 319
qualitative analysis, **49–55**
quality management, 94
quality of hire metric, 183
quality team structure, in Six Sigma, 207
quantitative analysis, **50–53**
question inconsistency bias of interviewer, 163
questionnaires, data collection from, 50
quid pro quo harassment, 335

R

rabbi trusts, 304
Radio Union v. Broadcast Services, Inc., 371
Ragsdale v. Wolverine, 292
Railroad Safety Act, 116
railroads, safety technology, 383
Railway Labor Act, 356, 439
Ramazzini, Bernardino, 399
random drug testing, 408
ranking method of performance appraisal,
    231, 274

ratios, 53
reaction evaluation method for training, 227
Reagan, Ronald, 294
realistic job preview, 164–165
reasonable expectation of privacy, 418
"reasonable person" standard, 420
reasonable suspicion drug testing, 409
recency bias of interviewer, 163
recent graduates, exam eligibility requirements, 9
recertification, **10**
recognition of employees, 97
recognitional picketing, 364
recordable case rate formula, 423
recruiting job candidates, **151–157**
    methods, **153–156**
        external recruiting, 154–156
        internal, 153
        succession planning, 154
    strategies, 151–152
red circle rate of pay, 279
reduced FMLA leave schedule, 291
reduction in force (RIF), in WARN Act, 181
reengineering, 105
    in workforce planning, 143
reference checks, 170
Refreezing stage of change, 199
Regents of California v. Bakke, **449**
regiocentric approach to international
    staffing, 185
Rehabilitation Act of 1973, 134, 136, 441, 451
    document retention requirements, 59, 64
relatedness in ERG theory, 35
reliability, of selection tests, 168
relocation, **175**
repatriation, **236–237**
repetitive stress injuries (RSI), 399
replacement chart, 154
replacement cost per employee, 184
reporting pay, 268
request for proposal (RFP), 26–27
research and development function in
    organizations, **95**
reserved rights doctrine, 368
resignations, 179
respondeat superior, 334
responsibilities, 5
rest periods, as compensable, 259
restricted stock options, 319
results evaluation method for training, 228
resumes, 158
retained earnings, 77
retained employment agencies, 156
retention bonuses, 272

retention programs, 179
  competition and, 255
  strategies, 348–349
retirement
  age increase for, 286, 287
  before ERISA, 298
Retirement Equity Act (REA), 303, 443
return on investment (ROI), 54
  for human resource development, 236
revenue, 77
Revenue Act of 1978, 303, 443
  and flexible spending accounts, 307–308
reverse discrimination, 452
reverse mentor, 213
rewards, in high-involvement organizations, 208
RFP (request for proposal), 26–27
"right to work" laws, 356
rightsizing, 105
risk assessment, 396–409
  safety and health risks, 396–402
Risk Management, 6, 79, 382
  core knowledge requirements and, 6
  federal legislation, 382–395
  global considerations, 423–424
  loss prevention, 409–417
  metrics, 422–423
  resources, 463
  risk assessment, 396–409
  workplace privacy, 417–421
risks, forecasting for organization, 110
ROI (return on investment), 54
rolling average, 53
Roosevelt, Frankline Delano, 285
Rosenfeld v. Southern Pacific, 447–448
RSI (repetitive stress injuries), 399

S

S-shaped learning curve, 220, *220*
sabbaticals, 312
safe harbor provision for payroll errors, 261
safety, 409
  training programs, 417
Safety and Health Achievement Recognition
  Program (SHARP), 393
safety and health management plan, 412–413
safety management programs, 409–410
safety needs in Maslow hierarchy, 34
St. Mary's Honor Center v. Hicks, 454–455
salary. *See* compensation

salary deductions, and FLSA exemption
  status, 260
salary range, 277
salary surveys, 275–276
sales and marketing function in organizations,
  94–95
salting, 363
same-sex harassment, 338
Sanitation standard, 403
Sarbanes-Oxley Act of 2002, 73, 114, 406, 447
SARS (severe acute respiratory syndrome), 402
satisfaction (motivation) factors, 34
Saturn Corporation, 208
SCA (Service Contract Act), 256, 440
  document retention requirements, 64
Scanlon, Joseph, 271
Scanlon plan, 271
scatter charts, 204
scheduled drug testing, 408
scheduling, 94
  for training program, 227
School Board of Nassau v. Arline, 451
scientific method, 49
"scoping" the project, 27
screening interviews, 160
seamless organizational structure, 71
searches of employee property, 419–420
seasonal workers, 147
secondary boycott, 371
secondary research, 49
Section 125 plans, 307–308
Securities and Exchange Commission (SEC),
  96, 116
Securities Exchange Act of 1934, 96
security risks, 405–409
  for financial assets, 406
  for human assets, 407–409
  for information assets, 406–407
  for physical assets, 406
selection tests
  legal issues, 166–167
  reliability and validity, 168
  types, 165–168
self-actualization needs in Maslow hierarchy, 34
self-assessment, in performance appraisal, 230
self-assessment test, xxv–xl, 14
self-directed work team, 344
self-employed individuals, 147
self-funded health insurance plan, 306
self-knowledge, 44
self-study, 17, 223
Selling style of leadership, 40
Selye, Hans, 399

Senge, Peter, *The Fifth Discipline*, 201–202
Senior Professional in Human Resources (SPHR), 5
   exam, 8
      eligibility requirements, **9**
     seniority-based compensation, 265–266
     seniority, rewards for, 252
      Service Contract Act (SCA), 256, 440
     document retention requirements, 64
severance package, 181
severe acute respiratory syndrome (SARS), 402
sexual harassment, **335–339**
   costs to employers, 337
   EEOC guidelines for preventing, 338–339
sexual orientation, prohibiting discrimination
   based on, 339
shared vision, 202
shareholders, 93, 113
SHARP (Safety and Health Achievement
   Recognition Program), 393
Sherman Anti-Trust Act, 356, 438
shift pay, 266–267
shift premium, 267
short-range plans, 101
short-term disability insurance, 307
SHRM (Society for Human Resource
   Management), xx, 4
   Code of Ethical and Professional Standards, 44
   Learning Center, 16
   lobbying by, 113
sick pay, 312
similar-to-me bias of interviewer, 163
simple linear regression, 53
simulation models, 53
simulation training, 223
single-unit bargaining, 367
sit-down strike, 372
situational theories of leadership, **39–40**
Six Sigma, **207**
skill set, and compensation, 281
skills inventory, 153
skills training, 211
Skinner, B.F., 36
skip-level interviews, 348
Small Business Job Protection Act of 1996,
   303, 445
Small Business Regulatory Enforcement Fairness
   Act, 445
SMART model for goals, 102
social environment, assessment, 74
social needs in Maslow hierarchy, 34
Social Security Act of 1935, 285
   document retention requirements, 64

Social Security Amendments of 1965, 285
Society for Human Resource Management
   (SHRM), xx, 4
   Code of Ethical and Professional Standards, 44
   Learning Center, 16
   lobbying by, 113
Socratic seminars, 223
sole proprietorships, 92
sourcing job candidates, **151–157**
span of control, 109
specialists, certification for, 4
Specifications for Accident Prevention Signs and
   Tags, 403–404
"SPHR Only" icon, 5
SPHR (Senior Professional in Human Resources), 5
   exam, 8
      eligibility requirements, **9**
staff functions, 109
staffing needs analysis, **148–150**, *149*
staffing programs, **151–179**
   activities following offer, **175–179**
   candidate selection tools, **157–173**
   employment offers, **173–175**
   planning for future needs, 107
   sourcing and recruiting, **151–157**
standards for professional behavior, **44–45**
startup phase in organization life cycle, 97
state requirements, and exam questions, 12
state unemployment insurance (SUI), 287
state worker compensation laws, 414
statement of cash flows, 76
statistical models, 72
statutory bar to union election, 365
STEP analysis, 72
stereotyping bias of interviewer, 163
stock options, **318–319**
stockholders, 93
stop-loss insurance, 306
straight line operations, 371
strategic interventions in organization
   development, **199–202**
   change management, **199–200**
   human process interventions, **208–210**
   human resource management
     interventions, **211**
   knowledge management, **201**
   learning organizations, **201–202**
   techno-structural interventions, **202–208**
strategic management, 5
   core knowledge requirements and, 5
   global considerations in, **119**
   resources, 459

strategic partnerships, 108, 394
strategic planning, **98–104**
    budget, 104
    environmental scanning, **101**
    evaluation, 104
    for human resources, **107–108**
    implementing, **102**
    planning to plan, **99–100**
    process, *100*
    real world scenario, 103–104
    strategy formation, **101–102**
strategic workforce planning, **143–151**
    job analysis and description, **144–145**
    labor market analysis, **150–151**
    organization goals translated to staffing plans,
        148–150
    qualified employees, **145–148**
    workforce goals and objectives, **143–144**
strategy, 99. *See also* business strategy
stratification charts, 204, *205*
strengths, in SWOT analysis, 72
stress, 399–401
    stages and symptoms, 400
    and workplace violence, 407
stress interviews, 160
strike price, 318
strikes, 357, **371–372**
structured interviews, 160
Studebaker Corporation, 298
students, exam eligibility requirements, 9
study plan, **14–15**
    options, **15–17**
Sturgis, Inc. (M.B.), 362–363, 446
subject matter experts (SME), 30
substance abuse, **408**
succession planning, **154**
suggestion boxes, 343
summary plan description (SPD), 297–298
supervisor assessment, in performance
    appraisal, 230
supervisory training, 212
suppliers, for external recruiting, 155
supply and demand, for skill set in labor
    market, 254
supportive leadership style, 39
surveillance cameras, in workplace, 118
suspension, 31
swing shift, 266
SWOT analysis, 72
systems thinking, 201

T

tactical accountability measures, *55*
    for human resource development, 237
    of human resource plans, 119
    for total rewards, 317
    for Workforce Planning and Employment,
        183–184
tactical goals, 102
Taft-Hartley Act, 356–357, 370
talent management, 67
target audience, for training program, 218
target benefit plan, 303
target market, demographics, 74
task force, 343
task inventory, in training design, 218
task level training, 215
Tax Reform Act, 443
Taxman v. Board of Education of Piscataway,
    182, 444
TCNs (third-country nationals), 184
team learning, 202
teambuilding activities, **209**
technical/professional skills labor market, 151
techno-structural interventions, **202–208**
technology, 94, 96
    rate of change, 74
telecommuting, 146–147, 348–349
telephone calls, employer monitoring of, 418
Telling style of leadership, 39
temp-to-perm arrangements, 146–147
temporary workers, 146
    and union election, **362–363**
tenure in position, 281
teratogens, 397
termination of employment, 31–32
    for misconduct, 455
    wrongful, 352
testing programs for job candidates, **165–168**
    legal issues, 166–167
Texas Department of Community Affairs v.
    Burdine, **450**, 455
theater-style seating for training, *225*
Theory X/Theory Y, 35
third-country nationals (TCNs), 184
third-party administrator (TPA), 306
third-party contract management, 26–28
threats, in SWOT analysis, 72
time-and-a-half, 258
time-off programs, **312**
time series forecasts, 53

time to hire metric, 184
timing
    for performance appraisal, **230–231**
    of termination meetings, 351
top-down budgeting, 78
"top-down" communication, 28, 29
"top hat" plans, 304
tort, 79, 332
total compensation, 249
total quality management (TQM), **202–206**
Total Rewards, 6, 248. *See also* compensation
    budget, 320
    communication about, **316**
    core knowledge requirements and, 6
    defining, **249–253**
    federal legislation, 248–249, **256–264**
    global considerations, 321
    metrics, **317**
    and recruiting, 152
    resources, 461–462
    strategy, **252–253**
total rewards philosophy, **250–252**
    external conditions, 251
    internal conditions, **250–251**
    organizational culture, **251–252**
town hall meetings, 344
Toxic Substances Control Act (TSCA), 116
    document retention requirements, 64
TQM (total quality management), **202–206**
trainers, selection, 227
training, 37, **214–228**
    delivery mechanism, **223–224**
    evaluation, **227–228**
    on foreign country culture, 185
    implementing, **224–227**
    instructional methods, **222–223**
    materials for, **221–222**
    objectives of, 219
    from OSHA, 393
    for performance evaluators, **233–235**
    on safety, 417
    skills, 211
    supervisory, 212
training cost per employee, 237
trait theory of leadership, 38
transactional leadership, 41
transfer of training, 227
transformational leadership, 41
travel time, payment for, 259
trend analysis, 53
trends, in executive compensation, 318
tripartite arbitration panel, 354

trust, 346
TSCA (Toxic Substance Control Act), document
    retention requirements, 64
tuberculosis, 402
turnover rate of employees, 184
two-factor theory, 34
Tyco, 114

U

U-shaped-style seating for training, *226*
undue hardship, 134
Unemployment Compensation Amendments of
    1992, 303, 444
unemployment insurance, 182, 285, **287–288**
unfair labor practices (ULP), **358–359**
    employer, **358**
    filing charges, **359–360**
    union, **358–359**
"unforeseeable business circumstance"
    exception, 181
Unfreezing stage of change, 199
"unholy trinity," 414
Uniform Guidelines on Employee Selection
    Procedures (UGESP), 65, **156–157**, 442
Uniformed Services Employment and
    Reemployment Rights Act (USERRA),
    340–341, 445
Union of Needletrades, Industrial, and Textile
    Employees (UNITE), 364
union shops, 356, 368
union unfair labor practices, **358–359**
unions
    avoidance strategies, **372**
    deauthorization, 366
    decertification, 366
    for external recruiting, 155
    organization, **360–372**
        avoidance strategies, **372**
        campaign tactics, **363–364**
        collective bargaining, **366–372**
        conditions for, 454
        employer options, 360
        organizing process, **361–366**
United Steelworkers v. Weber, 450
U.S. Citizenship and Immigration Services
    (USCIS), 176
U.S. Congress
    House and Senate websites, 113
    legislative process, **111–112**

U.S. President
  executive orders (EO), 112
    power of injunction ending strike or
      lockout, 357
    signature or veto of bill, 112
universities, recruiting on, 155
unlawful employment practices, 130
unlawful strikes, 357
USA Today, 318
utility patents, 198

V

vacation pay, 312
valence, in expectancy theory, 36
validity of selection tests, 168
  real world scenario, 169
values of organization, **114–115**
variable compensation, **269–272**
variances in production process, process control
    charts for displaying, 206, *206*
vendor qualifications, in proposal, 27
vendors, for external recruiting, 155
verbal warning, written record of, 31
vestibule training, 223
vesting, 299
  schedules, 297
veto of bill, 112
vicarious liability, 337
video surveillance, 417, 419
Vietnam Era Veterans' Readjustment Act
  (VEVRA), **136–137**, 441
  document retention requirements, 65
virtual work team, 343
visas, employment, 177–178
vision insurance, 306
vision statement, 101
visual learners, 218
vital processes, identifying in BCP, 416
voluntary arbitration, 353
voluntary assumption of risk, 414
Voluntary Protection Program (VPP), 394
voluntary-recognition bar to union election, 366
voluntary recognition of union, 361
voluntary subjects of collective bargaining, 368
VPP (Voluntary Protection Program), 394
Vroom, Victor, 36

W

wage compression, 279

wage garnishments, 314–315
Wagner Act, 356, 439
waiting time, as compensable, 258
walk-in candidates, 156
Walsh-Healey Public Contracts Act (PCA), 439
  document retention requirements, 65
Wards Cove Packing Co. v. Atonio, 134
Washington v. Davis, 167, 442
Watkins, Sherron, 116
weaknesses, in SWOT analysis, 72
web resources
  Age Discrimination in Employment Act
    (ADEA), 134
  Americans with Disabilities Act (ADA), **134**
  Balanced Scorecard Institute, 110
  Civil Rights Act of 1964, Title VII, 131
  on completing OSHA forms, 388
  Davis Bacon Act, 256
  Employee Polygraph Protection Act
    (EPPA), 173
  Equal Employment Opportunity Act
    of 1972, 132
  Family Medical Leave Act (FMLA), 293
  on FLSA exemption requirements, 264
  on imputed income, 307
  Mine Safety and Health Administration, 394
  on minimum wage, 257
  National Institute of Occupational Safety and
    Health (NIOSH), 385
  NIOSH study on stress at work, 401
  OASDI and Medicare tax rates, 286
  OFCCP (Office of Federal Contract
    Compliance Programs), 142
  OSHA ergonomic hazards checklist, 399
  OSHA standards, 405
  pandemic preparation, 402
  Pregnancy Discrimination Act of 1978, 132
  Service Contract Act (SCA), 256
  Uniformed Services Employment and
    Reemployment Rights Act
    (USERRA), 341
  U.S. Congress, 113
  World Health Organization (WHO), 423
Weeks v. Southern Bell Telephone Co., 448
weighted average, 53
weighted employment applications, 159
weighted moving average, 53
Weinberg, Raymond B., *HRCI Certification
  Guide*, 18
Weingarten, Inc. (J.), 350
Welfare and Pension Disclosure Act
  (WPDA), 297
wellness benefits, **310–311**
whipsawing, 367

whistle-blowing, 333, 352
  real world scenario, 116
Wigand, Jeffrey, 116
wildcat strike, 372
Wirtz, Willard, 383
women
  in business leadership, global
     considerations, 186
  glass ceiling, 339–340
word of mouth, 345
work, and health, 383
work-for-hire exceptions, in copyright, 197
work rule, 347
work slowdown, 370, 372
work team, 343
Worker Adjustment and Retraining Notification
  (WARN) Act of 1988, **180–181**, 443
workers compensation, 293–294
  laws, 414
workforce expansion, 105
workforce goals and objectives, **143–144**
Workforce Planning and Employment (WFP),
  6, 129
  core knowledge requirements and, 6
  federal employment legislation, **129–143**
  global considerations, **184–186**
  metrics, **183–184**
  organization exit processes, **179–183**
    involuntary exit, **180–183**
    voluntary exit, **179–180**
  resources, 460
  staffing programs, **151–179**
    activities following offer, **175–179**
    candidate selection tools, **157–173**
    employment offers, **173–175**
    sourcing and recruiting, **151–157**
  strategic workforce planning, **143–151**
    job analysis and description, **144–145**
    labor market analysis, **150–151**
    organization goals translated to staffing
     plans, **148–150**
    qualified employees, **145–148**
    workforce goals and objectives, **143–144**
  workforce reduction, 105
  workplace
accidents impact, 409
behavior issues, **352–353**
investigations, **421–422**
policies and procedures, **346–347**
privacy in, **417–421**
workplace violence, **407**
World Health Organization (WHO), 423
WorldCom, 114
Worley, Christopher, *Organization Development
  and Change*, 199
WPDA (Welfare and Pension Disclosure Act), 297
written contract, 26
written warnings, 31
wrongful termination, 352

X

xy chart, 204

Y

yellow dog contracts, 356

Z

zero-based budgeting (ZBB), 78
zipper clause, in collective bargaining agreement,
  369

The Best PHR/SPHR Study Combination Available!

Get ready for the new PHR or SPHR exams with the most comprehensive and challenging sample tests anywhere! The Sybex Test Engine includes the following features:

- Chapter-by-chapter exam coverage of all the review questions from the book
- Four bonus exams available only on the CD
- Supports question formats found on the actual exam.

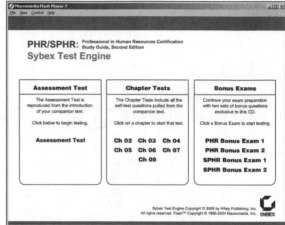

Search through the complete book in PDF!

- Access the entire PHR/SPHR: Professional in Human Resources Certification Study Guide, Second Edition complete with figures and tables, in electronic format.
- Search the PHR/SPHR: Professional in Human Resources Certification Study Guide, Second Edition chapters to find information on any topic in seconds.

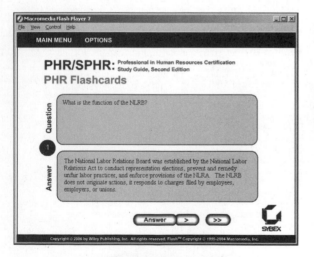

Use the Electronic Flashcards for PCs or Palm devices to jog your memory and prep for the exam at the last minute!

- Reinforce your understanding of key concepts.
- Download the Flashcards to your Palm device, and go on the road. Now you can study anywhere, anytime.